The Resourceful Reader

FIFTH EDITION

Readings to accompany
The Writer's Harbrace Handbook

✺

Suzanne Strobeck Webb
Texas Woman's University

with

Lou Ann Thompson
Texas Woman's University

HARCOURT COLLEGE PUBLISHERS
Fort Worth   Philadelphia   San Diego   New York   Orlando   Austin   San Antonio
Toronto   Montreal   London   Sydney   Tokyo

Publisher	Earl McPeek
Acquisitions Editor	Julie McBurney
Marketing Strategist	John Meyers
Developmental Editor	Michell Phifer
Project Manager	Angela Williams Urquhart

Cover image: Copyright © Photodisc

ISBN: 0-15-506979-9
Library of Congress Catalog Card Number has been requested.

Address for Domestic Orders
Harcourt College Publishers, 6277 Sea Harbor Drive, Orlando, FL 32887-6777
800-782-4479

Address for International Orders
International Customer Service
Harcourt College Publishers, 6277 Sea Harbor Drive, Orlando, FL 32887-6777
407-345-3800
(fax) 407-345-4060
(e-mail) hbintl@harcourtbrace.com

Address for Editorial Correspondence
Harcourt College Publishers, 301 Commerce Street, Suite 3700, Fort Worth, TX 76102

Web Site Address
http://www.harcourtcollege.com

Harcourt College Publishers will provide complimentary supplements or supplement packages to those adopters qualified under our adoption policy. Please contact your sales representative to learn how you qualify. If as an adopter or potential user you receive supplements you do not need, please return them to your sales representative or send them to:
Attn: Returns Department, Troy Warehouse, 465 South Lincoln Drive, Troy, MO 63379.

Printed in the United States of America

0 1 2 3 4 5 6 7 8 9   202   9 8 7 6 5 4 3 2 1

Harcourt College Publishers

✳

Preface

The Resourceful Reader, Fifth Edition, is designed expressly to accompany _The Writer's Harbrace Handbook._ This unique design provides a harmonious interaction between handbook and reader and, as a result, offers the instructor unprecedented efficiency in teaching. The sixty-six readings are arranged rhetorically in chapters according to the developmental strategies—namely, example, narration, description, process, cause and effect, comparison and contrast, classification and division, definition, and argument—outlined in Section 2e of _The Writer's Harbrace Handbook._ In four additional chapters, _The Resourceful Reader_ presents the arguments of a debate, the essay examination, the research paper, and a collection of classic essays. The readings balance classroom favorites with pieces seldom or never reprinted and amply represent a diversity of sources. Fifteen student essays appear throughout the book.

The Resourceful Reader offers numerous features that up to now have been lacking in the leading anthologies available for the teaching of writing:

- The pedagogical apparatus accompanying each reading focuses not only on meaning, purpose, audience, and rhetorical strategy in the whole essay but also on effective paragraphs, grammar, punctuation and mechanics, diction, effective sentences, and vocabulary building—all with references to pertinent discussions in _The Writer's Harbrace Handbook._
- "Argument" (Chapter 9) is followed by a minicasebook (Chapter 10) entitled "A Life-And-Death Issue Debated: The Environment," six short essays that present a variety of arguments, rhetorical strategies, and personal styles brought to bear on a single important issue.
- "The Essay Examination: A Student Writer across the Disciplines" (Chapter 11) allows students to follow one undergraduate, Anne Nishijima, as she responds to the special demands of the essay test in the social sciences, the humanities, and science.
- Four documented papers supplement those in _The Writer's Harbrace Handbook._ Two are by students (in Chapter 12, "Writing from Research") and follow the Modern Language Association's (MLA) and American Psychological Association's (APA) styles of documentation. Two in other sections are by professionals—one with MLA documentation in the text and one in an older documentation style that uses _Ibid._ and footnotes.

• "Building Vocabulary," a new feature in the fourth edition, offers questions that encourage students to discover the origin and meanings of words. Drawing from the vocabulary used in the professionally written readings, these questions not only ask students to define words but to isolate and combine prefixes, suffixes, and roots, to identify and define synonyms and antonyms, and to use new words in their own sentences.

The general introduction stresses the interaction between reading and writing, focusing first on how active, critical reading informs writing—"Reading To Write"—and then on the writing process—"Writing To Be Read." It concludes with "About This Book," some suggestions to the student for making the most of the various features of *The Resourceful Reader.*

Chapter introductions explain the rhetorical strategies exemplified by the readings. Within both the general introduction and the chapter introductions, as well as the questions after individual readings, references connect *The Resourceful Reader* with *The Writer's Harbrace Handbook.* Each chapter introduction concludes with an annotated student essay that illustrates the principles discussed in the introduction. Noteworthy features of the student essay are identified in the margin, and a subsequent commentary discusses the writer's strategies and choices. Though possible further improvements to student essays are sometimes noted, the emphasis in the commentaries is always positive, stressing the student's *achievement.* Each professionally written piece is introduced by a note that places the essay into a context, sometimes social, cultural, or biographical.

Throughout, *The Resourceful Reader* aims to demonstrate for students that "the rules"—necessarily presented concisely in a handbook—are not arbitrary but are simply principles that good writers apply in writing purposeful compositions. Each reading is followed by a strong pedagogical apparatus that includes two sets of questions keyed to *The Writer's Harbrace Handbook.* Questions under "Responding to the Whole Essay" ask students to consider audience, purpose, and other concerns of the "Writing" section (Chapters 1–10). References to the Handbook in the questions help students apply the Handbook principles to the readings. Questions under "Analyzing the Elements" explore the concerns of Handbook Chapters 11–35. Students are asked to consider grammatical issues (Chapters 11–17) in relation to *meaning,* not merely "the rules." "Effective Sentences" questions (referring to Chapters 18–23) often ask students to experiment with alternative structures of their own devising or to comment on the difference, in effect, between the writer's version and an alternative supplied in the question. "Diction" questions explore the concerns of Chapters 24–26, and "Punctuation and Mechanics" questions explore the concerns of Chapters 26–32. Questions under "Building Vocabulary" provide students with an opportunity to discover the origins and meanings of words and to practice using these words in their own sentences. Throughout, the questions in *The Resourceful Reader* emphasize *choice:* students are continually asked to put themselves in the writer's place and evaluate the writer's options. Finally, "Suggestions for Writing" are provided for each reading. These writing assignments are always related to the reading but are designed to afford students considerable freedom of choice.

A further advantage of *The Resourceful Reader* is that each reading observes as well as illustrates the principles in *The Writer's Harbrace Handbook:* no dangling modifiers, inexplicable fragments, or improper verb and case forms will crop up that the instructor has to excuse to the observant student. For example, where writers deliberately use fragments or where closely related independent clauses are connected by commas without a conjunction, the student is asked to analyze why and in each instance is also referred to the appropriate section of the handbook. Not even the best of writers, of course, is exempt from occasional infelicity, a pronoun reference that could be clearer, a modifier that squints a little. Where these rare lapses do appear, they are addressed—turned *to* pedagogical advantage in the questions—rather than left unnoted to perplex the alert student and mislead the unwary.

The alternate list of contents by subject is intended to enhance the book's flexibility and to suggest combinations of essays that can spark classroom discussion or further writing assignments. An author–title index makes selections easy to find. As a further aid to the busy instructor, an *Instructor's Manual* is available.

Acknowledgments.   Numerous people have rendered invaluable help and advice in the preparation of *The Resourceful Reader,* for which we are very grateful. Dr. Hilary Broadbent, formerly a student at Barnard College, provided help with student essays, as did Leslie Bivens, formerly a student at Texas Woman's University. Keisha Jackson wrote the new student essay illustrating comparison and contrast. My continuing thanks go to those students in previous classes whose essays were first printed in an earlier edition of this text: Jackie Nye, Roy Fowler, Lisa Garrett, Maya Ramirez, Nandina Brownell, Lauren Reismann, Tim Ellis, Carol Johnson, Oshunkentan Solomon, Anne Nishijima, Bill Wallace, and Barbara Kiger.

My continuing thanks go also to those who were particularly helpful and supportive with earlier editions: Kimberly Allison, Tom Broadbent, Marilyn Keef, Bob Miller, and Larry Mapp and Michael Rosenberg. Debts of other kinds are owed to James Galloway, Texas Woman's University Library, who rendered valuable assistance locating material in local libraries, and John Hepner, also of the TWU library, who proved repeatedly his uncanny ability to ferret out hard-to-locate facts.

At Harcourt College Publishers, my thanks go to senior developmental editor Michell Phifer, senior project manager Angela Urquhart, and sales managers Ellen Wynn and Tom Hall, all of whom have made valuable suggestions and given other kinds of useful help.

Special thanks go to Lou Thompson, my friend and colleague, without whose hard work I would still be looking for new essays, writing new exercises, trying to whip a manuscript into final shape, and struggling with permissions. For doing all that for me, she deserves not only to have her name appear in large type on the title page, but also to have profuse thanks in this preface. Her judgment and skill are apparent throughout the book. And of course, no set of acknowledgments would be complete without expressing my thanks to my family; to my husband, Dick, who takes care of everything else when I am in the midst of working on a book; and to Aaron and Karl, my grown sons of whom I am inordinately proud, who generously agree, edition after edition, to be guinea pigs for exercises, and who give good advice about essays and topics for student papers.

Contents

3 Description   85

4 Process   121

11 The Essay Examination: A Student Writer across the Disciplines   385

12 Writing from Research   397

*

Contents Arranged by Subject

Contemporary Issues

Cultural Values and Manners

Death

Education

Environment

Families

Growing Up

Philosophy and Belief

Places and Local Color

Politics

Psychology and Behavior

Science and Technology

Society and Morality

Tradition

War and Weapons

Women

Work and Business

The Resourceful Reader

FIFTH EDITION

Readings to accompany
The Writer's Harbrace Handbook

Introduction

Reading to Write, Writing to Be Read

Imagine you are digging on an archaeological site and one day you unearth a pot, intricately patterned, variously colored, miraculously whole after centuries of burial. As you hold the pot in your hand, your mind moves from admiration of the object to speculation about how, and by whom, it was created—an awareness that the pot is an artifact, something made by human hands and human intellect. Chances are, however, that it was not made on the first try. Not only did the potter probably have to make hundreds of pots to acquire the skill to produce those graceful lines, but also he or she undoubtedly shaped and reshaped the clay to get that very pot just right. Yet all you have is the pot. The earlier versions are gone, absorbed long ago into the final lovely thing you hold in your hand, and no record of the potter's labor to create it survives.

The essays in this book, too, are artifacts, things created by human intellect. The writers, like the potter, began with nothing more than their own hands and minds and experience. As readers, we see their finished creations, complete and as nearly perfect as the writers could make them—scarcely a seam anywhere, scarcely a lump or lopsidedness. Faced with a finished essay, readers seldom think much about the process (slow, seldom straightforward, often downright messy) that produced it—seldom are aware of how the writer may have labored to discover what was worth saying, then struggled to get the right words into phrases, clauses, sentences, paragraphs—that would enable the reader to re-create, from black marks on a page, the ideas that were in the writer's mind. Like anything made with skill and effort, the essay looks easy and natural—just as the writer wanted it to look.

But as you read the essays, you can reconstruct (though not perfectly) the process the writer went through, and in doing so learn much about writing well. This kind of reading requires the investment of time, effort, and attention, but it is an investment that will return a large profit because reading and writing go together: reading improves your writing, and writing makes you a better reader. When you tackle an essay as an active, involved reader, you go through much of the same process that you go through to write an essay, only in reverse. Beginning with the finished product, you take it apart to see how another writer met challenges similar to those you face when you write. As you analyze the many kinds of choices the writer made, you increase your understanding of the options available to you. Reading can be a rehearsal for writing. *The Resourceful Reader,* designed to be used along with the first edition of the *Writer's Harbrace Handbook,* provides the materials for that rehearsal. You, of course, must supply the effort.

Reading to Write.   To get the most from any essay, you should read it at least twice, the first time for a general idea of what the writer is saying, the second time—and perhaps more times—to see how the writer has gone about saying it, to examine all the means the writer used to make the essay work.

As you reread the essay, do so actively, pencil in hand to jot down notes in the margin or mark important ideas. Certain kinds of information you can look for will help you understand many of the decisions the writer made while writing. Perhaps the most basic consideration is *purpose*—what the writer intends to accomplish in the essay. Is the author's aim to inform the reader, focusing on the topic as objectively as possible, as John McPhee does in "Excerpt from *Assembling California*" (Chapter 3)? Or is the purpose to persuade, to sway the reader to take some action or adopt some point of view the writer considers desirable? For instance, "The Gift of Wilderness" (Chapter 9) is one of many pieces in which Wallace Stegner has argued eloquently that we must act now to preserve what wilderness we have left. And sometimes writers are not so much concerned to inform or persuade a reader as to express themselves—that is, to explore and share their own personal feelings and responses, as John Hockenberry does in his moving "The Hockenberry Files" (Chapter 2). But the question of purpose is not a simple one. As you read, bear in mind that in any effective piece of writing one purpose or another is likely to be dominant, but other purposes are sure to be present to some degree. Although Hockenberry's primary aim is to provide information, his essay certainly contains expressive elements, and unquestionably it aims to persuade us of something, too. And Stegner's "The Gift of Wilderness," though chiefly persuasive, is both informative and wonderfully expressive. (See 1g[1] for further discussion of purpose.)

Whatever the writer's purpose, to be successful in achieving it the writer must have a clear sense of *audience*—indeed, purpose and audience can scarcely be separated, since all writing is presumably meant to be read by someone (if only the writer, as with a diary or a grocery list). You can learn a great deal about writing effectively for your own audiences from considering how other writers have written for theirs. Occasionally you will find that the writer explicitly names the intended audience, but more often you will have to infer from clues what kind of audience the writer had in mind. (One possible clue is external: if what you are reading has been published in, for example, a magazine—as some of the reprinted essays in this book originally were—what kind of audience is that magazine aimed at?) Consider the tone of the essay, for tone reflects the writer's attitude toward the audience as well as toward the subject (see 1g[2]). Does the writer seem to assume that the audience will be sympathetic? Interested? Indifferent? Hostile? Consider, too, the writer's assumptions about the reader's knowledge. Does the writer either take pains to define specialized words or confine the vocabulary to words most general readers would be likely to understand? A piece written for specialists will assume considerable knowledge on the part of the reader and is likely to use a specialized vocabulary. (Although none of the essays in this book were written for highly specialized audiences, you can see a sample of such writing in 1g.)

With the writer's purpose and intended audience clearly in mind, you will be ready to focus more specifically on other elements of the essay. Look for the *thesis*—the central or controlling idea, the main point the writer is making. Being able to pick out and evaluate the thesis of a piece of writing is the very essence of active reading. Often the thesis is stated, but if it is not, it will be implicit in what the writer has to say about the subject. Even in a piece of writing that is mainly descriptive, there will be some focus or reason for describing, some dominant impression the writer means to create in the reader's mind; the details will not be randomly chosen. Similarly, in a narrative some attitude toward the events will be suggested—if not explicitly, then implicitly through the writer's choice of events and details and of language appropriate to the writer's view. (For more discussion of thesis, see 2b.)

One of the most practical things you can do as a reader trying to become a better writer is to pay attention to how other writers use the various *methods of development* (around which the first nine chapters of this book are organized): (1) example, (2) narration, (3) description, (4) process, (5) cause and effect, (6) comparison and contrast, (7) classification and division, (8) definition, and (9) argument. These are not hollow forms into which writers pour sentences to make essays; they are fundamental *thinking* strategies, basic ways human beings make sense of the world and communicate that sense to one another. Terms such as *narration* and *classification* may sound forbidding and technical, but if you run through the list of strategies again and consider the kinds of common questions each strategy answers, you will see how natural these methods are:

- What are some instances?—example
- What happened (or is happening)?—narration
- How does it look (feel, taste, smell, sound)?—description
- How does this work? How is this done?—process
- Why did this happen? What will be the result?—cause and effect
- What is it like? How is it different?—comparison and contrast
- What kinds are there?—classification and division
- What is it? What does it mean?—definition
- What should be done? What should we believe?—argument

Understanding and practicing these strategies will do more than teach you how to organize essays. You will use them every day, not only in all of your college courses but also in virtually every part of your life beyond the campus. (See also 2e.)

Consider an essay's introduction, conclusion, and title. Does the introduction arouse your interest and get you oriented in the essay by suggesting what it is about? Would you have introduced the essay differently? Why? Does the conclusion bring the essay to a satisfying close? Is the title appropriate? How does it serve (and reveal) the writer's purposes? Does it help to establish the tone of the essay? (See also 3b.)

Analyze the essay for logic and for unity and coherence. Has the writer avoided logical fallacies? (See also 1.) Are there digressions, irrelevancies? What kinds of signposts does the writer provide to help readers follow the thought from paragraph to paragraph and sentence to sentence? Are the ideas presented in the most effective order? Is each idea adequately developed? Try to see how the writer's concern about these issues has contributed to making the essay effective. If you find weaknesses (no writer is perfect), ask yourself how the writer might have done better. (See also 2a[1] and 3c.)

Consider the essay at the level of the sentence and the word, with an eye to what you can learn for your own use as a writer. How are sentences constructed to avoid monotony, to achieve the exact emphasis desired, to convey the relationships among ideas precisely? Is anything unclear—for instance, the reference of a pronoun or the relation of a modifier to what it modifies? Are there awkward constructions or inappropriate choices of words or of figurative language to distract or confuse the reader? Can you think of better choices the writer could have made? Conversely, where the writer has said something more effectively than you think you would have said it yourself, see if you can explain the difference. (As you think about such matters, you will find *Writer's* a useful reference, especially 11–17 and 18–26.)

The writer's choices regarding punctuation and mechanics are also worth studying. Even though punctuation and mechanics are governed to a considerable extent by convention, there are more choices to be made than you realize—including, of course, the choice to be "correct," to avoid violating the conventions in ways that would distract the reader and undermine your credibility, thereby interfering with communication. Ask questions as you read: Why has the writer chosen to set off a particular parenthetical expression with dashes instead of parentheses or commas, when either of these alternatives would also be acceptable? Why has the writer put that word in italics when regular type would also have been correct? Why did the writer choose a semicolon between two clauses instead of a period, or instead of a comma and a coordinating conjunction? Why is a colon better here than a semicolon? Why is this hyphen necessary? (Such decisions and many others are considered in 27–35.)

As you consider all the choices, large and small, that other writers have made, you are continually reconstructing the processes they went through and, in a very real sense, rehearsing for your own writing. Let's now focus on what happens when you write for other readers.

Writing to Be Read.   Writing is never done in a vacuum. When you write, you are always in a specific situation that involves an *audience* (that is, a known or perhaps hypothetical reader, whose background and interests you must consider); a *purpose* for writing, something you mean to accomplish; and a *subject*, something you will write about. Often your writing situation will clearly dictate your subject; for instance, essay examinations in college courses often specify a topic, and letters and reports written on the job usually deal with subjects that are either assigned or obvious. When the subject is given, your purpose may seem obvious, too, but you will usually find it worthwhile to consider your purpose a little more carefully: it may not be as simple as you think. Consider the essay examination again. If the question is "Explain the difference between the budget deficit and the national debt," your purpose seems clear enough: *to explain.* And explain you must, of course, if you want to receive credit. But consider: your instructor *knows* the difference between the budget deficit and the national debt; so your main purpose is to *convince* the instructor, by your explanation, that you have mastered certain basic concepts. Similarly, much business writing is devoted primarily to giving information, but if the writers were not just as much concerned with persuasive aims—giving a favorable impression and winning customers—as with conveying information, business letters might read like this: "Dear Client: The widgets cost $5.00. Yours truly."

In a college writing course, you may sometimes be entirely free to choose your own subject. If you are, you can write an interesting paper on almost any subject you care about. Think about your personal knowledge, interest, and beliefs. What have you read lately? Do you know an interesting character? Has some particular place made a special impression on you? What do you do when you're not in school? Do you work? Do you have some special interest such as photography or playing in a band? What ambitions do you have for yourself? What are your convictions? What makes you angry? You can find subjects in any of these questions for papers that will interest other people.

More often, however, your freedom to choose will be limited in some way. Outside a composition classroom, rarely will you be free to choose a subject drawn from your own experience. For instance, your geology professor may give you complete freedom to write on any aspect of geology that interests you, but you are expected to write a paper demonstrating your mastery of some part of the subject matter of the course. Geologists are interested in mountains, but a paper about the elation you experienced when you successfully completed a difficult ascent of Mount St. Helens, despite the fact that the mountain is an active volcano, will not do. In such a situation, instead of relying on personal experience, look for an interesting subject in your textbook, in your lecture notes, in the subject catalog in the library; talk to other students or to your professor.

Whatever your subject, your writing task will be easier and your finished composition more effective if you take some time to explore your subject and get it sharply in focus before you begin drafting. You can use a number of different methods to generate ideas about your subject: listing, questioning, applying different perspectives, and surveying possible development strategies. (See 2a[1].) Limiting and focusing a subject mean putting boundaries around it—perhaps reducing its scope—to make it manageable and, as with the subject of a photograph, deciding on the particular angle from which you will view it, what you will highlight and what you will eliminate as extraneous. (See 2a[2].) Constructing a clear, specific thesis statement can help you decide whether you have limited and focused your subject sufficiently and will also help you stay on the track as you draft the essay. (See 2b.)

If you have carefully considered your subject and purpose, chances are that the appropriate method of development will follow naturally. For instance, if exploring possible subjects for a history term paper led you to focus on striking similarities between two battles that occurred in different wars, the development strategy of comparison and contrast would suggest itself to you. If, however, your main interest was in discovering what events and conditions had led to these confrontations, you would quite naturally find yourself using the strategy of cause and effect. As we've noted, these development strategies are ways in which our minds naturally work. Your problem is rarely to choose appropriate development strategies but rather to employ them effectively. Reading and, above all, practice—writing—are the ways to learn.

Often—especially for a long paper—you may find it helpful to write down some kind of plan, an informal or even formal outline of your main ideas in what seems the most effective order, to guide you as you write (2c). Remember, however, that such a plan is not written in stone; you can change it if you need to, and you probably will. When you begin drafting your essay, try writing quickly, without much concern for matters such as spelling, punctuation, and usage, which you can revise later. Most writers find that this approach is the most productive. The point is to get your ideas to flow as freely as you can, while keeping your purpose and audience in mind. Incidentally, no law says that you must begin at the beginning and slog straight through to the end in spite of any difficulties you may encounter on the way. Some writers find that writing chunks or blocks of an essay without worrying about the order makes their ideas flow more freely; then they put the chunks together, reshaping and connecting them as necessary. If you run out of steam in one part of your essay, try moving to another part you feel more comfortable with. Also, some writers find that when they're stuck it may help to turn back to what they've already written and look for ways to improve it, correcting errors, finding more exact words, restructuring sentences, or making paragraphs more coherent. (This is revision, but you don't have to wait until you have a complete draft to engage in it. You are, in fact, revising all the time, even as you are planning.) The value of this procedure is that it keeps you engaged with the essay while your unconscious mind has a chance to work on the problem that stopped you. However, you may find that sometimes the best remedy is simply to take a break and think about something entirely different for a while—perhaps take a walk or cook dinner—to give your mental batteries an opportunity to recharge, and then come back fresh to the draft. Researchers on creativity have found that breakthroughs commonly occur when the individual has first struggled hard to solve a problem and then temporarily turned away from it to think of something else. Experiment and find a method that works for you. You aren't exactly like anyone else; your writing process won't be exactly like anyone else's, either. (See 2f.)

When you have a complete draft, set it aside for a time (if possible a few days, but at least overnight). When you come back to it, try to see it as though someone else had written it. Reading it aloud may help—or having someone else read it to you. Go over your draft several times, looking first at the larger elements—unity and coherence, the arrangement and development of ideas, logic, and so on. What, if anything, is irrelevant? If you find material that is unrelated to your central idea, be ruthless in cutting it out. Where could your reader have difficulty seeing how an idea is related to the ones before it? Supply a transitional expression. Where do you need to provide more details to make yourself clear, and where are you guilty of overkill? (See 3a.)

Once you are reasonably satisfied with the overall shape of the essay, turn to the smaller elements. (The reason for looking at large things first is that it is more efficient: solving large problems often eliminates many smaller problems, too.) Read your sentences over. What kinds of changes will make them more effective? Can any words be replaced with more appropriate or exact ones? Look for problems with grammar, punctuation, mechanics, and spelling, and make whatever changes are needed. (You may wish to read Donald M. Murray's "The Maker's Eye: Revising Your Own Manuscripts" in Chapter 4.)

When you have done your best, or the time comes when you must stop, put your essay into acceptable manuscript form. (See 4.) Except in special circumstances, such as when writing an in-class essay or taking an examination (see 8), make a clean copy, following your instructor's guidelines or those in 3 and 20. Even if you are writing in class, reserve time to make sure that your insertions and deletions are clear and that your paper is as neat as you can make it. A little forethought will go a long way here to avoid problems.

About This Book. Each of the first nine chapters of *The Resourceful Reader* focuses on one of the basic development strategies (or methods) that you will use in your college writing—and in all the writing you do. (These methods of development are also discussed in 2e in connection with paragraphs and in 2a as a tool for generating ideas about a subject.) The introduction to each chapter defines and explains the method, offers advice about using it, and concludes with an annotated student essay, illustrating it. Several essays from diverse sources follow. The authors of the selections have strikingly different personalities and voices, and they write on different subjects, with various purposes and for various audiences—but all use the particular development strategy being studied. A brief note that puts the essay into a social, cultural, or biographical context precedes each essay.

At the end of each selection, you will find several sets of questions. The first set, "Responding to the Whole Essay," directs your attention to overall considerations such as purpose, intended audience, and tone; thesis or central idea; method of development; coherence and unity; and so forth. This set of questions focuses on concerns treated in sections 1–10 of the *Writer's Harbrace Handbook*. The second set of questions, "Analyzing the Elements," is divided into four parts, corresponding to sections of the *Writer's Harbrace Handbook* as follows: grammar (11–17), effective sentences (18–22), punctuation and mechanics (27–35), diction (23–26). Most of the individual questions contain references to specific discussions in the *Handbook*, which you can turn to if you need background information or simply want to read further. Answering these questions will start you thinking about the kinds of choices writers make—choices that are sometimes conscious ones, but often are unconscious. A conscious awareness on your part of the decisions other writers made will help you when you are faced with similar choices. A new set of questions, "Building Vocabulary," will help you understand where words come from and what they mean.

Following the questions you will find "Suggestions for Writing"—ideas for writing projects (usually two) related in some way to the reading selection and designed to give you practice at meeting some of the challenges the author of the selection confronted.

Chapter 10, "A Life and Death Issue Debated: The Environment," is a special feature: a group of six essays all centering on a single controversial issue. The questions for this chapter are somewhat different in focus from those for Chapters 1 through 9.

Finally, Chapters 11 through 13 are entirely different from the chapters that precede them—and from each other. You may find Chapter 11 one of the most interesting and immediately useful in the book. Here we see one student, Anne Nishijima, coping successfully with essay examinations in three different college courses: humanities, social science, and natural science. This chapter, together with section 8 on writing under pressure, can be of immediate practical help to you in your various college courses, and you may want to look at it even before it is assigned.

Chapter 12 illustrates the documented research paper—of which you will probably have to write a considerable number in the course of your college work—with two student papers to supplement those in section 7 and 9. As you use this chapter, bear in mind that two of the essays in Chapters 1 through 9 are also documented papers, giving you a total—between *Writer's Harbrace Handbook* and *The Resourceful Reader*—of nine model research papers that you can consult for help with your own papers. (All nine are mentioned in the introduction to Chapter 12.)

Finally, no college writing anthology would be complete without some of the great pieces gathered in Chapter 13, "For Further Reading: Some Classic Essays." Your instructor may not be able to work all seven of these essays into the course, but try to read them on your own. These are great voices, some from the distant past, some more recent, that speak powerfully to us.

If the subject of a particular essay happens to interest you and you would like to find other pieces dealing with the same or a closely related subject, you may wish to consult the listings in "Contents Arranged by Subject," which follows the regular table of contents. You can get a further glimpse of the content of various essays by looking at the brief annotations after their titles in the table of contents. Incidentally, very interesting papers can often be written comparing essays that approach the same subject with different rhetorical strategies. If you find yourself looking for a writing topic, you might consider this possibility, especially later on in the course when you have read essays in several different sections of *The Resourceful Reader*.

However you use *The Resourceful Reader* in your particular writing course, its editor hopes that you will enjoy it and learn much from it—as she did in preparing it. Here's wishing you good reading and writing!

＊

Chapter 1

Example

One of the simplest but most effective ways for a writer to get an idea across clearly and forcefully is to provide a striking example or series of examples. In fact, a whole essay can be built with examples, as the readings in this chapter demonstrate.

An example may be as short as a word or two—for instance, a brief reference to a well-known figure (called an allusion):

> As Robin Hood and Baby Face Nelson show us, you don't always get what you pay for. Sometimes you get what others paid for. When a whole society begins to operate on that principle, that society is in trouble.
>
> —T. Breitfeld

Or a single example might extend to several pages. For instance (note that this phrase means "for *example*"), an essay aiming to persuade readers to support a program for the poor might rely on an account of one day in a family's struggle to live with dignity below the poverty line.

How will you know if you have used enough examples? There is no easy rule; perhaps the best advice is to put yourself in your reader's shoes and then ask yourself whether, from the reader's point of view, your points are as clear as they need to be. An essay discussing the horrors of college registration might benefit from two or three well-chosen examples but become tedious with more. On the other hand, an essay defining terrorism might require many examples to convey the complexity of that subject. The decision depends on your subject and purpose and, as always, the needs of your audience. In this chapter, Dave Barry's subject, the college experience, requires numerous brief examples, as does Jack Hitt's essay on SUVs. Eric Minton, however, combines short examples and extended ones in his essay about roller coasters and haunted houses.

A single striking example often makes an effective beginning for an essay, quickly capturing the reader's interest while it prepares the way for the writer's main idea, or thesis. Banesh Hoffmann begins "My Friend, Albert Einstein" with a memorable anecdote that establishes his main point: Einstein's astonishing simplicity. Once that idea has been stated, Hoffmann presents a number of other examples to develop it.

Sometimes you will want to give each example a paragraph of its own; at other times you may find that it works well to group several related examples in a single paragraph [2d(2)]. And of course an extended example may require several or even many paragraphs.

A danger in using examples is that they may be so engrossing that you lose sight of the point you are trying to make. Keep your purpose and your point in mind. Another danger is that just as too few examples can make an essay weak, too many can overload it. Be selective (even ruthless) in choosing which examples you will use. Keep only the best.

Choosing examples is only part of the battle; you must also arrange them effectively. Any of several organizing principles might be appropriate: time, space, complexity, or importance. For a fuller discussion, see [3c].

In the following essay, student Jackie Nye uses both brief and extended examples to explain how the reader might use relaxation techniques to reduce stress.

Stressed to the Max?

Major report due on Monday? Research project moving too slowly? Family making demands? Grade-point in jeopardy? In a hurry-up world where deadlines crowd the pages of our day planners and where the push to produce seems paramount, finding ways to relax becomes increasingly important. Whether we need to recover from a busy day at the office or unwind from a semester of nonstop study, relaxation techniques invariably offer effective therapy.

For instance, at day's end a long, leisurely soak in a warm eucalyptus-scented bath can loosen stiff, aching muscles, and a cup of good herbal tea can soothe the soul. A particularly stressful day may call for a deeper form of relaxation therapy, such as seeking a quiet place undisturbed by outside interruptions and influences and, once there, meditating to clear the mind. For many, meditation coupled with a few minutes of yoga exercises results in a refreshed mind and body.

No time to get away for that quiet cup of tea? Too overwhelmed for solitary meditation? Deep breathing exercises offer an impromptu way to relax any time. Inhale and exhale slowly. While inhaling, imagine breathing in all good, nurturing forces; while exhaling, picture the stream of exhaled air carrying away all the negative, unhappy, unproductive thoughts. Ten deep breaths are usually enough to produce renewed vigor and well-being.

Margin labels:

Generalization —thesis

Two brief examples

Third brief example

Transition

Extended example illustrating one method

Example 15

Topic, restriction, series of illustrations

Time and finances permitting, try a professional massage for an effortless way to relax. Feel the cares of the world melt away in the skilled hands of a massage therapist as warm oil is rubbed into the skin and muscles are gently kneaded. With such lavish attention, every muscle from the scalp to the toes tingles with increased circulation. In fact, massage can produce such a state of euphoria that some people report feeling as though they are floating on air. And experiencing the benefits of massage does not require the time and money to linger at a spa. This treatment can be enjoyed regularly by making a standing appointment with a local massage therapist or by learning massage basics with a friend or significant other.

Transition

For those with the time and the money, a residential spa may be the answer. Planned exercise, managed diet, massage, and cosmetic pampering can make the cares of the world disappear for a few days.

Brief example leading into an extended example illustrating a closely related point

For those who feel the need for an extended period to rest and relax, an ocean cruise is hard to beat. Experienced, efficient ship's crew members attend to mundane matters and the gentle rocking of the ship enhances nightly sleep. No ringing phones jangle the nerves, no business crises require immediate attention—just seabreezes, good food and entertainment, exotic ports of call, and best of all, isolation from everyday cares. A week of this kind of pampering is a sure way to relax and restore the body and mind for returning to the real world.

Extended transition to a new point

Everyone needs to relax at various times, but choosing an effective means depends on time, money, and physical ability. And it also depends upon the kind and degree of stress to be overcome. A few simple neck rolls may be enough to relieve the tense shoulder muscles that come from long hours at a

New point

desk. Life-threatening high stress from a major change in lifestyle or work environment can cause high blood pressure or other kinds of heart disease and calls for more drastic measures. A daily regimen of exercise and meditation combined with a good diet may be

Brief example

enough to keep stress-induced high blood pressure from rising beyond an acceptable level. A healthy body is a relaxed body.

Example using allusion

Health concerns give the art of relaxation new importance, so in the search for that perfectly relaxed state of balanced mind and muscle, it is worth remembering the wisdom of the Greek Stoic philosopher Epictetus. He taught that what affects us in life is not so much what happens to us as it is how we react to what happens to us.

Conclusion summarizes and points to future

While stress is inevitable, how to reduce or eliminate it to maintain health or simply avoid interference with daily living is a matter of individual choice. So choose well and choose often the way you wish to relax, and then the stress of hurrying to produce with deadlines to meet can work for you instead of against you.

Commentary.   Jackie Nye gets the reader's attention with a catchy opening sentence and keeps it by including interesting examples. Her introduction suggests that the stressful environment we all live in is reason enough to be interested in knowing more about managing stress.

Nye's organization is more complex than it may seem at first. She begins with simple, inexpensive remedies and then takes up the more expensive ones. And the simple remedies are, incidentally, those we can do for ourselves, whereas the expensive remedies require outside sources for fulfillment. In addition, Nye begins with remedies for relatively low levels of stress. As the essay moves along, the remedies address increasingly higher levels of stress. The climax of the essay is the paragraph in which she talks about the dangers to health that can result from unrelieved stress. Nye here points out that a change of lifestyle may be the necessary therapy for stress-induced hypertension.

Nye also uses a mix of brief and extended examples. In the second paragraph, she explains three ways to relax. The third paragraph focuses on a single technique, deep breathing. She signals that she is about to conclude when she refers to Epictetus, and then she sums up and challenges her readers to find suitable relaxation techniques.

My Friend, Albert Einstein
Banesh Hoffmann

Banesh Hoffmann (1906–1986) was born in England, the son of Polish immigrants, and educated at Oxford University and Princeton University. A distinguished mathematician and physicist, he taught briefly at the University of Rochester and then for forty years at Queens College of the City University of New York. He was also a member of Princeton's Institute for Advanced Study, and it was there, in 1935, that he came to know Albert Einstein, with whom he worked on a paper, "Gravitational Equations and the Problem of Motion." Author of numerous books during his long career, among them *The Strange Story of the Quantum* (1947) and *The Tyranny of Testing* (1962), Hoffmann wrote three books about Einstein: *Albert Einstein: Creator and Rebel* (1972) and *Albert Einstein: The Human Side* (1979), both with Einstein's personal secretary, Helen Dukas; and *Albert Einstein* (1975).

1   He was one of the greatest scientists the world has ever known, yet it I had to convey the essence of Albert Einstein in a single word, I would choose *simplicity*. Perhaps an anecdote will help. Once, caught in a downpour, he took off his hat and held it under his coat. Asked why, he explained, with admirable logic, that the rain would damage the hat, but his hair would be none the worse for its wetting. This knack for going instinctively to the heart of a matter was the secret of his major scientific discoveries—this and his extraordinary feeling for beauty.

2   I first met Albert Einstein in 1935, at the famous Institute for Advanced Study in Princeton, N.J. He had been among the first to be invited to the Institute, and was offered *carte blanche* as to salary. To the director's dismay, Einstein asked for an impossible sum: it was far too *small*. The director had to plead with him to accept a larger salary.

3   I was in awe of Einstein, and hesitated before approaching him about some ideas I had been working on. When I finally knocked on his door, a gentle voice said, "Come"—with a rising inflection that made the single word both a welcome and a question. I entered his office and found him seated at a table, calculating and smoking his pipe. Dressed in ill-fitting clothes, his hair characteristically awry, he smiled a warm welcome. His utter naturalness at once set me at ease.

4   As I began to explain my ideas, he asked me to write the equations on the blackboard so he could see how they developed. Then came the staggering—and altogether endearing—request: "Please go slowly. I do not understand things quickly." This from Einstein! He said it gently, and I laughed. From then on, all vestiges of fear were gone.

Einstein was born in 1879 in the German city of Ulm. He had been no   5
infant prodigy; indeed, he was so late in learning to speak that his parents
feared he was a dullard. In school, though his teachers saw no special talent
in him, the signs were already there. He taught himself calculus, for example,
and his teachers seemed a little afraid of him because he asked questions they
could not answer. At the age of sixteen, he asked himself whether a light wave
would seem stationary if one ran abreast of it. From that innocent question
would arise, ten years later, his theory of relativity.

Einstein failed his entrance examinations at the Swiss Federal Polytechnic   6
School, in Zurich, but was admitted a year later. There he went beyond his
regular work to study the masterworks of physics on his own. Rejected when
he applied for academic positions, he ultimately found work, in 1902, as a
patent examiner in Berne, and there in 1905 his genius burst into fabulous
flower.

Among the extraordinary things he produced in that memorable year were   7
his theory of relativity, with its famous offshoot, $E = mc^2$ (energy equals mass
times the speed of light squared), and his quantum theory of light. These two
theories were not only revolutionary, but seemingly contradictory: the former
was intimately linked to the theory that light consists of waves, while the latter said it consists somehow of particles. Yet this unknown young man boldly
proposed both at once—and he was right in both cases, though how he could
have been is far too complex a story to tell here.

Collaborating with Einstein was an unforgettable experience. In 1937, the   8
Polish physicist Leopold Infeld and I asked if we could work with him. He
was pleased with the proposal, since he had an idea about gravitation waiting to be worked out in detail. Thus we got to know not merely the man and
the friend, but also the professional.

The intensity and depth of his concentration were fantastic. When bat-   9
tling a recalcitrant problem, he worried it as an animal worries its prey. Often,
when we found ourselves up against a seemingly insuperable difficulty, he
would stand up, put his pipe on the table, and say in his quaint English, "I
will a little tink" (he could not pronounce "th"). Then he would pace up and
down, twirling a lock of his long, graying hair around his forefinger.

A dreamy, faraway and yet inward look would come over his face. There   10
was no appearance of concentration, no furrowing of the brow—only a placid
inner communion. The minutes would pass, and then suddenly Einstein would
stop pacing as his face relaxed into a gentle smile. He had found the solution
to the problem. Sometimes it was so simple that Infeld and I could have kicked
ourselves for not having thought of it. But the magic had been performed invisibly in the depths of Einstein's mind, by a process we could not fathom.

When his wife died he was deeply shaken, but insisted that now more than   11
ever was the time to be working hard. I remember going to his home to work
with him during that sad time. His face was haggard and grief-lined, but he
put forth a great effort to concentrate. To help him, I steered the discussion
away from routine matters into more difficult theoretical problems, and Einstein

gradually became absorbed in the discussion. We kept at it for some two hours, and at the end his eyes were no longer sad. As I left, he thanked me with moving sincerity. "It was fun," he said. He had had a moment of surcease from grief, and those groping words expressed a deep emotion.

Although Einstein felt no need for religious ritual and belonged to no   12
formal religious group, he was the most deeply religious man I have known. He once said to me, "Ideas come from God," and one could hear the capital "G" in the reverence with which he pronounced the word. On the marble fireplace in the mathematics building at Princeton University is carved, in the original German, what one might call his scientific credo: "God is subtle, but he is not malicious." By this Einstein meant that scientists could expect to find their task difficult, but not hopeless: the Universe was a Universe of law, and God was not confusing us with deliberate paradoxes and contradictions.

Einstein was an accomplished amateur musician. We used to play duets,   13
he on the violin, I at the piano. One day he surprised me by saying Mozart was the greatest composer of all. Beethoven "created" his music, but the music of Mozart was of such purity and beauty one felt he had merely "found" it—that it had always existed as part of the inner beauty of the Universe, waiting to be revealed.

It was this very Mozartean simplicity that most characterized Einstein's   14
methods. His 1905 theory of relativity, for example, was built on just two simple assumptions. One is the so-called principle of relativity, which means, roughly speaking, that we cannot tell whether we are at rest or moving smoothly. The other assumption is that the speed of light is the same no matter what the speed of the object that produces it. You can see how reasonable this is if you think of agitating a stick in a lake to create waves. Whether you wiggle the stick from a stationary pier, or from a rushing speedboat, the waves, once generated, are on their own, and their speed has nothing to do with that of the stick.

Each of these assumptions, by itself, was so plausible as to seem primi-   15
tively obvious. But together they were in such violent conflict that a lesser man would have dropped one or the other and fled in panic. Einstein daringly kept both—and by so doing he revolutionized physics. For he demonstrated they could, after all, exist peacefully side by side, provided we gave up cherished beliefs about the nature of time.

Science is like a house of cards, with concepts like time and space at the   16
lowest level. Tampering with time brought most of the house tumbling down, and it was this that made Einstein's work so important—and controversial. At a conference in Princeton in honor of his seventieth birthday, one of the speakers, a Nobel Prize winner, tried to convey the magical quality of Einstein's achievement. Words failed him, and with a shrug of helplessness he pointed to his wristwatch, and said in tones of awed amazement, "It all came from this." His very ineloquence made this the most eloquent tribute I have heard to Einstein's genius.

Although fame had little effect on Einstein as a person, he could not es- 17
cape it; he was, of course, instantly recognizable. One autumn Saturday, I was
walking with him in Princeton discussing some technical matters. Parents and
alumni were streaming excitedly toward the stadium, their minds on the coming football game. As they approached us, they paused in sudden recognition,
and a momentary air of solemnity came over them as if they had been reminded of a different world. Yet Einstein seemed totally unaware of this effect and went on with the discussion as though they were not there.

We think of Einstein as one concerned only with the deepest aspects of 18
science. But he saw scientific principles in everyday things to which most of
us would give barely a second thought. He once asked me if I had ever wondered why a man's feet will sink into either dry or completely submerged sand,
while sand that is merely damp provides a firm surface. When I could not answer, he offered a simple explanation.

It depends, he pointed out, on *surface tension,* the elastic-skin effect of a 19
liquid surface. This is what holds a drop together, or causes two small raindrops on a windowpane to pull into one big drop the moment their surfaces
touch.

When sand is damp, Einstein explained, there are tiny amounts of water 20
between grains. The surface tensions of these tiny amounts of water pull all
the grains together, and friction then makes them hard to budge. When the
sand is dry, there is obviously no water between grains. If the sand is fully
immersed, there is water between grains, but no water *surface* to pull them
together.

This is not as important as relativity; yet there is no telling what seeming 21
trifle will lead an Einstein to a major discovery. And the puzzle of the sand
does give us an inkling of the power and elegance of his mind.

Einstein's work, performed quietly with pencil and paper, seemed remote 22
from the turmoil of everyday life: But his ideas were so revolutionary they
caused violent controversy and irrational anger. Indeed, in order to be able to
award him a belated Nobel Prize, the selection committee had to avoid mentioning relativity, and pretend the prize was awarded primarily for his work
on the quantum theory.

Political events upset the serenity of his life even more. When the Nazis 23
came to power in Germany, his theories were officially declared false because
they had been formulated by a Jew. His property was confiscated, and it is
said a price was put on his head.

When scientists in the United States, fearful that the Nazis might develop 24
an atomic bomb, sought to alert American authorities to the danger, they were
scarcely heeded. In desperation, they drafted a letter which Einstein signed
and sent directly to President Roosevelt. It was this act that led to the fateful
decision to go all-out on the production of an atomic bomb—an endeavor in
which Einstein took no active part. When he heard of the agony and destruction that his $E = mc^2$ had wrought, he was dismayed beyond measure,
and from then on there was a look of ineffable sadness in his eyes.

There was something elusively whimsical about Einstein. It is illustrated   25
by my favorite anecdote about him. In his first year in Princeton, on Christmas
Eve, so the story goes, some children sang carols outside his house. Having
finished, they knocked on his door and explained they were collecting money
to buy Christmas presents. Einstein listened, then said, "Wait a moment." He
put on his scarf and overcoat, and took his violin from its case. Then, joining the children as they went from door to door, he accompanied their singing
·of "Silent Night" on his violin.

How shall I sum up what it meant to have known Einstein and his works?   26
Like the Nobel Prize winner who pointed helplessly at his watch, I can find
no adequate words. It was akin to the revelation of great art that lets one see
what was formerly hidden. And when, for example, I walk on the sand of a
lonely beach, I am reminded of his ceaseless search for cosmic simplicity—
and the scene takes on a deeper, sadder beauty.

✳

RESPONDING TO THE WHOLE ESSAY

1. This essay first appeared in *Reader's Digest*, a mass-circulation magazine with mil-
    lions of readers. What features in the essay appeal to such an audience? How do
    you think the essay might have changed if Hoffmann had written it for *Scientific
    American*? [1g]
2. What purpose can you discern in Hoffmann's reminiscences about Einstein? Is
    Hoffmann's aim primarily to entertain? To persuade the reader to a particular
    point of view? Explain. [1g]
3. How does Hoffmann's selection of details contribute to the development of his
    thesis? How do paragraphs 5–7 and 14–15 fit in? [2b]
4. What is interesting or arresting in Hoffmann's opening anecdote? Explain why
    this example entices the reader to keep reading. [3b(1)]
5. What other examples in the essay do you find most memorable? What does each
    contribute?
6. In paragraph 10, Hoffmann writes of Einstein in the process of solving a prob-
    lem: "There was no appearance of concentration, no furrowing of the brow—only
    a placid inner communion." In the very next paragraph, which discusses Einstein's
    grief following his wife's death, Hoffmann writes, "His face was haggard and grief-
    lined, but he put forth a great effort to concentrate." What do these opposing
    statements reveal?
7. What makes Hoffmann's final paragraph an effective conclusion? [3b(2)]

ANALYZING THE ELEMENTS

Grammar

1. In the second sentence of paragraph 2, what time relationship does the past per-
    fect tense of the first verb establish with the other verb? [17c]

2. In the next-to-last sentence of paragraph 3, Hoffmann writes, "Dressed in ill-fitting clothes, his hair characteristically awry. . . ." What word in the main clause do these phrases modify? What advantages does this phrasal construction have over separate sentences conveying the same information? [12a(1)]
3. The first sentence of paragraph 8 uses a gerund subject. Try rewriting the sentence to say the same thing without the gerund. Is the new version more or less successful than Hoffmann's? Why? [12a]
4. In the last sentence of paragraph 12, Hoffmann explains what Einstein meant when he said "God is subtle, but he is not malicious." Why does Hoffmann use the past tense for the part of the sentence following the colon? Would the meaning be different if he had used the present tense? [17c]

Effective Sentences

1. The final sentence of paragraph 3 contains the modifier "at once." Some writers might place that phrase at the end of the sentence. What would be the effect of such a move? Which way do you think the sentence works better? Why? [21a]
2. Paragraph 4 contains an inverted sentence—verb before subject. What is the inverted sentence, and what is the effect of that inversion? Explain the effect of inversion in the last sentence of paragraph 5. [21f]
3. Although needless shifts in the person and number of pronouns are to be avoided, in the second sentence of paragraph 12 Hoffmann deliberately chooses the impersonal pronoun *one*. Why is *one* better here than if Hoffmann had said, "*I* could hear the capital G"? [17g]

Punctuation and Mechanics

1. Explain why Hoffmann italicizes *simplicity* in the first sentence of the essay. [34f]
2. The fourth sentence of paragraph 1 contains an indirect quotation. Rewrite the sentence as it might have been if Hoffmann had used a direct quotation. [30a]
3. Explain the use of quotation marks in the last sentence of paragraph 25. [30b]

Diction

1. What is the meaning of *dullard* in the second sentence of paragraph 5? What other word could Hoffmann have used? Are there any advantages to using *dullard*? If so, what? [24a]
2. The first sentence of paragraph 9 contains the word *fantastic*. Write down what you think the word means and then look it up in your dictionary. What meaning do you think Hoffmann intended? [24a]
3. Hoffmann creates a new word to describe the kind of simplicity Einstein possessed—*Mozartean*. Explain what connotations Hoffmann probably intended to evoke by using this word. [24a]

BUILDING VOCABULARY

1. Define *recalcitrant*. From what Latin roots is *recalcitrant* borrowed? What do they mean? How did these roots change in Late Latin? Explain.

2. List and define two antonyms for *recalcitrant*. Write a sentence using each word you have listed.

SUGGESTIONS FOR WRITING

1. Write a character sketch of someone you know well, perhaps someone who has had an important influence on your life. As Hoffmann does, select examples that focus your essay on no more than one or two traits that have impressed you.
2. All of us—not only great geniuses—make our own discoveries of the natural world and experience a sense of wonder at its workings. Write a brief essay giving examples of your own discoveries and experiences.

Thrills and Chills
Eric Minton

Freelance writer Eric Minton covers the amusement park industry in his column in *Funworld Magazine*. He has also published articles in a number of trade magazines as well as in popular magazines such as *Good Housekeeping* and *Modern Maturity*. This essay appeared in *Psychology Today* with two other essays about roller coasters and haunted houses by Minton (included in this book; see "Beating Coasterphobia" in Chapter 2 and "Scaring Up Business" in Chapter 5).

In Orlando, Florida, David Clevinger stands in a back corridor of *Terror on Church Street* and listens expectantly as customers make their way through the haunted house's passages. Suddenly screams erupt, sending Clevinger, the attraction's artistic director and operations manager, into gales of glee. "I love that sound," he chortles. So does Dave Focke. Watching shrieking riders hurtle through the drops of *The Beast*, the massive wooden coaster at Paramount's Kings Island near Cincinnati, Ohio, Focke beams with pride. "Guests come off breathless, hearts pounding, scared out of their wits," exults Focke, the park's vice president of construction and maintenance. "And wanting to get in line to go again!" 1

Call them shock meisters, terror tacticians, spookologists and boo-ologists. 2 The small band of designers who create the roller coasters and haunted houses that are amusement parks' premier attractions are master manipulators of our deepest fears. They get us to walk through pitch black hallways and step into cutaway coaster cars that dangle our arms and legs. They exploit our most closely held vulnerabilities—and make us like it.

For designers, primarily engineers for coasters and theatrical artists for 3 haunted houses, turning fear into fun depends on illusion. No matter how precarious a roller coaster or alarming a haunted house may appear, it must be totally safe. "We always try to make them look and feel more dangerous than they really are," says Michael Boodley, president of Great Coasters International, Inc., of Santa Cruz, California.

Though the experience offered by roller coasters and haunted houses di- 4 verges dramatically—it's the difference between pushing a wagon over a steep hill versus telling campfire ghost stories—the attractions are constructed of common elements. Both draw on all our senses, both rely on surprise for their shocks and both quote heavily from the movies (coasters replicate action-adventure perils, a la *Indiana Jones* and *Star Wars*, and haunted houses feature quasi-Frankensteins and *Friday the 13th* Jasons).

But the biggest common denominator is that the two feed on the same 5
basic fear: loss of control. Once a coaster takes off, passengers can do nothing but sit or, on some rides stand, and scream. "The closest thing to compare it to is driving with an idiot," observes Boodley. Lynton Harris, director
of *Madison Scare Garden,* an annual fright fest in New York City, also uses
an auto analogy for haunted houses. "It's a hundred degrees outside, and you'd
expect to get in a car and have air conditioning, and all of a sudden the heater
gets turned on," he says. "Then the doors lock. Cocky as you are, you realize you're not in charge."

With roller coasters, the psychological games start before customers even 6
get into the train. Boodley purposely makes his wooden coasters as diabolical looking as possible. "It's kind of like a black widow spider web," he explains. "It's a very, very pretty thing, but when the black widow gets you..."
Queueing customers at *Outer Limits: Flights of Fear,* one of 12 coasters at
Kings Island, are treated to dim lights, alien noises and a video of a space station in the grip of a mysterious force. "Even after having ridden that ride
probably close to a hundred times, I sit there anticipating the start, and my
palms still sweat," says *Outer Limits* designer Jim Seay, president of Premier
Rides of Millersville, Maryland.

Whether the traditional chain-driven wooden or steel clackers or the newer 7
linear induction motor (LIM) rides that harness electromagnetic force to blast
off trains, all roller coasters play on two related—and universal—terrors: fear
of heights and fear of falling. "The loops and elements, they come and go,
but the coaster always has to have the big drop," says Focke of Kings Island.

Traditional coasters provide an excruciatingly slow buildup to the plunge. 8
"There's a lot of self-abuse on that chain lift," says Boodley. "Your own mind
puts you in a state of paralysis." (Wooden coasters also creak, rumble and
clickityclack naturally as they flex, but riders get a queasy feeling that the
structure is about to collapse. "That's probably one of the funniest things we
as designers get to appreciate," says Boodley.) LIMs, on the other hand, rocket
you into terror with trains that go from 0 to 60 mph in under four seconds.
The big drops are actually shorter on LIMs, but the sense of speed sets hearts
pounding.

Most coasters travel below 70 miles an hour, slower than many people 9
drive, but designers heighten the sense of speed and danger with close flybys
of terrain, buildings, people, even other trains. At Busch Gardens Tampa Bay,
Montu dives riders into five trenches, one of which emerges through the pa-
tio of an ersatz Egyptian temple. "Not knowing exactly where the bottom is
or where you come out is important," says Mark Rose, the park's vice president of design and engineering. "If you could see the whole thing, then you
could kind of play it out in your mind." Some coasters, like *Outer Limits* and
Disney World's *Space Mountain,* intensify the fear and suspense by keeping
passengers in the dark for the entire ride.

Upping the vulnerability quotient even further is a recent innovation: in- 10
verted coasters which suspend riders below the track and carve away as much

of the train as possible. "There is less fiberglass, less coach around you, so your feet are just hanging out there," notes Rose. During one stretch of track on *Montu,* passengers' soles skim just 24 inches above the ground. Riders also get dangled over a pit of live Nile crocodiles.

A coaster's effects, though, are not all illusory. Passengers pull close to 4   11 positive G's on some plummets. They turn upside down on loops and rotate head over heels through corkscrews. They literally feel the wind in their hair and, on a LIM coaster launch, the air in their eyes. Human bodies don't commonly experience such acrobatic maneuvers, and that in itself is psychologically disorienting. "Anytime you put a rider in a situation they're not used to, there's an element of the unknown," declares Boodley. "And for 80 percent of people, fear is the unknown."

The biggest unknown of all is death, and creators of haunted houses are   12 masters at exploiting our fear of dying, especially in a gruesome manner. To unnerve guests, designers depend on two elements. The first is setting a spooky mood with sights, sounds, smells and "feels"—"all the things that make you uneasy," says Drew Edward Hunter, co-chairman of the International Association of Haunted Attractions and design director of haunted attractions at Sally Corporation of Jacksonville, Florida. "Then you have the second part, the attack, the out-and-out scare. I don't think you can have one without the other."

For the "creep-out" effect, haunts are always dark; skeletons, skulls, fog,   13 ticking clocks and screaming ghouls abound. "On my sets, I try to capture a claustrophobic feeling," says *Terror on Church Street's* Clevinger. "I bring my ceilings low, the walls close." To further emphasize the sense of enclosure, he hangs tree branches, Spanish moss, rags and spider webs.

Just the suggestion of something loathsome will give customers the scream-   14 ing meemies. "Do the sounds of insects, and people scratch their heads all the way through," says John Denley, president and owner of Boneyard Productions of Salem, Massachusetts. Run a soundtrack that whispers of rats, turn on ankle-aimed air hoses and professional football players tap dance. A strong whiff of formaldehyde and you have the scent of death, "no matter what country you're in," says Clevinger.

The second part of the equation is the scare, which, say spookologists, is   15 really a "startle." "All scares are primarily based on two things," instructs Edward Marks, president of Jets Productions of Chatsworth, California. "One, it's there and does something you don't expect it to do, or two, it's not there and it appears."

In *Terror on Church Street,* customers come upon Hannibal Lecter, the   16 cannibal psychiatrist of *Silence of the Lambs.* He yells and lunges against his cell's bars, drawing yelps from viewers. The cries quickly subside into nervous tittering. As guests make their way around the bars, Lecter follows along inside. Then, just when viewers feel safest, Lecter opens the cage door and steps out. "The guys who were taunting him usually scream the loudest," observes Clevinger.

In the second type of gag, designers have people or objects suddenly emerge 17
from in front, beside, above or below patrons. A surefire gag—and the simplest
of all—is dropping a spider on a person's head. "We call that a $2 scare," says
Harris of *Madison Scare Garden.* "It's the best value-for-money scare we've
ever used."

Another never-fail gotcha goes by the generic term "UV Dot Man." Guests 18
enter a dark room with ultraviolet dots on the wall (variations would be skeletons or geometric patterns). A black-masked actor wearing a black bodysuit,
likewise bearing UV dots, stands against the wall and jumps out. "You are actually looking at him before he leaps out at you," Marks says. "It works every
time, and it's so simple." (Another certain scare that designers hate, but feel
compelled to use, is the hockey-masked goon waving a whirring chainsaw.
Customers complain if a haunted house doesn't have one.)

For designers, combining the two types of gags may be the most satisfying 19
scare of all. In his favorite trick, Denley once draped sheets over padding, topped
them with masked and wigged heads, and attached the forms to the caging on
oscillating fans. He plugged the fans into a power strip, but left the cords clearly
visible. These "monsters" started moving in unison when people entered the
room. After the initial surprise, guests noticed the power strip and began mock-
ing the amateurish set up. Suddenly, the middle white-sheeted monster—actually
a man with one of the plugged-in extension cords tied to his leg—leaped out.

"It was hilarious," recalls a chuckling Denley, who is also known as 20
Professor Nightmare. "We had a woman hyperventilate. We had people wet
themselves. They thought they knew the gag—and, bam! we hit them with something totally different." Guests losing control of their bladders is considered a
badge of honor among haunt producers. "We call it yellow control," Clevinger
says. Getting an entire group to cower on the ground is another measure of
success.

While the live actors who sometimes assume roles in haunted productions 21
are forbidden to touch patrons, they are encouraged to invade their personal
space. "Everybody's got this wonderful circle around them," says Denley, who
likes to have actors suddenly appear as close to a person as possible, then disappear. "We want to leave you thinking, 'What was that?'"

Designers also like to pick their victims. "We call it 'slicing the group,' " 22
says Marks at Jets Productions. "We actually can single out a person from 20
people. A guy and girl clinging together—I can slice them apart with the right
scare." A trained actor watches their body language, whether they tighten up,
stare him down, or avert their eyes.

Male customers are a favorite target. "We try to take the guys who are 23
hecklers and make examples of them," observes Denley. "If you nail them, the
rest of the group will follow." Men also pose a special challenge. "Guys
are harder to read than women," Denley explains. "They don't do body language as much. Women are more animated, more intent on being scared. Guys
play it cool." Designers usually get them with strikes from above or below, but
they're careful. Men sometimes lash out with their fists.

"The scariest things come from your mind," sums up Edward Hunter.   24
"With the right setup, the right imagination, the right story, your mind creates things we couldn't possibly show you." "No matter how good the makeup
or the costume, nothing is more effective than your imagination," echoes
Denley. One proof: guests at *Terror on Church Street* scream loud and long
when, at a particular point, they catch a glimpse of lurking monsters. The
fiends: themselves, reflected in strategically placed mirrors.

✱

RESPONDING TO THE WHOLE ESSAY

1. This essay was in *Psychology Today*. Why is this subject particularly suitable for
   the readership of this magazine? [1g(2)]
2. What is the primary purpose of this essay? [1g(1)]
3. Why are examples important for the development of the author's thesis? Are the
   examples well selected?
4. Consider the effectiveness of the opening of the essay. [3b(1)]
5. How does Minton use comparison and contrast in paragraph 4? [2e(5)]
6. How does Minton organize the essay? [2c]
7. Examine the two other essays in this book by the same author on roller coasters
   and haunted houses (Chapters 2 and 5).

ANALYZING THE ELEMENTS

Grammar

1. Why is the plural *are* used in the second sentence of paragraph 2? [16d]
2. What part of speech is *Upping* in paragraph 10? How does it function in the sentence? [11c]

Effective Sentences

1. How does the last sentence in paragraph 2 effectively support Minton's thesis? [21h]
2. Comment on the effective use of repetition in the last sentence of paragraph 4.
   [21e, 21g]

Punctuation and Mechanics

1. Why does Minton use the dash in the last sentence of paragraph 2? [31e]
2. Why is the first comma used in the second sentence of paragraph 3? [27b]

Diction

1. The words *shock meisters, spookologists* and *boo-ologists* (paragraph 2) have been
   created by the author. How do these words help him establish tone? [3a(3)]
2. How effective are the adjectives in the second sentence of paragraph 3? [24a]

BUILDING VOCABULARY

1. What is the origin of the word *precarious* (paragraph 3)?
2. Look up the suffix *-ologist* Minton uses in forming new words.

SUGGESTIONS FOR WRITING

1. Write an essay about one of your interests or hobbies, using a variety of examples.
2. Write an essay in which you observe the behavior of people at a particular event or type of event.

Just Walk on By: A Black Man Ponders His Power to Alter Public Space

Brent Staples

Born in 1951 in Chester, Pennsylvania, Brent Staples holds a bachelor's degree from Widener University and a Ph.D. in psychology from the University of Chicago. Currently a member of the editorial board of The *New York Times,* Staples began his work for the *Times* as the first assistant metropolitan editor in 1985. "Just Walk on By" first appeared in *Ms.* magazine in 1986.

My first victim was a woman—white, well dressed, probably in her early 1
twenties. I came upon her late one evening on a deserted street in Hyde Park, a relatively affluent neighborhood in an otherwise mean, impoverished section of Chicago. As I swung onto the avenue behind her, there seemed be a discreet, uninflammatory distance between us. Not so. She cast back a worried glance. To her, the youngish black man—a broad six feet two inches with a beard and billowing hair, both hands shoved into the pockets of a bulky military jacket—seemed menacingly close. After a few more quick glimpses, she picked up her pace and was soon running in earnest. Within seconds she disappeared into a cross street.

That was more than a decade ago. I was twenty-two years old, a gradu- 2
ate student newly arrived at the University of Chicago. It was in the echo of that terrified woman's footfalls that I first began to know the unwieldy inheritance I'd come into—the ability to alter public space in ugly ways. It was clear that she thought herself the quarry of a mugger, a rapist, or worse. Suffering a bout of insomnia, however, I was stalking sleep, not defenseless wayfarers. As a softy who is scarcely able to take a knife to a raw chicken— let alone hold it to a person's throat—I was surprised, embarrassed, and dismayed all at once. Her flight made me feel like an accomplice in tyranny. It also made it clear that I was indistinguishable from the muggers who occasionally seeped into the area from the surrounding ghetto. That first encounter, and those that followed, signified that a vast, unnerving gulf lay between nighttime pedestrians—particularly women—and me. And I soon gathered that being perceived as dangerous is a hazard in itself. I only needed to turn a corner into a dicey situation, or crowd some frightened, armed person in a foyer somewhere, or make an errant move after being pulled over by a policeman. Where fear and weapons meet—and they often do in urban America—there is always the possibility of death.

In that first year, my first away from my hometown, I was to become   3
thoroughly familiar with the language of fear. At dark, shadowy intersections
in Chicago, I could cross in front of a car stopped at a traffic light and elicit
the *thunk, thunk, thunk, thunk* of the driver—black, white, male, or female—
hammering down the door locks. On less traveled streets after dark, I grew
accustomed to but never comfortable with people who crossed to the other
side of the street rather than pass me. Then there were the standard unpleas-
antries with police, doormen, bouncers, cab drivers, and others whose business it is to screen out troublesome individuals *before* there is any nastiness.

I moved to New York nearly two years ago and I have remained an avid   4
night walker. In central Manhattan, the near-constant crowd cover minimizes
tense one-on-one street encounters. Elsewhere—visiting friends in SoHo,[1]
where sidewalks are narrow and tightly spaced buildings shut out the sky—
things can get very taut indeed.

Black men have a firm place in New York mugging literature. Norman   5
Podhoretz[2] in his famed (or infamous) 1963 essay, "My Negro Problem—And
Ours," recalls growing up in terror of black males; they "were tougher than
we were, more ruthless," he writes—and as an adult on the Upper West Side
of Manhattan, he continues, he cannot constrain his nervousness when he
meets black men on certain streets. Similarly, a decade later, the essayist and
novelist Edward Hoagland extols a New York where once "Negro bitterness
bore down mainly on other Negroes." Where some see mere panhandlers,
Hoagland sees "a mugger who is clearly screwing up his nerve to do more
than just *ask* for money." But Hoagland has "the New Yorker's quick-hunch
posture for broken-field maneuvering," and the bad guy swerves away.

I often witness that "hunch posture," from women after dark on the war-   6
renlike streets of Brooklyn where I live. They seem to set their faces on neutral and, with their purse straps strung across their chests bandolier style, they
forge ahead as though bracing themselves against being tackled. I understand,
of course, that the danger they perceive is not a hallucination. Women are
particularly vulnerable to street violence, and young black males are drasti-
cally overrepresented among the perpetrators of that violence. Yet these truths
are no solace against the kind of alienation that comes of being ever the suspect, against being set apart, a fearsome entity with whom pedestrians avoid
making eye contact.

It is not altogether clear to me how I reached the ripe old age of twenty-   7
two without being conscious of the lethality nighttime pedestrians attributed
to me. Perhaps it was because in Chester, Pennsylvania, the small, angry industrial town where I came of age in the 1960s, I was scarcely noticeable
against a backdrop of gang warfare, street knifings, and murders. I grew up
one of the good boys, had perhaps a half-dozen fist fights. In retrospect, my
shyness of combat has clear sources.

[1] A district of lower Manhattan known for its art galleries.
[2] A well-known literary critic and editor of *Commentary* magazine

Many things go into the making of a young thug. One of those things is the   8
consummation of the male romance with the power to intimidate. An infant discovers that random flailings send the baby bottle flying out of the crib and crashing to the floor. Delighted, the joyful babe repeats those motions again and again,
seeking to duplicate the feat. Just so, I recall the points at which some of my
boyhood friends were finally seduced by the perception of themselves as tough
guys. When a mark cowered and surrendered his money without resistance, myth
and reality merged—and paid off. It is, after all, only manly to embrace the
power to frighten and intimidate. We, as men, are not supposed to give an inch
of our lane on the highway; we are to seize the fighter's edge in work and in
play and even in love; we are to be valiant in the face of hostile forces.

Unfortunately, poor and powerless young men seem to take all this non-   9
sense literally. As a boy, I saw countless tough guys locked away; I have since
buried several, too. They were babies, really—a teenage cousin, a brother of
twenty-two, a childhood friend in his mid-twenties—all gone down in episodes
of bravado played out in the streets. I came to doubt the virtues of intimidation early on. I chose, perhaps even unconsciously, to remain a shadow—
timid, but a survivor.

The fearsomeness mistakenly attributed to me in public places often has   10
a perilous flavor. The most frightening of these confusions occurred in the late
1970s and early 1980s when I worked as a journalist in Chicago. One day,
rushing into the office of a magazine I was writing for with a deadline story
in hand, I was mistaken for a burglar. The office manager called security and,
with an ad hoc posse, pursued me through the labyrinthine halls, nearly to
my editor's door. I had no way of proving who I was. I could only move
briskly toward the company of someone who knew me.

Another time I was on assignment for a local paper and killing time be-   11
fore an interview. I entered a jewelry store on the city's affluent Near North
Side. The proprietor excused herself and returned with an enormous red
Doberman pinscher straining at the end of a leash. She stood, the dog extended toward me, silent to my questions, her eyes bulging nearly out of her
head. I took a cursory look around, nodded, and bade her good night.
Relatively speaking, however, I never fared as badly as another black male
journalist. He went to nearby Waukegan, Illinois, a couple of summers ago
to work on a story about a murderer who was born there. Mistaking the reporter for the killer, police hauled him from his car at gunpoint and but for
his press credentials would probably have tried to book him. Such episodes
are not uncommon. Black men trade tales like this all the time.

In "My Negro Problem—And Ours," Podhoretz writes that the hatred he   12
feels for blacks makes itself known to him through a variety of avenues—one
being his discomfort with that "special brand of paranoid touchiness" to which
he says blacks are prone. No doubt he is speaking here of black men. In time,
I learned to smother the rage I felt at so often being taken for a criminal. Not
to be so would surely have led to madness—via that special "paranoid touchiness" that so annoyed Podhoretz at the time he wrote the essay.

I began to take precautions to make myself less threatening. I move about   13
with care, particularly late in the evening. I give a wide berth to nervous people
on subway platforms during the wee hours, particularly when I have exchanged
business clothes for jeans. If I happen to be entering a building behind some people who appear skittish, I may walk by, letting them clear the lobby before I return, so as not to seem to be following them. I have been calm and extremely
congenial on those rare occasions when I've been pulled over by the police.

And on late-evening constitutionals along streets less traveled by, I em-   14
ploy what has proved to be an excellent tension-reducing measure: I whistle
melodies from Beethoven and Vivaldi and the more popular classical composers. Even steely New Yorkers hunching toward nighttime destinations seem
to relax, and occasionally they even join in the tune. Virtually everybody seems
to sense that a mugger wouldn't be warbling bright, sunny selections from
Vivaldi's *Four Seasons*. It is my equivalent of the cowbell that hikers wear
when they known they are in bear country.

✳

RESPONDING TO THE WHOLE ESSAY

1. What advantage does Staples gain by introducing his essay with an example of
    how one woman saw him as a threat? How does this example help Staples es-
    tablish his main idea? [2b]
2. Where is the main idea of paragraph 2 found? How do the examples that begin
    the paragraph prepare the reader for the main idea? [3c(1) and 3c(2)]
3. How does Staples achieve coherence in paragraph 13? Mark and label all the de-
    vices he uses.
4. What clues do the vocabulary and the details of "Just Walk on By" provide about
    Staples's intended audience? Describe the audience. [1g(2)]
5. Does Staples ever state his purpose for writing "Just Walk on By"? If so, where?
    If not, what do you think his purpose is? [1g(1)]
6. Comment on the tone of Staples's essay. What evidence do you find for your as-
    sessment of the tone Staples takes? [3a(3)]

ANALYZING THE ELEMENTS

Grammar

1. In the first sentence of paragraph 14, Staples uses the clause "what has proved to
    be an excellent tension-reducing measure: I whistle melodies from Beethoven and
    Vivaldi and the more popular classical composers." How does this clause function?
    As exactly as you can, explain how this clause advances Staples's main idea. [12b]
2. In the first sentence of paragraph 6, what advantage does Staples gain from us-
    ing *warrenlike* to modify *streets*? [24c]
3. In the final clause of the third sentence in paragraph 10, Staples uses the passive
    voice. Would the active voice be better? Explain your answer. [17c]

Effective Sentences

1. Paragraph 2 begins with the word *that*. What is the antecedent of this pronoun, and what advantage does Staples gain from beginning the paragraph this way? [16a]
2. Explain why rewriting the fourth sentence of paragraph 11 as follows has a different effect: She stood with the dog extended toward me. She was silent to my questions. Her eyes bulged nearly out of her head. [19b]
3. As fully as possible, explain what makes the fourth sentence of paragraph 13 effective.

Punctuation and Mechanics

1. Explain the reason for quotation marks around *hunch posture* in the first sentence of paragraph 6. Why is *before* italicized in the last sentence of paragraph 3? [30c and 34f]
2. Comment on the reason for each comma and each semicolon in the final sentence of paragraph 8. [27d and 28a]
3. Justify the capitalization of *Upper West Side* in the second sentence of paragraph 5. [33a]

Diction

1. How does Staples use the word *victim* in the first paragraph? Explain why he refers to the woman as a *victim*. [24c]
2. Look up the following words in your dictionary: *affluent* (paragraph 1), *quarry* and *dicey* (paragraph 2), *bandolier* (paragraph 6), *perilous* and *posse* (paragraph 10), *skittish* (paragraph 13), *warbling* (paragraph 14). What synonyms could Staples have used? In each case, which is better, the synonym or the word Staples uses? Why? [23a and 24a]
3. Staples's use of the phrase "less traveled" (paragraphs 3 and 14) seems to echo the language of Robert Frost's line, "I took the one less traveled by," from the poem, "The Road Not Taken." Comment on how that possible *allusion* contributes to Staples's main point. (You may find it helpful to look up the poem.) [24c]

BUILDING VOCABULARY

1. What are the Greek roots from which *paranoid* is borrowed? What do they mean? Write a sentence using a word derived from one of these Greek roots.
2. What is the meaning of the Latin suffix *-able*? List and define three words ending in this suffix. What is their grammatical function?

SUGGESTIONS FOR WRITING

1. Write an essay in which you use examples to describe how someone judged you unfairly and how you responded to the judgment.
2. Write an essay using examples to illustrate how you once had to alter your public behavior for reasons beyond your control. For instance, people often modify their public behavior because of the expectations of their families, because of peer group pressures, or because of standards imposed by an institution such as a school or the military.

The Myth of College
Dave Barry

Dave Barry is a Pulitzer Prize–winning journalist and syndicated humor columnist whose essays are published in nationwide and international newspapers and magazines. Additionally, Barry has gained recognition as an author, publishing a number of books, including his most recent titles, *Dave Barry's Guide to Guys, Dave Barry Is Not Making This Up,* and *Dave Barry in Cyberspace.* Many of his earlier books have become the subjects for the syndicated television show *Dave's World.* Barry currently works for the *Miami Herald's Tropic Magazine,* but in his spare time, he plays lead guitar in the rock band Rock Bottom Remainders, which is made up of distinguished writers, including Stephen King, Barbara Kingsolver, Amy Tan, and Robert Fulghum. In 1993, the band toured the United States, donating its profits to literacy and First Amendment causes. In "The Myth of College," Barry offers prospective students some humorous but insightful advice about choosing a major, using examples from his own experience and observations.

Many of you young persons out there are seriously thinking about going to college. (That is, of course, a lie. The only things you young persons think seriously about are loud music and sex. Trust me: these are closely related to college.) College is basically a bunch of rooms where you sit for roughly two thousand hours and try to memorize things. The two thousand hours are spread out over four years; you spend the rest of the time sleeping and trying to get dates.

Basically, you learn two kinds of things in college:

- *Things you need to know later in life (2 hours).* These include how to make collect telephone calls and get beer and crepe-paper stains out of your pajamas.
- *Things you will not need to know in later life (1,998 hours).* These are the things you learn in classes whose names end in "-ology", "-osophy", "-isty", "-ies", and so on. The idea is you memorize these things, then write them down in little exam books, then forget them. If you fail to forget them, you become a professor and have to stay in college for the rest of your life.

It's very difficult to forget everything. For example, when I was in college, I had to memorize—don't ask me why—the names of the metaphysical poets other than John Donne. I have managed to forget one of them, but I still remember that the other two were named Vaughan and Crashaw.

Sometimes, when I'm trying to remember something important, like   4
whether my wife told me to get tuna packed in oil or tuna packed in water,
Vaughan and Crashaw just pop up in my mind, right there in the supermarket. It's a terrible waste of brain cells.

After you've been in college for a year or so, you're supposed to choose   5
a major, which is the subject you intend to memorize and forget the most
things about. Here is a very important piece of advice: *be sure to choose a
major that does not involve Known Facts and Right Answers.*

This means that you must not major in mathematics, physics, biology, or   6
chemistry, because these subjects involve actual facts. If, for example, you major in mathematics, you're going to wander into class one day and the professor will say: "Define the cosine integer of the quadrant of the rhomboid
binary axis, and extrapolate your result to five significant vertices." If you
don't come up with exactly the answer the professor has in mind, you fail.
The same is true of chemistry: if you write in your exam book that carbon
and hydrogen combine to form oak, your professor will flunk you. He wants
you to come up with the same answer he and all the other chemists have
agreed on. Scientists are extremely snotty about this.

So you should major in subjects like English, philosophy, psychology, and   7
sociology—subjects in which nobody really understands what anybody else is
talking about, and which involve virtually no facts. I attended classes in all
these subjects, so I'll give you a quick overview of each:

English.   This involves writing papers about long books you have read little   8
snippets of just before class. Here is a tip on how to get good grades on your
English papers: never say anything about a book that anybody with any common sense would say. For example, suppose you are studying *Moby Dick.*
Anybody with any common sense would say that Moby Dick is a big white
whale, since the characters in the book refer to it as a big white whale roughly
eleven thousand times. So, in your paper, you say Moby Dick is actually the
Republic of Ireland. Your professor, who is sick to death of reading papers
and never liked *Moby Dick* anyway, will think you are enormously creative.
If you can regularly come up with lunatic interpretations of simple stories,
you should major in English.

Philosophy.   Basically, this involves sitting in a room and deciding there is   9
no such thing as reality and then going to lunch. You should major in philosophy if you plan to take a lot of drugs.

Psychology.   This involves talking about rats and dreams. Psychologists are   10
obsessed with rats and dreams. I once spent an entire semester training a rat
to punch little buttons in a certain sequence, then training my roommate to
do the same thing. The rat learned much faster. My roommate is now a doctor. If you like rats or dreams, and above all if you dream about rats, you
should major in psychology.

Sociology.   For sheer lack of intelligibility, sociology is far and away the number one subject. I sat through hours of sociology courses, and read gobs of sociology writing, and I never once heard or read a coherent statement. This is because sociologists want to be considered scientists, so they spend most of their time translating simple, obvious observations into scientific-sounding code. If you plan to major in sociology, you'll have to learn to do the same thing. For example, suppose you have observed that children cry when they fall down. You should write: "Methodological observation of the sociometrical behavior tendencies to prematurated isolates indicates that a causal relationship exists between groundward tropism and lachrimatory, or 'crying' behavior forms." If you can keep this up for fifty or sixty pages, you will get a large government grant.   11

✳

RESPONDING TO THE WHOLE ESSAY

1.   Which would you say predominates in this essay: the writer's interest in his own feelings, an interest in exploring the possibilities offered by an unusual topic, or a wish to persuade readers to think differently about their own lives? Do you discern other purposes? Point to evidence in this essay to support your answers. [1g]
2.   From the evidence in the essay, what can you infer about the audience for whom "The Myth of College" was written? [1g]
3.   Which paragraphs are built on a single example? Which contain clusters of examples? Explain. [2d(2)]
4.   How would you identify the tone of the essay? Be as specific as you can. [3a(3)]

ANALYZING THE ELEMENTS

Grammar

1.   Explain whether *this* in the third sentence of the last paragraph is a broad or explicit reference. Identify similar references for *this* in the essay. Are these references clear? Why or why not? [16e]
2.   The first sentence of paragraph 4 contains a verb with a particle: *pop up*. Explain why the particle belongs with the verb rather than serving as a preposition. Find at least one other verb with particle in the essay. [11a]

Effective Sentences

1.   In most sentences, the verb directly follows the subject. However, the subject and verb in the next-to-last sentence in paragraph 8 are separated by the clause "who is sick to death of reading papers and never liked *Moby Dick* anyway." Could this clause be moved to a different part of the sentence? Explain. [12b and 19a(4)]
2.   Comment upon the parallel structure of the clause following the colon in the first sentence of paragraph 2 and the fourth sentence of paragraph 2. What is the rhetorical effect of this parallelism? [20 and 21g]

Punctuation and Mechanics

1. Explain the use of dashes in the second sentence of paragraph 3. Could the author have used parentheses in place of the dashes, and if so, would the sentence have the same effect? Explain. [31e and 31f]
2. Following the colon in the sixth sentence of the last paragraph, Barry uses a combination of single and double quotation marks. Explain why both types of quotation marks are necessary. Be as specific as you can. [30a(1) and 30a(3)]
3. Notice that each of the last four paragraphs (8–11) begin with a word followed by a period. Because a colon has been used to begin this list, punctuating each of the listed items with a colon would be chancy. Usage is divided concerning this problem, so Barry has chosen the period as an alternative. What do you think of Barry's choice of punctuation? Do you find it effective or confusing? Explain.

Diction

1. In the second sentence of paragraph 6 and the sixth sentence of paragraph 11, Barry introduces technical jargon into the essay. What effect does Barry achieve by doing this? Explain. [23b(1)]
2. Look up each of the words in the following sentence from "The Myth of College" and rewrite the sentence without using technical jargon: "Methodological observation of the sociometrical behavior tendencies of prematurated isolates indicates that a causal relationship exists between groundward tropism and lachrimatory, or 'crying' behavior forms." Which sentence is easier to understand: the original or your revision? Explain. [23b(6)]

BUILDING VOCABULARY

1. Look up the meanings of the following words: *rhomboid, binary, vertices, cosine, integer.*
2. Create at least two words ending in each of the following suffixes: *-ology, -istry,* and *-ic.* Write sentences using each of the words that you have listed.

SUGGESTIONS FOR WRITING

1. Write an essay using examples to explain how most college students live.
2. Write an essay using examples to illustrate (and explain and justify) the myth of single or married life, or the myth of adulthood.

The Hidden Life of SUVs
Jack Hitt

Jack Hitt is a writer for *GQ* magazine and a contributing editor for Public Radio International and WBEZ's *This American Life*. His book, *Off the Road: A Modern-Day Walk Down the Pilgrim's Route into Spain,* was published by Simon and Schuster in 1994.

What's in a name? What do you make of a passenger vehicle called a 1 Bronco? Or one dubbed a Cherokee? How about a Wrangler? Are they just chrome-plated expressions of sublimated testosterone flooding the highways? Check out the herd that grazes the average car lot these days: Blazer, Tracker, Yukon, Navigator, Tahoe, Range Rover, Explorer, Mountaineer, Denali, Expedition, Discovery, Bravada. Besides signaling that we're not Civic or Gallant, they indicate there's something else going on here.

These are, of course, all names of sport utility vehicles, the miracle that has 2 resurrected Motown. Think back to the dark days of the previous decade when the Japanese auto industry had nearly buried Detroit. In 1981, only a relative handful of four-wheel-drives traveled the road, and the phrase "sport utility vehicle" hadn't entered the language. Today, they number more than 14 million, and that figure is growing fast. If you include pickups and vans, then quasi trucks now constitute about half of all the vehicles sold in America. Half. They're rapidly displacing cars on the highways of our new unbraking economy.

Go to any car lot and jawbone with a salesman, and you'll find that big 3 is once again better. Any savvy dealer (clutching his copy of Zig Ziglar's *Ziglar on Selling*) will try to talk you up to one of the latest behemoths, which have bloated to such Brobdingnagian dimensions as to have entered the realm of the absurd.

Ford, in fact, has unveiled a new monster, the Excursion, due to hit the 4 showrooms before the millennium. With a corporate straight face, its literature touts as selling points that the Excursion is "less than 7 feet tall...and less than 20 feet long" and is "more fuel efficient...than two average full-size sedans."

These Big Berthas have even spawned new vocabulary words. The biggest 5 of the big, for instance, can no longer fit comfortably in a standard-size garage or the average parking space. So salesmen will often sell you on one of the "smaller" SUVs by praising its "garageability."

What, then, explains the inexorable advance of these giant SUVs into our 6 lives? Why do we want cars that are, in fact, high-clearance trucks with four-wheel drive, an optional winch, and what amounts to a cowcatcher?

The answer, in part, lies in the vehicles themselves. Cars are not fickle   7
fashions. They are the most expensive and visible purchases in an economy
drenched in matters of status and tricked out with hidden meanings.

Some people will tell you that the shift from car to truck can be explained   8
simply: We Americans are getting, um, bigger in the beam. We aren't comfortable in those Camrys, so we trade up to a vehicle we can sit in without
feeling scrunched. Here's a new buzzword for Ziglar disciples: fatassability.

But I think the key is found not so much in their size or expense (although   9
both keep ballooning) but in those ersatz Western names. The other day, I
saw an acquaintance of mine in a boxy steed called a Durango. Say it out
loud for me: "Durango." Can you get the syllables off your tongue without
irony? In the post-"Seinfeld" era, can anyone say *Durango* without giving it
an Elaine Benes enunciation at every syllable? Doo-RANG-Go.

The true irony comes from the fact that this thoroughly market-researched   10
word no longer has any core meaning. No one comprehends its denotation
(Colorado town) but only its vague connotations (rugged individualism, mastery over the wilderness, cowboy endurance). The word does not pin down
meaning so much as conjure up images.

These names are only the end product of the intense buyer-profiling that   11
the car companies and the marketing firms continuously carry out. By the
time they make it to the lot, these cars are streamlined Frankensteinian con-
coctions of our private anxieties and desires. We consumers don't so much
shop for one of these SUVs as they shop for us.

A typical focus-group study might be one like the "cluster analysis" con-   12
ducted by college students for Washington, D.C.-area car dealers in 1994 and
reported in *Marketing Tools*. The analysts coordinated numerous databases,
mail surveys, and census information to profile the typical "Bill and Barb-
Blazers," whose consumer apprehensions can shift from block to block, but
can be pinpointed down to the four-digit appendix on the old zip code.

Each Bill and Barb then got tagged as "Young Suburbia" or "Blue-Collar   13
Nursery" or "Urban Gentry." Translation, respectively: "college-educated, up-
wardly mobile white" or "middle-class, small-town" or "educated black" people. The students next identified what images spoke to the underlying appeal
of an SUV for each group (prestige, child space, weekend leisure). Then they
developed targeted ads to run in the media most favored by each group: the
Wall Street Journal, National Geographic, Black Entertainment Television.

Many of the ads they developed were directed at women. For example,   14
the one meant for upscale homeowners depicted a "woman architect standing next to her four-door [Blazer] at a Washington-area construction site" and
"conveyed her professional leadership in a city with one of the highest rates
of labor force participation for women."

Sport utility vehicles are quickly becoming women's cars. In fact, current   15
statistics show that 40 percent of all SUV sales are to women, and the proportion is growing. (More men, on the other hand, are buying bigger, tougher
pickup trucks.) But one wonders what's going on in the mind of that female

architect or that soccer mom, high above the world in her soundproof, tinted-glass SUV, chatting on her cellular phone as she steers her mobile fortress down the street.

When GMC decided to launch the Denali (an SUV named for the Alaskan 16 mountain), the auto-trade papers discussed the subtleties of that outdoorsy name: Even though most buyers "will never venture into territory any less tram-pled than the local country club parking lot," wrote *Ward's Auto World*, "the important goal of the Denali marketing hype is to plant the image in customers' minds that they can conquer rugged terrain. The metaphor of Alaska is partic-ularly apt because SUVs, especially the larger of the species, depend on the myth that we have new frontiers yet to pave. Perhaps we're trying to tame a differ-ent kind of wilderness. Indeed, in an age of gated communities...the SUV is the perfect transportation shelter to protect us from fears both real and imagined."

In one focus group, female drivers confessed they hesitated even to exit 17 the interstate "because they are afraid of what they are going to find on some surface streets."

G. Clotaire Rapaille, a French medical anthropologist and student of the 18 consumer mind, practices a more advanced marketing technique called "ar-chetype research." In one session he has consumers lie on the floor and lulls them into a relaxed alpha state with soothing music. Then he asks them to free-associate from images of different vehicle designs and write stories about what they hoped the design would become. Overwhelmingly, Rapaille told the *Wall Street Journal,* his participants had the same reaction: "It's a jungle out there. It's Mad Max. People want to kill me, rape me. Give me a big thing like a tank."

More and more, SUVs give us that tank-like security, and part of the feel- 19 ing derives from their literal altitude. Down there is the old working class, the new peasants who haven't figured out how to snatch a six-figure income out of our roaring economy—the little people who don't own a single Fidelity fund. There's a brutal Darwinian selection at work: They huddle down in their wretched Escorts and their Metros—not merely because they are poor but be-cause they deserve to be.

These are the new savages: people who drive cars. They scrape and fetch 20 about in their tiny compacts, scuttling along on surface streets. But above it all, in their gleaming, skyscraping vehicles, is the new high society—the am-bitious, the exurban pioneers, the downtown frontiersmen.

It's been said that the most distinctive feature of the American character 21 is that we continually define ourselves as pilgrims facing a new frontier. In their darkest hearts, the members of the new-money bourgeoisie have con-vinced themselves that we live in an unforgiving wilderness of marauders and brutes. The hidden meaning of our new conveyances can be found right on the surface. Once upon a time, Trailblazers, Explorers, and Trackers tamed the Wild West. Now, through the sorcery of focus groups, the bull-market gentry have brought the Pathfinders and Mountaineers back into their lives in the belief that they need to conquer the savage land one more time.

✳

RESPONDING TO THE WHOLE ESSAY

1. What is Hitt's primary purpose? Is he against SUVs? [1g(1)]
2. What kinds of examples does Hitt use to support his thesis?
3. What authorities does Hitt cite? Are these the appropriate authorities for this topic? [6c, 6e]
4. Is beginning the essay with a series of questions effective? Does Hitt answer those questions? [3b(1)]
5. At what point does Hitt's essay go beyond the subject of vehicles and address more serious issues of economic class?

ANALYZING THE ELEMENTS

Grammar

1. What is the relative pronoun in the last sentence of paragraph 3? What is its antecedent? [16a(2)]
2. Explain the use of the singular *is* and the plural *are* in the second sentence of paragraph 15. [17e]
3. What part of speech is *jawbone* in paragraph 3? [11b]

Effective Sentences

1. How does Hitt use questions to make his essay more effective? [22e, 24d]
2. Explain the effective use of first person in the last sentence of paragraph 11. [24d]

Punctuation and Mechanics

1. *SUV* is an acronym. What does it stand for? [35f] Why is it capitalized? [33a(10)]
2. Why does *SUV* not contain periods? [31a(2)] How is *SUV* made plural? [29c]

Diction

1. What is accomplished by Hitt's language in phrases like *herd that grazes* (paragraph 1) and *boxy steed* (paragraph 9) in enhancing his thesis? [24a(4)]
2. What idea is conveyed by describing drivers of cars as *savages* (paragraph 20) and *maurauders and brutes* (paragraph 21)? [24a(2)]

BUILDING VOCABULARY

1. What is *Brobdingnagian* (paragraph 3)? Where does that word come from? [23a]
2. What is the origin of *behemoths* (paragraph 3)? [23a]

SUGGESTIONS FOR WRITING

1. Write an essay in which you look at the names of some other product and consider what qualities manufacturers and advertisers emphasize with these names.
2. Explain how the car you drive does or does not accurately reflect your personality and lifestyle.

*

Chapter 2

Narration

Narration is storytelling; that is, the writer of a narrative unfolds for the reader a sequence of events, either true or fictional. Although narratives usually proceed in chronological order, they may also begin in the middle or at the end of the story and provide "flashbacks" to earlier events. And occasionally a narrative recounts events in the order of their importance rather than in the time sequence in which they occurred.

Narratives come in all sizes and flavors: they may be short—jokes are often narratives—or long, as are Victorian novels. They may be humorous, as is Eric Minton's "Beating Coasterphobia" in this chapter, or serious, as is Darwin Turner's "The Harlem Renaissance."

Narratives often contain conflict and suspense. For instance, in this chapter all the writers—Minton and Turner as well as Maya Angelou, John Hockenberry, and Annie Dillard—present a conflict as the core of their tales. The conflict may be with oneself, as it is for Dillard and Minton, or with society, as in the essay by Angelou; or it may be with an idea, as it is in the essay by Turner. Hockenberry's essay presents a touching blend of conflicts.

Narratives have a point of view: they may be told in the first person ("I") or third person. First-person narratives are often deeply subjective (although they need not be), emphasizing the writer's reactions to events, as Angelou's, Minton's, Hockenberry's, and Dillard's do. Third-person narratives, on the other hand—although they may display the writer's feelings—are usually more objective. An example is Turner's "The Harlem Renaissance."

Narratives (excluding fictional narratives, which are beyond the scope of this book) may have an expressive, informative, or persuasive purpose or a combination of these. (For a full discussion of purpose, see [1g].) When a narrative is primarily expressive, it focuses on the writer's feelings about events; when primarily informative, it focuses on the events themselves; when primarily persuasive, it uses the events to influence the reader's opinion or to move the reader to some course of action. Evidence of all three purposes can be found in the readings in this section.

As you write narratives, always keep your purpose and your audience clearly in mind. Doing so will enable you to decide which events are significant and how they can best be arranged to achieve the effect you want, as well as help you choose the kinds of specific details that will make the events real for your reader.

Five questions that are sure to be in your reader's mind can help you plan your narrative strategy. In addition to learning *what* happens (action), your reader will want to know *who* is involved in the events (actors), and *when* (time) and *where* (place) the events occur (often referred to as the setting). Especially, the reader will be interested in *why* (cause).

Notice how Roy Fowler, a nontraditional student, provides answers to these questions as he recounts a frustrating experience.

Roadblocks

Introduction
Context

    Last week I arrived ten minutes late for a major anatomy exam. It wasn't my fault. I left my part-time job with plenty of time for driving to campus, parking, and getting to my seat in the classroom, but two trucks—a semi and a dump truck—collided on the interstate and stopped traffic for thirty

Point

minutes. It never fails. Why is it, whenever I really need to be somewhere, someone or something is

Setting—where
and when

always in my way, just like when I was on that Air Force training exercise in southern Germany.

    It was a very cold morning back in January 1990. The snow crunched beneath my feet, and the cold breeze stung my face as I quickly walked back from the breakfast tent to my sleeping tent where I removed my coat, gloves, scarf, and sweater and lay down on my cot trying to get warm. I only had an hour, and I wanted to soak up as much heat as possible before I had to go outside for the rest of the

Minor
conflict

day. As I drifted between sleep and wakefulness, someone roughly shook me back to consciousness. Had time passed that quickly? Surely my hour wasn't up. The captain was shaking me awake to congratulate me on becoming the father of a little girl. I became fully

Precipitating event

alert as I realized he was also holding something back: There were complications; my newborn daughter was in the intensive care unit in San Antonio, Texas; she might not live.

Background and
details
Event

    The military has a system for everything, even getting people home for emergencies. I quickly packed my bags, changed into civilian clothing, and hurried towards the administration tent to sign out of the unit before leaving for Frankfurt International Airport. But I had to wait nearly an hour until someone was

Event

available to drive me to the division support unit

(DSU) that handled all the Red Cross notifications for emergency leave. There, I completed leave forms and picked up plane tickets—paperwork required for me to leave Germany. But then, there I was, stuck sitting in another tent, waiting for another ride. Finally, after lunch, I got into an old army-green VW bus, top speed 80 kph—about 50 mph. Three hours dragged by as that old bus lumbered down the autobahn toward Frankfurt. I mentally cheered as we arrived at the U. S. Air Force side of the airport. I was ready to fly across the ocean to my gravely ill baby girl. I wasn't ready for the surprise that waited for me at the personnel office, though.

The last flight back to the States had left at two o'clock. I was so close, but I was not going home that day. The chaplain, there to give me support, said, "We'll get you out of here tomorrow morning." There was nothing to do but call the hospital in Texas to check on my family. My wife was fine, but my little girl was scheduled for surgery the next morning, surgery she had only a fifty-percent chance of surviving. I spent that evening sitting in the Air Force club, I soon realized that, though drinking myself to sleep might make the night seem to pass more quickly, it wouldn't bring me any closer to my wife and little girl in Texas. After all, there were no flights until the next day.

Early the next day one of the chaplain's drivers gave me a ride to the other side of the airport for my 10:00 flight. Ticket in hand, I checked in at the gate and boarded the plane. After everyone settled into their seats, I watched the flight attendant close the cabin door, felt the bump of the tug as it hooked to the plane, and rejoiced as it pushed us away from the gate. We taxied away from the terminal and traveled down the taxiway, feeling every crack in the asphalt, and lined up for takeoff. Waiting for the plane to take off, I drifted so deeply into thoughts of home and my baby daughter that I never felt the plane roar down the runway and leap into the air. I was startled when, ten minutes after the plane was in the air, the pilot announced, "We are having trouble with the landing gear. We can't make it retract, we do not have enough fuel to fly to the United States with the gear down, and we are too heavy to land back at Frankfurt. We are going to fly out over the ocean, and if we still cannot get the gear to retract, we will have to dump

Event

Event

Note expressive aim

Events

Note effect of details

First Set of complicating events

some fuel and return to Frankfurt." One moment my

stomach turned with anticipation, and the next it churned with frustration. Four hours later I was back at the Frankfurt terminal and no closer to home.

But I wasn't licked yet, and Delta was not the only American carrier in Frankfurt. I ran to the TWA ticket counter and exchanged my ticket for the 7:00 p.m. flight to London with an early-morning flight from there to the USA. The clock in the airport lounge where I waited slowly ticked away four hours before I stood in front of the departure gate ready to board

another plane. The gate attendant announced a delay. There was a problem with the fuel lines. I waited until 10:00 p.m. when it was announced that the repair could not be made and the flight was canceled. There were no flights to the States until the following day. The airline put us up at a small hotel an hour away from the airport.

Day three, six in the morning; I waited for a taxi to the airport to change my ticket yet again. And then I was back at the Delta departure gate waiting to board

for the third time. I entered the plane, located my seat, sat down, watched the flight attendant close the door, felt the tug connect to the plane, felt our movement away from the terminal. I was back on the runway waiting for takeoff, just as I had been the day before, but this day, this time, this plane was going to take me home even if I had to fly it myself. Once in the air and dreading an announcement that might cancel my flight home, I settled into my seat with a sigh of relief when I felt the landing gear thump into place and I began to compute my arrival time in Dallas.

Seven hours later the plane landed at DFW airport. At least I was in the United States; I could manage any roadblocks here. Once in the terminal, I called my home unit at Fort Hood to make arrangements to get to San Antonio. As the plane they booked me on taxied toward the Killeen terminal, I saw the turning rotor blades of the waiting army helicopter. I left the plane, ran across the ramp, boarded the helicopter, and ninety minutes later, landed on the grass in front of the army hospital in

San Antonio. My father and father-in-law greeted me and took me to see my wife. And then I went to ICU where my pretty baby girl fought for life. (Six years old now, with wheels, she gives perpetual motion a new definition.)

Conclusion—
Summarizes major
conflict, puts in
perspective, and
ties it to initial
minor conflict

In this supersonic age it had taken me three
days to fly from Germany to the USA. Roadblocks:
bureaucracy, scheduling problems, technical difficulties
all conspired to delay me in a time of serious family
crisis. Traffic jams, dead batteries, traffic lights—
they're still hidden behind every corner and
occasionally slow me down, but they can never hold
me back. I took my family home intact and I aced my
anatomy exam.

Commentary.   Fowler's introduction establishes the context for the essay; he
begins by recounting a recent event, being late for an exam. His analysis of
the source of his frustration provides a rationale for the essay. Then he moves
backward in time to a specific event in 1990.

From this point on, Fowler's essay is organized in straightforward chronological order, moving from the background events in Germany through the
events that followed. Within this chronological frame he establishes why the
events occurred at the same time that he makes the setting (the military and
other bureaucracies) concrete by offering details about how he continually
had to hurry up and then to wait. These details, as well as those he includes
to tell us about how worried he was about his newborn daughter, contribute
to his expressive aim.

Fowler's frustration about not getting to class on time is a conflict that
frames the primary conflict between Fowler and the roadblocks that delay him
on his journey home from Germany—bureaucracy, scheduling inadequacies,
and technical failures. Although how he misses his exam is not fully developed, this incident lends force to the main conflict by emphasizing his feelings of urgency and irritation as he discovers each successive delay.

Fowler makes skillful use of parallelism when he reports the sequence of
his actions as he boards each plane. In the first instance, the actions emphasize his worried anticipation; in the second they function almost as a scale
upon which he measures his frustration.

Note too how Fowler's reference to roadblocks in his conclusion echoes
his introduction. The essay ends snappily, tightly drawing together the two
events in a single sentence: "I took my family home intact and I aced my
anatomy exam."

Beating Coasterphobia
Eric Minton

Freelance writer Eric Minton covers the amusement park industry in his column, in *Funworld* magazine. He has also published articles in a number of trade magazines as well as in popular magazines such as *Good Housekeeping* and *Modern Maturity*. This essay appeared in *Psychology Today* with two other essays about roller coasters and haunted houses by Minton (included in this book; see "Thrills and Chills" in Chapter 1 and "Scaring Up Business" in Chapter 5).

1   Whenever I've been faced with riding a roller coaster, I'VE recalled the mythic Sirens' singing. I remember all too well that sailors lured by the beauty of the voices ended up crashing and perishing on the rocks.

2   My fear of roller coasters has been deeply ingrained. I suffer from acrophobia, which makes me certain I'll spill onto the ground a mile below, and a personal height (6-foot-2-inches) that makes me feel I have to scrunch down to avoid being scalped by girders. As if that isn't enough, I also suffer from motion sickness. Ironically, I'm a journalist who derives his living from writing about amusement parks, and I'm well aware of how safe these contraptions are (triple-redundancy security systems!), Still, I *know* that my ride will be the one time *all* the safety systems fail.

3   I'm not alone in that feeling, of course—and that concerns amusement parks who see dollars dribbling away. Now they're doing something about it. Universal Studios recently enlisted two psychologists, Brian Newmark and Michael Otto, to come up with a plan to help frightened riders at its new Orlando, Florida, theme park, Islands of Adventure. The park's biggest attractions are two next-generation coasters: *Dueling Dragons,* which sends two inverted trains on intertwining courses resembling the flight paths of the Navy's Blue Angels, and *The Incredible Hulk,* which catapults cars through a kelly green track that looks like gift-wrap ribbon gone berserk.

4   The psychologists' solution: the Coasterphobia Stress Management Program. As a diagnosis, the term "coasterphobia" is suspect, says Otto, Ph.D., director of the cognitive-behavior therapy program at Massachusetts General Hospital and an associate professor at Harvard Medical School. "A 'phobia' demands you have a serious life interference," he explains. "You can go through your whole life and not ride roller coasters and be perfectly fine." But to those who fear the pretzelated structures, life is often less enjoyable. In screening participants for the course's test run,

"coasterphobics" reported that their trepidations kept them from fully par-
ticipating in social outings to amusement parks, and parents felt that it
hindered their performance as mothers and fathers.

Fifteen coasterphobics were in the first class; I was one of them. The   5
goal: to learn techniques that we could use before and during the ride to
overcome the strain. "It's not about convincing people to get on the ride,"
stresses Newmark, Ph.D., a clinical psychologist in Wayland, Massachusetts.
"It's about reducing anxiety."

Newmark and Otto began by explaining to us how the mind and body   6
naturally respond to a coaster's speed and G forces, sensations coaster fans
channel into a thrill but the rest of us believe is real danger. We had to
learn to not listen to our instincts, said the pair. "Why do we tighten our
hold on the harness handles if we're sure the coaster car is going to fly off
the track?" asked Newmark "Do we think we can really pilot the car to
a safe landing by gripping harder?" I listened closely to their teachings to
approach the ride as fun. Engineers design these rides to thrill us, we were
told, and if we sit back and let their genius unfold, we'll enjoy the experience.

Then we trained. We tensed and untensed muscles to learn to relax.   7
We did breathing exercises. We circled our heads to induce dizziness. We
rocked back and forth in our chairs to simulate a coaster's motion. Then
we circled our heads while rocking. We screamed, which Otto pointed out
not only forces you to breathe on the coaster but is part of the ride's fun.
We watched a passenger perspective video of *The Incredible Hulk*, rocking as we did so. At this point the hitherto-willing participants started
swallowing hard. Eyes grew wide and wary, and when Otto turned the
video's sound on, one woman tensed up so much she forgot to rock.

Next came our graduation exercise: riding *The Incredible Hulk*. I set-   8
tled into my seat, the harness lowered over my shoulders and mechanically
locked into place. Have fun, I reminded myself, and instead of feeling
trapped or worrying that you're among the first people to ride this coaster
(guinea pig? sufficiently tested?), just let the adventure happen. With the
catapult up that first lift, I began a yelled-out running commentary that
continued through the ride's sudden rotating twists and countless loops,
corkscrews and dives, all the way back to the station. Sure it was gibberish,
but normally I ride coasters with clenched teeth.

To the psychologists' surprise, all 15 of us coasterphobics rode *The*   9
Hulk not once, but twice. Several even took a third turn, and one couple
hit the track five times. As for me, on both my trips I arrived back at the
station with a happy heart but a queasy stomach. Motion sickness isn't
imaginary, sad to say, and just writing this brings back that woozy feeling. Nevertheless, I no longer regard coasters with apprehension. I'm even
ready to take on *Dueling Dragons,* which looks even more diabolical than
The Hulk. Maybe I'll get a little ill from the motion, but now I can handle
the emotion.

✳

RESPONDING TO THE WHOLE ESSAY

1. What is Minton's primary purpose? [1g(1)]
2. What is the point of view of this essay? How does the point of view make this essay particularly effective, considering its purpose?
3. Who is Minton's audience? Find evidence in the essay that Minton is aware of his audience. [1g(2)]
4. How does Minton use humor effectively in his essay?
5. What order does Minton use to present the sequence of his events? [2c]
6. Read the other two essays in this book by Minton about roller coasters and haunted houses (Chapters 1 and 5).

ANALYZING THE ELEMENTS

Grammar

1. Examine the use of the passive voice in the first sentence of the essay. [21d(1)]
2. The first sentence of paragraph 3 contains a relative pronoun. What is the antecedent? [16a(2)]
3. Is the first sentence of paragraph 7 a complete sentence? [11a]

Effective Sentences

1. Examine the sequence of events outlined in paragraph 7. How does Minton use sentence variety and transition to present these events effectively? [22]
2. Is Minton's conclusion effective? Why or why not? [[3b(2)]

Punctuation and Mechanics

1. How is the colon used in paragraphs 4, 5, and 8? [31d]
2. Find three different uses of the comma in paragraph 8 [27]
3. Why are *The Incredible Hulk* and *Dueling Dragons* italicized? [34]
4. How is the parenthesis used in paragraph 8? [31f]

Diction

1. Paragaph 1 contains an allusion. Explain how the allusion helps to establish Minton's tone in the essay. [Glossary of Terms]
2. Find words that express the subjective feelings of the author. [24]

BUILDING VOCABULARY

1. What is *acrophobia* (paragraph 2)? How does Minton create the word *coaster-phobia* using the suffix *-phobia*?
2. Minton also creates the word *pretzelated* (paragraph 4). What does the suffix *-ated* mean?

SUGGESTIONS FOR WRITING

1. Write an essay in which you narrate an experience that frightened you or about which you had ambivalent feelings.
2. Write a narrative essay in which you describe your personal experience taking a class.

The Hockenberry File
John Hockenberry

John Hockenberry has established a respected reputation in all media—radio, television, and print. He has won Peabody Awards and Emmy Awards, and he was the first Western broadcast journalist to report directly from Kurdish refugee camps in Albania. Born in Dayton, Ohio, and educated at the University of Chicago and University of Oregon, Hockenberry has been paraplegic since a car accident at the age of nineteen. His memoir, *Moving Violations: War Zones, Wheelchairs, and Declarations of Independence* (Hyperion, 1995) outlines his experiences as a reporter in a wheelchair. He can be seen on NBC's *Dateline* and his own show *Hockenberry* on MSNBC. He lives in New York with his wife and two daughters.

A refugee camp has no stairs but in this one, just outside Kukes, Albania, 1 where it had rained the entire night before, stairs might have actually helped in getting through this mud. Rolling carefully to avoid the open toilets, I ventured into the center of the camp to speak with a group of families, carefully thinned of their adult males, huddled behind their tractor wagons draped with clear or occasionally green plastic. These convoys of red tractors full of weeping old women and smiling children have become the emblems of this, the last atrocity in an atrocity-filled century.

During my first three days, 25,000 Kosovar refugees had crossed the 2 Albanian border and an even greater number had crossed into Macedonia. People sat together on the ground anywhere they could find a rock or stump. The oldest and most frail were on brown blankets stained with dark puddles of rainwater. A tiny baby was wrapped tightly in a wooden cradle. A feeble old woman in a scarf rocked while gazing back at the mountain peaks she had so recently crossed. She had made it over. In her eyes was the disheartening assumption she would not be making the return trip in this lifetime.

Among the little piles of objects arranged at the back of each wagon, the 3 ornately carved cradle stood out. This was the one object that even allowed for the possibility that life was dedicated to something besides crude, pure necessity. Everything else, dented metal pots, rope, drab clothes, random pieces of flatware, plastic forks with metal spoons grabbed by the fistful, was absent of any decoration. All of it had been hastily collected in the rush to leave. Staying warm and dry over miles and weeks in the snow and rain was the only goal. Each family had its heroic inventory of the items within reach at the moment they became too terrified to stay. For these Kosovar Albanians, now home is no longer within reach.

I asked questions about places, dates. Probing to find a system behind this   4
mass exodus, a pattern emerged. Village by village, paramilitary police had
come. They marked the doors of each Albanian home and had ordered the
people to leave. Many used colorful language. *Go find your Clinton. He has
a home for you.* Or else it came out, *You belong to NATO now.*

Where were the men? There were various stories. "They stayed behind to   5
fight the Serbs," some said. "They fought and died already," said others. Most
said only, "They were taken away." Each family had pictures of its men and
laid them out for curious journalists to see. People and pictures together like
this made eerie gap-toothed family *tableaux* with blurry snapshots where the
brothers, fathers and sons should have been.

I knew this place. I had been to places like these before. This hasty hu-   6
manitarian retreat was an old story. The Kosovars were little different from
any people uprooted. As in Romania, Somalia, Iraq, Iran and Kurdistan, the
adults were the ones terrified and sad, their faces said "refugee." On the other
hand, their children seemed to be having the time of their lives. They ran wild.
Their faces said that the squalid camp had become in their innocent eyes a
place of adventure, the first in their young lives.

This was expressed in chilling contradictions. At the same moment one   7
family was sobbing about the loss of their sons, a young boy, the last son,
showed me his arm. On it was written UCK, the acronym of the Kosovo
Liberation Army. He marched back and forth in front of his family's tent anxious to go off and fight. "And if you don't come back?" I asked.

"I will go to heaven," was his joyous reply. His family watched vacantly.   8
His mother said to me, "These camps make our children into beggars and soldiers. Unless we go home they will be able to do nothing else."

Disability was something of an abstract concept here. From the height of   9
my wheelchair, which could have made the trip over the mountains more bear-
able for any pair of refugees, I towered over the people sitting on the ground.
My chair looked useful to them. But otherwise it was not important. I did not
stand out in any way. It was a welcome relief from the constant staring and
the day to day freak-show mentality in America whenever a wheelchair arrives on the scene. The same blessed anonymity I had known before, in feeding camps in Somalia or at a border checkpoint in Iraq crowded with Kurdish
refugees. One man who drove me from place to place in a large van had built
a wooden ramp for rolling me up and into his vehicle. He had painted it
proudly and affixed non-skid strips for my wheels. Osman was his name. He
wanted me to call him Señor Ramp. We soon became fast friends although
we knew not a syllable of each other's respective languages.

Going to Albania was a return to places I had not seen for many years.   10
In the beginning, as the first horrible reports began to filter out of Kosovo, I
went into a closet and pulled out a beat-up aluminum suitcase I had not looked
at for a decade. It had been my companion in the Middle East for the years
I lived in Jerusalem as a radio correspondent, during the Gulf War, Kurdistan,
and Somalia. Every person with a disability has such a case, a bag, a box in

which are stored those items which make an independent life safe, possible. Each case contains those items which an individual has tested through experience, each case as different as each independent life.

I opened my case. There were the spare inner tubes, wheelchair tires, hex wrenches, cans of motor oil, catheters, seven bottles of hydrogen peroxide, iodine solution, batteries, flashlights, hammers, files and dozens of small tools for any conceivable wheelchair repair. When I saw that it was ready to go, I knew I was.   11

Unlike any other time in a foreign war zone this time I would be broadcasting live television. The main risk of doing live TV from the middle of a refugee camp in Albania is that America will suddenly stop paying attention. At the end of the twentieth century, war is not a reliable story line for American television viewers anymore. I stayed in Albania for about three weeks. I left after two boys opened fire in a Colorado high school on April 20. America stopped paying attention. The refugee crisis goes on. I still miss my friend, Señor Ramp.   12

❋

RESPONDING TO THE WHOLE ESSAY

1. This essay appeared in *WE Magazine,* a journal that focuses on issues related to disabilities. Would it be of interest to a broader audience? [1g(2)]
2. What is the specific purpose of Hockenberry's narration? [1g(1)]
3. Find evidence that Hockenberry's disability informs his perspective.
4   How does this narration place the author in a conflict or create suspense?
5. How does Hockenberry focus on individual experiences? [2d(2)]

ANALYZING THE ELEMENTS

Grammar

1. What is the subject of the last sentence of paragraph 2? [11c]
2. Why is the plural *were* used in the second sentence of paragraph 11? [17e(5)]

Effective Sentences

1. How does Hockenberry use subordination and coordination to make his first sentence effective? [19]
2. Comment on the brevity of the first sentence of paragraph 6. [21]

Punctuation and Mechanics

1. How does Hockenberry use italics in paragraph 4? [34]
2. Why does Hockenberry use a comma in the first sentence of paragraph 4? [27c]

Diction

1. What image is created by use of words such as *heroic* (paragraph 3) and *exodus* (paragraph 4)? [24a]
2. Considering his audience, why does Hockenberry use the phrase *freak-show* in paragraph 9? [23d(3)]

BUILDING VOCABULARY

1. Look up the following words: *ornately* (paragraph 3), *tableaux* (paragraph 5), *abstract* (paragraph 9).

SUGGESTIONS FOR WRITING

1. Hockenberry describes his case that contains all the necessary things for wheelchair repair. The refugees similarly have had to leave their country with only the necessary "inventory" of objects. If you were forced to leave your home at short notice, what necessary things would you carry with you and why?
2. Hockenberry worries that Americans are no longer paying attention to the problems in Albania because our attention has been directed to other, more local problems. Write an essay in which you narrate your observation or experience of an event or situation that you would like others to pay more attention to.

Momma, the Dentist, and Me
Maya Angelou

Born Marguerite Johnson in St. Louis in 1928, Maya Angelou was raised
with her brother, Bailey, in Stamps, Arkansas, by her grandmother, who, with
Uncle Willie, operated a country store. After leaving Stamps, she lived in Los
Angeles, where she had a dancing career, and in New York, where she became an active worker in the civil rights movement. She has produced a series on Africa for PBS-TV and written three books of poetry as well as four
volumes of her autobiography. This selection is from the first of those autobiographical volumes, *I Know Why the Caged Bird Sings*.

The angel of the candy counter had found me out at last, and was exacting   1
excruciating penance for all the stolen Milky Ways, Mounds, Mr. Goodbars,
and Hersheys with Almonds. I had two cavities that were rotten to the gums.
The pain was beyond the bailiwick of crushed aspirins or oil of cloves. Only
one thing could help me, so I prayed earnestly that I'd be allowed to sit under the house and have the building collapse on my left jaw. Since there was
no Negro dentist in Stamps, nor doctor either, for that matter, Momma had
dealt with previous toothaches by pulling them out (a string tied to the tooth
with the other end looped over her fist), pain killers and prayer. In this particular instance the medicine had proved ineffective; there wasn't enough
enamel left to hook a string on, and the prayers were being ignored because
the Balancing Angel was blocking their passage.

I lived a few days and nights in blinding pain, not so much toying with   2
as seriously considering the idea of jumping in the well, and Momma decided
I had to be taken to a dentist. The nearest Negro dentist was in Texarkana,
twenty-five miles away, and I was certain that I'd be dead long before we
reached half the distance. Momma said we'd go to Dr. Lincoln, right in Stamps,
and he'd take care of me. She said he owed her a favor.

I knew there were a number of whitefolks in town that owed her favors.   3
Bailey and I had seen the books which showed how she had lent money to
Blacks and whites alike during the Depression, and most still owed her. But
I couldn't aptly remember seeing Dr. Lincoln's name, nor had I ever heard of
a Negro's going to him as a patient. However, Momma said we were going,
and put water on the stove for our baths. I had never been to a doctor, so she
told me that after the bath (which would make my mouth feel better) I had
to put on freshly starched and ironed underclothes from inside out. The ache
failed to respond to the bath, and I knew then that the pain was more serious
than that which anyone had ever suffered.

Before we left the Store, she ordered me to brush my teeth and then wash   4
my mouth with Listerine. The idea of even opening my clamped jaws increased
the pain, but upon her explanation that when you go to a doctor you have
to clean yourself all over, but most especially the part that's to be examined,
I screwed up my courage and unlocked my teeth. The cool air in my mouth
and the jarring of my molars dislodged what little remained of my reason. I
had frozen to the pain, my family nearly had to tie me down to take the tooth-
brush away. It was no small effort to get me started on the road to the dentist. Momma spoke to all the passers-by, but didn't stop to chat. She explained
over her shoulder that we were going to the doctor and she'd "pass the time
of day" on our way home.

Until we reached the pond the pain was my world, an aura that haloed   5
me for the three feet around. Crossing the bridge into whitefolks' country,
pieces of sanity pushed themselves forward. I had to stop moaning and start
walking straight. The white towel, which was drawn under my chin and tied
over my head, had to be arranged. If one was dying, it had to be done in style
if the dying took place in whitefolks' part of town.

On the other side of the bridge the ache seemed to lessen as if a white-   6
breeze blew off the whitefolks and cushioned everything in their neighborhood—including my jaw. The gravel road was smoother, the stones smaller
and the tree branches hung down around the path and nearly covered us. If
the pain didn't diminish then, the familiar yet strange sights hypnotized me
into believing that it had.

But my head continued to throb with the measured insistence of a bass   7
drum, and how could a toothache pass the calaboose, hear the songs of the
prisoners, their blues and laughter, and not be changed? How could one or
two or even a mouthful of angry tooth roots meet a wagonload of powhitetrash children, endure their idiotic snobbery and not feel less important?

Behind the building which housed the dentist's office ran a small path   8
used by servants and those tradespeople who catered to the butcher and
Stamps' one restaurant. Momma and I followed that lane to the backstairs of
Dentist Lincoln's office. The sun was bright and gave the day a hard reality
as we climbed up the steps to the second floor.

Momma knocked on the back door and a young white girl opened it to   9
show surprise at seeing us there. Momma said she wanted to see Dentist
Lincoln and to tell him Annie was there. The girl closed the door firmly. Now
the humiliation of hearing Momma describe herself as if she had no last name
to the young white girl was equal to the physical pain. It seemed terribly unfair to have a toothache and a headache and have to bear at the same time
the heavy burden of Blackness.

It was always possible that the teeth would quiet down and maybe drop   10
out of their own accord. Momma said we would wait. We leaned in the harsh
sunlight on the shaky railings of the dentist's back porch for over an hour.

He opened the door and looked at Momma. "Well, Annie, what can I do   11
for you?"

He didn't see the towel around my jaw or notice my swollen face.   12

Momma said, "Dentist Lincoln. It's my grandbaby here. She got two rot-   13
ten teeth that's giving her a fit."

She waited for him to acknowledge the truth of her statement. He made   14
no comment, orally or facially.

"She had this toothache purt' near four days now, and today I said, 'Young   15
lady, you going to the Dentist.'"

"Annie?"   16

"Yes, sir, Dentist Lincoln."   17

He was choosing words the way people hunt for shells. "Annie, you know   18
I don't treat nigra, colored people."

"I know, Dentist Lincoln. But this here is just my little grandbaby, and   19
she ain't gone be no trouble to you. . . ."

"Annie, everybody has a policy. In this world you have to have a policy.   20
Now, my policy is I don't treat colored people."

The sun had baked the oil out of Momma's skin and melted the Vaseline   21
in her hair. She shone greasily as she leaned out of the dentist's shadow.

"Seem like to me, Dentist Lincoln, you might look after her, she ain't noth-   22
ing but a little mite. And seems like maybe you owe me a favor or two."

He reddened slightly. "Favor or no favor. The money has all been repaid   23
to you and that's the end of it. Sorry, Annie." He had his hand on the doorknob. "Sorry." His voice was a bit kinder on the second "Sorry," as if he
really was.

Momma said, "I wouldn't press on you like this for myself but I can't take   24
No. Not for my grandbaby. When you come to borrow my money you didn't
have to beg. You asked me, and I lent it. Now, it wasn't my policy. I ain't no
moneylender, but you stood to lose this building and I tried to help you out."

"It's been paid, and raising your voice won't make me change my mind.   25
My policy . . ." He let go of the door and stepped nearer Momma. The three
of us were crowded on the small landing. "Annie, my policy is I'd rather stick
my hand in a dog's mouth than in a nigger's."

He had never once looked at me. He turned his back and went through   26
the door into the cool beyond. Momma backed up inside herself for a few
minutes. I forgot everything except her face which was almost a new one to
me. She leaned over and took the doorknob, and in her everyday soft voice
she said, "Sister, go on downstairs. Wait for me. I'll be there directly."

Under the most common of circumstances I knew it did no good to ar-   27
gue with Momma. So I walked down the steep stairs, afraid to look back and
afraid not to do so. I turned as the door slammed, and she was gone.

Momma walked in that room as if she owned it. She shoved that silly   28
nurse aside with one hand and strode into the dentist's office. He was sitting
in his chair, sharpening his mean instruments and putting extra sting into his
medicines. Her eyes were blazing like live coals and her arms had doubled
themselves in length. He looked up at her just before she caught him by the
collar of his white jacket.

"Stand up when you see a lady, you contemptuous scoundrel." Her tongue   29
had thinned and the words rolled off well enunciated. Enunciated and sharp
like little claps of thunder.

The dentist had no choice but to stand at R.O.T.C. attention. His head   30
dropped after a minute and his voice was humble. "Yes, ma'am, Mrs. Henderson."

"You knave, do you think you acted like a gentleman, speaking to me like   31
that in front of my granddaughter?" She didn't shake him, although she had
the power. She simply held him upright.

"No, ma'am, Mrs. Henderson."   32

"No, ma'am, Mrs. Henderson, what?" Then she did give him the tiniest   33
of shakes, but because of her strength the action set his head and arms to
shaking loose on the ends of his body. He stuttered much worse than Uncle
Willie. "No, ma'am, Mrs. Henderson, I'm sorry."

With just an edge of her disgust showing, Momma slung him back in his   34
dentist's chair. "Sorry is as sorry does, and you're about the sorriest dentist I
ever laid my eyes on." (She could afford to slip into the vernacular because
she had such eloquent command of English.)

"I didn't ask you to apologize in front of Marguerite, because I don't want   35
her to know my power, but I order you, now and herewith. Leave Stamps by
sundown."

"Mrs. Henderson, I can't get my equipment . . ." He was shaking terri-   36
bly now.

"Now, that brings me to my second order. You will never again practice   37
dentistry. Never! When you get settled in your next place, you will be a veg-
etarian caring for dogs with the mange, cats with the cholera and cows with
the epizootic. Is that clear?"

The saliva ran down his chin and his eyes filled with tears. "Yes, ma'am.   38
Thank you for not killing me. Thank you, Mrs. Henderson."

Momma pulled herself back from being ten feet tall with eight-foot arms   39
and said, "You're welcome for nothing, you varlet, I wouldn't waste a killing
on the likes of you."

On her way out she waved her handkerchief at the nurse and turned her   40
into a crocus sack of chicken feed.

Momma looked tired when she came down the stairs, but who wouldn't   41
be tired if they had gone through what she had. She came close to me and
adjusted the towel under my jaw (I had forgotten the toothache; I only knew
that she made her hands gentle in order not to awaken the pain). She took
my hand. Her voice never changed. "Come on, Sister."

I reckoned we were going home where she would concoct a brew to elim-   42
inate the pain and maybe give me new teeth too. New teeth that would grow
overnight out of my gums. She led me toward the drugstore, which was in
the opposite direction from the Store. "I'm taking you to Dentist Baker in
Texarkana."

I was glad after all that I had bathed and put on Mum and Cashmere   43
Bouquet talcum powder. It was a wonderful surprise. My toothache had

quieted to solemn pain, Momma had obliterated the evil white man, and we were going on a trip to Texarkana, just the two of us.

On the Greyhound she took an inside seat in the back, and I sat beside   44
her. I was so proud of being her granddaughter and sure that some of her magic must have come down to me. She asked if I was scared. I only shook my head and leaned over on her cool brown upper arm. There was no chance that a dentist, especially a Negro dentist, would dare hurt me then. Not with Momma there. The trip was uneventful, except that she put her arm around me, which was very unusual for Momma to do.

The dentist showed me the medicine and the needle before he deadened   45
my gums, but if he hadn't I wouldn't have worried. Momma stood right behind him. Her arms were folded and she checked on everything he did. The teeth were extracted and she bought me an ice cream cone from the side window of a drug counter. The trip back to Stamps was quiet, except that I had to spit into a very small empty snuff can which she had gotten for me and it was difficult with the bus humping and jerking on our country roads.

At home, I was given a warm salt solution, and when I washed out my   46
mouth I showed Bailey the empty holes, where the clotted blood sat like filling in a pie crust. He said I was quite brave, and that was my cue to reveal our confrontation with the peckerwood dentist and Momma's incredible powers.

I had to admit that I didn't hear the conversation, but what else could   47
she have said than what I said she said? What else done? He agreed with my analysis in a lukewarm way, and I happily (after all, I'd been sick) flounced into the Store. Momma was preparing our evening meal and Uncle Willie leaned on the door sill. She gave her version.

"Dentist Lincoln got right uppity. Said he'd rather put his hand in a dog's   48
mouth. And when I reminded him of the favor, he brushed it off like a piece of lint. Well, I sent Sister downstairs and went inside. I hadn't never been in his office before, but I found the door to where he takes out teeth, and him and the nurse was in there thick as thieves. I just stood there till he caught sight of me." Crash bang the pots on the stove. "He jumped just like he was sitting on a pin. He said, 'Annie, I done tole you, I ain't gonna mess around in no niggah's mouth.' I said, 'Somebody's got to do it then,' and he said, 'Take her to Texarkana to the colored dentist' and that's when I said, 'If you paid me my money I could afford to take her.' He said, 'It's all been paid.' I tole him everything but the interest been paid. He said ''Twasn't no interest.' I said, ''Tis now, I'll take ten dollars as payment in full.' You know, Willie, it wasn't no right thing to do, 'cause I lent that money without thinking about it.

"He tole that little snippety nurse of his'n to give me ten dollars and make   49
me sign a 'paid in full' receipt. She gave it to me and I signed the papers. Even though by rights he was paid up before, I figger, he gonna be that kind of nasty, he gonna have to pay for it."

Momma and her son laughed and laughed over the white man's evilness   50
and her retributive sin.

I preferred, much preferred, my version.   51

*

RESPONDING TO THE WHOLE ESSAY

1. How would you describe Angelou's purpose in "Momma, the Dentist, and Me"? Is it mainly to share an experience, to move her reader to indignation, or both? Point to evidence in the essay. [1g]
2. Comment on the difference in tone between the account of Momma's confrontation with the dentist given in italics and that given at the end of the essay. [3a(3)]
3. Although Angelou narrates the events involved in a trip to two dentists, the account deals with more than just the pain of a toothache. Explain.
4. What is Angelou's main point? How do you know? [2b]
5. In what kind of order does Angelou relate the event? Why is this organization appropriate? [2c]
6. Identify and account for any changes in the point of view Angelou uses in this essay.

ANALYZING THE ELEMENTS

Grammar

1. Why is *Negro's* in sentence 3 of paragraph 3 in the possessive case? [29a(5)]
2. The last sentence of paragraph 29 is elliptical; that is, an important grammatical element is implied rather than stated. Supply the omitted part and comment on the difference in the effect. [13]
3. The first sentence of "Momma, the Dentist, and Me" contains the verb *had found,* the fifth sentence contains the verb *had dealt,* and the second sentence of paragraph 3 contains the verb *had lent.* To what time sequence do these verbs refer? What would be the effect of rewriting each sentence using *found, dealt,* and *lent* instead? [17c]

Effective Sentences

1. This essay contains what appear to be two serious grammatical errors. One of these occurs in the fifth sentence of paragraph 1, and the other can be found in the second sentence of paragraph 5. Identify these errors and explain why you think they were not corrected. [15e(1) and 16e(3)]
2. Observe the parallelism Angelou uses in the third sentence of paragraph 28 and the fourth sentence of paragraph 37 (beginning "When you get settled"). Try to rewrite the second sentence of paragraph 6 so that all three elements described are parallel. What difficulties do you encounter? How would you resolve them? [20]
3. Comment upon how Angelou achieves sentence variety in paragraph 45. [22]

Punctuation and Mechanics

1. Account for why, in the second sentence of paragraph 3, *Blacks* is capitalized, whereas *whites* is not. Why is *Store* capitalized in sentence 1 of paragraph 4? [33]
2. Justify the lack of a comma following the introductory adverb clause in the first

sentence of paragraph 5 and before the last element of a series in the final sentence of paragraph 7. [27]
3. Explain the use of single and double quotation marks in paragraph 15. [30]

Diction

1. Angelou uses two kinds of vocabulary in "Momma, the Dentist, and Me." Dictionaries attach labels to words that are not in Edited American English. Use your dictionary to check for labels on the following words: *bailiwick* (paragraph 1), *calaboose* and *powhitetrash* (paragraph 7), *nigger* (paragraph 25), *knave* (paragraph 31), *sorriest* (paragraph 34), *epizootic* (paragraph 37), *varlet* (paragraph 39), *crocus* (paragraph 40), *peckerwood* (paragraph 46), *snippety* (paragraph 49), *retributive* (paragraph 50). If a word is not listed, what do you think that indicates? [24c]
2. Paragraphs 13 through 24 contain a number of expressions that would be grammatically incorrect in most written English. Why are they acceptable here? Are there any other instances in which these expressions might be acceptable in writing? Explain. [23]
3. "Momma, the Dentist, and Me" contains several similes. Find three and explain why each is appropriate. [24a(4)]

BUILDING VOCABULARY

1. Define *humiliate*. List and define two synonyms and two antonyms for *humiliate*. Write sentences using each of these words.
2. The verb *concoct* has two related meanings. What are they? List and define one synonym for each of the meanings of *concoct*.

SUGGESTIONS FOR WRITING

1. Write an essay about an event where someone was unthinkingly and unnecessarily cruel.
2. Write an essay in which you give two versions of a single event, each from a different point of view. You might do as Angelou did and write about the event as you wanted it to be and also as it actually was, or you might write about how you could look at a single event in two different ways depending upon external influences.

God in the Doorway
Annie Dillard

Annie Dillard, a writer and a naturalist, was born in 1945 in Pittsburgh, Pennsylvania. She has published several volumes of essays, among them *Pilgrim at Tinker Creek,* for which she received the Pulitzer Prize for nonfiction (1974), *Holy the Firm* (1978), and *Teaching a Stone to Talk* (1982). Leaving Virginia, where she had written *Pilgrim at Tinker Creek,* she taught writing at Western Washington University. She now makes her home in Connecticut and is a frequent contributor to *Atlantic, Harper's, Science,* and other magazines.

1 One cold Christmas Eve I was up unnaturally late because we had all gone out to dinner—my parents, my baby sister, and I. We had come home to a warm living room, and Christmas Eve. Our stockings dropped from the mantel; beside them, a special table bore a bottle of ginger ale and a plate of cookies.

2 I had taken off my fancy winter coat and was standing on the heat register to bake my shoe soles and warm my bare legs. There was a commotion at the front door; it opened, and cold wind blew around my dress.

3 Everyone was calling me. "Look who's here! Look who's here!" I looked. It was Santa Claus. Whom I never—ever—wanted to meet. Santa Claus was looming in the doorway and looking around for me. My mother's voice was thrilled: "Look who's here!" I ran upstairs.

4 Like everyone in his right mind, I feared Santa Claus, thinking he was God. I was still thoughtless and brute, reactive. I knew right from wrong, but had barely tested the possibility of shaping my own behavior, and then only from fear, and not yet from love. Santa Claus was an old man whom you never saw, but who nevertheless saw you; he knew when you'd been bad or good. He knew when you'd been bad or good! And I had been bad.

5 My mother called and called, enthusiastic, pleading; I wouldn't come down. My father encouraged me; my sister howled. I wouldn't come down, but I could bend over the stairwell and see: Santa Claus stood in the doorway with night over his shoulder, letting in all the cold air of the sky; Santa Claus stood in the doorway monstrous and bright, powerless, ringing a loud bell and repeating Merry Christmas, Merry Christmas. I never came down. I don't know who ate the cookies.

6 For so many years now I have known that this Santa Claus was actually a rigged-up Miss White, who lived across the street, that I confuse the *dramatis personae* in my mind, making of Santa Claus, God, and Miss White an awesome, vulnerable trinity. This is really a story about Miss White.

Miss White was old; she lived alone in the big house across the street. She 7
liked having me around; she plied me with cookies, taught me things about
the world, and tried to interest me in finger painting, in which she herself took
great pleasure. She would set up easels in her kitchen, tack enormous slick
soaking papers to their frames, and paint undulating undersea scenes: hori-
zontal smears of color sparked by occasional vertical streaks which were understood to be fixed kelp. I liked her. She meant no harm on earth, and yet
half a year after her failed visit as Santa Claus, I ran from her again.

That day, a day of the following summer, Miss White and I knelt in her 8
yard while she showed me a magnifying glass. It was a large, strong hand
lens. She lifted my hand and, holding it very still, focused a dab of sunshine
on my palm. The glowing crescent wobbled, spread, and finally contracted to
a point. It burned; I was burned; I ripped my hand away and ran home crying. Miss White called after me, sorry, explaining, but I didn't look back.

Even now I wonder: if I meet God, will he take and hold my bare hand 9
in his, and focus his eye on my palm, and kindle that spot and let me burn?

But no. It is I who misunderstood everything and let everybody down. 10
Miss White, God, I am sorry I ran from you. I am still running, running from
that knowledge, that eye, that love from which there is no refuge. For you
meant only love, and love, and I felt only fear, and pain. So once in Israel love
came to us incarnate, stood in the doorway between two worlds, and we were
all afraid.

*

RESPONDING TO THE WHOLE ESSAY

1. The first paragraph establishes the time and place of the action as well as introducing some of the actors—information commonly offered in introductions to narratives. How does Dillard make this information interesting and immediate for
   the reader? [3b(1)]

2. What time is being spoken of in each of paragraphs 5, 6, and 7? How does Dillard
   signal the time changes? [3d]

3. How does Dillard integrate the magnifying glass incident with the Santa Claus incident? What details tie them together? What do the two events have in common?
   What does she see as the meaning of the two events?

4. Is Dillard's conclusion effective? Why or why not? What is the effect of the final
   sentence of the essay? [3b(2)]

5. Identify as clearly as you can Dillard's primary purpose in "God in the Doorway."
   Then examine the essay to see whether other purposes might also be involved and
   how they might interact in the essay. [1g(1)]

6. In paragraph 6, Dillard says, "This is really a story about Miss White." Is it really a story about Miss White? Explain your answer.

ANALYZING THE ELEMENTS

Grammar

1. In the second sentence of paragraph 2, Dillard coordinates main clauses in two ways. Explain what relationships among the three clauses are established by this handling of coordination. [19b]
2. In the third sentence of paragraph 4, the coordinating conjunctions *but* and *and* help to establish certain relationships among a group of related ideas. Identify the ideas Dillard is presenting here, and explain the relationships among them. How are these relationships reflected in the rest of the essay? [3d and 19b(3)]
3. In the last sentence of paragraph 8, what do *sorry* and *explaining* modify? Explain why they are separated from the word they modify. [15a and 21f]

Effective Sentences

1. What is the effect of the repetition in the fourth and fifth sentences of paragraph 4? [21e]
2. Comment on Dillard's use of sentence variety in paragraph 5. [22a]
3. In the fifth sentence of paragraph 8, does "It burned; I was burned" achieve more than the mere repetition of an idea? If so, what?

Punctuation and Mechanics

1. What is the purpose of the dashes in the fifth sentence of paragraph 3? [31e]
2. Dillard makes frequent use of the semicolon throughout her essay. Explain her use of the semicolon in the first three sentences of paragraph 5, the second sentence of paragraph 7, and the next-to-last sentence of paragraph 8. [28]
3 Explain the commas in the third sentence of paragraph 10. [27]

Diction

1. In the third sentence of paragraph 5, Dillard combines the seemingly contradictory adjectives *monstrous, bright,* and *powerless* to describe Santa Claus. In paragraph 6 she combines *awesome* and *vulnerable.* Explain how this juxtaposition of seemingly contradictory qualities expands her meaning. [24a]
2. In the final sentence of the essay, Dillard uses the word *incarnate.* Look up the word in a good dictionary, and then explain what connotations it brings to the sentence. [24a(2)]
3. Also in the last sentence of the essay, Dillard tells us that love "stood in the doorway between two worlds." What kind(s) of figurative language does this phrase contain? What does she mean by "doorway between two worlds"? [24a(4)]

BUILDING VOCABULARY

1. *The American Heritage Dictionary* offers two distinct meanings for *kindle.* Dillard uses *kindle* as a transitive verb meaning "ignite or arouse." Explain the origin of this verb. How it is related to the intransitive verb *kindle,* meaning "to give birth to young?"
2. List and define two synonyms for the verb *try.* Write a sentence using each of these synonyms.

SUGGESTIONS FOR WRITING

1. Narrate an experience that you did not fully understand at the time it occurred but that you came to understand later.
2. Narrate an experience in which an irrational fear influenced your behavior.

Writing "God in the Doorway"
Annie Dillard

———————

Ten years ago, a magazine editor asked me to describe Christmas memo- 1
ries. At first I refused, thinking I couldn't come up with anything more original than the usual "we-all-sat-around-the-big-table-at-Grandma's," with its
usual overwritten descriptions of platters of food. Writing is tough. I don't
like to take pains to come up with the usual. I told the editor I was sorry.

But I no sooner got off the phone than I recalled this scene, this old, sore 2
business of Miss White's playing Santa Claus. I'd run from Miss White because, when I was small, I was afraid of the wrathful, omnipotent God: who
wants to meet the God who'll make you fry in hell for your sins? (My parents didn't give me these notions; I must have picked them up from the world
at large.) Now, when I was thirty, I saw I was still afraid of the forgiving God:
who wants to be on the receiving end of undeserved love? I was still running
from the vulnerable God whose love I'd refused, the God people hurt as I'd
hurt Miss White. Miss White forgave me, I believe, just as Santa Claus forgives bad children by bringing them presents anyway, and just as God, I'd
heard, forgives people. The trouble was, I hadn't forgiven myself. I was still
brooding over it all when I was thirty.

I began roughing out a draft of the incidents. First I'd tell the Santa Claus 3
story, then the magnifying glass story; at the end I'd swiftly make the point,
that we are still running from God's love, God's "eye." As I write this now,
at forty, it's still hard to see which is worse: God's eye which sees your sins
(all the times you've hurt people), or God's eye which seeks you out with its
forgiveness, when you haven't forgiven yourself.

The first draft started abstractly: "Like everyone in his right mind, I feared 4
Santa Claus. Maybe this is the beginning of every child's wisdom. Of course I
thought he was God. He was unseen but real and somehow omnipresent." . . .

Reading this over I saw how appallingly boring it was. Who would want 5
to read something that practically begins with the word "omnipresent"? Who
would want to read something so vague and drippy it uses the word "somehow"? Where are we, anyhow? What, if anything, is happening? So I chucked
all this and began with the scene: it's Christmas Eve, some time ago, in a living
room.

Even so, my description of this scene wandered off the point right away. 6
In the second draft there was extraneous speculation about what restaurant
the family might have gone to that night. There was extraneous description
of how my lined coat felt on my bare arms on the drive home from the restaurant. That's the trouble with writing about your life: you keep babbling

because you're so marvelously interested. You're always tempted to indulge yourself. The babbling does no real harm if you have sense enough to drag yourself back on course from time to time, and, more important, if you have sense enough to recognize and cut out all the babble before you let anyone read the thing.

In the course of the second or third draft I'd gotten interested not only in   7
my own irrelevant memories, but also in an abstract side issue: how a child shapes behavior. I went on for a page about this. Again I saw how boring readers would find it; it had little to do with the matter at hand, which was an image: Santa Claus in the doorway. I tossed this page and later used the ideas in another essay.

Almost everything I cut from the early drafts was too abstract. You don't   8
say, I was eagerly awaiting Santa Claus. You say, We'd set out ginger ale and cookies. When you're telling any kind of story, every sentence should be full of things to see, hear, smell, or touch.

It's important to cut out weak parts; it's even more important to strengthen   9
strong parts. I revised to strengthen the central image. Images are more powerful than ideas. They stick in the imagination. If they are good symbolic images, they carry ideas with them; they embody and vivify ideas.

The essay describes Santa Claus in the doorway twice. First it gives the   10
setting and lays out the picture plainly: Santa Claus was looming in the doorway and looking around for me. Then it explains why I was afraid of Santa Claus. Then it describes Santa Claus again (once more with feeling), hoping that the second time the same image would resound with multiple meanings: Santa Claus is like the omnipotent God we fear as we fear the cold abyss of eternal night, etc. To make an occasion for describing it twice, I had the narrator take another look at Santa Claus from upstairs.

This business of describing something more than once is effective. I learned   11
it from Faulkner. You give the picture, stop the action and fill in some background which invests the picture with a wealth of feeling and meaning, and then give the picture again. If I were writing this piece now, I'd go over it a third time, bringing out the contrast between the two worlds—the cold eternal night, and the warm bright room (like a stable with a manger) here on earth where loving people love imperfectly and Christmases are not always merry. There's a lot of meaning packed too tightly here; I didn't really develop it all.

The details of the second description suggest various aspects of the idea: 12
Santa Claus stood in the doorway with night over his shoulder, letting in all the cold air of the sky; Santa Claus monstrous and bright, powerless, ringing a loud bell and repeating Merry Christmas, Merry Christmas. I wanted the image to be paradoxical, nagging unresolved in the mind. "Bright" is usually a positive word, and ringing bells are usually cheerful things; together they set up a weird tension (a *frisson*) with "monstrous"—which in turn usually doesn't go with "powerless." Good description doesn't moronically insist on one simple mood—the lyric flowery meadow, the terrifying avalanche.

Interesting feelings are complex and contradictory; I try to evoke complex feelings by shading things with their opposites. (And of course good writing doesn't *describe* feelings at all; it evokes them in the reader by describing the observable world with vivid language.)

Miss White is an innocent. She gives cookies to a neighbor child; she enjoys finger painting. We hurt innocent people (or gods) because we are wrongly afraid they'll hurt us. I ran from Miss White as Santa Claus; I ran from her again when I fancied she'd burned me with her magnifying glass. In both cases the essay likens her to the omnipotent, angry God. But in both cases, it turns out, she is more like the innocent, vulnerable, forgiving God whose love we refuse—by crucifying Christ, you could say, or by hurting our innocent neighbor. 13

The essay draws parallels between Santa Claus and the omnipotent God through logic: He's an old man who knows when you've been bad or good. It draws parallels between Miss White and the omnipotent God through language: After describing the magnifying glass incident (with as many active verbs as I could muster), I skipped a few lines and used the same imagery to imagine God's burning me in hell. At its very end, the essay draws parallels between Miss White and the vulnerable God (of whom the familiar symbol is Christ) through the inner logic of imagery: So Santa Claus powerless in the doorway with night over his shoulder invokes (at least subconsciously) two other images: the infant Jesus in Bethlehem, and Christ crucified. Both are standard representations of love's vulnerability and ultimate triumph. 14

Note how remarkably less interesting all this is than the anecdotal essay itself. This is why no one reads literary criticism. This is also why writers are well advised to keep mum about what they've written. If they can please us with vivid little bits of story, who cares what weird ideas drove them to their typewriters in the first place? 15

The essay's last paragraph is crucial. It brings it all together nicely: So once in Israel love came to us incarnate, stood in the doorway between two worlds, and we were all afraid. The omnipotent God/Santa Claus becomes the vulnerable Christ/Miss White, the neighbor whom I failed to love. The fearful little girl on Christmas Eve becomes by implication the loud crowd on Good Friday crying "crucify him." And the adult who's writing the essay converges on past themes and writes in the present: I am still running. 16

But its tone is worrisome. It suddenly sounds too solemn; it sounds preachy and pious. It still bothers me. It sounds like an evangelist making a pitch: "You ever feel this way? You need Jesus Christ." 17

I thought a little intellectual Christianity wouldn't hurt a magazine's Christmas issue—but that's no excuse. More profoundly I hoped that the phrase "stood in the doorway between two worlds" would bring it all down to earth, and back to the essay's narrative surface. Right then, I fondly hoped, the reader would see in a flash how well the essay works; the metaphor holds. The reader would be so pleased, so positively stunned, he'd forgive the 18 pompous tone of "So once in Israel love came to us incarnate." I hoped he'd forgive it—but now, ten years later, I don't really think it's forgivable.

Annie Dillard, Easter Week, 1984

✳

RESPONDING TO THE WHOLE ESSAY

1. In paragraph 5, Dillard considers her original opening from the point of view of a reader. As a reader, do you agree with Dillard's judgments about the opening? Why or why not? What else do you see in it that you find either effective or ineffective? Note that Dillard says that she "chucked all this . . . ," but in fact she saved some of it and used it elsewhere in the final version. Is what she saved effective as she finally used it? [3a]
2. In retrospect, Dillard finds the final sentence of "God in the Doorway" pompous and doesn't "really think it's forgivable." On what grounds might a reader agree with her? Disagree with her?
3. Describe Dillard's intended audience for this essay. How is it different from the audience for "God in the Doorway"? What statements does Dillard make that show she is aware of both audiences? [1g(2)]
4. How does Dillard's purpose in this essay differ from that of "God in the Doorway"? What is her purpose in this essay? [1g(1)]

SUGGESTIONS FOR WRITING

1. Write an account of the process you used in writing an essay for your composition course or one of your other courses. If possible, choose an essay or paper you worked especially hard on. Here are a few questions to help you get started: What prompted you to write that particular essay on that particular subject, and to write it as you did? As you worked on it, did you encounter problems that were especially difficult to solve? What, if anything, came easily? As you reread the essay now, do you find things in it that especially please you? What parts, if any, do you now wish you'd written differently, and why? Attach a copy of the essay or paper you are writing about to your account of writing it.
2. Write an evaluation of one of the other narrative essays printed in this section. Consider the writer's apparent purpose and intended audience, and, in light of those, comment on such matters as the choice and ordering of events, the beginning and ending, the writer's attitude (tone), and words, phrases, or sentences that strike you as especially effective.

The Harlem Renaissance: One Facet of an Unturned Kaleidoscope

Darwin Turner

Holding bachelor's (1947) and master's (1949) degrees from the University of Cincinnati, Darwin Turner earned a Ph.D. from the University of Chicago. He taught English at several universities, including North Carolina Agricultural and Technical State, Indiana University, and the University of Michigan, and from 1980 until his death in 1992 served as chair of Afro-American Studies at the University of Iowa. His publications include *A Guide to Composition* (1960) and *In a Minor Chord: Three African American Writers and Their Search for Identity* (1971); he edited *Black Drama in America: An Anthology* (1971) and, with J. Sekona, *The Art of the Slave Narrative* (1983). Turner was born in Cincinnati, Ohio, in 1931.

Geraldine's brash cry, "What you see is what you get," is appropriate comment on the tendency of many Americans to fix their attention on only a particular aspect of Black life in America—usually the most spectacular aspect. If they would twist the base of the kaleidoscope of Black life, the multicolored fragments would rearrange themselves into different patterns, some of them startlingly different. But few viewers choose to adjust the kaleidoscope. 1

As a result, out of the many patterns of Black life during the 1920s, the dominant image emblazoned on the vision of America is the Harlem Renaissance. By the same process, from the Harlem Renaissance itself, a Jazzed Abandon has become the most memorable spectacle. James Weldon Johnson's description of reactions to Harlem summarizes the legend of the Harlem Renaissance: 2

It is known in Europe and the Orient, and it is talked about by natives in the interior of Africa. It is farthest known as being exotic, colourful [*sic*], and sensuous; a place of laughing, singing, and dancing; a place where life wakes up at night. This phase of Harlem's fame is most widely known because, in addition to being spread by ordinary agencies, it has been proclaimed in story and song. And certainly this is Harlem's most striking and fascinating aspect. New Yorkers and people visiting New York from the world over go to the night-clubs of Harlem and dance to such jazz music as can be heard nowhere else; and they get an exhilaration impossible to duplicate. Some of these seekers after new sensations go beyond the gay night-clubs; they peep in under the more seamy side of things; they nose down into lower strata of life. A visit to

Harlem at night—the principal streets never deserted, gay crowds skipping from one place of amusement to another, lines of taxicabs and limousines standing under the sparkling lights of the entrances to the famous night-clubs, the subway kiosks swallowing and disgorging crowds all night long—gives the impression that Harlem never sleeps and that the inhabitants thereof jazz through existence.[1]

Johnson continued, "But, of course, no one can seriously think that the two hundred thousand and more Negroes in Harlem spend their nights on any such pleasance."[2] So we too can say, "Surely, no one seriously thinks that this picture or even the entire 'Renaissance' constitutes the totality of the patterns housed in the kaleidoscope of Black life during the 1920s, the decade of the 'New Negro.'"   3

Even if one examines only the literary portraiture of the decade, one discerns more than a single image as the minute, tinted mirrors arrange and rearrange themselves into diverse patterns reflecting the actuality of Black life or reflecting the psyches of the Black and white artists who depicted that life. A knowledgeable individual twists the instrument to view the primitivism depicted by such white authors as Julia Peterkin, Eugene O'Neill, Sherwood Anderson, Dubose Heyward, Mary Wiborg, and William Faulkner, or the exotic abandon simulated by Carl Van Vechten. But a slight adjustment reshapes those images into the cultural elitism revealed by Van Vechten and cherished by W. E. B. DuBois. Another adjustment reveals the integrationist optimism of Langston Hughes, or the pan-Africanism of W. E. B. DuBois, or the Black nationalism of Marcus Garvey. Examine rural southern Blacks from the perspectives of Peterkin, Heyward, Faulkner, and Jean Toomer; or scrutinize the urban northerners of Toomer, Claude McKay, Rudolph Fisher, Langston Hughes, and Countée Cullen. Smile at the enthusiastic and naive Carl Van Vechtens, Mabel Dodges, and other white patrons as they prance about with their trophies collected on safaris into the Black jungles; then scowl at the lynchers painted by Claude McKay and photographed by Walter White. Admire the "patient endurance," with which William Faulkner colored his Dilsey; but do not overlook the militant impatience that inflames McKay's poetic voice. Consider the African nationalism vaguely sketched by Cullen, Hughes, and McKay; but compare it with Hughes' poetic demands for American integration and McKay's impressionistic sketches of the damnable siren, America, that fascinates, challenges, and captivates Blacks. Excite yourselves with sexual abandon garishly painted by Van Vechten, Anderson, McKay, and Toomer; but study also the conservative, often frustrated Blacks portrayed by Jessie Fauset and Toomer. Weep for the impotent failures depicted by O'Neill and Paul Green; but rejoice with the bold, determined aspirants of Fauset and Fisher. . . .   4

[1]James W. Johnson, *Black Manhattan* (New, 1968; originally published, 1930), pp. 160–161. [Author's note]

[2]Ibid., p. 161. [Author's note]

Such awareness of the multiplicity of patterns of Black life during the 1920s 5 justifies a reexamination, necessarily brief and somewhat superficial, of the Harlem Renaissance, particularly the literary Renaissance—to determine the reasons for its image as Jazzed Abandon, to trace more closely the more serious themes of the literature, and to reassess the significance of the Renaissance.

If we of the 1970s picture Black life in the 1920s as a riotous nightclub 6 tour, we cannot blame the best-known white writers for our misconception. Ironically, although Blacks became so popular as a subject that almost every prominent American author of the decade featured them in at least one major work, most of these authors ignored the Harlem scene in their literature. Such obvious neglect prompts speculation about the reasons: Were the authors describing the Afro-Americans they knew best? Or were they deliberately creating Black characters who would contrast with, and perhaps obscure, the image of the proud Renaissance Blacks?

Of course, in 1920, when O'Neill's *Emperor Jones* appeared, the Harlem 7 Renaissance was less than a flutter in the heart of Alain Locke, the Black philosopher and cultural historian who named that era. O'Neill cannot be accused of ignoring what he could not have been expected to see. Situating his Black on a Caribbean island, O'Neill showed how fear, stripping away civilized veneer, reduces a man—in this instance, a southern Black—to a primitive.

The contrast between the Renaissance and O'Neill's work, however, appears in *All God's Chillun Got Wings* (1924). This drama, necessarily set in 8 the North, describes the pathetic relationship between a Black man, who aspires to be a lawyer, and the "fallen" white woman whom he marries. The woman, betrayed and deserted by a white lover, marries the Black but becomes insane—or more insane, according to your view. The Black fails to become a lawyer partly because his wife, not wanting him to succeed, interferes with his study. The more crucial reason for his failure, however, is that whenever he is examined by whites, he forgets whatever he knows. In 1924, the year the play appeared, Jessie Fauset and Walter White published the first Black novels of the decade: *There Is Confusion,* which centers on the lives of middle-class Blacks in Philadelphia, among them a Black graduate of a white medical school, and *The Fire in the Flint,* a protest against lynching. For three years, Black musicals had been the rage of Broadway theater. BLACK was in, by 1924. The next year *Survey Graphic* would focus an entire issue on the "New Negro," James Weldon Johnson would hail Harlem as the capital of Black America, others would call it "Mecca." Despite these events, O'Neill provided New York theatergoers with a Black protagonist whose aspirations exceed his ability. Whatever O'Neill's reasons for the theme, the choice of an actor to portray the protagonist could not have been more ironic. The Black who panics when examined by whites was played by Paul Robeson, all-American football player (I believe that he was the first Black selected by Walter Camp as an all-American), a twelve-letter man in athletics, and a Phi Beta Kappa graduate, who earned one of the highest academic averages in the history of Rutgers University.

The spectacle of Black failure was continued by Paul Green, a North   9
Carolinian who wrote more plays about Blacks than any other white person
during the decade. In 1926 Green won the Pulitzer Prize for *In Abraham's
Bosom,* a drama in which Black Abe McCrannie, during Reconstruction, tries
futilely to establish a school for Blacks. In the same year, 1926, W. E. B. DuBois,
editor of *The Crisis,* the voice of the N.A.A.C.P., continuing a practice intended
to encourage Black scholarship, published the pictures of the year's Black college graduates. Within a few years, DuBois would proudly announce that the
large number of graduates prohibited his publishing the pictures of all.

Another memorable drama of the decade was Dubose Heyward's *Porgy,*   10
now an American "classic," a story of a Black and crippled junk dealer, who
strives to win Bess, a fallen woman, from Crown, a bad, bad man. Perhaps
the most appropriate evaluation of the drama comes from W. E. B. DuBois,
who insisted that he did not object to the play. Then, sniffing delicately from
the rarified atmosphere surrounding a New England Brahmin who was a Ph.D.
graduate from Harvard and had been a graduate student at Heidelberg, DuBois
explained that, although he did not doubt that Heyward's Blacks existed in
Charleston, South Carolina, he regretted Heyward's failure to portray the educated Blacks DuBois associated with when he visited that city.

During the 1920s William Faulkner foreshadowed his future stature with   11
The Sound and the Fury, located primarily in Mississippi, with a glance at
Cambridge, Massachusetts. Faulkner's major Black character in this novel is
Dilsey, prototype of "the Black who endures." Like Green and O'Neill,
Faulkner probably had not read Alain Locke's introduction to *The New Negro*
(1925). Locke asserted: "Sentimental interest in the Negro has ebbed. We used
to lament this as the falling off of our friends; now we rejoice and pray to be
delivered both from self-pity and condescension. The mind of each racial group
has had a better weaning, apathy or hatred on one side matching disillusion-
ment or resentment on the other; but they face each other today with the possibility at least of entirely new mutual attitudes."[3]

The decade ended with a production of the extraordinarily popular *Green*   12
Pastures (1930) by Marc Connelly. Based on Roark Bradford's *Ol' Man Adam
and His Chillun,* the drama seems to retell the Old Testament from the perspective of a Black child at a church fish-fry. The narrator is not a child, however; he is an adult.

However distorted their vision of Blacks may have been, well-known white   13
American authors of the 1920s cannot be blamed for the exotic image of the
nightclub Black. That image comes from Blacks themselves and from a few
whites who identified themselves as promoters of Blacks or as sympathizers.

The image may have begun with *Shuffle Along* (1921), a brilliant and   14
popular musical, written and directed by four Blacks—Flournoy Miller, Eubie
Blake, Noble Sissel, and Aubrey Lyles. In the same year, *Shuffle Along* was
succeeded by *Put and Take,* another musical by a Black—Irving C. Miller,

[3]Locke, "The New Negro," *The New Negro* (New York, 1968). [Author's note]

who also produced *Liza* (1923), which was followed in the same year by *Runnin' Wild* by Miller and Lyles. The beauty of Afro-American chorus girls such as Florence Mills and Josephine Baker, the exotic foreign settings, the gaiety and the frenzy of these musicals and their successors may have cultivated in Broadway audiences a taste for particular depictions of Black life. Furthermore, these musicals may have created an image difficult to change.

Although it is located in the South, Sherwood Anderson's *Dark Laughter* (1925) conjures up the image of a joyful, untroubled people who, themselves freed from the need to read Freud, laugh gently at frustrated whites, who repress their own sexual desires. The image of joy continues in Carl Van Vechten's novel, *Nigger Heaven* (1926), set in Harlem. Although Van Vechten later proclaimed his desire to familiarize white readers with a cultural Black society which gives soirées and speaks French, he glamorized the Scarlet Creeper, a "sweetman" (gigolo), and he depicted Black night life with an excitement certain to allure readers.   15

The exoticism and gaiety appear in the works of Black writers themselves. Even Countée Cullen, known to subsequent generations as a somewhat prim purveyor of high art, contrasted the warmth of Blacks with the coldness of whites, wrote atavistically of the African rhythm inherent in the walk of a Black waiter (in *Color,* 1925), and rhapsodized the wildness of the African heritage.   16

In his first collection, *The Weary Blues* (1926), Langston Hughes not only created jazz/blues poems but also wrote with an exuberance tending to promote the image of an uninhibited people: 17

DREAM VARIATION

> *To fling my arms wide*
> *In some place of the sun,*
> *To whirl and to dance*
> *Till the white day is done.*
> *Then rest at cool evening*
> *Beneath a tall tree*
> *While night comes on gently,*
>   *Dark like me,—*
> *That is my dream!*
> *To fling my arms wide*
> *In the face of the sun,*
> *Dance! whirl! whirl!*
> *Till the quick day is done.*
> *Rest at pale evening. . . .*
> *A tall, slim tree. . . .*
> *Night coming tenderly*
>   *Black like me.*[4]

[4]Hughes, *The Weary Blues* (New York, 1926). [Author's note]

Black novelists also contributed to the image of an uninhibited people whose lives are exotic whirls. In *Home to Harlem* (1928), Claude McKay, a Black West Indian, drowned social protest in a flood of night life—prostitutes, sweetmen, jazz, nightclub fights—as he told the story of a Black deserter from the armed services who searches through Harlem for the prostitute whom he loves. Succeeding novelists, such as Rudolph Fisher (*The Walls of Jericho,* 1928) and Wallace Thurman (*The Blacker the Berry,* 1929), seemed almost compelled to include irrelevant nightclub scenes as though they had become clichés of Black life.

It should not be wondered then that W. E. B. DuBois, editor of *The Crisis,*   18 reserved sections of several issues to question whether writers and publishers shared his fear that Black writers were being encouraged to create derogatory pictures of Blacks. Seriously concerned about respectable images of Blacks, DuBois, more than two decades earlier, had rationalized their enthusiasm as a primitivism promoted by the experience of slavery, a primitivism which would be modified when Black Americans matured into the sophistication of Euro-American society. Now that his "Talented Tenth" seemed to promote spectacles of frenzy, however, DuBois suspected that their desire to publish persuaded them to ignore the truth of Black life and to pander to whites by creating images designed to titillate.

Beneath the surfaces of gay abandon during the 1920s, however, are more   19 somber issues, more sober themes which should be examined more closely. The same writers who seem to rejoice in the enthusiasm of Black life also sounded what Langston Hughes described as "the sob of the jazz band"—the melancholy undertone of Black life, ever present but sometimes unheard by those who failed to listen carefully.

Claude McKay pictured a Harlem dancer who guards her soul from the   20 lascivious image suggested by her dance (*Harlem Shadows,* 1922), and Langston Hughes described the weariness of a jazz pianist (*The Weary Blues,* 1926). In The *Walls of Jericho* (1928) Fisher overshadowed the scenes of night life with a quieter depiction of the romance of two working people of Harlem. Thurman tempered his scenes of night life and dances in *The Blacker the Berry* by revealing that some Blacks visited dance halls not to gorge themselves with gaiety but to discover companionship to ease their loneliness. In the same novel a white Chicagoan confirms his impression that the exotic savagery of Harlemites is grossly exaggerated by their white press agents. While his actress-sister revels in what she considers the barbaric splendor of the Black club they visit, the Chicagoan sees a generally decorous behavior which assures him that Harlemites are no wilder than the Blacks he has known in Chicago (and perhaps not as wild as the whites in either city). Countée Cullen asserted that he wrote *One Way to Heaven* (1932) to counter Carl Van Vechten's *Nigger Heaven* by showing the humanity of Black life in Harlem. In scene after scene, Cullen balances superficial exuberance with sober explanation: The enthusiasm of a religious revival does not obscure the fact that in attendance also are some morally respectable Blacks who are not swept away by the emotion. The heroine, a morally circumspect, hard-working woman, has attended several revivals to which she has been indifferent. A male's illicit love affair is ascribed partly to the nature of the wandering male and partly to a desire to find companionship because his wife, who has become a religious fanatic, is engaged in an affair with Jesus.

These more serious vestiges of Black life in America should not be ignored [21] when one considers the literature of the Renaissance; for, far from being mere entertainers, many Black writers regarded literature as a means of seriously examining problems of living. Moreover, they did not restrict their examinations to problems of Blacks in an adversary relationship with white society. Almost from the first they were concerned with issues which might be considered universal if American critics were more willing to discover universality in the lives of Black people.

The interest in human conditions appears in Jean Toomer's *Cane* (1923), [22] the work of the Renaissance which is the best known and the most highly respected in academic circles. Toomer delineates many protagonists whose difficulties do not depend primarily upon their ancestry: Karintha has matured too soon sexually; Carma lives in a society which pretends that a woman should become sexless if her husband does not live with her; Esther cannot reconcile her sexual urges with the education by a society which has taught her that "good" girls do not feel such urges; John, in "Theater," cannot adapt his idealized romanticizing into a satisfactory relationship with an actual woman; Dorris, in "Theater," dreams of a companionship that will provide a real substitute for the artificiality of the theater; Muriel, in "Box Seat," fears to defy the little-minded, social regulators of the world; Avery finds it more pleasurable to be supported by men than to labor as a teacher in a normal school. The problems of these individuals may be complicated or intensified by their condition as Blacks in America, but the problems would exist regardless of their race.

Jessie Fauset, the too little-known author of *There Is Confusion* (1924), [23] *Plum Bun* (1929), *The Chinaberry Tree* (1933), and *Comedy: American Style* (1933), contrived her novels to focus on the problems of Blacks whose lives are not continuously affected by their interrelationships with whites. Most often their problems derive from their ambition or from a society excessively willing to evaluate individuals according to false criteria. In *There Is Confusion,* for example, an ambitious young Black protagonist disrupts and nearly destroys the people around her because she tries to regulate their lives according to her delusions. Because she believes that people should not marry outside their class, she interferes with her brother's romance with a young woman whose family background is different. Doing "the right thing," by withdrawing from the relationship, the second young woman then rushes into an unfortunate marriage. Because the protagonist believes that suitors must be trained into suitably devoted servants, she refused to apologize to the man she loves even though she is wrong. After he apologizes in order to effect a reconciliation, she delays a response with the deliberate intention of causing him to learn that he cannot win her too easily. She begins to realize her error only when he, jolted by her rebuff, proposes to a woman who offers him affection without reservation.

In stories which she published during the 1920s, Zora Neale Hurston of   24
Florida explores such an "in-group" issue as the manner in which townspeople affect individuals by forcing them to act out of character in order to maintain the respect of the mob ("Spunk"). In addition, she vividly revealed the problems which disturb male-female relationships: the alienation which develops when a naive wife is seduced by a traveling salesman ("The Gilded Six-Bits"); the tragic consequences when a self-centered husband who has exploited his wife tries to replace her ("Sweat").

Black dramatists, such as Willis Richardson and Georgia D. Johnson, pre-   25
pared domestic dramas for the Black community: the tensions between a man and his improvident brothers-in-law ("The Broken Banjo"); the pathos of a situation in which a child is permitted to die because the mother favors the healing power of faith above that of man's medicine.

In such ways as these, Black people of the Renaissance explored serious   26
issues involving Black people but not deriving primarily from the racial ancestry or from their relationship with whites. This statement, however, should not encourage a fallacious assumption that the Black writers evaded their racial identity or ignored problems which do derive from interracial conflict. To the contrary, Black Renaissance writers frequently expressed concerns which strikingly anticipate major themes identified with the revolutionary Black Arts writers of the 1960s: a search for and affirmation of ancestral heritage, a feeling of alienation from the white Euro-American world; a presentation of and protest against oppression; and even militant defiance of oppression. . . .

The serious themes that Renaissance writers explored most frequently, as   27
might be expected, are protests against oppression. The presence of such themes has been obscured by three facts: (1) many readers remember the glamorous gaiety and forget the serious comments; (2) some protests appear as brief asides rather than fully developed explanations; (3) some protests seem mild because, rather than directly assaulting whites, they adumbrate the manner in which external oppression causes Blacks to oppress themselves. The way that serious protest can be ignored is evidenced by the customary reactions of casual readers to McKay's *Home to Harlem* (1928), which appears, even in this paper, as a prototype of a Black work that promotes exoticism. The vividly exotic spectacles blind many readers to McKay's presentation of such facts as the following: During World War I many Black soldiers who enlisted to fight for democracy were restricted to service as laborers; during the 1920s some Harlem clubs, whether owned by whites or Blacks, discriminated against Blacks by refusing them admission—except as entertainers or waiters; in many occupations Black workers surrendered their dignity to the caprice of white supervisors.

It is true that no *Native Son* burst from the Renaissance to denounce   28
American oppression. But Walter White's novel *The Fire in the Flint* (1924)

decries the brutality of lynchings, as does Claude McKay's "The Lynching." Toomer's "Blood-Burning Moon" and "Kabnis" (*Cane*) reveal the powerlessness of Blacks to protect themselves from white brutality: a successful self-defense summons the lynch mob as quickly as a murder would.

Much more prevalent is the Renaissance writers' tendency to attack oppression indirectly by showing how it causes Blacks to turn against themselves. Because color, as an evidence of African ancestry, was a shibboleth of whites against Blacks, many Blacks used color as a criterion of intra-group evaluation. In *The Blacker the Berry* the protagonist, because of her dark skin, suffers within her family, in school and college, and in efforts to secure employment. Yet pathetically, as Thurman shows, the heroine cherishes the same criteria which have victimized her. She desires only men who are of lighter complexion and Caucasian appearance; and she undervalues herself, believing for a time at least that her Blackness is an ineradicable blot upon her record. In *Comedy: American Style* (1933), Fauset censured a Negro mother who values her children according to the degree of their approximation to Caucasian appearance. Walter White's *Flight* (1928) and Nella Larsen's *Passing* (1929) show the dilemmas of heroines who, repressed by the conditions of life as Blacks, attempt to improve their lot by passing for white. 29

In ironic repudiation of the images of Blacks as amoral beings, Jean Toomer repeatedly stressed the necessity for middle-class Negroes to liberate themselves from conscious imitation of the restrictive morality of Anglo-Saxons. "Esther," "Theater," and "Box-Seat" all reveal the frustrations of Black people who, desiring social approval, repress their emotions, their humanness. In "Kabnis" Carrie K., fearing censure by others, represses her instinctual attraction to Lewis. Paul ("Rona and Paul," *Cane*) loses a female companion because of his self-conscious desire to explain to a bystander that the relationship is not lustful. Toomer's most fully developed attack on middle-class morality appears in the unpublished drama "Natalie Mann." Mert, a school teacher, dies because she perceives too late that she must enjoy passion fully without concern for society's censure. Natalie, the protagonist, develops to this awareness only through the assistance of a Christ-like male who himself has experienced the rebukes of the middle class. 30

Toomer was not the only writer to question the excessive effort of Blacks to conform to the standards presumed to be those of whites. The protagonist in Walter White's *Flight* is forced to leave town and, temporarily, to deny her race because Blacks will not permit her to forget that she has had a child out of wedlock: her lover's proposal of abortion so diminished him in her esteem that she refused his subsequent efforts to marry her. 31

During the 1920s few writers reacted militantly to oppression with the kind of rhetoric for which Black revolutionary literature became notorious during the 1960s. There are several reasons. A generally optimistic faith that talented Blacks soon would emerge with the mainstream muted rhetorical violence and violent rhetoric. Furthermore, publishers during the 1920s did not permit the kind of language and the explicit description of violent action which 32 became almost commonplace in later decades. Third, the publishing houses were controlled by whites. It should be remembered that much of the Black revolutionary literature of the 1960s issued from Black publishers of poetry and in Black community drama.

Under the circumstances it is not surprising that the militant reaction of-   33 ten was expressed as self-defense, as in Claude McKay's well-known "If We Must Die" (*Harlem Shadows*). Less frequently came prayers for destruction, as in McKay's "Enslaved" (*Harlem Shadows*). Most often the militancy is a proud hostility toward whites. At the end of *Flight* the male protagonist learns why his father abhorred whites: they had deprived him of inheritance by refusing to recognize him as their offspring. In turn he refuses to permit an elderly white to ease his own conscience by making a monetary donation while continuing to ignore the blood relationship.

I cannot conclude without reassessing the significance of the literary   34 Harlem Renaissance. If it is remembered for expression of gaiety rather than for the serious concerns of the Black authors; if it was a movement which involved only talented artists in one segment of the Black American population; if it reflects primarily the life of only one part of one city inhabited by Blacks; if it evidences little awareness of such a significant issue for Blacks as DuBois' dreams and promotions of pan-Africanism and even less awareness of or respect for Marcus Garvey's Back-to-Africa movement—if the literary Renaissance is so limited, does it merit serious study? Was it, as Harold Cruse has suggested, an era to be examined only as a pathetic example of a time when Black artists might have established criteria for their art but failed to do so? Was it, as W. E. B. DuBois stated and as LeRoi Jones insisted more forcefully later, a movement that lost validity as it became a plaything of white culture? In fact, is the very attention given to it by historians of Black culture evidence of the willingness of Blacks and whites to glorify, or permit glorification of, inferior art by Blacks?

Each of these allegations has partial validity. But such objections based   35 on idealistic absolutes fail to consider the actual significances of the literary Renaissance. First, in no other decade had Black novelists been afforded such opportunity for publication. If fewer than twenty original, non–vanity-press novels appeared between 1924 and 1933, that figure nevertheless exceeded the number published by American commercial houses in all the years since the publication of the first Black American novel, Williams Wells Brown's *Clotel* (1853). Even the Depression and the closing of some outlets could not dispel the new awareness that possibilities existed for Blacks who wished to write novels. The field was open to many writers, not merely to the individual geniuses—the Paul Dunbar or the Charles Chesnutt of an earlier decade. This productivity, as well as the later success of Richard Wright, undoubtedly encouraged such novelists as Chester Hines, Ann Petry, Frank Yerby, and William G. Smith, who developed during the late 1930s and early 1940s.

The literary examples and inspirations were not limited to the novel. Only   36 a few serious Black dramas reached Broadway, but the enthusiastic establishment of Black community theaters during the 1920s furthered the creation of a Black audience for drama and promoted awareness of the need for writers to create material for that audience.

Perhaps the productivity in poetry had less significant influence because   37
Blacks previously had found outlets for poetry—the national reputation of Paul Laurence Dunbar was known by Blacks. Moreover, poetry was still to be considered an avocation which one supported by revenue derived from a stable vocation. But there was hope that Black writers might be able to sustain themselves partly through grants, for Countée Cullen had established a precedent by winning a Guggenheim Fellowship for his proposal of a poetry-writing project.

Of final benefit to future writers was the mere fact that entrées had been   38
established. A Langston Hughes or Wallace Thurman or Countée Cullen or, later, an Arna Bontemps knew publishers and knew other people who might be able to assist prospective authors. In all these senses, the Renaissance was not a rebirth but, in very significant ways, a first birth for Black Americans in literature.

A second significance of the literary Renaissance is its inspiration for   39
African and Caribbean poets such as Léopold Senghor, Aimé Césaire, and Léon Damas who, a generation later in the 1930s and 1940s, promoted Negritude, a literary-cultural movement which emphasized consciousness of African identity and pride in the Black heritage. More than a decade after the Negritude writers, newer Black American writers of the 1960s looked to African Negritude for inspiration. Thus, both directly and circuitously, the Renaissance promoted Black American literature and Black consciousness of future decades.

Finally, the Renaissance has importance as a symbol. In many respects, the   40
actuality of a culture is less important than the myth which envelops and extends from that culture. The memory that Black Americans had been recognized and respected for literary achievements, as well as other artistic achievements, established awareness that there could be a literary culture among Blacks. If the memory faded rapidly from the consciousness of white America, it did not fade from the minds of Blacks responsible for continuing the culture among their people. Marcus Garvey did not succeed in restoring Black Americans to Africa; consequently, he is remembered as a dream that faded. But the Renaissance, for Black Americans and others, has gained strength as the mythic memory of a time when Blacks first burst into national consciousness as a talented group that was young, rebellious, proud, and beautiful.

✳

RESPONDING TO THE WHOLE ESSAY

1. What is Turner's purpose in "The Harlem Renaissance"? Is the essay primarily an expression of Turner's feelings about the movement, a report detailing the main

features of the movement, or an argument that the movement should be seen as reflecting the realities of Black life? [1g(1)]

2. What does Turner assume his audience already knows? This essay may be difficult for readers who have a limited understanding of twentieth-century American literature. Is it, therefore, also ineffective for those readers? Why or why not? Assess and account for your own response to the essay. [1g(2)]
3. Notice that Turner maintains a third-person point of view throughout the essay. What is the relationship between that point of view and the purpose of the essay?
4. Explain how, in his introduction, Turner engages the reader's interest. [3b(1)]
5. Explain Turner's use of the kaleidoscope image as an organizing principle. [2c]
6. Explain how the conclusion, beginning with paragraph 38, ties together the various views of the Renaissance that Turner has offered. [3b(2)]

ANALYZING THE ELEMENTS

Grammar

1. Explain why, in the second sentence of paragraph 8, Turner uses *who* and *whom* as he does. Why does he not say "man, whom" or "woman who"? [16c]
2. Identify all of the verbs in the second sentence of paragraph 22. Then justify Turner's choice of singular or plural for each verb. [17a]
3. Why does Turner use the past perfect in sentence 7 of paragraph 8, the simple past in sentence 8, the future in sentence 9, and the present in sentence 10? Explain. [17c]

Effective Sentences

1. In the first sentence of paragraph 1, the subject and verb are divided by a parenthetical quotation. Is the effectiveness of the sentence increased or diminished? Explain. [22d]
2. Explain how Turner keeps the large number of details in paragraph 30 from appearing to be excessive. [18b]
3. Explain why the second sentence in paragraph 34 is periodic and comment upon its rhetorical effect. [21b]

Punctuation and Mechanics

1. Explain why Turner uses a colon before the long quotation in paragraph 2. [30]
2. Comment upon Turner's use of italics and parentheses in paragraph 20. [31f and 34]
3. The second sentence of paragraph 27 is long, but Turner makes it clear with careful punctuation. Explain the use of the following in that sentence: colon, semicolon, comma, and parentheses. [27d, 28a, 31d, and 31f]

Diction

1. Why are *non–vanity-press* (sentence 4, paragraph 35) and *poetry-writing* (sentence 3, paragraph 37) hyphenated? [32g]
2. Paragraph 4 contains a long catalogue of "literary portraiture . . . reflecting the actuality of Black life." Using more than a dozen synonyms for "look at," Turner

ingeniously relates the items in the catalogue while maintaining the reader's interest. Write a paragraph of your own in which you supply at least five synonyms for an action you want your reader to perform repeatedly. [24a]
3. Turner uses a rich and varied vocabulary in this essay. Look up the following words in your dictionary: *protagonist* (paragraph 8), *soirée* and *gigolo* (paragraph 15), *atavistically* (paragraph 16), *pander* (paragraph 18), *vestige* (paragraph 21), *improvident* (paragraph 25), *fallacious* (paragraph 26), *censure* (paragraph 30), *notorious* (paragraph 32). Explain how the connotations and denotations of these words are appropriate. [24a]

BUILDING VOCABULARY

1. Define *abhor*. From what Latin roots is *abhor* borrowed? What do they mean?
2. Identify and define the Latin roots that *circumspect* comes from. Write a sentence using a word derived from one of these Latin roots.

SUGGESTIONS FOR WRITING

1. Choose a particularly interesting recent event (a crime, a political confrontation, or a significant event in the life of a celebrity, for example) and read at least three articles about the event in such sources as *Time, Newsweek,* or the *New York Times.* Then write your own account of the event, maintaining an objective, third-person point of view. Be careful to give credit when quoting from your sources. (See 6 and 7 for help with handling sources.)
2. You are an editor for a popular magazine that prints condensed books and articles. You have been assigned to condense Turner's article to fewer than 1,000 words—that is, boil it down while retaining the author's own words and organization. Carry out the assignment. (You may make small changes and insertions for coherence since the author will be asked to approve your version before it is published.)

*

Chapter 3

Description

Description uses language to re-create for a reader what is experienced through the senses—sight, sound, taste, touch, and smell. Because it is grounded in the senses, description relies especially on concrete images. (For a discussion of concreteness, see [24a(4)].) This emphasis on concreteness and specificity is one of the things that make description so effective in bringing a story to life or making an argument persuasive. Indeed, description most often occurs in combination with other strategies, particularly narration; description can explain and expand a comparison, a process, a definition, an argument, a classification—any of the other strategies.

Whatever your purpose for writing, description helps you and your reader share an experience or an impression. If your purpose is to express your feelings, description can make those feelings tangible for your reader. This kind of description, often called *subjective,* emphasizes the personal response to an object rather than the characteristics of the object itself. In contrast to expressive writing, informative writing usually employs *objective* description, which relies on sensory data uncolored by the writer's feelings and attitudes. For example, if you were to write, "Pitted with tiny depressions, the skin of the orange exudes a pungent odor when scraped," you would have written an objective description. If, on the other hand, you were to write, "The scraped skin of the orange is redolent of lazy summer mornings," you would have a subjective description.

Sometimes the difference between objective and subjective description is mainly a matter of the connotations of the words the writer chooses: "The skin under her eyes crinkled into fine networks when she laughed, and delicate traces of powder dusted her withered cheeks" has a more subjective quality than "The skin under her eyes was crossed and recrossed by tiny lines, and her cheeks, which bore traces of powder, had lost their former firm roundness." Notice how words like *crinkled, networks, dusted,* and *withered* contribute to the subjective quality of the first description.

The main task in writing successful description is to make sure that all of the details you select will contribute to a single *dominant impression* that fulfills your purpose. If you are writing about your grandmother's face, you must decide whether you want to show her as she would appear in a harsh light to a stranger or whether you want to allow your feelings for her to soften the portrait. In either case, you would not include details of her dress or the timbre of her voice because they would tell the reader nothing about her face. Nor would you include every detail of her face. When describing, select only the best and most relevant details to convey the impression you want.

Your purpose will govern not only your selection of details but also your arrangement of them. You might arrange them spatially—near to far, top to bottom, left to right, and so forth—or in order of importance, or moving from larger to smaller or more general to more specific (or vice versa). But whatever pattern you choose, follow through with it; jumping back and forth without reason between different principles or arrangement can blur the impression you are trying to build.

A good way to begin a description is to jot down, either from observation or from recollection, as many details, however tiny or seemingly unimportant, as you can. Then, according to your purpose, you can select the most significant details and arrange them in the most effective pattern. As you read the description essay by Lisa Garrett, a student, notice that Garrett structures her description within an argumentative frame. Notice also the kinds of details she has chosen to convey her corollary point that natural beauty is one important way that nature feeds the senses and augments the reader's experience of scenery.

The Fragility of Natural Wonders

Introduction
establishes context

Details set broad
initial perspective

Narrows
perspective

Specific detail

Thesis

Visual images

My home state of Oregon is known for a kind of scenic beauty that is protected by its very grandeur. It is hard to credit that the carelessness and greed of humans could damage such beauty writ large: the majesty of Mount Hood, the splendor of the Columbia Gorge, the grandeur of the rugged coastline. Complacency is easy in the face of such hugeness. Mere scale disguises the fragility of diminutive gems such as Multnomah Falls, a ruined beauty nestled within the larger magnificence of the Gorge. Here the careless enthusiasm of tourists supports a blatant commercialism that mars the ethereal natural beauty formed by delicate waterfall traceries. Other gems have so far been more fortunate, but they are threatened by air, water, and people pollution. Where will we find the rare peace that only nature offers when these places are gone? Each time I visit one of my favorite spots I become acutely aware of this threat.

Here below the waterfall in Oneonta Gorge, the sunlight is diffused and the sky is just a thin blue strip between the black basalt walls of the gorge. At first the one-hundred-foot walls of the narrow gorge with their seventy-five-foot crowns of majestic old-growth Douglas fir seem to lean ominously over me. As I sit on my water-rounded basalt boulder a while longer, the walls of the gorge seem to offer protection rather than threat. To outsiders, this place seems isolated from things that might endanger it, but it is frighteningly attached to the polluted world and is precariously easy to spoil.

I breathe in the clean, cool air filtered through the mist from the falls and mingled with the scents of fir trees, rhododendron flowers, and clean soil. I listen to the gurgle of the water, the singing of robins, and rustle of the trees and shrubs above me as they are brushed by the breeze. I observe a nearby trout plucking its lunch of mayfly nymphs from the rocks, a few wild birds chasing mosquitoes, and a spider repairing its web. The bright, clear water of Oneonta Creek squeezes through thick cushions of moss and swirls through gracefully wavering strands of green algae.

On my way here I walked through a magnificent stand of Douglas fir, where each regal tree seemed to protect its small section of forest. I rested in a quiet and radiant meadow where the dead trees, gnarled and silvery, proudly guarded the sweetly fragrant huckleberry and wildflowers of the meadow.

Now, as I watch the water surge over the falls and into the gorge below, I wonder at the immense power of the countless raindrops that it took to carve this deep, narrow crevasse into the hard Oregon basalt. The uniqueness of this gorge is in its dimensions. It is only two miles in length and only thirty feet wide. But unfortunately, even this narrow opening cannot prevent pollutants borne by the air, the rain, and the groundwater from entering the gorge and these pollutants jeopardize several species of plant life that flourish in this gorge and are found nowhere else on earth.

I am calmed and refreshed by this powerful and lovely place, but at the same time I am frightened for my Oneonta Creek and for the many unusual places around the world that are similarly threatened. Will they remain the pure and vigorous places they are now or will polluted air and water destroy them?

Marginal annotations:

Spatial perspective
Visual images

Reference to thesis

Olfactory and tactile images
Perspective narrows
Auditory images

Visual images and very specific details

Adjusts temporal perspective

Visual image

Olfactory image

Visual image

Specific details

Perspective narrows

Refers to thesis

Return to frame established in first paragraph
Conclusion echoes thesis

Commentary. In the first paragraph, Garrett creates a frame for the description that follows, her expression of ecological concern. This frame also establishes the context that sparked the essay, her appreciation of the natural beauty of her home and her concern that it is in jeopardy. Garrett narrows the reader's view from the panoramic perspective of the introductory paragraph to the very minute focus on the trout catching a mayfly.

Throughout the essay, she emphasizes sensory details that show the reader exactly what she fears to lose, the clean air, the scents of flowers and trees, the sounds of water and wild life. In addition to her effective use of visual and auditory images, Garrett takes advantage of rarely used tactile and olfactory images that lend immediacy and richness to the picture she paints.

Her movement through the essay is not only a movement from large to small and near to far. She also includes a suggestion of chronological movement: what she saw on her way to Oneonta Creek, how time changed her perception of the brooding quality of the gorge, the eons it took to create this special place.

She also works at keeping her thesis before the reader by twice referring to the danger she senses and by giving additional specific details to muster the reader's concern as well, details such as the references to the unique plant life the gorge shelters. To conclude, Garrett recalls the sensory details by referring to their effects ("I am calmed and refreshed") and then reestablishes the environmental frame issue she established in the first paragraph.

The Way to Rainy Mountain
N. Scott Momaday

N. Scott Momaday (1934–) was awarded a Guggenheim Fellowship in 1966
and won a Pulitzer Prize in 1969 for his first novel, *House Made of Dawn*.
Born in Lawton, Oklahoma, of Kiowa and Cherokee ancestry, Momaday
graduated from the University of New Mexico and received a Ph.D. from
Stanford University. Momaday has taught English and comparative literature
at the University of California–Santa Barbara and at Stanford and has also
published two collections of poetry. *The Way to Rainy Mountain,* his second
book and the one from which this essay is taken, is a collection of legendary
Kiowa tales. Using time as an organizing principle for his description, in this
selection, Momaday evokes a sense of both the immediate and the remote past.

A single knoll rises out of the plain in Oklahoma, north and west of the 1
Wichita range. For my people, the Kiowas, it is an old landmark, and they
gave it the name Rainy Mountain. The hardest weather in the world is there.
Winter brings blizzards, hot tornadic winds arise in the spring, and in summer the prairie is an anvil's edge. The grass turns brittle and brown, and it
cracks beneath your feet. There are green belts along the rivers and creeks,
linear groves of hickory and pecan, willow and witch hazel. At a distance in
July or August the steaming foliage seems almost to writhe in fire. Great green
and yellow grasshoppers are everywhere in the tall grass, popping up like corn
to sting the flesh, and tortoises crawl about on the red earth, going nowhere
in the plenty of time. Loneliness is an aspect of the land. All things in the
plain are isolate; there is no confusion of objects in the eye, but *one* hill or
one tree or *one* man. To look upon that landscape in the early morning, with
the sun at your back, is to lose the sense of proportion. Your imagination
comes to life, and this, you think, is where Creation was begun.

I returned to Rainy Mountain in July. My grandmother had died in the 2
spring, and I wanted to be at her grave. She had lived to be very old and at
last infirm. Her only living daughter was with her when she died, and I was
told that in death her face was that of a child.

I like to think of her as a child. When she was born, the Kiowas were liv- 3
ing the last great moment of their history. For more than a hundred years they
had controlled the open range from the Smoky Hill River to the Red, from the
headwaters of the Canadian to the fork of the Arkansas and Cimarron. In al-
liance with the Comanches, they had ruled the whole of the Southern Plains.
War was their sacred business, and they were the finest horsemen the world
has ever known. But warfare for the Kiowas was preeminently a matter of

disposition rather than of survival, and they never understood the grim, unrelenting advance of the U.S. Cavalry. When at last, divided and ill provisioned, they were driven onto the Staked Plains in the cold of autumn, they fell into panic. In Palo Duro Canyon they abandoned their crucial stores to pillage and had nothing then but their lives. In order to save themselves, they surrendered to the soldiers at Fort Sill and were imprisoned in the old stone corral that now stands as a military museum. My grandmother was spared the humiliation of those high gray walls by eight or ten years, but she must have known from birth the affliction of defeat, the dark brooding of old warriors.

Her name was Aho, and she belonged to the last culture to evolve in North   4
America. Her forebears came down from the high country in western Montana nearly three centuries ago. They were a mountain people, a mysterious tribe of hunters whose language has never been classified in any major group. In the late seventeenth century they began a long migration to the south and east. It was a journey toward the dawn, and it led to a golden age. Along the way the Kiowas were befriended by the Crows, who gave them the culture and religion of the Plains. They acquired horses; and their ancient nomadic spirit was suddenly free of the ground. They acquired Tai-me, the sacred sun-dance doll, from that moment the object and symbol of their worship, and so shared in the divinity of the sun. Not least, they acquired the sense of destiny, therefore courage and pride. When they entered upon the Southern Plains they had been transformed. No longer were they slaves to the simple necessity of survival; they were a lordly and dangerous society of fighters and thieves, hunters and priests of the sun. According to their origin myth, they entered the world through a hollow log. From one point of view, their migration was the fruit of an old prophecy, for indeed they emerged from a sunless world.

Though my grandmother lived out her long life in the shadow of Rainy   5
Mountain, the immense landscape of the continental interior lay like memory in her blood. She could tell of the Crows, whom she had never seen, and of the Black Hills, where she had never been. I wanted to see in reality what she had seen more perfectly in the mind's eye, and drove fifteen hundred miles to begin my pilgrimage.

A dark mist lay over the Black Hills, and the land was like iron. At the   6
top of a ridge I caught sight of Devil's Tower upthrust against the gray sky as if in the birth of time the core of the earth had broken through its crust and the motion of the world was begun. There are things in nature that engender an awful quiet in the heart of man; Devil's Tower is one of them. Two centuries ago, because of their need to explain it, the Kiowas made a legend at the base of the rock. My grandmother said:

Eight children were there at play, seven sisters and their brother. Suddenly the boy was struck dumb; he trembled and began to run upon his hands and feet. His fingers became claws, and his body was covered with fur. There was a bear where the boy had been. The sisters were terrified; they ran, and the bear

after them. They came to the stump of a great tree, and the tree spoke to them,
It bade them climb upon it, and as they did so, it began to rise into the air.
The bear came to kill them, but they were just beyond its reach. It reared
against the tree and scored the bark all around with its claws. The seven sisters were borne into the sky, and they became the stars of the Big Dipper.

From that moment, and so long as the legend lives, the Kiowas have kinsmen
in the night sky. Whatever they were in the mountains, they could be no more.
However tenuous their well-being, however much they had suffered and would
suffer again, they had found a way out of the wilderness.

My grandmother had a reverence for the sun, a holy regard that now is   7
all but gone out of mankind. There was a wariness in her, and an ancient awe.
She was a Christian in her later years, but she had come a long way about,
and she never forgot her birthright. As a child she had been to the sun dances;
she had taken part in that annual rite, and by it she had learned the restoration of her people in the presence of Tai-me. She was about seven when the
last Kiowa sun dance was held in 1887 on the Washita River above Rainy
Mountain Creek. The buffalo were gone. In order to consummate the ancient
sacrifice—to impale the head of a buffalo bull upon the Tai-me tree—a delegation of old men journeyed into Texas, there to beg and barter for an animal from the Goodnight herd. She was ten when the Kiowas came together
for the last time as a living sun-dance culture. They could find no buffalo;
they had to hang an old hide from the sacred tree. Before the dance could begin, a company of soldiers rode out from Fort Sill under orders to disperse
the tribe. Forbidden without cause the essential act of their faith, having seen
the wild herds slaughtered and left to rot upon the ground, the Kiowas backed
away forever from the tree. That was July 20, 1890, at the great bend of the
Washita. My grandmother was there. Without bitterness, and for as long as
she lived, she bore a vision of deicide.

Now that I can have her only in memory, I see my grandmother in the   8
several postures that were peculiar to her: standing at the wood stove on a
winter morning and turning meat in a great iron skillet; sitting at the south
window, bent above her beadwork and afterwards, when her vision failed,
looking down for a long time into the fold of her hands; going out upon a
cane, very slowly as she did when the weight of age came upon her; praying.
I remember her most often at prayer. She made long, rambling prayers out of
suffering and hope, having seen many things. I was never sure that I had the
right to hear, so exclusive were they of all mere custom and company. The
last time I saw her she prayed standing by the side of her bed at night, naked
to the waist, the light of a kerosene lamp moving upon her dark skin. Her
long black hair, always drawn and braided in the day, lay upon her shoulders
and against her breasts like a shawl. I do not speak Kiowa, and I never understood her prayers, but there was something inherently sad in the sound,
some merest hesitation upon the syllables of sorrow. She began in a high and

descending pitch, exhausting her breath to silence; then again and again—and always the same intensity of effort, of something that is, and is not, like urgency in the human voice. Transported so in the dancing light among the shadows of her room, she seemed beyond the reach of time. But that was illusion; I think I knew then that I should not see her again.

Houses are like sentinels in the plain, old keepers of the weather watch.   9
There, in a very little while, wood takes on the appearance of great age. All colors wear soon away in the wind and rain, and then the wood is burned gray and the grain appears and the nails turn red with rust. The window panes are black and opaque; you imagine there is nothing within, and indeed there are many ghosts, bones given up to the land. They stand here and there against the sky, and you approach them for a longer time than you expect. They belong in the distance; it is their domain.

Once there was a lot of sound in my grandmother's house, a lot of coming   10
and going, feasting and talk. The summers there were full of excitement and reunion. The Kiowas are a summer people; they abide the cold and keep to themselves, but when the season turns and the land becomes warm and vital they cannot hold still; an old love of going returns upon them. The aged visitors who came to my grandmother's house when I was a child were made of lean and leather, and they bore themselves upright. They wore great black hats and bright ample shirts that shook in the wind. They rubbed fat upon their hair and wound their braids with strips of colored cloth. Some of them painted their faces and carried the scars of old and cherished enmities. They were an old council of warlords, come to remind and be reminded of who they were. Their wives and daughters served them well. The women might indulge themselves; gossip was at once the mark and compensation of their servitude. They made loud and elaborate talk among themselves, full of jest and gesture, fright and false alarm. They went abroad in fringed and flowered shawls, bright beadwork and German silver. They were at home in the kitchen, and they prepared meals that were banquets.

There was frequent prayer meetings, and nocturnal feasts. When I was a   11
child I played with my cousins outside, where the lamplight fell upon the ground and the singing of the old people rose up around us and carried away into the darkness. There were a lot of good things to eat, a lot of laughter and surprise. And afterwards, when the quiet returned, I lay down with my grandmother and could hear the frogs away by the river and feel the motion of the air.

Now there is a funeral silence in the rooms, the endless wake of some   12
final word. The walls have closed in upon my grandmother's house. When I returned to it in morning, I saw for the first time in my life how small it was. It was late at night, and there was a white moon, nearly full. I sat for a long time on the stone steps by the kitchen door. From there I could see out across the land; I could see the long row of trees by the creek, the low light upon the rolling plains, and the stars of the Big Dipper. Once I looked at the moon and caught sight of a strange thing. A cricket had perched upon the handrail, only a few inches away. My line of vision was such that the creature filled the

moon like a fossil. It had gone there, I thought, to live and die, for there, of all places, was its small definition made whole and eternal. A warm wind rose up and purled like the longing within me.

The next morning, I awoke at dawn and went out on the dirt road to   13
Rainy Mountain. It was already hot, and the grasshoppers began to fill the air. Still, it was early in the morning, and birds sang out of the shadows. The long yellow grass on the mountain shone in the bright light, and a scissortail hied above the land. There, where it ought to be, at the end of a long and legendary way, was my grandmother's grave. She had at last succeeded to that holy ground. Here and there on the dark stones were ancestral names. Looking back once, I saw the mountain and came away.

＊

RESPONDING TO THE WHOLE ESSAY

1. Discuss how "The Way to Rainy Mountain" is at once a memoir of Momaday's grandmother, a history of the Kiowas, and a chronicle of the author's own literal and spiritual journey. Using your discussion as a basis for judgment, point out where Momaday informs or persuades the reader, and where he expresses personal feelings. [1g(1)]
2. Find evidence in "The Way to Rainy Mountain" that suggests what kinds of readers Momaday was writing for. [1g(2)]
3. Descriptive details communicate by appealing to the senses: sight, sound, touch, taste, and smell. Comment on Momaday's use of concrete, sensory details to describe not only a place—the open range of Oklahoma—but also his grandmother and the Kiowas as a people. Which sense does Momaday rely on most frequently? What other senses does he invoke? (Look particularly at paragraphs 1 and 9.)
4. The concept of time is ever-present in "The Way to Rainy Mountain." Discuss Momaday's use in the essay of the present, the recent past, the historical past, and legendary time.
5. Is Momaday's discussion of Devil's Tower a digression, or is it relevant to the point of the essay? If it is a digression, why does he include it? If it is relevant to the point of the essay, explain how. [3c]
6. In his conclusion, Momaday says, "There, where it ought to be, at the end of a long and legendary way, was my grandmother's grave." How does this sentence summarize the essay? [3b(2)]

ANALYZING THE ELEMENTS

Grammar

1. Explain what time relationships are indicated by uses of the simple past and past perfect tenses in paragraph 2. [17c]
2. In the eighth sentence of paragraph 3 (beginning "In Palo Duro Canyon . . ."), the phrase "to pillage" could formally be either an infinitive or a prepositional phrase. Explain how the reader knows which was intended. [12a]

Effective Sentences

1. Comment on some of the various ways Momaday makes the fourth sentence of paragraph 1 effective. [20, 21d, and 24a(4)]
2. In paragraph 4, Momaday uses the word *acquired* near the beginning of three sentences—the seventh, eighth, and ninth. Comment on the effect of this repetition. [21e]
3. Explain what makes the eleventh sentence in paragraph 7 (beginning "Forbidden without cause . . .") and the next-to-last sentence in paragraph 8 effective. [22c]

Punctuation and Mechanics

1. Explain Momaday's use of the semicolon in the following sentences: the eleventh sentence of paragraph 4 (beginning "No longer . . ."); the first sentence of paragraph 8; the third sentence of paragraph 10. [28a]
2. How is the colon used in the first sentence of paragraph 8? Could any other mark of punctuation have been used? If so, what? [31d]

Diction

1. Comment on how figurative language contributes to the tone and the meaning of the essay. [14a(5)]
2. Look up the following words in your dictionary: *preeminently* and *pillage* (paragraph 3), *tenuous* (after the block quotation in paragraph 6), *consummate* and *deicide* (paragraph 7), *inherently* (paragraph 8), *nocturnal* (paragraph 11), *hied* (paragraph 13). With the aid, if necessary, of a dictionary of synonyms, find possible substitutes for as many of these words as you can; you may have to use a phrase instead of a single word. Then explain either why the word Momaday uses is more precise than the substitute or why the substitute is more precise. [24a(3)]

BUILDING VOCABULARY

1. Explain the origin of *imagine*. Does *imagine* come from a Latin or Greek root? If so, what is the root, what does it mean, and from which of these two languages does it originate? Can you find any indication of when this root was imported into the English language?
2. From what Old English word does *gossip* derive? What does this Old English word mean? What is the British meaning of the noun *gossip*? Can you find an American definition of *gossip* similar to that of the British definition? What is it? What is the meaning of *gossip* most often used in American English?

SUGGESTIONS FOR WRITING

1. Write an essay describing an elderly person and the place where he or she lives. Strive to show a relationship between the person and the place.
2. Using as many sensory details as you can muster, describe a natural (or urban) landscape that sticks in your memory. In your description, try to *show* rather than *tell* why the scene is memorable.

The Courage of Turtles
Edward Hoagland

Born in New York City, Edward Hoagland (1932–) was raised in Connecticut and educated at Harvard University. Hoagland has written for such periodicals as *Harper's, Commentary,* the *New Yorker,* and *Esquire.* Among the literary awards he has received are a Guggenheim Fellowship, an O. Henry Award, and an American Academy of Arts and Letters Travelling Fellowship. His books include *The Courage of Turtles, Walking the Dead Diamond River, Red Wolves and Black Bears,* and *African Calliope: A Journey to the Sudan.* A careful observer, Hoagland often exploits the dramatic quality of the struggle for survival, as he does in "The Courage of Turtles."

Turtles are a kind of bird with the governor turned low. With the same 1
attitude of removal, they cock a glance at what is going on, as if they need only to fly away. Until recently they were also a case of virtue rewarded, at least in the town where I grew up, because, being humble creatures, there were plenty of them. Even when we still had a few bobcats in the woods the local snapping turtles, growing up to forty pounds, were the largest carnivores. You would see them through the amber water, as big as green wash basins at the bottom of the pond, until they faded into the inscrutable mud as if they hadn't existed at all.

When I was ten I went to Dr. Green's Pond, a two-acre pond across the 2
road. When I was twelve I walked a mile or so to Taggart's Pond, which was lusher, had big water snakes and a waterfall; and shortly after that I was bicycling way up to the adventuresome vastness of Mud Pond, a lake-sized body of water in the reservoir system of a Connecticut city, possessed of cat-backed little islands and empty shacks and a forest of pines and hardwoods along the shore. Otters, foxes and mink left their prints on the bank; there were pike and perch. As I got older, the estates and forgotten back lots in town were parceled out and sold for nice prices, yet, though the woods had shrunk, it seemed that fewer people walked in the woods. The new residents didn't know how to find them. Eventually, exploring, they did find them, and it required some ingenuity and doubling around on my part to go for eight miles without meeting someone. I was grown by now, I lived in New York, and that's what I wanted on the occasional weekends when I came out.

Since Mud Pond contained drinking water I had felt confident nothing 3
untoward would happen there. For a long while the developers stayed away, until the drought of the mid-1960s. This event, squeezing the edges in, convinced the local water company that the pond really wasn't a necessity as a catch basin, however; so they bulldozed a hole in the earthen dam, bulldozed

the banks to fill in the bottom, and landscaped the flow of water that remained to wind like an English brook and provide a domestic view for the houses which were planned. Most of the painted turtles of Mud Pond, who had been inaccessible as they sunned on their rocks, wound up in boxes in boys' closets within a matter of days. Their footsteps in the dry leaves gave them away as they wandered forlornly. The snappers and the little musk turtles, neither of whom leave the water except once a year to lay their eggs, dug into the drying mud for another siege of hot weather, which they were accustomed to doing whenever the pond got low. But this time it was low for good; the mud baked over them and slowly entombed them. As for the ducks, I couldn't stroll in the woods and not feel guilty, because they were crouched beside every stagnant pothole, or were slinking between the bushes with their heads tucked into their shoulders so that I wouldn't see them. If they decided I had, they beat their way up through the screen of trees, striking their wings dangerously, and wheeled about with that headlong, magnificent velocity to locate another poor puddle.

I used to catch possums and black snakes as well as turtles, and I kept   4
dogs and goats. Some summers I worked in a menagerie with the big personalities of the animal kingdom, like elephants and rhinoceroses. I was twenty before these enthusiasms began to wane, and it was then that I picked turtles as the particular animal I wanted to keep in touch with. I was allergic to fur, for one thing, and turtles need minimal care and not much in the way of quarters. They're personable beasts. They see the same colors we do and they seem to see just as well, as one discovers in trying to sneak up on them. In the laboratory they unravel the twists of a maze with the hot-blooded rapidity of a mammal. Though they can't run as fast as a rat, they improve on their errors just as quickly, pausing at each crossroads to look left and right. And they rock rhythmically in place, as we often do, although they are hatched from eggs, not the womb. (A common explanation psychologists give for our pleasure in rocking quietly is that it recapitulates our mother's heartbeat *in utero.*)

Snakes, by contrast, are dryly silent and priapic. They are smooth movers,   5
legalistic, unblinking, and they afford the humor which the humorless do. But they make challenging captives; sometimes they don't eat for months on a point of order—if the light isn't right, for instance. Alligators are sticklers too. They're like war-horses, or German shepherds, and with their bar-shaped, vertical pupils adding emphasis, they have the *idée fixe* of eating, eating, even when they choose to refuse all food and stubbornly die. They delight in tossing a salamander up towards the sky and grabbing him in their long mouths as he comes down. They're so eager that they get the jitters, and they're too much of a proposition for a casual aquarium like mine. Frogs are depressingly defenseless: that moist, extensive back, with the bones almost sticking through. Hold a frog and you're holding its skeleton. Frogs' tasty legs are the staff of life to many animals—herons, raccoons, ribbon snakes—though they themselves are hard to feed. It's not an enviable role to be the staff of life, and after frogs you descend down the evolutionary ladder a big step to fish.

Turtles cough, burp, whistle, grunt and hiss, and produce social judgments. 6
They put their heads together amicably enough, but then one drives the other
back with the suddenness of two dogs who have been conversing in tones too
low for an onlooker to hear. They pee in fear when they're first caught, but
exercise both pluck and optimism in trying to escape, walking for hundreds of
yards within the confines of their pen, carrying the weight of the cumbersome
box on legs which are cruelly positioned for walking. They don't feel that the
contest is unfair; they keep plugging, rolling like sailorly souls—a bobbing, infirm gait, a brave, sea-legged momentum—stopping occasionally to study the
lay of the land. For me, anyway, they manage to contain the rest of the animal world. They can stretch out their necks like a giraffe, or loom underwa-
ter like an apocryphal hippo. They browse on lettuce thrown on the water like
a cow moose which is partly submerged. They have a penguin's alertness, combined with a build like a brontosaurus when they rise up on tiptoe. Then they
hunch and ponderously lunge like a grizzly going forward.

Baby turtles in a turtle bowl are a puzzle in geometrics. They're as deco- 7
rative as pansy petals, but they are also self-directed building blocks, prop-
ping themselves on one another in different arrangements, before upending
the tower. The timid individuals turn fearless, or vice versa. If one gets a bit
arrogant he will push the others off the rock and afterwards climb down into
the water and cling to the back of one of these he has bullied, tickling him
with his hind feet until be bucks like a bronco. On the other hand, when this
same milder-mannered fellow isn't exerting himself, he will stare right into the
face of the sun for hours. What could be more lionlike. And he's at home in
or out of the water and does lots of metaphysical tilting. He sinks and rises,
with an infinity of levels to choose from; or, elongating himself, he climbs out
on the land again to perambulate, sits boxed in his box, and finally slides
back in the water, submerging into dreams.

I have five of these babies in a kidney-shaped bowl. The hatchling, who 8
is a painted turtle, is not as large as the top joint of my thumb. He eats chicken
gladly. Other foods he will attempt to eat but not with sufficient perseverance
to succeed because he's so little. The yellow-bellied terrapin is probably a yearling, and he eats salad voraciously, but no meat, fish or fowl. The Cumberland
terrapin won't touch salad or chicken but eats fish and all of the meats except for bacon. The little snapper, with a black crenelated shell, feasts on any
kind of meat, but rejects greens and fish. The fifth of the turtles is African.
I acquired him only recently and don't know him well. A mottled brown, he
unnerves the green turtles, dragging their food off to his lairs. He doesn't seem
to want to be green—he bites the algae off his shell, hanging meanwhile at
daring, steep, head-first angles.

The snapper was a Ferdinand until I provided him with deeper water. 9
Now he snaps at my pencil with his downturned and fearsome mouth, his
swollen face like a napalm victim's. The Cumberland has an elliptical red mark
on the side of his green-and-yellow head. He is benign by nature and ought
to be as elegant as his scientific name (*Pseudemys scripta elegans*), except he

has contracted a disease of the air bladder which has permanently inflated it; he floats high in the water at an undignified slant and can't go under. There may have been internal bleeding, too, because his carapace is stained along its ridge. Unfortunately, like flowers, baby turtles often die. Their mouths fill up with a white fungus and their lungs with pneumonia. Their organs clog up from the rust in the water, or diet troubles, and, like a dying man's, their eyes and heads become too prominent. Toward the end, the edge of the shell becomes flabby as felt and folds around them like a shroud.

While they live they're like puppies. Although they're vivacious, they would   10
be a bore to be with all the time, so I also have an adult wood turtle about six inches long. Her shell is the equal of any seashell for sculpturing, even a Cellini shell; it's like an old, dusty, richly engraved medallion dug out of a hillside. Her legs are salmon-orange bordered with black and protected by canted, heroic scales. Her plastron—the bottom shell—is splotched like a margay cat's coat, with black ocelli on a yellow background. It is convex to make room for the female organs inside, whereas a male's would be concave to help him fit tightly on top of her. Altogether, she exhibits every camouflage color on her limbs and shells. She has a turtleneck neck, a tail like an elephant's, wise old pachydermatous hind legs and the face of a turkey—except that when I carry her she gazes at the passing ground with a hawk's eye and mouth. Her feet fit to the fingers of my hand, one to each one, and she rides looking down. She can walk on the floor in perfect silence, but usually she lets her shell knock portentously, like a footstep, so that she resembles some grand, concise, slow-moving id. But if an earthworm is presented, she jerks swiftly ahead, poises above it and strikes like a mongoose, consuming it with wild vigor. Yet she will climb on my lap to eat bread or boiled eggs.

If put into a creek, she swims like a cutter, nosing forward to intercept a   11
strange turtle and smell him. She drifts with the current to go downstream, maneuvering behind a rock when she wants to take stock, or sinking to the nether levels, while bubbles float up. Getting out, choosing her path, she will proceed a distance and dig into a pile of humus, thrusting herself to the coolest layer at the bottom. The hole closes over her until it's as small as a mouse's hole. She's not as aquatic as a musk turtle, not quite as terrestrial as the box turtles in the same woods, but because of her versatility she's marvelous, she's everywhere. And though she breathes the way we breathe, with scarcely perceptible movements of her chest, sometimes instead she pumps her throat ruminatively, like a pipe smoker sucking and puffing. She waits and blinks, pumping her throat, turning her head, then sets off like a loping tiger in slow motion, hurdling the jungly lumber, the pea vine and twigs. She estimates angles so well that when she rides over the rocks, sliding down a drop-off with her rugged front legs extended, she has the grace of a rodeo mare.

But she's well off to be with me rather than at Mud Pond. The other turtles   12
have fled—those that aren't baked into the bottom. Creeping up the brooks to sad, constricted marshes, burdened as they are with that box on their backs, they're walking into a setup where all their enemies move thirty times faster than they.

It's like the nightmare most of us have whimpered through, where we are weighted down disastrously while trying to flee; fleeing our home ground, we try to run.

I've seen turtles in still worse straits. On Broadway, in New York, there is a penny arcade which used to sell baby terrapins that were scrawled with bon mots in enamel paint, such as KISS MY BABY. The manager turned out to be a wholesaler as well, and once I asked him whether he had any larger turtles to sell. He took me upstairs to a loft room devoted to the turtle business. There were desks for the paper work and a series of racks that held shallow tin bins atop one another, each with several hundred babies crawling around in it. He was a smudgy-complexioned, serious fellow and he did have a few adult terrapins, but I was going to school and wasn't actually planning to buy; I'd only wanted to see them. They were aquatic turtles but here they went without water, presumably for weeks, lurching about in those dry bins like handicapped citizens, living on gumption. An easel where the artist worked stood in the middle of the floor. She had a palette and a clip attachment for fastening the babies in place. She wore a smock and a beret, and was homely, short and eccentric-looking, with funny black hair, like some of the ladies who show their paintings in Washington Square in May. She had a cold, she was smoking, and her hand wasn't very steady, although she worked quickly enough. The smile that she produced for me would have looked giddy if she had been happier, or drunk. Of course the turtles' doom was sealed when she painted them, because their bodies inside would continue to grow but their shells would not. Gradually, invisibly, they would be crushed. Around us their bellies—two thousand belly shells—rubbed on the bins with a mournful, momentous hiss.

Somehow there were so many of them I didn't rescue one. Years later, however, I was walking on First Avenue when I noticed a basket of living turtles in front of a fish store. They were as dry as a heap of old bones in the sun; nevertheless, they were creeping over one another gimpily, doing their best to escape. I looked and was touched to discover that they appeared to be wood turtles, my favorites, so I bought one. In my apartment I looked closer and realized that in fact this was a diamondback terrapin, which was bad news. Diamondbacks are tidewater turtles from brackish estuaries, and I had no sea water to keep him in. He spent his days thumping interminably against the baseboards, pushing for an opening through the wall. He drank thirstily but would not eat and had none of the hearty, accepting qualities of wood turtles. He was morose, paler in color, sleeker and more Oriental in the carved ridges and rings that formed his shell. Though I felt sorry for him, finally I found his unrelenting presence exasperating. I carried him, struggling in a paper bag, across town to the Morton Street Pier on the Hudson. It was August but gray and windy. He was very surprised when I tossed him in; for the first time in our association, I think, he was afraid. He looked afraid as he bobbed about on top of the water, looking up at me from ten feet below. Though we were both accustomed to his resistance and rigidity, seeing him still pitiful, I recognized that I must have done the wrong thing. At least the river was salty, but it was also bottomless; the waves were too rough for him, and the tide was coming in, bumping him against the pilings underneath the pier. Too late, I realized that he wouldn't be able to swim to a peaceful inlet in New Jersey, even if he could figure out which way to swim. But since, short of diving in after him, there was nothing I could do, I walked away.

✳

RESPONDING TO THE WHOLE ESSAY

1. Is Hoagland's purpose chiefly to give his reader information about turtles, to convey his own feelings toward them, or to persuade the reader to adopt his view of them? Support your answer with evidence. Whichever aim is primary, can you point to evidence of the others? [1g(1)]
2. What audience is Hoagland writing for? What elements of diction, tone, and organization help you to characterize the audience? [1g(2) and 3a(3)]
3. Descriptive writing is usually found in combination with other methods of development. What other methods does Hoagland rely on in "The Courage of Turtles"? Point to instances of each. [2e]
4. Who is the turtle's greatest enemy? How does that idea inform the entire essay? [2b]
5. Explain how "bucks like a bronco" and "What could be more lionlike?" in the fourth and sixth sentences of paragraph 7 establish a connection between that paragraph and the previous one. Find several other examples of Hoagland's picking up a thread from an earlier part of the essay and weaving it in. What quality does the essay gain from this technique? [3c]
6. Comment on the tone of this essay: How does Hoagland manage to convey his love of and admiration for turtles without falling into sentimentality? What keeps the conclusion from becoming maudlin? [3a(3) and 3b(2)]

ANALYZING THE ELEMENTS

Grammar

1. In the third sentence of paragraph 1, what does the phrase "being humble creatures" modify? What does it add to the sentence? [12a and 15a]
2. Explain why no coordinating conjunction is necessary between the last two independent clauses of the fifth sentence of paragraph 11. [27a]

Effective Sentences

1. In the third sentence of paragraph 3 Hoagland repeats the word *bulldozed*. What is the effect of this repetition? How is repetition used for effect in the fifth sentence of paragraph 5? [21e]
2. In the seventh sentence of paragraph 3 (beginning "But this time . . ."), how does coordination contribute to the force of the paragraph?
3. What effect does beginning the fourth sentence of paragraph 8 with the object rather than the subject have? Would the sentence have been as effective if it had been written in the normal order? Why or why not? [21f]

4. Explain how the participial phrases in the third sentence of paragraph 12 contribute to sentence variety. [22b]

Punctuation and Mechanics

1. Why is the last sentence of paragraph 4 in parentheses? Does the sentence contribute to the development of Hoagland's description of turtles' intelligence? How? What, if anything, would be lost by omitting the sentence? [31f]
2. Explain Hoagland's use of the colon in the eighth sentence of paragraph 5. [31d]
3. Why are italics used in the fourth sentence of paragraph 9? [34a]

Diction

1. In the last sentence of paragraph 3, how does the phrase "another poor puddle" contrast with the rest of the sentence? What is the effect of this contrast?
2. Figurative language plays a large part in creating the tone of Hoagland's essay. Explain how the following examples of figurative language contribute to the tone: "with the suddenness of two dogs who have been conversing in tones too low for an onlooker to hear," "rolling like sailorly souls—a bobbing, infirm gait, a brave, sea-legged momentum" (paragraph 6); "as decorative as pansy petals" (paragraph 7); "The snapper was a Ferdinand," "like a napalm victim's," "like flowers, baby turtles often die," "like a dying man's, their eyes and heads become too prominent," "folds around them like a shroud" (paragraph 9); "swims like a cutter" (paragraph 11); "It's like the nightmare most of us have whimpered through" (paragraph 12); "lurching about in those dry bins like handicapped citizens, living on gumption," "like some of the ladies who show their paintings in Washington Square in May" (paragraph 13); "as dry as a heap of old bones in the sun" (paragraph 14). [24a(4)]
3. Comment on the meaning and appropriateness of the following words: *carnivores* and *inscrutable* (paragraph 1, last two sentences); *untoward* (paragraph 3, first sentence); *cumbersome* and *apocryphal* (paragraph 6, third and sixth sentences); *metaphysical* (paragraph 7, next-to-last sentence); *carapace* (paragraph 9, fifth sentence); *canted, ocelli, portentously,* and *id* (paragraph 10, fourth, fifth, and tenth sentences); *ruminatively* (paragraph 11, sixth sentence); *gimpily, interminably,* and *morose* (paragraph 14, third, seventh, and ninth sentences). [24a]

BUILDING VOCABULARY

1. Define *voracious.* What Latin root does *voracious* come from? What does it mean?
2. List and define three synonyms for *voracious.* Write sentences using each of these synonyms.

SUGGESTIONS FOR WRITING

1. Write an essay describing some kind of creature you find especially appealing (for example, birds, cats, spiders, armadillos, dinosaurs). If no creature appeals to you, write on one you especially dislike. Try to write your description, as Hoagland does, with both facts and feelings, finding some personal perspective or angle that will help you achieve the tone you want.
2. Write an essay describing some occasion when, perhaps by accident or inattention, you unwittingly violated some principle you believed in strongly. Strive to maintain as matter-of-fact an approach as Hoagland does in his conclusion.

The Blobs
Patricia Brady

Patricia Brady writes speeches and op-ed pieces, produces multimedia presentations (including most recently a history of African-American activism in Boston), and cohosts a local affairs television program. She lives in Gloucester, Massachusetts.

It was a time to remember, the time the blobs came to Gloucester. The paper ran a front-page story headlined "The Blobs," describing local shores "carpeted with mysterious masses." A picture of a big hand showed something like a crystalline caterpillar creeping across the palm. 1

Gloucester is an old sea town on the north shore of Massachusetts. It was explored by Champlain, settled by Puritans, fished out of by generations of seafarers. But the blobs were a new experience for Gloucester, according to the *Gloucester Daily Times*. As one fisherman said, no one had ever seen anything like them. 2

They'd come silently upon the waves. Little jellylike creatures the size of your fingertip—some of them quite independent, others curiously stuck together in chains six inches long, or six feet, or maybe even sixteen feet. Clear as spring water, each little blob, with a thread of bluish purple winding deep within. What were they, everyone wanted to know. "Squid eggs," declared some. "Alien spawn," asserted others. Might they be poisonous? Dangerous? There were reports of boat engine intakes being clogged by them. People thought of birds flying into the engines of jet planes and wondered what toll the blobs might take. Harvard had been contacted, ditto the New England Aquarium, the National Marine Fisheries Service, Northeastern University. The top minds of a nation were homing in on the blobs of Gloucester. 3

Meanwhile, locals headed for the beach to experience the blobs personally. A brilliant morning revealed the creatures lying in long, snaky lines at the edge of the water, some rolling back and forth in the wash of the waves, others just lazing there on the beach, shining in the sun. And so many of them. Indeed, as the paper had reported, you could not walk along the water's edge without stepping on dozens of them. 4

But people at the beach were not stepping on the blobs. They were walking near them, touching them with the toes of their shoes, poking them gently, leaning down to peer at them. Some (the bolder) picked up a sampling to study it more closely; they stood still with heads bowed over open palms, like people reading their own fortunes. Strangers talked to one another, shaking their heads, testifying to the mysteriousness of it all. 5

102

No one knew what the blobs were, but one thing was certain: Everyone   6
liked them. Couldn't help it. They were simultaneously cute and strange, like
babies from outer space. Familiar in a way but refusing to divulge their name,
at once individuals and masses, very little and (those hooked together) pretty
big, maybe plants but could be animals: The blobs tapped into a deep human
curiosity that is indistinguishable from delight. They made the humans smile,
the blobs did. Shake their heads and smile.

Those little blobs had a powerful effect, it cannot be denied. They puzzled   7
the people on the beach, charmed them, tickled them, seduced them, lured them
sweetly out of their personal selves and into the mystery surrounding them. If
anything offers hope amid the dark complexities of our history-laden times, it
is the enduring connection between us and the natural world, the way it calls
to us and the way we answer it, the way we go on answering it, as helpless
against its appeal, as unthinking, as weak in the knees as lovers. Enthralled by
the blobs, the people on the beach in Gloucester lifted their gaze from the glis-
tening sand and stared out across the blue-and-white sea with the waves collapsing so delicately and gave themselves over, for a moment, to the larger reality that sang to them.

A week or two later, the blobs were gone, washed back into the sea. They   8
resurfaced briefly in the local paper, when the experts revealed them to be advanced invertebrates. It turned out that our little half-teaspoons of jelly had
muscles, nerves, pharynxes that were notably large, and hearts that had long
fascinated science with their ability to pump in both directions. Some had
green blood! People were naturally pleased to learn all of this, and pleased,
too, to discover that the scientific name of the blobs was *Thalia,* which is also
the name of the muse of comic poetry.

The blobs had struck a lot of us as both comical and poetic, so light they   9
seemed, and so finely put together. The word *thalia* means blooming, which
felt just as right, for the blobs had certainly bloomed upon our beaches—
bloomed and faded, and disappeared like the blossoms of spring and the generations that had stood and wondered on the beach before us. It all fit. Except the
common name, the name we were supposed to call the blobs, which is *salps.*

Salps? No. No one in Gloucester is ever going to call the blobs *salps.* It's   10
just not a name that covers the experience of encountering them on the beach,
lying and lolling and rolling in the surf, clean and bright and friendly as bubbles, and shining like the first day of creation. When the blobs returned for a
visit this fall, a fisherman who spotted them called the *Times* and said, "Those
frog eggs are back." You could tell he was pleased.

*

RESPONDING TO THE WHOLE ESSAY

1. Is this essay written primarily for the purpose of expressing, informing, or
   persuading? [1g(1)]

2. How early in the essay do you realize that the blobs are not threatening? [2b]
3. Are the images mostly visual? What other senses are depicted? [2e]
4. What is accomplished by including descriptions of the reactions of the townspeople? [2e]
5. What is accomplished by including the scientific data? [2d, 23b]

ANALYZING THE ELEMENTS

Grammar

1. Comment on the use of sentence fragments in paragraph 6. Are they justified? [13]
2. In the fifth sentence of paragraph 6, why is *that* used instead of *which?* [G]

Effective Sentences

1. How effective is the opening sentence? [3b(1)]
2. Observe the sentence variety in paragraph 3. Identify two different types of sentences in this paragraph. [22, 12c]

Punctuation and Mechanics

1. Why is *Thalia* italicized and capitalized in paragraph 8 but not capitalized in paragraph 9? [33a(10), 34e]
2. Why is *blobs* not italicized in paragraph 9 but *salps* is? [34e]

Diction

1. What image is conjured up with the word *blob?* [24a]
2. Find the descriptive words that suggest the blobs are not dangerous. Can you find any words that are threatening? [24a]
3. Find words that emphasize the mysterious quality of the blobs.

BUILDING VOCABULARY

1. Find synonyms for *crystalline.* Would any of these synonyms have been a better choice?
2. How can blobs be "poetic" (paragraph 9)?

SUGGESTIONS FOR WRITING

1. Write an essay in which you describe something mysterious.
2. Write an essay in which you describe something very common, but try to describe it in very exotic or mysterious details.

Singing with All the Saints
Aaron McCarroll Gallegos

Aaron McCarroll Gallegos is a freelance writer who lives in Toronto. Formerly an editor for *Sojourner* magazine, he is working on a book on Latino youth and alternatives to gang violence.

By the time my wife and I arrived for morning worship at St. John Coltrane   1
African Orthodox Church, waves of intense sound were already flowing from the Divisadero Street storefront. Located in San Francisco's Western Addition district, between the gritty Tenderloin and groovy Haight-Ashbury neighborhoods, St. John's has a powerful witness the local community can't ignore. Even the most jaded pedestrians were poking their heads in the door to see what all the racket was about.

In spite of the church's huge reputation, the sanctuary is only the size of   2
your average living room, and it feels even smaller because of the radiant Byzantine-style icons that cover the walls: Jesus the Alpha and Omega, Mary the Mother of God, the Tree of Life, and, above the altar, the icon that testifies to the uniqueness of this congregation—a noble image of the church's patron saint, jazz musician John Coltrane, complete with golden halo and holy fire streaming from his saxophone.

While some might find it odd that a church would so honor a jazz mu-   3
sician, this diverse gathering of church members, music lovers, tourists, and the spiritually curious didn't seem to mind. Throughout several hours of worship, the brilliantly colored church pulsated with Coltrane's music, led by a drumly-beating, sax-playing team of clergy. Shouts of "Hallelujah!" "Amen!" and "Praise God!" punctuated chants and melodies from Coltrane's masterwork, *A Love Supreme*.

Some recent accounts in the press about this church have missed the point,   4
mistakenly concluding that the church worships Coltrane himself. In fact, its theology is quite traditional. What makes this church wildly different—and somewhat controversial—is its use of the music and words of a jazz musician to express devotion to God. But something else is going on at St. John's as well. I believe their unique form of worship raises important issues about the changing nature of modern American religion, especially mainstream Christianity, as we enter the twenty-first century.

John Coltrane is certainly not the most likely candidate for Christian saint-   5
hood. He wasn't a conventional Christian, nor was he a conventional musician. Until his death in 1967, "Trane," an endless seeker, pursued an eclectic spiritual path influenced by Christianity, Islam, Hinduism, the Kabbalah,

astrology, and Einstein's theory of relativity. He expressed this spiritual search in his music, and he invited his listeners along on the pilgrimage.

Coltrane had a strong Christian upbringing in the North Carolina home   6
of his minister grandfather, but music—not religion—was his life's passion. He took up the clarinet and saxophone in high school, then moved to Philadelphia in search of work. Coltrane practiced hard, often silently fingering his sax late into the night in the boardinghouse room he shared with his cousin Mary.

After a short stint in the navy, Coltrane became deeply involved with the   7
postwar jazz scene, backing some of the era's top performers, including Dizzy Gillespie, Johnny Hodges, and Miles Davis. But jazz wasn't the only thing consuming Trane. Like Charlie Parker, one of his idols, he got hooked on both heroin and alcohol. While opinions vary as to how severely Coltrane's addictions affected his music, he did get fired from several gigs, including his most prominent one, with trumpeter Davis.

In 1957 Coltrane overcame his addictions and, like many others who con-   8
quer their personal demons, found his way to a greater spiritual depth. "I experienced, by the grace of God," he later wrote, "a spiritual awakening which was to lead me to a richer, fuller, more productive life. At that time, in gratitude, I humbly asked to be given the means and privilege to make others happy through music." Coltrane produced an amazing amount of work in the 10 years he had left to live. By the time he died of liver cancer in 1967 at age 40, he had taken the saxophone, and jazz itself, to new places, raising the art of improvisation to a level that few if any have equaled.

Coltrane's hallowed status at St. John's is largely the work of the church's   9
founder and bishop, Franzo Wayne King. King founded the church in 1971 as the One Mind Temple Evolutionary Transitional Body of Christ. In 1982 the church joined the African Orthodox Church, a small denomination started by African Americans who had been drawn to aspects of Greek, Russian, and Coptic Orthodox liturgy. Appointed the church's bishop, King dropped its old name and chose Coltrane as its patron saint. As a young man, King—not unlike Coltrane—had fled the religion of his Pentecostal parents for the jazz clubs. Seeing Coltrane play in 1965 was the "sound baptism" that started King on a "very serious and earnest journey to seek out God." At St. John's, he hoped to lead others to the transformative spiritual experience he had encountered in Coltrane's music.

St. John's attracts a diverse group of seekers: disaffected Gen-Xers, affluent   10
African-American businesspeople, dreadlocked hippies, aging beats. Even those who are familiar with Coltrane's music may not be prepared for the positive vibrations of "St. John, the sound Baptist," as the church calls him. On the Sunday I attended, the tiny chapel was nearly full when the service began, but within minutes people started slipping out. The din of saxophones, drums, congas, bass, and percussion quickly overwhelmed the uninitiated. A trumpet inches from the back of my head screeched and honked the artist's avant-garde music

throughout the service. But the worship style, flowing out of the Pentecostal and black church traditions, is as fervent and powerful as you'll find anywhere.

Many Christians have criticized St. John's for granting sainthood to a jazz   11 musician and former addict; but given Coltrane's spiritual impact on the African-American community and beyond, the decision isn't so strange. In many ways, mainstream Christianity's refusal to consider canonizing exceptional people like Coltrane parallels the dominant Western culture's assertion that the only truly "classical" music is by Beethoven, Mozart, and other white Europeans. Yet the music of Duke Ellington, Miles Davis, Billie Holiday, Bob Marley, and, yes, John Coltrane is equally "classic"—or more so, some would argue.

On another level, the service at St. John's challenges mainstream as-   12 sumptions about worship itself. While people around the world spend hours, if not days, celebrating their spiritual traditions, North American churchgo-ers often get irritable if services last more than an hour. At St. John's, the hours of worship filled with unsettling sounds are a challenge to mainstream churches that have conformed in many ways to the dominant paradigms of Western society: consumerism instead of personal sacrifice, entertainment in-stead of prophecy, the individual instead of community.

In the coming decades, as the center of Christianity moves from Europe   13 and North America to Africa, Asia, and Latin America, other cultural ex-pressions of worship are destined to become more influential. St. John's is an indication of that trend. Indeed, the cultural reshaping of spiritual expres-sion has been going on as long as humans have gathered for religious wor-ship. Still, many find it hard to equate worship with "ugly" music, which is how some would describe much of Coltrane's later work. Can art that chal-lenges our sense of aesthetics be said to inspire us? Or can only the art we consider beautiful and attractive lift our hearts and souls toward the divine?

Coltrane's later work is, in fact, beautiful, at least for many who have   14 delved deeply into it. Some Coltrane critics have called it "anti-jazz," but oth-ers would disagree. In his recent biography, *John Coltrane: His Life and Music* (University of Michigan, 1998), Lewis Porter, professor of jazz theory at Rutgers University, explores one of Coltrane's most obtuse works, "Venus," recorded in 1966 with drummer Rashied Ali. Porter concludes that "Venus" is an exceedingly complex study of chord contortions based on systematic, al-most mathematical, musical theory.

But what Coltrane was doing went far beyond technical virtuosity. After   15 recording *A Love Supreme* in 1964 (a work he said had come to him as a vision from God), Coltrane stated that 90 percent of his playing was actu-ally prayer. "I know there are bad forces, forces that bring suffering to oth-ers and misery to the world," he once said, "but I want to be the opposite force, I want to be the force which is truly for good." By all accounts a humble and gentle man, Coltrane no doubt would have been uncomfort-able being called a saint. But he surely would have been happy to hear his music moving people toward a deeper relationship with the divine.

*

RESPONDING TO THE WHOLE ESSAY

1. Is this essay primarily for description, or does it have another purpose? [1g(1)]
2. In describing the church of St. John Coltrane, does Gallegos draw comparisons with other churches? Why or why not?
3. What kind of concrete details does Gallegos use? How do these details make the essay more effective? [2e(2)]
4. Which of the senses does Gallegos draw on for his description? [2e(2)]
5. Is this description more objective or subjective? Find evidence in the essay which supports your answer.

ANALYZING THE ELEMENTS

Grammar

1. Find examples of Gallegos's use of active verbs in paragraph 3. [21d]
2. Why is the plural pronoun *their* used in the fifth sentence of paragraph 4? [16d(3)]

Effective Sentences

1. Comment on the parallelism of the last sentence of paragraph 11. [20a(1)]
2. Comment on the use of rhetorical questions in paragraph 12. [Glossary of Terms]

Punctuation and Mechanics

1. Why are dashes used in paragraph 6? Would any other punctuation work as well or better? [31e(2)]
2. Comment on the use of numerals in paragraph 7. [35h]

Diction

1. Why is the Haight-Ashbury neighborhood described as "groovy"? [23a]
2. Find words in the essay that you would expect to find in a description of a church. Are there any words that you would not expect to find in such a description?

BUILDING VOCABULARY

1. What is the Greek origin of the word *eclectic?* Use the word in a sentence.
2. Look up the following words: *Byzantine, icon, hallowed.*

SUGGESTION FOR WRITING

1. Write an essay in which you describe an unusual event or place.
2. Write an essay describing your first visit to a place.

Excerpt from Assembling California
John McPhee

John McPhee (1931–) has been recognized as a key innovator of nonfiction writing. McPhee brought to nonfiction writing the objectivity of a journalist, a keen eye for detail, and an ability to arrange information so that it shows a story rather than tells it. His distinction as a writer became apparent as early as 1965, when the *New Yorker* published McPhee's creative profile of basketball player Bill Bradley. Shortly after the publication of this article, McPhee, then a writer for *Time* magazine, accepted the position of staff writer at the *New Yorker*. McPhee continues to write for the *New Yorker* and teaches a course entitled "The Literature of Fact" as Ferris Professor of Journalism at Princeton University. In addition, McPhee has written a number of best-selling books, including *Coming into the Country* and his four-book series about geology, collectively known as *Annals of the Former World*. In this selection, from *Assembling California,* the fourth book of the geology series, McPhee explains how the Loma Prieta earthquake of 1989 came to be and how it affected the people and landscape of California.

There is a swerve in the San Andreas Fault where it moves through the Santa Cruz Mountains. It bends a little and then straightens again, like the track of a tire that was turned to avoid an animal. Because deviations in transform faults retard the sliding and help strain to build, the most pronounced ones are known as tectonic knots, or great asperities, or prominent restraining bends. The two greatest known earthquakes on the fault occurred at or close to prominent restraining bends. The little jog in the Santa Cruz Mountains is a modest asperity, but enough to tighten the lock. As the strain rises through the years, the scales of geologic time and human time draw ever closer, until they coincide. An earthquake is not felt everywhere at once. It travels in every direction—up, down, and sideways—from its place and moment of beginning. In this example, the precise moment is in the sixteenth second of the fifth minute after five in the afternoon, as the scales touch and the tectonic knot lets go.

The epicenter is in the Forest of Nisene Marks, a few hundred yards from Trout Creek Gulch, five miles north of Monterey Bay. The most conspicuous nearby landmark is the mountain called Loma Prieta. In a curving small road in the gulch are closed gates and speed bumps. PRIVATE PROPERTY. KEEP OUT. This is steep terrain—roughed up, but to a greater extent serene. Under the redwoods are glades of maidenhair. There are fields of pampas grass, stands of tan madrone. A house worth two million dollars is under construction, and will continue when this is over. BEWARE OF DOG.

Motion occurs fifty-nine thousand eight hundred feet down—the deepest   3
hypocenter ever recorded on the San Andreas Fault. No drill hole made anywhere on earth for any purpose has reached so far. On the San Andreas, no
earthquake is ever likely to reach deeper. Below sixty thousand feet, the rock
is no longer brittle.

The epicenter, the point at the surface directly above the hypocenter, is   4
four miles from the fault trace. Some geologists will wonder if the motion occurred in a blind thrust, but in the Santa Cruz Mountains the two sides of
the San Andreas Fault are not vertical. The Pacific wall leans against the North
American wall at about the angle of a ladder.

For seven to ten seconds, the deep rockfaces slide. The maximum jump   5
is more than seven feet. Northwest and southeast, the slip propagates an ag-
gregate twenty-five miles. This is not an especially large event. It is nothing
like a plate-rupturing earthquake. Its upward motion stops twenty thousand
feet below the surface. Even so, the slippage plane—where the two great slant-
ing faces have moved against each other—is an irregular oval of nearly two
hundred square miles. The released strain turns into waves, and they develop
half a megaton of energy. Which is serious enough. In California argot, this
is not a tickler—it's a slammer.

The pressure waves spread upward and outward about three and a half   6
miles a second, expanding, compressing, expanding, compressing the crystal
structures in the rock. The shear waves that follow are somewhat slower.
Slower still (about two miles a second) are the surface waves: Rayleigh waves,
in particle motion like a rolling sea, and Love waves, advancing like snakes.
Wherever things shake, the shaking will consist of all these waves. Half a
minute will pass before the light towers move at Candlestick Park. Meanwhile,
dogs are barking in Trout Creek Gulch. Car alarms and house alarms are
screaming. If, somehow, you could hear all such alarms coming on throughout the region, you could hear the spread of the earthquake. The redwoods
are swaying. Some snap like asparagus. The restraining bend has forced the
rock to rise. Here, west of the fault trace, the terrain has suddenly been elevated a foot and a half—a punch delivered from below. For some reason, it
is felt most on the highest ground.

On Summit Road, near the Loma Prieta School, a man goes up in the air   7
like a diver off a board. He lands on his head. Another man is thrown sideways through a picture window. A built-in oven leaves its niche and shoots
across a kitchen. A refrigerator walks, bounces off a wall, and returns to its
accustomed place. As Pearl Lake's seven-room house goes off its foundation,
she stumbles in her kitchen and falls to the wooden floor. In 1906, the same
house went off the same foundation. Her parents had moved in the day before. Lake lives alone and raises prunes. Ryan Moore, in bed under the covers, is still under the covers after his house travels a hundred feet and ends
up in ruins around him.

People will come to think of this earthquake as an event that happened   8
in San Francisco. But only from Watsonville to Santa Cruz—here in the region

of the restraining bend, at least sixty miles south of the city—will the general intensity prove comparable to 1906. In this region are almost no freeway overpasses, major bridges, or exceptionally tall buildings. Along the narrow highland roads, innumerable houses are suddenly stoop-shouldered, atwist, bestrewn with splinters of wood and glass, even new ones "built to code." Because the movement on the fault occurs only at great depth, the surface is an enigma of weird random cracks. Few and incongruous, they will not contribute to the geologic record. If earthquakes like Loma Prieta are illegible, how many of them took place through the ages before the arrival of seismographs, and what does that do to geologists' frequency calculations?

Driveways are breaking like crushed shells. Through woods and fields, a ripping fissure as big as an arroyo crosses Morrill Road. Along Summit Road, a crack three feet wide, seven feet deep, and seventeen hundred feet long runs among houses and misses them all. Roads burst open as if they were being strafed. Humps rise. Double yellow lines are making left-lateral jumps. (Left-lateral: either way you look at it, the far side of the jump appears to have moved to the left.)

|| ||

Cracks, fissures, fence posts are jumping left as well. What is going on? The San Andreas is the classic right-lateral fault. Is country going south that should be going north? Is plate tectonics going backward? Geologists will figure out an explanation. With their four-dimensional minds, and in their interdisciplinary ultraverbal way, geologists can wiggle out of almost anything. They will say that while the fault motion far below is absolutely right lateral, blocks of rock overhead are rotating like ball bearings. If you look down on a field of circles that are all turning clockwise, you will see what the geologists mean.

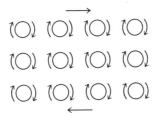

Between one circle and the next, the movement everywhere is left lateral. But the movement of the field as a whole is right lateral. The explanation has legerdemain. Harry Houdini had legerdemain when he got out of his ropes, chains, and handcuffs at the bottom of the Detroit River.

All compression resulting from the bend is highest near the bend, and the compression is called the Santa Cruz Mountains. Loma Prieta, near four thousand feet, is the highest peak. The words mean Hill Dark. This translation will gain in the shaking, and appear in the media as Dark Rolling Mountain.

At the University of California, Santa Cruz, three first-year students from   11
the East Coast sit under redwoods on the forest campus. As the shock waves reach them and the trees whip overhead, the three students leap up and spontaneously dance and shout in a ring. Near the edge of town, a corral disintegrates, horses run onto a highway, a light truck crashes into them and the driver is killed. Bicyclists are falling to the streets and automobiles are bouncing. Santa Cruz has been recovering from severe economic depression, in large part through the success of the Pacific Garden Mall, six blocks of old unreinforced brick buildings lately turned into boutiques. The buildings are contiguous and are of different heights. As the shock waves reach them, the buildings react with differing periods of vibration and knock each other down. Twenty-one buildings collapse. Higher ones fall into lower ones like nesting boxes. Ten people die. The Hotel Metropol, seventy years old, crashes through the ceiling of the department store below it. The Pacific Garden Mall is on very-young-floodplain river silts that amplify the shaking—as the same deposits did in 1906.

Landslides are moving away from the epicenter in synchrony with the car   12
alarms. As if from explosions, brown clouds rise into the air. A hundred and eighty-five acres go in one block slide, dozens of houses included. Hollister's clock tower falls. Coastal bluffs fall. Mountain cliffs and roadcuts fall.

The shock waves move up the peninsula. Reaching Los Gatos, they give   13
a wrenching spin to houses that cost seven hundred and fifty thousand dollars and have no earthquake insurance. A man is at work in a bicycle shop. In words that *Time* will print in twenty-four-point type, he will refer to the earthquake as "my best near-death experience." (For a number of unpublished fragments here, I am indebted to editors at Time Warner, who have shared with me a boxful of their correspondents' files.)

Thirteen seconds north of the epicenter is Los Altos, where Harriet and   14
David Schnur live. They grew up in New York City and have the familiar sense that an I.R.T. train is passing under their home. It is a "million-dollar Cape Cod," and glass is breaking in every room. This is scarcely their first earthquake.

David: "Why is it taking so long?"   15

Harriet: "This could be the last one. Thank God we went to *shul* during   16
the holidays."

The piano moves. Jars filled with beans shatter. Wine pours from break-   17
ing bottles. A grandfather clock, falling—its hands stopping at 5:04—lands on a metronome, which begins to tick.

The shock reaches Stanford University, and sixty buildings receive a hun-   18
dred and sixty million dollars' worth of damage. The university does not have earthquake insurance.

The waves move on to San Mateo, where a woman in a sixteenth-floor apart-   19
ment has poured a cup of coffee and sat down to watch the third game of the World Series. When the shock arrives, the apartment is suddenly like an airplane

in a wind shear. The jolt whips her head to one side. A lamp crashes. Books fall. Doors open. Dishes fall. Separately, the coffee and the cup fly across the room.

People are dead in Santa Cruz, Watsonville has rubble on the ground, and   20 San Francisco has yet to feel anything. The waves approach the city directly from the hypocenter and indirectly via the Moho. Waves that begin this deep touch the Moho—the geophysical boundary between crust and mantle—at so slight an angle that they carom upward, a phenomenon known as critical reflection. As the shaking begins in San Francisco, it is twice as strong as would generally be expected for an earthquake of this magnitude at that distance from the epicenter.

Two men are on a motor scooter on Sixteenth Street. The driver, glanc-   21 ing over his shoulder, says, "Michael, stop bouncing." A woman walking on Bush Street sees a Cadillac undulating like a water bed. She thinks, What are those people *doing in there?* Then the windows fall out of a nearby café. The sidewalks are moving. Chimneys fall in Haight-Ashbury, landing on cars. In Asbury Heights, a man is watering his patch of grass. He suddenly feels faint, his knees weaken, and his front lawn flutters like water under wind. Inside, his wife is seated at her seven-foot grand. The piano levitates, comes right up off the floor as she plays. She is thinking, I'm good but not this good. A blimp is in the air above. The pilot feels vibration. He feels four distinct bumps.

In Golden Gate Park, high-school girls are practicing field hockey. Their   22 coach sees the playing field move, sees "huge trees . . . bending like windshield wipers." She thinks, This is the end, I'm about to fall into the earth, this is the way to go. Her players freeze in place. They are silent. They just look at one another.

In the zoo, the spider monkeys begin to scream. The birdhouse is full of   23 midair collisions. The snow leopards, lazy in the sun with the ground shaking, are evidently unimpressed. In any case, their muscles don't move. Pachy, the approximately calico cat who lives inside the elephant house, is outside the elephant house. She refused to enter the building all day yesterday and all day today. When someone carried her inside to try to feed her, she ran outside, hungry.

At Chez Panisse, in Berkeley, cupboard doors open and a chef's personal   24 collection of pickles and preserves crashes. The restaurant, renowned and booked solid, will be half full this evening. Those who come will order exceptionally expensive wine. Meanwhile, early patrons at a restaurant in Oakland suddenly feel as if they were in the dining car of a train that has lurched left. When it is over, they will all get up and shake hands.

In the San Francisco Tennis Club, balls are flying without being hit.   25 Players are falling down. The ceilings and the walls seem to be flowing. Nearby, at Sixth and Bluxome, the walls of a warehouse are falling. Bricks crush a car and decapitate the driver. Four others are killed in this avalanche as well.

In the hundred miles of the San Andreas Fault closest to San Francisco,   26 no energy has been released. The accumulated strain is unrelieved. The U.S. Geological Survey will continue to expect within thirty years an earthquake in San Francisco as much as fifty times as powerful. In the Survey's offices in

Menlo Park, a seismologist will say, "This was not a big earthquake, but we hope it's the biggest we deal with in our careers." The Pacific Stock Exchange, too vital to suffer as much as a single day off, will trade by candlelight all day tomorrow.

Passengers on a rapid-transit train in a tube under the bay feel as if they had left the rails and were running over rocks. The Interstate 80 tunnel through Yerba Buena Island moves like a slightly writhing hose. Linda Lamb, in a sailboat below the Bay Bridge, feels as if something had grabbed her keel. Cars on the bridge are sliding. The entire superstructure is moving, first to the west about a foot, and then back east, bending the steel, sending large concentric ripples out from the towers, and shearing through bolts thicker than cucumbers. This is the moment in which a five-hundred-ton road section at one tower comes loose and hinges downward, killing the driver of a car below and breaking open the lower deck, so that space gapes to the bay. Heading toward Oakland on the lower deck, an Alameda County Transit driver thinks that all his tires have blown, fights the careening bus for control, and stops eight feet from a plunge to the water. Smashed cars vibrate on the edge but do not fall. Simultaneously, the Golden Gate Bridge is undulating, fluctuating, oscillating, pendulating. Daniel Mohn—in his car heading north, commuting home—is halfway across. From the first tremor, he knows what is happening, and his response to his situation is the exact opposite of panic. He feels very lucky. He thinks, as he has often thought before, If I had the choice, this is where I would be. Reporters will seek him later, and he will tell them, "We never close down." He is the current chief engineer of the Golden Gate Bridge. 27

Peggy Iacovini, having crossed the bridge, is a minute ahead of the chief engineer and a few seconds into the Marin Headlands. In her fluent Anglo-Calif she will tell the reporters, "My car jumped over like half a lane. It felt like my tire blew out. Everybody opened their car doors or stuck their heads out their windows to see if it was their tires. There were also a couple of girls holding their chests going oh my God. All the things on the freeway were just blowing up and stuff. It was like when you light dynamite—you know, on the stick—it just goes down and then it blows up. The communication wires were just sparking. I mean my heart was beating. I was like oh my God. But I had no idea of the extent that it had done." 28

At Candlestick Park, the poles at the ends of the foul lines throb like fishing rods. The overhead lights are swaying. The upper deck is in sickening motion. The crowd stands as one. Some people are screaming. Steel bolts fall. Chunks of concrete fall. A chunk weighing fifty pounds lands in a seat that a fan just left to get a hot dog. Of sixty thousand people amassed for the World Series, not one will die. Candlestick is anchored in radiolarian chert. 29

The tall buildings downtown rise out of landfill but are deeply founded in bedrock, and, with their shear walls and moment frames and steel-and-rubber isolation bearings, they sway, shiver, sway again, but do not fall. A woman forty-six floors up feels as if she were swinging through space. A woman twenty-nine floors up, in deafening sound, gets under her desk in fetal position 30 and thinks of the running feet of elephants. Cabinets, vases, computers, and law books are flying. Pictures drop. Pipes bend. Nearly five minutes after five. Elevators full of people are banging in their shafts.

On the high floors of the Hyatt, guests sliding on their bellies think of it 31 as surfing.

A quick-thinking clerk in Saks herds a customer into the safety of a door- 32 jamb and has her sign the sales slip there.

Room service has just brought shrimp, oysters, and a bucket of champagne 33 to Cybill Shepherd, on the seventh floor of the Campton Place Hotel. Foot of Nob Hill. Solid Franciscan sandstone. Earthquakes are not unknown to Shepherd. At her home in Los Angeles, pictures are framed under Plexiglas, windowpanes are safety glass, and the water heater is bolted to a wall. Beside every bed are a flashlight, a radio, and a hard hat. Now, on Nob Hill, Shepherd and company decide to eat the oysters and the shrimp before fleeing, but to leave the champagne. There was a phone message earlier, from her astrologer. Please call. Shepherd didn't call. Now she is wondering what the astrologer had in mind.

A stairway collapses between the tenth and eleventh floors of an office 34 building in Oakland. Three people are trapped. When they discover that there is no way to shout for help, one of them will dial her daughter in Fairfax County, Virginia. The daughter will dial 911. Fairfax County Police will teletype the Oakland police, who will climb the building, knock down a wall, and make the rescue.

Meanwhile, at sea off Point Reyes, the U.S. naval ship *Walter S. Diehl* is 35 shaking so violently that the officers think they are running aground. Near Monterey, the Moss Landing Marine Laboratory has been destroyed. A sea cliff has fallen in Big Sur—eighty-one miles south of the epicenter. In another minute, clothes in closets will be swinging on their hangers in Reno. Soon thereafter, water will form confused ripples in San Fernando Valley swimming pools. The skyscrapers of Los Angeles will sway.

After the earthquake on the Hayward Fault in 1868, geologists clearly 36 saw that dangers varied with the geologic map, and they wrote in a State Earthquake Investigation Commission Report, "The portion of the city which suffered most was . . . on made ground." In one minute in 1906, made ground in San Francisco sank as much as three feet. Where landfill touched natural terrain, cable-car rails bent down. Maps printed and distributed well before 1989—stippled and cross-hatched where geologists saw the greatest violence to come—singled out not only the Nimitz Freeway in Oakland but also, in San Francisco, the Marina district, the Embarcadero, and the Laocosnic freeways near Second and Stillman. Generally speaking, shaking declines with distance from the hypocenter, but where landfill lies on loose sediment the shaking can amplify, as if it were an explosion set off from afar with a plunger and a wire. If a lot of water is present in the sediment and the fill, they can be changed in an instant into gray quicksand—the effect known as liquefaction. Compared with what happens on bedrock, the damage can be something like a hundredfold, as it was on the lakefill of Mexico City in 1985, even though the hypocenter was far to the west, under the Pacific shore.

In a plane that has just landed at San Francisco International Airport,   37
passengers standing up to remove luggage from the overhead racks have the luggage removed for them by the earthquake. Ceilings fall in the control tower, and windows break. The airport is on landfill, as is Oakland International, across the bay. Sand boils break out all over both airfields. In downtown San Francisco, big cracks appear in the elevated I-280, the Embarcadero Freeway, and U.S. 101, where they rest on bayfill and on filled-in tidal creek and filled-in riparian bog. They do not collapse. Across the bay, but west of the natural shoreline, the Cypress section of the Nimitz Freeway—the double-decked I-880—is vibrating at the same frequency as the landfill mud it sits on. This coincidence produces a shaking amplification near eight hundred percent. Concrete support columns begin to fail. Reinforcing rods an inch and a half thick spring out of them like wires. The highway is not of recent construction. At the tops of the columns, where they meet the upper deck, the joints have inadequate shear reinforcement. By a large margin, they would not meet present codes. This is well known to state engineers, who have blueprinted the reinforcements, but the work has not been done, for lack of funds.

The under road is northbound, and so is disaster. One after the last, the   38
slabs of the upper roadway are falling. Each weighs six hundred tons. Reinforcing rods connect them, and seem to be helping to pull the highway down. Some drivers on the under road, seeing or sensing what is happening behind them, stop, set their emergency brakes, leave their cars, run toward daylight, and are killed by other cars. Some drivers apparently decide that the very columns that are about to give way are possible locations of safety, like doorjambs. They pull over, hover by the columns, and are crushed. A bank customer-service representative whose 1968 Mustang has just come out of a repair shop feels the jolting roadway and decides that the shop has done a terrible job, that her power steering is about to fail, and that she had better get off this high-speed road as fast as she can. A ramp presents itself. She swerves onto it and off the freeway. She hears a huge sound. In her rearview mirror she sees the upper roadway crash flat upon the lower.

As the immense slabs fall, people in cars below hold up their hands to   39
try to stop them. A man eating peanuts in his white pickup feels what he thinks are two flat tires. A moment later, his pickup is two feet high. Somehow, he survives. In an airport shuttle, everyone dies. A man in another car guns his engine, keeps his foot to the floor, and races the slabs that are successively falling behind him. His wife is yelling, "Get out of here! Get out of here!" Miraculously, he gets out of here. Many race the slabs, but few escape. Through twenty-two hundred yards the slabs fall. They began falling where the highway leaves natural sediments and goes onto a bed of landfill. They stop where the highway leaves landfill and returns to natural sediments.

Five minutes after five, and San Francisco's Red Cross Volunteer Disaster   40
Services Committee is in the middle of a disaster-preparedness meeting. The Red
Cross Building is shivering. The committee has reconvened underneath its table.

In yards and parks in the Marina, sand boils are spitting muds from ori-   41
fices that resemble the bell rims of bugles. In architectural terminology, the
Marina at street level is full of soft stories. A soft story has at least one open
wall and is not well supported. Numerous ground floors in the Marina are
garages. As buildings collapse upon themselves, the soft stories vanish. In a
fourth-floor apartment, a woman in her kitchen has been cooking Rice-A-Roni.
She has put on long johns and a sweatshirt and turned on the television to
watch the World Series. As the building shakes, she moves with experience into
a doorway and grips the jamb. Nevertheless, the vibrations are so intense that
she is thrown to the floor. When the shaking stops, she will notice a man's legs,
standing upright, outside her fourth-story window, as if he were floating in air.
She will think that she is hallucinating. But the three floors below her no longer
exist, and the collapsing building has carried her apartment to the sidewalk.
Aqueducts are breaking, and water pressure is falling. Flames from broken gas
mains will rise two hundred feet. As in 1906, water to fight fires will be scarce.
There are numbers of deaths in the Marina, including a man and woman later
found hand in hand. A man feels the ground move under his bicycle. When he
returns from his ride, he will find his wife severely injured and his infant son
dead. An apartment building at Fillmore and Bay has pitched forward onto
the street. Beds inside the building are standing on end.

The Marina in 1906 was a salt lagoon. After the Panama Canal opened,   42
in 1914, San Francisco planned its Panama–Pacific International Exposition
for the following year, not only to demonstrate that the city had recovered
from the great earthquake to end all earthquakes but also to show itself off
as a golden destination for shipping. The site chosen for the Exposition was
the lagoon. To fill it up, fine sands were hydraulically pumped into it and
mixed with miscellaneous debris, creating the hundred and sixty-five dry acres
that flourished under the Exposition and are now the Marina. Nearly a minute
has passed since the rock slipped at the hypocenter. In San Francisco, the
tremors this time will last fifteen seconds. As the ground violently shakes and
the sand boils of the Marina discharge material from the liquefying depths,
the things they spit up include tarpaper and bits of redwood—the charred remains of houses from the earthquake of 1906.

✳

RESPONDING TO THE WHOLE ESSAY

1. Would you say that McPhee's purpose in this essay is primarily expressive, informative, or persuasive? Cite evidence to support your answer. [1g(1)]
2. What kinds of readers does McPhee seem to have in mind? Is he writing for
   people with knowledge of geology and the geological workings of earthquakes?

Does he expect that his readers have experienced an earthquake? Use evidence in the essay to comment on the assumptions he appears to make about his audience. [1g(2)]

3. Comment upon paragraph 2 as an example of a description arranged spatially. [2e and 18b]

4. How does McPhee link the first five sentences of paragraph 6 and the last five sentences of paragraph 27? [3d and 21e]

5. Analyze paragraph 9 as an example of question-answer development. Does McPhee answer these questions or are they rhetorical questions? What does McPhee achieve by developing the paragraph in this way? [2c and Glossary of Usage]

6. Notice that the verb tense in paragraph 41 is not consistent. Present, past perfect, and future tenses are all present in this paragraph. Explain whether the shifts in verb tense in sentences 1–6 are necessary. Be as specific as you can. [17c]

ANALYZING THE ELEMENTS

Grammar

1. Explain the grammatical function of *whose* in the eighth sentence of paragraph 38. To what does *whose* refer? [16]

2. What does the phrase *One after the last* modify in the sentence of paragraph 38? Why? [15b]

3. What is the mood of *come* in the third sentence of paragraph 24? How can you tell? [17d]

Effective Sentences

1. The third sentence of paragraph 8 could be rewritten: *Almost no freeway overpasses, major bridges, or exceptionally tall buildings are in this region.* What does McPhee achieve by writing the sentence as he does? Explain as well as you can. [21f]

2. McPhee makes effective use of parallel structure of several kinds, including balanced parts, repeated words, correlatives. Find at least one example of each. [20]

3. How does McPhee achieve emphasis in the seventh sentence of paragraph 27 and the first sentence of paragraph 30? How do these sentences add to the emphatic tone of the essay? [21c]

4. Throughout the essay, McPhee uses fragments for emphasis. The two fragments in paragraph 33 could be added to the sentence that precedes them: *Room service has just brought shrimp, oysters, and a bucket of champagne to Cybill Shepherd, on the seventh floor of the Campton Place Hotel, a hotel made of solid Franciscan sandstone and located at the foot of Nob Hill.* Does this sentence retain the urgency conveyed by McPhee's use of fragments? Try to explain why or why not. [13]

5. Notice that the seventh sentence of paragraph 9 and the last sentence of paragraph 13 are enclosed in parentheses. Try to explain the purpose of each of these sentences. Why does McPhee choose to enclose them in parentheses? [31f]

Punctuation and Mechanics

1. Comment upon the use of the apostrophe in *dollars'* in the first sentence of paragraph 18. How might the sentence be rewritten to clarify the relationship indicated by this apostrophe? [29]
2. Explain the capitalization of *Franciscan* in the third sentence of paragraph 33; *Plexiglas* in the fifth sentence of paragraph 33, and *San Francisco's Red Cross Volunteer Disaster Services Committee* in the first sentence of paragraph 40. Why do you think McPhee capitalizes each word in the fragments that make up the fourth, fifth, and last sentences of paragraph 2? [33]
3. Explain why McPhee chooses commas, rather than semicolons, to separate the main clauses that make up the fourth sentence of paragraph 13. [27a and 28a]
4. Double quotation marks generally set off thoughts from other text. Why do you think McPhee avoids using double quotation marks in the fourth and twelfth sentences of paragraph 21, the third sentence of paragraph 22, and the thirteenth sentence of paragraph 27? How might this choice have influenced McPhee to italicize *doing* in the fourth sentence of paragraph 21? Explain. [30a(5) and 34]
5. The second sentence of paragraph 28 ("In her fluent . . .") begins a quotation that extends throughout the remainder of the paragraph. If this essay were written in the MLA style of documentation, how would this quotation be handled? in APA style of documentation? Write a paraphrase of this long quotation. Is the paraphrase as effective as McPhee's original use of direct quotation? Why or why not? [30b and 7h]

Diction

1. Throughout the essay, McPhee uses words that are exact, idiomatic, and fresh. Comment upon the effectiveness of each of the following words: *stoop-shouldered, atwist, bestrewn* in the fourth sentence of paragraph 8 and *undulating, fluctuating, oscillating, pendulating* in the ninth sentence of paragraph 27. [24c]
2. Paragraph 20 includes several technical terms: *hypocenter, geophysical boundary, crust, mantle, critical reflection,* and *epicenter.* Justify this use of jargon and explain how it contributes to the overall tone of the essay. [23c and 3a(3)]
3. Why does McPhee use *lies* instead of *lays* in the fifth sentence of paragraph 36? Explain. [23b]

BUILDING VOCABULARY

1. From what Greek roots do the words *epicenter* and *hypocenter* originate? What do these roots mean? List two words derived from each of these roots and write sentences using each.
2. Explain the meanings and origin of the prefixes *super-, ultra-,* and *trans-.* Make a list of six words, including two words beginning with each of these prefixes. Write a sentence with each of the words you have listed.

SUGGESTIONS FOR WRITING

1. Using concrete details, describe an earthquake or other natural disaster that you have witnessed (for example, a blizzard, tornado, heat wave, flood, hurricane, or thunderstorm).
2. Write a short essay describing your anticipation of or preparation for a natural disaster or extreme change in the weather.

*

Chapter 4

Process

Process explanations are of two kinds: those that tell a reader how to perform some task and those that simply explain how something works. In both kinds, a writer describes a sequence of steps, generally in chronological order, one step leading to the next. As you might suppose, therefore, process is closely related both to narration and to cause and effect.

In this chapter, Alexander Petrunkevitch's "The Spider and the Wasp" explains a process that occurs in nature, a process humans cannot duplicate. Garrison Keillor's "How to Write a Letter" humorously describes letter writing from the point of view of a shy person, encouraging his readers to make their marks upon the world through letters. In "Sugaring" Marguery Guest explains the intricate details of tapping trees for maple syrup. In "The Maker's Eye: Revising Your Own Manuscripts," Donald M. Murray aims to give his readers practical advice, as his subtitle indicates, though the process Murray writes about is not straightforward and varies greatly from writer to writer and from project to project, so its steps cannot be set down in any firm order. Mummifying a corpse is a process more clearly structured: you *must* do some things before others. Adam Goodheart, in "Mummy Arts," gives step-by-step directions (don't try this at home). Similarly, Michael Kernan's essay on medical technology used in caring for the animals at the National Zoo is more informational than instructional. Most readers would not have the equipment or the expertise to follow the process.

In writing about a process, be very careful to explain the steps in the proper order and to omit no steps that are necessary. An awareness of your reader is supremely important in writing about processes—especially if you are giving directions. As you write, continually ask yourself what your readers already know and what they need to be told. Must terms be defined, parts described, steps illustrated? Crucial, too, is the way you make time relationships clear for the reader. Special care with verb tenses [17c] and transitional devices [3d] is part of the key to success here.

In the following student essay, Maya Ramirez gives directions for playing the Irish bagpipes. Notice how she combines explanation with instructions, describing each part of the instrument before telling the reader exactly what to do. Notice, too, how she uses verb tenses and transitional expressions signaling time to keep the sequence of steps clear.

Playing the Irish Bagpipes

Introduction—list of materials and comment on circumstances

If you want to play the Irish bagpipes, you need a set of pipes, a lot of time and patience, and, if you live in an apartment building, neighbors who are hard of hearing. Since Irish pipes are bellows-blown rather than mouth-blown, you do not need the powerful lungs required for the more familiar Scottish bagpipes. There is an adage that it takes seven years to make a piper, and the first year or two can be a little excruciating; once the worst is over, however, the instrument is a joy to play.

Informative process— description of instrument

Start with a practice set. You will have a chanter, bag, and bellows. The chanter is the part that actually makes sound. As you examine it, you will see that it is a long wooden tube with finger holes cut in it like a recorder, and it has a closed brass tube mounted on the end. Inside the brass tube is the reed, which vibrates to produce the sound, but the reed is very fragile and the brass tube should not be removed except with extreme caution. From the brass tube a smaller, shorter tube, called the input tube, protrudes at an angle. This is the part you will insert into the bag.

Now examine the bag. It is made of leather (or vinyl), usually covered with fabric, and is shaped like the letter P. In the end of the stem of the P you will find a fitting to receive the input tube of the chanter. Sticking out of the side of the fat part of the P is a tube called the blowstick, to which you will eventually attach the bellows.

Next, therefore, examine the bellows. It resembles a fireplace bellows without handles. One cheek of the bellows has a short leather strap and an air valve, through which air can enter the bellows as you pump. The other cheek has a long leather strap and a flexible tube (often made of a piece of bicycle inner tube). Air comes out of this tube when you pump.

Descriptive process—how to hold the pipes

Now you are ready to strap the thing on and begin to play. First, strap the bellows to your body. The long strap goes around your body at about rib height with the bellows itself on the right side, and

First step

Second step

Third step

Fourth step

How to prepare
the pipes for
making sound

Fifth step

Sixth step

Seventh step

the short strap goes around your right arm just above
the elbow. When the bellows is on in this fashion, the
flexible tube will pass in front of your body extending
about halfway across. Try pumping the bellows with
your elbow (the motion is rather like imitating a
chicken flapping its wings). Next, tuck the bag under
your left arm with the fat part of the bag under the
elbow and the long narrow part on top, jutting forward.
If the bag is placed properly, the blowstick will project
halfway across in front of your body and be in just the
right place to plug into the tube that sticks out of the
bellows. Plug the blowstick into the tube.

If you now pump the bellows, air coming into
the bellows on the upstroke of your right elbow will,
on the downstroke, pass through the tube and
blowstick in front of you into the bag under your left
arm. Several strokes with the bellows should begin to
fill the bag, and if you then squeeze the bag with your
left elbow, air will come out the long narrow neck that
sticks out in front of you. Into the fitting at the end
of this neck, insert the input tube of the chanter. Now
the air, instead of passing uselessly out of the bag,
passes through the chanter, causing the reed to
vibrate and make a horrible noise. As you master the
instrument, this noise will gradually be transformed
into music.

How to adjust
sound quality

Eighth step

Ninth step

Tenth step

Eleventh step

Twelfth step

Conclusion

Sit down, if you are not already sitting, and
place the open end of the chanter against your right
leg a couple of inches above the knee. Pump the
bellows with long, steady strokes and, as the bag fills,
apply steady gentle pressure to the bag with the left
elbow. You can get a second, higher octave by forcing
a little extra air from the bag through the chanter.
Lifting the chanter off the knee gives a louder, wailing
tone for variety. Closing the chanter against the knee
and covering all the finger holes between notes stops
the sound and allows you to play staccato. With a
fingering chart handy, you will be able to play
different notes of the scale, and as you become
accustomed to the simultaneous actions of pumping,
squeezing, and fingering, you will soon be playing
tunes. At that point, you will be well on your way to
becoming a piper.

Commentary. Maya Ramirez begins her process essay with a nod to the
convention of listing the equipment necessary—and brings a little humor to

the subject as she does so. Her equipment list includes not only the requisite pipes, but also the necessary lifestyle (one with considerable free time), the best kind of personality (a patient one), and the right kind of neighbors (ones who are hard of hearing). To allay any apprehensions the reader may have developed through a minimal familiarity with Scottish pipes, she also points out, again with some levity, that Irish pipes require no extraordinary physical ability.

Ramirez assumes that her audience knows little about the Irish pipes—a fairly exotic instrument. Accordingly, she makes her description unusually detailed. If one had never seen a set of these pipes, one could readily recognize them from having read her description. Furthermore, she makes the description a part of the process of learning to play the pipes. Essentially Ramirez is saying, "Familiarize yourself with this instrument. Look at the parts and let me explain what those parts do," defining the function of each part of the instrument so that when she actually sets forth the steps involved in playing the pipes, the reader can more readily follow the instructions.

When she has described the form and the function of each part of the instrument (and also told the reader how to handle each part and which parts to be especially careful with), Ramirez begins her instructions: "Now you are ready to strap the thing on and begin to play." It is worth noting that these instructions are organized into three sets. First she tells the reader how to put the instrument on and connect the bellows and the bag. Next she explains how to ready the instrument so that it can make a sound: pump air into the bag with the bellows and fit the chanter to the bag. Finally, she tells the reader how to adjust the quality of the sound that comes out of the instrument. Her conclusion suggests that the reader use a fingering chart and practice the motions required to play the pipes.

This process essay is especially clear and direct, providing all the information the rank novice needs to begin with. But Ramirez did not simply sit down and produce this kind of clarity and simplicity straight off. As the rough draft that follows will show, she had to do considerable cutting and simplifying for her uninformed audience, and she also radically reorganized the essay. Originally, she did not give step-by-step directions, nor did she take an encouraging approach. For example, the second paragraph of the draft would be enough to scare any prospective piper, and so she simplified it by deleting her explanation of the difference between a full set of pipes and a practice set. She also deleted extraneous (though interesting) information about the name of the pipes, and transferred to the introduction the information about how Irish pipes are blown.

To avoid getting the reader tangled in all the information about what the straps do and where to put them, she separated those ideas, explaining the bellows and the bag before addressing what to do with the straps. She also separated the instructions about how to manipulate the instrument from those about how it works and amplified the information about the chanter.

First Draft of "Playing the Irish Bagpipes"
by Maya Ramirez

If you want to play the Irish bagpipes, you need a set of pipes, a lot of time and patience, and, if you live in an apartment building, neighbors who are hard of hearing. There is an adage that it takes seven years to make a piper, and the first one or two can be somewhat excruciating; once the worst is over, however, the instrument is a joy to play.

Irish bagpipes are blown with a bellows, rather than by mouth. In fact, there are those who believe that "Uilleann" pipes, the Gaelic term, means "elbow pipes" because it is with the elbow that the bellows is pumped. Because there is so much to coordinate, with the bellows being pumped with the right arm, the bag being squeezed with the left arm, and the chanter, which is the melody pipe, being played with the fingers, it is best to start with a practice set, composed only of these pieces. A full set also includes drones, low pipes that play a steady note behind the melody, and regulators, which play chords when their metal keys are pressed with the right wrist—usually while both hands are being used on the chanter. A practice set is quite enough to wrestle with in the beginning.

There is a long strap on one face of the bellows. This strap goes around your waist, to hold the contraption stationary against your right side, nestled against the bottom of your ribs. A shorter strap on the other face buckles around your upper arm. You can practice pumping the bellows with your right elbow. (If there isn't any padding for your elbow on the bellows, add some, or your elbow will be extremely sore in no time at all.)

Now take the bag and tuck it under your left elbow. Protruding from one side of the bag is a hollow stick, called the blowstick. The blowstick is inserted into the tube that protrudes from the inner face of the bellows, so that air pumped by the bellows passes through the tube in front of you into the bag under your left arm. Pump the bellows a few times and make sure there are no leaks in the connections of the bellows to blowstick, and blowstick to bag. As you pump, you should feel the bag fill with air.

Now you are ready for the chanter. In the end of the narrow neck of the bag, there is a round piece of wood with a hole in it. This is called the chanter-stock. Near the top end of the chanter itself there is a narrow angled tube, usually made of brass, that fits into the holes. Again, make sure there is no leak in the joint, or much of your laborious bellows-pumping will be wasted. Once you are sure everything is more or less airtight, you are ready to play music.

Sit down, if you are not already sitting, and place the open end of the chanter against your right leg a couple of inches above the knee. With the chanter thus closed, you can get a second, higher octave by forcing a little extra air from the bag through the chanter. Popping the chanter off the knee gives a louder, wailing sound for variety. You will need a chart for the fingering, but with a fingering chart handy you can begin exploring notes and scales. At first, the sensation will be like wrestling with an octopus, but soon you will get the hang of pumping in long, steady strokes with the right arm, maintaining pressure on the bag with the left arm and raising and lowering the chanter off your knee as you finger the notes. You will find that by closing the chanter entirely between notes, with all fingers down and the end of the pipe against your leg, you can play staccato, or put rests in the music for phrasing. By rolling your fingers off the holes, rather than just lifting them, you can "bend" notes, sliding from one pitch to another. If the chanter is slightly out of tune, and nearly all of them are, you can sometimes keep the notes truer by varying the pressure of your left arm. When all that finally becomes second nature, you will be well on your way to becoming a piper.

How to Write a Letter
Garrison Keillor

Writer and broadcaster Garrison Keillor was born in Anoka, Minnesota, in 1942. A graduate of the University of Minnesota, Keillor published his first story in 1969 in the *New Yorker.* Keillor is best known as the host of the popular National Public Radio program *Prairie Home Companion,* which aired between 1974 and 1987, when Keillor left the program to write. Keillor has also published *Happy to Be Here* (1982), *Lake Wobegon Days* (1985), and *Leaving Home: A Collection of Lake Wobegon Stories* (1987). "How to Write a Letter," which Keillor wrote as an advertisement for the International Paper Company, offers humorous, but insightful, advice to help shy people make their mark upon the world.

1   We shy persons need to write a letter now and then, or else we'll dry up and blow away. It's true. And I speak as one who loves to reach for the phone, dial the number, and talk. I say, "Big Bopper here—what's shakin,' babes?" The telephone is to shyness what Hawaii is to February, it's a way out of the woods, *and yet:* a letter is better.

2   Such a sweet gift—a piece of handmade writing, in an envelope that is not a bill, sitting in our friend's path when she trudges home from a long day spent among yahoos and savages, a day our words will help repair. They don't need to be immortal, just sincere. She can read them twice and again tomorrow: *You're someone I care about, Corinne, and think of often and every time I do you make me smile.*

3   We need to write, otherwise nobody will know who we are. They will have only a vague impression of us as A Nice Person, because frankly, we don't shine at conversation, we lack the confidence to thrust our faces forward and say, "Hi, I'm Heather Hooten, let me tell you about my week." Mostly we say "Uh-huh" and "Oh really." People smile and look over our shoulder, looking for someone else to talk to.

4   So a shy person sits down and writes a letter. To be known by another person—to meet and talk freely on the page—to be close despite distance. To escape from anonymity and be our own sweet selves and express the music of our souls.

5   Same thing that moves a giant rock star to sing his heart out in front of 123,000 people moves us to take ballpoint in hand and write a few lines to our dear Aunt Eleanor. *We want to be known.* We want her to know that we have fallen in love, that we quit our job, and we're moving to New York, and we want to say a few things that might not get said in casual

conversation: *thank you for what you've meant to me, I am very happy
right now.*

The first step in writing letters is to get over the guilt of *not* writing. You   6
don't "owe" anybody a letter. Letters are a gift. The burning shame you feel
when you see unanswered mail makes it harder to pick up a pen and makes
for a cheerless letter when you finally do. *I feel bad about not writing, but
I've been so busy,* etc. Skip this. Few letters are obligatory, and they are *Thanks
for the wonderful gift* and *I am terribly sorry to hear about George's death*
and *Yes, you're welcome to stay with us next month,* and not many more than
that. Write those promptly if you want to keep your friends. Don't worry
about the others, except love letters, of course. When your true love writes
*Dear Light of My Life, Joy of My Heart, O Lovely Pulsating Core of My
Sensate Life,* some response is called for.

Some of the best letters are tossed off in a burst of inspiration, so keep your   7
writing stuff in one place where you can sit down for a few minutes and *Dear
Roy, I am in the middle of an essay for International Paper but thought I'd drop
you a line. Hi to your sweetie too* dash off a note to a pal. Envelopes, stamps,
address book, everything in a drawer so you can write fast when the pen is hot.

A blank white 8" × 11" sheet can look as big as Montana if the pen's   8
not so hot—try a smaller page and write boldly. Or use a note card with a
piece of fine art on the front; if your letter ain't good, at least they get the
Matisse. Get a pen that makes a sensuous line, get a comfortable typewriter,
a friendly word processor—whichever feels easy to the hand.

Sit for a few minutes with the blank sheet in front of you, and mediate on   9
the person you will write to, let your friend come to mind until you can almost
see her or him in the room with you. Remember the last time you saw each
other and how your friend looked and what you said and what perhaps was
unsaid between you, and when your friend becomes real to you, start to write.

Write the salutation—*Dear You*—and take a deep breath and plunge in.   10
A simple declarative sentence will do, followed by another and another and
another. Tell us what you're doing and tell it like you were talking to us. Don't
think about grammar, don't think about lit'ry style, don't try to write dramatically, just give us your news. Where did you go, who did you see, what
did they say, what do you think?

If you don't know where to begin, start with the present moment: *I'm sit-*   11
*ting at the kitchen table on a rainy Saturday morning. Everyone is gone and
the house is quiet.* Let your simple description of the present moment lead to
something else, let the letter drift gently along.

The toughest letter to crank out is one that is meant to impress, as we all   12
know from writing job applications; if it's hard work to slip off a letter to a
friend, maybe you're trying too hard to be terrific. A letter is only a report to
someone who already likes you for reasons other than your brilliance. Take
it easy.

Don't worry about form. It's not a term paper. When you come to the   13
end of one episode, just start a new paragraph. You can go from a few lines

about the sad state of rock'n roll to the fight with your mother to your fond memories of Mexico to your cat's urinary tract infection to a few thoughts on personal indebtedness to the kitchen sink and what's in it. The more you write, the easier it gets, and when you have a True True Friend to write to, a *compadre*, a soul sibling, then it's like driving a car down a country road, you just get behind the keyboard and press on the gas.

Don't tear up the page and start over when you write a bad line—try to write your way out of it. Make mistakes and plunge on. Let the letter cook along and the let yourself be bold. Outrage, confusion, love—whatever is in your mind, let it find a way to the page. Writing is a means of discovery, always, and when you come to the end and write *Yours ever* or *Hugs and Kisses,* you'll know something you didn't when you wrote *Dear Pal.* 14

Probably your friend will put your letter away, and it'll be read again a few years from now—and it will improve with age. And forty years from now, your friend's grandkids will dig it out of the attic and read it, a sweet and precious relic of the ancient Eighties that gives them a sudden clear glimpse of you and her and the world we old-timers knew. You will then have created an object of art. Your simple lines about where you went, who you saw, what they said, will speak to those children and they will feel in their hearts the humanity of our times. 15

You can't pick up a phone and call the future and tell them about our times. You have to pick up a piece of paper. 16

✹

RESPONDING TO THE WHOLE ESSAY

1. Keillor wrote this essay as an advertisement for International Paper Company. Use evidence in the essay to comment on Keillor's assumptions about his audience. [1g(2)]
2. Would you say Keillor's purpose in writing this essay is mainly to express his feelings about writing, to inform the reader, or to persuade the reader? Can you find evidence of aims other than the one you chose as primary? Explain. [1g(1)]
3. Could a reader use this essay as a guide for writing a personal letter? Why or why not?
4. Explain what Keillor accomplishes in his introduction. Where does he establish a context for the essay? [1g(3)]
5. Keillor's conclusion accomplishes more than simply telling how to end a personal letter. Explain what else it accomplishes and how it does so. [3b(2)]
6. Comment on the use of humor in this essay. [3a(3)]

ANALYZING THE ELEMENTS

Grammar

1. Notice that most of the verbs in Keillor's essay are in the present tense. What does he accomplish by using the present tense throughout the essay? Try converting the

verbs in one paragraph to past tense. In what ways does the past tense change the effect of the essay? [17c]
2. The first sentence in paragraph 7 begins with a passive construction. Try to rewrite the sentence so that both independent clauses are in the active voice. What difficulties do you encounter? [17]
3. Keillor uses a fragment as the last sentence of paragraph 7. Explain why this fragment is justifiable. [13]

Effective Sentences

1. The second sentence of paragraph 9 consists of a number of coordinate clauses linked by *and*. What keeps this sentence from being "stringy"? [19b]
2. Comment on the parallel structure of the third sentence in paragraph 5. [20]
3. Find three examples of sentences in which Keillor has used forceful verbs. Comment on the effect of those verbs. [21d]

Punctuation and Mechanics

1. Justify Keillor's use of commas to link independent clauses in the fifth sentence of paragraph 1. [27a]
2. Why is "A Nice Person" capitalized in the second sentence of paragraph 3? What would be the effect of not capitalizing the phrase? [33a]
3. What is the function of the italics in the first sentence of paragraph 7? [34]

Diction

1. Keillor uses a word (*ain't,* second sentence of paragraph 8) referred to in the *American Heritage Dictionary* as "nonstandard" and "beyond rehabilitation." What justification can you find for his using this word? [23b]
2. Paragraph 8 begins with a simile. Explain why the comparison is humorous. [24a(4)]

BUILDING VOCABULARY

1. List and define three synonyms of the present-tense verb *read.* Write sentences using each of these synonyms.
2. What is the Greek root from which *letter* is derived? What does it mean? Through what other languages and roots can *letter* be traced?

SUGGESTIONS FOR WRITING

1. Take Keillor's advice as you write a personal letter.
2. Using Keillor as a loose model, write an essay explaining how to accomplish some common, but unpleasant, daily task that requires mainly mental effort, such as paying bills, planning menus, scheduling appointments.

Mummy Arts
Adam Goodheart

Adam Goodheart is the senior editor of and columnist for the Library of
Congress's *Civilization,* a magazine devoted to the discussion of history, culture, social issues, and literature. In his column, "Lost Arts," Goodheart explores such historical and cultural phenomena as witch-hunting and dueling.
Writing from a twentieth-century perspective, Goodheart creates, in "Mummy
Arts," a humorous yet informative account of the ancient Egyptians' method
of preparing corpses for the afterlife. Through his combination of detailed
instructions and witty commentary, Goodheart emphasizes the religious and
cultural significance of the ancient Egyptians' ritual of mummification.

Old pharaohs never died—they just took long vacations. Ancient Egyptians 1
believed that at death a person's spirit, or *ka,* was forcibly separated from the
body. But it returned now and then for a visit, to snack on the food that had
been left in the tomb. It was crucial that the body stay as lifelike as possible
for eternity—that way, the *ka* (whose life was hard enough already) would
avoid reanimating the wrong corpse. These days, dead pharaohs are admittedly a bit hard to come by. If you decide to practice mummification on a
friend or relative, please make sure that the loved one in question is fully de-
ceased before you begin.

    1. Evisceration Made Easy. The early stages of the process can be a bit 2
malodorous, so it's recommended that you follow the ancient custom of re-
locating to a well-ventilated tent. (You'll have trouble breathing anyway, since
tradition also prescribes that you wear a jackal-head mask in honor of Anubis,
god of the dead.) After cleansing the body, break the nose by pushing a long
iron hook up the nostrils. Then use the hook to remove the contents of the
skull. You can discard the brain (the ancient Egyptians attributed no special
significance to it).

    Next, take a flint knife and make a long incision down the left side of the 3
abdomen. Actually, it's best to have a friend do this, since the person who
cuts open the body must be pelted with stones to atone for the profanation.
After you've stoned your friend, use a bronze knife to remove the internal organs through the incision. Wash them in palm wine as a disinfectant and set
them aside to inter later in separate alabaster jars. Leave the heart in place
(Egyptians believed it was the seat of consciousness).

    2. Salting and Stuffing. Once the abdominal cavity is empty, fill it with 4
natron, a natural salt found at the Wadi Natrun in the western Nile delta.
Heap more natron on top of the body until it is completely covered. According

to a papyrus in the Louvre, it should then be left for 42 days, after which it will be almost totally desiccated. Having removed the natron, anoint the head with frankincense and the body with sacred oil. Pack the skull and abdomen with myrrh and other spices, and cover the incision with a sheet of gold.

For an extra-lifelike effect, you can stuff the corpse's skin with a compound of sawdust, butter, and mud. Don't overdo it, though. Queen Henettowey, wife of Pinedjem I, was so overstuffed that when archaeologists found her, her face had split open like an old sofa.   5

3. Wrapping Up. If you thought mummies wrapped in bedsheets were the stuff of B movies, think again: Even pharaohs were usually wound in strips cut from household linens. Pour molten pine resin over the body; in the course of centuries this will turn the flesh black, glassy, and rock-hard. While the resin's still tacky, bandage each of the extremities separately, including fingers and toes. Then brush on another coat and repeat. (Go easy on the resin—Tutankhamen stuck to his coffin and had to be chipped out piece by piece.) Amulets can be placed between the layers of bandages; a scarab over the heart is the minimum. The last layers should secure the arms and legs to the body. Your mummy is now ready to be entombed in grand style.   6

A note on sarcophagi: Careful labeling will prevent embarrassing mix-ups later on. A mummy long thought to be Princess Mutemhet of the twenty-first dynasty was recently x-rayed and found to be a pet baboon.   7

✳

RESPONDING TO THE WHOLE ESSAY

1. What is Goodheart's primary purpose in "Mummy Arts"? Does he focus mainly on the information itself, on amusing his readers, or on moving his audience to a particular action or point of view? Does he have a secondary purpose? If so, how is it revealed? [1g(1)]
2. Explain how Goodheart unifies paragraph 4 and makes it coherent. [3c]
3. For what audience does Goodheart appear to write? What evidence can you muster to support your answer? [1g(2)]

ANALYZING THE ELEMENTS

Grammar

1. What kind of verbal phrase is *reanimating the wrong corpse* in the fourth sentence of paragraph 1? How does it function in this sentence? [12a]
2. What advantage does Goodheart's use of *can* rather than *may* bring to the first sentence of paragraph 2 and the first sentence of paragraph 5? Would *may* be a better choice in either of these sentences? Why or why not? [23 and 24]

Effective Sentences

1. Compare the use of *it* in the third sentence of paragraph 1 with the use of *it* in the following sentence. What does *it* refer to in the third sentence? How is *it* used in the fourth sentence? [16]
2. Explain why the participial phrase in the fourth sentence of paragraph 4 is not a dangling modifier. [12a and 15e]
3. In what ways does Goodheart add variety to the sentences of paragraph 1? Find and discuss at least two ways. [22]

Punctuation and Mechanics

1. Explain Goodheart's use of the semicolon in the second and sixth sentences of paragraph 6. Rewrite these sentences without using the semicolon. [28]
2. What purpose is served by using a colon in the first sentence of paragraph 6 rather than punctuating the clauses as separate sentences? [31d]
3. Comment upon the use of the apostrophe in *you'll* in the second sentence of paragraph 2, *it's* in the second sentence of paragraph 3, *corpse's* in the first sentence of paragraph 5, and *resin's* in the third sentence of paragraph 6. [29]

Diction

1. The last sentence of paragraph 5 contains figurative language. Comment upon how the splitting of an overstuffed corpse might resemble the splitting of an old sofa. [24a(4)]
2. The first sentence of this essay alludes to a well-known pattern of expression (old . . . never die—they just . . .). How does this opening cliché influence the overall tone of the essay? [24c]

BUILDING VOCABULARY

1. What are the Latin roots from which the word *evisceration* is derived? What do they mean? Write a sentence using a word derived from one of the Latin roots you identified.
2. What are the Greek roots from which the words *sarcophagus* and *scarab* are borrowed? What do each of these roots mean? How do the meanings of the Greek and Latin roots differ from the meanings of the words derived from them? Are the English borrowings more or less descriptive?

SUGGESTIONS FOR WRITING

1. Think of something that you do or have done that most people have little experience in doing (for example, coloring hair, rebuilding an engine, catering a party, skydiving). Using plenty of specific details, explain to a stranger how to perform this activity.
2. Write a process essay giving instructions for preparing a food or beverage you enjoy (for example, baking bread, cooking spaghetti, making cocoa, broiling steak).

Sugaring
Margery Guest

Margery Guest (1946–) is a columnist and travel writer who was born in
Detroit, Michigan, and now resides in Grand Rapids. She came to writing
about twenty years ago and has published her work in regional and national
magazines such as *Reader's Digest* and *Travel & Leisure*. She has a B.A. in
English from Western Michigan University.

When I was a kid growing up in Michigan, Dad made pancakes every   1
Sunday. "Golden blacks!" he'd holler out as a way of calling us to the table.
The pancakes were rarely black, but he liked them on the dark side, and he
always encouraged us to like what he liked. Some Sundays he made buck-
wheat pancakes and, in that case, "Buckwheats!" was the call to action.

We behaved like hungry prospectors at a mining camp during these pan-   2
cake feasts even though we'd just come from doing nothing more industrious
than watching cartoons and playing Lincoln Logs in our pajamas. On the
table would be stacks of fluffy pancakes, enough for all five of us to have as
many as we wanted, and always a pitcher of hot maple syrup. At the end of
the table, there'd be a bottle of this other stuff. It had a red label and the *fifth*
ingredient listed on it was maple syrup. It was never heated because Dad was
trying to make a point. Too indulgent to simply *not offer* this alternative, he
was expressing how utterly incomprehensible it was to him that anyone could
actually prefer it. It was my favorite.

Part of becoming an adult is learning how good *real* spaghetti, *real* mac-   3
aroni and cheese, and *real* maple syrup are compared to the stuff we liked
as kids. I grew up late, came to real maple syrup late. Because I'd been such
a stubborn kid, refusing to even taste the real stuff, I had a lot of catching
up to do. My knowledge of maple syrup involved a sizable gap: I knew it
began with a maple tree and somehow wound up poured from a colorful
tin container onto my pancakes. But how did it get from the tree to my
table?

Mother Nature is in Charge   Over 80 percent of the world's maple syrup   4
production comes from the province of Quebec, with the largest export market being the States. Ten percent more is produced in Ontario and the remaining 10 percent in our country. Of that 10 percent, Vermont, New York,
Wisconsin, Ohio, and my home state of Michigan are all large contributors.
However, Vermont is the place with the reputation, the mystique, the tall
tales, the state that produces a half million gallons in an average year, and

the one of the few states that actually *grades* its syrup. To fully experience "sugaring," I knew I had to visit Vermont.

I began my quest at Shaker Maple Farm, owned by Steve and Leah Willsey. It's in Starksboro, Vermont, up in the Green Mountains. Vermont natives refer to sugaring time as the "fifth season"—mud season. The maple syrup season can last from three to six weeks, but no one can rush it, push it, delay it, or alter it in any way. The maple syrup farmer is at the mercy of Mother Nature. He or she knows this and has the utmost respect for it. As it has always been since before recorded history and will always be, Mother Nature runs this operation.

Because the process depends so much on nature's whim, it hasn't changed much in hundreds of years. When spring comes and temperatures begin to rise above freezing during the day, the maple trees (*Acer saccharum*) begin to unfreeze from the outside in. The "sap-flow mechanism" remains a mystery to even educated scientists, but remember phloem and xylem from eighth grade science?: It works something like that. The sap begins to run up and down the inside of the tree to nourish the buds. Meanwhile, carbon dioxide gas is forming inside the tree and needs to escape. Any opening will begin to leak sap. As the temperature drops during the day, the sap stops running and begins again on the next day of thawing temperatures.

When the sap begins to run, or shortly beforehand, it's time to tap the trees. With an old-fashioned brace and bit drill (or a gas-powered one for modern operations) a hole is made 7/16 of an inch in diameter and two or three inches deep into the trunk of the tree. This tap is actually a wound in the tree. Then a "tap," "spout," or "spile" is placed inside the hole and tapped in with a hammer, just until it's sitting nicely in the tree and sap starts to run out like from a faucet. A tree with a diameter of ten to eighteen inches can have one tap; nineteen to twenty-four inches, two taps; and so on. Too many taps will take too much sap from the tree and thus harm it. Steve Willsey hugs the tree to determine how many taps he'll use. If his fingers don't touch, it gets two taps. If they touch, only one. Then, for the trees around the farmhouse, he hooks a bucket onto the spile, covers it with a lid, and moves on.

Instead of buckets, most modern operations (including Steve's) use plastic tubing strung elaborately around the hillsides to carry the sap by force of gravity right into the sugarhouse. Some (either purists or gluttons for punishment) still do it the old-fashioned way, attaching buckets by hand, checking them daily and making the rounds, sometimes with horse-drawn drays, to gather the sap.

When the sap comes out of the tree it's clear. That's because it's about two percent sap and 98 percent water. When enough sap is gathered into the sugarhouse it's time for boiling. It will take forty gallons of boiled sap to produce one gallon of syrup.

The sugarhouse is usually a small, wooden cabin. An enormous wood "arch" (stove) called an evaporator takes up most of the room inside and when boiling begins, will demand constant stoking. Pallets of lumber are stacked outside to feed a roaring fire huge enough to thrill Sam McGee.

On top of the evaporator are large partitioned stainless pans with boil-   11
ing sap reaching several different stages on its way to becoming syrup. When the temperature of the sap hits 219 degrees, it's syrup. The density of the syrup must be checked with a hydrometer to make sure it's exactly right. Too soon and bacteria survives, with its attendant risk of fermentation; too late and it's overboiled and begins to crystallize.

Boiling is an exciting social event. Some Vermonters say it serves to wake   12
people up after the long cold winter. Neighbors gather when they see steam rising from the sugarhouse and know they'll be welcomed. The phone rings constantly with the question, "You boiling tonight?"

Hazardous Duty   Although everyone at Shaker Maple Farm assured me there   13
was absolutely no danger, they couldn't fool me. Think about it: you're in a tiny *wooden* building with an enormous *raging* fire inside and sparks flying around the opening of a huge furnace. A crowd of men heaves logs through the open doors of this furnace, while several large dogs wander around. (Their purpose still escapes me except that *everyone* in Vermont owns a large dog.) Once in a while, someone revs up a huge tractor and backs it noisily into the sugarhouse to dump a pallet full of wood. The men holler and lift, lift and holler, until the tractor is freed of the pallet. On top of the evaporator is a 16-foot-long by six-foot wide pan filled with hundreds of gallons of froth-ing, hot sticky liquid, threatening to bubble over at any moment. Extra peo-ple mill about, chatting, laughing, eating, drinking, and generally getting in the way.

This whole operation is done in steam so thick you often can't see the   14
face of the person next to you. And it's not done in the morning when every-one is fresh and alert—oh no. It's done at night, often after a full day's work. Why have we never seen this headline: "Thirty-five Die in Latest Maple Syrup Mishap?" Leah Willsey assured me there was nothing to worry about. Well, there was that one time her hair caught on fire. "What did you do?" I asked, horrified. "I put it out," she said. Vermonters are a calm lot.

There is controversy about how the making of maple syrup began in   15
America. Its origins have been lost because they go so far back. Instead, we have an abundance of theories. Some think French explorers or missionaries taught the native Iroquois, Micmac, Huron, Ojibway, and Abenaki Indians to boil sap. Others insist it was the other way around. Still others prefer the squirrel theory: the common squirrel was often seen biting into maple trees, then returning later to savor the sugar crust that had dried at the wound. All humans did was watch the squirrel and improve on the method a bit.

Know Your Terms   If you go to Vermont, or any sugaring state, you do not   16
want to appear a bumpkin. I've put together a brief lexicon from my experi-ence in Vermont to prevent this from happening:

- *Maple sugaring*—the process of turning sap into syrup
- *Sugarbush*—the maple grove
- *Sugarhouse*—the wooden building where all this alchemy takes place
- *Running*—during thaws, the time when sap is coursing through the trees
- *Tapping*—pounding taps into trees
- *Boiling*—the process of reducing the water content of the sap and thickening it to syrup
- *Run*—one start and stop of the entire syrup-making process (a good year might have twenty-five separate runs)
- *Ayup*—a northern New England term meaning, *that's correct;* same as yes in all other states. (e.g., *"Are you boiling?" "Ayup."*)

Having witnessed this process first-hand, and learned what is involved, I would never begrudge the price of real maple syrup. Making maple syrup may be the most labor-intensive job a person could have, particularly for those who do it the old-fashioned way with buckets and horses. Most producers have other jobs, so sugaring is an exhausting labor of love. It's terrifically hard work, but it keeps them close to their families, close to their neighbors, close to the basics of life. It keeps them tough. Perhaps it contributes to the stoical, laid-back attitude I noticed among Vermonters. *Mother Nature will either cooperate this year or she won't.* Don't get uptight over what you can't control.   17

I'm all through making golden blacks for my kids and look forward to making them for my grandkids. But I'm going to make one change: I won't even put that other stuff on the table. I'll be tough, like those Vermonters. I'll serve only real maple syrup and if any of my hypothetical grandkids have the nerve to ask, *"Is this all we've got?"* I'll just stare 'em down and answer, *ayup.*   18

✳

RESPONDING TO THE WHOLE ESSAY

1. Is Guest's primary purpose in writing this essay expressive, informative, or persuasive? [1g(1)]
2. Find evidence in this essay of Guest's awareness of her audience. [1g(2)]
3. Is the essay designed to instruct its readers so that they can follow the process? [2e(3)]
4. What purpose does the introduction serve in establishing a context for the essay? [3b(1)]
5. In addition to describing the process of sugaring, what attitude about the process does this essay develop? [2b]
6. Comment on the use of humor in this essay.

ANALYZING THE ELEMENTS

Grammar

1. Guest uses several contractions (*there'd, it's*). Identify these contractions and comment on their appropriateness to this essay. [29b]
2. Does the last sentence in paragraph 4 contain a split infinitive? Can its use be justified? [5a(5)]

Effective Sentences

1. The last sentence of paragraph 2 is very brief. Explain how that sentence is an effective ending to the paragraph. Find other examples of Guest's use of short sentences for effect. [21h]
2. Comment on the parallel structure of the fourth sentence of paragraph 4. [20a(10)]
3. Find three examples of complex sentences and comment on their effectiveness. [12c(3)]

Punctuation and Mechanics

1. Find two different uses of quotation marks in Guest's essay. [30]
2. Comment on the use of the semicolon in the last sentence of paragraph 11. What other ways could that sentence be punctuated? [28a]
3. Comment on Guest's use of italics. [34]

Diction

1. Explain how the word "stuff" in paragraph 2 prepares the reader for the tone of the essay. [24a]
2. What is the effect of using technical terms like *sap-flow mechanism* and *hydrometer?*
3. Find three words that lend an informal tone to Guest's essay.

BUILDING VOCABULARY

1. Find synonyms for *bumpkin.*
2. What is a *hydrometer?* What do the roots of the word mean?

SUGGESTIONS FOR WRITING

1. Using Guest's essay as a loose model, write an essay in which you examine two ways of doing something (the traditional way and the modern way, your way and someone else's way).
2. Write an essay in which you describe how learning about a process made you appreciate something more.

The Maker's Eye: Revising Your Own Manuscripts

Donald M. Murray

Donald M. Murray (1924–) teaches writing at the University of New Hampshire. Before entering teaching, he was a professional journalist, serving as an editor for *Time* and winning the Pulitzer Prize for his editorials in the *Boston Globe*. In recent years Murray has published several books that have influenced the teaching of writing: *A Writer Teaches Writing* and *Learning by Teaching* are both addressed to his fellow teachers; *Write to Learn* is a textbook for students. In "The Maker's Eye: Revising Your Own Manuscripts," Murray focuses on revising as a part of the writing process.

When students complete a first draft, they consider the job of writing 1 done—and their teachers too often agree. When professional writers complete a first draft, they usually feel that they are at the start of the writing process. When a draft is completed, the job of writing can begin.

That difference in attitude is the difference between amateur and pro- 2 fessional, inexperience and experience, journeyman and craftsman. Peter F. Drucker, the prolific business writer, calls his first draft "the zero draft"—after that he can start counting. Most writers share the feeling that the first draft, and all of those which follow, are opportunities to discover what they have to say and how best they can say it.

To produce a progression of drafts, each of which says more and says it 3 more clearly, the writer has to develop a special kind of reading skill. In school we are taught to decode what appears on the page as finished writing. Writers, however, face a different category of possibility and responsibility when they read their own drafts. To them the words on the page are never finished. Each can be changed and rearranged, can set off a chain reaction of confusion or clarified meaning. This is a different kind of reading, which is possibly more difficult and certainly more exciting.

Writers must learn to be their own best enemy. They must accept the crit- 4 icism of others and be suspicious of it; they must accept the praise of others and be even more suspicious of it. Writers cannot depend on others. They must detach themselves from their own pages so that they can apply both their caring and their craft to their own work.

Such detachment is not easy. Science fiction writer Ray Bradbury sup- 5 posedly puts each manuscript away for a year to the day and then rereads it as a stranger. Not many writers have the discipline or the time to do this. We must read when our judgment may be at its worst, when we are close to the euphoric moment of creation.

Then the writer, counsels novelist Nancy Hale, "should be critical of every-   6
thing that seems to him most delightful in his style. He should excise what he most admires, because he wouldn't thus admire it if he weren't . . . in a sense protecting it from criticism." John Ciardi, the poet, adds, "The last act of the writing must be to become one's own reader. It is, I suppose, a schizophrenic process, to begin passionately and to end critically, to begin hot and to end cold; and, more important, to be passion-hot and critic-cold at the same time."

Most people think that the principal problem is that writers are too proud   7
of what they have written. Actually, a greater problem for most professional writers is one shared by the majority of students. They are overly critical, think everything is dreadful, tear up page after page, never complete a draft, see the task as hopeless.

The writer must learn to read critically but constructively, to cut what is   8
bad, to reveal what is good. Eleanor Estes, the children's book author, ex-plains: "The writer must survey his work critically, coolly, as though he were a stranger to it. He must be willing to prune, expertly and hard-heartedly. At the end of each revision, a manuscript may look . . . worked over, torn apart, pinned together, added to, deleted from, words changed and words changed back. Yet the book must maintain its original freshness and spontaneity."

Most readers underestimate the amount of rewriting it usually takes to   9
produce spontaneous reading. This is a great disadvantage to the student writer, who sees only a finished product and never watches the craftsman who takes the necessary step back, studies the work carefully, returns to the task, steps back, returns, steps back, again and again. Anthony Burgess, one of the most prolific writers in the English-speaking world, admits, "I might revise a page twenty times." Roald Dahl, the popular children's writer, states, "By the time I'm nearing the end of a story, the first part will have been reread and altered and corrected at least 150 times. . . . Good writing is essentially rewrit-ing. I am positive of this."

Rewriting isn't virtuous. It isn't something that ought to be done. It is   10
simply something that most writers find they have to do to discover what they have to say and how to say it. It is a condition of the writer's life.

There are, however, a few writers who do little formal rewriting, prima-   11
rily because they have the capacity and experience to create and review a large number of invisible drafts in their minds before they approach the page. And some writers slowly produce finished pages, performing all the tasks of revi-sion simultaneously, page by page, rather than draft by draft. But it is still possible to see the sequence followed by most writers most of the time in rereading their own work.

Most writers scan their drafts first, reading as quickly as possible to catch   12
the larger problems of subject and form, then move in closer and closer as they read and write, reread and rewrite.

The first thing writers look for in their drafts is *information*. They know that a good piece of writing is built from specific, accurate, and interesting information. The writer must have an abundance of information from which to construct a readable piece of writing.   13

Next writers look for *meaning* in the information. The specifies must build to a pattern of significance. Each piece of specific information must carry the reader toward meaning.   14

Writers reading their own drafts are aware of *audience*. They put themselves in the reader's situation and make sure that they deliver information which a reader wants to know or needs to know in a manner which is easily digested. Writers try to be sure that they anticipate and answer the questions a critical reader will ask when reading the piece of writing.   15

Writers make sure that the *form* is appropriate to the subject and the audience. Form, or genre, is the vehicle which carries meaning to the reader, but form cannot be selected until the writer has adequate information to discover its significance and an audience which needs or wants that meaning.   16

Once writers are sure the form is appropriate, they must then look at the *structure*, the order of what they have written. Good writing is built on a solid framework of logic, argument, narrative, or motivation which runs through the entire piece of writing and holds it together. This is the time when many writers find it most effective to outline as a way of visualizing the hidden spine by which the piece of writing is supported.   17

The element on which writers may spend a majority of their time is *development*. Each section of a piece of writing must be adequately developed. It must give readers enough information so that they are satisfied. How much information is enough? That's as difficult as asking how much garlic belongs in a salad. It must be done to taste, but most beginning writers underdevelop, underestimating the reader's hunger for information.   18

As writers solve development problems, they often have to consider questions of *dimension*. There must be a pleasing and effective proportion among all the parts of the piece of writing. There is a continual process of subtracting and adding to keep the piece of writing in balance.   19

Finally, writers have to listen to their own voices. *Voice* is the force which drives a piece of writing forward. It is an expression of the writer's authority and concern. It is what is between the words on the page, what glues the piece of writing together. A good piece of writing is always marked by a consistent, individual voice.   20

As writers read and reread, write and rewrite, they move closer and closer to the page until they are doing line-by-line editing. Writers read their own pages with infinite care. Each sentence, each line, each clause, each phrase, each word, each mark of punctuation, each section of white space between the type has to contribute to the clarification of meaning.   21

Slowly the writer moves from word to word, looking through language to see the subject. As a word is changed, cut, or added, as a construction is   22 rearranged, all the words used before that moment and all those that follow that moment must be considered and reconsidered.

Writers often read aloud at this stage of the editing process, muttering or whispering to themselves, calling on the ear's experience with language. Does this sound right—or that? Writers edit, shifting back and forth from eye to page to ear to page. I find I must do this careful editing in short runs, no more than fifteen or twenty minutes at a stretch, or I become too kind with myself. I begin to see what I hope is on the page, not what actually is on the page.   23

This sounds tedious if you haven't done it, but actually it is fun. Making something right is immensely satisfying, for writers begin to learn what they are writing about by writing. Language leads them to meaning, and there is the joy of discovery, of understanding, of making meaning clear as the writer employs the technical skills of language.   24

Words have double meanings, even triple and quadruple meanings. Each word has its own potential for connotation and denotation. And when writers rub one word against the other, they are often rewarded with a sudden insight, an unexpected clarification.   25

The maker's eye moves back and forth from word to phrase to sentence to paragraph to sentence to phrase to word. The maker's eye sees the need for variety and balance, for a firmer structure, for a more appropriate form. It peers into the interior of the paragraph, looking for coherence, unity, and emphasis, which make meaning clear.   26

I learned something about this process when my first bifocals were prescribed. I had ordered a larger section of the reading portion of the glass because of my work, but even so, I could not contain my eyes within this new limit of vision. And I still find myself taking off my glasses and bending my nose towards the page, for my eyes unconsciously flick back and forth across the page, back to another page, forward to still another, as I try to see each evolving line in relation to every other line.   27

When does this process end? Most writers agree with the great Russian writer Tolstoy, who said, "I scarcely ever reread my published writings, if by chance I come across a page, it always strikes me: all this must be rewritten; this is how I should have written it."   28

The maker's eye is never satisfied, for each word has the potential to ignite new meaning. This article has been twice written all the way through the writing process, and it was published four years ago. Now it is to be republished in a book. The editors make a few small suggestions, and then I read it with my maker's eye. Now it has been re-edited, re-revised, re-read, re-re-edited, for each piece of writing to the writer is full of potential and alternatives.   29

A piece of writing is never finished. It is delivered to a deadline, torn out of the typewriter on demand, sent off with a sense of accomplishment and shame and pride and frustration. If only there were a couple more days, time for just another run at it, perhaps then . . .   30

✳

RESPONDING TO THE WHOLE ESSAY

1. Is Murray writing primarily for college students or for anyone who wants to improve as a writer? How do you know? How useful is the essay for college students? For others? [1g]
2. Is Murray's purpose in "The Maker's Eye" primarily to express himself about writing, to provide information about writing, or to persuade the reader to adopt certain writing procedures? If the essay has more than one of these aims, point to evidence of each one. [1g(1)]
3. What characteristics of a good introduction does Murray's first paragraph display? Explain. [3b(1)]
4. Explain why Murray's conclusion is effective. [3b(2)]
5. After rereading paragraph 20, explain what methods Murray uses to define *voice*. [3c(7)]
6. What are the steps in the writing process that Murray describes? Will the process work if some steps are performed out of sequence? Which steps (if any) can be omitted? Will following these steps guarantee better writing? Why or why not?

ANALYZING THE ELEMENTS

Grammar

1. Identify the subordinate clauses in the second sentence of paragraph 15 and explain specifically how each one functions in the sentence. [12b]
2. In paragraphs 16, 17, and 18 (and in a number of other paragraphs as well) Murray uses the passive voice. In each of these paragraphs, find the sentence in which the verb is passive, and rewrite the sentence with an active verb. What problems do you encounter? In each sentence, what problem did Murray's choice of the passive solve? Explain. [21d]

Effective Sentences

1. Comment on at least two ways in which Murray makes the first sentence in paragraph 3 effective. [21b and 21e]
2. Examine the second sentence of paragraph 4. Explain its structure and the effect. [20a]

Punctuation and Mechanics

1. Explain the uses of the commas, quotation marks, and ellipsis points in the first two sentences of paragraph 6. [27, 30a, and 31i]
2. Explain the uses of the commas, colon, and quotation marks in the second sentence of paragraph 8. [27, 31d, and 30a]

Diction

1. Examine Murray's use of figurative language—for example, "the hidden spine" (paragraph 17) and "writers rub one word against the other" (paragraph 25). Point to several instances of figurative language and explain what each one adds to the essay. [24a(4)]
2. Murray repeats the word *each* seven times in the last sentence in paragraph 21. What is gained by the repetition? Is the repetition necessary? Why do we not perceive it as wordy? [20a and 21e]

BUILDING VOCABULARY

1. From what Latin roots is *manuscript* derived? What do they mean? Write a sentence using a word derived from one of these Latin roots.
2. List and define two synonyms for *revise*. Write sentences using each of these synonyms.

SUGGESTIONS FOR WRITING

1. Write a process essay explaining how to acquire a certain skill (such as riding a bicycle or skateboard, windsurfing, skiing, swimming, playing a certain musical instrument, juggling).
2. Write a process essay explaining how to solve a particular problem (selecting a course of study, overcoming stage fright, breaking a bad habit).

The Spider and the Wasp

Alexander Petrunkevitch

Born in Russia and educated there and in Germany, Petrunkevitch (1875–1964) emigrated to America in 1903. He taught for many years at Yale University, and while on that faculty published the books that made him an internationally recognized authority on spiders: *Index Catalogue of Spiders of North, Central, and South America* (1911) and *An Inquiry into the Natural Classification of Spiders* (1933). Petrunkevitch was also well known for his translations of English and Russian poetry, and he was a historian and philosopher as well as a scientist. This essay, written for *Scientific American,* reflects his lifelong interest in insects and his gifts as a writer.

In the feeding and safeguarding of their progeny insects and spiders exhibit some interesting analogies to reasoning and some crass examples of blind instinct. The case I propose to describe here is that of the tarantula spiders and their arch-enemy, the digger wasps of the genus Pepsis. It is a classic example of what looks like intelligence pitted against instinct—a strange situation in which the victim, though fully able to defend itself, submits unwittingly to its destruction. 1

Most tarantulas live in the tropics, but several species occur in the temperate zone and a few are common in the southern U.S. Some varieties are large and have powerful fangs with which they can inflict a deep wound. These formidable looking spiders do not, however, attack man; you can hold one in your hand, if you are gentle, without being bitten. Their bite is dangerous only to insects and small mammals such as mice; for man it is no worse than a hornet's sting. 2

Tarantulas customarily live in deep cylindrical burrows, from which they emerge at dusk and into which they retire at dawn. Mature males wander about after dark in search of females and occasionally stray into houses. After mating, the male dies in a few weeks, but a female lives much longer and can mate several years in succession. In a Paris museum is a tropical specimen which is said to have been living in captivity for 25 years. 3

A fertilized female tarantula lays from 200 to 400 eggs at a time; thus it is possible for a single tarantula to produce several thousand young. She takes no care of them beyond weaving a cocoon of silk to enclose the eggs. After they hatch, the young walk away, find convenient places in which to dig their burrows and spend the rest of their lives in solitude. The eyesight of tarantulas is poor, being limited to a sensing of change in the intensity of light and to the perception of moving objects. They apparently have little or no sense 4

145

of hearing, for a hungry tarantula will pay no attention to a loudly chirping cricket placed in its cage unless the insect happens to touch one of its legs.

But all spiders, and especially hairy ones, have an extremely delicate sense   5 of touch. Laboratory experiments prove that tarantulas can distinguish three types of touch: pressure against the body wall, stroking of the body hair, and riffling of certain very fine hairs on the legs called trichobothria. Pressure against the body, by the finger or the end of a pencil, causes the tarantula to move off slowly for a short distance. The touch excites no defensive response unless the approach is from above where the spider can see the motion, in which case it rises on its hind legs, lifts its front legs, opens its fangs and holds this threatening posture as long as the object continues to move.

The entire body of a tarantula, especially its legs, is thickly clothed with   6 hair. Some of it is short and wooly, some long and stiff. Touching this body hair produces one of two distinct reactions. When the spider is hungry, it responds with an immediate and swift attack. At the touch of a cricket's antennae the tarantula seizes the insect so swiftly that a motion picture taken at the rate of 64 frames per second shows only the result and not the process of capture. But when the spider is not hungry, the stimulation of its hairs merely causes it to shake the touched limb. An insect can walk under its hairy belly unharmed.

The trichobothria, very fine hairs growing from disclike membranes on   7 the legs, are sensitive only to air movement. A light breeze makes them vibrate slowly, without disturbing the common hair. When one blows gently on the trichobothria, the tarantula reacts with a quick jerk of its four front legs. If the front and hind legs are stimulated at the same time, the spider makes a sudden jump. This reaction is quite independent of the state of its appetite.

These three tactile responses—to pressure on the body wall, to moving of   8 the common hair, and to flexing of the trichobothria—are so different from one another that there is no possibility of confusing them. They serve the tarantula adequately for most of its needs and enable it to avoid most annoyances and dangers. But they fail the spider completely when it meets its deadly enemy, the digger wasp Pepsis.

These solitary wasps are beautiful and formidable creatures. Most species   9 are either a deep shiny blue all over, or deep blue with rusty wings. The largest have a wing span of about four inches. They live on nectar. When excited, they give off a pungent odor—a warning that they are ready to attack. The sting is much worse than that of a bee or common wasp, and the pain and swelling last longer. In the adult stage the wasp lives only a few months. The female produces but a few eggs, one at a time at intervals of two or three days. For each egg the mother must provide one adult tarantula, alive but paralyzed. The mother wasp attaches the egg to the paralyzed spider's abdomen. Upon hatching from the egg, the larva is many hundreds of times smaller than its living but helpless victim. It eats no other food and drinks no water. By the time it has finished its single Gargantuan meal and become ready for wasphood, nothing remains of the tarantula but its indigestible chitinous skeleton.

The mother wasp goes tarantula-hunting when the egg in her ovary is al- 10
most ready to be laid. Flying low over the ground late on a sunny afternoon,
the wasp looks for its victim or for the mouth of a tarantula burrow, a round
hole edged by a bit of silk. The sex of the spider makes no difference, but the
mother is highly discriminating as to species. Each species of Pepsis requires
a certain species of tarantula, and the wasp will not attack the wrong species.
In a cage with a tarantula which is not its normal prey, the wasp avoids the
spider and is usually killed by it in the night.

Yet when a wasp finds the correct species, it is the other way about. To 11
identify the species the wasp apparently must explore the spider with her
antennae. The tarantula shows an amazing tolerance to this exploration. The
wasp crawls under it and walks over it without evoking any hostile response.
The molestation is so great and so persistent that the tarantula often rises on
all eight legs, as if it were on stilts. It may stand this way for several minutes.
Meanwhile the wasp, having satisfied itself that the victim is of the right
species, moves off a few inches to dig the spider's grave. Working vigorously
with legs and jaws, it excavates a hole eight to ten inches deep with a diameter slightly larger than the spider's girth. Now and again the wasp pops out
of the hole to make sure that the spider is still there.

When the grave is finished, the wasp returns to the tarantula to complete 12
her ghastly enterprise. First she feels it all over once more with her antennae.
Then her behavior becomes more aggressive. She bends her abdomen, protruding her sting, and searches for the soft membrane at the point where the
spider's legs join its body—the only spot where she can penetrate the horny
skeleton. From time to time, as the exasperated spider slowly shifts ground,
the wasp turns on her back and slides along with the aid of her wings, trying
to get under the tarantula for a shot at the vital spot. During all this maneuvering, which can last for several minutes, the tarantula makes no move to
save itself. Finally the wasp corners it against some obstruction and grasps
one of its legs in her powerful jaws. Now at last the harassed spider tries a
desperate but vain defense. The two contestants roll over and over on the
ground. It is a terrifying sight and the outcome is always the same. The wasp
finally manages to thrust her sting into the soft spot and holds it there for a
few seconds while she pumps in the poison. Almost immediately the tarantula falls paralyzed on its back. Its legs stop twitching; its heart stops beating. Yet it is not dead, as is shown by the fact that if taken from the wasp
it can be restored to some sensitivity by being kept in a moist chamber for
several months.

After paralyzing the tarantula, the wasp cleans herself by dragging her 13
body along the ground and rubbing her feet, sucks the drop of blood oozing
from the wound in the spider's abdomen, then grabs a leg of the flabby, helpless animal in her jaws and drags it down to the bottom of the grave. She
stays there for many minutes, sometimes for several hours, and what she does
all that time in the dark we do not know. Eventually she lays her egg and attaches it to the side of the spider's abdomen with a sticky secretion. Then she

emerges, fills the grave with soil carried bit by bit in her jaws, and finally tramples the ground all around to hide any trace of the grave from prowlers. Then she flies away, leaving her descendant safely started in life.

In all this the behavior of the wasp evidently is qualitatively different from   14 that of the spider. The wasp acts like an intelligent animal. This is not to say that instinct plays no part or that she reasons as man does. But her actions are to the point; they are not automatic and can be modified to fit the situation. We do not know for certain how she identifies the tarantula—probably it is by some olfactory or chemo-tactile sense—but she does it purposefully and does not blindly tackle a wrong species.

On the other hand, the tarantula's behavior shows only confusion. Evidently   15 the wasp's pawing gives it no pleasure, for it tries to move away. That the wasp is not simulating sexual stimulation is certain because male and female tarantulas react in the same way to its advances. That the spider is not anesthetized by some odorless secretion is easily shown by blowing lightly at the tarantula and making it jump suddenly. What, then, makes the tarantula behave as stupidly as it does?

No clear, simple answer is available. Possibly the stimulation by the wasp's   16 antennae is masked by a heavier pressure on the spider's body, so that it reacts as when prodded by a pencil. But the explanation may be much more complex. Initiative in attack is not in the nature of tarantulas; most species fight only when cornered so that escape is impossible. Their inherited patterns of behavior apparently prompt them to avoid problems rather than attack them. For example, spiders always weave their webs in three dimensions, and when a spider finds that there is insufficient space to attach certain threads in the third dimension, it leaves the place and seeks another, instead of finishing the web in a single plane. This urge to escape seems to arise under all circumstances, in all phases of life, and to take the place of reasoning. For a spider to change the pattern of its web is as impossible as for an inexperienced man to build a bridge across a chasm obstructing his way.

In a way the instinctive urge to escape is not only easier but often more   17 efficient than reasoning. The tarantula does exactly what is most efficient in all cases except in an encounter with a ruthless and determined attacker dependent for the existence of her own species on killing as many tarantulas as she can lay eggs. Perhaps in this case the spider follows its usual pattern of trying to escape, instead of seizing and killing the wasp, because it is not aware of its danger. In any case, the survival of the tarantula species as a whole is protected by the fact that the spider is much more fertile than the wasp.

*

RESPONDING TO THE WHOLE ESSAY

1. What kind of audience is Petrunkevitch writing for in this essay? What evidence in the essay reveals the audience Petrunkevitch envisions? [1g(2)]

2. "The Spider and the Wasp" is primarily a minutely observed factual account, but its power as an essay depends on the author's fascination with his subject. What evidence of this personal involvement can you point to? Are Petrunkevitch's feelings ever explicitly stated? If so, where? [3a]
3. Analyze paragraph 12 for ways in which Petrunkevitch links sentences to make time relationships clear and form a coherent sequence. Mark the kinds of transitional devices you discover in the paragraph. [3d]
4. Point throughout the essay to examples of inductive reasoning. [5h(1)]
5. What kinds of transitions does Petrunkevitch use to move from paragraph to paragraph? Explain the transition from paragraph 15 to paragraph 16. [3d]
6. What central idea gives unity to the essay? Show how the essay is unified. [2b]

ANALYZING THE ELEMENTS

Grammer

1. In the first sentence of paragraph 1, what is the grammatical function of each of these words: *feeding safeguarding, interesting, reasoning*? [11 and 15a]
2. What is the grammatical function of each *which* in the first sentence of paragraph 3? What is the antecedent? Explain your reasons for preferring the sentence as it is written rather than writing it as follows: *burrows which they emerge from at dusk and which they retire into at dawn.* [11]
3. What reason can you give for the use of the passive voice in the final sentence in paragraph 10? Try rewriting the sentence so that the verbs are all in the active voice. What difficulties do you encounter? [21d]
4. What is the subject of each of the following verbs in the first sentence of paragraph 13: *cleans, sucks, grabs, drags*? [11]

Effective Sentences

1. In the first sentence of the essay, how does Petrunkevitch let the reader know which kinds of characteristics insects exhibit and which kinds spiders exhibit? [20a]
2. The last sentence in paragraph 3 is inverted. Why? [21f]
3. In the first sentence of paragraph 8, are the elements of the series contained within the dashes parallel? If so, explain why. If not, how could the sentence be written to make them parallel? [20a]

Punctuation and Mechanics

1. Explain the uses of the dash and the commas in the final sentence of paragraph 1. Would other punctuation have served as well? Why or why not? [31e and 27d]
2. What use of the semicolon is found in the last two sentences of paragraph 2? How are the parts of the sentences on either side of each semicolon related to each other? [28a]
3. Why is the colon in the second sentence of paragraph 5 appropriate? What other marks of punctuation could have been used? Which is most effective? Why? [31d]

Diction

1. What is the meaning of the following words: *progeny, crass,* and *unwittingly* (paragraph 1); *riffling* (paragraph 5); *tactile* (paragraph 8); *formidable* and *pungent* (paragraph 9); *tramples* (paragraph 13)? Explain how these words are more exact choices than their synonyms would be. [24a]
2. Find examples of technical vocabulary in the essay. What reasons did Petrunkevitch probably have for using these words? Do they interfere with your understanding of the essay? Why or why not? [23b]
3. Throughout the essay, Petrunkevitch uses several informal words and expressions. How do they contribute to or detract from the success of the essay? [23b(1)]
4. Petrunkevitch uses an allusion, *Gargantuan,* in the final sentence of paragraph 9. To what does he allude? Is the allusion effective? Why or why not? [23a]

BUILDING VOCABULARY

1. A secondary definition offered in *The American Heritage Dictionary* describes the tarantula as "a large wolf spider (*Lycosa tarentula*) of southern Europe, once thought to cause tarantism." Look up the word *tarantism* in your dictionary. What does it mean? What is the primary definition of *tarantula*?
2. The word *cylindrical* is the adjectival form of *cylinder*. Notice that *cylinder* is defined according to three different academic disciplines. What are they? How is *cylinder* defined within each of these disciplines?

SUGGESTIONS FOR WRITING

1. Consider the ritual of the spider and the wasp, as Petrunkevitch reports it. Then, as a detached but fascinated observer, write a short process essay (under 1,000 words) describing in meticulous detail some human ritual. Here are a few suggestions:

   Commuting
   Going to the laundromat
   Celebrating a birthday
   Eating a lobster or an artichoke
   High school graduation
   College registration
   Calling for a date
   Shopping at the supermarket

2. Closely observe your pet or another animal in some typical behavior, such as eating, begging, or stalking, and write a short process essay describing the behavior in great detail.

Zoo Medicine
Michael Kernan

Since graduating with a B.A. from Harvard in 1949, Michael Kernan (1927–)
has had a varied and distinguished career in journalism. He wrote for the
Washington Post for over twenty years, and since 1994 has penned the reg-
ular column, "Around the Mall and Beyond," for *Smithsonian Magazine*.
Kernan has also published two novels, *The Lost Diaries of Frans Hals,* and
The Violet Dots, as well as articles in *Life, Reader's Digest, National
Geographic, Traveler,* and other magazines.

Question: How do you give a 448-pound gorilla an EKG? 1

Answer: With a lot of help. 2

It takes ten people to lift a sedated hulk named Mopie onto the operat- 3
ing table at the National Zoological Park hospital. Actually, the 24-year-old
silver-back is getting much more than an electrocardiogram. For over an hour
he will be put through some of the most sophisticated heart tests we have, including an exam with a transesophageal ultrasonic scope, part of a Doppler
echocardiograph machine.

The scope is a silvery L-shaped tube, hardly a foot long, and it costs 4
$48,000. It is hand-built, with 64 crystals that can be fired in phased sequence
to vibrate and thus send sound waves into the heart; the waves that bounce
back are digitally reconstructed into a video image. Inserted into the esopha-
gus next to the heart, the instrument provides an extraordinary picture of that
organ, its valves, the aorta and everything else, as it pumps away. What we
have here is a charming switch: the latest developments in human medicine
being used to benefit animals.

"Cardiovascular disease is a significant problem in orangutans and goril- 5
las, especially male gorillas," Dr. Richard Cambre, head of the Zoo's
Department of Animal Health, tells me, "We've done all nine of our orangutans and now are working on the nine gorillas with echocardiograms, blood
pressure exams and blood workups for cholesterol and lipid levels."

Though zoo animals live longer than wild ones as a rule—35 years is the 6
average age for gorillas; the record is 54—they tend to develop heart trouble. No one knows just why. Is it hypertension? Arteriosclerosis? And why
the high cholesterol? Though the Zoo provides the apes with a diet that is
as close as possible to what they would eat in the wild, are the apes missing
some trace item, some leaf or plant that they find in the lowlands of Zaire
and Cameroon?

151

"These exams will give us baseline stats," Cambre says, "so we can fol-   7
low them in later years. One thing: we don't have heart data on gorillas while
they're awake. We might be able to train orangutans to accept a blood pressure cuff, but gorillas, I don't know."

They are not ideal patients. When Dr. Lucy Spelman, associate veterinar-   8
ian at the Zoo, approached Mopie earlier this morning with the dart gun that
would anesthetize him, Cambre recalls, "he figured out what was going on
before she had a chance to fire the dart, though he'd never seen this particular type of equipment before. He knew what was going to happen to him."
So Mopie produced from the source a gigantic handful of fresh gorilla ma-
nure and hurled it at Dr. Spelman, spattering her from hair to heels.

Undaunted, she is in the operating room working away on Mopie with   9
the rest of the doctors when I arrive. She has wiped the stuff off her glasses
but is otherwise concentrating on what she has come here to do. All in a day's
work. The place has a pungent smell, somewhat like a bad case of halitosis.
The vets tell me this is the normal scent of a gorilla when he's scared.

The dart, fired from an air pistol, goes into the leg muscles and puts a   10
gorilla down in 15 minutes or so. After that he is kept under anesthesia with
isoflurane gas, inhaled through a tube.

Now Mopie lies there with his silverhaired knees splayed and his giant   11
paws curled like a sleeping child's fingers. A transducer clipped to his tongue
tracks his blood oxygen saturation and pulse rate. His eyes are slightly open.
The doctors bustle around him in their surgical masks and gloves, taking notes,
checking the video monitors, moving probes about on his vast chest.

When I ask how she got into doing this, Dr. Spelman says simply that   12
she always wanted to be a zoo vet. She was in private practice but prefers
the variety of experience in a zoo. In one day she may help with a cardiac
workup on a gorilla, do a root canal on a Sumatran tiger, take blood from
a sea lion.

As Mopie's heart thumps away in living color on the Doppler machine,   13
a frighteningly accomplished trunkful of electronics costing six figures and
loaned by Hewlett-Packard as a friendly gesture, I talk to Dr. Steven Goldstein,
one of three Washington cardiologists who have given up this Sunday and vol-
unteered to help. I ask if Mopie's heart rate of 123 beats per minute, duly
recorded on the monitor, is very bad.

"It would be bad for a human but might be not so bad for an ape. This   14
may be mild for him." Goldstein does, however, see what appears to be a
problem in the main pumping chamber, the left ventricle. Normal human
ventricles eject 60 to 70 percent of the blood in a given contraction. In
orangutans, the efficiency is down to 55 to 65 percent. Mopie's is as low as
35 percent.

"I think it's abnormal, but I've only seen 10 or 11 great apes," says   15
Goldstein, who has been volunteering at the Zoo since September 1995. "He's
the second gorilla that I've seen with this condition. His father died at 37 of

a heart problem, but then his father was born in the wild. Apes do live artificially long in captivity."

The beauty of the Doppler machine, National Zoo primates curator Lisa   16
Stevens tells me, is that you can literally watch and videotape the heart at work. A conventional heart x-ray might be obscured by the ribs and, besides, is two-dimensional and static. When the ultrasonic scope is inserted, you can see everything in motion, even the aortic valve opening and closing.

Stevens came to the National Zoological Park straight from Michigan State,   17
18 years ago. "I thought I'd do this for a few years, but then I realized that this was it. I started with cats, then bears, seals and sea lions. You become specialized eventually, but most people are very versatile. You work with all the animals, from elephants to fish. And you appreciate and respect them all."

Dr. Cambre, who came here two years ago after 15 years at the Denver   18
Zoo, says that being a zoo veterinarian gets into your blood. "Animal personalities are fascinating. We have Ph.D. curators here and a keeper staff that's mostly college educated. We depend on them to report unusual behavioral patterns for individual animals to us. Sometimes these are early warning signs of illness. It takes a team effort to figure out what's going on." Without an owner to tell them what an animal's problem is, Zoo people have to rely on their own close observations. Is an animal eating well? Defecating normally? Moody? Under stress?

On another of my visits to the Zoo, Azy, a large male orangutan, spot-   19
ted Cambre as we strolled past. Azy rushed back and forth in his cage, pushing a huge barrel before him in an impressive display of power. "It's a lot of bluster," Cambre said. "He's trying to intimidate me. He knows who I am. He knows who's going to win if I get my dart gun. So he's bluffing. Of course, if I was stupid enough to wander into his cage, he'd kill me. They're forgiving up to a point. But they don't like us, because if they're sick we've got to dart 'em."

After the heart exam, as Mopie lies on his back, half covered by a blan-   20
ket and breathing peacefully, Dr. Spelman cleans the gorilla's wicked-looking teeth with dental tools. Yes, even apes are prone to cavities and gum disease.

Now Mopie is being unplugged from the monitors and transferred to an   21
x-ray table for a complete set of pictures. Even moving him from one table to another takes a half-dozen people hauling on the heavy canvas netting he's lying in.

"We'll take him off anesthesia when he's back in a cage," explains Stevens.   22
"He'll recover pretty fast. He'll be groggy for the rest of the day, but awake and eating. He might be a little cross. He's into that role of being the big dominant male. Mopie can be sullen, but he has his light moments. By tomorrow he'll be back to normal."

The team struggles through narrow doorways with Mopie and deposits   23
him in a van for the trip back to the ape house. There they tug and push him through barred passageways to a cage, where the anesthesia tube is removed. Immediately he begins to clear his throat, sounding exactly like may father in

the morning. In a minute he starts to move, and the staff leaves to give the same round of tests to another gorilla.

I hear some serious screams and the pounding of bare feet as a large fe-   24
male named Mesou flees down a runway. Following her, holding a long dart gun, comes the interpid Dr. Spelman in clean coveralls, her brown hair pulled back in a ponytail. She moves with deliberation, intent and calm.

The CO_2 gun pops. "There," she says. "That was a good one." Mesou   25
sits down with a philosophic grunt.

✳

RESPONDING TO THE WHOLE ESSAY

1. What is the primary purpose of this essay? [1g(1)]
2. Is this essay expressive, informative, or persuasive? [1g(1)]
3. Would the reader be able to follow this process? Why or why not?
4. Find examples of comparison and contrast in the essay. [2e(5)]
5. How does Kernan make the animals seem more "human"? Why would he do this?
6. Does Kernan use adequate examples? [2d(2)]

ANALYZING THE ELEMENTS

Grammar

1. Justify the use of a fragment in the answer to the opening question. [13]
2. Comment on the agreement in the relative clause in the paragraph 13. [17e(6)]

Effective Sentences

1. What is effective about the "switch" described in the last sentence of paragraph 4?
2. Comment on the incorporation of direct quotations in paragraphs 5, 7, 8, 14, 15, 19, and 22. [7c, 30f]

Punctuation and Mechanics

1. Why is a colon used in the last sentence of paragraph 4? [31d(1)]
2. Why is *zoo* capitalized (paragraphs 5, 6, 8, and 19) but not in paragraphs 12 and 18? Is the distinction correct? [33a(4)]

Diction

1. What is accomplished by including a number of technical terms in the essay? Does the reader need to know them in order to understand the essay?
2. Find words used to describe Mopie the gorilla. Which of these words make him seem almost human? Which of these words emphasize his brutishness?
3. Find words which emphasize the difficulty of the process.

BUILDING VOCABULARY

1. What is the Latin origin of *halitosis*?
2. What is a *curator*? Where besides a zoo might a curator work?

SUGGESTIONS FOR WRITING

1. Describe a process that requires the participation and cooperation of a team of people.
2. Write an essay in which you explain to someone how to take a child to the zoo for the first time.

*

Chapter 5

Cause and Effect

Cause and *effect* are complementary terms: *cause* refers to what makes things happen (reasons); *effect* refers to what happens (results). A cause always presupposes one or more effects; an effect has one or more causes. Cause-and-effect essays can focus on exploring either causes or effects, or they may analyze a causal chain, in which an effect becomes the cause of an effect that in turn also is a cause, and so on. In this chapter, for example, Rachel L. Jones's "The Price of Hate: Thoughts on Covering a Ku Klux Klan Rally" predicts effects, and both John Williams's "And Here's the Pitch" and Eric Minton's "Scaring Up Business" explore causal chains.

Although cause-and-effect essays occasionally have a mainly expressive aim, emphasizing the writer's personal responses, usually they are intended to be informative or persuasive. An informative essay focuses on causal relationships objectively, simply as facts the reader will find useful or interesting. A persuasive essay explores causal relationships in order to sway the reader to the writer's point of view or to move the reader to some kind of action— for instance, to correct some condition that has undesirable effects. (For further discussion of purpose, see 1g.)

Causal relationships are rarely simple. Any given effect is likely to have several causes, some more immediate than others, and of course each of those causes may have produced a variety of effects besides the one under consideration. Consider all of the following statements:

I'm cold because it's only 30 degrees Fahrenheit.

I'm cold because it's winter.

I'm cold because I left my coat on the bus.

I'm cold because a friend was talking to me on the bus and made me forget my coat.

I'm cold because I live in Bemidji, Minnesota, rather than near the equator.

I'm cold because heat is being exchanged between my body and the atmosphere in accordance with the second law of thermodynamics.

I'm cold because the metabolic processes of human beings do not produce enough heat to keep them warm in Bemidji.

I'm cold because I don't have fur.

All of these causes can be true simultaneously. And note that every one of them has effects besides making me cold. Even leaving my coat on the bus has other effects: I'll have to go to the bus company's lost-and-found room (a nuisance that will cause me to miss doing something else), and if the coat hasn't been turned in I'll have to buy another one (which in turn will cause me to forgo something else I could have bought with the money). Yet this example, my shivering in Bemidji, is a very simple one. Imagine, then, how long a possible list might be constructed for something really complicated, such as the causes of crime.

So writers must guard against oversimplifying. Discovering the immediate cause of an event may be easy, but other more remote causes may be more important. The firing on Fort Sumter is often seen as the immediate cause of the Civil War. But of course the issue of slavery was far more basic, and slavery was in turn causally related to economic factors such as Northern control of banking and Southern control of cotton supplies for the Northern fabric mills, as well as to political factors such as the Southern championship of states' rights and the Northern commitment to federalism. All of these things contributed to the conflict, though some more immediately and more visibly than others.

The complexity of events is not the only difficulty the writer faces in cause-and-effect analysis. Vested interests sometimes deliberately obscure causal relationships for their own benefit. For instance, when the Warren Commission investigated the cause of President John F. Kennedy's assassination, one of the obstacles it met was that certain government agencies pointed the finger of blame at each other to avoid having it pointed in their own direction.

Finally, in assigning causes to effects, writers must be not only objective but rational. It is all too easy to ignore evidence that points to a cause we do not wish to consider. And even the most fair-minded writer can still fall into those logical traps, to which we are all vulnerable, called fallacies. (See 5i.)

In the following essay, Nandina Brownell, a student, develops her analysis of causes and effects into an effective argument. Note especially how Brownell addresses both the immediate and remote causes.

Control

Establishes context

A family boards a transport shuttle at the Orlando airport. Mother, father, son, and daughter chatter animatedly about their day at Disneyworld. Ten-year-old Ray Junior wears a Donald Duck sweatshirt and is laden with Disney souvenirs. His six-year-old sister, Amy, wears a hat with Mickey ears and clutches her own small bag of memorabilia. All the seats are filled, so the four of them stand around the chromium support poles in the car, smiling, happy, and tired. As the car lurches to a start, Amy

stumbles. Her father shoots a disapproving glance and
thunders, "Watch what you're doing, you clumsy fool!"
Amy silently grabs the support pole, and her large
eyes sweep the carful of strangers now staring at her.
She blinks once, twice, three times as the tears well in
her eyes and her face flushes scarlet. She lowers her
head, and her Mickey ears tumble to the floor of the
car. Clutching the pole, she picks up the hat and puts
it back on her head akimbo. The family, and the entire
car, falls silent. Finally, the family reaches its stop
and gets off. The incident is over. The family walks in
silence to their departure gate, their Disney regalia
now a bizarre counterpoint.

Analysis of causes   You have all witnessed an Amy. Most of you
have done nothing. And most of you regret it long
after. Interestingly, Amy's case is not strictly child
abuse. The casual observer may rightly interpret this
as a single act of a loving but tired father at the end
of a long day. Nevertheless, Amy is a victim of
something that may be far more insidious than overt
abuse. Amy is clearly a victim of inappropriate
control. And she is not alone. Like Amy we have all
been victims of inappropriate control. Worse, we have
all been perpetrators.

Transition to   At a time when issues such as child and
argument   spousal abuse, sexual harassment, police brutality, and
human rights violations are at the American fore, it
may seem frivolous to talk about such a minor issue
as control. Nevertheless, it is clearly time to talk,
because each of those larger issues, each of these
incursions into the well-being of another, is clearly the
result of inappropriate control.

Even more than the stuff of media events—
children and spouses not interactively part of a
family, students disenfranchised from their own
learning process, a national work force made up of
the robotically disempowered—the result of
inappropriate control is the death of personal, social,
and political autonomy. We are at least nominally a
nation where all are created equal and all are entitled
to "life, liberty, and the pursuit of happines." To begin
to turn these constitutional guarantees into a personal
reality, we need to find solutions to the problem of
inappropriate control, solutions that may lie in the
causes.

Illustration   Ben is a 34-year-old systems analyst. Raised
alternately by an occasionally institutionalized

Remote causes

schizophrenic mother, then his domineering father and
acquiescent stepmother, Ben had to make his own
way for as long as he could remember: he set his own
bedtimes, took his baths, packed his own peanut
butter sandwiches for school, ordered his own
existence. Following in his father's footsteps, he
worked as a roofer for ten years after high school and
just recently graduated with a B.S. degree. He has
gladly turned in his hard hat for a white shirt and
dark tie. He has been married for about a year to
Lisa, who quit her job at Ben's request. For the first
month or so, Lisa spent time decorating their new

Immediate causes

home and enjoying her unstructured time. Ben would
often make what seemed like simple requests: don't
tuck the sheets in at the foot of the bed, keep the
thermostat at 70 degrees at all times. On their three-
month anniversary, Ben joined Lisa in the shower—to
explain the waste involved in shampooing her hair
twice every time she washed it. Ben now insists that
his shirts be laundered once a week and all hung with
the second button buttoned and fronts facing left in
the closet. He insists that Lisa have a hot meal on the
table at 6 p.m. but chides her when she uses more
than one pan to prepare the meal—one-pot meals are
more efficient. He wants Lisa to finish the dishes by 7
so she can sit beside him in front of the television.
They go to bed at 11 because they have to be up at
6:30—Ben to get dressed for work, Lisa to fix his
breakfast and pack his mid-morning snack: peanut
butter and honey sandwiches without the crusts.
Every Saturday, they go to the mall, where Ben looks
for office attire, soliciting Lisa's opinion, but seldom
buying. When they argue, Ben frequently compares
Lisa to his mentally ill mother and attacks her
competency as a wife and potential mother. He always
makes up the next day with flowers.

Effect

Lisa, after a year, is abjectly unhappy. It's
obvious in many ways that Ben loves her, and she's
sure she loves him. She wants to please and to do
right by him as a wife. His requests are simple, but
she just can't seem to keep them all straight. She's
confused and occasionally thinks she may be losing

Immediate cause

her mind. But as any counselor can tell her, she's not
losing her mind, she's lost control over her own life.

Remote causes

The causes of that lost control—and the
concomitant loss of power and self-esteem—lie in both
Lisa and Ben. First, out of a sense of love and wifely

duty, Lisa has abdicated control, and her attempts at regaining control erupt into arguments, recriminations, and then a return to the established controller-controlled roles. Second, Ben's need for control has two causes: he thinks he is making an honest attempt to keep the chaos of the world out of his home, and he needs to feel important.

Generalizes to all

Many deny they could ever be like Ben or Lisa. However, each one of us dons and doffs these roles often: we become the obsequious pleaser to avoid rocking the boat; we see the world as a dangerous and chaotic place and order our existences accordingly; and we often put ourselves and others through strange psychological gyrations so we can feel important.

Remedies

But when we slip into these roles, what can we do? First, do a control-check periodically. Looking at the large picture, do you still feel in control of your own existence? If not, quickly find the source. Is it your job? your family? yourself? If you can push the control reset button yourself, do so: talk to your supervisor about your need to feel some ownership over your projects; talk to your spouse and family about your need to do a fair share of things "your way"; convince yourself that making your own decisions benefits you and those around you. If the reset button seems inaccessible, seek professional help: the office industrial psychologist, a family counselor, a personal psychologist. Clearly the longer you give up control, the more difficult it is to regain it.

Problems

What about those occasions when we slip into the controller role: when we are on the verge of ridiculing our child, of blabbing an embarrassing anecdote about a co-worker, of badgering our spouse, of imposing order on others? The first step is to stop before speaking or acting. The next step is to think. Will there be any losers if I say or do what I'm planning? If the answer is yes, don't do it. Rather, begin searching for win-win strategies. Does your five-year-old have an affinity for matches? Supervise his or her candle-lighting at dinner time. Are two valuable employees always battling for power? Make them co-leaders on a project and reward them equally. Does your near-perfect spouse's lip-smacking during meals drive you crazy? Focus on the half-full glass, count your blessings, count to ten, and think of his or her last act of kindness to you.

Summary   Granted, stamping out child and spousal abuse,
          sexual harassment, police brutality, and human rights
          violations may seem a near impossibility. And it may
Effects   be. But we can't eliminate national and global woes
          when the seeds of them thrive in our own homes and
          communities. If each of us learns to give and take
Causes   control appropriately, we may, in a small and
          important way, make this a better, more egalitarian
          world.

Commentary. Nandina Brownell's essay is both an analysis of cause and effect and an argument proposing a solution to the problem. She begins with a calculated bid for the reader's sympathy: she tells a tale of a father's callous and public criticism of his young daugther—an event that she sees as the effect of an inappropriate exercise of control, the primary cause she analyzes in the essay. Following the narrative, Brownell analyzes its causes: potential, immediate, and remote. She makes a transition to her argument by claiming that several national, social, and political issues also result from the same cause and that dealing with that cause as individuals may reduce its effect nationally.

To illustrate her point and to make the problem more immediate for the general reader, Brownell devotes the next three paragraphs to a narrative of events occurring in the lives of a newly married couple, Ben and Lisa, presenting a chain of causes and effects. Brownell then generalizes the causes of such marital disruptions to all people, who seek to please, to impose order on our own lives, and to feel important. Next, she offers a way to take control of our own lives and suggests how to relinquish control of others' lives. Her conclusion derives directly from this proposal: by controlling ourselves rather than others we may begin to take small steps toward resolving some of our major social problems—a new set of causes and effects.

Brownell's essay is an ambitious effort, but it suffers from oversimplification, though she is apparently aware of that problem and attempts to handle it in her conclusion. She is to be commended, however, for taking the risk and for maintaining enough distance from her own writing to notice and attempt to correct a potential problem which would qualify her success.

Scaring Up Business
Eric Minton

A freelance writer, Eric Minton covers the amusement park industry in his column, "The Loop" for *Funworld* Magazine. He has also published articles in a number of trade magazines and in popular magazines *Good Housekeeping* and *Modern Maturity*. This essay appeared in *Psychology Today* with two other essays about roller coasters and haunted houses by the same author (included in this volume, see "Thrills and Chills" in Chapter 1 and "Beating Coasterphobia" in Chapter 2).

To consumers, roller coasters and haunted houses ARE fright fests. To the 1
proprietors, they're a business, and however much designers delight in their craft, they ultimately must make sure the attraction turns a profit. Many haunted houses are stand-alone attractions and get their income from direct ticket sales. Some houses—as well as virtually all coasters—are included in the single-price admission at most amusement parks. In that case, whether or not the customer rides a coaster or visits a haunted house has no direct impact on that day's income. A dazzling attraction, however, drives up the season's gate by creating good word-of-mouth publicity that entices new customers to come and try it out. It also draws repeat customers who want to relive the thrills and chills.

Quality, therefore, counts. "We have found through experience that some 2
coasters are so rough people will ride them once and not want to get back on," says Mark Rose, vice president of design and engineering for Busch Gardens Tampa Bay. "We want to have a ride that's smooth and comfortable. Our experience here is when it's done right, people do it 10 times a day." The park has set two parameters for its major coasters: to reach a maximum of 3.85 vertical G's (the gravitational force that pushes riders back into their seats) and a maximum of 0.5 lateral G's (the side-to-side force). Keeping the lateral forces to a half G makes the ride smooth, and engineers further assure the effect by adjusting the track's tilt by millimeters.

Length of ride is another issue. The laws of physics determine that coaster 3
trains can only go so far powered by gravity (and after their initial blastoff, Linear Induction Motor coasters rely on gravity to complete the course), so no matter how tall the track, rides can only last about one minute from the first drop to last brake. This can be lengthened by extending the time to the first drop or after the last brake, though doing the latter tends to dilute the ride's overall thrill. *The Beast* at Paramount's Kings Island uses two lifts to double the length of the average ride to just under five minutes.

Designers must weigh three factors in determining a ride's length. Customers   4
who have queued for up to an hour want to get their wait's worth. Second,
a person can tolerate only so much fright time. "The one thing that gets people on is they know there's a limit to how long it lasts," says Michael Boodley,
president of Great Coasters International, Inc. "It's like they have this threshold to a fear that they normally wouldn't want to experience, but because
they know there's an end in sight they're willing to go for it."

Finally, operators want to move as many customers as quickly as possi-   5
ble through the ride. That not only shortens patrons' wait, keeping tempers
in check, it also gets them—and their wallets—circulating in the park. People
standing in line can't spend money on souvenirs or food. To maximize the
flow, some larger coasters, like *The Beast,* stagger runs by two trains.

"Throughput" is also essential to a haunted house's economic success; the   6
faster groups exit, the faster more paying customers can enter. As much as designers love to see terrified guests fall on the floor, they know such halts cut
into an attraction's bottom line. For designers, the trick is to keep guests moving without making them feel rushed. To do this, the theatrical wizards often
employ the "scare-forward" precept: startling groups from the rear or sides
sends them plunging ahead rather than drawing back. A frontal strike, on the
other hand, will cause a person to veer left or right—perfect for when the
exit lies laterally. To vary patrons' pace, designers use light (people naturally
move faster when visibility is good) or darkness (they slow down). Similarly,
curtains will retard movement; people approach them hesitatingly. Edward
Marks, president of Jets Productions, Inc., says he first used drapes as a barrier for light, sound and smoke between scenes, but in high-flow houses he
removes them altogether.

No topic is totally off limits for a haunted house, but regional differences   7
and local demographics may temper presentations. Religious matter is generally taboo in all American haunts. "I'm lucky I have a cross in the cemetery,"
says David Clevinger, artistic director and operations manager of *Terror on
Church Street* in Orlando, Florida. Topical subjects can strike too close a
chord, too. "We wouldn't have a locker room with a dead kid on the ground
and another one holding a gun," notes Marks, referring to the recent spate of
school shootings. "That's real, not escapism." To make sure people know a
fright is staged, Marks sometimes goes over the top in his presentations. For
example, if he does a car wreck, he'll put zombies in the seats.

Another no-no is touching the customer. Squirting or dripping warm wa-   8
ter on a guest is acceptable, and people bump into hanging corpses in *Terror
on Church Street's* morgue, but actors are uniformly coached that no matter
how close they want to get to a customer, they cannot make physical contact.
Nor can the fake cleaver or bladeless chainsaw they sometimes wield. You
can scare people witless, stress designers, you just can't mess with their safety.

✳

RESPONDING TO THE WHOLE ESSAY

1. Though this essay is primarily to inform the reader of the commercial interest of those in the business of haunted houses and roller coasters, look for evidence of persuasive and expressive writing. [1g(1)]
2. Is this essay objective or subjective? Find evidence of the author's opinion.
3. Does Minton use examples effectively? Find three examples. [2d(2)]
4. Does Minton use a balance of examples from both roller coasters and haunted houses? Note the transition in paragraph 6.
5. Does the essay focus more on causes or on effects?
6. This essay was published in *Psychology Today*. Why would the readers of this magazine be interested in this essay? [1g(2)]

ANALYZING THE ELEMENTS

Grammar

1. Examine the use of plural and singular references to customers in paragraph 4. [16d]
2. Examine the consistency in tenses used in paragraph 4. [17c]

Effective Sentences

1. Note the short sentences which begin paragraphs 2 and 3. How are these effective? [21b]
2. How do the sentences in paragraphs 4 and 5 work together effectively as a unit? [3d]

Punctuation and Mechanics

1. Why is *word-of-mouth* hyphenated in paragraph 1? [32g]
2. Why does *G's* contain an apostrophe in paragraph 2? [29c]

Diction

1. What is *throughput* (paragraph 6)? Is a definition necessary? Why is it sometimes effective to use jargon?
2. What is the distinction in paragraph 1 between *proprietors* and *designers*?

BUILDING VOCABULARY

1. Define *queued* (paragraph 4).
2. What is the origin of *taboo* (paragraph 7)?

SUGGESTIONS FOR WRITING

1. Write an essay in which you discuss the causes and/or effects of the popularity of a particular phenomenon, such as an activity or celebrity.
2. Examine your own consumerism in terms of cause and effect. How do you respond to advertising, displays, or other marketing techniques?

The Price of Hate: Thoughts on Covering a Ku Klux Klan Rally

Rachel L. Jones

Rachel Jones was born in 1961 in Cairo, Illinois, and attended Northwestern University and Southern Illinois University. Having served internships at the *New York Times* and *Washington Post*, she writes for the *Miami Herald*. Jones explains that she has always been fascinated with words "and the images they could evoke, how they could make you feel, hear, smell and taste power there," and so she chose writing as a profession to "translate events—everyday and extraordinary—into digestible bites" so that people become aware that "their world is growing and changing." "The Price of Hate" chronicles one event that resulted in the world changing for Jones herself.

I was sitting at my computer terminal when I overheard someone in the   1
office mention his concern because he thought a black couple was moving into a house on his street.

He was standing only four feet away from me, yet lacked a mechanism   2
that would prevent him from making racist statements in front of a black person. I stopped typing and stared at his back. He froze momentarily, and the woman he was talking to glanced at me.

I didn't confront him. I had to transmit copy to St. Petersburg and then   3
leave to cover a graduation. Besides, my stomach was churning. Just seven days earlier, at a Ku Klux Klan rally in Clearwater, I had stood only four feet away from a Tarpon Springs man who told me he was tired of "the n———s getting everything."

I'd be lying if I said that the possibility of covering a Ku Klux Klan rally   4
didn't cause me a few moments' concern about my physical well-being. But when another reporter came over to tell me about the May 28th Klan rally in front of Clearwater City Hall, I reasoned, "It's just another assignment. I am a reporter, and I know my life isn't all budget meetings."

I must also admit to a curiosity about the Klan, and it seemed a good op-   5
portunity to take a look at that sideshow of human nature. Now, I *could* have asked to be excused from that particular assignment. As a police reporter, my Saturdays are sometimes very busy. Had I approached my editor to delicately decline, we could have both made ourselves believe it was only natural to send a burly young man into the fray. Anything could have happened that day—traffic accidents, drownings, first-degree murders at the jail.

167

I couldn't be two places at once, could I?

But two days before the event, I turned to my editor and asked, "I AM   7
covering the rally on Saturday, aren't I?"

She didn't miss a beat. Yes, of course. Just a short story, unless the streets   8
were running with blood or something.

I jokingly told her about the only slightly feigned horror of my older sis-   9
ter, who shrieked into the phone, "They're letting a black reporter cover the
KLAN?"

At the Klan rally, the man from Tarpon Springs saw my press badge and   10
figured I was a part of something he called the "Black Associated Press," which
he swore was denying white journalism graduates jobs. Mr. Tarpon told me
that n———s weren't qualified to get the jobs they were getting through affirmative action, and that America is for white people.

I paused momentarily and asked what he thought should be done about   11
black people. He didn't know or care.

"Send 'em all to hell," he said, while I took notes.   12

It's funny—it was all so clinical. My voice held an even tone, and while   13
he talked I searched his contorted face for some glimmer of recognition on his
part that *I* was a human being, and the words that he spat just might hurt me.

Just as I later waited for Mr. Welcome Wagon to turn around and apol-   14
ogize for his blunder, I waited for the Tarpon Springs man to show some spark
of humanity, but he finished his conversation and walked away.

My stomach was still churning hours later as I relived that rally. The whole   15
experience was like being scalded, like having something sharp raked over my
flesh until it was raw.

After it was over I went home and drank a shot from the bottle of brandy   16
I'd bought last Christmas. In Harlequin romances, handsome princes always
proffered hard liquor to soothe the jangled nerves of a distraught heroine.

But I was alone, and I was no heroine. That night, every noise from the   17
apartment upstairs made me jump, and the pattern of trees against the curtains frightened me as I tossed and turned. I called three of my siblings, but
other than offering sympathy, they felt helpless to ease my trauma.

I had been so naive about the whole assignment. The thing is, I never   18
thought it would change me. I figured it would be difficult, but I didn't want
it to *change* me.

What you must understand about the Klan is that its members and sup-   19
porters have been stripped of their humanity. I gained that insight and feel
stronger for it. It was easy enough on one level to say, "These people are stupid, so I shouldn't be bothered by what they say."

But that was cold comfort as I walked across the City Hall parking lot,   20
feeling a numbness creep through my arms and legs. I thought I must have
been walking like the Scarecrow in *The Wizard of Oz,* but figured if I could
just make it to the church across the street, I'd be fine.

At the church, I asked to use the phone and was sent down a hall and to 21
the left. My fingers felt like sausages as I tried to use the rotary dial, muttering curses as I fouled up several times. Finally managing to reach an editor, I was coherent enough to give her information for a brief summary of the rally.

But when the next editor picked up the phone, I dissolved in tears after 22
three words. He was puzzled, and I think unaware of what was wrong at first. I whimpered that I was sorry and didn't know what was wrong, either. I gasped and caught a few breaths before describing in a wavering voice what had happened.

He tried calming me down to discuss the facts. How many people at- 23
tended? Had there been any clashes? What did police have to say? I planned to write a full story.

The editor said maybe we should just ignore the event. He asked if any 24
of the Klan members had been abusive to me. I mumbled, "Uh hum," and the tears flowed fresh. He told me to get as much police information as I could and to call him back later.

I placed the phone on the hook and buried my face in my hands, letting 25
the sobs come freely. The man who had let me use the church phone brought me a box of tissues and a Coke.

After I splashed my face with cold water and controlled the sobs, I headed 26
back to the rally, just as the Klansmen were loading up to leave. Shouts of "white supremacy" rang through the air as they rolled out, and my photographer walked over to give me the Klansmen's names. I turned away, telling her that I probably wouldn't use them anyway.

"I didn't think it would affect me," I whispered. 27

"Don't cry. They aren't worth it, Rachel," she said. 28

But even then, it had started to change me . . . 29

When you have stared into the twisted face of hate, you *must* change. I 30
remember watching the documentary *Eyes on the Prize*, in particular the segment on the desegregation of Little Rock High School in 1957, and being disturbed by the outpouring of rage against those nine students.

The whites who snarled into the camera back then had no explanation 31
for their vitriol and violence other than that the students were black, and they didn't care who knew it. They weren't going to let those n———s into the school, no matter what.

I've struggled all my life against a visceral reaction to that kind of racism. 32
I have been mistreated because of my color, but nothing ever came near to what those students went through on a daily basis.

That and countless other examples let me know what I'd been spared, 33
and I decided to choose the path of understanding, realizing that some people are always going to fear or even hate me because of my color alone.

It's a burden blacks must carry no matter how high a level of achieve- 34
ment they reach, and I sought to incorporate that into my own striving. Watching films of what hate turned those people into made me choose to

reject it, to deal with people individually and not tarnish all whites with the same obscene images. *I would not hate.*

But as one Klan supporter muttered, "N——b——," at me as I   35
weaved my way through the crowd, that resolve crumbled. It stung as much as if he *had* slapped me or thrown something.

The leader shouted taunts and epithets at a black woman who was infu-   36
riated by the proceedings, and who had even lunged at several people in the small group of supporters.

As the black woman walked away, the leader shouted, "Why don't you   37
go back to Nee-gor Africa where you came from!" I laughed because he sounded foolish, but he saw me and sent a fresh stream of obscenity my way.

A Jewish woman who came to protest was heaped with stinging abuse,   38
and the rabble was ingenious in its varied use of sexual and racial obscenities directed toward her.

Other reporters and photographers eyed me warily throughout the rally,   39
watching for my reactions to the abuse. When the leader started passing out leaflets and avoided my outstretched hand, a photographer asked for two and brought me one.

I said thank you. He said quietly, "You're very, very welcome," and was   40
embarrassed when I caught his eye.

When it was all over, several police officials called me brave. But I felt   41
cold, sick and empty. I felt like such a naive fool. I felt bitter. So this is what it feels like, I thought. Why *shouldn't* I just hate them right back, why couldn't I diffuse this punch in the gut?

What is noble about not flinching in the face of hate? Slavery, lynchings,   42
rape, inequality, was that not enough? If they want to send me to hell, shouldn't I want to take them along for the ride?

But I still couldn't hate. I was glad I had cried, though. It defied their de-   43
mented logic. It meant I was human.

✳

RESPONDING TO THE WHOLE ESSAY

1. What is Jones's primary purpose in writing "The Price of Hate: Thoughts on Attending a Ku Klux Klan Rally"? How can you discern that purpose? Is there evidence of a secondary purpose? If so, what? [1g(1)]
2. What audience is Jones writing for? Present evidence to support your answer. [1g(2)]
3. What is Jones's basic plan of organization? Is she concerned with both immediate and remote causes? If so, what are they and where are they mentioned?
4. Jones introduced her essay by briefly relating an incident that occurred at her office. How is that incident related to the rest of the essay? [1g and 2b]
5. Explain why the paragraphs in "The Price of Hate" are so short and comment on how Jones links them so that her essay flows smoothly. [3c]
6. Jones divided her essay into four sections. Why? [2c]

ANALYZING THE ELEMENTS

Grammar

1. The second sentence of paragraph 8 is a virtual sentence. Rewrite the sentence supplying the missing elements(s). Which is more effective? Why? [13]
2. Examine the tenses of the verbs in the final sentence of paragraph 10 and compare with the tenses of the verbs in the preceding sentences. Why do you think Jones changed the tense? Is the change effective? [17c]

Effective Sentences

1. What elements in the second sentence of paragraph 15 are parallel? How else might the sentence be written? Which is more effective? Why? [20]
2. The first sentence of paragraph 33 begins with the relative pronoun *that*. What does *that* refer to? How do you know? [16a]
3. Comment on the structure of the second sentence of paragraph 42. Is it effective? Why or why not? [22]

Punctuation and Mechanics

1. Comment on Jones's use of italics in the second sentence of paragraph 5. [34]
2. Justify the omission of the comma following the introductory adverbial clause in the first sentence of paragraph 16. [27]

Diction

1. In the first sentence of paragraph 35, Jones uses *weaved* rather than *wove*. Explain this usage. Consult your dictionary if necessary. [23b]
2. Jones uses the phrase "on a daily basis" in paragraph 32. Explain why this phrase could be considered wordy and rewrite the sentence. [25a and 25b]
3. The first sentence of paragraph 30 contains a personification. Explain. [24c]

BUILDING VOCABULARY

1. Find two synonyms for *proffer*. How is *proffer* different from *offer*?
2. What is the source of the word *jangle*?

SUGGESTIONS FOR WRITING

1. Write an essay about an event that made you change your view of yourself or your world, explaining why you changed.
2. Write an essay about an event or circumstance in your life (or the life of someone you know) that resulted in a chain of causes.

On Warts
Lewis Thomas

Born in New York in 1913, Lewis Thomas was educated at Princeton
University and Harvard Medical School. He has served on the faculties of
several medical schools and is still engaged in the practice of medicine as
president of the Memorial Sloan-Kettering Cancer Clinic. Since 1971 he has
been writing columns for the *New England Journal of Medicine*, many of
which have been collected in three books: *The Lives of a Cell: Notes of a
Biology Watcher*, for which Thomas won the National Book Award in 1974;
The Medusa and the Snail: More Notes of a Biology Watcher, for which he
won the American Book Award in 1979; and *Late Night Thoughts on
Listening to Mahler's Ninth Symphony* (1983). These collections have established Thomas's reputation as an essayist of extraordinary lucidity and grace—
qualities exemplified in the essay that follows.

Warts are wonderful structures. They can appear overnight on any part 1
of the skin, like mushrooms on a damp lawn, full grown and splendid in the
complexity of their architecture. Viewed in stained sections under a micro-
scope, they are the most specialized of cellular arrangements, constructed as
though for a purpose. They sit there like turreted mounds of dense, impene-
trable horn, impregnable, designed for defense against the world outside.

In a certain sense, warts are both useful and essential, but not for us. As 2
it turns out, the exuberant cells of a wart are the elaborate reproductive apparatus of a virus.

You might have thought from the looks of it that the cells infected by the 3
wart virus were using this response as a ponderous way of defending themselves against the virus, maybe even a way of becoming more distasteful, but
it is not so. The wart is what the virus truly wants; it can flourish only in cells
undergoing precisely this kind of overgrowth. It is not a defense at all; it is
an overwhelming welcome, an enthusiastic accommodation meeting the needs
of more and more virus.

The strangest thing about warts is that they tend to go away. Fully grown, 4
nothing in the body has so much the look of toughness and permanence as a
wart, and yet, inexplicably and often very abruptly, they come to the end of
their lives and vanish without a trace.

And they can be made to go away by something that can only be called 5
thinking, or something like thinking. This is a special property of warts which
is absolutely astonishing, more of a surprise than cloning or recombinant DNA
or endorphin or acupuncture or anything else currently attracting attention in

the press. It is one of the great mystifications of science: warts can be ordered off the skin by hypnotic suggestion.

Not everyone believes this, but the evidence goes back a long way and   6
is persuasive. Generations of internists and dermatologists, and their grandmothers for that matter, have been convinced of the phenomenon. I was once told by a distinguished old professor of medicine, one of Sir William Osler's original bright young men, that it was his practice to paint gentian violet over a wart and then assure the patient firmly that it would be gone in a week, and he never saw it fail. There have been several meticulous studies by good clinical investigators, with proper controls. In one of these, fourteen patients with seemingly intractable generalized warts on both sides of the body were hypnotized, and the suggestion was made that all the warts on one side of the body would begin to go away. Within several weeks the results were indisputably positive; in nine patients, all or nearly all of the warts on the suggested side had vanished, while the control side had just as many as ever.

It is interesting that most of the warts vanished precisely as they were in-   7
structed, but it is even more fascinating that mistakes were made. Just as you might expect in other affairs requiring a clear understanding of which is the right and which the left side, one of the subjects got mixed up and destroyed the warts on the wrong side. In a later study by a group at the Massachusetts General Hospital, the warts on both sides were rejected even though the instructions were to pay attention to just one side.

I have been trying to figure out the nature of the instructions issued by   8
the unconscious mind, whatever that is, under hypnosis. It seems to me hardly enough for the mind to say, simply, get off, eliminate yourselves, without providing something in the way of specifications as to how to go about it.

I used to believe, thinking about this experiment when it was just pub-   9
lished, that the instructions might be quite simple. Perhaps nothing more detailed than a command to shut down the flow through all the precapillary arterioles in and around the warts to the point of strangulation. Exactly how the mind would accomplish this with precision, cutting off the blood supply to one wart while leaving others intact, I couldn't figure out, but I was satisfied to leave it there anyhow. And I was glad to think that my unconscious mind would have to take the responsibility for this, for if I had been one of the subjects I would never have been able to do it myself.

But now the problem seems much more complicated by the information   10
concerning the viral etiology of warts, and even more so by the currently plausible notion that immunologic mechanisms are very likely implicated in the rejection of warts.

If my unconscious can figure out how to manipulate the mechanisms   11
needed for getting around that virus, and for deploying all the various cells in the correct order for tissue rejection, then all I have to say is that my unconscious is a lot further along than I am. I wish I had a wart right now, just to see if I am that talented.

There ought to be a better word than "Unconscious," even capitalized,   12
for what I have, so to speak, in mind. I was brought up to regard this aspect
of thinking as a sort of private sanitarium, walled off somewhere in a suburb
of my brain, capable only of producing such garbled information as to keep
my mind, my proper Mind, always a little off balance.

But any mental apparatus that can reject a wart is something else again.   13
This is not the sort of confused, disordered process you'd expect at the hands
of the kind of Unconscious you read about in books, out at the edge of things
making up dreams or getting mixed up on words or having hysterics. Whatever,
or whoever, is responsible for this has the accuracy and precision of a surgeon.
There almost has to be a Person in charge, running matters of meticulous detail beyond anyone's comprehension, a skilled engineer and manager, a chief
executive officer, the head of the whole place. I never thought before that I
possessed such a tenant. Or perhaps more accurately, such a landlord, since I
would be, if this is in fact the situation, nothing more than a lodger.

Among other accomplishments, he must be a cell biologist of world class,   14
capable of sorting through the various classes of one's lymphocytes, all with
quite different functions which I do not understand, in order to mobilize the
right ones and exclude the wrong ones for the task of tissue rejection. If it
were left to me, and I were somehow empowered to call up lymphocytes and
direct them to the vicinity of my wart (assuming that I could learn to do such
a thing), mine would come tumbling in all unsorted, B cells and T cells, sup-
pressor cells and killer cells, and no doubt other cells whose names I have not
learned, incapable of getting anything useful done.

Even if immunology is not involved, and all that needs doing is to shut   15
off the blood supply locally, I haven't the faintest notion how to set that up.
I assume that the selective turning off of arterioles can be done by one or another chemical mediator, and I know the names of some of them, but I wouldn't
dare let things like these loose even if I knew how to do it.

Well, then, who does supervise this kind of operation? Someone's got to,   16
you know. You can't sit there under hypnosis, taking suggestions in and having them acted on with such accuracy and precision, without assuming the
existence of something very like a controller. It wouldn't do to fob off the
whole intricate business on lower centers without sending along a quite detailed set of specifications, way over my head.

Some intelligence or other knows how to get rid of warts, and this is a   17
disquieting thought.

It is also a wonderful problem, in need of solving. Just think what we   18
would know, if we had anything like a clear understanding of what goes on
when a wart is hypnotized away. We would know the identity of the cellular
and chemical participants in tissue rejection, conceivably with some added information about the ways that viruses create foreignness in cells. We would
know how the traffic of these reactants is directed, and perhaps then be able
to understand the nature of certain diseases in which the traffic is being conducted in wrong directions, aimed at the wrong cells. Best of all, we would

be finding out about a kind of superintelligence that exists in each of us, infinitely smarter and possessed of technical know-how far beyond our present understanding. It would be worth a War on Warts, a Conquest of Warts, a National Institute of Warts and All.

✱

RESPONDING TO THE WHOLE ESSAY

1. What can you say about the audience for whom Lewis Thomas wrote "On Warts"? Can you point to evidence that he was writing for his fellow physicians? Does anything in the essay seem to indicate that Thomas also had a wider audience in mind? [1g(2)]
2. How would you characterize Thomas's purpose or purposes in "On Warts"? Is his aim chiefly expressive, informative, or persuasive? Can you point to evidence of all three aims? [1g(1)]
3. Where in the essay does Thomas state causes? What effects does he assign to those causes? Which are immediate (direct) causes? How does Thomas deal with remote causes?
4. Point to examples of inductive reasoning in the essay. Would you expect to find inductive reasoning in many essays that involve cause and effect? Why or why not? [1e]
5. Where does Thomas make clear what his thesis is? [2c]
6. How is Thomas's conclusion (paragraph 18) related to the rest of the essay? Does it summarize the essay? Does it indicate new directions for exploration? Point out how each sentence in the conclusion is prepared for earlier in the essay. [28f(2); 32f]
7. How would you describe the tone of "On Warts"? How is the tone related to Thomas's audience and purpose? [29a; 33a]

ANALYZING THE ELEMENTS

Grammar

1. Explain why the correlatives *both . . . and* are appropriate to link *useful* and *essential* in the first sentence of paragraph 2. [20d]
2. Can the sentence fragment that follows the first sentence in paragraph 9 be justified? Would Thomas have done better to attach it to the preceding sentence? How else might he have rewritten it? Would one tactic have been better than the other? [13]

Effective Sentences

1. Analyze the first sentence in paragraph 3. How does the imbalance in the length of the two main clauses contribute to the effectiveness of the sentence? Compare the third sentence of paragraph 9. [22a]
2. The final sentence of paragraph 14 contains many details. Explain how Thomas establishes the relationships among those details and thus keeps them from overpowering the sentence. [19a]

Punctuation and Mechanics

1. Thomas uses semicolons to separate independent clauses in the last two sentences in paragraph 3, but a colon to separate the independent clauses in the last sentence of paragraph 5. Account for the differences. [28a and 31d]
2. Thomas capitalized *unconscious* in the first sentence of paragraph 12, and *mind* in the last. What does this capitalization indicate about how Thomas wants the reader to understand the sentence? [33a]

Diction

1. Thomas makes frequent and effective use of similes and metaphors. Find as many as you can, and explain why each is appropriate. [24a(4)]
2. Thomas occasionally uses medical terms in "On Warts" and also words that are not part of most people's everyday vocabulary. Look up the following medical terms (using a medical dictionary if necessary): *cloning, recombinant DNA,* and *endorphin* (paragraph 5); *gentian violet* (paragraph 6); *precapillary arterioles* (paragraph 9); *etiology* (paragraph 10); and *lymphocytes* (paragraph 14). Then explain the probable reason Thomas used *impregnable* (paragraph 1) instead of *unconquerable; ponderous* (paragraph 3) instead of *heavy; meticulous* instead of *careful; intractable* instead of *stubborn* (paragraph 6); and *plausible* instead of *believable* (paragraph 10). [23 and 24]

BUILDING VOCABULARY

1. What elements is the word *architecture* made up of? List as many words as you can think of using the first two roots.
2. What are the sources of the words *meticulous, exuberant,* and *fob*? What does each mean?

SUGGESTIONS FOR WRITING

1. Select some illness or other unwelcome condition, and in a short essay explain the cause(s). Consider both immediate and (if possible) remote causes. Some possibilities: sunburn, near- (or far-) sightedness, tooth decay, a hangover, sneezing, yawning, snoring, blushing, hiccups.
2. Write a short essay exploring probable effects, taking as your topic "If____could be cured by hypnosis. . . ." (You fill in the blank, possibly with one of the conditions referred to in question 1.)
3. Write a cause-and-effect essay explaining how current medical thinking validates some old-fashioned explanation of illness or cure for illness. (For example, the old-fashioned belief that chicken soup is good for what ails you has been validated by the discovery of minute amounts of penicillin in chicken soup.)

And Here's the Pitch
John M. Williams

John M. Williams publishes *Assistive Technology News* and writes a biweekly assistive technology column for *Business Week Online*.

There is a quiet, politically correct revolution taking place on our TV screens. It is led by more than 100 high-profile corporations eager to tap a new market and willing to cough up around $150 million in creative and developmental costs with major ad agencies to do so, according to *Advertising Age*, the industry's publication of record. Some are doing it to soften their hard-core image as greedy corporate monoliths. Others are aiming to attract new customers. They all recognize that the time is right to buck the ad industry's long-held tendency to show only "perfect" people on TV commercials.

What's up in ad land? Agencies are using people with a wide range of disabilities in TV spots, plugging everything from Internet search engines to Oreos. The emotionally charged commercials feature shopping, eating, using assistive technology in the workplace, traveling, playing, skiing, driving, drinking soft drinks, eating snacks, teaching, learning and doing the full range of activities that traditional ads have used. The commercials are running during prime time and top-rated sports events in major markets. They are getting high marks from industry insiders, consumers and advocates in the disability movement for the indelible, positive images of ability they portray and their contribution to the progress of mainstreaming.

The ads arrive on a breath of fresh air that is filling the sails of an industry so vast ($79.3 billion a year in the U.S. in 1998 and growing at an 8.3% clip each year, with $1.92 billion a year in Internet advertising alone, according to a recent report from PricewaterhouseCoopers) that it takes quite a breeze to get it moving on a new course. With a few notable exceptions— the classic DuPont spot of over a decade ago that featured double amputee Bill Demby on the basketball court stands out—agencies and marketing experts have stayed close to the shoreline on the issue of showing people with disabilities. This reflects their adherence to the received wisdom that only the image of the ideal, as determined by demographic studies, now outdated, could move product. "Madison Avenue has always been scared of alienating the largest population in the country and so has always been behind the social times," admits Thomas Learner, a 15-year veteran of the industry. "We were creative in our messages, but we believed our audience was the same—white, able-bodied and perfect. I was Wall Street accounts during an era when we

177

did not show a black person in an ad. When we did, we sanitized them. To show a disabled person using products went against the mainstream Madison Avenue's paternalistic view."

The social and economic crosscurrents propelling this change are known to the vanguard of the disability community, but are still news to marketing experts. One important motive is the dire need for corporations to discover new markets, and the recognition that the 54 million Americans with disabilities have never been targeted in campaigns as rigorous and sophisticated as those used to reach smaller minority groups based on ethnicity or gender. The ads, which follow the paradigmatic shift from cause to customer marketing as pioneered by business strategy expert Jeannette Harvey, show that corporate America is waking up to the power of people with disabilities as consumers and borrowers. A second force is the rapid rise to social acceptability, and higher visibility, of celebrities, athletes and business leaders with disabilities. Cynics say that this is coupled with the need to clean up corporate images and present an aspect that is more caring and human. The fourth element is the movement toward reality and the use of actual people with experiences closer to our own in an effort to shake up the typical utopian expectations of what an ad will show and hold up the mirror to who we are.   4

The multimillion-dollar campaigns that massive corporations launch—as a rule of thumb, ad budgets equal between 3% and 10% of annual sales, and the world's leading advertiser, Procter & Gamble, spends over $5 billion annually—are moving rapidly into these waters. Just ask David Matthews, senior manager in charge of affirmative action at Nabisco, a food giant based in Parsippany, New Jersey, with $8 billion in sales, that is running a terrific new spot featuring a hard-of-hearing kid enjoying Oreos. He notes, "I think society's attitude toward people with disabilities has changed. The ADA has had impact in this field. We see more people with disabilities in the mainstream, and because we do, they are no longer the invisible consumers." Ann Smith, a company spokesperson, says, "We use people with disabilities in our Oreo ads because the message has impact. A commercial showing a deaf child signing to his mother communicates the power of the moment."   5

One of the real success stories has been a great spot for Internet search engine Snap.com, launched earlier this year to combat the wacky, bold commercials of rival Yahoo. To make users feel better and smarter than Yahoo-types, Snap.com turned to the concept of people helping people. A talented NBC scriptwriter named Mark Bennett, whose experience with an autistic relative gave him a window into the world of disability, created a touching ad in which a deaf boy boards a school bus in the morning and sits alone, under the watchful eye of a classmate who rushes to the computer that evening to learn how to sign so that on the ride the next morning they can communicate. One decision was a snap: Casting insisted that an actual deaf child star in the ad. As Bertina Ciccerelli, an NBC exec, says, "We took the high road. We wanted realism in the ad, and we achieved it." After the ad ran during NBC's prime time at the breaks in *Dateline* and *Providence*, Snap.com was   6 deluged with thousands of positive responses from the hard-of-hearing community.

By the year 2000, the spending power of people with disabilities will reach 7
the trillion-dollar mark. That's enough to catch the interest of automotive giant GM, where the disability angle is the frontier in a demographic landscape that has been mapped, sliced and diced so finely when it comes to minorities that it is a wonder there was this large a chunk left. Ken Tregenza, employment relations administrator at General Motors, Detroit, says, "Using people with disabilities in ads is becoming part of our institutionalized thinking at GM and of course we see it at other companies. We now recognize there is a market out there for accessible vans and other products. We recognize them as consumers." Keeping up the pace, Saturn, Ford and Chrysler have also turned to ads featuring people with disabilities.

Beyond Nabisco, Microsoft and the Big Three, ads have either appeared 8
or are in the works at IBM, McDonald's, AT&T, Bell Atlantic, Pacific Bell, Chevron, Campbell's, Target, Gatorade, Nike, VISA, General Mills, Wal-Mart, K-Mart, Coca Cola, Pepsi, Disney, Hallmark, DuPont, JC Penney, Sears, Bank of America, The Gap, Charles Schwab, Starbucks, NationsBank and Unum. Ad industry insiders, including sources at NW Ayers, J.Walter Thompson and BBDO, three of the major agencies, project that the current ads are only the tip of the iceberg.

Change of this magnitude usually comes from the top. Getting the CEO's 9
commitment to use people with disabilities counts for winning more than half the battle, particularly in a tradition-bound field such as advertising where the rank and file have to be kicked and dragged into giving up their familiar fare. Charles Schwab's name is on the door, and he happens to have a disability (dyslexia), so it is not surprising that the brokerage's ads, including one very powerful spot currently running that features a blind investor, are disability friendly. Another force is the focus groups composed either of people with disabilities or those who work with them. Eventually, their responses make it to the small screen. "We must develop ads that include disabled people in the mainstream of the community's perception of the abilities a disabled person has," says Tregenza. "Our ads cannot be so narrow that they only appeal to disabled consumers. The able-bodied population must be able to identify with the product being promoted, too."

The ratings are already coming in, and the scores are high. McDonald's, 10
one of the first companies to show people signing in their ads, reports a marked increase in business from the blind, hard-of-hearing and wheelchair-using public. K-Mart and Wal-Mart have reported similar increases in their stores. It also shows in their hiring. McDonald's note that more than 70 percent of their restaurant managers report hiring a disabled worker. "We value our customers and workers with disabilities. We have gained from using people with disabilities in our ads, and we are better and stronger for doing so," says Rogercarole Rogers of McDonald's. Microsoft, GM, Boeing, Wal-Mart, K-Mart, IBM are inundated with resumes from people with disabilities applying for

jobs. At IBM, Paul Luther, a specialist in assistive technology based in Austin, Texas, says, "When we advertise people with disabilities using our products, we sell more of those products."

One of the most dramatic instances of the direct lift given to brand aware- 11
ness by an ad featuring people with disabilities came from a spot for U.S. Robotics featuring the great astrophysicist Stephen Hawking. According to Michael Diedrich of the boutique advertising firm Leap Frog, when U.S. Robotics conducted the "pre-post" study to measure impact, showed that over the course of just four months after the ads appeared, brand awareness leaped from 36 percent to 48 percent, an increase that Diedrich calls "significant." In the all-important category of recall, the jump from 52 percent to 67 percent was considered by Diedrich to be (excuse the pun) astronomical. The positive effect on brand awareness was directly traced to a similar dramatic increase in advertising awareness, which jumped from 19 percent to 39 percent. Diedrich, who created the campaign, was ecstatic. "Talk about a breakthrough! These are tremendous gains, particularly in light of the loud 'noise' in the modem category of late. In short, the results are phenomenal."

The community's response to using the ads is enormous and positive. 12
Companies receive hundreds and sometimes thousands of favorable letters from people with disabilities, and their parents, relatives and friends after an ad is shown. Smith says, "People tell us in their letters they remember our ads with disabled people in them because it shows a special bond between the people in the ads. Their responses are what we are looking for." When DuPont debuted the Bill Demby basketball spots in 1987, the thousands of letters they received in the first week prompted the company to pull the rest of its other commercials for an entire season.

Just about the only downside to the trend is grumbling from those in the 13
disability community who find the images too glossy and upbeat. The executive director of a well-known national service organization in the Midwest, speaking on condition of anonymity, complains, "There is a problem showing the positive images of disabled people on TV. In raising money, we appeal to the paternalism of the giver. If that paternalism is not there, we have more trouble raising money to find cures." But the United Way, beset by a bout of bad publicity amid charges of corruption five years ago, made a comeback with a series of TV ads that depict the people with disabilities who have been the beneficiaries of their funding. Audience studies showed a marked increase in the reputation of United Way for doing so, according to Mario Pellegrini, who writes and directs the ads for Vital Productions. They run as public service announcements during broadcasts of NFL games as well as in movie theaters.

The darker side to the phenomenon is the latent fear of reprisal from a 14
minority group that, so far, has not been known for its consumer activism. In the boardrooms of major American companies, memories of the ethnic boycots of the 60s die hard. While most disability advocacy groups focus their attention on government, the prospect of pickets in wheelchairs, backed by

family and friends, is daunting. A bitter foretaste of how this could happen was experienced a decade ago when country and western singer Mel Tellis, who stutters, was used in a humorous ad campaign by Petrofina promoting oil and gas products. The backlash from disability organizations was fast and furious, and the ads were pulled within a week, in part because of the picketing and boycots. That kind of painfully negative spin is yet another reason to keep the new ad campaigns disability-friendly. As they say on Madison Avenue, where disability is hot, we'll run it up the flagpole and see who salutes.

✳

RESPONDING TO THE WHOLE ESSAY

1. This essay was published in a magazine about disabilities. Would it require any changes to be published for a more general audience? [1g(2)]
2. Does the essay focus primarily on causes or effects?
3. Does the author reveal any bias toward his subject? Explain. [31(3)]
4. Does the author use adequate examples? Are they well selected? [2d(2)]
5. Is Williams's comparison of the depiction of the disabled in advertising to that of ethnic minorities appropriate? Why or why not? [2e(5)]

ANALYZING THE ELEMENTS

Grammar

1. In the third sentence of paragraph 6, find all the pronouns. Are they in the correct case and number? [16]
2. Identify the subject and the predicate in the first sentence of paragraph 9. [11a]

Effective Sentences

1. Is the opening sentence effective? Why or why not? [3b(1)]
2. What is the metaphor in paragraph 3? Is it effective? Why or why not? [24a(4)]

Punctuation and Mechanics

1. Why does Williams include the word *perfect* in quotation marks in paragraph 1? [30d]
2. How does Williams punctuate the titles of television programs? [34a]

Diction

1. How many acronyms can you find in this essay? Does Williams identify them all, or does he expect the reader to recognize them? [35f]
2. How many different disabilities does Williams refer to specifically? How does he refer to them? Does he use the language you are accustomed to? Is his language "politically correct"?

BUILDING VOCABULARY

1. What does *paternalistic* mean? Does Williams use the word accurately in paragraph 3?
2. What is *mainstreaming*? How is that word used specifically in talking about people with disabilities?
3. Look up the following words: *monoliths* (paragraph 1), *paradigmatic* (paragraph 4), *beneficiaries* (paragraph 13), *boycotts* (paragraph 14).

SUGGESTIONS FOR WRITING

1. Watch television over a period of a few days and observe the commercials shown either during a specific time (after school, during sports events, etc.). Describe how well the commercials reflect their intended audience. Do they show the viewers as they are or as they want to be?
2. Write an essay in which you reflect on a typical day and how it would be different if you had a physical disability.

Growing Up in Black and White
Jack E. White

Jack White, author of the "Dividing Line" column and national correspondent for *Time* magazine, is the first African-American journalist to rise to the
high-ranking positions of nation editor with *Time* and senior producer for
domestic news for ABC News *World News Tonight*, as well as the first to
become a columnist for a national newsweekly. Beginning in 1972, White's
career with *Time* exceeds a quarter of a century and is marked by increasingly responsible posts: Nairobi bureau chief in 1980, correspondent for the
presidential campaign and member of the panel of journalists at the 1984
vice-presidential debate, Midwest bureau chief in 1985, and deputy chief of
correspondents in 1987, with responsibility for supervising 51 correspondents
in the magazine's ten domestic bureaus across the United States.

Before joining *Time*, White was a general assignments reporter for the
Washington Post and later for Tennessee's *Race Relations Reporter*. His articles have appeared in the *Columbia Journalism Review*, the *Progressive*,
Ebony Magazine, and *Our World News*, an online version of a forthcoming
black-controlled national newspaper. Among his numerous journalism awards
is the National Association of Black Journalists' First Place for Magazines,
the Griot Award from the New York Association of Black Journalists, and
the Unity Award from Lincoln University for commentary. He has also appeared on NBC's *Today Show*, PBS's *Washington Week in Review* and *Charlie
Rose* shows, BET's *Our Voices* and *Lead Story*, CNBC's *Equal Time* and
CNN's *Both Sides with Jesse Jackson* and the *McLaughlin Group*.

A native of North Carolina, White attended Swarthmore College and in
1976–1977 was a Nieman Fellow at Harvard University with a concentration on African affairs and American ethnic politics. He is married and the
father of three sons and a daughter.

"Mommy, I want to be white."   1

Imagine my wife's anguish and alarm when our beautiful brown-skinned   2
three-year-old daughter made that declaration. We thought we were doing
everything right to develop her self-esteem and positive racial identity. We
overloaded her toy box with black dolls. We carefully monitored the racial
content of TV shows and videos, ruling out *Song of the South* and *Dumbo*,
two classic Disney movies marred by demeaning black stereotypes. But we
saw no harm in *Pinocchio* which seemed as racially benign as *Sesame Street*
or *Barney* and a good deal more engaging. Yet now our daughter was saying
she wanted to be white, to be like the puppet who becomes a real boy in the
movie. How had she got that potentially soul-destroying idea and, even more
important, what should we do about it?

That episode was an unsettling reminder of the unique burden that haunts   3
black parents in America: helping their children come to terms with being black
in a country where the message too often seems to be that being white is better. Developing a healthy self-image would be difficult enough for black children with all the real-life reminders that blacks and whites are still treated differently. But it is made even harder by the seductive racial bias in TV, movies
and children's books, which seem to link everything beautiful and alluring with
whiteness while often treating blacks as afterthoughts. Growing up in this all-
pervading world of whiteness can be psychologically exhausting for black children just as they begin to figure out who they are. As a four-year-old boy told
his father after spending another day in the overwhelmingly white environment
of his Connecticut daycare facility, "Dad, I'm tired of being black."

In theory it should now be easier for children to develop a healthy sense   4
of black pride than it was during segregation. In 1947 psychologists Kenneth
and Mamie Clark conducted a famous experiment that demonstrated just how
much black children had internalized the hatred that society directed at their
race. They asked 253 black children to choose between four dolls, two black
and two white. The result: two-thirds of the children preferred white dolls.

The conventional wisdom had been that black self-hatred was a by-product   5
of discrimination that would wither away as society became more tolerant.
Despite the civil rights movement of the 1960s, the black-is-beautiful movement of the '70s, the proliferation of black characters on television shows
during the '80s and the renascent black nationalist movement of the '90s, the
pro-white message has not lost its power. In 1985 psychologist Darlene Powell-
Hopson updated the Clarks' experiment using black and white Cabbage Patch
dolls and got a virtually identical result: 65% of the black children preferred
white dolls. "Black is dirty," one youngster explained. Powell-Hopson thinks
the result would be the same if the test were repeated today.

Black mental-health workers say the trouble is that virtually all the   6
progress the U.S. has made toward racial fairness has been in one direction.
To be accepted by whites, blacks have to become more like them, while many
whites have not changed their attitudes at all. Study after study has shown
that the majority of whites, for all the commitment to equality they espouse,
still consider blacks to be inferior, undesirable and dangerous. "Even though
race relations have changed for the better, people maintain those old stereotypes," says Powell-Hopson. "The same racial dynamics occur in an integrated
environment as occurred in segregation; it's just more covert."

Psychiatrists say children as young as two can pick up these damaging   7
messages, often from subtle signals of black inferiority unwittingly embedded
in children's books, toys and TV programs designed for the white mainstream.
There are many more positive images about black people in the media than
there used to be, but there's still a lot that says that white is more beautiful
and powerful than black, that white is good and black is bad, says James P.
Comer, a Yale University psychiatrist who collaborated with fellow black psychiatrist Alvin F. Poussaint on *Raising Black Children* (Plume).

The bigotry is not usually as blatant as in Roald Dahl's *Charlie and the*   8
Chocolate Factory. When the book was published in 1964, the *New York Times* called it a "richly inventive and humorous tale." Blacks didn't see anything funny about having the factory staffed by "Oompaoompas," pygmy workers imported in shipping cartons from the jungle where they had been living in the trees.

Today white-controlled companies are doing a better job of erasing racially   9
loaded texts from children's books and movies. But those messages still get through, in part because they are at times so subtle even a specialist like Powell-Hopson misses them. She recently bought a book about a cat for her six-year-old daughter, who has a love of felines. Only when Powell-Hopson got home did she discover that the beautiful white cat in the story turns black when it starts behaving badly. Moreover, when the products are not objectionable, they are sometimes promoted in ways that unintentionally drive home the theme of black inferiority. Powell-Hopson cites a TV ad for dolls that displayed a black version in the background behind the white model "as though it were a second-class citizen."

Sadly, black self-hatred can also begin at home. Even today, says Powell-   10
Hopson, "many of us perpetuate negative messages, showing preference for lighter complexions, saying nappy hair is bad and straight hair is good, calling other black people 'niggers,' that sort of thing." This danger can be greater than the one posed by TV and the other media because children learn so much by simple imitation of the adults they are closest to. Once implanted in a toddler's mind, teachers and psychologists say, such misconceptions can blossom into a full-blown racial identity crisis during adolescence, affecting everything from performance in the classroom to a youngster's susceptibility to crime and drug abuse. But they can be neutralized if parents react properly.

In their book, Comer and Poussaint emphasize a calm and straightfor-   11
ward approach. They point out that even black children from affluent homes in integrated neighborhoods need reassurance about racial issues because from their earliest days they sense that their lives are "viewed cheaply by white society." If, for example, a black little girl says she wishes she had straight blond hair, they advise parents to point out "in a relaxed and unemotional manner...that she is black and that most black people have nice curly black hair, and that most white people have straight hair, brown, blond, black. At this age what you convey in your voice and manner will either make it O.K. or make it a problem."

Powell-Hopson, who along with her psychologist husband Derek, has   12
written *Different and Wonderful: Raising Black Children in a Race-Conscious Society* (Fireside), takes a more aggressive approach, urging black parents in effect to inoculate their children against negative messages at an early age. For example, the authors suggest that African-American parents whose children display a preference for white dolls or action figures should encourage them to play with a black one by "dressing it in the best clothes, or having it sit next to you, or doing anything you can think of to make your child

sense that you prefer that doll." After that, the Hopsons say, the child can be offered a chance to play with the toy, on the condition that "you promise to take the very best care of it. You know it is my favorite." By doing so, the Hopsons claim, "most children will jump at a chance to hold the toy even for a second."

White children are no less vulnerable to racial messages. Their reactions   13
can range from a false sense of superiority over blacks to an identification with sports superstars like Michael Jordan so complete that they want to become black. But if white parents look for guidance from popular child-care manuals, they won't find any. "I haven't included it because I don't feel like an expert in that area," says T. Berry Brazelton, author of *Infants and Mothers* and other child-care books. "I think it's a very, very serious issue that this country hasn't faced up to." Unless it does, the U.S. runs the risk of rearing another generation of white children crippled by the belief that they are better than blacks and black children who agree.

As for my daughter, we're concerned but confident. As Comer says, "In   14
the long run what children learn from their parents is more powerful than anything they get from any other source." When my little girl expressed the wish to be white, my wife put aside her anguish and smilingly replied that she is bright and black and beautiful, a very special child. We'll keep telling her that until we're sure she loves herself as much as we love her.

✳

RESPONDING TO THE WHOLE ESSAY

1. White establishes the context for "Growing Up in Black and White" in paragraph 1. What event occasioned the essay and what were the circumstances surrounding that event? [1g(3)]
2. What is White's main point and where does he state it? How is information about the relative numbers of positive black and white images related to the main idea? How is information about approaches to parenting related to the main idea? [2b]
3. Pointing to specific evidence in the essay, comment on White's purpose in "Growing Up in Black and White." To what extent can the essay be said to be expressive, informative, or persuasive? [1g(1)]
4. White indicates a number of causes, both immediate and remote, that contribute to the negative image African-Americans internalize about blackness. What are three of these causes? Which does White identify as immediate and which as remote causes?
5. For what kind of audience would you say White is writing? Does anything in the essay reveal or suggest the intended audience? Be specific. Might any particular group or groups find the essay offensive? If so, which, and why? [1g(2)]
6. What devices does White use to achieve coherence in paragraph 6? paragraph 12? [3c]

ANALYZING THE ELEMENTS

Grammar

1. What is the grammatical function of the infinitive phrase *To be accepted by whites* in the second sentence of paragraph 6? Of *embedded* in the first sentence of paragraph 7? [11]
2. In the second sentence of paragraph 7, the subject and the verb appear not to agree. Is there in fact a problem? If so, what is it? If not, why not? [17c]
3. How many separate simple sentences can you derive from the fourth sentence of paragraph 11? Has White gained anything by combining all of these ideas in a single sentence? If so, what? If not, why not? [21 and 25]

Effective Sentences

1. Rewrite the first sentence of paragraph 4 removing both instances of *it* as the subject. What would you say is accomplished by this revision? Which is better, the revision or the sentence as White wrote it? Explain. [25a(3)]
2. In the second sentence of paragraph 5, White employs two techniques that contribute to sentence effectiveness. Identify each technique and explain what it offers. [20a and 22e]
3. The fourth sentence of paragraph 9 is inverted. Explain what this inversion contributes to the effectiveness of the sentence. [21f]

Punctuation and Mechanics

1. Explain why White uses a colon in sentence 1 of paragraph 3, the final sentence of paragraph 4, and sentence 3 of paragraph 5. What other mark could he have used? [31d]
2. In paragraph 5, White uses two different styles to refer to dates. He also spells out some numbers but states others using Arabic numerals. Explain these practices. [35f]
3. In the first sentence of paragraph 6, the words following *say* are not enclosed in quotation marks. What reason can you give for that? [30a]

Diction

1. The word *virtual* is becoming quite common as a result of the contemporary interest in virtual reality. Dilbert once introduced his virtual girlfriend to his mother, philosophers of the Internet refer to virtual machines, and one wag wrote "virtual" when asked to state his place of employment. White uses *virtually* twice in "Growing Up in Black and White." Look the word up in a recent dictionary. Which meaning does White intend for *virtually* in paragraph 5? In paragraph 6? [24a]
2. Look up *O.K.* in at least three different dictionaries (such as *Webster's Collegiate Dictionary,* 10th edition, *The American Heritage Dictionary,* 3rd edition, or the *Random House Dictionary*). What does each give as its origin? Do any of the dictionaries comment on usage? If so, which one(s) and what do they say? [23a]
3. In "Growing Up in Black and White," three different terms refer to black people. Identify each of these terms and justify its use in its context. Is this usage racist? Why or why not?

BUILDING VOCABULARY

1. Look up the following words and note their etymology: *demeaning* (paragraph 2), *espouse* (paragraph 6), *covert* (paragraph 6), and *blatant* (paragraph 8). Comment on the role of the prefix or suffix (if any) in determining the meaning of the word.
2. Look carefully through "Growing Up in Black and White" to find at least three words formed using each of the following suffixes: *-ance*, *-ation*, *-ity*, and *-ment*. What are the words from which these are created? What class of words (part of speech) do these suffixes create?

SUGGESTIONS FOR WRITING

1. Write an essay in which you identify at least two influences in society that positively or negatively affected your own upbringing.
2. White describes how subtle elements in our society conspire to foster an unhealthy self-image in children. Write an essay in which you identify, describe, and explain the effect of such an element or combination of elements in your own life or in that of a person you know well. (The emphasis on slenderness or on keeping a stiff upper lip could be examples of such elements.)

✳

Chapter 6

Comparison and Contrast

Should you walk or take the bus? Vote Democratic or Republican (or not vote)? Major in classics or accounting? Watch the news or a comedy rerun? Order a pizza or cook? Such decisions—and hosts of others both trivial and important that you confront every day—require you to *compare* and *contrast* alternatives. You continually set objects, ideas, or possible courses of action side by side in your mind and consider their similarities and their differences in order to understand them better and make wise choices. And since understanding and intelligent decision-making are two of the most important goals of writing, comparison and contrast are important in your writing—especially college writing—as well as in your other activities.

Comparing, which focuses on similarities, and contrasting, which focuses on differences, may sound like contrary tasks, but in practice the two cannot be divorced (and so they are often referred to by the single term *comparison,* as we shall do in the following discussion). The reason is that only things that are likely to exhibit both similarities and differences are worth considering in a side-by-side, comparative way. What could be the point of enumerating the similarities of two things that are known to be identical, whether they are two identical spoons in a drawer or identical positions on a social issue? Conversely, why examine the differences between two things known to have *nothing* in common? Examining the merits of the electric shaver versus the "safety" razor can be productive because both are devices for separating hair from skin; exploring whether to shave with a blade or with a banana is not likely to be, shall we say, fruitful (except, perhaps, in the hands of an absurdist such as Steve Martin or Woody Allen). There must be some significant similarity in order for differences to be meaningful. In short, there must be a *basis for comparison.* When writing a comparison-and-contrast paper, always ask yourself, "Have I chosen for comparison two things whose similarities and differences are sufficient to make the comparison worthwhile for me and my readers?" The basis for comparison need not be obvious, however; you can *make* it clear. Separated by five hundred years, Christopher Columbus and the U.S. astronauts may seem to have little in common; yet in "Columbus and the Moon," in this section, Tom Wolfe finds and develops a strong basis for comparison in the fact that both were explorers and especially in the public response to the adventures of both. When the basis for comparison is not obvious, involving two essentially unlike things, it is a special kind of comparison called *analogy.* Analogy depends on pointing out uncommon or uncanny likenesses between two dissimilar things, usually one familiar and one unfamiliar.

Comparison can be useful for many purposes, as we have already hinted. Certainly it is an important tool for clarifying decisions for oneself: "Shall I major in classics or accounting? Let's see: here are the advantages of the one . . . and of the other. But on the other hand, these are the disadvantages of the one . . . and of the other." But a decision need not be at stake; writers often engage in comparison because what may be revealed is interesting or important in itself. When you consider two objects side by side, each emphasizes certain features of the other that would not be as evident if you examined the objects individually. That is why instructors in college courses so often give assignments that are comparative: compare two poems or two characters in a story or play; compare two biological specimens; compare two historic documents, such as the Magna Carta and the Constitution, or two figures, such as Ben Franklin and Thomas Jefferson, or conditions in the North and those in the South; and so forth. (Notice in Chapter 11, "The Essay Examination," that all three of Anne Nishijima's essay examination answers—in literature, history, and zoology—involve comparison to a significant degree.) Comparison can also be a powerful persuasive strategy: for example, a writer might contrast the conditions of life of a wealthy person with those of a poor or homeless person to dramatize the plight of the latter.

Basically, a comparison paper can be organized in either of two ways—*subject by subject* or *point by point*—or a combination of the two. A subject-by-subject comparison (also called a "whole-by-whole" or "block" comparison) is divided into two major blocks (plus, usually, an introduction and conclusion): the first block considers one of the items (ideas, courses of action) being compared and examines all the pertinent points; the second block then does the same for the other item (idea, course of action). A point-by-point (also called "part-by-part") comparison reverses this pattern; the points of comparison rather than the items themselves are the main basis or organization. One point or feature is raised at a time, and the items are compared in relation to that point before the next point is raised. An illustration will help to make this clear: a comparison of typical families in the 1950s with those in the 1990s. We can use either a block structure or a point-by-point structure. Thus a general outline of block structure would look something like the one on the left below. For point-by-point structure, the outline would look like the one on the right.

Subject by Subject	*Point by Point*
Fifties families [1st subj.]	Mothers' role [point 1]
Mothers' role [point 1]	Fifties families [1st subj.]
Fathers' role [point 2]	Nineties families [2nd subj.]
Children's role [point 3]	Fathers' role [point 2]

Nineties families [2nd subj.]   Fifties families [1st subj.]
   Mothers' role [point 1]   Nineties families [2nd subj.]
   Fathers' role [point 2]   Children's role [point 3]
   Children's role [point 3]   Fifties families [1st subj.]
                          Nineties families [2nd subj.]

Each of these arrangements has its advantages and disadvantages. The subject-by-subject organization has the advantage of helping the reader keep each subject in mind *as a whole*. But if this organization is used in a long, complex comparison, one with many points, the reader may have a hard time keeping all the points in mind until it is time to turn from one subject to the other. So the subject-by-subject arrangement is usually best suited to short, simple comparisons involving only a few points. The disadvantage of the point-by-point arrangement has already been implied: the reader tends to lose sight of the whole while focusing on the parts; but when the parts being examined are numerous, point-by-point is usually the practical choice. You can greatly diminish the drawbacks of either strategy if you include appropriate transitional devices to keep your reader "on the track" and if you supply reminders from time to time to help the reader see how your various points are related.

Subject-by-subject and point-by-point strategies can sometimes be combined in the same essay, as they are in Bruce Catton's "Grant and Lee: A Study in Contrasts." Catton employs a subject-by-subject approach in revealing the numerous differences between the two great Civil War generals—presenting first a full-length picture of Lee, then one of Grant. But he then shifts to a point-by-point approach in showing their similarities.

Balance is very important in writing comparisons. This does not mean that you are obliged to devote equal space and emphasis to every point or even to both of your subjects; your purpose will determine what should be emphasized. But your reader is certain to be puzzled, and perhaps confused, if you raise points about one subject that you ignore altogether in writing about the other.

In the following essay, notice how Keisha Jackson establishes fundamental similarities—a basis for comparison—as well as fundamental differences—a basis for contrast—before she develops each, using a subject-by-subject approach.

The Real Truth About Cats and Dogs

Context

Basis for
comparison

At least once a week I get an e-mail from a friend listing the undesirable qualities of cats. These examples of "humor" always come from dog people, who insist, in ignorance, that cats are lazy and selfish and have made fools of their owners. As the owner of a dog and two cats, I think I can make a more informed judgment about which makes the better pet.

Thesis

And for me, at least, cats are better than dogs.

Subject—
cleanliness

First of all, cats are clearly cleaner and easier to take care of than dogs. Rocky, my eight-year-old Golden Lab, has to be washed regularly. Every time it rains Rocky is covered in mud. I have to stop everything I'm doing and clean him up before he gets on my mom's furniture. I can't just leave him outside because he will bark and whine and annoy all the neighbors. Not only do I not have to clean my cats, they wouldn't permit it if I wanted to. They clean themselves several times a day. And they wouldn't go near mud.

Subject—
convenience in
maintenance

Although some might argue that litter boxes are inconvenient, I would much rather clean the litter box once a day than get out of bed in the middle of the night to let the dog out. Cats are self-maintaining when it comes to doing their business. They can stay in bed as long as I can. And I don't have to get up to feed them either. I leave water and dry food out so they can help themselves. Unlike dogs, cats will pace themselves when it comes to eating. If I left a week's worth of food out for Rocky, he would eat it all at once and then really need to go outside. As a result, I can be gone overnight or even for two nights and my cats will be okay, but Rocky requires maintenance throughout the day.

Subject—affection

Another myth about cats and dogs is that dogs are more affectionate than cats. Of course, cats are not as demonstrative as dogs are about showing you how much they love you, but I could do without the slobbering eighty pounds of love that is Rocky. He seems to love me the most when I'm all dressed up to go out. My two cats, Whitney and Mariah, on the other hand, are content to sleep in my lap while I'm reading or watching television. Cats are smart. They know you can have too much of a good thing.

Subject—laziness

Anyone who thinks cats are lazy and not playful has never seen a cat in the presence of a paper bag. My cats play several times a day. They chase each other around the house and they play with me, but they do not have to rely on anyone else for their amusement. They can turn anything into a toy. My cats love the little plastic rings that come around milk jugs. Sometimes Rocky's tail is the favored toy. But I've seen them play with toys and chase critters that I couldn't see. Rocky has to have a playmate, and that playmate is usually yours truly. Rocky doesn't care if I'm busy doing something else. And he would play all day if I would only cooperate. Sometimes I think Rocky would chase his tennis ball until he dropped dead. A cat would never do that. They know when to rest.

Conclusion— restatement of thesis

Don't get me wrong. I love my dog, but even Rocky—with the cat scratch across his nose—even Rocky would have to agree that cats are superior to dogs.

Commentary. Jackson introduces her essay by telling us what occasion stimulated her thinking on the subject—that is, that she receives regular e-mails from "dog people" that malign cats as lazy and selfish. She then draws a basis of comparison and cites her own authority, as an owner of both a dog and cats. Then she states her thesis: for her, cats are the superior pets. She devotes the next two paragraphs to explaining how cats pose less inconvenience than dogs. She uses the examples of their cleanliness and the convenience of feeding the cats and maintaining their litter box. She balances these details with contrasting details that support her thesis that dogs are more trouble.

Jackson then dispels the idea that cats are not affectionate. Again she uses details to describe both dogs and cats so that the reader can clearly see the basis of her preference for cats. The next paragraph argues that cats are not lazy as they are purported to be; Jackson uses the contrasting idea of cats' pacing themselves in terms of physical activity to point out that cats are generally smarter than dogs. This provides an effective transition to a humorous restatement of her thesis.

Grant and Lee: A Study in Contrasts
Bruce Catton

Bruce Catton (1899–1978) began his career as a journalist and worked for several newspapers, including the *Cleveland Plain Dealer*. His abiding interest in history, however, led to his becoming a noted authority on the Civil War, about which he published more than a dozen books. In 1954 he received both the Pulitzer Prize and the National Book Award for one of these, *A Stillness at Appomattox*. Among the others—all good reading for the nonspecialist as well as the historian—are *Mr. Lincoln's Army* (1960), *Never Call Retreat* (1965), *Terrible Swift Sword* (1967), *This Hallowed Ground* (1969), and *Gettysburg: The Final Fury* (1974). The essay that follows, "Grant and Lee: A Study in Contrasts," first appeared in a collection of historical essays written by prominent historians, *The American Story* (1956), and has been widely reprinted since. In it Catton compares and contrasts the two greatest Civil War generals in terms of the different traditions they represented.

When Ulysses S. Grant and Robert E. Lee met in the parlor of a modest house at Appomattox Court House, Virginia, on April 9, 1865, to work out the terms for the surrender of Lee's Army of Northern Virginia, a great chapter in American life came to a close, and a great new chapter began. 1

These men were bringing the Civil War to its virtual finish. To be sure, other armies had yet to surrender, and for a few days the fugitive Confederate government would struggle desperately and vainly, trying to find some way to go on living now that its chief support was gone. But in effect it was all over when Grant and Lee signed the papers. And the little room where they wrote out the terms was the scene of one of the poignant, dramatic contrasts in American history. 2

They were two strong men, these oddly different generals, and they represented the strengths of two conflicting currents that, through them, had come into final collision. 3

Back of Robert E. Lee was the notion that the old aristocratic concept might somehow survive and be dominant in American life. 4

Lee was tidewater Virginia, and in his background were family, culture, and tradition . . . the age of chivalry transplanted to a New World which was making its own legends and its own myths. He embodied a way of life that had come down through the age of knighthood and the English country squire. America was a land that was beginning all over again, dedicated to nothing much more complicated than the rather hazy belief that all men had equal rights, and should have an equal chance in the world. In such a land Lee stood 5 for the feeling that it was somehow of advantage to human society to have a pronounced inequality in the social structure. There should be a leisure class, backed by ownership of land; in turn, society itself should be keyed to the land as the chief source of wealth and influence. It would bring forth (according to this ideal) a class of men with a strong sense of obligation to the community; men who lived not to gain advantage for themselves, but to meet the solemn obligations which had been laid on them by the very fact that they were privileged. From them the country would get its leadership; to them it could look for the higher values—of thought, of conduct, of personal deportment—to give it strength and virtue.

Lee embodied the noblest elements of this aristocratic ideal. Through him, 6 the landed nobility justified itself. For four years, the Southern states had fought a desperate war to uphold the ideals for which Lee stood. In the end, it almost seemed as if the Confederacy fought for Lee; as if he himself was the Confederacy . . . the best thing that the way of life for which the Confederacy stood could ever have to offer. He had passed into legend before Appomattox. Thousands of tired, underfed, poorly clothed Confederate soldiers, long-since past the simple enthusiasm of the early days of the struggle, somehow considered Lee the symbol of everything for which they had been willing to die. But they could not quite put this feeling into words. If the Lost Cause, sanctified by so much heroism and so many deaths, had a living justification, its justification was General Lee.

Grant, the son of a tanner on the Western frontier, was everything Lee 7 was not. He had come up the hard way, and embodied nothing in particular except the eternal toughness and sinewy fiber of the men who grew up beyond the mountains. He was one of a body of men who owed reverence and obeisance to no one, who were self-reliant to a fault, who cared hardly anything for the past but who had a sharp eye for the future.

These frontier men were the precise opposites of the tidewater aristocrats. 8 Back of them, in the great surge that had taken people over the Alleghenies and into the opening Western country, there was a deep, implicit dissatisfaction with a past that had settled into grooves. They stood for democracy, not from any reasoned conclusion about the proper ordering of human society, but simply because they had grown up in the middle of democracy and knew how it worked. Their society might have privileges, but they would be privileges each man had won for himself. Forms and patterns meant nothing. No man was born to anything, except perhaps to a chance to show how far he could rise. Life was competition.

Yet along with this feeling had come a deep sense of belonging to a na- 9 tional community. The Westerner who developed a farm, opened a shop or set up in business as a trader, could hope to prosper only as his own community prospered—and his community ran from the Atlantic to the Pacific and from Canada down to Mexico. If the land was settled, with towns and highways and accessible markets, he could better himself. He saw his fate in terms of the nation's own destiny. As its horizons expanded, so did his. He

had, in other words, an acute dollars-and-cents stake in the continued growth
and development of his country.

And that, perhaps, is where the contrast between Grant and Lee becomes   10
most striking. The Virginia aristocrat, inevitably, saw himself in relation to
his own region. He lived in a static society which could endure almost anything except change. Instinctively, his first loyalty would go to the locality in
which that society existed. He would fight to the limit of endurance to defend it, because in defending it he was defending everything that gave his own
life its deepest meaning.

The Westerner, on the other hand, would fight with an equal tenacity for   11
the broader concept of society. He fought so because everything he lived by
was tied to growth, expansion, and a constantly widening horizon. What he
lived by would survive or fall with the nation itself. He could not possibly
stand by unmoved in the face of an attempt to destroy the Union. He would
combat it with everything he had, because he could only see it as an effort to
cut the ground out from under his feet.

So Grant and Lee were in complete contrast, representing two diametri-   12
cally opposed elements in American life. Grant was the modern man emerging; beyond him, ready to come on the stage, was the great age of steel and
machinery, of crowded cities and a restless, burgeoning vitality. Lee might have
ridden down from the old age of chivalry, lance in hand, silken banner fluttering over his head. Each man was the perfect champion of his cause, drawing both his strengths and his weaknesses from the people he led.

Yet, it was not all contrast, after all. Different as they were—in background,   13
in personality, in underlying aspiration—these two great soldiers had much in
common. Under everything else, they were marvelous fighters. Furthermore,
their fighting qualities were really very much alike.

Each man had, to begin with, the great virtue of utter tenacity and fi-   14
delity. Grant fought his way down the Mississippi Valley in spite of acute personal discouragement and profound military handicaps. Lee hung on in the
trenches at Petersburg after hope itself had died. In each man there was an
indomitable quality . . . the born fighter's refusal to give up as long as he can
still remain on his feet and lift his two fists.

Daring and resourcefulness they had, too; the ability to think faster and   15
move faster than the enemy. These were the qualities which gave Lee the dazzling campaigns of Second Manassas and Chancellorsville and won Vicksburg
for Grant.

Lastly, and perhaps greatest of all, there was the ability, at the end, to turn   16
quickly from war to peace once the fighting was over. Out of the way these two
men behaved at Appomattox came the possibility of a peace of reconciliation.
It was a possibility not wholly realized in the years to come, but which did, in
the end, help the two sections to become one nation again . . . after a war whose
bitterness might have seemed to make such a reunion wholly impossible. No
part of either man's life became him more than the part he played in their brief
meeting in the McLean house at Appomattox. Their behavior there put all

succeeding generations of Americans in their debt. Two great Americans, Grant and Lee—very different, yet under everything very much alike. Their encounter at Appomattox was one of the great moments of American history.

✳

RESPONDING TO THE WHOLE ESSAY

1. Is Catton's purpose in "Grant and Lee: A study in Contrasts" primarily expressive, informative, or persuasive? What evidence can you find to support your answer? Is there evidence of all three purposes? [1g(1)]
2. What kind of audience do the details in "Grant and Lee: A Study in Contrasts" lead you to imagine Catton had in mind? In what way(s) are you or are you not a member of that audience? [1g(2)]
3. What advantage does Catton gain by contrasting the two generals before he compares them? What would have been the effect of approaching the subject the other way?
4. Analyze Catton's use of both subject-by-subject (whole-by-whole or block) organization and point-by-point (part-by-part) organization (explained in the introduction to this section). Where, and for what kind of information, is each pattern used? Might alternative arrangements have been as effective? Why or why not?
5. Analyze Catton's use of various transitional devices throughout the essay to help readers keep their bearings. In particular, comment on the functions of paragraphs 12 and 13 within the whole essay and on the transition between these two paragraphs. [3d]
6. Explain how the introduction and conclusion frame the essay, providing and reinforcing the basis for Catton's comparison. [3b]

ANALYZING THE ELEMENTS

Grammar

1. In the third sentence of paragraph 6, Catton writes "for which Lee stood." Would the meaning of the sentence change if Catton had instead written "which Lee stood for"? To what does *which* refer in both versions? What is the probable reason Catton preferred the former? Is that choice obligatory? [11c and 11d]
2. The next-to-last sentence of the essay is a deliberate fragment. What reason might Catton have had for using it? Had Catton written a complete sentence instead, what would it have been? How would the effect have been different? [13]

Effective Sentences

1. Comment on the use and effectiveness of parallel structure in the last sentence of paragraph 5. [20a]
2. Explain how Catton's inversion of normal sentence order in the first sentence of paragraph 15 contributes to the effectiveness of the sentence. [21f]

Punctuation and Mechanics

1. Explain the use of the semicolon in the sixth sentence of paragraph 5 and the fourth sentence of paragraph 6. What other mark of punctuation could have been used? Explain what advantage(s) the semicolon offers. [28b]
2. Explain Catton's use of ellipsis points in paragraphs 5, 6, 14, and 16. What other kinds of punctuation might he have used? Would other punctuation have made the sentences more or less effective? Why? [31i]

Diction

1. Explain the meaning (both the denotation and connotations) of *tidewater* in the first sentences of paragraph 5 and paragraph 8. [24a(1) and 24a(2)]
2. Examine the ways in which Catton's use of images and figurative language contributes to the effectiveness of the essay—for example, the image of Lee "lance in hand, silken banner fluttering over his head" (paragraph 12) and of Grant embodying "the eternal toughness and sinewy fiber of the men who grew up beyond the mountains" (paragraph 7). [24a(4)]

BUILDING VOCABULARY

1. Look up *static, sinewy, fidelity,* and *daring* and state the meaning of each. What are their antonyms?
2. What are the sources of *poignant* and *chivalry*? Approximately when did each word come into the English language?

SUGGESTIONS FOR WRITING

1. Write an essay comparing and contrasting two professionals you know (for instance, teachers, ministers, doctors) who represent different professional styles but who are both excellent in their work.
2. Report an imaginary encounter between two figures who have something in common but whose differences are striking enough to make the meeting interesting to observe. Locate your characters wherever it suits you: at a party, in adjacent airplane seats on a long flight, in the dentist's waiting room, or even in a chance encounter in heaven (or elsewhere, as may be appropriate). A few possibilities: Citizen Kane and Mike Wallace; George Washington and Yasser Arafat; John Lennon and Caruso; Charlie Brown and Doonesbury; General Patton and Barry Switzer; Babe Ruth and Nolan Ryan; Beethoven and Mozart; Wyatt Earp and J. Edgar Hoover.

Columbus and the Moon
Tom Wolfe

A Virginian who attended Washington and Lee University and then earned a Ph.D. in American studies from Yale University, Tom Wolfe turned to journalism instead of the academic world, working first as a reporter for the *Washington Post* and then as a feature writer for *Esquire* and *New York* (when it was still the Sunday magazine of the late *New York Herald Tribune* and also afterward). He is a frequent contributor to *Harper's* and other magazines. Wolfe is one of the most gifted practitioners of "the new journalism"—a style of reporting in which the writer's personality is given full sway. His books (whose titles reflect his unusual style) include *The Kandy-Colored Tangerine-Flake Streamline Baby*, *The Electric Kool-Aid Acid Test*, and *The Pump House Gang* (all 1968); *Radical Chic and Maumauing the Flak Catchers* (1970); *The Bonfire of the Vanities* (1985); two books on art and architecture, *The Painted Word* (1975) and *From Bauhaus to Our House* (1981); and *The Right Stuff* (1979), which won him the American Book Award. In "Columbus and the Moon," Wolfe traces the similarities and differences between the space explorations through the 1970s and the explorations of Columbus in the fifteenth century.

The National Aeronautics and Space Administration's moon landing ten   1
years ago today was a Government project, but then so was Columbus's voyage to America in 1492. The Government, in Columbus's case, was the Spanish Court of Ferdinand and Isabella. Spain was engaged in a sea race with Portugal in much the same way that the United States would be caught up in a space race with the Soviet Union four and a half centuries later.

The race in 1492 was to create the first shipping lane to Asia. The   2
Portuguese expeditions had always sailed east, around the southern tip of Africa. Columbus decided to head due west, across open ocean, a scheme that was feasible only thanks to a recent invention—the magnetic ship's compass. Until then ships had stayed close to the great land masses even for the longest voyages. Likewise, it was only thanks to an invention of the 1940s and early 1950s, the high-speed electronic computer, the NASA would even consider propelling astronauts out of the Earth's orbit and toward the moon.

Both NASA and Columbus made not one but a series of voyages. NASA   3
landed men on six different parts of the moon. Columbus made four voyages to different parts of what he remained convinced was the east coast of Asia. As a result both NASA and Columbus had to keep coming back to the Government with their hands out, pleading for refinancing. In each case the

reply of the Government became, after a few years: "This is all very impressive, but what earthly good is it to anyone back home?"

Columbus was reduced to making the most desperate claims. When he   4
first reached land in 1492 at San Salvador, off Cuba, he expected to find gold, or at least spices. The Arawak Indians were awed by the strangers and their ships, which they believed had descended from the sky, and they presented them with their most prized possessions, live parrots and balls of cotton. Columbus soon set them digging for gold, which didn't exist. So he brought back reports of fabulous riches in the form of manpower; which is to say, slaves. He was not speaking of the Arawaks, however. With the exception of criminals and prisoners of war, he was supposed to civilize all natives and convert them to Christianity. He was talking about the Carib Indians, who were cannibals and therefore qualified as criminals. The Caribs would fight down to the last unbroken bone rather than endure captivity, and few ever survived the voyages back to Spain. By the end of Columbus's second voyage, in 1496, the Government was becoming testy. A great deal of wealth was going into voyages to Asia, and very little was coming back. Columbus made his men swear to return to Spain saying that they had not only reached the Asian mainland, they had heard Japanese spoken.

Likewise by the early 1970s, it was clear that the moon was in economic   5
terms pretty much what it looked like from Earth, a gray rock. NASA, in the quest for appropriations, was reduced to publicizing the "spinoffs" of the space program. These included Teflon-coated frying pans, a ballpoint pen that would write in a weightless environment, and a computerized biosensor system that would enable doctors to treat heart patients without making house calls. On the whole, not a giant step for mankind.

In 1493, after his first voyage, Columbus had ridden through Barcelona   6
at the side of King Ferdinand in the position once occupied by Ferdinand's late son, Juan. By 1500, the bad-mouthing of Columbus had reached the point where he was put in chains at the conclusion of his third voyage and returned to Spain in disgrace. NASA suffered no such ignominy, of course, but by July 20, 1974, the fifth anniversary of the landing of Apollo 11, things were grim enough. The public had become gloriously bored by space exploration. The fifth anniversary celebration consisted mainly of about 200 souls, mostly NASA people, sitting on folding chairs underneath a camp meeting canopy on the marble prairie outside the old Smithsonian Air Museum in Washington listening to speeches by Neil Armstrong, Michael Collins, and Buzz Aldrin and watching the caloric waves ripple.

Extraordinary rumors had begun to circulate about the astronauts. The most   7
lurid said that trips to the moon, and even into earth orbit, had so traumatized the men, they had fallen victim to religious and spiritualist manias or plain madness. (Of the total seventy-three astronauts chosen, one, Aldrin, is known to have suffered from depression, rooted, as his own memoir makes clear, in matters that had nothing to do with space flight. Two teamed up in an evangelical organization, and one set up a foundation for the scientific study of psychic phenomena—

interests the three of them had developed long before they flew in space.) The NASA budget, meanwhile, had been reduced to the light-bill level.

Columbus died in 1590, nearly broke and stripped of most of his honors 8 as Spain's Admiral of the Ocean, a title he preferred. It was only later that history began to look upon him not as an adventurer who had tried and failed to bring home gold—but as a man with a supernatural sense of destiny, whose true glory was his willingness to plunge into the unknown, including the remotest parts of the universe he could hope to reach.

NASA still lives, albeit in reduced circumstances, and whether or not his- 9 tory will treat NASA like the admiral is hard to say.

The idea that the exploration of the rest of the universe is its own reward is 10 not very popular, and NASA is forced to keep talking about things such as bigger communications satellites that will enable live television transmission of European soccer games at a fraction of the current cost. Such notions as "building a bridge to the stars for mankind" do not light up the sky today—but may yet.

✳

RESPONDING TO THE WHOLE ESSAY

1. To what extent is Wolfe concerned here with informing and to what extent with persuading the reader? Which aim is dominant? How does Wolfe's choice of subjects to compare serve this aim? Is that an expressive dimension in the essay as well? Point to evidence. [1g(1)]
2. Wolfe takes pains to provide background information about his two subjects. What does this effort tell us about the audience he had in mind as he wrote? [1g(2)]
3. What is Wolfe's basis for comparing Columbus and NASA? How is the essay organized? How else might it have been organized? What advantage did arranging the essay as it appears offer?
4. Comment on the title of Wolfe's essay. What does it promise the reader? How does it reflect the approach Wolfe takes in the essay? [3b(3)]
5. How does Wolfe accomplish transitions between paragraphs? Explain, giving specific examples. [3d]
6. Explain how Wolfe's introduction arouses the reader's interest at the same time that it announces the subject of the essay. What is the effect of Wolfe's conclusion? [3b(1) and 3b(2)]

ANALYZING THE ELEMENTS

Grammar

1. The third sentence in paragraph 4 and the first sentence in paragraph 10 are both compound-complex sentences. Explain what a compound-complex sentence is, and, as fully as you can, comment on what rhetorical advantages these sentences offer Wolfe. [12c(4)]
2. The final sentence in paragraph 4 may appear at first glance to be a comma splice; however, it is not. Explain why a comma between *mainland* and *they* is sufficient

and why it is unnecessary to add a coordinating conjunction. How does handling the sentence this way make it more effective? [14a]

3. The last sentence of paragraph 5 is a fragment. What reason might Wolfe have had for using it here? [13]

Effective Sentences

1. How does parallel structure contribute to the effectiveness of the final sentence in paragraph 6? [20a]
2. Wolfe could have begun the second sentence of paragraph 8 as follows: "Only later did history begin to look upon him. . . ." Is Wolfe's actual beginning better? Why or why not?

Punctuation and Mechanics

1. Justify Wolfe's capitalization of *Government* in the first sentence of paragraph 1 and *Court* in the second. [33a]
2. Explain why it is unnecessary to use quotation marks in the second sentence of paragraph 7. What advantage does this method of quotation offer Wolfe? What disadvantage would the use of quotation marks have entailed? [30a]

Diction

1. Explain how the following words and phrases contribute to the tone Wolfe establishes in the essay: *their hands out* (paragraph 3), *testy* (paragraph 4), *badmouthing* (paragraph 6), *light-bill level* (paragraph 7), *broke* (paragraph 8). [24a]
2. Wolfe uses two different kinds of allusions in "Columbus and the Moon." Explain what "a giant step for mankind" (paragraph 5) alludes to. Then explain what "in reduced circumstances" (paragraph 9) alludes to. How do these allusions differ? How does each expand the meaning of the essay?

BUILDING VOCABULARY

1. List at least five other words that are derived from the same root word as *expedition*.
2. What does the prefix *circum-* mean? List at least three words that begin with it.

SUGGESTIONS FOR WRITING

1. Considering either your college career or your working career as a kind of voyage, think of two different directions in which you could go and contrast them.
2. Both explorations Wolfe describes consumed enormous sums of money that conceivably could have been used for human benefit in other ways. Think of an alternative program the United States could establish with the vast funds it spends on the space program, or that it spends on some particular aspect of the space program, and compare and contrast the space program and your alternative in terms of the benefits and sacrifices entailed. For example, you might think of medical or educational programs, economic subsidies of various kinds, and so forth.

And Now, the Salmon Wars
Robert Sullivan

Robert Sullivan (1963–) lives in Portland, Oregon. His book, *The Meadowlands: Wilderness Adventures at the Edge of a City*, was published in 1998.

Unlike other environmental crises in the Pacific Northwest, the salmon 1
crisis is one none of us who live here can escape. What I mean is that the recent decision by the federal government to order new protections for nine
types of Northwest salmon is a problem that urbanites and suburbanites can't
take care of neatly, or at least not in the manner of past environmental crises
here.

Back when the controversy over old-growth logging was at its height, you 2
could sit at home and write a check (preferably printed on recycled paper)
and vote for a forestry-reform candidate. Then, at backyard Gardenburger
barbecues, you could feel good about having done your part.

Now, with the salmon crisis, you step out the door and the rain that's 3
running off your front lawn, awash in fertilizer, is a problem. You drive to
work (alone) and you are adding to the oil and other chemicals that all eventually drain into the streams.

You work for a company that wants to expand its offices into what is a 4
salmon habitat, which describes just about every wetland within a day's drive
of Seattle. At home, you turn on a light that is fed cheaply by the very dams
that make it nearly impossible for salmon to swim upstream.

For us to change this chain of events requires more than just writing checks. 5
It requires changing our life-styles, which is something most Northwesterners
have always seemed loath to do. We'll happily buy coffee from farmers who
pay the Central American pickers a decent wage, but we don't want anyone
to tell us what to do with our lot size or with that instrument that is most integral to life here: the sport utility vehicle.

After all, we're here for the life-style, for the trees, for the fact that it's 6
not so crowded (even if it is starting to look kind of crowded after all). We're
here to recreate, to enjoy. We're here for us.

During the spotted owl "war," the fight often was between the people 7
who lived in the cities and the people who lived in the rest of the Northwest.
The rural people resented a bunch of out-of-towners telling them how to go
about their jobs, not to mention their lives. The city side held distinct advantages: It vastly outnumbered the rural side, and a slowdown of logging

203

didn't necessarily affect city businesses—the water-exploiting computer-chip factories, for instance, or car commuter-intensive industries.

This new debate will be different. Many of the threatened salmon runs   8 go through urban and suburban areas, so all of a sudden being for the salmon means being against building a new home wherever you'd like, being for increased taxes, being prepared to change suburban life.

Of course, the fact that the crisis is so enormous and that we're all at   9 fault will be used as an excuse to do nothing at all. If it's not just clear-cutting that is killing the fish (the bare hillsides erode, sending silt into clear streams), then the logging companies can say, well, we should be able to keep logging. The prodam contingent—farmers and farm corporations that rely on barge traffic and dam-powered irrigation—may blame housing development.

But these arguments are as easy to see through as a clear stream in a pro-   10 tected forest, if for no other reason than this: Before the Columbia River and its tributaries were blocked with dozens of dams, 10 million to 16 million salmon made the annual run back up to their spawning grounds; in 1996, a little less than a million did.

Likewise, as this new debate continues, the phrase "putting salmon be-   11 fore people" will be heard over and over, but even the young people growing up here today—the wannabe kayaking champions, fishing guides and future water drinkers—know that somehow the people need to line up behind the fish that the fish, are like the canary in the coal mine.

For a long time, we tried in vain to jury-rig the system with huge hatch-   12 eries that churned out weak genetic Xerox copies of the wild fish, with concrete fish ladders that simulate the submerged waterfalls that salmon need to commute up the Columbia to spawn and die.

Now the salmon are making us look not just at what we can do with the   13 rivers but at what we can do with the way we commute and choose our homes and shop and live. The question is, will it be too much of a hassle for us to look at ourselves?

*

RESPONDING TO THE WHOLE ESSAY

1. Is Sullivan's primary purpose expressive, informative, or persuasive? [1g(1)]
2. What is Sullivan's primary topic? To what is he comparing and contrasting his topic?
3. What is Sullivan's role in the topic at hand; in other words, is he a part of the audience he is addressing? Describe this audience and cite evidence. [1g(2)]
4. Does Sullivan use a point-by-point or a subject-by-subject organization? Why is this more effective?
5. Is it appropriate for Sullivan to use the second person pronoun? What purpose could this serve? [1g(2)]

ANALYZING THE ELEMENTS

Grammar

1. In paragraph 5 the first sentence begins a prepositional phrase, but how does the phrase function in the sentence? [12a]
2. Why does Sullivan use the plural form of *to be* with the subject of *salmon*? [17e]

Effective Sentences

1. The last sentence of paragraph 11 contains a simile. Identify it and explain its effectiveness. [Glossary of Terms]
2. Comment on the parallelism of the last sentence of paragraph 8. [20]

Punctuation and Mechanics

1. Comment on Sullivan's use of dashes in paragraphs 7, 9, and 11. Does he use them the same way in each case? Would another form of punctuation be more appropriate or effective? [31e]
2. Why does Sullivan use parentheses in the first sentence of paragraph 6?

Diction

1. Why does Sullivan refer to the salmon concern as a "crisis" but the earlier spotted owl concern as a "war"?
2. What is effective about specifying that the barbecues in paragraph 2 are "Gardenburger"?

BUILDING VOCABULARY

1. Look up the origin of environment. Has the meaning changed?
2. The word "jury-rig" is relatively new (it does not appear in dictionaries from twenty years ago). What does it mean? Why do some people use the nonstandard "jerry-rig" instead of the recognized "jury-rig"?
3. What does *recreate* mean? Look at the roots of the word.

SUGGESTIONS FOR WRITING

1. Write an essay about an environmental issue that has an immediate effect in your life.
2. Write an essay directed to your peers in which you argue that they should be more involved in a particular social or political concern.

Small Is Still Beautiful
David Morris

David Morris is vice president of the Minneapolis- and Washington, D.C.-based Institute for Local Self-Reliance. He also directs the Institute's New Rules Project: "designing rules as if community matters." This article was adapted from an address to the Place Matters Conference in St. Paul, Minnesota, on November 12, 1998.

"The real voyage of discovery," wrote Marcel Proust, "lies not in seeking new lands but in seeing with new eyes." Seeing with new eyes requires challenging the conventional wisdom that bigger is better, that separating the producer from the consumer, the banker from the depositor, the worker from the owner, the government from its citizens is a necessary requirement for achieving a prosperous economy and a healthy society. 1

Seeing with new eyes means rediscovering the importance of place. Perhaps the finest empirical analysis of the relationship between local institutions and community life was conducted 50 years ago by Walter Goldschmidt, then a researcher for the U.S. Department of Agriculture. Goldschmidt examined two remarkably similar farm communities in California's San Joaquin Valley. Dinuba and Arvin had the same volume of crop production, comparable soil quality, and similar climate. The communities were equidistant from major urban areas and were similarly served by highways and rail lines. They differed in only one major respect: The Dinuba economy was based on many small family farms, while the town of Arvin depended on a few large-scale agribusiness operations. Goldschmidt discovered that Dinuba's family farm economy provided its residents with a substantially higher median income and standard of living. Moreover, the citizens of Dinuba, to a far greater extent than their counterparts in Arvin, were involved in building a strong community. 2

For example, the quality and quantity of projects that benefited the entire community, like paved streets and sidewalks and garbage and sewage disposal, were far superior in Dinuba. The agribusiness town had no high school and only one elementary school. Dinuba provided its citizens with four elementary schools in addition to a high school. The family farm town had three public parks. The corporate farm town had a single playground, donated by a corporation. 3

Dinuba's residents not only invested their money in expanding their community's physical infrastructure, they also invested their time in building its civic infrastructure. Dinuba had more than twice the number of civic 4 associations as Arvin. In Dinuba, there were various governmental bodies that enabled residents to make decisions about the public welfare through direct popular vote. No such bodies existed in Arvin.

You would think that the government would have been delighted by 5 Goldschmidt's findings, for he had empirically validated the uniquely American belief that the key to a healthy society is the broadest possible ownership of productive assets. You would be wrong.

For 30 years the USDA suppressed the report. Indeed, under pressure from 6 industry, it abolished Goldschmidt's position and, later, the entire office that studied agriculture's impact on communities.

Hearing the story of Dinuba 50 years later, it seems Goldschmidt must 7 have been describing a mythical town—or a scenario long since relegated to the dustbins of history. After all, that's what reading the daily headlines and watching the evening news would lead us to conclude.

The statistics are indeed sobering. A thousand farms a week have gone 8 out of business since 1950. Community pharmacies have been closing their doors at a rate of about 1,000 per year for the past five year. In 1972, independent booksellers claimed 58 percent of all book sales. By 1997 their share had fallen to 17 percent. Almost 5 percent of all retail spending today is captured by a single company, Wal-Mart.

It's getting scary out there. Last September, the federal government gave 9 its stamp of approval to the merger of Travelers Group and Citicorp, giving birth to Citigroup, a financial enterprise with $700 billion in assets that serves 100 million customers in 100 countries. In November, Cargill announced that it would purchase the grain operations of Continental Grain, reportedly allowing Cargill to control as much as 70 percent of the world's grain market.

These figures cannot be ignored. But they should not be overstated. The 10 independent sector is under attack and has ceased to be the dominant organizational form, but it isn't dead.

Consider the following statistics from Minnesota, a state with a popula- 11 tion (4.5 million) less than half that of Los Angeles, and typical of most U.S. states:

- More than 500 independent community pharmacies still exist.
- Almost 40 percent of all electricity customers own their own electric company, in the form of either a municipally owned or a cooperatively owned utility.
- Some 400 community banks and credit unions control more than 25 percent of all bank assets.
- More than 20,000 independent farmers dot the countryside.
- More than 30,000 second-generation family-owned businesses and 13,000 third-generation enterprises continue to compete successfully.

Place-based enterprises need not simply tap into our nostalgic yearning 12 for a simpler and more rooted yesteryear. They can make a powerful case that humanly scaled institutions are the most effective way to go. In every sector of the economy, the evidence yields the same conclusion: Small is efficient, dynamic, democratic, and cost effective.

Consider education. Exhaustive studies have found that small schools have　13 less absenteeism, lower dropout rates, fewer disciplinary problems, higher teacher satisfaction, and higher test scores than big schools. The evidence is so compelling that big cities like Chicago and Philadelphia and New York literally have begun down-sizing their schools by subdividing existing school buildings into two or three or even four completely independent schools. And the most impressive results have occurred when the school district not only shrinks the size of the school but also shrinks the distance between authority and responsibility by delegating decision-making power to the individual school.

The same scale of institution that best cares for our children best cares　14 for our money. In 1990, 92 percent of the nation's 12,165 banks had assets under $300 million, and two-thirds had assets under $100 million. Happily, the Federal Reserve has found that there are no efficiencies to be gained by banks any larger than this. In the 1980s, researchers found that savings and loans that stuck to their knitting and lent close to home did not, on average, require a federal bailout.

Community banks also serve their communities best. A 1996 Federal　15 Reserve study found that small banks made 82 percent of all commercial loans to very small business borrowers. And fees for checking accounts and other basic services were, on average, 15 percent lower at small banks than at large, multistate institutions, according to a 1997 study by the U.S. Public Interest Research Group.

In manufacturing, too, small scale pertains. Small manufacturers consti-　16 tute more than 98 percent of the 360,000 U.S. manufacturing enterprises. Two-thirds have fewer than 20 employees. From 1979 to 1989, small- and medium-sized manufacturing businesses created more than 20 million new jobs while the Fortune 500 lost almost 4 million jobs.

Place-based enterprises are not only efficient, they are also wildly popu-　17 lar. Poll after poll concludes that the vast majority of the population supports community team policing, home-based health care, community banks, neighborhood schools, and local businesses.

In brief, community-based enterprises and institutions still command con-　18 siderable resources and even more considerable respect and admiration. Today, individually and collectively, these enterprises are building on this foundation to survive in the age of planetary corporations and electronic commerce.

Meanwhile, communities around the country are looking for ways to en-　19 courage local ownership without interfering with the dynamism and entrepreneurialism of the private sector. Kent County in Maryland, Cape Cod towns in Massachussetts, and other communities have adopted comprehensive plans that explicitly call for planning bodies to support "locally owned businesses." On the West Coast, five cities, including Carmel, California, have adopted bans on the "formula restaurant" (defined as a restaurant "required by contractual or other arrangements to offer standardized menus, ingredients, food preparation, employee uniforms, interior decor, signage, or exterior design" or "adopt a name, appearance, or food presentation format which causes it to be substantially identical to another restaurant"). Carmel is not prohibiting McDonald's from setting up shop; it just can't look like a McDonald's. In essence, Carmel is outlawing uniformity—and thereby encouraging local ownership.

Since the 1970s, Congress has provided handsome tax incentives to com- 20 panies that give stock to their employees. More than a thousand companies are now majority-owned by their workers. These firms must operate in the same competitive marketplace as investor-owned firms, but they tend to have a different decision-making calculus. Absentee owners might well decide to close a profitable operation if they can make more money in another location. Such a decision would be unlikely at an employee-owned firm.

And Congress last year debated a bill that would have abolished the in- 21 heritance tax on family-owned farms and businesses bequeathed to family members who continued to operate them.

We live in an era of great change. But change is not necessarily progress. 22 As Bertrand Russell said, change is inevitable, while progress is problematic. Change is scientific while progress is ethical. We will have change, whether we will it or not. But we will have progress only if we develop strategies that channel investment capital and entrepreneurial energies and scientific genius in directions compatible with our dearly held values. This means strategies that defend and nurture place-based enterprises as the building blocks and lifeblood of dynamic, self-conscious, and healthy communities.

✳

RESPONDING TO THE WHOLE ESSAY

1. Does this essay focus more on comparison or on contrast? Support your answer.
2. What is the primary purpose of the essay? [1g(1)]
3. Morris's major study on which he bases his argument is fifty years old. Does that present any problems for his credibility?
4. Does Morris use point-by-point or subject-by-subject organization?
5. Does Morris provide a variety of examples? Can you think of any major areas he might have used to strengthen his argument?

ANALYZING THE ELEMENTS

Grammar

1. What kind of word is "Seeing" (first sentence of paragraph 2)? How does the phrase "Seeing with new eyes" function in that sentence? [11]
2. Is the first sentence of paragraph 13 a complete sentence? Why or why not? [12]

3. What is the correlative conjunction in the fourth sentence of paragraph 13? [Glossary of Terms]
4. Comment on Morris's use of "less" and "fewer" in paragraph 13. [Glossary of Usage]

Effective Sentences

1. Find two good transitional sentences in this essay. [3d]
2. Comment on the parallelism of the last sentence of paragraph 18. [20]

Punctuation and Mechanics

1. Comment on Morris's use of numerals. [35b]
2. In the third sentence of paragraph 22, why does Morris not use quotation marks? [30a]

Diction

1. What is the difference between *change* and *progress*?
2. Find words in the essay that depict the environment Morris favors.

BUILDING VOCABULARY

1. What is the meaning of the word *empirical*? What is its origin? [23a]
2. Some words are formed by combining elements of two or more words. In paragraph 2, what is the effect of combining two words to form "*agribusiness*"? [23a]

SUGGESTIONS FOR WRITING

1. Write an essay in which you discuss the advantages (or disadvantages) of living in a small town (or large city).
2. Compare and contrast two places, one small and one large.
3. Choose a different cliché (Morris uses the idea that "bigger is better") and argue that it is not true.

Cyberpunk R.I.P.
Paul Saffo

Paul Saffo delves into recent literary and social history to explore the similarities he notes between the cyberpunk movement of the early 1990s and the
beatnik movement of the late 1950s. In each movement, Saffo sees the seeds
of a coming revolution in mass culture, and indeed, if his analysis is correct,
we might all want to heed Bette Davis's command in *All About Eve:* "Fasten
your seatbelts! It's going to be a bumpy night." A frequent contributor to
such computer magazines as *Wired, Windows,* and *PC Computing,* Saffo
(psaffo@MCImail.com) is a research fellow at the Institute for the Future in
Menlo Park, California.

Like a sun-grazing comet on a deep-space trajectory, the cyberpunk move-   1
ment is disappearing as quickly as it arrived just a few years ago. Moreover,
the movement was hardly more substantial than a comet's fuzzy tail when it
came to numbers—there were never more than 100 hardcore cyberpunks at
any time before the term hit the mainstream press.

But don't sell cyberpunks's social impact short, for insubstantial comets   2
have long served as messengers. I suspect that cyberpunks are to the 1990s
what the beatniks were to the '60s—harbingers of a mass movement waiting
in the wings. Just as the beatniks anticipated the hippies, cyberpunks are setting the stage for a coming digital counterculture that will turn the '90s zeitgeist utterly on its head. This movement in the making has yet to be described,
much less named, but eerie parallels between the beatnik and cyberpunk movements offer strong hints of what is to come.

For starters, both movements were given focus by literary fiction. The   3
beatniks took their cue from a handful of "beat writers" (Jack Kerouac, Alan
Ginsberg, Gregory Corso, and William S. Burroughs), while cyberpunks found
their identity in the cyberpunk science fiction genre defined by writers such
as William Gibson, Rudy Rucker, Bruce Sterling, and John Shirley. Moreover,
the lead works in both traditions orbited emerging infrastructures: Kerouac's
On the Road played off the concrete mobility enabled by the Interstate
Highway Act, while Gibson's *Neuromancer* portrayed a future world wrapped
around vast information highways. Eager readers never realized that neither
writer was really one of them: Kerouac disliked driving; Gibson banged out
Neuromancer on a 1927 Hermes typewriter.

Like the cyberpunks, there were never more than a handful of true beat-   4
niks—less than 120 in all before the movement hit the media in the late 1950s,
according to essayist George Leonard. Leonard's descriptions of the North

211

Beach beatnik milieu parallel today's cyberpunk culture. Word got out on the grapevine of parties at people's "pads," and, like raves, these happenings quickly evolved into underground quasi-commercial events. Just as cyberpunks carry their network identities into the physical world, the beatniks were fond of pseudonyms. "Everyone had a name, like in a Damon Runyon novel," observes Leonard. Ironically, neither group named its own movement, for just as the cyberpunks were so dubbed by a literary interloper, the term "beatnik" was coined by *San Francisco Chronicle* columnist Herb Caen.

Once labeled, both movements quickly surrendered their visual archetypes   5
to the cultural mainstream. In 1960, youths the world over were aping the goateed, cool-shades beatnik look, while today, PDBs (people dressed in black) affecting electronic lifestyles are more numerous than network nodes. This surrender would send both movements into the black hole of history, but not before they inspired larger movements to come. Just five years after the beatniks's demise in 1960, the hippies emerged from the Haight Ashbury to change our cultural landscape forever.

Like cyberpunks, the beatniks were for the most part low-key, slightly   6
mournful loners. Beatnik individualism was a sullen and stubborn reaction to the optimistic company-man materialism of the Eisenhower era, just as the cyberpunks stand in stark contrast to the antiseptic military-industrial orderliness of the Reagan-Bush years.

But Kerouac later concluded that beat also meant beatific—imbued with   7
joy or blessedness—and it was this aspect of the beatniks that became the germ of the hippie movement, according to Leonard. "It was a time of grace," he told me, referring to the early days of the Haight-Ashbury, when it seemed that a new age of cultural consciousness truly was dawning.

Optimism and a sense of community distinguished the hippies from the   8
beatniks, and will also distinguish the cyberpunks from the coming digital counterculture. The cyberpunk world is starkly non-utopian, serving up the same sort of intimate but uneasy accommodation with technology portrayed in the movie *Blade Runner*. I will bet that the digital counterculture will reject this bleak vision of a future in which technology enlarges the human spirit as a new tool for consciousness in much the same way that the hippies appropriated the psychoactive chemical spin-offs of the military-industrial complex. This new movement will be cyberpunk imbued with human warmth, substituting a deep sense of interdependence in place of lone wolf isolationism. Cyberpunks envision humans as electronic cyber-rats lurking in the interstices of the information mega-machine; the gospel of the post-cyberpunk movement will be one of machines in the service of enlarging our humanity.

It is too early to tell what the digital counterculture will call itself, but   9
the history of the hippies offers a clue. "Hippie" traces its origins to "hipster," slang for a cruel and cynical 1950s subculture that predated the beats. The digital counterculture thus is likely to appropriate an older term for its own, in the same way that the hippies appropriated and turned "hipster" into something entirely new. I'll bet that they call themselves something like "tekkies,"

consciously adopting the scornful '80s slang for nerds, stripping the word of its industrial coldness and making it synonymous with the human control of technology.

Hippies appeared in 1965, several years after the beatnik movement had gone 10 public. Given this chronology, the tekkies will arrive sometime in the mid-1990s, if not sooner. Watch the skies for a new comet—it will be digital, and its tail is likely to glow in Technicolor swirls. Its arrival will change our lives forever.

✳

RESPONDING TO THE WHOLE ESSAY

1. What basis for comparison does Saffo use for this essay? Does he state it? If so, where? [2d]
2. With what literary device does Saffo introduce and conclude this essay? Why is this kind of device particularly appropriate in a comparison-contrast essay? [24a(3)]
3. Comment upon the organization of this essay—part by part, whole by whole, or a combination? [2c]
4. Analyze sentence by sentence the organizational strategy used in paragraph 3. [2d]

ANALYZING THE ELEMENTS

Grammar

1. Why is the first sentence of paragraph 2 not a comma splice? [12b(3)]
2. Explain what makes the first sentence in paragraph 8 a grammatically simple sentence. [12c(1)]
3. Comment upon the use of the infinitive in the final sentence of paragraph 5. [12a]
4. The final sentence in paragraph 9 is a complex sentence. Explain what a complex sentence is and find at least one more in this essay. Then, as fully as you can, comment on what rhetorical advantages these sentences offer Saffo. [12c(3)]

Effective Sentences

1. How does parallel structure contribute to the effectiveness of the second sentence of paragraph 6? [20a]
2. Saffo could have begun the second sentence of paragraph 8 as follows: "Starkly non-utopian, the cyberpunk world serves up the same sort of intimate. . ." Is Saffo's actual beginning better? Why or why not? [22b]

Punctuation and Mechanics

1. There is a small difference in meaning between "a sullen and stubborn reaction," as Saffo writes in paragraph 6, and the more common approach of separating these coordinate adjectives with a comma—"a sullen, stubborn reaction." What does Saffo gain by separating them with a conjunction? [27c]

2. Justify the use of a semicolon in the last sentence in paragraph 8. What do you think was Saffo's reason for not making separate sentences? [28a]
3. Why are the following italicized: *Neuromancer* (paragraph 3), *On the Road* (paragraph 3), *Blade Runner* (paragraph 8)? [34a]
4. Comment upon Saffo's use of numbers in paragraph 2. [35f]

Diction

1. What is the origin of the phrase *to sell something short* (paragraph 2)? What does it mean? [23ac]
2. Look up the following words in a good desk dictionary, write down the etymology (history) of each one, and then write an explanation of how the meaning of each word is probably related to its history: *harbinger* (paragraph 2), *dubbed* (paragraph 4), *milieu* (paragraph 4), *interloper* (paragraph 4), *archetype* (paragraph 5). [23a]

BUILDING VOCABULARY

1. *Zeitgeist* (paragraph 2) is a German word made by combining the words *Zeit* and *Geist*. Look each word up in a German-English dictionary and write down the meanings. Then, considering the meanings of those two words as well as the way the word is used in the essay, explain the meaning of *Zeitgeist*.
2. *Goateed* is used as an adjective in paragraph 5. The word is easily recognizable as a relative of the noun, *goatee,* but what steps had to occur for it to be used as an adjective?

SUGGESTIONS FOR WRITING

1. Write a short essay in which you compare behaviors and attitudes in high school with those in college. For instance, you might compare the behaviors of students studying for final exams or their attitudes toward homework.
2. Write an essay in which you suggest a new term for the coming cyberculture, comparing and contrasting it to Saffo's term, *tekkies.*

Anglo vs. Chicano: Why?

Arthur L. Campa

Arthur L. Campa (1905–1975) was the author of more than seventy mono-
graphs and articles for professional journals as well as of several books:
Acquiring Spanish, *Spanish Folk-Poetry in New Mexico*, and *Treasure of the
Sangre de Cristos*. Born in Guaymas, Mexico, he was educated at the University
of New Mexico and Columbia University and for many years he was chair-
man of the modern language department at the University of Denver and directed the Center for Latin American Studies there. He also served as a U.S.
State Department lecturer in Spain, as cultural attaché to the U.S. Embassy
in Peru, and as training project director in Denver for the Peace Corps. Among
his many awards were a Rockefeller research grant and a Guggenheim fellowship. First published in *Western Review*, "Anglo vs. Chicano: Why?" takes
an anthropological view of the conflict between the two cultures.

The cultural differences between Hispanic and Anglo-American people   1
have been dwelt upon by so many writers that we should all be well informed
about the values of both. But audiences are usually of the same persuasion
as the speakers, and those who consult published works are for the most part
specialists looking for affirmation of what they believe. So, let us consider
the same subject, exploring briefly some of the basic cultural differences that
cause conflict in the Southwest, where Hispanic and Anglo-American cultures
meet.

Cultural differences are implicit in the conceptual content of the languages   2
of these two civilizations, and their value systems stem from a long series of
historical circumstances. Therefore, it may be well to consider some of the
English and Spanish cultural configurations before these Europeans set foot
on American soil. English culture was basically insular, geographically and
ideologically; was more integrated on the whole, except for some strong theological differences; and was particularly zealous of its racial purity. Spanish
culture was peninsular, a geographical circumstance that made it a catchall of
Mediterranean, central Europe and north African peoples. The composite nature of the population produced a marked regionalism that prevented close
integration, except for religion, and led to a strong sense of individualism.
These differences were reflected in the colonizing enterprise of the two cultures. The English isolated themselves from the Indians physically and culturally; the Spanish, who had strong notions about *pureza de sangre* [purity
of blood] among the nobility, were not collectively averse to adding one more
strain to their racial cocktail. Cortés led the way by siring the first *mestizo* in

215

North America, and the rest of the conquistadores followed suit. The ultimate products of these two orientations meet today in the Southwest.

Anglo-American culture was absolutist at the onset; that is, all the dom-   3
inant values were considered identical for all, regardless of time and place. Such values as justice, charity, honesty were considered the superior social order for all men and were later embodied in the American Constitution. The Spaniard brought with him a relativistic viewpoint and saw fewer moral implications in man's actions. Values were looked upon as the result of social and economic conditions.

The motives that brought Spaniards and Englishmen to America also dif-   4
fered. The former came on an enterprise of discovery, searching for a new route to India initially, and later for new lands to conquer, the fountain of youth, minerals, the Seven Cities of C'bola and, in the case of the missionaries, new souls to win for the Kingdom of Heaven. The English came to escape religious persecution, and once having found a haven, they settled down to cultivate the soil and establish their homes. Since the Spaniards were not seeking a refuge or running away from anything, they continued their explorations and circled the globe 25 years after the discovery of the New World.

This peripatetic tendency of the Spaniard may be accounted for in part   5
by the fact he was the product of an equestrian culture. Men on foot do not venture far into the unknown. It was almost a century after the landing on Plymouth Rock that Governor Alexander Spotswood of Virginia crossed the Blue Ridge Mountains, and it was not until the nineteenth century that the Anglo-American began to move west of the Mississippi.

The Spaniard's equestrian role meant that he was not close to the soil, as   6
was the Anglo-American pioneer, who tilled the land and built the greatest agricultural industry in history. The Spaniard cultivated the land only when he had Indians available to do it for him. The uses to which the horse was put also varied. The Spanish horse was essentially a mount, while the more robust English horse was used in cultivating the soil. It is therefore not surprising that the viewpoints of these two cultures should differ when we consider that the pioneer is looking at the world at the level of his eyes while the *caballero* [horseman] is looking beyond and down at the rest of the world.

One of the most commonly quoted, and often misinterpreted, character-   7
istics of Hispanic peoples is the deeply ingrained individualism in all walks of life. Hispanic individualism is a revolt against the incursion of collectivity, strongly asserted when it is felt that the ego is being fenced in. This attitude leads to a deficiency in those social qualities based on collective standards, an attitude that Hispanos do not consider negative because it manifests a measure of resistance to standardization in order to achieve a measure of individual freedom. Naturally, such an attitude has no *reglas fijas* [fixed rules].

Anglo-American who achieve a measure of success and security through   8
institutional guidance not only do not mind a few fixed rules but demand them. The lack of a concerted plan of action, whether in business or in politics, appears unreasonable to Anglo-Americans. They have a sense of

individualism, but they achieve it through action and self-determination. Spanish individualism is based on feeling, on something that is the result not of rules and collective standards but of a person's momentary, emotional re-action. And it is subject to change when the mood changes. In contrast to Spanish emotional individualism, the Anglo-American strives for objectivity when choosing a course of action or making a decision.

The Southwestern Hispanos voiced strong objections to the lack of cour-   9
tesy of the Anglo-Americans when they first met them in the early days of the Santa Fe trade. The same accusation is leveled at the *Americanos* today in many quarters of the Hispanic world. Some of this results from their differ-ent conceptions of polite behavior. Here too one can say that the Spanish have no *reglas fijas* because for them courtesy is simply an expression of the way one person feels toward another. To some they extend the hand, to some they bow and for the more *'ntimos* there is the well-known *abrazo*. The concepts of "good or bad" or "right and wrong" in polite behavior are moral consid-erations of an absolutist culture.

Another cultural contrast appears in the way both cultures share part of   10
their material substance with others. The pragmatic Anglo-American con-tributes regularly to such institutions as the Red Cross, the United Fund and a myriad of associations. He also establishes foundations and quite often leaves millions to such institutions. The Hispano prefers to give his contribution di-rectly to the recipient so he can see the person he is helping.

A century of association has inevitably acculturated both Hispanos and   11
Anglo-Americans to some extent, but there still persist a number of culture traits that neither group has relinquished altogether. Nothing is more dis-quieting to an Anglo-American who believes that time is money than the time perspective of Hispanos. They usually refer to this attitude as the "*mañana* psychology." Actually, it is more of a "today psychology," be-cause Hispanos cultivate the present to the exclusion of the future; because the latter has not arrived yet, it is not a reality. They are reluctant to relin-quish the present, so they hold on to it until it becomes the past. To an Hispano, nine is nine until it is ten, so when he arrives at nine-thirty, he jubilantly exclaims: "*¡Justo!*" [right on time]. This may be why the clock is slowed down to a walk in Spanish while in English it runs. In the United States, our future-oriented civilization plans our lives so far in advance that the present loses its meaning. January magazine issues [including ID's] are out in December, 1973 cars have been out since October; cemetery plots and even funeral arrangements are bought on the installment plan. To a person engrossed in living today the very idea of planning his funeral sounds like the tolling of the bells.

It is a natural corollary that a person who is present oriented should be   12
compensated by being good at improvising. An Anglo-American is told in ad-vance to prepare for an "impromptu speech," but an Hispano usually can im-provise a speech because "*Nosotros lo improvisamos todo*" [we improvise everything].

Another source of cultural conflict arises from the difference between *being*   13
and *doing*. Even when trying to be individualistic, the Anglo-American
achieves it by what he does. Today's young generation decided to be themselves, to get away from standardization, so they let their hair grow, wore
ragged clothes and even went barefoot in order to be different from the
Establishment. As a result they all ended up doing the same things and created another stereotype. The freedom enjoyed by the individuality of *being*
makes it unnecessary for Hispanos to strive to be different.

In 1963 a team of psychologists from the University of Guadalajara in   14
Mexico and the University of Michigan compared 74 upper-middle-class students from each university. Individualism and personalism were found to be
central values for the Mexican students. This was explained by saying that a
Mexican's value as a person lies in his *being* rather than, as in the case of the
Anglo-Americans, in concrete accomplishments. Efficiency and accomplishments are derived characteristics that do not affect worthiness in the Mexican,
whereas in the American it is equated with success, a value of highest prior-
ity in the American culture. Hispanic people dissociate themselves from material things or from actions that may impugn a person's sense of being, but
the Anglo-American shows great concern for material things and assumes responsibility for his actions. This is expressed in the language of each culture.
In Spanish one says, *"Se me cayó la taza"* [the cup fell away from me] instead
of "I dropped the cup."

In English, one speaks of money, cash and all related transactions with   15
frankness because material things of this high order do not trouble Anglo-
Americans. In Spanish such materialistic concepts are circumvented by referring to cash as *efectivo* [effective] and when buying or selling as something *al
contado* [counted out], and when without it by saying *No tengo fondos* [I
have no funds]. This dissociation from material things is what produces
sobriedad [sobriety] in the Spaniard according to Miguel de Unamuno, but in
the Southwest the dissociation from materialism leads to *dejadez* [lassitude]
and *desprendimiento* [disinterestedness]. A man may lose his life defending his
honor but is unconcerned about the lack of material things. *Desprendimiento*
causes a man to spend his last cent on a friend, which when added to lack of
concern for the future may mean that tomorrow he will eat beans as a result
of today's binge.

The implicit differences in words that appear to be identical in meaning are   16
astonishing. Versatile is a compliment in English and an insult in Spanish. An
Hispano student who is told to apologize cannot do it, because the word
doesn't exist in Spanish. *Apología* means words in praise of a person. The Anglo-
American either apologizes, which is a form of retraction abhorrent in Spanish,
or compromises, another concept foreign to Hispanic culture. *Compromiso*
means a date, not a compromise. In colonial Mexico City, two hidalgos once
entered a narrow street from opposite sides, and when they could not go around,
they sat in their coaches for three days until the viceroy ordered them to back
out. All this because they could not work out a compromise.

It was that way then and to some extent now. Many of today's conflicts   17
in the Southwest have their roots in polarized cultural differences, which need
not be irreconcilable when approached with mutual respect and understanding.

✳

RESPONDING TO THE WHOLE ESSAY

1. What primary purpose can you ascertain for Campa's writing "Anglo vs. Chicano: Why?" What features in the eassy make the purpose clear? [1g(1)]
2. How does the essay reveal the nature of the audience Campa was writing for? Does knowing that the essay was written twenty or more years ago influence your understanding of Campa's audience? Would the essay need to be modified to appeal to the same group of readers today? If so, how and why? If not, why not? [1g(2)]
3. Does Campa organize this eassy subject by subject or point by point? What advantages does his chosen method offer? What would be the effect of using the other method?
4. Campa makes frequent use of examples to develop his ideas. Explain how examples develop the ideas in paragraphs 4, 10, 11, 13, and 16. [2e]
5. Where does Campa make clear that he is focusing on *why* there are cultural differences between Hispanic and Anglo-American cultures? Explain how the rest of the eassy maintains that focus. [2b]
6. What solution to the problems raised in the eassy does Campa's concluding paragraph suggest? Comment on the effectiveness of this strategy for a conclusion. [3b]

ANALYZING THE ELEMENTS

Grammar

1. Explain how the phrase "the superior social order for all men" is used in the second sentence of paragraph 3. [15a]
2. Campa uses a fragment to conlude paragraph 16. Why? [13]

Effective Sentences

1. Explain the probable reason for Campa's use of the passive in the first sentence of the essay. How does this sentence establish a pattern for the rest of the essay? Is the use of passive voice here effective? Why or why not? [21d(1)]
2. In the fourth sentence of paragraph 14, to what does *it* refer? Explain why the reference is clear and the antecedent need not be repeated. [16b]

Punctuation and Mechanics

1. Examine the use of commas in the last sentence of paragraph 1 and the seventh sentence of paragraph 2 (beginning "The English isolated. . ."). Is each comma necessary? Why or why not? Would the meaning of the sentence change if the

comma(s) were eliminated from the sentence in paragraph 1? In paragraph 2? [27d and 27f]
2. Explain the use of semicolons in the third sentence of paragraph 2. What other method of punctuation could have been used, if any? [28b]

Diction

1. Campa incorporates a number of Spanish words and expressions into "Anglo vs. Chicano: Why?" Considering Campa's audience, comment on whether these expressions contribute to or detract from the essay.
2. Campa's vocabulary is varied and precise. Check your dictionary for the meanings of the following words and explain how each is appropriate in its context: *insular* and *peninsular* (paragraph 2), *absolutist* (paragraph 3), *peripatetic* (paragraph 5), *incursion* and *collective* (paragraph 7), *pragmatic* (paragraph 10), *acculturated* (paragraph 11), and *corollary* (paragraph 12). [24a(2)]

BUILDING VOCABULARY

1. What is the meaning of the prefix *pen-*? How does it alter the meaning of the word *insular*? List at least two other words beginning with the prefix *pen-*. Explain the way it alters the root word in each case.
2. The following words are frequently confused: *disinterested* and *uninterested*, *pragmatic* and *practical*, *prevaricate* and *procrastinate*. Look up each word and state its meaning.

SUGGESTIONS FOR WRITING

1. Write an essay in which you compare and contrast two families you know well.
2. Contrast two culturally different communities from your own region as Campa does for the Southwest. These communities need not be ethnically different, but may be socially or religiously different, or different for other reasons. Take care to maintain, as Campa does, a spirit of fairness and objectivity as you account for the cultural differences you discuss.

Chapter 7

Classification and Division

W hen you group ideas or objects into categories, you are classifying. When you separate ideas or objects into parts, you are dividing. Classifying and dividing are complementary. They are both important strategies in writing, but they are far more than that; they are fundamental to how people understand and organize information to make it useful. For instance, if you have to buy grapes, hamburger, cheese, tomatoes, milk, chicken, and butter at the supermarket, you'll proceed most efficiently through the store if you consider the categories into which the management has classified those items: produce, meats, and dairy products. But at the dairy counter you will also want to consider whether to buy whole, lowfat, or skimmed milk.

Classification is important in every field, but perhaps especially in science, which often progresses by refining categories and establishing new ones. Think of the great classification systems that enable botanists and zoologists to find order in, and write intelligibly about, the staggering diversity of living things on the earth. Or consider, for that matter, how astronomers classify the earth itself, as a *planet,* one of several classes of heavenly bodies that make up our solar system, which in turn belongs to a larger star system we call a *galaxy;* galaxies themselves are classified in four categories on the basis of their form: elliptical, spiral (ours is spiral, as is Andromeda), barred spiral, and irregular.

Classification, obviously, involves recognizing common characteristics that diverse items share (and therefore is closely related to comparison and contrast, dealt with in Chapter 6). Galaxies, as we noted, are normally classified on the basis of shape. Stars, however, can be classified on many different bases— for instance, size, composition, color, brightness, age, distance; the choice of a basis depends on the classifier's immediate purpose. The point is that in writing an essay or other paper, you may be able to classify your subject in several different ways, some of which will serve your purpose better than others; you must choose the *basis of classification* that is best for your purpose. To return to the supermarket for a moment, the management (though it might not remain the management very long) could choose an alphabetical basis of classification and arrange everything on the shelves accordingly—the apples next to the antacids, the bread between the beans and the brooms, and so forth.

Such an arrangement works fine, after all, in the telephone directory, where "your fingers do the walking." Or the merchandise could be classified according to the type of package: bottled things in aisle 1, canned things in aisle 2, boxed things in aisle 3, bagged things in aisle 4, loose things in aisle 5. Obviously, not all bases of classification are equally valuable. To return from shopping to writing, if you were writing with the purpose of showing that certain types of folk legends are found over and over again in many different cultures, you might classify legends by their content: creation legends, flood legends, and so on. For a different purpose—for instance, to emphasize the distinctive qualities of legends from different cultures—you might classify legends according to where they originated—Greek legends, American Indian legends, Japanese legends, and so on. Whenever you classify, have a clear idea of your purpose and your *basis* for classifying.

Once you have a basis clearly in mind, make sure that all of your categories stick to that basis. It is all too easy to fall into the trap of creating overlapping, illogical categories. Do not, that is, classify dogs as large, medium, small, and unfriendly. The last is a category formed on a different basis from the others—degree of friendliness rather than size. (Friendliness could, of course, be the basis for a classification—in, for example, an entertaining essay on the dogs you have known; friendly to a fault, affable but reserved, indifferent, and downright hostile.) All of this may seem too obvious—and indeed, if you were writing about newspapers, you probably would not fall into the error of classifying them as conservative, moderate, liberal, or weekly. But it's not hard to imagine a writer's illogically grouping newspapers into two classes such as these: papers interested in promoting the good of the public and papers interested in making a profit for themselves—as if these two interests could not be combined. When you classify, be sure your categories are consistent, established on the same basis.

Finally, be sure your classification does not omit any important categories. This does not mean that you must give equal attention to every category as you write; that decision will depend on your purpose. It does mean that your readers are likely to wonder whether you have both oars in the water if you appear to have overlooked a category they regard as significant in the context of your discussion. For instance, if you were writing about the ways in which oppressed people might respond to oppression, as Martin Luther King, Jr., does in this chapter, and you failed to consider the possibility of people's simply giving in to oppression, accepting their situation as hopeless, readers who have given in and lost all hope might be justified in feeling that your essay was not intended for them—that you do not understand or perhaps even care about their plight.

Division (also called analysis) is a mode of thought—and of writing—that breaks things down into their parts for a purpose, usually to understand them better, and often in preparation for putting the elements together again in new ways (called synthesis). As a user of this book, you have continually been engaged in division, analyzing elements of the essays printed here in order to understand what makes the essays successful. Having analyzed the many individual choices the various writers have made, you will be prepared to put this information together in a new synthesis: your own, unique writing. Division helps us understand almost any subject—objects, ideas, emotions, processes, texts, and so forth. Consider, for example, the diverse subjects of the analyses that follow in this chapter: good writing, contemporary American men, our response to music.

For analytical essays, as for other kinds, purpose and audience may vary greatly. For instance, the audience for an analysis might be exclusively oneself—as in a diary entry written to sort out the writer's feelings or ideas about some experience. It should be stressed that analytical writing does not merely report the findings of finished investigations; even when you begin your writing with the sense that you have already investigated your subject thoroughly, you are quite likely to make further discoveries as you write about it. That is the nature of analysis, and is the reason analytical writing is so often called for in college courses, where the objective is learning. You might divide a poem into it parts for a literature course, consider the various parts that make up the structure of a bridge for an engineering course, or analyze a business situation for a management course. Beyond the campus, analysis usually serves very immediate practical ends; nurses and doctors analyze patients; lawyers analyze briefs; politicians analyze voters; coaches analyze teams; business people analyze products, competitors, problems; and so forth.

Division is a powerful tool not only for discovering but also for explaining—and here, of course, is where the question of audience becomes crucial. Consider, for example, "How We Listen to Music" by Aaron Copland, printed in this chapter. Though Copland, one of America's most distinguished symphonic composers, certainly is capable of writing at an extremely high level of technical sophistication, notice how his purpose in this essay requires that he write in simple, nontechnical language that will be understood by an audience of nonmusicians.

Especially if you are writing on a subject that is complex, you may need to give considerable thought to the *basis* of your analysis—your reason for dividing it in a particular way. For example, Jacqueline Berke's essay in this chapter seeks to discover the qualities of good writing. To proceed, however, Berke finds that she must first establish what she means by *good*: "pungent, vital, moving, memorable." This definition, focusing on the effect of the writing on the reader, provides the basis for an investigation that leads Berke to certain qualities in the writing itself: economy, simplicity, and clarity. However, the story editor of a television soap opera might define good writing in a quite different way: writing for which sponsors will pay a high price in order to sell their products during the commercial breaks. An analysis on this basis might reveal the qualities of "good" writing to be that it always keeps the viewers wondering what will happen next so they'll stay tuned, punishes the bad characters and rewards the good ones, and has plenty of romance—and plenty of breaks for commercials.

Five of the seven essays reprinted in this chapter illustrate classification, and two illustrate analysis. One of the essays is by a scientist writing with a primarily informative aim: Desmond Morris's "Territorial Behavior" examines the ways in which human beings establish and protect three types of "territories"—tribal, familial, and personal. Martin Luther King, Jr., makes classification a powerful tool for persuasion, arguing to his readers that nonviolent resistance in the face of oppression is the only choice that can work. Ron Geraci and Scott Adams—both humorists with widely different temperaments and styles—demonstrate still other uses of classification. Jacqueline Berke and Aaron Copland—a writer and a musician, respectively—analyze their arts for the purpose of explaining them to novices.

Two student essays illustrate the principles expressed in this section. Both students were given complete freedom of subject, but Lauren Reismann's assignment was to write a classification paper and Timothy Ellis's was to write an analytical essay. Reismann chose a subject she was familiar with, one which she could assume any reader would have at least a glancing acquaintance. She shows her reader how the various kinds of houses fall into clear categories related to how the features of each category fit her family. Ellis takes a different approach. He assumes the reader knows virtually nothing about his subject. As you read each of the essays and the commentary that follows, consider how these writers attempt to adhere to the principles just explained.

A House Is Not a Home

Introduction—reason for classifying	My family's recent move from Omaha to Dallas revealed to me that houses come in three main categories—houses that my family can afford but wouldn't live in, houses that we can't afford but would
Identification of classes	die to live in, and houses that will do. I base my observation upon the fact that we looked at over a hundred houses, but we never saw any that would not
Completeness	fit into one of these classifications. I am a little nervous, however, because one of the categories— houses that will do—is very small, whereas the other two categories are very large.
First class—implies basis for classification	We found a large number of houses we cannot afford but which we absolutely love. After exhausting the real estate agent, my family and I generally spent the rest of the afternoon looking at model homes in elegant subdivisions. We contended that doing so would give us many ideas about what we really wanted in the home we would eventually live in; and we were right. We got hundreds of ideas, none of which we could afford. We particularly like the houses with

elevated ceilings and large, elaborate leaded windows. Those windows sparkled in the afternoon sun like jewels. Built-in Jacuzzi tubs and private saunas in the master bathrooms sang a siren's song to my father, and my mother was enamored of the large, separate walk-in closets and the fireplaces in the master bedrooms. I, myself, was partial to the upstairs arrangements—large book-lined game rooms from which enough bedrooms with private bathrooms for me and each of my sisters and brothers opened. My brothers were enchanted by the swimming pools and the mirrored exercise rooms. Nobody cared much about the kitchens, although they were large, contained built-in barbecue grills, silent dishwashers and Sub-Zero refrigerators, not to mention enough cabinets to store dishes for a large restaurant and a pantry that would hold enough food for a small army.

Implies basis for classification

Second class

The real estate agent, a nice woman named Loretta, tirelessly showed us used houses. Although we expressed to her our desires for saunas, pools, fireplaces, and lots of bathrooms, she insisted upon showing us houses that did not meet those simple requirements (except that we could afford them). The typical house sat on what she insisted upon calling a "sunlight" lot which was distinguished by lacking any shade whatsoever. Not only that, but my brothers were discouraged by the large expanses of grass these houses displayed. My sister and I found the bathroom arrangements unacceptable—one for my parents, one for my brothers, and one for my sister and me. Not only that, but Eileen and I would have to share a bedroom—a small bedroom, the closet to which would not hold all of my clothes let alone hers. (Besides, the single closet would make it all too easy for her to raid my wardrobe.) The undersized two-car garages couldn't hold a wrench to the spacious garage with workbench that my Dad longed for. And the kitchens! Their only virtue is that they would accommodate only one person at a time, thus protecting my siblings and me from KP. My parents were only induced to look at these shacks for two reasons: the school district was reputed to be a good one and they were concerned about my younger brothers and sister getting a decent education and the locations were within easy reach of my parents' offices.

Third class— implies basis for classification

Finally, Loretta got wise. She showed us some houses in a suburb where the prices were only about two-thirds of those in the fancy school district but where the education was adequately maintained thanks to the presence of two state universities in the town (one of which I now attend). My parents would have to commute only about an hour each way. There were two acceptable houses, although they lacked what my sister and I had come to think of as basic luxuries. We bought the cheaper one. My sister and I still have to share a bathroom, but we each have our own bedroom; my brothers lack a pool, but the yard has plenty of trees. My parents got the Jacuzzi in the master bathroom and separate closets, but had to forgo the sauna and the fireplace in the bedroom. Although my brothers still have to share a bedroom, the kitchen has two pantries so that they won't starve, and there is enough cabinet space for my grandmother's china and crystal which my mother has kept packed away most of my life. Dad has an oversized two-car garage to play in, and there's lots of storage space in the attic. It will do.

Commentary.   In her introduction, Reismann comments briefly on why she wants to classify the kinds of houses that are for sale—to explain why her family bought the house they did. She first identifies houses that her family cannot afford as a class—mainly houses that are expensively built with many high-priced options. She then further divides this category by explaining what each family member liked about the expensive houses.

Then she identifies the class of houses which her family can afford but which are unsuitable. Again, she applies her test—how does this house fit the way the family lives? Although she had referred to location in her discussion of the previous category (elegant subdivisions), she makes a stronger point about location in her discussion of this category. It is, after all, the reason that the real estate agent shows them houses that are unsuitable even though the family makes their desires known.

In discussing her final category, Reismann takes up only those elements about which the family has had to compromise, thus fulfilling her focus on the category of "houses that will do." She concludes her essay with a curt statement emphasizing that point.

A Brief Beginner's Guide to Reference Sources

Introduction

Recently, I was required to write a lengthy paper for my history class, and after much deliberation, I decided to write about the events that prompted the Germans to destroy the Berlin Wall.

Because I had not currently seen news on this subject in popular publications, I realized that my topic would require a great deal of research. Unfortunately, I had no idea where to begin my study; therefore, this project became very intimidating. Then at the suggestion of a friend, I asked a reference librarian for assistance. The librarian told me about reference materials available at most libraries that aid in the location of published documents and learning aids on a variety of subjects. The librarian's suggestions reduced my research time—time that I, otherwise, would have spent searching aimlessly through magazines and books for information. Consequently, I became interested in learning more about reference materials that could make my college and business research more efficient.

Thesis   Reference sources offer a wealth of information, and are helpful tools for beginning any study.

Primary division

First major part

Reference sources are available in print and microfilm formats as well as in on-line formats. They are divided into two categories: control-access and information sources. Control-access sources, primarily bibliographies and indexes, direct the researcher to documents and materials necessary for extensive study.

First minor part

For most people, the mention of bibliographies brings to mind a list of books; however, bibliographies also inventory audiovisual materials, periodicals, software programs, movies, reports, and studies. Due to the recent information explosion, bibliographies play a vital role in research because they compile available resources and offer necessary facts for finding these items for further research.

Further subdivision

Bibliographies that contain information not restricted by time, territory, language, subject, or form are referred to as universal bibliographies. One example of a universal bibliography is the National Union Catalog compiled by the Library of Congress. This catalog describes information sources held by libraries throughout the United States. Obviously, universal bibliographies are difficult to compile; therefore, most bibliographies are limited in scope. Often these bibliographies are limited to a particular subject, country, or trade. These limited bibliographies are generally good sources to use for studies in a particular discipline such as history, the humanities, and science.

Second minor part

Indexes are also good sources for locating information on a particular subject, especially information published in current magazines. Indexes contain listings that are analyzed by the name and subject of the document and then listed under the author's name and all other subject headings that apply. Indexes are traditionally divided into periodical indexes, newspaper indexes, and serial indexes which provide citations including the name of the author, the subject of the document, and the name of the publisher.

Further subdivision

The Reader's Guide to Periodical Literature is an index consisting of periodical citations in broad and specific subject fields. This annually published reference guide is useful in locating magazine articles published on current social issues and events. To locate information in particular subject areas such as the humanities or science, subject indexes are also available. Historical Abstracts is one such publication; it offers a short brief summary of journals, books, and other related materials concentrating on world history.

Second major part

Although bibliographies and indexes are essential tools for beginning research, many factual questions arise that can easily be answered by the second type of reference source, the information source or ready-reference. Most people have used a ready-reference source sometime in their life. Ready-

Further subdivision

reference sources are divided into encyclopedias, dictionaries, geographical sources, fact sources and government documents. Ready-reference sources are necessary materials for the better understanding of the subject studied. While researching a subject, most people encounter new terms that they must understand before they can continue their study. New words may be found quickly in a dictionary—an alphabetical listing of words, pronunciations, and meanings. Geographical sources such as atlases and guidebooks offer information about place names that the researcher has never before encountered, and statistics and other factual information is available in fact sources such as yearbooks, almanacs, and directories.

Conclusion

The collection and synthesis of information are two of the greatest challenges of the college experience. Knowledge of both control-access and ready-reference materials makes the collection of information much easier and significantly reduces research time. In fact, just knowing that these materials are available increases the researcher's confidence in his or her ability to complete a project and, as a result, allows the researcher more time for synthesizing the information located.

Commentary. Tim Ellis sets an ambitious agenda for himself by proposing to analyze basic reference sources. His clear sense of audience contributes much to the accomplishment of that purpose. He views his readers as those who feel lost when they walk into a library, and so he assumes that they know virtually nothing of how to find information on a subject.

To identify with his audience, Ellis begins with an account of how he was overwhelmed by the prospect of trying to locate information for a history paper he had to write, explaining that all he knew to do was to page through magazines trying to find something on his subject. But with the help of a reference librarian he learns how to start.

His guide breaks the subject—reference sources—into parts and analyzes each of those parts so that the neophyte researcher knows where to begin. For instance, in the second paragraph he divides reference sources into two groups and then defines those groups—those which enable access to sources and so give the researcher some control over the process, and those which furnish information.

Ellis subdivides his first group of sources into bibliographies and indexes and describes some bibliographies and indexes available to search for specific kinds of information. He then takes up the next group and suggests some general information sources in particular fields. He concludes by reemphasizing the value of knowing how to handle sources.

Three Types of Resistance to Oppression
Martin Luther King, Jr.

Martin Luther King, Jr., was born in Atlanta, Georgia, in 1929, and assassinated in Memphis, Tennessee, in 1968—four years after he was awarded the Nobel Peace Prize. The son of a Baptist minister, he himself was ordained to the ministry at the age of eighteen and subsequently graduated from Morehouse College and Crozer Theological Seminary. He received a Ph.D. in systematic philosophy from Boston University in 1954. King became nationally prominent as a result of his activities in the Montgomery, Alabama, bus boycott in 1955, and for the rest of his life was an advocate of nonviolent resistance to racial injustice and a powerful voice for the Civil Rights Movement—as president of the Southern Christian Leadership Conference and as a charismatic and persuasive speaker. Among his writings are *Why We Can't Wait* (1964) and *Where Do We Go From Here? Chaos or Community* (1968). The following selection is from his first book, *Stride Toward Freedom* (1958).

Oppressed people deal with their oppression in three characteristic ways. 1 One way is acquiescence: the oppressed resign themselves to their doom. They tacitly adjust themselves to oppression, and thereby become conditioned to it. In every movement toward freedom some of the oppressed prefer to remain oppressed. Almost 2800 years ago Moses set out to lead the children of Israel from the slavery of Egypt to the freedom of the promised land. He soon discovered that slaves do not always welcome their deliverers. They become accustomed to being slaves. They would rather bear those ills they have, as Shakespeare pointed out, than flee to others that they know not of. They prefer the "fleshpots of Egypt" to the ordeals of emancipation.

There is such a thing as the freedom of exhaustion. Some people are so 2 worn down by the yoke of oppression that they give up. A few years ago in the slum areas of Atlanta, a Negro guitarist used to sing almost daily: "Ben down so long that down don't bother me." This is the type of negative freedom and resignation that often engulfs the life of the oppressed.

But this is not the way out. To accept passively an unjust system is to co- 3 operate with that system; thereby the oppressed become as evil as the oppressor. Noncooperation with evil is as much a moral obligation as is cooperation with good. The oppressed must never allow the conscience of the oppressor to slumber. Religion reminds every man that he is his brother's keeper. To accept injustice or segregation passively is to say to the oppressor that his actions are morally right. It is a way of allowing his conscience to fall asleep. At this moment the oppressed fails to be his brother's keeper. So acquiescence—while often the easier way—is not the moral way. It is the way of the coward. The Negro cannot win the respect of his oppressor by acquiescing; he merely increases the oppressor's arrogance and contempt. Acquiescence is interpreted as proof of the Negro's inferiority. The Negro cannot win the respect of the white people of the South or the peoples of the world if he is willing to sell the future of his children for his personal and immediate comfort and safety.

A second way that oppressed people sometimes deal with oppression is   4
to resort to physical violence and corroding hatred. Violence often brings about momentary results. Nations have frequently won their independence in battle. But in spite of temporary victories, violence never brings permanent peace. It solves no social problem; it merely creates new and more complicated ones.

Violence as a way of achieving racial justice is both impractical and immoral.   5
It is impractical because it is a descending spiral ending in destruction for all. The old law of an eye for an eye leaves everybody blind. It is immoral because it seeks to humiliate the opponent rather than win his understanding; it seeks to annihilate rather than to convert. Violence is immoral because it thrives on hatred rather than love. It destroys community and makes brotherhood impossible. It leaves society in monologue rather than dialogue. Violence ends by defeating itself. It creates bitterness in the survivors and brutality in the destroyers. A voice echoes through time saying to every potential Peter, "Put up your sword." History is cluttered with the wreckage of nations that failed to follow this command.

If the American Negro and other victims of oppression succumb to the   6
temptation of using violence in the struggle for freedom, future generations will be the recipients of a desolate night of bitterness, and our chief legacy to them will be an endless reign of meaningless chaos. Violence is not the way.

The third way open to oppressed people in their quest for freedom is the   7
way of nonviolent resistance. Like the synthesis in Hegelian philosophy, the principle of nonviolent resistance seeks to reconcile the truths of two opposites—acquiescence and violence—while avoiding the extremes and immoralities of both. The nonviolent resister agrees with the person who acquiesces that one should not be physically aggressive toward his opponent; but he balances the equation by agreeing with the person of violence that evil must be resisted. He avoids the nonresistance of the former and the violent resistance of the latter. With nonviolent resistance, no individual or group need submit to any wrong, nor need anyone resort to violence in order to right a wrong.

It seems to me that this is the method that must guide the actions of the   8
Negro in the present crisis in race relations. Through nonviolent resistance the Negro will be able to rise to the noble height of opposing the unjust system while loving the perpetrators of the system. The Negro must work

passionately and unrelentingly for full stature as a citizen, but he must not use inferior methods to gain it. He must never come to terms with falsehood, malice, hate, or destruction.

Nonviolent resistance makes it possible for the Negro to remain in the   9
South and struggle for his rights. The Negro's problem will not be solved by running away. He cannot listen to the glib suggestion of those who would urge him to migrate en masse to other sections of the country. By grasping his great opportunity in the South he can make a lasting contribution to the moral strength of the nation and set a sublime example of courage for generations yet unborn.

By nonviolent resistance, the Negro can also enlist all men of good will   10
in his struggle for equality. The problem is not a purely racial one, with Negroes set against whites. In the end, it is not a struggle between people at all, but a tension between justice and injustice. Nonviolent resistance is not aimed against oppressors but against oppression. Under its banner consciences, not racial groups, are enlisted.

If the Negro is to achieve the goal of integration, he must organize him-   11
self into a militant and nonviolent mass movement. All three elements are indispensable. The movement for equality and justice can only be a success if it has both a mass and militant character, the barriers to be overcome require both. Nonviolence is an imperative in order to bring about ultimate community.

A mass movement of militant quality that is not at the same time com-   12
mitted to nonviolence tends to generate conflict, which in turns breeds anarchy. The support of the participants and the sympathy of the uncommitted are both inhibited by the threat that bloodshed will engulf the community. This reaction in turn encourages the opposition to threaten and resort to force. When, however, the mass movement repudiates violence while moving resolutely toward its goal, its opponents are revealed as the instigators and practitioners of violence if it occurs. Then public support is magnetically attracted to the advocates of nonviolence, while those who employ violence are literally disarmed by overwhelming sentiment against their stand.

*

RESPONDING TO THE WHOLE ESSAY

1. What categories does King establish? What is the basis of the classification? Has King omitted any categories that ought to appear in this particular classification? If so, what? If not, show how the classification is complete.
2. What is King's primary purpose in the essay? How does classification help him accomplish that purpose? [1g(1)]
3. From evidence in the essay, try to describe the audience King was writing for. What kinds of language help you to identify that audience? What allusions does King make in the essay, and how do they contribute to your understanding of King's

audience? You are now also part of King's audience. How successful are King's rhetorical strategies for you? Explain. [1g(2)]

4. Paragraphs 1 and 2 are similar in two ways: both are arranged according to the topic-restriction-illustration pattern, and both are developed by examples. In each paragraph, what is the topic? The restriction? How do the examples develop the ideas? [3d]

5. Comment upon King's use of transitional devices to ensure coherence in paragraph 3. [3de]

6. King's skillful use of various devices to establish clear transitions between paragraphs makes the reader's task of following the essay almost effortless. Show how King achieves this coherence. [3d]

ANALYZING THE ELEMENTS

Grammer

1. In the third sentence of paragraph 2, what is the subject of the clause "'that down don't bother me'"? Usually, what part of speech is that word? What does this use tell you about rigid classifications of parts of speech? In standard English, the verb here would be *doesn't* rather than *don't*. How can *don't* be justified in this context? Do the same considerations apply to the deliberate misspelling of *been*? [23b]

2. The final sentence of paragraph 7 summarizes King's discussion to that point. Analyze the sentence to show how the various grammatical elements contribute to the summary.

3. What is the mood of the verb in the last sentence of paragraph 7? What reason might King have had for choosing that mood? What is the grammatical function of *individual, group,* and *anyone*? [11c and 17d]

4. In the second sentence of paragraph 8, King uses a series of prepositional phrases to clarify what he means by "noble height." Show how each prepositional phrase contributes to this classification. What part of speech is the object of each preposition? [11 and 12]

Effective Sentences

1. Compare the ninth sentence of paragraph 3 with the tenth, and the first sentence of paragraph 6 with the second. What strategies for making sentences effective do these comparisons reveal? [20b, 21e, and 21h]

2. Analyze King's use of parallel structure in paragraph 5. Point to effective uses of parallelism elsewhere in the essay. [20a and 20b]

Punctuation and Mechanics

1. Explain the use of the colon in the second sentence of paragraph 1. Could King have used a semicolon? Why or why not? What would be the effect of using a semicolon rather than a colon? [28 and 31d]

2. Explain the use of the semicolon in the third sentence of paragraph 11. How would the effect have been different had King used a period and then started a new sentence instead? [28]

Diction

1. Check the meaning of the following words in your dictionary: *tacitly* and *acquiescence* (paragraph 1), *corroding* (paragraph 4), *desolate* and *legacy* (paragraph 6), *synthesis* (paragraph 7), *malice* (paragraph 8), *sublime* (paragraph 9), *imperative* (paragraph 11), *anarchy, inhibited,* and *repudiates* (paragraph 12). Explain how each word helps to make precise the meaning of the sentence in which it appears. In each instance, can you think of any other word that would have served as well? [24a]
2. Explain the effect of the figurative language King uses in the first sentence of paragraph 6. [24a(4)]
3. King makes an allusion to the philosophy of Hegel in the second sentence of paragraph 7. Must the reader be familiar with Hegelian philosophy to grasp the meaning of this sentence? Why or why not? Why do you suppose King included the allusion?

BUILDING VOCABULARY

1. Identify the elements from which each of the following is derived: *tacit, acquiesce, corrode, overwhelm.* What does each word mean? What other word or words are derived from the same root?
2. What words are derived from the root *-habit*? What does each mean? What does *-hibit* mean?

SUGGESTIONS FOR WRITING

1. Consider some obstacle, limiting circumstance, or other frustration with which you are (or have been) confronted in your life—for instance, at work, at school, or at home—and write an essay in which you classify the possible responses and then argue that one of these is best. If you prefer, or if your life seems to have been free of obstacles and frustrations, write the same kind of essay about possible responses to some opportunity.
2. Write an essay classifying the kinds of action that may be taken to accomplish a purpose (such as purchasing a car or a home, getting a raise in pay, changing someone's attitude toward you).

Territorial Behavior
Desmond Morris

Desmond Morris, noted British zoologist, is the author of several widely acclaimed studies aimed at the general reader explaining human behavior from a zoological perspective: *The Naked Ape, The Human Zoo, Intimate Behavior,* and *Manwatching.* A graduate of Oxford University, Morris has taught at Oxford and worked as a research fellow of the university; he is presently affiliated with the department of psychology. He has contributed to a number of journals, among them *Behavior, British Birds, New Scientist,* and *Zoo Life.* "Territorial Behavior," from *Manwatching,* describes man's behavior by classifying it according to the kinds of territory being defended.

A territory is a defended space. In the broadest sense, there are three kinds 1
of human territory: tribal, family, and personal.

It is rare for people to be driven to physical fighting in defense of these 2
"owned" spaces, but fight they will, if pushed to the limit. The invading army encroaching on national territory, the gang moving into a rival district, the trespasser climbing into an orchard, the burglar breaking into a house, the bully pushing to the front of a queue, the driver trying to steal a parking space, all of these intruders are liable to be met with resistance varying from the vigorous to the savagely violent. Even if the law is on the side of the intruder, the urge to protect a territory may be so strong that otherwise peaceful citizens abandon all their usual controls and inhibitions. Attempts to evict families from their homes, no matter how socially valid the reasons, can lead to siege conditions reminiscent of the defence of a medieval fortress.

The fact that these upheavals are so rare is a measure of the success of 3
Territorial Signals as a system of dispute prevention. It is sometimes cynically stated that "all property is theft," but in reality it is the opposite. Property, as owned space which is *displayed* as owned space, is a special kind of sharing system which reduces fighting much more than it causes it. Man is a cooperative species, but he is also competitive, and his struggle for dominance has to be structured in some way if chaos is to be avoided. The establishment of territorial rights is one such structure. It limits dominance geographically. I am dominant in my territory and you are dominant in yours. In other words, dominance is shared out spatially, and we all have some. Even if I am weak and unintelligent and you can dominate me when we meet on neutral ground, I can still enjoy a thoroughly dominant role as soon as I retreat to my private base. Be it ever so humble, there is no place like a home territory.

Of course, I can still be intimidated by a particularly dominant individ-   4
ual who enters my home base, but his encroachment will be dangerous for
him and he will think twice about it, because he will know that here my urge
to resist will be dramatically magnified and my usual subservience banished.
Insulted at the heart of my own territory, I may easily explode into battle—
either symbolic or real—with a result that may be damaging to both of us.

In order for this to work, each territory has to be plainly advertised as   5
such. Just as a dog cocks its leg to deposit its personal scent on the trees in
its locality, so the human animal cocks its leg symbolically all over his home
base. But because we are predominantly visual animals we employ mostly visual signals, and it is worth asking how to do this at the three levels: tribal,
family, and personal.

First: The Tribal Territory. We evolved as tribal animals, living in com-   6
paratively small groups, probably of less than a hundred, and we existed like
that for millions of years. It is our basic social unit, a group in which everyone knows everyone else. Essentially, the tribal territory consisted of a home
base surrounded by extended hunting grounds. Any neighboring tribe in-
truding on our social space would be repelled and driven away. As these early
tribes swelled into agricultural super-tribes, and eventually into industrial nations, their territorial defence systems became increasingly elaborate. The tiny,
ancient home base of the hunting tribe became the great capital city, the primitive warpaint became the flags, emblems, uniforms, and regalia of the specialized military, and the war-chants became national anthems, marching songs
and bugle calls. Territorial boundary-lines hardened into fixed borders, often
conspicuously patrolled and punctuated with defensive structures—forts and
lookout posts, checkpoints and great walls, and, today, customs barriers.

Today each nation flies its own flag, a symbolic embodiment of its terri-   7
torial status. But patriotism is not enough. The ancient tribal hunter lurking
inside each citizen finds himself unsatisfied by membership in such a vast con-
glomeration of individuals, most of whom are totally unknown to him personally. He does his best to feel that he shares a common territorial defence
with them all, but the scale of the operation has become inhuman. It is hard
to feel a sense of belonging with a tribe of fifty million or more. His answer
is to form sub-groups, nearer to his ancient pattern, smaller and more personally known to him—the local club, the teenage gang, the union, the specialist society, the sports association, the political party, the college fraternity,
the social clique, the protest group, and the rest. Rare indeed is the individual
who does not belong to at least one of these splinter groups, and take from it
a sense of tribal allegiance and brotherhood. Typical of all these groups is the
development of Territorial Signals—badges, costumes, headquarters, banners,
slogans, and all the other displays of group identity. This is where the action
is, in terms of tribal territorialism, and only when a major war breaks out does
the emphasis shift upwards to the higher group level of the nation.

Each of these modern pseudo-tribes sets up its own special kind of home   8
base. In extreme cases non-members are totally excluded, in others they are

allowed in as visitors with limited rights and under a control system of special rules. In many ways they are like miniature nations, with their own flags and emblems and their own border guards. The exclusive club has its own "customs barrier": the doorman who checks your "passport" (your membership card) and prevents strangers from passing in unchallenged. There is a government: the club committee; and often special displays of the tribal elders: the photographs or portraits of previous officials on the walls. At the heart of the specialized territories there is a powerful feeling of security and importance, a sense of shared defence against the outside world. Much of the club chatter, both serious and joking, directs itself against the rottenness of everything outside the club boundaries—in that "other world" beyond the protected portals.

In social organizations which embody a strong class system, such as military units and large business concerns, there are many territorial rules, often unspoken, which interfere with the official hierarchy. High-status individuals, such as officers or managers, could in theory enter any of the regions occupied by the lower levels in the peck order, but they limit this power in a striking way. An officer seldom enters a sergeant's mess or a barrack room unless it is for a formal inspection. He respects those regions as alien territories even though he has the power to go there by virtue of his dominant role. And in businesses, part of the appeal of unions, over and above their obvious functions, is that with their officials, headquarters, and meetings they add a sense of territorial power for the staff workers. It is almost as if each military organization and business concern consists of two warring tribes: the officers versus the other ranks, and the management versus the workers. Each has its special home base within the system, and the territorial defence pattern thrusts itself into what, on the surface, is a pure social hierarchy. Negotiations between managements and unions are tribal battles fought out over the neutral ground of a boardroom table, and are as much concerned with territorial display as they are with resolving problems of wages and conditions. Indeed, if one side gives in too quickly and accepts the other's demands, the victors feel strangely cheated and deeply suspicious that it may be a trick. What they are missing is the protracted sequence of ritual and counter-ritual that keeps alive their group territorial identity.

Likewise, many of the hostile displays of sports fans and teenage gangs are primarily concerned with displaying their group image to rival fan-clubs and gangs. Except in rare cases, they do not attack one another's headquarters, drive out the occupants, and reduce them to a submissive, subordinate condition. It is enough to have scuffles on the borderlands between the two rival territories. This is particularly clear at football matches, where the fan-club headquarters becomes temporarily shifted from the club-house to a section of the stands, and where minor fighting breaks out at the unofficial boundary line between the massed groups of rival supporters. Newspaper reports play up the few accidents and injuries which do occur on such occasions, but when these are studied in relation to the total numbers of displaying fans involved it is clear that the serious incidents represent only a tiny fraction of the overall group behavior. For every actual punch or kick there are a thousand war-cries, war-dances, chants, and gestures.

Second: The Family Territory. Essentially, the family is a breeding unit and the family territory is a breeding ground. At the center of this space, there is the nest—the bedroom—where, tucked up in bed, we feel at our most territorially secure. In a typical house the bedroom is upstairs, where a safe nest should be. This puts it farther away from the entrance hall, the area where contact is made, intermittently, with the outside world. The less private reception rooms, where intruders are allowed access, are the next line of defence. Beyond them, outside the walls of the building, there is often a symbolic remnant of the ancient feeding grounds—a garden. Its symbolism often extends to the plants and animals it contains, which cease to be nutritional and become merely decorative—flowers and pets. But like a true territorial space it has a conspicuously displayed boundary-line, the garden fence, wall, or railings. Often no more than a token barrier, this is the outer territorial demarcation, separating the private world of the family from the public world beyond. To cross it puts any visitor or intruder at an immediate disadvantage. As he crosses the threshold, his dominance wanes, slightly but unmistakably. He is entering an area where he senses that he must ask permission to do simple things that he would consider a right elsewhere. Without lifting a finger, the territorial owners exert their dominance. This is done by all the hundreds of small ownership "markers" they have deposited on their family territory: the ornaments, the "possessed" objects positioned in the rooms and on the walls; the furnishings, the furniture, the colors, the patterns, all owner-chosen and all making this particular home base unique to them.

It is one of the tragedies of modern architecture that there has been standardization of these vital territorial living units. One of the most important aspects of a home is that it should be similar to other homes only in a general way, and that in detail it should have many differences, making it a *particular* home. Unfortunately, it is cheaper to build a row of houses, or a block of flats, so that all the family living-units are identical, but the territorial urge rebels against this trend and house-owners struggle as best they can to make their mark on their mass-produced properties. They do this with garden-design, with front-door colors, with curtain pattern, with wallpaper and all the other decorative elements that together create a unique and different family environment. Only when they have completed this nest-building do they feel truly "at home" and secure.

When they venture forth as a family unit they repeat the process in a minor way. On a day-trip to the seaside, they load the car with personal belongings and it becomes their temporary, portable territory. Arriving at the beach they stake out a small territorial claim, marking it with rugs, towels, baskets, and other belongings to which they can return from their seaboard wanderings. Even if they all leave it at once to bathe, it retains a characteristic territorial quality and other family groups arriving will recognize this by setting up their own "home" bases at a respectful distance. Only when the whole beach has filled up with these marked spaces will newcomers start to position themselves in such a way that the inter-base distance becomes reduced. Forced to pitch between several existing beach territories they will feel a momentary sensation of intrusion, and the established "owners" will feel a similar sensation of invasion, even though they are not being directly inconvenienced.

The same territorial scene is being played out in parks and fields and on 14 riverbanks, wherever family groups gather in their clustered units. But if rivalry for spaces creates mild feelings of hostility, it is true to say that, without the territorial system of sharing and space-limited dominance, there would be chaotic disorder.

Third: The Personal Space. If a man enters a waiting-room and sits at one 15 end of a long row of empty chairs, it is possible to predict where the next man to enter will seat himself. He will not sit next to the first man, nor will he sit at the far end, right away from him. He will choose a position about halfway between these two points. The next man to enter will take the largest gap left, and sit roughly in the middle of that, and so on, until eventually the latest newcomer will be forced to select a seat that places him right next to one of the already seated men. Similar patterns can be observed in cinemas, public urinals, airplanes, trains, and buses. This is a reflection of the fact that we all carry with us, everywhere we go, a portable territory called a Personal Space. If people move inside this space, we feel threatened. If they keep too far outside it, we feel rejected. The result is a subtle series of spatial adjustments, usually operating quite unconsciously and producing ideal compromises as far as this is possible. If a situation becomes too crowded, then we adjust our reactions accordingly and allow our Personal Space to shrink. Jammed into an elevator, a rush-hour compartment, or a packed room, we give up altogether and allow body-to-body contact, but when we relinquish our Personal Space in this way, we adopt certain special techniques. In essence, what we do is to convert these other bodies into "nonpersons." We studiously ignore them, and they us. We try not to face them if we can possibly avoid it. We wipe all expressiveness from our faces, letting them go blank. We may look up at the ceiling or down at the floor, and we reduce body movements to a minimum. Packed together like sardines in a tin, we stand dumbly still, sending out as few social signals as possible.

Even if the crowding is less severe, we still tend to cut down our social 16 interactions in the presence of large numbers. Careful observations of children in play groups revealed that if they are high-density groupings there is less social interaction between the individual children, even though there is theoretically more opportunity for such contacts. At the same time, the high-density groups show a higher frequency of aggressive and destructive behavior patterns in their play. Personal Space—"elbow room"—is a vital commodity for the human animal, and one that cannot be ignored without risking serious trouble.

Of course, we all enjoy the excitement of being in a crowd, and this re-   17
action cannot be ignored. But there are crowds and crowds. It is pleasant
enough to be in a "spectator crowd," but not so appealing to find yourself in
the middle of a rush-hour crush. The difference between the two is that the
spectator crowd is all facing in the same direction and concentrating on a distant point of interest. Attending a theatre, there are twinges of rising hostility toward the stranger who sits down immediately in front of you or the one
who squeezes into the seat next to you. The shared armrest can become a polite, but distinct territorial boundary-dispute region. However, as soon as the
show begins, these invasions of Personal Space are forgotten and the attention is focused beyond the small space where the crowding is taking place.
Now, each member of the audience feels himself spatially related, not to his
cramped neighbors, but to the actor on the stage, and this distance is, if anything, too great. In the rush-hour crowd, by contrast, each member of the
pushing throng is competing with his neighbors all the time. There is no escape to a spatial relation with a distant actor, only the pushing, shoving bodies all around.

Those of us who have to spend a great deal of time in crowded condi-   18
tions become gradually better able to adjust, but no one can ever become completely immune to invasions of Personal Space. This is because they remain
forever associated with either powerful hostile or equally powerful loving feelings. All through our childhood we will have been held to be loved and held
to be hurt, and anyone who invades our Personal Space when we are adults
is, in effect, threatening to extend his behavior into one of these two highly
charged areas of human interaction. Even if his motives are clearly neither
hostile nor sexual, we still find it hard to suppress our reactions to his close
approach. Unfortunately, different countries have different ideas about exactly
how close is close. It is easy enough to test your own "space reaction": when
you are talking to someone in the street or in any open space, reach out with
your arm and see where the nearest point on his body comes. If you hail from
western Europe, you will find that he is at roughly fingertip distance from
you. In other words, as you reach out, your fingertips will just about make
contact with his shoulder. If you come from eastern Europe you will find you
are standing at "wrist distance." If you come from the Mediterranean region
you will find that you are much closer to your companion, a little more than
"elbow distance."

Trouble begins when a member of one of these cultures meets and talks   19
to one from another. Say a British diplomat meets an Italian or an Arab diplomat at an embassy function. They start talking in a friendly way, but soon
the fingertips man begins to feel uneasy. Without knowing quite why, he starts
to back away gently from his companion. The companion edges forward again.
Each tries in his way to set up a Personal Space relationship that suits his own
background. But it is impossible to do. Every time the Mediterranean diplomat advances to a distance that feels comfortable for him, the British diplomat feels threatened. Every time the Briton moves back, the other feels rejected.

Attempts to adjust this situation often lead to a talking pair shifting slowly across a room, and many an embassy reception is dotted with western-European fingertip-distance men pinned against the walls by eager elbow-distance men. Until such differences are fully understood and allowances made, these minor differences in "body territories" will continue to act as an alienation factor which may interfere in a subtle way with diplomatic harmony and other forms of international transaction.

If there are distance problems when engaged in conversation, then there are clearly going to be even bigger difficulties where people must work privately in a shared space. Close proximity of others, pressing against the invisible boundaries of our personal body-territory, makes it difficult to concentrate on non-social matters. Flat-mates, students sharing a study, sailors in the cramped quarters of a ship, and office staff in crowded work-places, all have to face this problem. They solve it by "cocooning." They use a variety of devices to shut themselves off from the others present. The best possible cocoon, of course, is a small private room—a den, a private office, a study, or a studio—which physically obscures the presence of other nearby territory-owners. This is the ideal situation for non-social work, but the space-sharers cannot enjoy this luxury. Their cocooning must be symbolic. They may, in certain cases, be able to erect small physical barriers, such as screens and partitions, which give substance to their invisible Personal Space boundaries, but when this cannot be done, other means must be sought. One of these is the "favored object." Each space-sharer develops a preference, repeatedly expressed until it becomes a fixed pattern, for a particular chair, or table, or alcove. Others come to respect this, and friction is reduced. This system is often formally arranged (this is my desk, that is yours), but even where it is not, favored places soon develop. Professor Smith has a favorite chair in the library. It is not formally his, but he always uses it and others avoid it. Seats around a mess-room table, or a boardroom table, become almost personal property for specific individuals. Even in the home, father has his favorite chair for reading the newspaper or watching television. Another device is the blinkers-posture. Just as a horse that over-reacts to other horses and the distractions of the noisy race-course is given a pair of blinkers to shield its eyes, so people studying privately in a public place put on pseudo-blinkers in the form of shielding hands. Resting their elbows on the table, they sit with their hands screening their eyes from the scene on either side.

A third method of reinforcing the body-territory is to use personal markers. Books, papers, and other personal belongings are scattered around the favored site to render it more privately owned in the eyes of companions. Spreading out one's belongings is a well-known trick in public-transport situations, where a traveller tries to give the impression that seats next to him are taken. In many contexts carefully arranged personal markers can act as an effective-territorial display, even in the absence of the territory owner. Experiments in a library revealed that placing a pile of magazines on the table in one seating position successfully reserved that place for an average of 77 minutes. If a sports-jacket was added, draped over the chair, then the "reservation effect" lasted for over two hours.

In these ways, we strengthen the defences of our Personal Spaces, keep-   22
ing out intruders with the minimum of open hostility. As with all territorial behavior, the object is to defend space with signals rather than with fists and at all three levels—the tribal, the family, and the personal—it is a remarkably efficient system of space-sharing. It does not always seem so, because news-papers and newscasts inevitably magnify the exceptions and dwell on those cases where the signals have failed and wars have broken out, gangs have fought, neighboring families have feuded, or colleagues have clashed, but for every territorial signal that has failed, there are millions of others that have not. They do not rate a mention in the news, but they nevertheless constitute a dominant feature of human society—the society of a remarkably territorial animal.

✳

RESPONDING TO THE WHOLE ESSAY

1. What purpose is most evident in "Territorial Behavior"? Explain with evidence from the essay. What evidence of a secondary purpose, if any, does the essay contain? [1g(1)]
2. What evidence in "Territorial Behavior" indicates the audience for which Morris was writing? Describe that audience. [1g(2)]
3. What is the tone of the essay? Does the tone influence the reader's perception of the information the essay provides? If so, how? [3a(3)]
4. What basis for classification does Morris use? Where does he state it? What kinds of background information does he offer for his classification?
5. Explain how Morris introduces his subject and arouses the reader's interest in it in the first five paragraphs of the essay. [3b(1)]
6. Morris develops paragraphs 11, 17, 18, and 20 in different ways. Comment on his use of these different patterns of development. [2e]

ANALYZING THE ELEMENTS

Grammar

1. What form of the verb is used in the first clause of the final sentences of paragraph 3? Why is this form used? [17d]
2. The phrase following *unit* in the second complete sentence of paragraph 6 in an appositive. Check the glossary, "Grammatical and Rhetorical Terms," in *Writer's* for an explanation of appositives, and then comment on what this appositive adds to *unit*, the noun it is in apposition to. Do the modifiers of *unit* need to be taken into consideration?
3. Justify the use of a comma to separate the independent clauses in the second sentence of paragraph 8. [27a]

Effective Sentences

1. Analyze the techniques for ensuring sentence variety that Morris uses in each main clause of the first sentence of paragraph 2. [22]
2. How does the absolute phrase that begins the fifth sentence of paragraph 17 contribute to its effectiveness? [12a]

Punctuation and Mechanics

1. Explain the use of a comma after *space* in the second sentence of paragraph 2. What other mark of punctuation could have been used? What is the difference in effect between the two marks of punctuation in this context? [27d and 31d]
2. Explain why the three independent clauses in the sixth complete sentence of paragraph 6 are separated by commas. [27c]
3. Explain the difference between the ways Morris uses quotation marks (as in the first sentence of paragraph 2) and italics (as in the third sentence of paragraph 3). Is this distinction maintained throughout the essay? [30d and 34e]

Diction

1. Examine the use of hyphenated words in the last sentence of paragraph 11 and throughout paragraph 12. Why are these words hyphenated? Do all of them need to be? Why or why not? [32g]
2. In the last sentence of paragraph 15, Morris uses a cliché: "like sardines in a tin." Explain why this cliché is or is not effectively used. [24c]

BUILDING VOCABULARY

1. In Britain, the following words have meanings different from those they have in the United States: *bathe, football, cinema, flat, garden.* What are the American equivalents?
2. What is the source of the word *fan* in its informal meaning? List at least two other words with the same source.

SUGGESTION FOR WRITING

1. Classify and describe the kinds of territorial behavior you have observed at one or more events (for example, at basketball games, in classrooms, in elevators, in your living quarters, at parties, in meetings, and so on).

Which Stooge Are You?
Ron Geraci

Ron Geraci is a senior editor for *Men's Health* Magazine and edits the "Malegrams" section.

Men spend millions of dollars on psychotherapy trying to figure out why 1
they're unhappy, why their kids don't respect them, why women treat them
like idiots. Perhaps shrinks help some men, but for many others, it's money
that would have been better spent on popcorn and videotapes. To solve many
of life's problems, all you really need to do is watch the *Three Stooges*.

Call It Stooge Therapy. We're all variations of Moe, Larry, or Curly, and 2
our lives are often short subjects filled with cosmic slapstick. When Moe (your
boss) hits Curly (your buddy) with a corporate board and then blindsides you
when you try to make it all nice, you're living a Stooge moment. Here you'll
find the personality type each Stooge represents. Once you determine which
Stooge you are, you'll better understand the problems you bring on yourself—
and how you can be a generally happier, more successful knucklehead.

Are You a Moe? Everyone knows more than one Moe. These men are the 3
insufferable know-it-alls who become driving instructors, gym teachers, and
divorce attorneys. The coach who had you do pushups in front of the team?
He was a Moe. So was that boss who made you carry his golf bag.

In short, Moes are hot-tempered men who intimidate people with verbal 4
slaps and managerial eye pokes, according to Stuart Fischoff, Ph.D., a psychologist at California State University. "Moe has a paternalistic personality,
which is pretty common among men," Fischoff says. "He treats everyone like
a child and bullies people to keep them off balance." Being a temperamental
loudmouth also helps Moe scare off critics who might expose his little secret:
He's no smarter than the saps he terrorizes. Moe himself proved that point.
Although he served up most of the nose gnashings and belly bonks in 190
shorts, he always ended up back in the mud with Larry and Curly.

Even if you've never actually threatened to tear somebody's tonsils out, 5
there are a few other clues that can tag you as a Moe. First, naturally, Moes
are explosive hotheads who storm through life constantly infuriated by other
people. "These men suffer from classic low frustration tolerance," says Allen
Elkin, Ph.D., a psychologist in New York. "This not only makes them difficult to work with, but it also gives them high blood pressure, high cholesterol,

244

and a much greater risk of heart attack." In fact, Moes often end up seeking counseling to control their anger, usually after it costs them a job, a marriage, or a couple of good pals. "I tell them to just get away from infuriating situations quickly," says Elkin. "Remember, you don't *have* to poke Curly in the eye because he destroyed the plumbing."

Second, in the likely event that a Moe manages to foul things up himself, he'll find a way to blame his mistakes on other people, says Fischoff. In *Healthy, Wealthy, and Dumb* (1938), for example, Moe breaks a $5,000 vase with a 2-by-4 and screams at Larry, "Why didn't you bring me a softer board?!" 6

Your habits on the job are the most telling signs. If you're a Moe, you're probably the hardest-driving wise guy at work. "High-strung, bossy men with Moe personalities tend to live at their jobs," says Elkin. To help stop overloading themselves with work they can't possibly finish (a common Moe peccadillo), workaholic Moes should make a list of projects they *won't* do each day—and then make sure they keep their hands off those folders. 7

Moe Howard (1897–1975) had a classic Moe personality. Even offscreen, he was the fiery, short-fused leader of the trio who made all the decisions. Of course, this put a lot of worries on Moe's shoulders. "My father was an anxiety-ridden, nervous man," says Paul Howard, Moe's son. "He didn't have much patience. He always worried about his kid brother Curly, and if Larry flubbed a line, my father could become upset and criticize him almost like a director." Larry probably shaped up fast; Moe could always put some English into the next eye gouge. 8

Now, in fairness to all men with bowl cuts and bad attitudes, there are some big advantages to having a Moe personality. "If I could choose my Stooge, I'd sure as hell be a Moe," says Fischoff. Because they're usually so domineering and assertive, Moes are often able to bark their way into leadership positions quickly. (Kennedy and Nixon were Moes; Carter was a Larry.) If you crammed all the *Fortune*-100 CEOs into one Bennigan's, you'd have Moe Central with a wet bar. 9

Another Moe perk: Women flock to you like geeks to a *Star Trek* premiere. Moe is an aggressive, tenacious SOB, and women are genetically programmed to find those traits sexually attractive, says Barbara Keesling, Ph.D., a Southern California sex therapist. That's because prehistoric Moes used their superior eye-poking abilities to scare off those wise-guy tigers. It's why that Moe who gave you noogies in high school went through skirts faster than J. Edgar Hoover—and why he's probably divorced now. 10

"Moes are control freaks," says Keesling. "That can be sexually exciting at first, but women get tired of it very quickly. I know—I've dated examples of all three Stooges. I'm thankful they didn't all try to sleep in my bed at once." 11

The Classic Larry Personality. Larry is the passive, agreeable fellow who scrapes through life by taking his licks and collecting his paycheck. "Generally, things happen *to* a Larry; he doesn't make them happen," says Alan Entin, 12

Ph.D., a psychologist with the American Psychological Association. Larry is the ubiquitous "nice guy" who commutes to his mediocre job, congenially tries to cover Curly's ass, and spends his day trying to avoid getting whacked in the nose by Moe.

That's right: John Q. Taxpayer is a Larry.   13

A subtle testosterone shift, though, can make all the difference in what   14
kind of life this lovable sap leads. Give the classic Larry a little more testicularity, and you have a good-natured man who isn't a biological doormat. He'll kick a wino off your lawn but won't fink on your free cable. That makes him a perfect coworker, neighbor, and pal.

But subtract a little gonad power, and a Larry can be an indecisive wimp   15
whose greatest ambition in life is to watch *Everybody Loves Raymond*. These pitiful, wishy-washy slobs constantly get clobbered for being—as Larry would put it—"a victim of soicumstance," and that typically makes them passive-aggressive, says Fischoff.

"A Larry doesn't have the nerve to be assertive, so he protests by not do-   16
ing something," Fischoff says: not securing the ladder on the triple-bunk bed, or not mentioning that the coffee is actually rat poison. Consequently, Larrys are rarely promoted. If a Larry actually does work up the courage to ask for a raise, the Moe he works for will usually give him a meaningless title upgrade—or say, "Get outta here before I murder ya."

To determine if you're an overly passive Larry, answer these three ques-   17
tions.

What's new? If you're a classic Larry, nothing is new. Your answer will   18
be the latest yarn about the office Curly who once photocopied his own butt. "Larrys live vicariously through Moes and Curlys," says Fischoff. "They don't really have a strong identity of their own."

Still dream about writing a screenplay? "Larrys don't have a life plan," says   19
Fischoff. They bumble from one opportunity to the next while awaiting their "break"; a Moe plots his life like a war and a Curly flatly avoids challenges.

Do you weasel out of big projects? Larrys become good at deflecting re-   20
sponsibility. This lets them avoid the risk of failure (and success) without looking like a bum. In *Idiots Deluxe* (1945), as Curly is being attacked by a giant bear, Moe screams, "Go out there and help him!" "The bear don't need no help!" Larry yells back.

The chief bonus in being a Larry, of course, is that almost everyone thinks   21
you're a swell chum. The dames eventually warm up to you, too, although it might take a few decades. Women reeling from years of turbulent relationships with Moes and Curlys often settle down with a Larry, says Keesling, because he's a stable, predictable, okeydokey guy who won't mind heading to the 7-Eleven for tampons. That makes him husband material. "I'd date Moe and Curly, but I'd marry Larry," confided several women we asked.

Like most Larrys, Larry Fine (1902–1975) spent his career following Moe   22
and his free time ducking him. "Larry and Moe weren't friends," says Lyla Budnick, Larry's sister. "Their dealings were all business." Like any good Larry,

he found passive-aggressive ways to make Moe fume. "My father would be at an airport hours early," says Joan Maurer, Moe's daughter, "but Larry would show up 5 minutes before the plane took off. This made my dad very upset." For Larry, making Moe sweat in a crowded airport terminal was probably a tiny payback for the daily humiliations.

The Curly Syndrome.   In *the Sweet Pie and Pie* (1941), Curly tries to throw 23
a pie at the usual gang of rich idiots but gets nailed with a pastry each time he cocks his arm. Finally he bashes himself with the pie to deprive others of the satisfaction. This illustrates Curly's strategy for life. "These men laugh at themselves so other people can't ridicule them first," says Elkin. "It comes across as funny, but this kind of defense mechanism really stems from a large reservoir of anger and resentment."

Curly had what's called an oral personality, and a particularly self- 24
destructive one. Boisterous, attention-seeking men, especially those who are secretly ashamed of something, like a beer gut or a bald head, often feel that they must perform in order to be liked, says Keesling. "These guys always come in for counseling, because they experience mood swings and addiction problems. It's what killed Curly and his modernday version, Chris Farley."

Men with Curly personalities are almost always fat, says Fischoff, because 25
they live to binge. They overdose on food, booze, gambling, drugs, or sex—and sometimes on all five in one badly soiled hotel bed. Curly, a consummate binger, even out-lined his plans for a utopian life in *Healthy, Wealthy, and Dumb*: "Oh boy! Pie à la mode with beer chasers three times a day!"

On the job, Curlys pride themselves on providing comedic relief. "A Curly 26
senses he's no leader, so he garners attention by being a fool," says Fischoff. This nets him no respect, but it does defuse criticism. Who can fire a guy when he's down on the carpet running in circles?

Just like his two nitwit cohorts, Curly Howard's offscreen personality was 27
pretty similar to that of the Stooge he portrayed. He drank heavily, overate, and smoked several cigars a day. "He would always be out carousing and drinking, and playing the spoons in nightclubs," remembers Paul Howard, his nephew.

"I've heard stories that my father sometimes had to pay for the damage 28
Curly caused while drinking," says Joan Maurer, Moe's daughter. If woo-wooing was enough to get Curly belted onscreen, can you imagine what Moe dished out over a real-life antic like this?

Curly's lifestyle apparently made him foggy at work, too. When he barked 29
at women or said "nyuk-nyuk-nyuk!" it was often because he had forgotten his lines. After having a series of obvious mini-strokes (he could barely grumble out his woos in 1945's *If a Body Meets a Body*), Curly had a career-ending stroke in 1946 and died in 1952 at age 48.

He had a hoot along the way, of course. Everybody loves a clown, so 30
Curlys get plenty of party invites—and nightcaps with attractive women. "If each of the Stooges were to flirt with a woman, Curly would probably take her home, because his humor radiates confidence," Keesling says. (And what

woman could resist an opener like "Hiya, Toots"?) But a Curly's neuroses usually shine through within a few dates, which explains why Curlys tend to have few long-term sex partners, says Keesling.

Curly Howard was married four times. "With the exception of his fourth 31
marriage, his best relationship was with his dogs," says Paul Howard. Curly expressed his marital outlook pretty clearly in 1941's *An Ache in Every Stake*, as he shaved a lathered block of ice with a razor: "Are you married or happy?"

✳

RESPONDING TO THE WHOLE ESSAY

1. This article was originally published in *Men's Health* magazine. Who is his audience? What is Geraci's relationship to that audience? [1g(2)]
2. How does Geraci establish tone in the essay? [31(3)]
3. Consider the order in which Geraci presents his three classifications. Would another order be as effective?
4. Find evidence of Geraci's use of other expository techniques (definition, comparison, contrast, examples). [2e]
5. Are there any weaknesses in his classification system?
6. Can you find an explicit thesis statement in this essay? [2b]

ANALYZING THE ELEMENTS

Grammar

1. In the second sentence of paragraph 8, what is the antecedent of the pronoun? [16d]
2. What does *This* refer to in paragraph 23? [16d]

Effective Sentences

1. Explain the effectiveness of the last sentence of paragraph 1.
2. How does Geraci use questions effectively? [22e]

Punctuation and Mechanics

1. How does Geraci make proper names plural? [32]
2. Explain the use of hyphens in paragraph 6. [32g]

Diction

1. Explain how the following words contribute to Geraci's tone: *shrinks* (paragraph 1), *knucklehead* (paragraph 2), *soicumstance* (paragraph 15), *dames* (paragraph 21).
2. What is accomplished by the figurative expression "like Geeks to a Star Trek premiere" in paragraph 10? [24a(4)]

BUILDING VOCABULARY

1. Provide definitions for the following words in the essay: *pecadillo* (paragraph 7), *workaholic* (paragraph 7), *English* (paragraph 8), *ubiquitous* (paragraph 12).

SUGGESTIONS FOR WRITING

1. Write an essay in which you classify a large group of people according to their similarity to another popular group of characters, possibly the characters on a television show like *Friends*, or characters from a cartoon.
2. Write an essay (either serious or humorous) classifying the different varieties of an emotion or attitude—for example, different kinds of frustration, anger, happiness, love, envy, or excitement.

Computer Skills Mean Sex Appeal
Scott Adams

Scott Adams was an applications engineer at Pacific Bell in the Bay Area when he created his very successful comic strip, "Dilbert," which satirizes modern office life. Certainly the fact that, like Dilbert, most of us have had to deal with incompetent authority figures accounts for at least part of the success of the strip. Dilbert is Everyman (as Dogbert is Everydog); he's an ordinary guy who does what we do, and occasionally what we would like to do. In this essay, by equating Dilbert's nerdiness with the sexual mystique most of us would like to have—a nerdiness with which most of us fear we may be overly well endowed—Adams lends substance to daydreams we may have of becoming fabulously attractive to potential significant others.

1   I get about a hundred e-mail messages a day from readers of my comic strip "Dilbert." Most are from disgruntled office workers, psychopaths, stalkers, comic-strip fans—that sort of person. But a growing number are from women who write to say they think Dilbert is sexy. Some say they've already married someone like Dilbert and couldn't be happier.

2   If you're not familiar with Dilbert, he's an electrical engineer who spends most of his time with his computer. He's a nice guy but not exactly Kevin Costner.

3   Okay, Dilbert is polite, honest, employed, and educated. These are good traits, but they don't explain the incredible sex appeal. So what's the attraction?

4   I think it's a Darwinian thing. We're attracted to people who have the best ability to survive and thrive. In the old days it was important to be able to run down an antelope and kill it with a single blow to the forehead. But that skill is becoming less important every year. Now all that matters is if you can install your own Ethernet card without having to call tech support and confess your inadequacies to a stranger.

5   It's obvious that the world today has three distinct classes of people, each with its own evolutionary destiny:

- KNOWLEDGEABLE COMPUTER USERS who will evolve into godlike noncorporeal beings who rule the universe (except for those who work in tech support).
- COMPUTER OWNERS who try to pass as knowledgeable but secretly use hand calculators to add totals to their Excel spreadsheets. This group will gravitate toward jobs as high school principals and operators of pet crematoriums. Eventually they will become extinct.
- NON-COMPUTER USERS who will grow tails, sit in zoos, and fling dung at tourists.

Obviously, if you're a woman and you're trying to decide which evolu- 6
tionary track you want your offspring to take, you don't want them on the
luge ride to the dung-flinging Olympics. You want a real man. You want a
knowledgeable computer user with real evolutionary potential.

And women prefer men who listen. Computer users are excellent listen- 7
ers because they can look at you for long periods of time without saying anything. Granted, early in a relationship it's better if the guy actually talks. But
men use up all the stories they'll ever have after six months. If a woman marries a guy who's in, let's say, retail sales, she'll get repeat stories starting in the
seventh month and lasting forever. Marry a computer programmer and she
gets a great listener for the next 70 years.

Plus, with the ozone layer evaporating, it's good strategy to mate with 8
somebody who has an indoor hobby. Outdoorsy men are applying suntan lo-
tion with SPF 10,000 and yet by the age of 30 they still look like dried chili
peppers in trousers. Compare that with the healthy glow of a man who spends
12 hours a day in front of a video screen.

It's also well established that computer users are better lovers. If you doubt 9
the sexiness of male PC users, consider their hair. They tend to have either (1)
male pattern baldness—a sign of elevated testosterone—or (2) unkempt jungle hair—the kind you see only on people who just finished a frenzied bout
of lovemaking.

In less enlightened times, the best way to impress women was to own a 10
hot car. But women wised up and realized it was better to buy their own hot
cars so they wouldn't have to ride around with such jerks. Information technology has replaced hot cars as the new symbol of robust manhood. Men
know that unless they get a digital line to the Internet no woman is going to
look at them twice.

Finally there is the issue of mood lighting. Nothing looks sexier than a 11
man in boxer shorts illuminated only by a 15-inch SVGA monitor. If we agree
that this is every woman's dream scenario, then I think we can also agree that
it's best if the guy knows how to use the computer. Otherwise, he'll just look
like a loser sitting in front of a PC in his underwear.

In summary, it's not that I think non–PC users are less attractive. It's just 12
that I'm sure they won't read this article.

✷

RESPONDING TO THE WHOLE ESSAY

1. Adams uses the first four paragraphs of his essay to establish a context—the occasion, place, or intellectual climate influencing a piece of writing. What does he
   give as the occasion for writing this essay? [1g(3)]
2. What is Adams's main purpose in writing "Computer Skills Mean Sex Appeal"?
   Is there evidence of other aims? Is there a relationship between the occasion and
   the purpose of this essay? Explain. [1g(1)]

3. Comment on the audience Adams probably envisioned for this essay, which was originally published in *Windows Magazine*, a publication dedicated to news and commentary regarding the Windows computer operating system. [1g(2)]
4. Adams identifies "three distinct classes of people, each with its own evolutionary destiny." What basis for classification does Adams use here? Does it make useful distinctions? Explain. [2e]

ANALYZING THE ELEMENTS

Grammar

1. In the second sentence of paragraph 1, what is the grammatical function of the phrase "that sort of person"? Comment on Adams's use of this phrase to achieve his purpose. [12]
2. In the first sentence of paragraph 9, Adams comments that computer users are "better lovers." How can this incomplete comparison be justified? [26c]

Effective Sentences

1. Success in telling jokes often depends upon the ability to know just how long to pause before saying the punch line. Similarly, in written humor much depends upon making two incongruous statements appear to be related. Comment on how Adams accomplishes this feat with the final phrase of the second sentence in paragraph 1 and with the third and fourth sentences of paragraph 4.
2. What does the parallel structure in the third sentence of paragraph 11 contribute to the humor of the essay? [20, 26]

Punctuation and Mechanics

1. What reasons can you give for Adams's omitting a comma after *Internet* in the last sentence of paragraph 10? [27f]
2. Comment upon Adams's use of abbreviations and acronyms in paragraph 11. [35]

Diction

1. Adams uses casual, informal language in this essay. What does he gain (or lose) by doing so? Give two examples of casual language. [23]
2. What is a *luge ride* (paragraph 6)? What does it mean in the context of the rest of the sentence and of the last sentence of paragraph 5? [24c].

BUILDING VOCABULARY

1. Look up *frenzy* (*frenzied,* paragraph 9) in a desk or unabridged dictionary. Write one sentence in which you use the word as a noun and another in which you use it as an adjective.
2. According to *Webster's Collegiate Dictionary,* 10th edition, the word *robust* (paragraph 10) derives from a Latin word for "the strength of an oak." What are the modern meanings for the word?

SUGGESTIONS FOR WRITING

1. Write an essay classifying people you have met while doing something you enjoy. Make sure you state your basis for classification clearly.
2. Write an essay concerning college life that might have a title such as "Three (or Four) Kinds of_____."

The Plot against People
Russell Baker

After graduating from Johns Hopkins University, Russell Baker worked as a reporter for the *Baltimore Sun* and *The New York Times*. Since 1962, he has written "The Observer," a syndicated newspaper column of humorous social criticism, which appears several times a week. He was awarded the Pulitzer Prize in 1979 for distinguished commentary. He has also contributed to a number of magazines including *Ladies' Home Journal, McCall's, Saturday Evening Post,* and *The New York Times Magazine.* In addition to collections of his columns—*Poor Russell's Almanac, The Upside Down Man,* and *So This Is Depravity*—Baker has published two autobiographical works, *Growing Up* and *The Rescue of Miss Yaskell and Other Pipe Dreams.* Typical of Baker's wry view of the world, "The Plot against People" is a humorous classification of inanimate objects according to a very surprising principle.

Inanimate objects are classified scientifically into three major categories— 1
those that break down, those that get lost, and those that don't work.

The goal of all inanimate objects is to resist man and ultimately to defeat 2
him, and the three major classifications are based on the method each object
uses to achieve its purpose. As a general rule, any object capable of breaking
down at the moment when it is most needed will do so. The automobile is
typical of the category.

With the cunning peculiar to its breed, the automobile never breaks down 3
while entering a filling station which has a large staff of idle mechanics. It
waits until it reaches a downtown intersection in the middle of the rush hour,
or until it is fully loaded with family and luggage on the Ohio Turnpike. Thus
it creates maximum inconvenience, frustration, and irritability, thereby reducing its owner's lifespan.

Washing machines, garbage disposals, lawn mowers, furnaces, TV sets, 4
tape recorders, slide projectors—all are in league with the automobile to take
their turn at breaking down whenever life threatens to flow smoothly for their
enemies.

Many inanimate objects, of course, find it extremely difficult to break 5
down. Pliers, for example, and gloves and keys are almost totally incapable
of breaking down. Therefore, they have had to evolve a different technique
for resisting man.

They get lost. Science has still not solved the mystery of how they do it, 6
and no man has ever caught one of them in the act. The most plausible theory

is that they have developed a secret method of locomotion which they are able to conceal from human eyes.

It is not uncommon for a pair of pliers to climb all the way from the cel- 7 lar to the attic in its single-minded determination to raise its owner's blood pressure. Keys have been known to burrow three feet under mattresses. Women's purses, despite their great weight, frequently travel through six or seven rooms to find hiding space under a couch.

Scientists have been struck by the fact that things that break down virtu- 8 ally never get lost, while things that get lost hardly ever break down. A furnace, for example, will invariably break down at the depth of the first winter cold wave, but it will never get lost. A woman's purse hardly ever breaks down; it almost invariably chooses to get lost.

Some persons believe this constitutes evidence that inanimate objects are 9 not entirely hostile to man. After all, they point out, a furnace could infuriate a man even more thoroughly by getting lost than by breaking down, just as a glove could upset him far more by breaking down than by getting lost.

Not everyone agrees, however, that this indicates a conciliatory attitude. 10 Many say it merely proves that furnaces, gloves and pliers are incredibly stupid.

The third class of objects—those that don't work—is the most curious of 11 all. These include such objects as barometers, car clocks, cigarette lighters, flashlights and toy-train locomotives. It is inaccurate, of course, to say that they *never* work. They work once, usually for the first few hours after being brought home, and then quit. Thereafter, they never work again.

In fact, it is widely assumed that they are built for the purpose of not 12 working. Some people have reached advanced ages without ever seeing some of these objects—barometers, for example—in working order.

Science is utterly baffled by the entire category. There are many theories 13 about it. The most interesting holds that the things that don't work have attained the highest state possible for an inanimate object, the state to which things that break down and things that get lost can still only aspire.

They have truly defeated man by conditioning him never to expect any- 14 thing of them. When his cigarette lighter won't light or his flashlight fails to illuminate, it does not raise his blood pressure. Objects that don't work have given man the only peace he receives from inanimate society.

✳

RESPONDING TO THE WHOLE ESSAY

1. What is Baker's purpose in "The Plot against People"? Is there evidence of a secondary purpose? Explain. [1g]
2. Comment on the appropriateness of the essay for an audience of college students, giving reasons for your view. What other groups would find the essay appealing? Is there any group of readers who would not be likely to appreciate this essay? If so, which group and why? If not, why not? [1g]

3. Baker intends to be illogical in certain ways in this essay, yet in other ways he is rigorously logical. Point to examples and explain the effect. [5h-i]
4. A standard method of organizing a classification essay is to begin by stating the categories that will be discussed and then to establish the basis for classification used to arrive at those categories. Explain how Baker's use of this method helps to establish the tone of his essay.
5. In a successful classification, categories must be exclusive rather than overlapping; in other words, items in one category may not also be placed in another category within the same classification. How well does Baker fulfill this requirement?
6. What do things that break down, things that get lost, and things that don't work have in common? Is the order in which Baker discusses these categories meaningful? Explain. [2c]

ANALYZING THE ELEMENTS

Grammar

1. Explain the grammatical function of *scientifically* in the first sentence of paragraph 1 and explain how the word influences the reader's expectations about how the essay will proceed. [15b]
2. In the first sentence of paragraph 12, what purpose is served by the use of the passive voice? [17c]

Effective Sentences

1. Explain the parallel structure of the second sentence of paragraph 9. How does the parallelism contribute to the tone? [20a]
2. To what does *it* in the second sentence of the final paragraph refer? Can this broad reference be justified? Explain. [16e]

Punctuation and Mechanics

1. What use of the dash is illustrated by the first sentence of paragraph 4? Could the sentence be structured more effectively any other way? Explain your answer. [31e]
2. What justification can be given for the italics in the third sentence of paragraph 11? [34f]

Diction

1. Notice the combination of an inanimate object as subject with a verb of action in paragraph 7. Explain the effect of this incongruity.
2. How does Baker's imitation of scientific language (even of jargon) contribute to the effect of the essay? Find several examples of this kind of parody.

BUILDING VOCABULARY

1. Words with sources in Old English are so common that we rarely notice them. Look up the following words and state the meaning of the Old English word from which they are descended: *blood, breed, cunning, guest, light, work, woman.*

2. Words for objects are borrowed from other languages at least as often as they derive from earlier English words. Which of the following are borrowed and which are native: *pliers, furnace, purse, luggage, glove, couch, mattress?*

SUGGESTIONS FOR WRITING

1. Classify some ordinary group of people or things (for example, automobile drivers, retail clerks, grocery store paperbacks, horror movies, fast foods) into categories, and write a humorous essay showing how each category represents a different approach in a secret plot to destroy our sanity, our digestion, or even our lives.
2. Write an essay (either serious or humorous) classifying the different varieties of an emotion or attitude—for example, different kinds of frustration, anger, happiness, love, envy, or excitement.

The Qualities of Good Writing
Jacqueline Berke

Jacqueline Berke is a professor of English at Drew University, where she teaches both introductory and advanced writing courses and various courses in literature. A widely published writer herself, she has contributed to many journals and magazines, has been a fellow of the MacDowell Colony for artists and writers, and is the author of a widely used writing textbook, *Twenty Questions for the Writer.* "The Qualities of Good Writing" is reprinted here from that book. (The speech by Patrick Henry from which Berke quotes in her first two paragraphs is printed in full in Chapter 13 of *The Resourceful Reader.*)

Even before you set out, you come prepared by instinct and intuition   1
to make certain judgments about what is "good." Take the following familiar sentence, for example: "I know not what course others may take, but as for me, give me liberty or give me death." Do you suppose this thought of Patrick Henry's would have come ringing down through the centuries if he had expressed this sentiment not in one tight, rhythmical sentence but as follows:

> It would be difficult, if not impossible, to predict on the basis of my limited information as to the predilections of the public, what the citizenry at large will regard as action commensurate with the present provocation, but after arduous consideration I personally feel so intensely and irrevocably committed to the position of social, political, and economic independence, that rather than submit to foreign and despotic control which is anathema to me, I will make the ultimate sacrifice of which humanity is capable—under the aegis of personal honor, ideological conviction, and existential commitment, I will sacrifice my own mortal existence.

How does this rambling, "high-flown" paraphrase measure up to the   2
bold "Give me liberty or give me death"? Who will deny that something is "happening" in Patrick Henry's rousing challenge that not only fails to happen in the paraphrase but is actually negated there? Would you bear with this long-winded, pompous speaker to the end? If you were to judge this statement strictly on its rhetoric (its choice and arrangement of words), you might aptly call it more boring than brave. Perhaps a plainer version will work better:

Liberty is a very important thing for a person to have. Most people—at least the people I've talked to or that other people have told me about—know this and therefore are very anxious to preserve their liberty. Of course I can't be absolutely sure about what other folks are going to do in this present crisis, what with all these threats and everything, but I've made up my mind that I'm going to fight because liberty is really a very important thing to me; at least that's the way I feel about it.

This flat, "homely" prose, weighted down with what Flaubert called "fatty   3
deposits," is grammatical enough. As in the pompous paraphrase, every verb agrees with its subject, every comma is in its proper place; nonetheless it lacks the qualities that make a statement—of one sentence or one hundred pages—pungent, vital, moving, memorable.

Let us isolate these qualities and describe them briefly. . . . The first quality   4
of good writing is *economy*. In an appropriately slender volume entitled *The Elements of Style,* authors William Strunk and E. B. White stated concisely the case for economy: "A sentence should contain no unnecessary words, a paragraph no unnecessary sentences, for the same reason that a drawing should have no unnecessary lines and a machine no unnecessary parts. This requires not that the writer make all his sentences short or that he avoid all detail . . . but that every word tell." In other words, economical writing is *efficient* and *aesthetically satisfying.* While it makes a minimum demand on the energy and patience of readers, it returns to them a maximum of sharply compressed meaning. You should accept this as your basic responsibility as a writer: that you inflict no unnecessary words on your readers—just as a dentist inflicts no unnecessary pain, a lawyer no unnecessary risk. Economical writing avoids strain and at the same time promotes pleasure by producing a sense of form and right proportion, a sense of words that fit the ideas that they embody—with not a line of "deadwood" to dull the reader's attention, not an extra, useless phrase to clog the free flow of ideas, one following swiftly and clearly upon another.

Another basic quality of good writing is *simplicity*. Here again this does   5
not require that you make all your sentences primerlike or that you reduce complexities to bare bone, but rather that you avoid embellishment or embroidery. The natural, unpretentious style is best. But, paradoxically, simplicity or naturalness does not come naturally. By the time we are old enough to write, most of us have grown so self-conscious that we stiffen, sometimes to the point of rigidity, when we are called upon to make a statement in speech or in writing. It is easy to offer the kindly advice "Be yourself," but many people do not feel like themselves when they take a pencil in hand or sit down at a typewriter. Thus during the early days of the Second World War, when air raids were feared in New York City and blackouts were instituted, an anonymous writer—probably a young civil service worker at City Hall—produced and distributed to stores throughout the city the following poster:

> Illumination
> is Required
> to be
> Extinguished
> on These Premises
> After Nightfall

What this meant, of course, was simply "Lights Out After Dark"; but ap-   6
parently that direct imperative—clear and to the point—did not sound "official" enough; so the writer resorted to long Latinate words and involved syntax (note the awkward passives "*is* Required" and "*to be* Extinguished") to
establish a tone of dignity and authority. In contrast, how beautifully simple
are the words of the translators of the King James Version of the Bible, who
felt no need for flourish, flamboyance, or grandiloquence. The Lord did not
loftily or bombastically proclaim that universal illumination was required to
be instantaneously installed. Simply but majestically "God said, Let there be
light: and there was light. . . . And God called the light Day, and the darkness he called Night."

Most memorable declarations have been spare and direct. Abraham   7
Lincoln and John Kennedy seemed to "speak to each other across the span of
a century," notes French author André Maurois, for both men embodied noble themes in eloquently simple terms. Said Lincoln in his second Inaugural
Address: "With malice towards none, with charity for all, with firmness in
the right as God gives us the right, let us strive on to finish the work we are
in. . . ." One hundred years later President Kennedy made his Inaugural ded-
ication: "With a good conscience our only sure reward, with history the final
judge of our deeds, let us go forth to lead the land we love. . . ."

A third fundamental element of good writing is *clarity*. Some people   8
question whether it is always possible to be clear; after all, certain ideas
are inherently complicated and inescapably difficult. True enough. But the
responsible writer recognizes that writing should not add to the complications nor increase the difficulty; it should not set up an additional road-
block to understanding. Indeed, the German philosopher Wittgenstein went
so far as to say that "whatever can be said can be said clearly." If you understand your own idea and want to convey it to others, you are obliged
to render it in clear, orderly, readable, understandable prose—else why
bother writing in the first place? Actually, obscure writers are usually confused, uncertain of what they want to say or what they mean; they have
not yet completed that process of thinking through and reasoning into the
heart of the subject.

Suffice it to say here that whatever the topic, whatever the occasion, ex-   9
pository writing should be readable, informative, and, wherever possible, engaging. At its best it may even be poetic, as Nikos Kazantzakis suggests in
Zorba the Greek, where he draws an analogy between good prose and a beautiful landscape:

To my mind the Cretan countryside resembled good prose, carefully ordered, sober, free from superfluous ornament, powerful and restrained. It expressed all that was necessary with the greatest economy. It had no flippancy nor artifice about it. It said what it had to say with a manly austerity. But between the severe lines one could discern an unexpected sensitiveness and tenderness; in the sheltered hollows the lemon and orange trees perfumed the air, and from the vastness of the sea emanated an inexhaustible poetry.

Even in technical writing, where the range of styles is necessarily limited (and poetry is neither possible nor appropriate), you must always be aware of "the reader over your shoulder." Take such topics as how to follow postal regulations for overseas mail, how to change oil in an engine, how to produce aspirin from salicylic acid. Here are technical expository descriptions that defy a memorable turn of phrase; here is writing that is of necessity cut and dried, dispassionate, and bloodless. But it need not be difficult, tedious, confusing, or dull to those who want to find out about mailing letters, changing oil, or making aspirin. Those who seek such information should have reasonably easy access to it, which means that written instructions should be clear, simple, spare, direct, and most of all, *human*: for no matter how technical a subject, all writing is done *for* human beings *by* human beings. Writing, in other words, like language itself, is a strictly human enterprise. Machines may stamp letters, measure oil, and convert acids, but only human beings talk and write about these procedures so that other human beings may better understand them. It is always appropriate, therefore, to be human in one's statement. 10

Part of this humanity must stem from your sense of who your readers are. You must assume a "rhetorical stance." Indeed this is a fundamental principle of rhetoric: *nothing should ever be written in a vacuum.* You should identify your audience, hypothetical or real, so that you may speak to them in an appropriate voice. A student, for example, should never "just write," without visualizing a definite group of readers—fellow students, perhaps, or the educated community at large (intelligent nonspecialists). Without such definite readers in mind, you cannot assume a suitable and appropriate relationship to your material, your purpose, and your audience. A proper rhetorical stance, in other words, requires that you have an active sense of the following: 11

1. Who you are as a writer.
2. Who your readers are.
3. Why you are addressing them and on what occasion.
4. Your relationship to your subject matter.
5. How you want your readers to relate to the subject matter.

✳

RESPONDING TO THE WHOLE ESSAY

1. Would you say that Berke's primary purpose in "The Qualities of Good Writing" is expressive, informative, or persuasive? Does knowing that the selection comes

from a textbook on writing influence your judgment? Why or why not? What evidence can you find of purposes other than the one you named as primary? [1g(1)]

2. Reread Berke's final paragraph, which concludes with a list of five things the writer must have actively in mind in order to have a "rhetorical stance." What do you suppose Berke's own answers to these five questions were as she wrote "The Qualities of Good Writing"?

3. Analyze Berke's essay for its use of examples. Are any important points made that are not illustrated?

4. From a consideration of Berke's first two paragraphs, how would you describe Berke's attitude toward her reader and the kind of relationship she wishes to establish with the reader? [1g(2)]

5. Analyze the use of transitional devices in paragraph 8. [27b]

6. Find and discuss examples in Berke's own writing of the qualities of good writing she identifies: economy, simplicity, clarity.

ANALYZING THE ELEMENTS

Grammar

1. The third sentence of paragraph 8 is actually an intentional sentence fragment. How might Berke justify using the fragment? [13]

2. The first sentence of paragraph 9 is a complex sentence, comprising a main clause and a subordinate clause. What is the verb of the main clause? Comment on the verb's number, tense, voice, and mood. [17, especially 17d]

Effective Sentences

1. Consider the second sentence of paragraph 4 and the first sentences of paragraph 5 and 8:

The first quality of good writing is *economy.*
Another basic quality of good writing is *simplicity.*
A third fundamental element of good writing is *clarity.*

In the context of the essay, how would the effect be different if these three sentences had been written as follows?

Economy is the first quality of good writing.
Simplicity is another basic quality of good writing.
Clarity is a third fundamental element of good writing.

2. Analyze the use of parallelism in the last three sentences of paragraph 4, and comment on its effectiveness. [20a]

Punctuation and Mechanics

1. Give reasons for Berke's uses of italics in paragraph 4. Are any of the italics optional (that is, not required by rules of correctness)? Might the fact that this selection was written for a textbook have any bearing on Berke's use of italics? [34a and 34f]

2. The use of capital letters in the first sentence of paragraph 6 is unusual. Normally it would not be necessary to capitalize all the words in a phrase such as "Lights Out After Dark," or to capitalize "Required" and "Extinguished" in such phrases as "is required" and "to be extinguished." Why has Berke done so here?

Diction

1. Paragraph 4 contains several striking comparisons that lend force to points being made—both in the quotation from Strunk and White (drawing, machine) and in Berke's own subsequent discussion (dentist, lawyer). Comment on the appropriateness and effect of each comparison.
2. Using your dictionary if necessary, comment on the meaning and appropriateness of *Latinate*, *grandiloquence*, and *bombastically* in paragraph 6 and of *spare* in the first sentence of paragraph 7. [24a(2)]

BUILDING VOCABULARY

1. What is the usual meaning of the word *homely*? What word do we generally use to mean "having the qualities of home"?
2. Look up the meaning of the prefix *para-*. Find three words in Berke's essay that begin with this prefix. What is the meaning of each?

SUGGESTIONS FOR WRITING

1. Analyze some academic field of study—perhaps the one you expect to choose as your major—dividing it into its main parts or subfields, and write an essay explaining it for a reader (such as a friend or parent or some other relative) who knows little about it. Unless your instructor prefers otherwise, such an essay could be in the form of a letter, which you might actually wish to send (thus getting a double benefit) after it has served its purpose in your writing course.
2. Write an essay analyzing in detail the wordiness and other weaknesses in Berke's long, windy paraphrase in paragraph 1 of Patrick Henry's statement, "Give me liberty or give me death." (You may find it helpful first to review 23, 24, and 25. If you need assistance with the mechanics of quoting, see 30.)

How We Listen to Music
Aaron Copland

Pianist and composer of music for orchestra, ballet, stage, film, and voice, Aaron Copland (1900–1990) was the first composer to receive a Guggenheim fellowship, and he has been awarded the Pulitzer Prize in music, the New York Music Critics Circle Award twice, and an Oscar for his musical score for *The Heiress*. He received the Gold Medal of the American Academy of Arts and Letters in 1956. Copland holds honorary degrees from many colleges and universities, including Brandeis University, the University of Hartford, Harvard University, Illinois Wesleyan University, Oberlin College, Princeton University, and Temple University. He has appeared extensively in the United States and Europe as a lecturer and as a conductor, and he has also taught musical composition at Harvard and the New School for Social Research. Among his books are *What to Listen for in Music*, *Our New Music*, *Music and Imagination*, and *Copland on Music*. "How We Listen to Music" is from *What to Listen for in Music* (1957).

1   We all listen to music according to our separate capacities. But, for the sake of analysis, the whole listening process may become clearer if we break it up into its component parts, so to speak. In a certain sense we all listen to music on three separate planes. For lack of a better terminology, one might name these: (1) the sensuous plane, (2) the expressive plane, (3) the sheerly musical plane. The only advantage to be gained from mechanically splitting up the listening process into these hypothetical planes is the clearer view to be had of the way in which we listen.

2   The simplest way of listening to music is to listen for the sheer pleasure of the musical sound itself. That is the sensuous plane. It is the plane on which we hear music without thinking, without considering it in any way. One turns on the radio while doing something else and absent-mindedly bathes in the sound. A kind of brainless but attractive state of mind is engendered by the mere sound appeal of the music.

3   You may be sitting in a room reading this book. Imagine one note struck on the piano. Immediately that one note is enough to change the atmosphere of the room—proving that the sound element in music is a powerful and mysterious agent, which it would be foolish to deride or belittle.

4   The surprising thing is that many people who consider themselves qualified music lovers abuse that plane in listening. They go to concerts in order to lose themselves. They use music as a consolation or an escape. They enter an ideal world where one doesn't have to think of the realities of everyday

life. Of course they aren't thinking about the music either. Music allows them to leave it, and they go off to a place to dream, dreaming because of and apropos of the music yet never quite listening to it.

Yes, the sound appeal of music is a potent and primitive force, but you 5
must not allow it to usurp a disproportionate share of your interest. The sensuous plane is an important one in music, a very important one, but it does not constitute the whole story.

There is no need to digress further on the sensuous plane. Its appeal to 6
every normal human being is self-evident. There is, however, such a thing as becoming more sensitive to the different kinds of sound stuff as used by various composers. For all composers do not use that sound stuff in the same way. Don't get the idea that the value of music is commensurate with its sensuous appeal or that the loveliest sounding music is made by the greatest composer. If that were so, Ravel would be a greater creator than Beethoven. The point is that the sound element varies with each composer, that his usage of sound forms an integral part of his style and must be taken into account when listening. The reader can see, therefore, that a more conscious approach is valuable even on this primary plane of music listening.

The second plane on which music exists is what I have called the 7
expressive one. Here, immediately, we tread on controversial ground. Composers have a way of shying away from any discussion of music's expressive side. Did not Stravinsky himself proclaim that his music was an "object," a "thing," with a life of its own, and with no other meaning than its own purely musical existence? This intransigent attitude of Stravinsky's may be due to the fact that so many people have tried to read different meanings into so many pieces. Heaven knows it is difficult enough to say precisely what it is that a piece of music means, to say it definitely, to say it finally so that everyone is satisfied with your explanation, but that should not lead one to the other extreme of denying to music the right to be "expressive."

My own belief is that all music has an expressive power, some more and 8
some less, but that all music has a certain meaning behind the notes and that that meaning behind the notes constitutes, after all, what the piece is saying, what the piece is about. This whole problem can be stated quite simply by asking, "Is there a meaning to music?" My answer to that would be, "Yes." And "Can you state in so many words what the meaning is?" My answer to that would be, "No." Therein lies the difficulty.

Simple-minded souls will never be satisfied with the answer to the second 9
of these questions. They always want music to have a meaning, and the more concrete it is the better they like it. The more the music reminds them of a train, a storm, a funeral, or any other familiar conception the more expressive it appears to be to them. This popular idea of music's meaning—stimulated and abetted by the usual run of musical commentator—should be discouraged wherever and whenever it is met. One timid lady once confessed to me that she suspected something seriously lacking in her appreciation of music because

of her inability to connect it with anything definite. That is getting the whole thing backward, of course.

Still, the question remains, How close should the intelligent music lover   10
wish to come to pinning a definite meaning to any particular work? No closer than a general concept, I should say. Music expresses, at different moments, serenity or exuberance, regret or triumph, fury or delight. It expresses each of these moods, and many others, in a numberless variety of subtle shadings and differences. It may even express a state of meaning for which there exists no adequate word in any language. In that case, musicians often like to say that it has only a purely musical meaning. They sometimes go farther and say that *all* music has only a purely musical meaning. What they really mean is that no appropriate word can be found to express the music's meaning and that, even if it could, they do not feel the need of finding it.

But whatever the professional musician may hold, most musical novices   11
still search for specific words with which to pin down their musical reactions. That is why they always find Tschaikovsky easier to "understand" than Beethoven. In the first place, it is easier to pin a meaning-word on a Tschaikovsky piece than on a Beethoven one. Much easier. Moreover, with the Russian composer, every time you come back to a piece of his it almost always says the same thing to you, whereas with Beethoven it is often quite difficult to put your finger right on what he is saying. And any musician will tell you that that is why Beethoven is the greater composer—because music which always says the same thing to you will necessarily soon become dull music, but music whose meaning is slightly different with each hearing has a greater chance of remaining alive.

Listen, if you can, to the forty-eight fugue themes of Bach's *Well Tempered*   12
Clavichord. Listen to each theme, one after another. You will soon realize that each theme mirrors a different world of feeling. You will also soon realize that the more beautiful a theme seems to you the harder it is to find any word that will describe it to your complete satisfaction. Yes, you will certainly know whether it is a gay theme or a sad one. You will be able, in other words, in your own mind, to draw a frame of emotional feeling around your theme. Now study the sad one a little closer. Try to pin down the exact quality of its sadness. Is it pessimistically sad; is it fatefully sad or smilingly sad?

Let us suppose that you are fortunate and can describe to your own   13
satisfaction in so many words the exact meaning of your chosen theme. There is still no guarantee that anyone else will be satisfied. Nor need they be. The important thing is that each one feel for himself the specific expressive quality of a theme or, similarly, an entire piece of music. And if it is a great work of art, don't expect it to mean exactly the same thing to you each time you return to it.

Themes or pieces need not express only one emotion, of course. Take such   14
a theme as the first main one of the *Ninth Symphony,* for example. It is clearly made up of different elements. It does not say only one thing. Yet anyone hearing it immediately gets a feeling of strength, a feeling of power. It isn't a

power that comes simply because the theme is played loudly. It is a power inherent in the theme itself. The extraordinary strength and vigor of the theme results in the listener's receiving an impression that a forceful statement has been made. But one should never try to boil it down to "the fateful hammer of life," etc. That is where the trouble begins. The musician, in his exasperation, says it means nothing but the notes themselves, whereas the nonprofessional is only too anxious to hang on to any explanation that gives him the illusion of getting closer to the music's meaning.

Now, perhaps, the reader will know better what I mean when I say that 15 music does have an expressive meaning but that we cannot say in so many words what that meaning is.

The third plane on which music exists is the sheerly musical plane. Besides 16 the pleasurable sound of music and the expressive feeling that it gives off, music does exist in terms of the notes themselves and of their manipulation. Most listeners are not sufficiently conscious of this third plane.

Professional musicians, on the other hand, are, if anything, too conscious 17 of the mere notes themselves. They often fall into the error of becoming so engrossed with their arpeggios and staccatos that they forget the deeper aspects of the music they are performing. But from the layman's standpoint, it is not so much a matter of getting over bad habits on the sheerly musical plane as of increasing one's awareness of what is going on, in so far as the notes are concerned.

When the man in the street listens to the "notes themselves" with any degree 18 of concentration, he is most likely to make some mention of the melody. Either he hears a pretty melody or he does not, and he generally lets it go at that. Rhythm is likely to gain his attention next, particularly if it seems exciting. But harmony and tone color are generally taken for granted, if they are thought of consciously at all. As for music's having a definite form of some kind, that idea seems never to have occurred to him.

It is very important for all of us to become more alive to music on its 19 sheerly musical plane. After all, an actual musical material is being used. The intelligent listener must be prepared to increase his awareness of the musical material and what happens to it. He must hear the melodies, the rhythms, the harmonies, the tone colors in a more conscious fashion. But above all he must, in order to follow the line of the composer's thought, know something of the principles of musical form. Listening to all of these elements is listening on the sheerly musical plane.

Let me repeat that I have split up mechanically the three separate planes 20 on which we listen merely for the sake of greater clarity. Actually, we never listen on one or the other of these planes. What we do is to correlate them—listening in all three ways at the same time. It takes no mental effort, for we do it instinctively.

Perhaps an analogy with what happens to us when we visit the theater 21 will make this instinctive correlation clearer. In the theater, you are aware of the actors and actresses, costumes and sets, sounds and movement. All these give one the sense that the theater is a pleasant place to be in. They constitute the sensuous plane in our theatrical reactions.

The expressive plane in the theater would be derived from the feeling that 22 you get from what is happening on the stage. You are moved to pity, excitement, or gayety. It is this general feeling, generated aside from the particular words being spoken, a certain emotional something which exists on the stage, that is analogous to the expressive quality in music.

The plot and plot development is equivalent to our sheerly musical plane. 23 The playwright creates and develops a character in just the same way that a composer creates and develops a theme. According to the degree of your awareness of the way in which the artist in either field handles his material will you become a more intelligent listener.

It is easy enough to see that the theatergoer never is conscious of any of 24 these elements separately. He is aware of them all at the same time. The same is true of music listening. We simultaneously and without thinking listen on all three planes.

In a sense, the ideal listener is both inside and outside the music at the 25 same moment, judging it and enjoying it, wishing it would go one way and watching it go another—almost like the composer at the moment he composes it; because in order to write his music, the composer must also be inside and outside his music, carried away by it and yet coldly critical of it. A subjective and objective attitude is implied on both creating and listening to music.

What the reader should strive for, then, is a more *active* kind of listen- 26 ing. Whether you listen to Mozart or Duke Ellington, you can deepen your understanding of music only by being a more conscious and aware listener— not someone who is just listening, but someone who is listening *for* something.

❋

RESPONDING TO THE WHOLE ESSAY

1. From reading the essay, how would you characterize the audience for whom it was written? Point to evidence in support of your answer. [1g(2)]
2. What is Copland's primary purpose in "How We Listen to Music"? Where does he state or strongly imply this purpose? [1g(1)]
3. Copland announces in his introduction the strategy he will use to develop his essay. Explain how the introduction reflects the organization of the essay as a whole. [3b]
4. What is Copland's basis for division in "How We Listen to Music"?
5. What problem with his analysis does Copland acknowledge? Why does he bring it up where he does?
6. How does Copland establish the conversational tone of the essay? [3a(3)]

ANALYZING THE ELEMENTS

Grammar

1. The fourth sentence of paragraph 11 is an intentional sentence fragment. What reason might Copland have had for using it? [13]
2. In paragraph 13 Copland uses verbs with three different moods—imperative, indicative, and subjunctive. Point to the shifts, and explain what Copland accomplishes by this variation. [17c]
3. The last sentence of paragraph 19 contains two gerund phrases. What are they, and how does each function in the sentence? [12a]

Effective Sentences

1. Explain how parallelism helps to make the last sentence of paragraph 4 effective. [20]
2. In paragraph 14 a number of the sentences could be combined to make longer sentences. Which ones lend themselves easily to combination? What rhetorical purpose is served by not combining them? [19a and 19b]

Punctuation and Mechanics

1. Explain why the first sentence of paragraph 10 ends with a question mark rather than with a period. [31b]
2. Explain the function of the dash in the last sentence of paragraph 11. [31e]

Diction

1. Look up the following words in your dictionary and consider their appropriateness in the essay: *sensuous* (paragraph 1), *deride* (paragraph 3), *apropos* (paragraph 4), *usurp* (paragraph 5), *commensurate* and *integral* (paragraph 6), *intransigent* (paragraph 7), and *arpeggios* and *staccatos* (paragraph 17). [23a and 24a(1)]
2. Comment on whether, in the fifth sentence of paragraph 6, the connotations of *commensurate* fit with the tone established by "Don't get the idea. . . ." [24a(2)]

BUILDING VOCABULARY

1. What are the three meanings of the adjective *sheer?*
2. *Concert, compose,* and *commensurate* all use the same prefix. What is that prefix? Why is this prefix sometimes spelled *com-* and sometimes *con-?*

SUGGESTIONS FOR WRITING

1. Consider carefully your own response to some work of art other than a musical work—a painting, statue, or work of architecture, a poem or short story, a film or play—and write an essay in which you analyze your response, dividing it into different aspects or levels. Alternatively, write such an essay analyzing your response to a person—either a real person or a character in a book or film—toward whom

your attitude is complex. (*Caution:* Do not choose your composition instructor, no matter what your feelings may be; this is never successful.)

2. Although Copland excludes no kind of music, he focuses on classical music. Write a brief "listening guide" to another kind of music you like—such as jazz (or a particular kind of jazz), country, rock (either soft rock or heavy metal), or folk—analyzing it for a reader who has little or no knowledge of it. Or instead you may write such a guide to appreciating the music of a particular instrument—guitar, trombone, flute, whatever.

＊

Chapter 8

Definition

When you say, "I mean . . . ," you are defining. A definition, whether it is a short dictionary definition or an entire essay, explains what something is. Formal definitions—the kind you most often find in your dictionary—follow a classic three-part pattern, naming the object or concept to be defined, placing it in a class, and then differentiating it from other members of that class. See 23a for some samples, or refer to your own dictionary.

You will find that you often need to use formal definitions in your writing. But the dictionary does not restrict itself to such definitions, and you need not do so either. In fact, a definition essay may involve many of the strategies discussed in this book, as the essays in this chapter show. Kathleen Murphy defines *romantic hero* by giving examples. John R. Erickson begins his definition of *cowboy* with a short narrative, compares and contrasts the cowboy with the rancher and with other workers, and also relies on examples and description.

Since you write a definition to explain some concept or object to your reader, obviously you must consider what the reader already knows before you can decide what kinds of details and examples you need to supply and what kind of vocabulary you should use—or whether you need to define at all. For instance, if you were writing about a *rumble seat*, you would have to give much more explanation for readers under sixty than for readers who are older, since such open passenger seats were not used in cars manufactured much after World War II. And older readers could simply be expected to know what a rumble seat is without explanation—very likely having sat in the rumble seat as a child or as a teenager out on a double date.

An awareness not only of your readers' background and interests but also of your purpose in writing for those readers is crucial to the decisions you will make. Are you writing primarily to convey information to a reader who you can safely assume is interested in learning more about your subject? If so, you may have the luxury of taking time and space to explore your subject in considerable depth, as Kathleen Murphy does in "The Good, The Bad, and The Ugly: Clint Eastwood as Romantic Hero." On the other hand, you might be writing with a strongly persuasive aim, hoping to win over skeptical readers to your point of view—and you might therefore try to be as brief as possible

271

and to rely on a few striking examples and carefully chosen details so as not to exhaust your readers' patience while you make your case.

As you write definitions, a few special cautions are worth bearing in mind. Be careful with your logic; one of the most frequent traps writers fall into with definition is circularity. You don't help your reader much when you define a Cistercian monk as a monk belonging to the Cistercian order. Also avoid the awkward and illogical use of *is when* or *is where* in definitions that do not involve time or place. For instance, do not write "Terrorism *is where* [or *is when*] violence and intimidation are used for some political purpose." Terrorism is neither a place (*is where*) nor a time (*is when*). Instead, write "Terrorism is the use of violence and intimidation for some political purpose."

In the following essay, student Carol Johnson, defines "feminist." As you read the essay, notice the kinds of information Johnson provides and the various development strategies she employs.

What Is a Feminist?

Term to be defined	The term "feminist" has been used to batter or applaud so many women and movements in our society that it is easily one of the most misunderstood adjectives of the century. So, what is a feminist? Is it a woman who hates men? Is it a woman who wants only women to run the country? Is it a woman with short cropped hair wearing comfortable shoes? I don't
Reason for definition	think there is an easy answer; an understanding of the word "feminist," I believe, requires an understanding of the political, social, and economic issues that form its origination.
Historical context	First, historically and politically speaking, there were some women who saw the role women played in society and were concerned; they felt women needed the right to vote. These women questioned why society, at that time almost entirely represented by men, did not consider them equal to men. These women interpreted the U.S. Constitution to affirm that it was not God's intention to enslave men, so they wanted to know why women were being enslaved. Also, these women knew that if they ever hoped to influence the laws that oppressed them, women must have the right to vote.
Historical definition	For women in this country in the early part of this century were pitifully oppressed both economically and socially. Because they were not allowed to receive the same education men were given, if a woman had to earn her living, she was forced into low-paying service jobs or low-level factory

positions that required long hours of tedious labor under horrendous conditions. The majority of women lacked the ability to exercise any control over their circumstances. These women were not women of influence, but women of the working class, overworked, underpaid, and without a voice—the majority of women!

Political definition

Women from all classes protested these abusive and discriminatory practices. These protesters banded together and marched through the streets of their country demanding equality with men. And these women were labeled feminists. They wanted the right to vote, they wanted the right to fair working conditions and fair wages, and they wanted the right to live their lives in the manner they chose without ostracism from society. Yes, these women (and a few like-minded men) were called feminists.

Modern feminist agenda

Today, feminists come in all shapes, sizes, races, ages, and sexes. Today, the word "feminist" still implies a political agenda. But do we really need to have feminists and a feminist agenda today? The answer is a definite yes. Why? Because women still make only 70 cents on the dollar men earn doing similar jobs; because women single heads of households and their children are the fastest growing segment of the homeless population; because abuse of women by their fathers, husbands, and boyfriends is still happening and on the increase—the truth is, feminists must continue to work every day to make equality a reality.

Term and class differentia

These feminists are men and women who actively promote the political, economic, and social equality of women. Some feminists may be gay; far more are heterosexual. But all feminists believe in the undeniable fact that men and women are equal under

Expansion of class

our Constitution.

Commentary. Johnson sets up the essay as a question to be answered by the definition. She begins by presenting several commonly held, but patently false, views of what a feminist is and notes that the true definition must be understood in a historical and political context; hence her essay is also an argument for feminism.

The body of her essay first offers a historical context, giving background information about the plight of ordinary women at the turn of the century and about the early feminists who protested against discrimination against women. This information leads to her historical definition of a feminist.

However, since her purpose is to present a definition of the modern feminist, she then identifies how a feminist looks and follows that information with a statement of how a feminist thinks. To justify the need for feminists, Johnson states several ways in which women are oppressed today.

Her essay concludes with her statement of term, class, and differentiating characteristics—the elements of a formal definition. The term is *feminist*; the class is *men* and *women*; and the differentiating characteristic is *who actively promote the political, economic, and social equality of women.*

Johnson's strategy is interesting. Because the essay is an argument as well as a definition essay, Johnson defers her strongest evidence. As she draws to a close, she points out how in several ways life has changed little for the working-class woman. She also deflects a standard, but ignorant, criticism of feminists by pointing out that sexual preference is not relevant. Structuring the essay in this way allows Johnson to make her point strongly.

The "Perfect" Trap

Monica Ramirez Basco

Monica Ramirez Basco is a researcher and psychologist at the University of Texas Southwestern Medical Center at Dallas. Her book, *Never Good Enough: Freeing Yourself from the Chains of Perfectionism*, was published in 1999. She also co-authored *Cognitive-Behavioral Therapy for Bipolar Disorder* with A. John Rush.

Susan, an interior designer, had been working frantically for the last month 1
trying to get her end-of-the-year books in order, keep the business running, and plan a New Year's Eve party for her friends and her clients. Susan's home is an advertisement of her talent as a designer, so she wanted to make some changes to the formal dining room before the party that would be particularly impressive. It all came together in time for the party and the evening seemed to be going well, until her assistant, Charles, asked her if Mrs. Beale, who owned a small antique shop and had referred Susan a lot of business, and Mr. Sandoval, a member of the local Chamber of Commerce and a supporter of Susan's, had arrived.

Susan felt like her head was about to explode when she realized that she 2
had forgotten to invite them to the party. "Oh, no," she moaned. "How could I be so stupid? What am I going to do? They'll no doubt hear about it from someone and assume I omitted them on purpose. I may as well kiss the business good-bye." Though Charles suggested she might be overreacting a little, Susan spent the rest of the night agonizing over her mistake.

Susan is an inwardly focused perfectionist. Although it can help her in 3
her work, it also hurts her when she is hard on herself and finds error completely unacceptable. Like many people, she worries about what others will think of her and her business. However, in Susan's case her errors lead to humiliation, distress, sleepless nights and withdrawal from others. She has trouble letting go and forgiving herself because, in her mind, it is OK for others to make mistakes, but it is not OK for her to make mistakes.

Tom, on the other hand, is an outwardly focused perfectionist. He feels 4
OK about himself, but he is often disappointed in and frustrated with others who seem to always let him down. Quality control is his line of work, but he cannot always turn it off when he leaves the office.

Tom drove into his garage to find that there was still a mess on the work- 5
bench and floor that his son Tommy had left two days ago. Tom walked through door and said to his wife in an annoyed tone of voice, "I told Tommy to clean up his mess in the garage before I got home." His wife defended their

son, saying, "He just got home himself a few minutes ago." "Where is he now?" Tom demanded. "He better not be on the phone." Sure enough, though, Tommy was on the phone and Tom felt himself tensing up and ordering, "Get off the phone and go clean up that mess in the garage like I told you." "Yes, sir," said Tommy, knowing that a lecture was coming.

For Tom, it seems like every day there is something new to complain   6
about. Tommy doesn't listen, his wife doesn't take care of things on time, and there is always an excuse. And even when they do their parts it usually isn't good enough, and they don't seem to care. It is so frustrating for Tom sometimes that he does the job himself rather than ask for help, just so he doesn't have to deal with their procrastination and excuses.

Tom's type of perfectionism causes him problems in his relationships with   7
others because he is frequently frustrated by their failure to meet his expectations. When he tries to point this out in a gentle way, it still seems to lead to tension, and sometimes to conflict. He has tried to train himself to expect nothing from others, but that strategy doesn't seem to work either.

The Personal Pain of Perfectionists.   The reach for perfection can be painful   8
because it is often driven by both a desire to do well and a fear of the consequences of not doing well. This is the double-edged sword of perfectionism.

It is a good thing to give the best effort, to go the extra mile, and to take   9
pride in one's performance, whether it is keeping a home looking nice, writing a report, repairing a car, or doing brain surgery. But when despite great efforts you feel as though you keep falling short, never seem to get things just right, never have enough time to do your best, are self-conscious, feel criticized by others, or cannot get others to cooperate in doing the job right the first time, you end up feeling bad.

The problem is not in having high standards or in working hard.   10
Perfectionism becomes a problem when it causes emotional wear and tear or when it keeps you from succeeding or from being happy. The emotional consequences of perfectionism include fear of making mistakes, stress from the pressure to perform, and self-consciousness from feeling both self-confidence and self-doubt. It can also include tension, frustration, disappointment, sadness, anger or fear of humiliation. These are common experiences for inwardly focused perfectionists.

The emotional stress caused by the pursuit of perfection and the failure   11
to achieve this goal can evolve into more severe psychological difficulties. Perfectionists are more vulnerable to depression when stressful events occur, particularly those that leave them feeling as though they are not good enough. In many ways, perfectionistic beliefs set a person up to be disappointed, given that achieving perfection consistently is impossible. What's more, perfectionists who have a family history of depression and may therefore be more biologically vulnerable to developing the psychological and physical symptoms of major depression may be particularly sensitive to events that stimulate their self-doubt and their fear of rejection or humiliation.

The same seems to be true for eating disorders, such as anorexia nervosa 12 and bulimia. Several recent studies have found that even after treatment, where weight was restored in malnourished and underweight women with anorexia, their perfectionistic beliefs persisted and likely contributed to relapse. Perfectionism also seems to be one of the strongest risk factors for developing an eating disorder.

Sometimes the pain of perfectionism is felt in relationships with others. 13 Perfectionists can sometimes put distance between themselves and others unintentionally by being intolerant of others' mistakes or by flaunting perfect behavior or accomplishments in front of those who are aware of being merely average. Although they feel justified in their beliefs about what is right and what is wrong, they still suffer the pain of loneliness. Research suggests that people who have more outwardly focused perfectionism are less likely than inwardly focused perfectionists to suffer from depression or anxiety when they are stressed. However, interpersonal difficulties at home or on the job may be more common.

How Did I Get This Way? There is considerable scientific evidence that many 14 personality traits are inherited genetically. Some people are probably born more perfectionistic than others. I saw this in my own children. My oldest son could sit in his high chair, happily playing with a mound of spaghetti, his face covered with sauce. My second son did not like being covered in goo. Instead, he would wipe his face and hands with a napkin as soon as he was old enough to figure out how to do it. As he got a little older, he kept his room cleaner than his brother. When he learned to write he would erase and rewrite his homework until it was "perfect."

Parental influences can influence the direction or shape that perfection- 15 ism takes. Many perfectionists, especially inwardly focused perfectionists, grew up with parents who either directly or indirectly communicated that they were not good enough. These were often confusing messages, where praise and criticism were given simultaneously. For example, "That was nice, but I bet you could do better." "Wow, six As and one B on your report card! You need to bring that B up to an A next time." "Your choir performance was lovely, but that sound system is really poor. We could hardly hear you."

Unfortunately, with the intention of continuing to motivate their children, 16 these parents kept holding out the emotional carrot: "Just get it right this time and I will approve of you." Some psychological theories suggest over time the child's need to please her parents becomes internalized, so that she no longer needs to please her parents; she now demands perfection from herself.

Some perfectionists tell stories of chaotic childhoods where they never 17 seemed to have control over their lives. Marital breakups, relocations, financial crises, illnesses and other hardships created an environment of instability. One of the ways in which these people got some sense of order in their otherwise disordered lives was to try to fix things over which they had some control, such as keeping their rooms neat and tidy, working exceptionally hard on schoolwork, or attempting to control their younger brothers and sisters. As adults, however, when their lives were no longer in flux, they may have continued to work hard to maintain control.

Are You A Perfectionist?   Perfectionists share some common characteristics.   18
They are usually neat in their appearance and are well organized. They seem to push themselves harder than most other people do. They also seem to push others as hard as they push themselves. On the outside, perfectionists usually appear to be very competent and confident individuals. They are often envied by others because they seem to "have it all together." Sometimes they seem perfect. On the inside they do not feel perfect, nor do they feel like they always have control over their own lives.

Let's look at some of these characteristics more closely and how they in-   19
terfere with personal and professional life. Terry, 34, a divorced working mother of two, is a high achiever with high career ambitions. But she can sometimes get hung up on the details of her work. She is not good with figures, but does not trust her staff enough to use their figures without checking them herself. She gets frustrated with this mundane work and makes mistakes herself and then becomes angry with her subordinates for doing poor work.

Perfectionists also tend to think there is a right way and wrong way to   20
do things. When Joe, a retired Marine Corps drill sergeant, takes his boys fishing they have a routine for preparation, for fishing and for cleanup. It is time-efficient, neat, organized. The boys think the "fishing ritual" is overdone and they resent having to comply.

Expecting people to do their best is one thing. Expecting perfection from   21
others often means setting goals that can be impossible to achieve. Brent, 32 and single, has been looking for Ms. Right for 12 years but cannot seem to find her. He does not have a well-defined set of characteristics in mind. He just has a general impression of an angel, a sexual goddess, a confident, independent, yet thoroughly devoted partner. Blond is preferable, but he's not that picky.

Perfectionists can have trouble making decisions. They are so worried   22
about making the wrong one that they fail to reach any conclusion. If the person is lucky, someone else will make the decision for them, thereby assuming responsibility for the outcome. More often the decision is made by default. A simple example is not being able to choose whether to file income tax forms on time or apply for an extension. If you wait long enough, the only real alternative is to file for an extension.

Along with indecision, perfectionists are sometimes plagued by great dif-   23
ficulty in taking risks, particularly if their personal reputations are on the line. Brent is in a type of job were creativity can be an asset. But coming up with new ideas rather than relying on the tried and true ways of business means making yourself vulnerable to the criticism of others. Brent fears looking like an idiot should an idea he advances fail. And on the occasions when he has

gone out on a limb with a new concept he has been overanxious. Brent's perfectionism illustrates several aspects of the way that many perfectionists think about themselves. There can be low self-confidence, fear of humiliation and rejection, and an inability to attribute success to their own efforts.

Breaking Free.   To escape the tyranny of perfectionism, you need to understand and challenge the underlying beliefs that drive you to get things "just right."   24

Each of us has a set of central beliefs about ourselves, other people and   25
the world in general and about the future. We use these beliefs or schemas to interpret the experiences in our life, and they strongly influence our emotional reactions. Schemas can also have influence on our choice of actions.

Under every perfectionist schema is a hidden fantasy that some really good   26
thing will come from being perfect. For example, "If I do it perfectly, then . . . I will finally be accepted . . . I can finally stop worrying . . . I will get what I have been working toward . . . I can finally relax." The flip side of this schema, also subscribed to by perfectionists, is that "If I make a mistake," there will be a catastrophic outcome ("I will be humiliated. . . . I am a failure . . . I am stupid . . . I am worthless").

Changing these schemas means taking notice of the experiences you have   27
that are inconsistent with, contrary to, or otherwise do not fit with them. June, who prides herself on being a "perfect" homemaker and mother, believed with 90 percent certainty that "If I do it perfectly, I will be rewarded." Yet she does a number of things perfectly that others do not even notice. June would tell herself that there would be a reward from her husband or her children for taking the extra time to iron their clothes perfectly. Her son did not even realize his shirts had been ironed. When Mother's Day came, she got the usual candy and flowers. No special treats or special recognition for her extra efforts.

When June begins to notice the inaccuracy of her schema, she begins to   28
reevaluate how she spends her time. She decides that if it makes her feel good, then she will do it. If it is just extra work that no one will notice, then she may skip it. She is certain that there are some things she does, such as iron the bedsheets, which no one really cares about. As a matter of fact, June herself doesn't really care if the sheets are ironed. However, she does like the feel of a freshly ironed pillow cover, so she will continue that chore. June has modified her schema. Now she believes that "If you want a reward, find a quicker and more direct way to get it."

If your schema centers around more existential goals, like self-acceptance,   29
fulfillment or inner peace, then you must employ a different strategy. If you believe that getting things just right in your life will lead to acceptance, then you must not be feeling accepted right now. What are the things you would like to change about yourself? What could you do differently that would make you feel better about who you are? If you can figure out what is missing or needs changing, you can focus your energies in that direction.

Or you may be motivated to take a different, less absolute, point of view.   30
Instead of "I must have perfection before I can have peace of mind," consider
"I need to give myself credit for what I do well, even if it is not perfect." Take
inventory of your accomplishments or assets. Perhaps you are withholding approval from yourself.

If your schema is that other people's opinions of you is a mirror of your   31
self-worth, you must ask yourself if you know when you have done something well, if you are able to tell the difference between a good performance
and a poor performance. If you are capable of evaluating yourself, you do not
really need approval from others to feel like you are a valuable worker or a
good romantic partner.

In general, you must treat your perfectionistic schemas as hypotheses   32
rather than facts. Maybe you are right or maybe you are wrong. Perhaps they
apply in some situations, but not in others (e.g., at work, but not at home),
or with some people, such as your uptight boss, but not with others, such as
your new boyfriend. Rather than stating your schema as a fact, restate it as
a suggestion. Gather evidence from your experiences in the past, from your
observations from others, or by talking to other people. Do things always happen in a way that your schemas would predict? If not, it is time to try on a
new basic belief.

One of my patients described the process as taking out her old eight-track   33
tape that played the old negative schemas about herself and replacing it with
a new compact disc that played her updated self-view. This takes some practice, but it is well worth the effort.

✷

RESPONDING TO THE WHOLE ESSAY

1. What is Basco's purpose in this essay? [1g(1)]
2. Who is the intended audience? [1g(2)]
3. In addition to the definition of perfectionism, find evidence of Basco's use of comparison or contrast. [2e(5)]
4. Find examples of Basco's use of cause and effect. [2e(4)]
5. How does the use of subtitles make the essay more effective?

ANALYZING THE ELEMENTS

Grammar

1. Does the pronoun agree in number with its antecedent in the last sentence of paragraph 16? [16d]
2. Does the pronoun agree in number with its antecedent in the third sentence of
   paragraph 22? [16d]

Effective Sentences

1. How effective is the parallelism of the last sentence of paragraph 9? [20]
2. Why is the third sentence of paragraph 20 effective? [22]

Diction

1. Are clichés used excessively in Basco's essay? Find three examples of clichés. [24c]
2. Define the connotations of the following words: *goo* (paragraph 14), *tyranny* (paragraph 24). [24a(2)]

Punctuation and Mechanics

1. Comment on the spelling of *OK* in paragraphs 3 and 4. [35 and Glossary of Usage]
2. In the last sentence of paragraph 14, why is "perfect" in quotation marks? [30d]

BUILDING VOCABULARY

1. What does *evolve* mean? Is it used correctly in paragraph 11? [24a]
2. Look up the roots of the following: *anorexia nervosa, bulimia, malnourished.* [23a]

SUGGESTIONS FOR WRITING

1. Write an essay about either your tendencies or someone else's toward perfectionism or some other personality struggle.
2. Examine society's emphasis upon perfectionism as it is reflected in the media.

Is It Reverse Discrimination?
Ruben Navarrette, Jr.

Born in 1967 in Fresno, California, Ruben Navarrette was valedictorian of his high school class in Sanger, California, the small town in the San Joaquin Valley where he has lived all his life except for the years he spent pursuing a bachelor's degree at Harvard University and graduate study at UCLA. Navarrette taught briefly at Fresno State University, and he has also taught kindergarten, an experience that provided him with what he calls the "most humbling experience of my life." Now a full-time writer, Navarrette is editor of *Hispanic Student,* a magazine for high school students. He writes regularly for the *Los Angeles Times,* the *Arizona Republic,* the *San Antonio Light,* and occasionally for the *San Francisco Chronicle.* He has also authored a book about being a Mexican-American at Harvard, *The Darker Shade of Crimson: Reflections of a Harvard Chicano,* published in 1993 by Bantam.

1   Their young eyes stare at me with a hint of skepticism, and perhaps a bit of anger I have come as a guest speaker to a government class at the high school in Sanger, California, I attended not long ago. Invited to defend an educational program that is continually under siege by those who want racial equity without sacrifice, I have come to confront an old friend—Allan Bakke.

2   It was six years ago, as a high-school senior, that I first met the spirit of the 33-year-old NASA engineer who, a decade earlier, had decided to become a doctor. After being rejected by 12 medical schools, he had challenged the admissions policy at the University of California, Davis' medical school. Bakke charged that the school's special admissions program, which reserved 16 of 100 places for "economically and educationally disadvantaged" applicants, violated his 14th Amendment right to equal protection.

3   Though, in 1978, the U.S. Supreme Court, by 5-4, eventually ordered his admission to Davis, it also allowed—indeed encouraged—colleges and universities to consider the race and sex of its applicants in order to bring diversity and racial parity to U.S. higher education.

4   None of this seemed important to me at the beginning of my senior year in high school, when I was setting my sights on applying to some of the top colleges in the United States.

5   Not everyone shared my confidence. In the middle of the application process, my high school principal counseled me that it was "fine" that I was applying to schools like Harvard, Yale, and Princeton, but that I should also consider applying to Fresno State nearby "just in case." I thanked him for his concern and promptly disregarded his advice.

Rebuffed, he cast the first spear of a bitter attack that was to be taken over   6
by my Anglo classmates and maintained through spring. "You may be right,"
he conceded with insincerity. "After all, your race should help you a lot. . . ."
In five minutes, he had dismissed four years of hard work and perfect grades.

My white classmates, many of them with grades not as good as mine and   7
reeling from rejections by the schools that were admitting me, were far more
direct. "Now, you know if you hadn't been Mexican . . . ." one of them said.
And it was then that I met Allan Bakke.

He was there in the eyes of my classmates, clutching in their fists letters   8
of rejection from Stanford. "It's not fair," I remember one of them saying.
"They turned me down because I was white."

I half-expected to find huge clusters of Mexican students at Harvard, but   9
I was one of only 35 Mexican-Americans in the school. Did this signify the
alleged "darkening" of higher education?

This is the legacy with which I entered the high school government class   10
and confronted Bakke. "Granted, racial discrimination was wrong back then
(presumably pre-civil rights movement)," a student conceded "But now that
that's over with, shouldn't we get rid of affirmative action?"

The first time I'd heard this line was from Nathan Glazer, a professor of   11
mine at Harvard, who some say coined the phrase "reverse discrimination."
Once a society has liberated its employment and educational opportunities
and fully met the burden of its democratic principles, Glazer argues, any further tampering with the laws of appropriation through race-preference programs constitutes impermissible "reverse discrimination."

My dispute with my old professor is that U.S. society has not yet reached   12
Glazer's window of equal opportunity.

I suggested to the students that they needed only to look at their imme-   13
diate surroundings. Sanger is, I reminded them, 72.8 percent Mexican-
American. The fire chief, the police chief, the mayor, the city attorney, the city
manager, and the majority of the City Council are white. The dropout rate of
Latino students from the school system that produced me is consistent with
the distressing national figure of 50 percent to 60 percent.

Clearly, no matter how slick and seductive the rhetoric about the suffer-   14
ing of "new victims," the reality of American society is that, as we enter the
year 2000, we have not yet ended the suffering of our old victims.

❋

RESPONDING TO THE WHOLE ESSAY

1. Does the fact that this essay first appeared in a newspaper help you to explain why Navarrette's paragraphs are so short? How? [2d]
2. Is Navarrette's purpose in "Is It Reverse Discrimination?" predominantly expressive, informative, or persuasive? Explain how the essay reveals Navarrette's purpose. [1g(1)]

3. In paragraph 1 Navarrette explains the situation that motivated his definition of *reverse discrimination*. Does this explanation provide necessary information—for example, would the essay be as effective if it began with the information in paragraph 3? Why or why not?

4. To define *reverse discrimination*, Navarrette uses both functional and stipulative kinds of definition. From evidence in the essay, what part(s) of the definition are functional, and what part(s) stipulative? You may need to look up *stipulative* in your dictionary. [2e]

5. Comment on how the rhetorical situation and the occasion influence the reader's understanding of Navarrette's essay. [1g(3)]

ANALYZING THE ELEMENTS

Grammar

1. Explain the time relationships among the tenses of the verbs in the first sentence of paragraph 1. [17]

2. What is the grammatical function of the clause "that U.S. society has not yet reached Glazer's window of equal opportunity" in paragraph 12? What are the implications of equating that clause with the subject of the sentence? [12b]

Effective Sentences

1. Comment on how Navarrette achieves sentence variety in paragraph 7. [21]

2. To what does *this* in the first sentence of paragraph 4 refer? Is the reference clear? Explain. [16b]

Punctuation and Mechanics

1. Comment on Navarrette's use of numbers in paragraph 2. Which, if any, need not be spelled out because the essay appeared in a newspaper but should be under other circumstances? [35]

2. Explain what Navarrette probably intended to convey by his use of ellipsis points in paragraphs 6 and 7. [31i]

Diction

1. In paragraph 11 Navarrette significantly changes tone. How does he accomplish this change? What do you think Navarrette's reason for the change was? [3a(3)]

2. What is the "spear" that Navarrette says his principal "cast"? Comment on any similar similes or metaphors in the rest of the essay. [24a]

BUILDING VOCABULARY

1. A euphemism is an inoffensive word that substitutes for one that might be considered offensive. Traditionally, euphemisms have referred to body functions and parts: a hundred years ago, tables were said to have *limbs* rather than *legs*—a body part that might give rise to salacious thought. Today, euphemisms often refer

to two kinds of potentially offensive language: words that identify various ethnic groups (as *minority* replaces *Native American*, for example) and words that refer to deplorable social conditions (as *disadvantaged* replaces *poor*). List at least five euphemisms that you encounter in one 24-hour period and state the word that each replaces.

2. What is the meaning of *equity*? Of *parity*? In what discipline are they most commonly used?

SUGGESTIONS FOR WRITING

1. Write a brief essay (500–750 words) defining a kind of behavior (*procrastination, prevarication, exaggeration,* and so on).

2. Define an object according to what it *does* (for example, *nuclear warhead, computer, automobile*).

Land of Identities
Bhikshuni Thubten Chodron

Bhikshuni Thubten Chodron was raised as a Jew and named Hannah Greene. After earning a degree in history from UCLA and teaching elementary school, she became a Buddhist in 1975 and was later ordained as a nun in the Tibetan tradition, studying with the Dalai Lama. She now lives in Seattle, where she teaches Buddhism at Dharma Friendship Foundation. Her books include *Open Heart, Clear Mind* (1990), *What Color Is Your Mind?* (1993), *Taming the Monkey Mind* (1999), *Transforming the Heart: The Buddhist Way to Joy and Courage* (1999), and *Modern Blossoms: Living as a Buddhist Nun* (2000).

1 The headline of the article in the major Israeli newspaper read, "My Name is Hannah Greene and I'm a Tibetan Nun." Interesting, I thought, those are two labels I don't usually apply to myself. "Hannah" is my Jewish name, not one many people know me by, and I'm not Tibetan. At least I was able to answer when the journalists asked, "What is your Jewish name?" Their second question stumped me. "Are you Jewish?"

2 What does being Jewish mean? I remember discussing it in Sunday school, and when the rabbi asked that on a test, I managed to pass. Am I Jewish because my ancestors were? Because I have dark curly hair (or at least used to before it got shaved twenty-one years ago when I ordained as a Buddhist nun), brown eyes, a "noticeable nose" (as my bother politely puts it)? Am I Jewish because I was confirmed and Rabbi Nateev no longer had to face my persistent questions?

3 But now I was stumped. I hadn't thought about whether or not I was Jewish. I just am. Am what? The interviewer tried another tack, "You're American. What does being American mean to you?" I couldn't answer that satisfactorily either. "I'm American because I have an American passport." They looked at me quizzically. Am I American because I grew up with "Mickey Mouse" and "I Love Lucy"? Because I protested the Vietnam War? (Some would say that made me un-American.) Because I was born the grandchild of immigrants who fled the pogroms, on a certain plot of land called Chicago?

4 How could I not know my identity? They were puzzled. As my fifteen days in Israel unfolded, the issue of identity became a recurring theme. I realized how much my views had changed. I had been studying and practicing the Buddha's teaching and thus had spent years trying to deconstruct my identity, to see it as something merely labeled, not as something fixed, not something I truly was. So many of our problems—personal, national, and international—come from clinging to these erroneous, solid identities. Thus in Buddhism, we are not trying to find out who we are but who we aren't.

286

We work to free ourselves from all our erroneous and concrete conceptions about who we are.

My Israeli host understood what the journalists were getting at: "If there were another Holocaust and you were arrested for being Jewish, would you protest saying you're not Jewish, you're Buddhist?" I was baffled. "There is so much suffering in the world right now," I responded, "and I'd rather focus on doing something about that than on thinking up and solving future problems that may not even occur."

"Your mother is Jewish. You could go to the immigration office and within an hour be an Israeli," I was told. "Would you want to do that?" What does being an Israeli mean? I wondered.

Everywhere I went people wanted to know my identity; they cared deeply about the labels I attached to myself, thinking that if they knew all the labels, they'd know me. Israel is a land of identities. At the Ulpan Akiva, a unique language school in Natanya where Israelis can learn Arabic and Palestinians can learn Hebrew, some Palestinians said, "We're Muslims. We hope you can come to our new country, Palestine, someday." More identities. When they heard I follow Tibetan Buddhism, they said, "The Tibetans' situation is similar to ours. We sympathize with them." This startled me because in the Jewish-Tibetan dialogue I had been involved with until then, we had focused on the commonalities of two peoples in exile trying to maintain their unique religions and cultures. But the Palestinians were right: Their situation is like that of the Tibetans, for both live in occupied lands.

In a Reform synagogue in Jerusalem, I participated in a Jewish-Buddhist dialogue. A rabbi and I began to discuss meditation, but the subject changed when the moderator asked, "Can one be Jewish and Buddhist at the same time? Or must one be either a Jew or a Buddhist?" The Orthodox rabbi on my left said, "There are various Buddhist schools and yours may not be one of them, but in general, Buddhists are idolaters." My eyes opened wide. Being an idolater was not an identity with which I associated myself. The Reform rabbi on my left, an American, said, "I agree; Buddhists worship idols." I was stunned. Calling someone an idol worshiper was about the worst insult a Jew could give someone, something tantamount to a Christian saying to a Jew, "You killed Christ." The Orthodox rabbi on my right added his view: "The various religions are like the colors of the rainbow. They all have their function. Many Jews are at the leading points of new religious movements, and it must be God's wish that there are many faiths." He turned to me smiling, and sincerely wishing me well, he said, "But remember, you're still Jewish."

By the time the moderator asked me to respond, I was so shocked that I was almost speechless. "To me, Jewish and Buddhist are merely labels. It is not important what we call ourselves. It is important how we live, how we treat others." Some people applauded.

I asked my Israeli Buddhist friends what they'd thought of the dialogue. "Oh, it was great," they responded. "We were afraid that the rabbis would be really judgmental and argumentative, but they were more open than we expected. It's remarkable that the two Orthodox rabbis came to the Reform synagogue. Many won't, you know."

Some people who thought one could be a Jew and a Buddhist told me, 11 "We have a Jewish soul, and we use Buddhist mindfulness meditation to bring out the best of it." Perplexed, because the Buddha refuted the idea of a permanent soul, let alone one that was inherently Jewish, I had asked what they meant. "We are part of the Jewish people. Our ancestors lived and thought in a particular way, and this culture and this way of looking at life are part of who we are." I wondered: Does their perspective mean that if you're born with "Jewish genes" in a Jewish family that you automatically have a certain identity? That you cannot escape some fixed place in history as the descendant of everything that happened to your ancestors before you even existed?

As a child, I was aware of aspects of Jewish culture that I loved and re- 12 spected, such as the emphasis on morality and treating all beings with equal respect. But I was also acutely aware of how the Jewish identity was shaped by persecution: "We are a unique group—look at how many times throughout history others have seen us as singular and have persecuted us even until death because of it." From early on, I had reflected on having an identity based on others' hate and injustice. I refused to be suspicious of people in the present simply because of experiences that my ancestors had in the past. Even as a child I wanted to have a positive view of humanity and not be shackled by keeping history's ghosts alive.

A ghost that haunts the Jews today is the Holocaust. They are a trauma- 13 tized people, and the Holocaust seemed to permeate almost everything in Israel. As a child I'd read a lot about the Holocaust, and it had taught me compassion, morality, being fair, not discriminating against an entire group of people, sticking up for the persecuted and downtrodden, and living honestly and with a clear conscience. Learning about the Holocaust had shaped many of the positive attitudes that eventually led me to Buddhism.

But I could never—either as a child or now as an adult—think that Jews 14 had the corner on suffering. In the Galilee, I led a weeklong meditation retreat. In one session, we had a spontaneous, heartfelt discussion about the Holocaust. One woman spoke about attending a gathering of second-generation Holocaust survivors and children of Nazis. When she listened to children of SS officers talk, she came to understand the deep guilt, suffering, and confusion they carry. How can you reconcile the memory of a loving father who cuddled you with the knowledge that he sanctioned the murder of millions of human beings? We talked about the parallels between the genocide of Jews and the more recent one of Tibetans by Chinese Communists. As Buddhists, how did the Tibetans view what happened to them? Why do we meet many Tibetans who experienced atrocities and do not seem to be emotionally scarred by the experience? Does forgiving mean forgetting? Shouldn't the world remember so that we can prevent genocide in the future?

Yes, we need to remember, but that remembering does not necessitate 15 keeping pain, hurt, resentment, and anger alive in our hearts. We can remember with compassion, and that is more powerful. By forgiving, we let go of our anger, and by doing that, we cease our own suffering.

That night, as we did a meditation on Chenresig, the Buddha of Compassion, out of my mouth—rather, out of my heart—came the words, "When you visualize Chenresig, bring him into the concentration camps. Imagine him in the trains, prisons, gas chambers. Visualize Chenresig in Auschwitz, Dachau. And as we recite the compassion mantra, imagine the brilliant light of compassion radiating from Chenresig and permeating every atom of these places and the people who were in them. This light of lovingkindness purifies the suffering, hate, and misconceptions of all beings—Jews, political prisoners, gypsies, Nazis, ordinary Germans who turned a blind eye to save their own skin—and heals all that pain." We chanted the mantra together for over half an hour, and the room was charged. Very few times have I meditated with so concentrated a group. 16

The next day a young man asked, "Most of the people who operated or lived in the concentration camps died many years ago. How could our meditation purify all of them?" There was a pause, and I responded: "We are purifying the effect that their lives have on us. By doing this, we let go of our pain, anger, and paranoia, so that we can bring compassion to the world in the present and future. We are preventing ourselves from living in deluded reaction to the past. We are stopping ourselves from creating a victim mentality that draws others' prejudice to us. We are ceasing the wish for revenge that makes us mistreat others. And although we cannot understand it intellectually, in a subtle way we do influence all the prisoners and Nazis in whatever form they are currently born in. We have to heal." 17

One day I went to the Wailing Wall to pray. For a while I recited the mantra of Chenresig and visualized purifying light healing the centuries of suffering in the Middle East. From a Buddhist view, the cause of all suffering lies in our minds and the disturbing attitudes and emotions that motivate us to act in destructive ways, even though we all long to be happy. From my heart, I made strong prayers that all beings, and especially people in this part of the world, be able to generate the three principal aspects of the path to enlightenment—the determination to be free from the cycle of constantly recurring problems, the altruistic intention to benefit all living beings, and the wisdom that realizes reality. I then put my head to the Wailing Wall in concentration. Suddenly I felt a "plop!" as something damp hit my cap. A bird was flying overhead. Recounting the episode to my friends, they informed me that it is said that if a bird poops on one's head at the Wailing Wall, it indicates one's prayers will be actualized! 18

＊

RESPONDING TO THE WHOLE ESSAY

1. What is Chodron trying to define in this essay? What is her primary purpose? [1g(1)]

2. Who is her audience? How does she take audience into consideration in her essay? [1g(2)]
3. What initiates Chodron's examination of the labels that are assigned to her?
4. How does Chodron define by exclusion?
5. How is her essay organized? In what order does she present her ideas? How is this effective? [2c]
6. What is Chodron's conclusion regarding the questions she has asked?

ANALYZING THE ELEMENTS

Grammar

1. Why is the verb *were* istead of *was* used in the first sentence of paragraph 5? [17d]
2. Justify the sentence fragment in paragraph 2. [13]

Effective Sentences

1. How effective are the questions in paragraphs 2 and 3? Are these rhetorical questions? [22e and Glossary of Terms]
2. Comment on the effectiveness of the second sentence of paragraph 7. [22a]

Diction

1. How is the word occupied used in paragraph 7?
2. In paragraph 16 Chodron uses the word *lovingkindness*. Why is this word appropriate for this essay?

Punctuation and Mechanics

1. Why is the word *rabbi* capitalized in paragraph 2, but not in paragraph 8?
2. Why are *Orthodox* and *Reform* capitalized in paragraph 8?

BUILDING VOCABULARY

1. Look up the following words: *pogroms* (paragraph 3), *genocide* (paragraph 14), *mantra* (paragraph 16).
2. What is the exact definition of *Holocaust*? [23a]
3. What is the definition of *deconstruct* as Chodron uses it in paragraph 4?

SUGGESTIONS FOR WRITING

1. Is there a label that others tend to ascribe to you that you find limiting or otherwise uncomfortable? Write an essay in which you define this label, using yourself as the main example to clarify the limitations.
2. Write an essay in which you describe how you have redefined yourself as a result of your travels, a significant experience, or through someone you have met.

What Is a Cowboy?

John R. Erickson

John R. Erickson (1943–) wrote "What Is a Cowboy?" in a barn in Beaver County, Oklahoma, in January, wearing gloves, a down vest, and a coat. In addition to battling the cold, Erickson fought daily with the barn mice over possession of his typewriter, which the mice found ideal to build nests in. The essay was published as the first chapter of Erickson's book *The Modern Cowboy* (1981), which grew out of Erickson's two-year experience working on an Oklahoma ranch, as did another book, *Panhandle Cowboy*. He is also author of *Through Time and the Valley* and other works of Western non-fiction, as well as a series of humorous novelettes about Hank the Cow Dog—spoofs of both detective fiction and old-fashioned Westerns. In "What Is a Cowboy?" Erickson shows how the real modern cowboy differs from the myth.

In 1978 and 1979 I was working as a cowboy on a ranch in Beaver County, Oklahoma. In the depths of January, I drove over to the next ranch and found my good friend and cowboy companion, Jake Parker. "Jake," I said, "we're about to starve out. We just can't make it on six hundred dollars a month. Inflation is killing us and I'm so danged tired of feeding cattle seven days a week that I could scream." Jake nodded.

In February I caught Jake as he was coming in from his feed run. "Jake," I said, "we're just barely getting by. If everyone stays healthy and the car doesn't break down, we'll make it. But if something goes wrong . . . I guess I'd better start looking around for another line of work."

Jake nodded. He understood.

In March I helped Jake do some cattle work. It was the first time we had been a-horseback since January. The day was warm and most of the snow had melted off the sandhills. Our horses felt good and so did we. "Parker," I said, "I'm looking forward to spring roundup season, aren't you?" He smiled and said, "You bet."

In April we were riding on a roundup crew, laughing and joking with the other cowboys, drinking in the spring air, working our horses, and playing with our ropes. And I said, "You know, Parker, we're damned lucky that somebody will pay us money for doing this." Jake laughed and said, "Yalp."

I have met the American cowboy on ranches in the Texas and Oklahoma Panhandles. I have ridden with him and worked beside him. I have eaten lunch with him on the ground and drunk water from his cup. I am tempted to describe him as I have seen him described in several books: "Merely folks, just

291

a plain everyday bowlegged human." It is a marvelous description, and very quotable. However, the temptation to use it merely points out the degree to which, on the subject of cowboys, we have come to rely on books and observations of the past. The fact is—and I rather hate to admit this—that I have known only one bowlegged cowboy, and I think he was born that way. Legend tells us that cowboys are supposed to have legs warped by long days in the saddle, and maybe fifty years ago they did. Today they don't. We can begin our description of the modern cowboy with the observation that, at least on one point of anatomy, he ain't what he used to be.

The cowboy I know is a workingman. He is defined by his work, which   7 should not be confused with the term "job." Cowboy work is more than a job; it is a life-style and a medium of expression. Remove the cowboy from his working environment and you have someone else, someone who resembles a cowboy in outward appearance but who, to one degree or another, is an imposter. Standing on a street corner, the cowboy is just an ordinary human. But out in the pasture, when he's a-horseback and holds a rope in his hands, he assumes the qualities that have made him a legend.

The fact that the cowboy is defined by his work has made him a difficult   8 subject to study. To see him at his best, you almost have to work with him day after day, and to understand what he does in his work, you almost have to possess a fundamental knowledge of the skills of his profession. Perhaps the people who are in the best position to observe and discuss the working cowboy are the men who work with him every day—other cowboys. Unfortunately, most cowboys don't write, and most writers don't work on ranches.

The cowboy does not own property. Owners of ranchland go by various   9 titles, among them rancher, cattleman, and stockman. The rancher owns the land, manages the operation, and makes decisions about buying and selling. Of course you can find instances where the two roles overlap. Some ranchers work beside their cowboys, and some cowboys are permitted to make management decisions, and in small ranching operations family members function in both capacities. But as a general rule it is safe to say that ranchers and cowboys are not the same breed. The term *cowboy,* as I use it, means a workingman who has mastered the skills needed in working around cattle, while the term *rancher* implies ownership and management.

In the cow lot or on a roundup crew the social differences between rancher   10 and cowboy don't mean much, but elsewhere they are clearly defined. Ranchers are often prominent leaders in the community; cowboys are not. Ranchers often sit on governing boards of businesses, churches, and schools; cowboys do not. Ranchers are frequently the subject of articles in livestock journals, while the cowboys are rarely mentioned. The rancher and his wife may belong to the country club, but the cowboy and his wife won't. The rancher has his circle of friends, the cowboy has his, and they do not often overlap.

There is one difference between them that goes right to the heart of the   11 matter: the rancher can take the day off or go into town whenever he wishes, but the cowboy can't. The cowboy's life is tied to the rhythms and patterns of animals: a cow that must be milked twice a day, chickens that must be turned out in the morning and shut up at night, horses that must be fed and watered, pregnant heifers that must be watched, and, in winter, cows that must be fed seven days a week. The rancher and the cowboy may dress alike, talk alike, and even think alike, but at six o'clock in the evening, one goes down to the milking barn while the other attends a meeting in town.

The cowboy is a workingman, yet he has little in common with the urban blue-collar worker. In the first place, as we have already observed, cowboy work is not just a job, with established work days, certain hours, and guaranteed holidays. Since he lives where he works, and since he deals with animals instead of machines, the cowboy is never really off work. He is on call 24 hours a day, 7 days a week, 365 days a year. The work is not always hard, but as a friend once observed to me, "It's damned sure steady." A calving heifer, a prairie fire, a sick horse may have him up at any hour of the day or night, and in this business there is no such thing as time-and-a-half for overtime. 12

In the second place, cowboys, unlike urban blue-collar workers, do not belong to a union, and they probably never will. The cowboy life attracts a special type of individual, one who can shift for himself and endure isolation, and one who thrives on physical hardship, a certain amount of danger, and low wages. These are not the qualities of a joiner, but of a loner. You might even go so far as to say that there is a little bit of outlaw in most of them— not that they are dishonest or deceitful, but rather that they are incorrigible like a spirited horse that is never quite broke and gentle, even though he may take the bit and saddle. Some cowboys stay in the profession simply because they don't fit anywhere else. They tried other jobs and couldn't adapt, or they went into business for themselves and failed. They returned to cowboying because it was in their bones and blood. 13

This stubborn, independent quality of the cowboy has fascinated the American public and has contributed to his status as a myth and a legend. We like to think of ourselves as a free and independent people, ready at any moment to tell the boss, the mayor, or the president himself to go straight to hell. Of course this is more a dream than a reality. Most of us are indentured to mortgage payments and car payment and live in terror of an IRS audit. Perhaps the cowboy, riding his horse across an endless prairie, has become a symbol of what we used to be—or at least what we *think* we used to be— and of what we would be if we could. He doesn't have to punch a time clock, drive through snarls of traffic every morning and afternoon, shave or wear a tie to work, or participate in hollow rituals in order to gain advancement. When he gets tired of the scenery, or if the boss crowds him too close, he packs his few possessions in a pickup and horse trailer and moves on to another ranch. In the American cowboy we find qualities we deeply admire— simplicity, independence, physical strength, courage, peace of mind, and self-respect—but which, to one degree or another, we have surrendered in order to gain something else. These qualities have made the cowboy the most 14 powerful mythical character in our folklore, and one which reaches to the very core of our identity as a people.

The typical cowboy, if we may speak of such an animal, does not carry   15 a pistol, strum a guitar, or burst into song at the end of the day. He has never rescued a maiden in distress or cleaned the outlaws out of a saloon. He can ride a bucking horse, but he can also get piled. He can rope a calf in the pasture, but he can also burn three loops before he makes the catch. In his working environment, he is dressed in blue jeans, a long-sleeved shirt, boots, western hat, and a vest. He looks good in these clothes, like an animal in its skin. In his work he moves with ease and grace, and sitting astride his horse he exudes confidence and authority. We are tempted to say that he is handsome, even though he might lack the physical endowments that we usually associate with that term.

But take him off his horse, throw him into a bathtub, scrub him down,   16 put him in a set of "good" clothes, and send him to town, and we will meet an entirely different man. All at once he becomes graceless and awkward. He isn't wearing his work hat and we see that he is getting bald, or if he has a good head of hair, it looks as though he has plastered it with lard and run a rake through it. His eyes, which outside are naturally set into a squint, seem puffy in the fluorescent light, and they do not sparkle. His "good" clothes are appalling, and we can hardly keep from laughing at him.

The mythology and legend of the Cowboy begin in this humble human   17 vessel. But the working cowboy is neither a myth nor a legend. He is an ordinary mortal. If we stopped at this point, we would have performed the ritual known as debunking, wherein a notable figure is taken like a buck deer, strung up, skinned and gutted, and held up naked for all to see. But I'm not setting out to debunk the cowboy. If he sometimes falls short of our expectations, he will surpass them when we see him at his best. And he is at his best when he is at his work. Ultimately, the cowboy *is* what he *does*.

So what is a cowboy? Is he a heroic figure or just a common laborer? It's   18 hard to say. I've seen both sides, and I think it would be a mistake to place too much emphasis on one side or the other. If we view him only as a symbol and a mythical figure, then we lose contact with his humanness and fall into the kind of sentimentality that allows some observers to ignore the poverty, the loneliness, the exploitation of cowboys, and to gloss over the darker side of the cattle industry with little homilies about the "honor" of being a cowboy. But neither do we want to strip him down to enzymes and electrons or to present him as just another human fop doomed to mediocrity and failure, for this view would deny that he can rise above himself through displays of skill, strength, and courage. And that would be false.

If the cowboy is a hero, then we will want to know the price he pays for   19 this honor. If he is a common man, then we will want to know why he has fascinated our people for a hundred years. For the moment let us content ourselves with this definition: The cowboy is a common laborer with heroic tendencies and a sense of humor.

*

RESPONDING TO THE WHOLE ESSAY

1. Is Erickson's purpose mainly to inform the reader about cowboy life, to express his own feelings about the cowboy, or to persuade the reader to adopt a more realistic view? To what extent are all three purposes present? [1g(1)]
2. Describe the audience Erickson appears to have had in mind. Use evidence from the essay to support your assumptions about Erickson's intended audience. [1g(2)]
3. "What Is a Cowboy?" can be viewed as an expansion of the classic three-part formal definition, which names the thing to be defined, puts it into a class, and then differentiates it from the rest of the class. Analyze the essay, showing where each kind of information appears.
4. What rhetorical purpose is served by beginning with a series of examples illustrating the lifestyle of the cowboy? Is this an effective introduction to a definition of a cowboy? Why or why not? [3b(1)]
5. Extended definitions often make use of several strategies of development: *examples, narration, comparison, description, classification,* and so forth. How many different development strategies can you find at work in "What Is a Cowboy"? [2a and 2e]
6. Erickson offers what might be called a negative definition of *cowboy* in paragraph 6. Is the technique effective? Why or why not?
7. Comment on how coherence is achieved in paragraph 10. [3d]

ANALYZING THE ELEMENTS

Grammar

1. In the third sentence of paragraph 6, why does Erickson use *drunk* rather than *drank?* [17b]
2. The second sentence of paragraph 11 contains a passive construction. Try rewriting this sentence in the active voice. What are the difficulties? Which sentence is more effective? Why? [17c]

Effective Sentences

1. Compare the second sentence and the last sentence of paragraph 8. In what way are the sentences alike? In what way do the two sentences differ? What makes each of them effective? [20a and 20b]
2. Explain how coordination and subordination contribute to the effectiveness of the first sentence in paragraph 11. [19]
3. To what does *one* in the last sentence of paragraph 14 refer? Try reading the sentence without the *and* before *one.* How does the meaning change?

Punctuation and Mechanics

1. Explain the use of the dash in the fourth sentence of paragraph 13. Is that use of the dash different from the way the dash is used in paragraph 6? Explain. What other kind of punctuation might be used in place of these dashes? Which would be more effective? Why? [31e]

2. Why is *Cowboy* capitalized in the first sentence of paragraph 17? Does it need to be? Why or why not? [33a]

Diction

1. In the final sentence of paragraph 6, Erickson writes, "he ain't what he used to be." Does Erickson's language throughout the rest of the essay indicate that this use of *ain't* is the result of ignorance, or does he have a rhetorical purpose for its use? Explain. [1g(1) and 23]
2. Explain why *blue-collar* in the first sentence of paragraph 12 and *long-sleeved* in the fifth sentence of paragraph 15 are hyphenated. [32g]
3. Erickson uses cowboy jargon in paragraph 15. Explain what *piled*, *burn*, and *catch* mean as he uses them and why their use is justifiable. [23c]
4. Explain Erickson's figurative definition of debunking in paragraph 17. Why is it effective here? [24a(4)]

BUILDING VOCABULARY

1. In a sentence or two, write down a plausible origin for the word *cowboy*. Take into consideration both parts of the word. What do you make of the use of *boy*?
2. What is the origin of the word *fop* and what does it mean? Of *job*?

SUGGESTIONS FOR WRITING

1. Write an essay in which you define the practitioner of an occupation that you think has been overvalued, undervalued, or misunderstood (for example, physician, nurse, teacher, minister, salesperson, farmer, waiter, taxi driver, soldier, flight attendant, housekeeper).
2. Write an essay in which you use examples to define the popular view of a cowboy, senator, astronaut, police officer, movie star, sports hero, or other "larger-than-life" figure.

The Good, the Bad, and the Ugly:
Clint Eastwood as Romantic Hero
Kathleen Murphy

Formerly head of a cinema studies program at the University of Washington, film critic Kathleen Murphy is writer-in-residence at the Film Society of Lincoln Center. Her work as a film critic has been collected in several book-length studies and appears regularly in *Film Comment*, to which she is a contributing editor, as well as in various periodicals. The essay which follows was written on the occasion of Eastwood's being honored by the Film Society of Lincoln Center. In it, Murphy attempts to define what a romantic hero is by giving examples of the various kinds of such heroes played by veteran actor/director/writer Clint Eastwood during his long and successful career.

Topped by an assertive crest of tawny hair, a lanky cowboy edges his way 1
to the head of the chow-line for the lion's share of grub. It's 1959, the first episode of "Rawhide," a TV series debuting in a season that favors Westerns, and the hungry young man is, of course, Clint Eastwood as Rowdy Yates, trail boss Gil Favor's sidekick. "Rawhide" would run for seven seasons, but before its demise the brash, fresh-faced Rowdy had already metamorphosed into a Man with No Name, the burnt-out hardcase who shot a trilogy of Sergio Leone's famously bloody Westerns into the money. And by 1968, little more than a decade into his accidental acting career, Clint Eastwood had formed Malpaso, his own production company, cannily taking early control of his filmmaking destiny.

From the first, Eastwood demonstrated a remarkable shrewdness, a tal- 2
ent for the kind of focused observation that has translated into a consistently enlarging vision of a potent off-and on-screen persona. At 13, he taught himself to write music and play the piano; Eastwood the man clearly kept an eye out for anything—narrative motif, directorial style, genre convention, character components—that might be taken in and reconceived to expedite his ambitious ascent up the Hollywood foodchain. He saw the vein that worked for him as a performer, and mined it, sculpting variations for the better part of four decades. He's aimed that same control and cinematic intelligence at the business of directing. Eastwood's craft and art have always derived from informed, instinctive taste, most notably in the fabrication of an idiosyncratic, strangely durable romantic hero—a lover whose masks have been that of artist, angel, demon, death, holy fool, and even, on occasion, endearing dolt.

That first "Rawhide" episode, "Incident of the Tumbleweed Wagon," fea-   3
tured a paradigmatic Fifties sexpot, pouting, curvaceous Terry Moore, wearing heels, low-cut blouse, and manacles for her transport by prison wagon
through the wilderness. Dallas has exacted revenge—"an eye for an eye"—on
a townful of people who hanged her innocent, half-blind father. "There were
a lot of empty chairs at the dinnertable before I was through. . . ." At first
glimpse of this cactus Antigone, Rowdy Yates whistles wholehearted appreciation, prompting a caveat from Favor: "You haven't seen a woman in trouble yet that you haven't fallen for." Redemption for past-haunted Dallas is
death, taking a bullet meant for the good guys. One wonders if somewhere
in the babydoll vulgarity of Moore's expressions of vengeance lies recombinant DNA for Eastwood's innocent man hanged for rustling, resurrected for
revenge, and mirrored by Inger Stevens's raped and widowed huntress in *Hang
'Em High* (Ted Post, '68). Or for Evelyn Draper (Jessica Walter), Clint's mur-
derously outraged castoff in *Play Misty for Me* (Eastwood, '71). Or for the
coven of betrayed bacchantes in *The Beguiled* (Don Siegel, '74). Or even for
the actor's first full-fledged revenant, carrier of hellish retribution to a whole
guilty town in *High Plains Drifter* (CE, '73). Or Sondra Locke's violated Fury,
Harry's Dirty Harriet, in *Sudden Impact* (CE, '83).

In seminal collaboration with Leone, Eastwood forged a masculine pres-   4
ence predicated on the strictest conservation of energy and emotion, a contraction of character so severe that its *primum mobile* must remain mystery.
As with Robert Mitchum, that deep reserve is a come-on, provoking the
desire—in men and women—to agitate, to assult the still, unmoved flesh.
Disengaged and deracinated, he is given to intense watchfulness from some
inner coign of vantage—hell, grave, or madness. Confronted, his head turns
slowly, eyes narrowing into scorched-earth fury, as steady and deadly as a
swiveling gun turret. The thin lower lip curls upward to sign dismay or disgust, like a cat grimacing at a bad smell.* Fine lines already ray out from the
corners of the early Eastwood's fierce eyes, his forehead is vertically furrowed
and veined, and the very shock of his hair seems to spring thickly up along
those same rising vectors. It's as though whatever imploded the soul of the
Man with No Name scarred permanent blastlines into the desiccated landscape of his face.

His gait is that of a ghost or a predator, his poncho'd torso remaining   5
strangely still, propelled ahead by the long legs, as though swimming upright
in slowmotion. Paradoxically, the hands of the remorseless gunfighter are those
of a musician or a painter: elegant, long-fingered, with graceful wrists. In these
formative stages of the Eastwood persona, his often nearly whispered vocal
tones seem too pressured for ordinary speech. The silky, then increasingly

---

*Twenty-eight years later, in Wolfgang Petersen's *In the Line of Fire*, Eastwood plays at being Bogart, whose teeth-baring, berserker rages may have inspired his "spaghetti Western" variation. Sharing his piano bench with Rene Russo, he faces down his soon-to-be-lover by kidding
his own style: "Sometimes a glare is as good as a gun."

abrasive sibilance of his drawl, like sand or gravel shifting in water, works best for epigrams, cryptic ripostes, up-close seduction.

In Leone's *A Fistful of Dollars* ('64), Eastwood is enigma but not yet a dead man walking: he concentrates and reflects the town's amorality, as well as incarnating the unspoken prayer of Marisol (Marianne Koch), the faithful wife and mother held prisoner by the worst of a wolfish lot (Gian Maria Volonté). Riding down *Fistful's* main drag on his mule, this cold Christ come to harrow hell pauses to pass a dim smile on to the woman jailed for her desirability. A past crucifixion is hinted: when he takes the time to rescue Marisol, he recalls that "I knew someone like you once . . . there was no one to help her." 6

Similarly, there is no one to help the young sheriff (Eastwood) whipped to death in *High Plains Drifter*, a Grand Guignol Golgotha witnessed by two very different "Marys." When the lawman's unquiet shade returns to paint the town red, he uses his allure as demon lover to strip each woman down to her true soul, damning the pretty, young creature of vicious appetite (Mariana Hill) and saving the earthy, older Verna Bloom. Before disappearing into a horizon of shimmering heat waves, he stops to share that complicit smile—born of more than carnal knowledge—with Bloom, the only distaff survivor of his retribution. Later, in *Pale Rider* (CE, '85), Eastwood's supernatural Shane materializes in his funereal *Drifter* frock coat to protect both virgin and a last Western paradise from rape, to renew and confirm Carrie Snodgress's abandoned womanhood as well as miner Michael Moriarty's uncertain masculinity. 7

In *Coogan's Bluff* ('68) and *The Beguiled*, Eastwood took tutelage under director Don Siegel, his American film-father. Interestingly, in both films, The Man with No Name's existential arrogance shades into specific sexual insolence, erotic allure used as lethally as a gun. Arizona stud Coogan, abroad in the Big Apple, seduces with too-practiced ease a social worker (Susan Clark) committed to a program of "self-regeneration" for bad girls. Gentling her body as he might a skittish horse, whispering her into sensual trance, Coogan doesn't miss a beat when, having rifled her files of the information he's after, he walks out—without a word—on his unsuspecting prey. Scarcely hours later, he deliberately beds down a sociopathic hippie to con her into giving up a killer's whereabouts. It's probable that Siegel and Eastwood aren't consciously exposing manipulative machismo as a species of whoring. Still, when a slutty hotel-tart, way past her prime, tries to run an obvious scam on Coogan, his response is excessively ugly: there's a cruel, cracked mirror here, but the rest of *Coogan's Bluff* doesn't really support such reflections. 8

No question, though, that *The Beguiled*, the third film by Siegel and Eastwood, does—with a vengeance. In this Grimm fairy tale, Corporal John McBurney is a wounded Yankee deserter who stumbles on to a Southern seminary housing a tribe of girls and women as perversely neurasthenic as any out of Tennessee Williams's imagining. McBurney's first act is to passionately soul-kiss 12-year-old Amy (Pamelyn Ferdin), diverting her attention from an approaching Confederate column. An adept sexual performer, he plays to each seminarian's script: Geraldine Page's bisexual headmistress, seething with hot 9 memories of incestuous lovemaking with her brother; Elizabeth Hartman's repressed virgin, man-shy courtesy of a promiscuous father; Jo Ann Harris's self-serving Lolita; and little Amy's budding bad seed. "I wonder," he purrs into spinster Hartman's ear, "if you don't think of yourself as a Sleeping Beauty in a castle waiting for a handsome prince to free you with a kiss."

Could be a 19th-century Coogan, working his main chance, but *Beguiled*   10
has more in common with *Boxing Helena*, genders reversed. The dominant POV keeps shifting between McBurney and his avid auditors. When the young soldier is first brought in, unconscious, Page gazes hungrily down at the handsome head at her breast, savoring eyelashes on cheek, fine mouth relaxed in almost feminine curves, unruly blonde mane. It's the kind of titillating shot that in most movies (especially soft-porn and splatter flicks) would frame the face of a beautiful sleeping woman, helpless and vulnerable to rape.

Later, much recovered, McBurney leans back smiling, smug in his sexual   11
power, to indulge in a fantasy that stars him as each woman's lover. This rather conventional casting segues into Page's more outré dream: she, McBurney, and Hartman in a sexual romp, climaxing with his naked body sprawled across her lap in perfect reflection of the painting of a Pietà that hangs beside her bed.

Though he's the source of reawakened fertility (in women and chickens),   12
the ravaged McBurney ends up a symbolically castrated gigolo, "planted"—in parts—by *The Beguiled*'s convent of twisted sisters. Not until *The Rookie* (CE, '90) will such physical violation by a woman be visited on an Eastwood hero. Amazonian Sonia Braga, bad guy Raul Julia's second in command, cuts and caresses the handcuffed Eastwood's bared flesh with a razor blade; moving down toward his groin: "I hate anything useless," she growls. "Something is no good to me, I cut it off and throw it away." In this truly disturbing sequence, echoed many times over in a bank of video monitors, the sadistic Braga mounts and rides the unblinking Eastwood to climax. It's as though he's trying the experience on for size—playing the role from which he's rescued so many virgins and hookers in his films (*Two Mules for Sister Sara, The Outlaw Josey Wales, The Gauntlet, Sudden Impact, Tightrope, Pale Rider, Bronco Billy*). Braga is unfettered succubus, and her genealogy leads straight back to nightmare Evelyn Draper in *Play Misty for Me*, the film that followed hard upon *The Beguiled*, and Eastwood's directorial debut.

As The Man with No Name seemed a fatal projection of his enemies' own   13
amorality, so too is Evelyn Draper a Dantean retribution for the casual promiscuity practiced by Eastwood's Carmel disc jockey. She comes out of nowhere, her only I.D. "Annabel Lee," a Poe poem about two lovers so attached not even death can separate them. Like Eastwood's gunfighter revenant in *High Plains Drifter*, this unforgiving one-night stand lives to send those who sinned against her to hell. Despite Eastwood's soft-focus vision of Carmel's paradisiacal landscape through which he and the blonde artist who settles him down (Donna Mills) walk, swim, and make love, it's Walter's dark, unrelenting Lilith who steals the show until her directorial doppelgänger rubs her out.

There's something of unregenerate Evelyn abroad in *Tightrope* (Richard   14
Tuggle, '84), a film in which Eastwood's bitterly divorced cop, father of two
little girls (the older played by his own daughter Alison), takes a dangerous
dive into the belly of the sexual beast. Eastwood acts out his authentic, am-
biguous rage at the woman who abandoned him, handcuffing hookers in kinky,
sado-masochistic psychodramas. Shadowed, even directed, by a clown-masked
serial killer–rapist, the cop's dangerous play brings his darkside home, into
his girls' lives—despite the framed unicorn that guards their chaste beds. (In
Sudden Impact, shot just the year before *Tightrope,* the trauma caused by brutal sexual assult in her youth brings a woman round to an antique carousel,
on which she is stalked by her old tormentors. The most psychotic of the
rapists is ultimately impaled on the horn of a maddened unicorn.)

Tightrope is punctuated by genuinely disquieting moments, suggestive   15
of deeper sexual waters than are usually plumbed in the traditional cop story.
Eastwood lounges in a doorway, eyeing Geneviève Bujold—a woman who
sees through his conflicted psyche—as she demonstrates to a class how to
disable a rapist. When she kicks the dummy in the crotch, its eyes light up,
its tongue pops out, and tennis balls shoot across the gym straight at her
male audience of one. It's grotesque slapstick, and draws real blood from
wounded manhood. Later, Eastwood's daughter finds her dead-drunk dad
sprawled facedown on the livingroom couch, a wedding photograph clutched
in his hand. Her delicate features very grave, the prepubescent child climbs
aboard her father, warming with her tomgirl body the man her mother has
rejected.

Not much later, the cop's crazed-clown alter ego deposits this same child,   16
bound and gagged, in her father's bed, and her violation there is barely
thwarted. In the aftermath of her rescue, Eastwood explodes in purgative rage,
tearing up the offending bed and bellowing "You mother . . . !" at his own—
possessed—reflection. By film's end, the sexually shattered cop's reformation
is signaled when he flings away a severed arm, all that remains of the creature that acted out what Eastwood only dreamed of.

Sudden Impact introduced Dirty Harry Callahan to his vigilante coun-   17
terpart (Sondra Locke), a woman taking revenge on the thugs who raped her
and her younger sister years ago. As director and star, Eastwood can be remarkably generous with actresses in his films, and here he mostly steps back
to give the steely Locke, her hairstyle verging on Veronica Lake, room to play
out her version of *The Bride Wore Black.* What's of particular interest in
Sudden Impact is its mating of illness and creativity—the obsessed Locke paints
anguished self-portraits when she's not aiming crotch-shots at the men who
fractured her own innocence and her fragile sister's sanity. During the Eighties,
in *Bronco Billy* ('80), *Honky Tonk Man* ('82), *Sudden Impact,* TV's "Vanessa
in the Garden" ('85), and *Bird* ('88), director Eastwood signposted intriguing
intersections between assault on the mind or body and the generation of some
form of art, between muses and mirrored selves, between mostly male artists
or performers and their enabling lovers.

Eastwood directed "Vanessa in the Garden" for Steven Spielberg's short-   18
lived TV series *Amazing Stories*. Written by Spielberg and featuring Harvey
Keitel as a 19th-century impressionist, Sondra Locke as his wife, and Beau
Bridges as agent and family friend, this half-hour effort suffers from woeful
miscasting and awkward performances by the two male leads. But at the heart
of its oddly hallucinatory narrative lies a striking evocation of the power of
the imagination and the nature of the creative process.

Wife, subject, and muse, Vanessa is truly the artist's "godsend," an Eve   19
who composes his real and painted gardens and makes them fruitful. After
her accidental death, Keitel burns every canvas that bears her likeness—with
the inadvertent exception of the garden portrait—and sinks into drunken despair. One morning he wakes to a painting emptied of its central figure, and
Vanessa's sweet humming outside his window. In a stunning elision, the camera moves rightward from the abandoned canvas to catch Keitel's reflection
in a mirror; then tracks into the mirror to frame—through window panes—
the white-clad woman posed among her flowers; then, using the edge of the
actual painting as a wipe, drives leftward to confirm the scene in reality; returns to the artist's reflection, followed by a reprise of the ghost in the garden. When Keitel plunges outdoors, the vision dissolves away. (In *Sudden
Impact*, made just two years before, Locke played the despairing artist—as
well as murderess—firing her gun into a glass that mirrors her own face and
one of the grotesque self-portraits she has painted.)

It's irrelevant whether Keitel has gone mad, conjured his very own "pale   20
rider," or somehow found a way back to the spiritual source of his creativity:
that audacious camera sequence precisely diagrams a syntax of the imagination
at work. "It cannot be unless you create it," Vanessa whispers, and through the
art of making pictures, Keitel resurrects his wife and all their past and future
times. That phrase—"making pictures"—is Robert Kincaid's from *The Bridges
of Madison County* ('95), Eastwood's celebration of love as an expression of
passionate creativity. Kincaid explicitly identifies the aesthetic impulse to make
pictures with "making his way" to Francesca (Meryl Streep), and takes into exile the faith that they "are hardly two separate people now." Through the look-
ing-glass of "Vanessa in the Garden," Francesca and her godsend can be seen
creating a durable illusion to sustain them for the rest of their separated lives.

At the beginning of *Bronco Billy*, Eastwood's camera locates a circus big-   21
top in the middle of heartland fields, and time—dissolving ever deeper into
evening, closes slowly in on the set where a New Jersey shoe salesman directs
a sweetly communal fantasy of an heroic Wild West. The brightly lighted island inside the tent where Billy and his crew present their *tableaux vivants*
often seems to float in an ocean of darkness—indeed, at film's end, Billy and
his "family" of costumed misfits disappear into that darkness. As long as
"orphaned" heiress-on-the-run Antoinette Lilly (Sondra Locke) insists on poking holes in Billy's creation, she's the author of "bad luck" that literally brings
down the show. This gentle screwball comedy is a remarkably self-aware take
on Eastwood's career, and the art of the Western: even the director's reputed

need and ability to control every aspect of a shoot may be referenced in Billy's hot-tempered insistence on being "head ramrod." Eastwood's contemporary "Western" shapes up as a much lighter, self-reflexive version of *The Outlaw Josey Wales* (CE, '76): both Billy and Josey lose their wives under traumatic conditions, turning outlaw as a result; collect a ragtag family of mixed race, gender, and age; save from rape a girl (Sondra Locke, in both cases) who redeems the outsider-—or is herself redeemed—through love and enlistment in the hero's cause; and find a home in unexpected "paradise," Billy's American Flag circus tent and Josey's democratic ranch.

In the richly imagined *Bird*, a well-meaning psychiatrist recommends shock 22 therapy for lifetime drug-addict Charlie Parker (Forest Whitaker), who, recently confronted by his sorry soul in a bathroom mirror, has downed a bottle of iodine. When Chan (Diane Venora), the jazzman's wife and best audience, expresses concern about the effect of ECT on Bird's creativity, the doctor suggests that she may have to choose either husband or musician. Venora's red-hot Chan lays it on the line: "Husband *and* musician—they do not separate!" As though her words called up a home-movie memory, the space behind camera-facing Chan slowly blacks out. In that darkness materializes a "street of dreams," a neon-lit big-city strip of pulsing jazz joints down which a young, vibrant woman strides on her way to fall for Bird and his music. Chan's remembrance of a (flawed) paradise lost is as potent and seductive as Bronco Billy's Wild West bigtop, as Red Stovall's Grand Ole Opry, the "heart's desire" of a country singer in *Honky Tonk Man*, and yes, even Vanessa in her quiet garden.

That garden has turned nearly Fordian grave in *Unforgiven*, Eastwood's 23 masterpiece. William Munny's lost wife, marrying beneath her, reformed a devil of a man. In turn, after Claudia Feathers dies of smallpox, Munny makes her his guardian angel, an internalized ethic. Her chaste and aging knight—"I don't miss it much"—is drawn into a rather lowdown quest, inspired more by money than a lady's honor. But William Munny rises from pigshit to apotheosis when he lays his ghostly superego long enough to exact terrible revenge on men for whom slashing a woman's face or whipping a good man to death count less than civic peace and prosperity. (Shades of guilty Lago in *High Plains Drifter.*)

Wracked by fever-chills and a brutal beating by Sheriff Daggett (Gene 24 Hackman), Munny passes through the little death that often precedes the transformation of an Eastwood hero into a killing-machine. That transformation is triggered by a spiritual dissolve of three visages into one: his hallucinated vision of Claudia, her face eaten by worms; the white-blonde whore (Anna Thomson), her face crisscrossed by scars; and his own, its marred flesh skinned back to show a true death's head. "I thought you was an angel," says Munny to the woman who set this story in motion. Then: "I must look kinda like you."

It's not that William Munny reverts to his former drunken, demonic state, 25 during which he annihilated "everything that walked or crawled." Wearing the "colors" of both Claudia Feathers, "a comely young woman . . . not without prospects," and Delilah Fitzgerald, "damaged property," he becomes a force for something like divine retribution. Drifter, pale rider, barest bones of Bronco Billy's fairy tale, William Munny reshapes the ignominious stuff of actuality (Little Bill's eyewitness account of how English Bob came to kill Two-Gun Corky Corcoran) and cheap fiction (dime-novelist Beauchamp's Duke of Death, avenger of a woman's slighting) into purely clarifying myth. Afterwards, Claudia Feather's faithful husband disappears into vague, mundane history: "There was nothing on [her grave] marker to explain why [she] had married William Munny. . . ."

Reportedly, Eastwood planned early on to make a "romance" for his fifti- 26
eth film. *The Bridges of Madison County* stands as a love story for adults, unreeling in brave slowness (given contemporary popcult pulse rates). As in *Bird*, his lovers talk their way toward touching, exploring each other—mostly during and after meals at a kitchen table—through easy, sometimes heated conversational rhythms. A convention of many previous Eastwood films is the hero's uncanny ability to establish immediate, wordless rapport with women of all ages; here and in 1993's *In the Line of Fire*, he reveals a truly irresistible gift for gab and self-revelation. The intensely focused, yet mercilessly imper-sonal, attention with which he has always seared his enemies becomes, in *Bridges*, generous, erotic apprehension of Otherness. Always unusually par-tial to less-than-conventional beauty, more idiosyncratic, authentically lived-in-faces—Jessica Walter, *Breezy's* Kay Lenz, Verna Bloom, Sondra Locke, Alexa Kenin (*Honky Tonk Man*), Carrie Snodgress, Diane Venora, Rene Russo—*Bridges'* director virtually celebrates the seasoned character and flesh of Meryl Street's earthy Francesca.

In *The Bridges of Madison County*, Eastwood once more plays a sexual 27
savior of sorts, but through some alchemy of imagination and style, transub-stantiates a four-day love affair between an Iowa farmwife and a footloose pho-tographer, played by two stars beyond their physical prime, into the kind of newness we yearn to confer on sexual—and emotional—experience, if only for the space of a movie. As director and actor, Eastwood has rarely rested on his laurels, has always pushed toward new ground: when he turns his haggard vis-age to the camera in his last scene in *Bridges*, his hair lankly plastered down by pouring rain, his face is as open in its naked age and pain as any seen in the cinema. It's a courageous exposure, an opening of the soul, something few could have visualized when he was The Man with No Name. But this late divestiture of the mystery he took to the bank for so long, of any mask and armor, has been earned by four decades of accumulating assuance and self-knowledge as director, star, and man. They do not separate in this shootist for all seasons.

✳

RESPONDING TO THE WHOLE ESSAY

1. In an allusion to the title of Eastwood's early hit, the title of Murphy's essay sug-gests that some of Eastwood's romantic heroes are good, some are bad, and some are ugly. Identify which of Eastwood's heroes fit each of these categories and ex-plain the contribution of each to Murphy's definition of "romantic hero."

2. What technique does Murphy use to catch the reader's attention in her introductory paragraph? Why does this technique work? [3b(1)]
3. What kinds of assumptions does Murphy appear to have made about the background, interests, and needs of her intended audience? Point to evidence in the essay. [1g(2)]
4. What is the purpose of Murphy's essay? Does she appear to be primarily concerned with exploring her own perceptions about her subject, with exploring the subject itself, or with attempting to sway the reader to a particular point of view or course of action? Can you discern several purposes? [1g(1)]
5. Murphy employs a number of different development strategies in this essay. Find and discuss examples of each. [2a]
6. What transitional devices does Murphy use to make paragraph 21 coherent? Which device is most frequently used? [3d]

ANALYZING THE ELEMENTS

Grammar

1. Explain the use of "erotic allure used as lethally as a gun" in the second sentence of paragraph 8. [12a]
2. Determine the function of each clause in the final sentence of paragraph 8. Rewrite the sentence as two separate sentences. Which is better, the sentence as Murphy wrote it or the revised sentence? Why? [12b]
3. The first sentences of both paragraph 9 and paragraph 10 are elliptical; what is understood? Should either sentence have been rewritten? Why or why not? [13]
4. Explain what completes the comparison in the first sentence of paragraph 15. [12]

Effective Sentences

1. Comment on whether the passive voice used in the last sentence of paragraph 6 does or does not contribute to the effectiveness of the sentence. [21d]
2. Explain the advantages Murphy gains from repetition in the last sentence of paragraph 17. [21e]
3. What makes each of the following sentences effective: sentence 4 in paragraph 19, sentence 6 in paragraph 22, the final sentence of paragraph 26, and the second sentence of paragraph 27. [20a, 21g, and 22a]

Punctuation and Mechanics

1. What reason may Murphy have had for capitalizing *Fury* in the last sentence of paragraph 3? [33a]
2. Murphy uses two acronyms without giving the full form first: *POV* in sentence 2 of paragraph 10 and *I.D.* in sentence 2 of paragraph 13. What does each of these stand for? What reason can you think of for not first giving the full form? [35e]
3. Explain the use of semicolons in sentence 4 of paragraph 19. [28a and 28b]
4. What do the brackets in the last sentence of paragraph 25 indicate? [31g]
5. Explain the use of commas in the next-to-last sentence in paragraph 27. [27c]

Diction

1. What is meant by the following phrases borrowed from other languages: *primum mobile* (paragraph 4), *tableaux vivants* (paragraph 21)? [23a]
2. Write two sentences, one using *predicate* (paragraph 4) as a verb, the other using it as a noun. [24a]
3. Murphy uses a rich vocabulary peppered with words not commonly encountered. Look up the following terms and find a synonym for each: *caveat* (paragraph 3), *revenant* (paragraph 3), *seminal* (paragraph 4), *coign* (paragraph 4), *tutelage* (paragraph 8), *elision* (paragraph 19). [24c]
4. Explain the following allusions: *Grand Guignol* and *Golgotha* (paragraph 7), *Grimm* and *Tennessee Williams* (paragraph 9), *Pietá* (paragraph 11). [24a(4)]
5. *Flick* appears in the last sentence of paragraph 10. Check the current edition of a good desk dictionary to determine whether this word is slang or has come into common usage. [23b(2)]

BUILDING VOCABULARY

1. The following words have been borrowed from other languages. Look up each word in an unabridged dictionary and state its language of origin and its meaning: *segue* and *outré* (paragraph 11), and *doppelgänger* (paragraph 13).
2. Look up *deracinate* and *desiccate* in a good desk dictionary. What are the roots of each word? What does each root mean? What does the prefix *de-* mean?

SUGGESTIONS FOR WRITING

1. You are a reporter for a small cable company magazine that features commentary on actors starring in films that will be shown in the coming week. Do some research (see *Writer's* 6 and 7) and write an essay of about 1,000 to 1,200 words presenting a particular actor (male or female) as the virtual definition of a role (for example, tough cop, wise mother, wisecracking juvenile delinquent).
2. Write an essay in which you begin with a commonly accepted definition (such as a definition for friend) which you reject in favor of a more meaningful one.

✳

Chapter 9

Argument

Argument can be difficult to write well—in fact, it may be the most difficult of the many kinds of writing considered in this book (partly because it can include all those other kinds). But, although difficult, argument is worth the trouble; it is a kind of writing that very directly aims to make a difference, that gets things done.

By *argument* we do not mean quarreling or bickering—the meaning often given the term in everyday speech. Rather, argument is a method (or set of methods) for convincing readers of the rightness of an opinion or of a course of action that the writer considers desirable. Any or all of the other development strategies discussed in this book may be employed in writing arguments.

An argument may rely on several different kinds of appeals: appeals to the writer's own credibility or authority (sometimes called *ethical appeals*); appeals to reason (*logical appeals*); and appeals to the reader's emotions, values, or attitudes (*pathetic* or *affective appeals*). Writers appeal to their own credibility by demonstrating that they are knowledgeable about the subject and fair-minded in their argumentative approach, that they understand and respect the reader's viewpoint. They appeal to reason by being logical—that is, by reasoning properly themselves and supporting their assertions with good evidence—and by using development strategies appropriate to the material they are presenting. They appeal to emotions, values, and attitudes by choosing examples and raising issues about which the reader is likely to have strong feelings and by using language with connotations that are favorable to the writer's purpose (see 24a[2]).

As you plan an argument, consider how each kind of appeal can help you achieve your purpose. Often it is useful to emphasize one kind more than the others. For example, Aurora Levins Morales's "Liberation Geneology" appeals to the emotions and values of her audience as well as to logic. In contrast, Wallace Stegner, in "The Gift of Wilderness," stresses the appeal to his own credibility or authority: because he has experience, he expects his reader to grant that he knows what he's talking about.

Be careful, however, not to rely on one appeal too heavily. Too great a reliance on an appeal to your own credibility can give the impression that you are indifferent to the reader's values or that you have doubts about the reader's ability to reason logically. Relying exclusively on logical appeals may make you seem cold-blooded, heartless. Relying too much on appeals to the reader's emotions may make you seem unreasonable or softheaded.

The reasoning processes underlying an argument may be either inductive or deductive; more often they are both. Induction draws conclusions from amassed evidence; deduction applies a general truth to a particular case to reach a conclusion. Either method, if pursued carelessly, can lead the unwary writer into reasoning errors called fallacies. (See 5h and 5i for discussions of induction, deduction, and common fallacies.)

The basic formal elements of most arguments are (1) the *thesis*, a statement of the position or proposition the reader is being urged to accept (see 2b); (2) the presentation of *evidence* supporting the thesis; (3) consideration of *opposing arguments* (if appropriate); and (4) a *conclusion* emphasizing the thesis. These elements can be organized in various ways, depending on the situation and the writer's purpose. One classic pattern, often useful, begins by stating the thesis (and, if necessary, establishing the writer's credentials) in the introduction, goes on to present the evidence in favor of the thesis, next raises and refutes any likely objections, and concludes with a restatement of the thesis or perhaps with a recommendation or call to action based upon it. However, you may not always wish to open with a statement of your thesis. For example, if—as may often occur—you are arguing in response to someone else's argument, it may be best to begin by summarizing the other person's position and then presenting your own. Or if you are arguing in favor of some policy or course of action that you believe will solve a problem, you may need to begin by showing that there *is* a problem before you go on to present and defend your solution. Sometimes—especially if your thesis is one your reader might find distasteful enough to dismiss without giving you a chance to defend it—you may be wise to postpone a direct statement of the thesis until the end of your essay, after you have presented your evidence. Wherever you decide to state the thesis itself, the case you build for it will usually be most effective if you present your specific supporting points in increasing order of importance—strongest points last. (However, note the word "usually"; there are exceptions.)

The effectiveness of argument, perhaps more than of any other kind of writing you will do, depends on your consideration of the nature, needs, and interests of your intended audience, the reader (or readers) whom you are trying to convince. If you present too little evidence, the reader can justifiably dismiss your argument as weak. If you rely on evidence that the reader cannot understand or that is not pertinent to the reader's own interests, the reader can dismiss your argument as irrelevant. If you make mistakes in logical reasoning, the reader can dismiss your argument as false. If you adopt, or lapse into, an inappropriate tone, your reader can dismiss your argument as tactless, insensitive. Try hard to put yourself in your reader's place, to see your argument from the reader's point of view. (For help in analyzing audiences, see 1g(2).)

Not all arguments are serious. Argumentative writing can also be light-hearted, as Roxana Barry Robinson's "The Horse as Heater" demonstrates. Nevertheless, arguments often deal with matters of considerable gravity—even with issues of life and death, as a number of essays in this chapter do. In the following essay, student Oshunkentan Solomon argues movingly against capital punishment.

Death Penalty

Introduction: statement of the issue

The death penalty is not justice; this state-inflicted death is, rather, an act of hate and vengeance which chiefly succeeds in reminding us of how close we are to the jungle. The death penalty is retribution, and retribution is one of the most appealing arguments for the death penalty—so says Mencken. Yet, retribution cannot be considered a legitimate goal of criminal law.

Evidence: need for some remedy

We live in days of turbulence. Violence is common; murder is an hourly occurrence. Scarcely a day goes by that the evening news fails to report a tale of murder or other evidence of humankind's

Appeal to values

disdain for life. In the midst of all this anxiety and fear, perhaps our greatest need is reverence for life—mere life, our lives, the lives of others, and all life. Life is an end in itself. A humane and generous concern for every individual, for his safety, his health, and his fulfillment is and should be a legitimate goal of every law. It is this basic premise with which the concept of retribution—the death penalty—is at war.

Appeal to logic

Indeed, murder and capital punishment are not opposites that cancel one another, but similarities that breed their kind. From the perspective of reverence

Evidence: an execution

for life, how is the state's execution of mass-murderer Ted Bundy different from Bundy's own execution of dozens of women? And how can Bundy's state-inflicted death deter other murderers? When the state itself kills, the mandate "thou shalt not kill" loses the force of the absolute.

Proposed remedy

Surely, the abolition of the death penalty is a major achievement in the long road up from

Evidence: history

barbarism. Earlier societies excused themselves by pleading that self-preservation necessitated the imposition of capital punishment and, as cruelty begets cruelty, the number of crimes deemed capital offenses increased. But it was for the public good; too bad if in the process of isolating dangerous persons from the public, some innocents were executed for crimes they did not commit. Modern civilization has no such excuse.

Appeal to
credibility and
call to action

Our difficult days call for rare courage, the willingness to disenthrall ourselves to think and act anew. There is no justification for the death penalty. It cheapens life. Its injustices and inhumanity raise basic questions about our institutions and our purpose as a people. Why must we kill? What do we fear? What do we accomplish beside our own embitterment? Why cannot we revere life and in doing so create in the hearts of our people a love for mankind that will finally still violence?

Conclusion:
statement of
position

A responsible society wants protection, not revenge. It does not need to avenge itself, nor should it want to do so. Punishment for punishment's sake is not justice and is repugnant to civilized peoples. The death penalty is not only unnecessary and futile; it is barbaric and brutal.

Commentary.   Oshunkentan Solomon's argument falls into three main parts. He introduces the the issue essay by naming and stating his position on it—the death penalty's most appealing justification is not a legitimate concern of the law. The body of the essay presents Solomon's argument that the death penalty could not exist if humankind valued life. His conclusion restates his position.

The most obvious kind of reasoning in Solomon's argument is deductive; he has read about the violence in society, seen the death penalty enacted, and noted that it is not effective in preventing further violence. This leads him to reason that the death penalty should be abolished. Beginning his argument with a commentary on the barbaric nature of the death penalty—that its chief value is reminding us "how close we are to the jungle"—Solomon makes the telling point that it is not a legitimate means for law to take. The rest of the essay explains why the death penalty is not a legitimate means for controlling violence in the society. Solomon uses several appeals, the most effective being the appeal to the reader's attitudes and values. He also appeals to the lessons of history and to credibility—and invites the reader to join him in his call for courage and commitment to think and act anew. Having stated his case and made an impassioned emotional appeal, though he has brought logic and history to bear, Solomon restates his position, this time not his alone but that of every civilized person.

Cinderella's Stepsisters
Toni Morrison

One of our most-honored contemporary writers is Toni Morrison, born in Ohio in 1931. She won the Pulitzer Prize for fiction for *Beloved* (1988) and the National Book Award for *Song of Solomon* (1977). Her other novels include *The Bluest Eye* (1970), *Tar Baby* (1981), and *Jazz* (1992). A graduate of Cornell University (M.A., 1955), Morrison taught English and worked for Random House as an editor before she began teaching fiction writing and Black literature at Yale and at Barnard. She has also edited a collection of commentaries upon the Clarence Thomas–Supreme Court confirmation hearings (**Race-***ing* **Justice,** *En-***gender***ing* **Power:** *Essays on Anita Hill, Clarence Thomas, and the Construction of Social Reality,* 1992). This version of "Cinderella's Stepsisters," adapted from a commencement address Morrison delivered at Barnard College, was first published in *Ms.* magazine.

Let me begin by taking you back a little. Back before the days at college. To nursery school, probably, to a once-upon-a-time time when you first heard, or read, or, I suspect, even saw "Cinderella." Because it is Cinderella that I want to talk about; because it is Cinderella who causes me a feeling of urgency. What is unsettling about that fairy tale is that it is essentially the story of a household—a world, if you please—of women gathered together and held together in order to abuse another woman. There is, of course, a rather vague absent father and a nick-of-time prince with a foot fetish. But neither has much personality. And there are the surrogate "mothers," of course (god- and step-), who contribute both to Cinderella's grief and to her release and happiness. But it is her stepsisters who interest me. How crippling it must have been for those young girls to grow up with a mother, to watch and imitate that mother, enslaving another girl.

I am curious about their fortunes after the story ends. For contrary to recent adaptations, the stepsisters were not ugly, clumsy, stupid girls with outsize feet. The Grimm collection describes them as "beautiful and fair in appearance." When we are introduced to them they are beautiful, elegant, women of status, and clearly women of power. Having watched and participated in the violent dominion of another woman, will they be any less cruel when it comes their turn to enslave other children, or even when they are required to take care of their own mother?

It is not a wholly medieval problem. It is quite a contemporary one: feminine power when directed at other women has historically been wielded in what has been described as a "masculine" manner. Soon you will be in a position to do the very same thing. Whatever your background—rich or poor—whatever the history of education in your family—five generations or one—you have taken advantage of what has been available to you at Barnard and you will therefore have both the economic and social status of the step-sisters *and* you will have their power.

I want not to *ask* you but to *tell* you not to participate in the oppression   4
of your sisters. Mothers who abuse their children are women, and another woman, not an agency, has to be willing to stay their hands. Mothers who set fire to school buses are women, and another woman, not an agency, has to tell them to stay their hands. Women who stop the promotion of other women in careers are women, and another woman must come to the victim's aid. Social and welfare workers who humiliate their clients may be women, and other women colleagues have to deflect their anger.

I am alarmed by the violence that women do to each other: professional   5
violence, competitive violence, emotional violence. I am alarmed by the willingness of women to enslave other women. I am alarmed by a growing absence of decency on the killing floor of professional women's worlds. You are the women who will take your place in the world where *you* can decide who shall flourish and who shall wither; you will make distinctions between the deserving poor and the undeserving poor, where you can yourself determine which life is expendable and which is indispensable. Since you will have the power to do it, you may also be persuaded that you have the right to do it. As educated women the distinction between the two is first-order business.

I am suggesting that we pay as much attention to our nurturing sensibil-   6
ities as to our ambition. You are moving in the direction of freedom and the function of freedom is to free somebody else. You are moving toward self-fulfillment, and the consequences of that fulfillment should be to discover that there is something just as important as you are and that just-as-important thing may be Cinderella—or your stepsister.

In your rainbow journey toward the realization of personal goals, don't   7
make choices based only on your security and your safety. Nothing is safe. That is not to say that anything ever was, or that anything worth achieving ever should be. Things of value seldom are. It is not safe to have a child. It is not safe to challenge the status quo. It is not safe to choose work that has not been done before. Or to do old work in a new way. There will always be someone there to stop you. But in pursuing your highest ambitions, don't let your personal safety diminish the safety of your stepsister. In wielding the power that is deservedly yours, don't permit it to enslave your stepsisters. Let your might and your power emanate from that place in you that is nurturing and caring.

Women's rights is not only an abstraction, a cause; it is also a personal af-   8
fair. It is not only about "us"; it is also about me and you. Just the two of us.

＊

RESPONDING TO THE WHOLE ESSAY

1. What evidence do you see in "Cinderella's Stepsisters" that Morrison wrote it as a commencement address? Explain. [1g(3)]
2. Explain the appropriateness of Morrison's title, "Cinderella's Stepsisters." [3b(3)]
3. Is the first sentence of paragraph 1 an effective introduction? Why or why not? [3b(1)]
4. Analyze Morrison's argument identifying her basic claim and the assumptions (stated or unstated) that she makes.
5. What is Morrison's purpose in "Cinderella's Stepsisters"? [1g(1)]
6. What would you say are the characteristics of the audience for whom Morrison is writing? What evidence within the essay helps you define the audience? [1g(2)]

ANALYZING THE ELEMENTS

Grammar

1. Sentences 2, 3, and 4 of paragraph 1 are fragments. What rhetorical effect does Morrison achieve by using these fragments? [13]
2. Comment on the agreement of the subject and verb in the first sentence of paragraph 8. [17e]

Effective Sentences

1. Find at least two groups of sentences in which Morrison uses parallel structure and comment on what contribution parallelism makes. [20]
2. Explain why the phrase, *As educated women*, in the last sentence of paragraph 5 may be a dangling modifier, and justify its use. [15e]

Punctuation and Mechanics

1. Comment on Morrison's use of commas in the fourth sentence of paragraph 2. [27a, b, and c]
2. What message does Morrison's use of the colon in the first sentence of paragraph 5 send the reader? [31d]

Diction

1. Explain why *once-upon-a-time* and *nick-of-time* in paragraph 1 are hyphenated. [32g]
2. In the fourth sentence of paragraph 5, Morrison says, "you can determine who shall flourish and who shall wither." Why do you think she uses *shall* here, rather than *will*? [24a]

3. Morrison comments that it must have been *crippling* for the stepsisters to see Cinderella abused. What elements of the story does the word *crippling* evoke? [24a]

BUILDING VOCABULARY

1. *Status quo* is a phrase borrowed from Latin. Look it up in a good desk dictionary. What do the Latin words mean? What does the phrase signify in English? What other phrases borrowed from other languages can you think of that have become commonly used English ones?
2. Find at least three hyphenated adjectives in Morrison's "Cinderella's Stepsisters." What does each mean? What single-word synonym (if any) exists for these adjectives?

SUGGESTIONS FOR WRITING

1. Imagine that you are giving an address to a group of people just beginning their chosen careers. Write an essay arguing for or against the "feminine" or "masculine" use of power.
2. Write an essay in which the basic claim for your argument is Morrison's statement that "the function of freedom is to free somebody else" (paragraph 6).

The Horse as Heater

Roxana Barry Robinson

Born in Pine Mountain, Kentucky, Roxana Barry Robinson (1946–) was educated at Bennington College and the University of Michigan, from which she holds a B.A. degree. A recipient of a creative writing fellowship from the National Endowment of the Arts, Robinson has published her first novel, *Summer Light* (1988), and a biography titled *Georgia O'Keeffe: A Life* (1989). Her work has appeared in such diverse publications as the *New Yorker*, *Southern Review*, *New York Times*, *House and Garden*, *Arts*, *Artnews*, and *McCall's*. "The Horse as Heater" was first published in the *Patent Trader*, a newspaper serving Upper Westchester County, New York, where Robinson lives.

As fuel costs continue to spiral upwards, the householder must continue   1
his search for a reasonable and effective means of heating his establishment. Solar, or "passive," heating and woodburning stoves are popular alternatives to oil- and coal-burning systems; however, no discussion of modern heating methods would be complete without mention of the horse.

Horses may be used in a variety of ways as heating units. All of these are   2
simpler than existing mechanical methods, and surprisingly effective. The average 1,200-pound horse has a caloric production rate of 600 therms per minute, and double that if he is angry or unsettled. The fuel-calorie conversion rate is extremely favorable, being about one to eight, which means that the standard four-bedroom house, with snacking center and media room, can be heated by one healthy horse and eight bales of hay per week: an appealing statistic and a soothing prospect. As there are a number of horse-heating methods available, it is wise to examine each to determine which will fit your particular needs the best.

One common practice is the installation of a very large horse (a Percheron   3
or other heavy draft type is popular) in the basement of the house. Hot air ducts lead off the Percheron and act as conduits throughout the house. This is a safe and reliable method, as Percherons are mild and ruminative by nature, and fond of basements. In the event that your basement has been turned into a family recreation center, this should not adversely affect your Percheron system: many Percherons are ardent ping-pong spectators, and some are interested in taking up the game themselves. If the prospect of a blue-roan gelding playing round-robin in your basement unsettles you, remember this: even the most ineffectual efforts on the Percheron's part to join in family ping-pong games will raise the heat production in your home by a tremendous factor.

Encouraging the horse in any sort of physical activity, even charades, should enable your entire family and the close neighbors of your choice to take hot showers as a result.

A drawback of the central-heating Percheron is that it heats the entire   4
house regardless of which rooms are being used, and some homeowners prefer a more adaptable system which will heat only the rooms that are routinely occupied. Many people find that stationing Thoroughbred mares throughout the house is an attractive alternative to the heavy draft cellar horse. The Thoroughbred is an extremely energetic breed, and its heat production is enormous, owing to its highly developed capillary system, which is a relatively new feature in equine design. The dainty Thoroughbred foot, another hallmark of this fine breed, ensures minimum damage to your flooring and fine carpets. Thoroughbreds are, however, emotionally unstable, and more care and attention must be paid them than the placid draft horse. This maintenance may be more than the average homeowner is willing to provide: soothing words must be used, idle or vicious gossip must be eschewed, and a friendly greeting must be offered daily, incorporating the correct name of the horse (not some jocular substitute), to maintain psychic order. Failure to follow these rules may result in "sulk-outs," and a general lowering of temperature. Mares are more effusive than geldings, and they make particularly good heat producers, but they tend to shy at mice and violence, so geldings are recommended for kitchen and TV room use.

A third, and highly recommended, plan is to give each member of the   5
family a Shetland pony of his own. These tiny ponies are docile creatures, with thick coats and long manes which will double as bathmats. If properly trained, these nimble creatures will follow their receptors eagerly and unselfishly about the house, producing a steady stream of therms. They can be trained as well to make beds and wash sweaters; the drawback is, of course, that they are such terrible liars.

Besides the practical attractions of the horse, there is his great aesthetic   6
appeal. Durably made and skillfully designed, the horse is available in a handsome selection of coordinated earth tones, ranging from white to black and including brown. He also comes in a wide assortment of body styles, from the trim and compact Shetland, through the rugged, all-purpose Quarter horse, whose stylish white trim and abstract patterning make him a popular favorite with decorators, to the massive, heavy-duty Percheron or Clydesdale, who can heat an entire convention without moving a fetlock.

The horse is clean, docile, thrifty, and cheerful. He is biodegradable, non-   7
carcinogenic, and produces no long-term side effects. His own needs are modest: he requires only sweet sun-cured timothy hay and a double-handful of dry oats daily. Clearly, the record of the horse as a reliable and valuable helpmate to man continues, and the horse takes his place beside the stove, the sun, and the furnace.

✳

RESPONDING TO THE WHOLE ESSAY

1. How and where does Robinson let her readers know exactly what she is arguing for in this essay?
2. Robinson defines her rhetorical situation for the reader in the first paragraph. Identify her announced audience, explain what her purpose is, and comment on what lets the reader know that she intends to make her point through humor. [1g(2)]
3. Comment on the tone of this essay and how Robinson's use of logic—or lack of it—contributes to the tone. [3a(3)]
4. Would you say that Robinson's method in this essay is mainly deductive or inductive? Explain. [5h]
5. Does Robinson refute objections to her argument? If so, where and how? If not, why not?
6. Examine how Robinson connects paragraphs to give coherence to this essay, and comment on the techniques she uses. [3d]

ANALYZING THE ELEMENTS

Grammar

1. In the first sentence of the essay, Robinson refers to "the householder" as *he*. Rewrite the sentence to make the language inclusive. [23d]
2. In the third sentence of paragraph 3, what is the grammatical relationship between the clause beginning "as Percherons . . ." and the rest of the sentence? [12b]

Effective Sentences

1. Writers generally try to avoid frequent use of the passive voice, but Robinson turns such usage to her advantage. Comment on how her use of passive constructions contributes to the effectiveness of the essay. [21d]
2. Analyze Robinson's use of coordination and subordination in the third sentence of paragraph 4. What does subordination contribute to the general effectiveness of the sentence? [19]

Punctuation and Mechanics

1. Robinson uses colons in a number of sentences in "The Horse as Heater." Comment on her use of the colon in the fourth sentence of paragraph 2 and in the fourth and fifth sentences of paragraph 3. [31d]
2. Explain Robinson's use of quotation marks in the next-to-last sentence of paragraph 4. What other method could Robinson have used to accomplish this effect? [30d]

Diction

1. Explain the reason for each hyphen in *oil- and coal-burning* (paragraph 1), *fuel-calorie* (paragraph 2), *blue-roan* and *ping-pong* (paragraph 3), *central-heating* (paragraph 4), and *heavy-duty* (paragraph 6). [32g]
2. Comment on how Robinson's choice of words contributes to the humorous effect of the essay, paying particular attention to the fifth sentence of paragraph 3 and the final sentence of paragraph 5.

BUILDING VOCABULARY

1. The terms *blue-roan, gelding,* and *fetlock* refer specifically to attributes of horses. What does each term mean? Can you think of instances in which you might use one or more of these terms to refer to something other than a horse? Explain.
2. The following words are not frequently used in most writing, but they all have the advantage of being exceedingly precise: *ruminative, hallmark, eschew, docile.* What does each mean? Write a sentence using each word.

SUGGESTIONS FOR WRITING

1. Reflect carefully on some problem that you think needs a solution but for which ordinary solutions are not easily available. Write your own modest proposal in which you offer a startling—and potentially ridiculous—solution to the problem.
2. Write an essay in which your goal is to persuade an unbeliever of the value of some labor-saving gadget—microwave ovens, computers, power saws, battery-operated personal fans, and so on. Your essay might be serious or humorous, as you wish.

Liberation Genealogy
Aurora Levins Morales

Aurora Levins Morales, poet, essayist, and historian, was raised a "red-diaper baby" in the hills of Puerto Rico by her Jewish and Puerto Rican parents. She is the author of *Getting Home Alive*, a multigenre work co-written with her mother, Rosario Morales, and *Remedios*, a prose-poetry retelling of the history of the Atlantic world, through the lives of Puerto Rican women. Her essays have appeared in *Ms.*, *Woman's Review of Books*, and numerous anthologies. She holds a doctorate in women's studies and history and lectures nationally. She lives in San Francisco and Minneapolis. This selection is from *Medicine Stories: History, Culture and the Politics of Integrity.*

Raicism—from *raices* or roots—is the practice of rooting ourselves in the 1 real, concrete histories of our people: our families, our local communities, our ethnic communities. It is radical genealogy, history made personal. It is a keeping of accounts. Its intent is to pierce the immense, mind-deadening denial that permeates daily life, that drowns our deepest grief and horror about the founding and ongoing atrocities of racism, class, and patriarchy in endless chatter about trivialities. Oppression buries the actual lives of real and contradictory people in the crude generalizations of bigotry and punishes us for not matching the caricature, refusing all evidence of who we actually are in defiance of its tidy categories. It is a blunt instrument, used for bashing not only our dangerous complexities, but also the ancient and permanent fact of our involvement with each other.

Raicism, or rootedness, is the choice to bear witness to our specific, con- 2 tradictory historical identities in relationship to one another. It is an accounting of the debts and assets we have inherited, and acknowledging the precise nature of that inheritance is an act of spiritual and political integrity.

I grew up on stories of my mother's barrio childhood in Spanish Harlem 3 and the Bronx, of near starvation in the early years of the Depression, of my grandmother's single dress. It was not until I went to the small Puerto Rican town of Toa Alta and examined the parish registers that I discovered five generations of slave-holding ancestors among the petty landed gentry of northeast Puerto Rico. A handful of families held political and economic power, married their children to each other, and consolidated their wealth with the purchase of enslaved human beings. I remember the feelings, as this reality dawned on me, of shame, but also of excitement. Over the years I had found peasants, small farmers, revolutionaries in my family tree. This was the thing I had not wanted to find. If I could figure out how to face it and consciously carry it, how to transform shame and denial into wholeness, perhaps I could find a way out of the numbness of privilege, not only for myself, but also for the people I worked with in classes and workshops who came asking to learn.

So that day I wrote down the name of each and every slave held by my ancestors. I have used my own family history to break silence: to acknowledge publicly and repeatedly my family debt to their coerced labor, to expose and reject family mythology about our "kind" treatment of slaves as a step in challenging the generalized myth of kind slavery in Puerto Rico, and to decide that although none of these people had chosen me as a descendant, I owed them the respect one gives to ancestors because their labor had made it possible for my forebears to grow up and thrive. I have also made it my responsibility to make African people visible in every discussion of Puerto Rican history in which I participate.

Taking full responsibility for this legacy of relationships is empowering and radical. Guilt and denial and the defensive pull to avoid blame require immense amounts of energy and are profoundly immobilizing. Giving them up can be a great relief. Deciding that we are in fact accountable frees us to act. Acknowledging our ancestors' participation in the oppression of others (and this is ultimately true of everyone if you really dig) and deciding to balance the accounts on their behalf leads to greater integrity and less shame; less self-righteousness and more righteousness, humility, and compassion; and a sense of proportion.

At the same time, uncovering the credit side of the accounts not the suffering but the solidarity, persistence, love, hard work, creativity, and soul of our forebears, is also an obligation. We are responsible for carrying that forward into our own time and for calling on our kin to do likewise. For people committed to liberation to claim descent from the perpetrators is a renewal of faith in human beings. If slavers, invaders, committers of genocide, inquisitors can beget abolitionists, resistance fighters, healers, community builders, then any one can transform an inheritance of privilege or of victimization into something more fertile than either.

One of the rewards of discovering exactly who our people have been— and how and with whom they have lived—is the possibility of unimagined kinship. My Jewish ancestors were settled in the Ukraine as a buffer against Turkish invasion, alongside German Mennonites brought in to teach formerly landless Jews about farming. At a talk in Wichita, Kansas, I was able to thank their descendants and claim a relationship between us, as Eastern European Jew and German Christian; other than that of genocidal anti-Semitism.

Mapping the specificity of our ethnicity also reveals hidden relationships. European Americans in this country need to find out in relationship to whom they became white. The answers will be very different for the descendants of a Scot from Iowa, an Irishwoman from Alabama, a New York Pole, a Louisiana French-Spanish Creole, a Texan with roots in 17th-century England and 19th-century Austria, and a Romanian Jew who settled in turn-of-the-century San Francisco. Questions about our place within the megastructures of racism become intimate and carry personality. It becomes possible to see the choices we make right now as extensions of those inherited ones, and to choose more courageously as a result.

✳

RESPONDING TO THE WHOLE ESSAY

1. What is Morales' primary purpose in this essay? [1g(1)]
2. What expository techniques does Morales use to develop her thesis? [2e]
3. What is Morales' tone? Is she hostile or accusatory? Find evidence to support your answer. [3a(3)]
4. Morales relies heavily on one personal example to support her argument. Is this one example sufficient for the purposes of this essay?
5. Does Morales essay end on a negative or positive note? [3a(2)]

ANALYZING THE ELEMENTS

Grammar

1. Is the last sentence of the first paragraph parallel? [20d]
2. What is the antecedent of *It* in the last sentence of the first paragraph? [16e]
3. What is the antecedent to the pronoun *This* in the sixth sentence of paragraph 3? [16e]

Effective Sentences

1. How does Morales use sentence variety in the first paragraph? [22]
2. How does she use repetition in the first paragraph? [21e]

Punctuation and Mechanics

1. Why is *Raicism* in paragraphs 1 and 2 italicized? [34]
2. Why does Morales use semicolons in the last sentence of paragraph 5? [28b]

Diction

1. What is the effect of the words *chatter* and *trivialities* in the fourth sentence of the first paragraph? [24a(2)]
2. What does Morales mean by *Mapping* in the first sentence of paragraph 8? [24a(4)]

BUILDING VOCABULARY

1. Look up the definitions and the origins of the following words: *genealogy, barrio, genocide, anti-Semitism.* [23a]
2. Look up the definitions of *radical* and *caricature.* Do they mean what you thought they meant?

SUGGESTIONS FOR WRITING

1. Write an essay in which you argue that the federal government should *or* should not make payments of restitution to the heirs of slaves.
2. Do some research into your own genealogy, and write an essay in which you examine the effects of your family history on your current quality of life.

You Can't Judge a Crook by His Color
Randall Kennedy

Randall Kennedy is a professor at Harvard Law School. He is the author of *Race, Crime, and the Law* (1998).

In Kansas City, a Drug Enforcement Administration officer stops and questions a young man who has just stepped off a flight from Los Angeles. The officer has focused on this man because intelligence reports indicate that black gangs in L.A. are flooding the Kansas City area with illegal drugs. Young, toughly dressed, and appearing nervous, he paid for his ticket in cash, checked no luggage, brought two carry-on bags, and made a beeline for a taxi when he arrived. Oh, and one other thing: The young man is black. When asked why he decided to question this man, the officer declares that he considered race, along with other factors, because doing so helps him allocate limited time and resources efficiently.

Should we applaud the officer's conduct? Permit it? Prohibit it? This is not a hypothetical example. Encounters like this take place every day, all over the country, as police battle street crime, drug trafficking, and illegal immigration. And this particular case study happens to be the real-life scenario presented in a federal lawsuit of the early '90s, *United States v. Weaver*, in which the 8th U.S. Circuit Court of Appeals upheld the constitutionality of the officer's action.

"Large groups of our citizens," the court declared, "should not be regarded by law enforcement officers as presumptively criminal based upon their race." The court went on to say, however, that "facts are not to be ignored simply because they may be unpleasant." According to the court, the circumstances were such that the young man's race, considered in conjunction with other signals, was a legitimate factor in the decision to approach and ultimately detain him. "We wish it were otherwise," the court maintained, "but we take the facts as they are presented to us, not as we would like them to be." Other courts have agreed that the Constitution does not prohibit police from considering race, as long as they do so for bona fide purposes of law enforcement (not racial harassment) and as long as it is only one of several factors.

These decisions have been welcome news to the many law enforcement officials who consider what has come to be known as racial profiling an essential weapon in the war on crime. They maintain that, in areas where young African American males commit a disproportionate number of the street crimes, the cops are justified in scrutinizing that sector of the population more closely than others—just as they are generally justified in scrutinizing men more closely than they do women.

As Bernard Parks, chief of the Los Angeles Police Department, explained   5 to Jeffrey Goldberg of *The New York Times Magazine*: "We have an issue of violent crime against jewelry salespeople. . . . The predominant suspects are Colombians. We don't find Mexican Americans, or blacks, or other immigrants. It's a collection of several hundred Colombians who commit this crime. If you see six in a car in front of the Jewelry Mart, and they're waiting and watching people with briefcases, should we play the percentages and follow them? It's common sense."

Cops like Parks say that racial profiling is a sensible, statistically based tool.   6 Profiling lowers the cost of obtaining and processing crime information, which in turn lowers the overall cost of doing the business of policing. And the fact that a number of cops who support racial profiling are black, including Parks, buttresses claims that the practice isn't motivated by bigotry. Indeed, these police officers note that racial profiling is race-*neutral* in that it can be applied to persons of all races, depending on the circumstances. In predominantly black neighborhoods in which white people stick out (as potential drug customers or racist hooligans, for example), whiteness can become part of a profile. In the southwestern United States, where Latinos often traffic in illegal immigrants, apparent Latin American ancestry can become part of a profile.

But the defenders of racial profiling are wrong. Ever since the Black and   7 Latino Caucus of the New Jersey Legislature held a series of hearings, complete with testimony from victims of what they claimed was the New Jersey state police force's overly aggressive racial profiling, the air has been thick with public denunciations of the practice. In June 1999, at a forum organized by the Justice Department on racial problems in law enforcement, President Clinton condemned racial profiling as a "morally indefensible, deeply corrosive practice." Vice President Al Gore has promised that, if he is elected president, he will see to it that the first civil rights act of the new century would end racial profiling. His rival for the Democratic nomination, Bill Bradley, has countered that Gore should prepare an executive order and ask the president to sign it *now.*

Unfortunately, though, many who condemn racial profiling do so without   8 really thinking the issue through. One common complaint is that using race (say, blackness) as one factor in selecting surveillance targets is fundamentally racist. But selectivity of this sort can be defended on nonracist grounds. "There is nothing more painful to me at this stage in my life," Jesse Jackson said in 1993, "than to walk down the street and hear footsteps and start to think about robbery and then look around and see somebody white and feel relieved." Jackson was relieved not because he dislikes black people, but because he estimated that he stood a somewhat greater risk of being robbed by a black person than by a white person. Statistics confirm that African Americans—particularly young black men—commit a dramatically disproportionate share of street crime in the United States. This is a sociological fact, not a figment of a racist media (or police) imagination. In recent years, victims report blacks as perpetrators of around 25 percent of violent crimes, although blacks constitute only about 12 percent of the nation's population.

So, if racial profiling isn't bigoted, and if the empirical claim upon which   9
the practice rests is sound, why is it wrong?

Racial distinctions are and should be different from other lines of social   10
stratification. That is why, since the civil rights revolution of the 1960s, courts have typically ruled—based on the 14th Amendment's equal protection clause—that mere reasonableness is an insufficient justification for officials to discriminate on racial grounds. In such cases, courts have generally insisted on applying "strict scrutiny"—the most intense level of judicial review—to government actions. Under this tough standard, the use of race in governmental decision making may be upheld only if it serves a compelling government objective and only if it is "narrowly tailored" to advance that objective.

A disturbing feature of this debate is that many people, including judges,   11
are suggesting that decisions based on racial distinctions do not constitute unlawful racial discrimination—as long as race is not the only reason a person was treated objectionably. The court that upheld the DEA agent's action at the Kansas City airport, for instance, declined to describe it as racially discriminatory and thus evaded strict scrutiny.

But racially discriminatory decisions typically stem from mixed motives.   12
For example, an employer who prefers white candidates to black candidates—except for those black candidates with superior experience and test scores—is engaging in racial discrimination, even though race is not the only factor he considers (since he selects black superstars). In some cases, race is a marginal factor; in others it is the only factor. The distinction may have a bearing on the moral or logical justification, but taking race into account at all means engaging in discrimination.

Because both law and morality discourage racial discrimination, propo-   13
nents should persuade the public that racial profiling is justifiable. Instead, they frequently neglect its costs and minimize the extent to which it adds to the resentment blacks feel toward the law enforcement establishment. When O.J. Simpson was acquitted, many recognized the danger of a large sector of Americans feeling cynical and angry toward the system. Such alienation creates witnesses who fail to cooperate with police, citizens who view prosecutors as the enemy, lawyers who disdain the rules they have sworn to uphold, and jurors who yearn to get even with a system that has, in their eyes, consistently mistreated them. Racial profiling helps keep this pool of accumulated rage filled to the brim.

The courts have not been sufficiently mindful of this risk. In rejecting a   14
1976 constitutional challenge that accused U.S. Border Patrol officers in California of selecting cars for inspection partly on the basis of drivers' apparent Mexican ancestry, the Supreme Court noted in part that, of the motorists passing the checkpoint, fewer than 1 percent were stopped. It also

noted that, of the 820 vehicles inspected during the period in question, roughly 20 percent contained illegal aliens.

Justice William J. Brennan dissented, however, saying the Court did not 15 indicate the ancestral makeup of *all* the persons the Border Patrol stopped. It is likely that many of the innocent people who were questioned were of apparent Mexican ancestry who then had to prove their obedience to the law just because others of the same ethnic background have broken laws in the past.

The practice of racial profiling undercuts a good idea that needs more 16 support from both society and the law: Individuals should be judged by public authorities on the basis of their own conduct and not on the basis of racial generalization. Race-dependent policing retards the development of bias-free thinking; indeed, it encourages the opposite.

What about the fact that in some communities people associated with a 17 given racial group commit a disproportionately large number of crimes? Our commitment to a just social order should prompt us to end racial profiling even if the generalizations on which the technique is based are supported by empirical evidence. This is not as risky as it may sound. There are actually many contexts in which the law properly enjoins us to forswear playing racial odds even when doing so would advance legitimate goals.

For example, public opinion surveys have established that blacks distrust 18 law enforcement more than whites. Thus, it would be rational—and not necessarily racist—for a prosecutor to use ethnic origin as a factor in excluding black potential jurors. Fortunately, the Supreme Court has outlawed racial discrimination of this sort. And because demographics show that in the United States, whites tend to live longer than blacks, it would be perfectly rational for insurers to charge blacks higher life-insurance premiums. Fortunately, the law forbids that, too.

The point here is that racial equality, like all good things in life, costs 19 something. Politicians suggest that all Americans need to do in order to attain racial justice is forswear bigotry. But they must also demand equal treatment before the law even when unequal treatment is defensible in the name of nonracist goals—and even when their effort will be costly.

Since abandoning racial profiling would make policing more expensive and 20 perhaps less effective, those of us who oppose it must advocate a responsible alternative. Mine is simply to spend more money on other means of enforcement— and then spread the cost on some nonracial basis. One way to do that would be to hire more police officers. Another way would be to subject everyone to closer surveillance. A benefit of the second option would be to acquaint more whites with the burden of police intrusion, which might prompt more of them to insist on limiting police power. As it stands now, the burden is unfairly placed on minorities—imposing on Mexican Americans, blacks, and others a special kind of tax for the war against illegal immigration, drugs, and other crimes. The racial element of that tax should be repealed.

I'm not saying that police should never be able to use race as a guideline. 21 If a young white man with blue hair robs me, the police should certainly be able to use a description of the perpetrator's race. In this situation, though, whiteness is a trait linked to a particular person with respect to a particular incident. It is not a free-floating accusation that hovers over young white men practically all the time—which is the predicament young black men currently face. Nor am I saying that race could never be legitimately relied upon as a signal of increased danger. In an extraordinary circumstance in which plausible alternatives appear to be absent, officials might need to resort to racial profiling. This is a far cry from routine profiling that is subjected to little scrutiny.

Now that racial profiling is a hot issue, the prospects for policy change have improved. President Clinton directed federal law enforcement agencies to determine the extent to which their officers focus on individuals on the basis of race. The Customs Service is rethinking its practice of using ethnicity or nationality as a basis for selecting subjects for investigation. The Federal Aviation Administration has been re-evaluating its recommended security procedures; it wants the airlines to combat terrorism with computer profiling, which is purportedly less race-based than random checks by airport personnel. Unfortunately, though, a minefield of complexity lies beneath these options. Unless we understand the complexities, this opportunity will be wasted.   22

To protect ourselves against race-based policing requires no real confrontation with the status quo, because hardly anyone defends police surveillance triggered *solely* by race. Much of the talk about police "targeting" suspects on the basis of race is, in this sense, misguided and harmful. It diverts attention to a side issue. Another danger is the threat of demagoguery through oversimplification. When politicians talk about "racial profiling," we must insist that they define precisely what they mean. Evasion—putting off hard decisions under the guise of needing more information—is also a danger.   23

Even if routine racial profiling is prohibited, the practice will not cease quickly. An officer who makes a given decision partly on a racial basis is unlikely to acknowledge having done so, and supervisors and judges are loath to reject officers' statements. Nevertheless, it would be helpful for President Clinton to initiate a strict anti-discrimination directive to send a signal to conscientious, law-abiding officers that there are certain criteria they ought not use.   24

To be sure, creating a norm that can't be fully enforced isn't ideal, but it might encourage us all to work toward closing the gap between our laws and the conduct of public authorities. A new rule prohibiting racial profiling might be made to be broken, but it could set a new standard for legitimate government.   25

✳

RESPONDING TO THE WHOLE ESSAY

1. Find Kennedy's thesis statement. [2b]
2. This essay was originally published in the *New Republic*, a liberal magazine. Does Kennedy consider his audience? [1g(2)]

3. Why is cause and effect an important developmental tool for Kennedy's purpose? [2e]
4. Find evidence that Kennedy anticipates the arguments of those opposed to his thesis. [5e]
5. Does Kennedy attempt an argument that he cannot prove? [5d]

ANALYZING THE ELEMENTS

Grammar

1. Justify the sentence fragments in paragraph 2. [13]
2. Identify the clauses in the first sentence of paragraph 13. [12b]

Effective Sentences

1. Examine the sentence variety in paragraph 1. [22]
2. How does Kennedy use questions effectively throughout his essay? [5d, 5e, and 22e]

Punctuation and Mechanics

1. Why does Kennedy capitalize *Mexican* and *Colombian* but not *white* and *black*?
2. Why does Kennedy use a dash in the last sentence of paragraph 23? [31e(2)]

Diction

1. Explain Kennedy's use of figurative language in the last sentence of paragraph 13. [24a(4)]
2. Why does Kennedy use *fewer* instead of *less* in the second sentence of paragraph 14? [Glossary of Usage]
3. Explain Kennedy's use of figurative langauge in the sixth sentence of paragraph 20? [24a(4)]

BUILDING VOCABULARY

1. What is the origin of the word *hooligan*? Might this word be offensive to some readers? [23a]
2. What is the origin of *bona fide*? Name three synonyms for *bona fide*. [23a]

SUGGESTIONS FOR WRITING

1. Write an argument in which you dispel the stereotype of a group of which you are a member.
2. Write an essay in which you explore how generalizations about a particular group of people have created hardship for that group.

"'We can't dance together'"[1]

María Rosa Menocal

Born in 1953, María Rosa Menocal grew up along with rock and roll. She earned a Ph.D. in Romance philology, and she is a professor in the Department of Spanish and Portuguese at Yale University. Among her other academic writings, she has authored two books: *The Arabic Role in Medieval Literary History* (1987) and *Writing in Dante's Cult of Truth from Borges to Boccaccio* (1991). The original version of this essay, which was first published in *Profession 88*, a journal "of opinion about and for the modern language profession," contained a number of quotations from rock lyrics which could not be included because of copyright restrictions.

> Maybe this small attachment to my past is only another case of what Frank Zappa calls a bunch of old guys sitting around playing rock 'n' roll. But as we all know, rock 'n' roll will never die, and education too, as Henry Adams always sez, keeps going on forever.
>
> —*Thomas Pynchon, Introduction to* Slow Learner, *xxxiv*

Anyone who teaches Petrarch's lyric magnum opus, vulgarly known as the *Canzoniere*, is eventually bound to reveal to his or her students the rather delicious irony that Petrarch actually thought—or at least said, repeatedly—that writing in the vernacular, the language of the masses and the vulgar, was not a particularly worthwhile or dignified enterprise. I, at least, get a somewhat malicious pleasure from pointing out that it is, of course, because of his magnificently "vulgar" collection of love songs that Petrarch is at all remembered—and that he is such an integral part of canonical Western culture. The irony is a double one: first, if his statements can be taken at face value, Petrarch was terribly wrong in his assessments of the relative merits of his vernacular versus his "classical" writings; second, we have now, following his obviously misguided thinking on the matter and in blatant disregard of the historical lesson, "classicized" the love songs—which were so successful precisely because

This paper is written in memory of Clifton Cherpack, who did not quite make it to sixty-four. [Au.]

[1]Steely Dan, "Hey Nineteen."

they weren't "classical" in the first place.[2] When one reads Allan Bloom's derisive comments about music in *The Closing of the American Mind,* which are characterized by a remarkably similar disdain for popular love lyrics and the accompanying reverence for the "great tradition," one can't help but wonder, at least for a split second, if Bloom doesn't have a manuscript of rock lyrics stashed away someplace. Well, it was just a split second.

In fact, a first reading of Bloom, of the chapter entitled "Music" in particular, should logically lead one merely to shrug one's shoulders at his stereotypically retrograde views. I spent several months ticking off all the reasons why writing a response to Bloom's book was, is, even on the face of it, a waste of time and a somewhat self-indulgent exercise. It struck me as significant, however, that other reviewers, no matter how negative, rarely mentioned his ravings about music, tending to be concerned with more "serious" issues about education he raises. Even the witty and intelligent review in *Rolling Stone,* which lays many of Bloom's pretenses bare ("he is peddling fundamentalism for highbrows" [Greider 39]) essentially passes over Bloom's substantive comments about music—in great measure, no doubt, because for anyone reading that journal his comments are too ludicrous even to require a response, their silliness exposed just by their being quoted. But because, as the example of Petrarch so clearly indicates, the multiple and complex issues revolving around the question of "vulgar" love lyrics and the canonical literary tradition are much too important to and central in our profession to be left to the occasional college newspaper refutation by a student music reviewer, I decided to respond.

I do so acknowledging the following limitations. First, I do not pretend to be in any way comprehensive or systematic in my treatment of rock, and the examples I have chosen are idiosyncratic, personal, and relatively random, the music that happened to come to mind. I am not a scholar or an expert in this area, nor is this a research paper on rock.[3] I am a middling to average, at best, connoisseur of the genre. But my examples are not unrepresentative (although

2

3

---

[2]See Vickers's extraordinary article for a much fuller discussion of these issues. Her appreciation of the parallels between Petrarch's work and that of one rock group, Survivor, as well as her detailed and sensitive exploration of the complexities of the relationship between popular and "classical" culture is exemplary. I am indebted to her for allowing me to read a prepublication version of the article. [Au.]

[3]Nevertheless, I have been asked to provide scholarly documentation for the songs and lyrics I quote. This is both perfectly reasonable and appropriate, given that I am, in part, claiming that much of rock and its lyrics is a cultural phenomenon to be treated like any other—and thus a song should be quoted as we would quote a poem. It is also true, however, and also part of my argument, that "everyone" knows that, for example, "When I'm Sixty-Four" is on the Beatles's *Sgt. Pepper* that came in 1967 and that the lyrics of a remarkable body of rock are part of the active memory of many people. Thus the citations and quotations that follow are representative of the communal knowledge and memory of rock—a reflection of the living lyrical tradition. The "Works Cited" listings reflect ex post facto documentation, in some cases incomplete. Note that many artists avoid putting dates on their albums. [Au.]

they in fact represent a minuscule selection of the full range), and someone else's personal sampling would have comparable validity. Second, I will not address in any great detail the much larger issues Bloom raises, although they are, perforce, the backdrop for the music chapter and, more important, they reflect an ideology within which his rejection of rock must be understood. But those are other reviews.[4] And for the sake of my argument—in sum, that Bloom is, from a scholarly point of view, wrong about what rock and roll is—I will attempt to suspend any sustained rebuttal that involves opinion as to what culture (and thus rock and roll) ought to be.

Bloom's argument about rock has three major elements: (1) that rock music and its lyrics are limited to "sex, hate and a smarmy, hypocritical version of brotherly love" (74), with an emphasis on sex: "rock music has one appeal only, a barbaric appeal, to sexual desire—not love, not *eros*, but sexual desire undeveloped and untutored" (73); (2) that rock's values (or lack thereof) are, at worst, antagonistic to fundamental cultural values and, at best, lie well outside other lasting cultural pursuits: "Rock music encourages passions and provides models that have no relation to any life the young people . . . can possibly lead, or to the kinds of admiration encouraged by liberal studies. . . . [A]s long as they have the Walkman on, they cannot hear what the great tradition has to say" (80–81); (3) that rock is a musical lyrical genre that concerns youth and children overwhelmingly: "Never was there an art form directed so exclusively to children" (74). Let's take these elements in that order.

Bloom's assertions about the poverty and limitations of rock's themes are perhaps the most excruciating in their simple lack of factualness—and there is such an embarrassment of riches available as counterargument that it is difficult to know where to start. What *is* true, certainly, is that the richest thematic mine is that of love—and more often than not, love that is in some way unsatisfying, unhappy, or unfulfilled. But many, if not most, of rock's classic love songs are about a great deal more—or less—than sex. From the Beatles' basically silly "Michelle" . . . (which reveals the metaliterary preoccupation of rock as well) to Dylan's charming ditty "You're Gonna Make Me Lonesome When You Go," which includes a refusal of other types of love poetry . . . , to the troubled and tortured love of Neil Young's "Now that you've made yourself love me . . ." there are few, if any, of the variations and variegations of "classical" love poetry that have not found lyrics in the rock canon.

Even if we limit ourselves to the writing of the artists mentioned above, Bloom's generalization not only crumbles but has to be replaced by the realization that rock's obsession with love and with its own expressions of the longing for love are next of kin to those same obsessions in all other lyrical schools. Thus, the Beatles's hymn to enduring, perfect, and as yet unfound love in "I Will" . . . is neatly counterbalanced by their wistful and hopeful

4

5

6

---

[4]See especially David Rieff's scathing comments about Bloom's cultural-ideological posture. [Au.]

projection about a perhaps nonexistent future in the classic "When I'm Sixty-Four." . . . Dylan's repertoire of love songs (although it is fair to say that he is far from being known as a love lyricist) is scarcely less representative of these ties to lyric antecedents. From the early, bittersweet "Don't Think Twice It's All Right" about the pain of failed love . . . to the famous "Just like a Woman" (satirized by Woody Allen in *Annie Hall*) to other, much more difficult and hermetic songs such as "Queen Jane Approximately" . . . , his long and varied career as a lyricist is reminiscent of a poetic ancestry he is quite conscious of following.⁵ And the centrality of the broken heart to the lyric tradition is simply and touchingly reflected in Neil Young's "Only Love Can Break Your Heart." . . .

The interesting question, of course, is why and how the preoccupation   7
with love and its expression in rock is so reminiscent of other lyrical traditions, so like other schools and canons that are now studied, by and large, in a more rarefied atmosphere. From twelfth-century Persian courtly poetry to Petrarchism in Renaissance Europe to opera in the last century, love and its many problems—sometimes sexual, sometimes not—are of overwhelming and enduring fascination and are perhaps the ultimate inspiration for poetry and lyrics—an inspiration that all these lyrical schools are also explicitly conscious of and that is often the focus of metaliterary interest itself. Taken as a whole, rock exhibits, theme for theme, much the same concerns as those of the traditions we have now classicized. In one example, the preoccupation with unsatisfactory love becomes the subject or object of poetry and creates, in turn, the association between the lyricist or singer and the lover. Self-reflection and metalyrical concerns include the glory and fame that will be achieved through the singing or poetry: some examples are "So You Want to Be a Rock 'n' Roll Star," "Do You Believe in Magic?" and that early and enduring anthem of rock, "Johnny B. Goode." . . . Thus, what is critical is not merely that Bloom (and others) have got it wrong but that ignorance prevents them from seeing that rock is in so many ways like parts of the "great tradition." And one is then, indeed, led to the question of whether rock resembles these traditions because it is descended from them or because some sort of universal parallelism is at work—a question that, because of our Bloom-like prejudices, has scarcely been asked, let alone answered.⁶ As for the sexuality, well, indeed, some rock lyrics are sexual, even, perhaps, exclusively and pointedly and vulgarly sexual. But sexuality, too, is far from uniquely modern, and Mick Jagger's "Satisfaction" and "Let's Spend the Night Together" pale, in both vulgarity and explicitness, beside some of the songs of the venerated William of Aquitaine.

---

⁵Dylan, who changed his name from Robert Zimmerman to one that linked him explicitly with the great tradition, has written dozens of songs whose lyrics explicitly harken back to all manner of poetic schools, from the Bible . . . to Petrarch . . . to the great poetic struggle of modernism. . . . [Au.]

⁶The one exception I know of is Vickers's article. [Au.]

But while rock may thus mimic earlier lyric schools in its fascination with   8
the generative power of unhappy love, it has exploited a much fuller range of
themes, including the historicopolitical one that Bloom dismisses as "a smarmy,
hypocritical version of brotherly love." Once again the generalization alarm-
ingly misrepresents the remarkable range of topics covered and views expressed.
Many of rock's earliest masterpieces, written in the late sixties and early sev-
enties, were, in fact, politically committed, and opposition to the war (and the
draft) and sympathy for the civil rights movements were major conditioning
and influential currents. But as often as not, the lyrics produced in this climate
were most conspicuously informed by and interwoven with the other musical
and lyrical traditions that are such important components of rock: black, particularly spiritual, music and the sort of folk tradition that Joan Baez's songs
rely on so heavily. Remnants of these strains, pervasive in rock even today, explain the centrality of the Talking Heads's "Take Me to the River" and Eric
Clapton's (and others') recordings of "Swing Low, Sweet Chariot." And while
there are plenty of examples of virtually unmediated protest (Country Joe and
the Fish's "What are we fighting for? . . ." is a classic, certainly, as is Dylan's
even more famous "The Times They Are a-Changin'"), much of the "political"
lyrics of rock are infinitely more complex.

The Band, for example, specialized in songs that reflected back on the   9
Civil War South, and by giving the poet a Confederate voice in "The Night
They Drove Old Dixie Down," they brilliantly underscored, without ever being explicit, the universal tragedy of war. The currently popular U2 plumbs
the complex problems and no-win situation of Northern Ireland in equally
subtle ways. Finally, many rock lyricists have made their points by merely taking over or only slightly rewriting "classics" from other traditions: Prince sings
the Lord's Prayer with remarkable effect; the Byrds sang Ecclesiastes in "Turn,
Turn, Turn." If these are smarmy versions of brotherly love, so be it. In fact,
what is stunning here is that rock's connections with the "great tradition" are
often quite explicit, markedly intertextual, and ultimately impossible to ignore. The extent to which Bloom's second major objection to rock—that it
has no cultural ties or links or avenues beyond itself—is simply mistaken comes
very much to the fore here.[7]

But above and beyond specific songs that are strictly and obviously tied,   10
intertextually, to any number of classic texts outside the rock tradition, rock's
place in contemporary society is a major link to a number of cultural phenomena that we now, from a safe distance, view as canonical. In fact, it is
telling that Bloom does acknowledge the great impact of rock: at the outset
of the chapter he goes on at some length, and with considerable accuracy,

---

[7]The British punk tradition, which I know scarcely at all and thus do not discuss more fully,
includes a number of "singings" of important texts. I am grateful to a student, Kirsten Thorne,
for bringing to my attention "The Wasteland," by the Mission U.K., and *"In Dulce Decorum,"*
by the Damned, where the text is a speech of Winston Churchill's. [Au.]

about the unique role rock plays in society and about rock's importance, unparalleled in recent history. He begins the chapter, in fact, noting that "[n]othing is more singular about this generation than its addiction to music. This is the age of music and the states of soul that accompany it. To find a rival to this enthusiasm, one would have to go back at least a century to Germany and the passion for Wagner's operas" (68). And, having remarked that one crucial difference between rock and the German passion of the last century is that rock is much less elitist (i.e., it cuts across class boundaries more), he goes on to note the great change that has occurred in the role music and its lyrics play in this century: "The power of music in the soul . . . has been recovered after a long period of desuetude" (69). In acknowledging this rather remarkable turn of events, this existence in the late twentieth century of a status for music and its lyrics that did not always exist and when it did was a major cultural institution and a central part of the culture, Bloom is implicitly recognizing what he will explicitly deny later on: the cultural centrality of the rock phenomenon. In fact, Bloom even goes on to note that this is the first generation he has taught that fully understand Plato's opposition to music, something earlier generations, for whom music was "background," were incapable of understanding. And since Bloom explicitly recognizes the enormous impact per se of the phenomenon, his refusal to see its cultural impact is grounded, explicitly, in what he sees as its failure to address issues other than sex—an opinion that, as I have tried to suggest, cannot be substantiated.

What can be substantiated is the perhaps radical-sounding assertion, already implicit in Bloom's comments, that the rock phenomenon is a twentieth-century version, in many if not in most of its details, of what at other times and in other places have been major lyrical schools with resounding impact in the cultures that produced them. Poetry, after all, had long ago ceased to be "lyrical" in the etymological sense of the word, an integral part of music. For most people—and many scholars—poetry is what was and is written down to be read and what is published in poetry journals or in the *New Yorker* or in anthologies. Poetry in that form not only is substantively different from lyrics but is rarely (and then only for a minuscule percentage of the population, now or in any other period of history) a living part of one's cultural or spiritual experience. But rock is much like opera and even more like the phenomenon of the troubadours in twelfth- and thirteenth-century Europe, when lyricists started singing in the vernaculars rather than in the long-dead Latin. Rock is poetry that is aggressively and self-consciously a part of the living tradition that, in great measure because it is attached to music, plays a fundamental and vital cultural role for many more people. In this regard, as in various others, Bloom's assertion that rock makes it difficult for young people to have a passionate relationship to the art and thought that are the substance of a liberal education is almost perversely skewed.

The truth is the opposite: the person, young or otherwise, for whom poetry is a living form that resonates daily in the mind and soul is quite capable of appreciating not only the poetry of the troubadours or of Petrarch, so

11

12

similar in other ways, but, more important, the great lyrical power of poetry in and of itself. Members of this generation, as Bloom likes to put it, are the first in a long time, thanks to rock, to be in a position to understand the impact and repercussions of many earlier lyrical phenomena. They should be able to grasp, for example (particularly if we as mediators can simply pull out the parallels), what is moving, rather than dusty and mechanical and arcane, in a previous generation's songs—much more so, I would argue, than people who don't know why tears have been shed at Lennon's "Imagine" or who don't think of love in the haunting structures of "Here, There, and Everywhere," or who might not hear the ecstasy and triumph of the Grateful Dead's "Touch of Grey" . . . , so often sung last summer by Jerry Garcia, who could have been grandfather to many in the audience. For those whose poetic sensibilities have incubated in the heart and soul and tapping feet, Puccini's sentimental arias can be truly moving and Verdi's triumphal choruses can stir, vicariously if nothing else, the same sentiments stirred at Woodstock.[8] The list of ways in which the experience of rock is enlightening vis-à-vis the "great tradition" is seemingly endless: students who know full well that a strong lyric tradition thrives on the seemingly paradoxical combination of parameters and restraints, and the individual creativity that thrives within the tradition and the repetition of commonplaces, can eventually read the medieval and Renaissance lyric traditions with a fuller appreciation of their astonishing repetitiousness. And those same "students" of rock, because rock has included, and continues to include, a substantial "trobar clus"[9] strain, those students who have learned instinctively to appreciate everything from "Lucy in the Sky with Diamonds" . . . to "Third World Man," by Steely Dan . . . , bring an important background to the study of the myriad canonical schools of hermetic lyrics that have produced poets as varied as Arnaut Daniel, the Spanish mystics, Mallarmé, and that fellow splicer of lines from the Italian, Ezra Pound.

Bloom's third major misapprehension is actually rather touching—or pathetic: that rock's appeal is exclusively to the young, that rock is a phenomenon of a "generation," that it affects his "students," and so on. This notion is belied by the simple facts of chronologies, celebrated every year as one great rock star after another turns forty or fifty and as those who grew up on rock are now bringing up children of their own. Toward the end of this chapter Bloom depicts a pathetic scenario where the poor parents who have struggled to provide a good life and who wish only the best for their child watch on, terrified and helpless, as their thirteen-year-old boy is mesmerized by MTV and its attendant horrors. This is a remarkable fantasy; the parents are, likely as not, especially if they are highbrow and college-educated, the ones who watch MTV and who introduced rock to their child in the first place. And

13

---

[8]Lest the connection appear farfetched I note that in the movie *The Killing Fields* the two most emotionally wrenching scenes are accompanied by Puccini's "Nessun dorma" and Lennon's "Imagine." [Au.]
[9]A complicated style used by some medieval Provençal poets.

while they may care less for their child's currently preferred groups and lyrics than for their own classics, they are probably not much concerned since it has become clear that their classics are becoming *the* classics and that their child will be listening to the Beatles, as well as to the Beatles's progeny. But more telling than even those fundamentals are columns on contemporary music that now appear regularly in the *New Yorker*, that holy sanctum of haute culture, and articles in academic journals that reflect the extent to which the centrality of rock can no longer be defined in generational terms at all.[10]

In fact, many of Bloom's (and others') misapprehensions about rock and   14
its impact are rooted in remarkably clichéd notions about the general poverty of "youth culture" and a commensurate (and I believe equally illusory) aggrandizement of the degree of "high culture" in earlier societies and generations. Thus, to take but one example, Bloom dismisses the powerful argument that, in fact, there is a significant revival of interest in classical music by saying that even if there is, only 5 to 10 percent of the population is affected. Does he believe that much more than that has ever had a serious interest in classical music? The serious listener does, indeed, listen seriously to all sorts of music. And not only is "Roll Over, Beethoven" tongue-in-cheek, ultimately, but twenty or so years down the line it may well end up on the same shelf as the Ninth. Likewise, it is obvious that, as with all other schools or cultural phenomena, there is a lot of trash out there and a part of the audience at every concert has never heard of Ecclesiastes. So what else is new? Are we to pretend that everyone who listened avidly to Wagner knew all the allusions? Don't we all know that for every Mozart there were hundreds of Salieris? Rock is no better and probably no worse. There is little doubt that many people who listen to much that is marvelously lyrical in rock, that is poetic and moving, never get past the beat, and, also undoubtedly, much of what has been written and will continue to be written will never amount to anything in posterity.

But it is nonsense—or wishful thinking—to say, as Bloom does, that when   15
we take the Walkmans off after years of listening to rock there will be nothing left. *Au contraire*. It is a pity Bloom has listened so little, for, given the great concern for culture and the educational tradition he claims to be championing, he is thus almost perversely depriving himself of access to a richly variegated and (in the very cultural terms he wishes to see the "liberal tradition") an enormously influential phenomenon. We cannot afford to ignore Bloom's misapprehensions about music, because the nature of his misunderstanding is so intimately tied with the debates now raging, not just at Stanford but nearly everywhere, about what constitutes the canon of "Western civilization." And the educator, particularly in the field of literature and literary culture, who like Bloom walks about deaf to our living lyric tradition is a less able explicator and mediator of the literary traditions and canonized poets

---

[10]A recent issue of *Stanford French Review* contains an article entitled "The Grateful Dead: Corneille's Tragedy and the Illusion of History." [Au.]

that are the fundamental intertexts for the troubadours of our own time. It might alter both the tenor and the substance of these discussions considerably if we were to recognize that a great deal of what is being listened to on the Walkmans is the great tradition very much alive and well—and as Pynchon sez, rock 'n' roll will never die, and education keeps going on forever.

Works Cited

The Band. "The Night They Drove Old Dixie Down." *The Band.* Capitol, CDP 7 46493 2, n.d. on original album.

Beatles. "Here, There and Everywhere." *Revolver.* Capitol, CDP 7 46441 2, 1966.

———. "I Will." No title [*White Album*]. EMI-Capitol, CDP 7 46443 2, 1968.

———. "Michelle." *Rubber Soul.* EMI-Capitol, CDP 7 46440 2, 1965.

———. "When I'm Sixty-Four." "Lucy in the Sky with Diamonds." *Sgt. Pepper's Lonely Hearts Club Band.* EMI, CDP 7 46442 2, 1967.

Berry, Chuck. "Johnny B. Goode."

———. "Roll Over, Beethoven."

Bloom, Allan. *The Closing of the American Mind: How Higher Education Has Failed Democracy and Impoverished the Souls of Today's Students.* New York: Simon, 1987.

Byrds. "So You Want to Be a Rock 'n' Roll Star." *The Byrds.* Columbia, G 30127, n.d.

———. "Turn, Turn, Turn." *Turn, Turn, Turn.* Columbia, CG 33645, n.d.

Clapton, Eric. "Swing Low, Sweet Chariot." *Time Pieces,* RSO, 800 014-2, 1975.

Country Joe McDonald. "I-Feel-like-I'm-Fixin'-to-Die Rag." *Woodstock.* Atlantic-Cotillion, SD 3-500, 1970.

Dylan, Bob. "Don't Think Twice It's All Right." *The Freewheelin' Bob Dylan.* Columbia, CK 8786, n.d.

———. "Queen Jane Approximately." *Highway 61 Revisited.* Columbia, CK 9189, 1965.

———. "Just like a Woman." *Blonde on Blonde.* Columbia, CK 841, n.d.

———. "You're Gonna Make Me Lonesome When You Go." *Blood on the Tracks.* Columbia, X 698, 1974.

———. "The Times They Are a-Changin'."

Grateful Dead. "Touch of Grey." *In the Dark.* Arista, ARCD 8452, 1987.

Greider, William. "Bloom and Doom." *Rolling Stone* 8 Oct. 1987:39–40.

Lennon, John. "Imagine."

Lovin' Spoonful. "Do You Believe in Magic?"

Pynchon, Thomas. *Slow Learner.* New York: Bantam, 1984.

Rieff, David. "The Colonel and the Professor." *Times Literary Supplement* 4–11 Sept. 1987:950, 960.

Rolling Stones. "Let's Spend the Night Together." *Flowers.* Abkco, 75092, 1966.

———. "Satisfaction."

Steely Dan. "Hey Nineteen." "Third World Man." *Gaucho.* MCA Records, MCAD-37220, 1980.

Talking Heads. "Take Me to the River." *Stop Making Sense.* Sire, 25186-1, 1984.

Vickers, Nancy. "Vital Signs: Petrarch and Popular Culture." *Romantic Review.* January 1988:184–95.

Young, Neil. "Only Love Can Break Your Heart." "I Believe in You." *After the Gold Rush.* Reprise, 2283-2, 1970.

✳

RESPONDING TO THE WHOLE ESSAY

1. Comment as fully as you can on Menocal's audience. What evidence can you find to show that she writes with her audience in mind? How might this essay be different if Menocal had written it for *Rolling Stone*? [1g(2)]
2. Why do you think Menocal begins her essay with a long paragraph discussing Petrarch's attitudes about his love poetry? What does this paragraph contribute to her argument? [3b(1)]
3. What is Menocal's purpose for writing "'We can't dance together'" and where does she state it? [1g(1)]
4. Analyze the structure of Menocal's argument in "'We can't dance together'" and answer the following: What case does she wish to make? How does she present her evidence? What concessions does she make, and why does she place them where she does? Does she refute possible objections? If so, where and how? What solution does she offer? Where does she state it? Does she urge the reader to take action? If so, what kind?
5. Is Menocal's reasoning in this essay primarily inductive or deductive? Support your answer with evidence from the essay. [5h]
6. What are the premises on which Menocal bases her argument? Where and how does she make them clear to the reader? [5e]
7. Paragraph 4 consists almost entirely of a single sentence. Justify both the length of the sentence and Menocal's choice to devote the entire paragraph to that sentence. [2d]
8. Given the fact that Menocal uses footnotes in her essay, why are her sources indicated in parentheses rather than in footnotes? [7]

ANALYZING THE ELEMENTS

Grammar

1. In the first sentence of paragraph 2, Menocal writes "should logically lead one merely to shrug one's shoulders." Why do you think Menocal chose to write the sentence as she did, rather than to write "should logically lead a person merely to shrug his shoulders"? What other choices did she have? [16d]
2. The second sentence of footnote 3 contains the statement, "much of rock and roll and its lyrics is a cultural phenomenon." Comment on the agreement of subject and verb in this statement. [17a]
3. Comment on the time relationships represented by the sequence of tenses in the sixth and seventh sentences of paragraph 10. [17c]

Effective Sentences

1. Analyze the fourth sentence of paragraph 5 as a periodic sentence. [21b]
2. The third sentence of paragraph 1 is very long and involved. Rewrite this sentence for a less academic audience. [22a]
3. Rewrite the sixth sentence of paragraph 14 and the final sentence of paragraph 15 to remove expletive constructions. [22b]

Punctuation and Mechanics

1. Why is each word of the title of this essay not capitalized? [33c]
2. In view of the fact that some lyrics have been deleted from this version of Menocal's essay, what do you make of the use of ellipses in paragraph 6? Are all of the ellipses used to indicate the same kind of omission? [30a and 31i]
3. Analyze the use of parentheses in paragraph 4. [31f]
4. Why does Menocal place the *n* in brackets in the third sentence of paragraph 10? [31g]

Diction

1. What is the plural of *Walkman* (sentences 1 and 6, paragraph 15)? [32]
2. Justify Menocal's misspelling, *sez,* in the final sentence of paragraph 15. [32]
3. Comment on Menocal's use of *back* with *reflected.* [25d]
4. Look up the following words in your dictionary and comment on the appropriateness (or lack of appropriateness) of diction in "'We can't dance together'": *stashed* (paragraph 1), *retrograde* (paragraph 2), *perforce* (paragraph 3), *metaliterary* and *ditty* (paragraph 5), *hermetic* (paragraph 6), *historicopolitical* and *smarmy* (paragraph 8), *intertextual* (paragraph 9), *telling* and *desuetude* (paragraph 10), *vis-à-vis* (paragraph 12), *haute culture* (paragraph 13), *commensurate* and *aggrandizement* (paragraph 14), *explicator* (paragraph 15). Which expressions could accurately be termed "academic jargon"? Why? [23b, 23c, and 24]
5. Comment on whether "not unrepresentative" (sentence 5, paragraph 3) is a double negative. If so, is it justified? Why or why not? [25a]

BUILDING VOCABULARY

1. What do *vulgar* and *vernacular* mean? What is the source of each word? What do they have in common?
2. Look up each of the following words and note (1) its source, (2) meaning, (3) synonym(s), (4) usage notes, and (5) other words made from the same root: *blatant, ludicrous, smarmy, arcane, sanctum, canonical.*

SUGGESTIONS FOR WRITING

1. Write an essay in which you argue that the attitude(s) of a particular authority group (for instance, parents, supervisors, internal revenue agents) is based on unsubstantiated beliefs rather than on fact.
2. Write an essay in which you argue for the appeal of a particular kind of music or performer (for instance, classical music or jazz, a specific "sound" like the Seattle sound or the Nashville sound, or a group like Soundgarden or the Oak Ridge Boys).

The Wrong Spin
Mike Godwin

In July of 1995 *Time* magazine published an article showcasing "a new study, *Marketing Pornography on the Information Superhighway*, purportedly by a team of researchers at Carnegie Mellon University"[1] and accepted for publication by the *Georgetown Law Journal*. As it turns out, the study was conducted primarily by an undergraduate at Carnegie Mellon, Marty Rimm. Donna Hoffman and Thomas Novak, associate professors of management at Vanderbilt University, claim that Rimm "grossly exaggerated the extent of pornography on the Internet by conflating findings from private adult-bulletin-board systems that require credit cards for payments (and are off-limits to minors) with those from the public networks (which are not)." Hoffman and Novak argue further that Rimm's statistics, particularly his "claim that 83.5 percent of the images stored on the Usenet newsgroups are pornographic," are so inaccurate as to be meaningless, and they point out that pornographic files comprise "less than one half of one percent of all messages posted on the Internet." Three weeks after publication of the article, *Time* noted that Rimm himself may not be what he had seemed, apparently having conducted a questionable survey that concluded that nearly two-thirds of his former fellow high school students had gambled at Atlantic City casinos. *Time* also reported that Rimm authored two books: one titled *The Pornographer's Handbook: How to Exploit Women, Dupe Men & Make Lots of Money*, which Rimm says is a satire, and the other a privately published novel titled *An American Playground* and based on his casino experiences. Godwin's essay takes the position that since the *Time* article fueled the hysteria begun by the radical right using tainted data, the magazine has a responsibility to fulfill its stated mission to help readers "think clearly about the legal issues of online life." It is important to know that Godwin (mnemonic@well.com) is staff counsel for the Electronic Frontier Foundation in San Francisco, an organization dedicated to ensuring that new communications technologies have the benefit of constitutional civil liberties.

Here's an interesting experiment. Try combining the topics of sex, children, and the Net in a magazine or newspaper story, or even in an online discussion. Amazingly, this combination will almost invariably cause ostensibly intelligent people to shut down their higher thinking centers. Let's hope this column proves an exception to the rule.

[1]Quotations in this note are from *Time*, July 24, 1995.

For me, the most recent example of this rule appeared on America Online 2
in *Time* magazine's online forum, Time Online. Generally, *Time* has done a
good job of creating a lively and interesting discussion forum, but sometimes
the corporate interests of Time Warner skew the discussion. Take, for example, the following post by RPTime (Robert Pondiscio, a public relations persons for *Time*) in the topic dedicated to discussion and criticism of the magazine's now-notorious "Cyberporn" cover story. Shortly after the national
press reported that the U.S. Justice Department had announced a dozen arrests in a two-year investigation into the use of commercial online services to
distribute child porn and seduce minors into sex, the following message appeared in the Cyberporn topic in Time Online:

Subj: Arrests 95-09-14 10:20:08 EDT
From: RPTime
Posted on: America Online

Looks like the FBI has arrested a dozen people in connection with the biggest
non-problem in cyberspace. The feds have reportedly seized digitized pornographic images of children as young as two years old from members of this
very online service.

I'll be interested in the reactions of our First Amendment absolutist friends.
Perhaps they will argue the arrested should be released, and the parents of
children involved should be charged with neglect for not adequately supervising their kids' online activities.

Robert

Analyzed rhetorically and legally, this is a fascinating post. In Pondiscio's 3
defense, it must be said that he's had to work overtime in defending *Time's*
decision to hype the fraudulent "Carnegie Mellon" study authored by Martin
Rimm. Given the flood of criticism of both the story and the study itself, you
can understand if Pondiscio is feeling a bit fried. So you may be able to forgive his over-the-top rhetorical strategy of classing critics of the cover story
as "First Amendment absolutists" who are blasé about child pornography or
the victimization of children.

From a legal standpoint, however, the post is even more interesting and far 4
less forgivable, given that Pondiscio, in both his public role and as a private individual, has touted *Time's* strength in explaining the issues to its readers. You
see, by posting this message in the topic dedicated to discussion of the
"Cyberporn" cover story, Pondiscio is implying that the FBI raids somehow vin-
dicate *Time's* decision to run the story. Yet even if we accept the (false) implication that the cover story was not primarily about Marty Rimm and his
Georgetown Law Journal article, Pondiscio's post demonstrates confusion about
what the legal and factual issues relating to porn, the Net, and children really are.

Defining the Terms.   When talking about pornography and child safety on   5
the Net, you'll often see several different terms bandied about as if they were
interchangeable. They're not. Here are some basic definitions.

Pornography: In general, material that presents sexual content of some   6
sort, with the intent of being arousing. *Playboy* and *Penthouse* could be included under this definition, and, like any other uses of the press, such material is presumptively legal under the First Amendment. To be illegal, pornography either must be found to be "obscene" (see below) or "child pornography"
(see below).

Obscenity: To be "obscene," pornography must meet all parts of a three-   7
part test designed by then-Chief Justice Warren Burger in 1973 in a case called
Miller v. California. This is normally a question of *content*. The three parts
of the so-called "Miller test" are as follows:

- *State statute*. Normally, there must be a state statute in place that
describes with specificity the particular sexual (or excretory) acts that
cannot be depicted.
- *Community standards*. The depiction of the sexual acts must be
"patently offensive" and "appeal to the prurient interest," as judged by
a reasonable man applying the standards of the community.
- *The escape clause*. To be obscene, the material must fail to meet the
requirements of the *Miller v. California* "escape clause." That is, must
lack "serious" literary, artistic, scientific, political, or other social value.

Child Pornography: This material is illegal regardless of whether it is ob-   8
scene, which means you don't even bother to ask any questions about "community standards." Under federal law, "child pornography" is any *visual* material that depicts a child either engaging in explicit sexual acts or posing in
a "lewd and lascivious" manner, when the manufacture of such material involves the actual use of a real child. Thus, verbal material can't be child porn
under federal law, although it could be obscene.

Similarly, computer-generated material that seems to depict children en-   9
gaged in sexual activity but does not use real children would not be child
porn, although it almost certainly would be obscene. In short, this category
is defined not primarily in terms of *content* ("offensive" depictions) but in
terms of *conduct* (the victimization of actual children).

Child Sexual Abuse: Sometimes children are abused sexually, yet no one   10
takes any pictures of it. This is not child porn, although of course it is illegal.

Child Seduction: Sometimes child abusers (see above) will attempt to se-   11
duce new victims. They may try to contact such victims via an online service.
Note: Despite the commonly repeated claim that pedophiles rely on pornography to seduce children, it is possible to engage in child seduction without
ever using pornography, obscenity, or child pornography.

Exposure to Inappropriate Materials: Most states make it illegal to expose   12
minors to sexually explicit material—even when such material is otherwise legal.

It is *this* issue that has been the primary subject of the "indecency" legislation that we've seen so much of in Congress this year.

Indecency: This is a special term for content that, up to now, has been   13
regulated only in two special areas of federal jurisdiction—broadcasting and so-called "dial-a-porn" services, both currently under the jurisdiction of the Federal Communications Commission (FCC). In those contexts, "indecency" normally means "patently offensive" sexual content or profane language.

When you're talking about media that are not under FCC jurisdiction—   14
newspaper and book publication, say, or the movie industry—the term "indecency" has no legal meaning. One of the strategies that lobbyists for the Christian Coalition and associated groups have been employing to limit sexual content online has been to ask Congress to expand FCC jurisdiction (and the FCC's definition of "indecency") to cover the Internet. In previous columns, I've argued that this would be unconstitutional.

Children First.   With our primer in hand, we can return to Robert Pondiscio's   15
posting above. And once you're clear on the different meanings of the terms and concepts I've outlined here, you can note that the FBI raids primarily involve material described as child pornography.

Yet the critics of *Time*'s "Cyberporn" cover story have been addressing   16
issues under pornography, obscenity, child seduction, and exposure to inappropriate materials—and primarily as they relate to *Time*'s coverage or to Martin Rimm's fraudulent study. What the critics were saying was a "non-problem" was the *Time*/Rimm implication that children (and others) were routinely stumbling, unwittingly, across pornographic images, which *Time* had described as "pervasive."

They were also arguing that, despite scary anecdotes about pedophiles   17
e-mailing pornography to children online, it's common for minors to spend years online without ever encountering a child predator or having any inappropriate material sent to them.

It was this argument that Pondiscio transmuted into a claim that child   18
predation in cyberspace was a "non-problem"—an especially adroit rhetorical move, given that Philip Elmer-DeWitt's story for *Time* had said the danger was minimal. Elmer-DeWitt wrote, "While groups like the Family Research Council insist that online child molesters represent a clear and present danger, there is no evidence that it is any greater than the thousand other threats children face every day."

That consideration aside, no one has ever denied that child sexual abuse   19
is a problem, whether in cyberspace or out of it. And neither *Time* nor its PR director are doing anyone any favors by distorting the arguments of the magazine's critics.

What *Time* could do, if Pondiscio and his employers were interested in   20
correcting the damage done by the "Cyberporn" article, would be to repeat a few basic and irreducible facts that have gotten lost in all the sensationalism—such as the fact that there's arguably less of a threat to your child online than

there is on the corner across from the schoolyard. After all, even the most determined child predator can't reach through the screen.

Time also could underscore the fact that the National Center for Missing   21
and Exploited Children has developed some excellent guidelines for parents and children. The NCMEC pamphlet entitled *Child Safety on the Information Superhighway* is available on America Online and just about everywhere else in cyberspace. If you and your children follow those guidelines, the Internet is a far safer place than is Disney World.

Unfortunately, the Net still isn't safe place for the Constitution. And that   22
won't change until we solve two problems. First, we've got to teach ourselves to think clearly about the legal issues of online life, regardless of the willingness of anti-porn activists and the mainstream media—including *Time*—to confuse them. Secondly, we've got to remember, come election time, that we need to protect ourselves against the "clear and present danger" of rogue senators who've forgotten the meaning of the Constitution they've sworn to uphold.

✸

RESPONDING TO THE WHOLE ESSAY

1. What is Godwin's probable reason for including the seven definitions cited in paragraphs 6 through 13? What would be the effect of leaving them out?
2. Comment on the transition from paragraph 21 to 22. Is it effective? Why or why not? [3d]
3. Where does Godwin let his readers know what his essay is about? How does he let us know his purpose? [1g(1)]
4. The essay was first published in *Internet World* magazine, a publication read by people interested in and knowledgeable about the Internet. With that in mind, comment on the characteristics of the audience Godwin was writing for. [1g(2)]

ANALYZING THE ELEMENTS

Grammar

1. Examine the uses of the past and past perfect tenses in the fourth sentence in paragraph 2. Which event referred to in the sentence happened first and which happened last? How do you know? [17c]
2. Comment upon the use of *you* as the world modified by the participial phrase *When talking* in the first sentence of paragraph 5. [15b]
3. Can the sentence fragment that begins paragraph 6 be justified? Would Godwin have done better to insert an innocuous verb such as *is*? Why or why not? [13]
4. Why does Godwin use *are* instead of *is* to agree with *that* in the first sentence of paragraph 14? [17e]

5. Rewrite the first sentence of paragraph 20 to remove all verbs in the subjunctive mood. What is the effect of rewriting the sentence this way? [17d]

6. In the first sentence of paragraph 19, what is the grammatical function of the phrase "That consideration aside"? [12a]

Effective Sentences

1. Consider Godwin's use of the first-person pronoun in paragraphs 2, 4, 14, 15, and 22 and of the second-person pronoun in paragraphs 3, 4, 5, 14, 15, 20, and 21. Comment on how this practice contributes to or detracts from sentence effectiveness. [17g]

2. To what does *this* in the last sentence of paragraph 14 refer? To understand clearly the effect of broad reference, first justify the sentence as Godwin wrote it, and then rewrite the sentence making the reference more specific. [16e]

3. Examine the relationships between coordinate and subordinate clauses in sentence 2 of paragraph 16. Explain as well as you can how these relationships contribute to making the sentence effective. [21g]

4. Comment on what makes sentence 1 in paragraph 18 effective or not effective. [21c]

5. What does repetition contribute to the effectiveness of the third and fourth sentences of paragraph 22? [21e]

Punctuation and Mechanics

1. Is the final clause in the first sentence of paragraph 8 restrictive or nonrestrictive? How can you tell? What does it modify? [12b]

2. Why does Godwin use the full name of the FCC in paragraph 13 but not in paragraph 14? [35e]

3. What do you think the quotation marks around *Carnegie Mellon* in sentence 2 of paragraph 3 mean? What other choice did Godwin have? [30c]

Diction

1. Using synonyms for the following words, rewrite the sentences in which each appears: *bandied* (paragraph 5), *presumptively* (paragraph 6), *prurient* (paragraph 7), *lascivious* (paragraph 8), *pedophile* (paragraph 11), *fraudulent* (paragraph 16), *adroit* (paragraph 28), *irreducible* (paragraph 20), *rogue* (paragraph 16). [23a]

2. Is the use of words such as *hype* and *fried* (paragraph 3) appropriate in an essay in which words such as *bandied*, *prurient*, and *adroit* are also used? Why or why not? [1g and 23b]

BUILDING VOCABULARY

1. Identify the base form (prefix 1 root) from which the adverb *presumptively* is made. How many other words can be made from the same base form? What are they?

2. What other words can be formed by combining various prefixes with the root form for *presumptively*? How does each prefix change the word?

SUGGESTIONS FOR WRITING

1. Identify an issue that you think has been irresponsibly reported. Write an essay arguing that the media have an obligation to make amends for the problems their irresponsibility has created.
2. Write an essay arguing for or against the proposition that one of the most pernicious effects of pornography is the way it demeans those who read (view) it.

The Gift of Wilderness
Wallace Stegner

Wallace Stegner (1909–1993) has written an impressive body of fiction and nonfiction. Among his many novels are *The Big Rock Candy Mountain, All the Little Live Things, Angle of Repose,* for which he received the Pulitzer Prize for fiction, and *The Spectator Bird,* for which he received the National Book Award. He is also the author of many nonfiction works, including *The Writer in America, Wolf Willow: A History, a Story, and a Memory of the Last Plains Frontier, The Uneasy Chair: A Biography of Bernard DeVoto,* and *One Way to Spell Man.* Born in Iowa and educated at the University of Iowa and the University of Utah, Stegner most often writes—in his nonfiction as well as his fiction—of how the good person lives responsibly in this world. That theme is reflected in "The Gift of Wilderness," in which Stegner calls attention to the responsibility we have not only to ourselves and to each other, but also to future generations and to the land itself.

Once, writing in the interests of wilderness to a government commission, I quoted a letter from Sherwood Anderson to Waldo Frank, written in the 1920s. I think it is worth quoting again. "Is it not likely," Anderson wrote, "that when the country was new and men were often alone in the fields and forest they got a sense of bigness outside themselves that has now in some way been lost? . . . I am old enough to remember tales that strengthen my belief in a deep semireligious influence that was formerly at work among our people. . . . I can remember old fellows in my home town speaking feelingly of an evening spent on the big empty plains. It had taken the shrillness out of them. They had learned the trick of quiet." 1

I have a teenaged granddaughter who recently returned from a month's Outward Bound exposure to something like wilderness in Death Valley, including three days alone, with water but no food, up on a slope of the Panamints. It is a not-unheard-of kind of initiation—Christ underwent it; Indian youths on the verge of manhood traditionally went off alone to receive their visions and acquire their adult names. I don't know if my granddaughter had any visions or heard the owl cry her name. I do know *she* cried some; and I know also that before it was over it was the greatest experience of her young life. She may have greater ones later on, but she will never quite get over this one. 2

It will probably take more than one exposure to teach her the full trick of quiet, but she knows now where to go to learn it, and she knows the mood to go in. She has felt that bigness outside herself; she has experienced the birth of awe. And if millions of Americans have not been so lucky as she, why, all the 3 more reason to save intact some of the places to which those who are moved to do so may go, and grow by it. It might not be a bad idea to require that wilderness initiation of all American youth, as a substitute for military service.

I, too, have been one of the lucky ones. I spent my childhood and youth in wild, unsupervised places, and was awed very early, and never recovered. I think it must have happened first when I was five years old, in 1914, the year my family moved to the remote valley of the Frenchman River, in Saskatchewan. The town was not yet born—we were among the first fifty or so people assembled to create it. Beaver and muskrat swam in the river, and ermine, mink, coyotes, lynx, bobcats, rabbits, and birds inhabited the willow breaks. During my half dozen years there, I shot the rabbits and trapped the fur-bearers, as other frontier boys have done, and I can remember buying Canadian Victory Bonds, World War I vintage, with the proceeds from my trapline. I packed a gun before I was nine years old. But it is not my predatory experiences that I cherish. I regret them. What I most remember is certain moments, revelations, epiphanies, in which the sensuous little savage that I then was came face to face with the universe. And blinked.

I remember a night when I was very new there, when some cowboys from the Z-X hitched a team to a bobsled and hauled a string of us on our coasting sleds out to the Swift Current hill. They built a fire on the river ice above the ford, and we dragged our sleds to the top of the hill and shot down, blind with speed and snow, and warmed ourselves a minute at the fire, and plowed up the hill for another run.

It was a night of still cold, zero or so, with a full moon—a night of pure magic. I remember finding myself alone at the top of the hill, looking down at the dark moving spots of coasters, and the red fire with black figures around it down at the bottom. It isn't a memory so much as a vision—I don't remember it, I *see* it. I see the valley, and the curving course of the river with its scratches of leafless willows and its smothered bars. I see the moon reflecting upward from a reach of wind-blown clear ice, and the white hump of the hills, and the sky like polished metal, and the moon; and behind or in front of or mixed with the moonlight, pulsing with a kind of life, the paled, washed-out green and red of the northern lights.

I stood there by myself, my hands numb, my face stiff with cold, my nose running, and I felt very small and insignificant and quelled, but at the same time exalted. Greenland's icy mountains, and myself at their center, one little spark of suffering warmth in the midst of all that inhuman clarity.

And I remember that evening spent on the big empty plains that Sherwood Anderson wrote about. In June of 1915 my father took my brother and me with him in the wagon across fifty miles of unpeopled prairie to build a house on our homestead. We were heavily loaded, the wagon was heavy and the team light, and our mare Daisy had a young foal that had a hard time keeping up. All day we plodded across nearly trackless buffalo grass in dust and heat, under siege from mosquitoes and horseflies. We lunched beside a slough where in the shallow water we ignorantly chased and captured a couple of baby mallards. Before I let mine go, I felt the thumping of that wild little heart in my hands, and that taught me something too. Night overtook us, and we camped on the trail. Five gaunt coyotes watched us eat supper, and later serenaded us. I went to sleep to their music.

Then in the night I awoke, not knowing where I was. Strangeness flowed around me; there was a current of cool air, a whispering, a loom of darkness overhead. In panic I reared up on my elbow and found that I was sleeping beside my brother under the wagon, and that night wind was breathing across me through the spokes of the wheel. It came from unimaginably far places, across a vast emptiness, below millions of polished stars. And yet its touch was soft, intimate, and reassuring, and my panic went away at once. That wind knew me. I knew it. Every once in a while, sixty-six years after that baptism in space and night and silence, wind across grassland can smell like that to me, as secret, perfumed, and soft, and tell me who I am.

It is an opportunity I wish every American could have. Having been born lucky, I wish we could expand the opportunities I benefited from, instead of extinguishing them. I wish we could establish a maximum system of wilderness preserves and then, by a mixture of protection and eduction, let all Americans learn to know their incomparable heritage and their unique identity.

We are the most various people anywhere, and every segment of us has to learn all anew the lessons both of democracy and conservation. The Laotain and Vietnamese refugees who in August 1980 were discovered poaching squirrels and pigeons in San Francisco's Golden Gate Park were Americans still suffering from the shock and deprivation of a war-blasted homeland, Americans on the road of learning how to be lucky and to conserve their luck. All of us are somewhere on a long arc between ecological ignorance and environmental responsibility. What freedom means is freedom to choose. What civilization means is some sense of *how* to choose, and among what options. If we choose badly or selfishly, we have, not always intentionally, violated the contract. On the strength of the most radical political document in human history, democracy assumes that all men are created equal and that given freedom they can learn to be better masters for themselves than any king or despot could be. But until we arrive at a land ethic that unites science, religion, and human feeling, the needs of the present and the claims of the future, Americans are constantly in danger of being what Aldo Leopold in an irritable moment called them: people remodeling the Alhambra with a bulldozer, and proud of their yardage.

If we conceive development to mean something beyond earth-moving, extraction, and denudation, America is one of the world's most undeveloped nations. But by its very premises, learned in wilderness, its citizens are the only proper source of controls, and the battle between short-range and long-range goals will be fought in the minds of individual citizens. Though it is entirely proper to have government agencies—and they have to be federal—to manage the residual wild places that we set aside for recreational, scientific, and spiritual reasons, they themselves have to be under citizen surveillance, for government agencies have been known to endanger the very things they ought to protect. It was San Francisco, after all, that dammed Hetch Hetchy, it was the Forest Service that granted permits to Disney Enterprises for the resortification of Mineral King, it is Los Angeles that is bleeding the Owens Valley dry and destroying Mono Lake, it is the Air Force that wants to install the MX Missile tracks under the Utah-Nevada desert and in an ecosystem barely hospitable to man create an environment as artificial, sterile, and impermanent as a space shuttle.

We need to learn to listen to the land, hear what it says, understand what it   13
can and can't do over the long haul; what, especially in the West, it should not be asked to do. To learn such things, we have to have access to natural wild land. As our bulldozers prepare for the sixth century of our remodeling of this Alhambra, we could look forward to a better and more rewarding national life if we learned to renounce short-term profit, and practice working for the renewable health of our earth. Instead of easing air-pollution controls in order to postpone the education of the automobile industry; instead of opening our forests to greatly increased timber cutting; instead of running our national parks to please and profit the concessionaires; instead of violating our wilderness areas by allowing oil and mineral exploration with rigs and roads and seismic detonations, we might bear in mind what those precious places are: playgrounds, schoolrooms, laboratories, yes, but above all shrines, in which we can learn to know both the natural world and ourselves, and be at least half reconciled to what we see.

❋

RESPONDING TO THE WHOLE ESSAY

1. How do the first nine paragraphs of the essay contribute to Stegner's persuasive purpose? [1g(1)]
2. Who are the people Stegner aims to persuade in "The Gift of Wilderness"? Does he hope to move his audience to a change of attitude, to action, or to both? Explain. [1g(2)]
3. Where does Stegner reveal what he arguing for? Is his logical strategy primarily inductive or deductive? Explain. [1b and 5h]
4. Which kinds of appeals discussed in the introduction to this chapter does Stegner use in "The Gift of Wilderness"? Trace the appeals in the essay and explain how they strengthen the argument. [5f]
5. Explain how Stegner uses a combination of methods to develop paragraph 11. [3c]
6. How does the title of Stegner's essay fit the subject matter? What does the title reveal of Stegner's attitude about his approach to his subject: [3b(3)]

ANALYZING THE ELEMENTS

Grammar

1. In paragraph 4, why has Stegner chosen to set off the final phrase as a deliberate sentence fragment rather than include it in the previous sentence? What considerations might help a writer decide whether this technique will be effective? [13]

2. Stegner uses an intentional sentence fragment in paragraph 7. What might his reason(s) have been? [13]

Effective Sentences

1. Discuss the effect of sentence length in paragraph 9. [22a]
2. Analyze and explain the effectiveness of the last sentence of the essay. [20a, 22a, and 30b]

Punctuation and Mechanics

1. Explain how the dash and the semicolon in the second sentence of paragraph 2 help to make the sentence more emphatic than three separate sentences would be. [28a and 31e]
2. Explain why the third sentence of paragraph 8 is punctuated with commas rather than with semicolons. [27c]

Diction

1. Discuss Stegner's use of concrete details and of figurative language in paragraph 6. [2d and 24a(4)]
2. What is the Alhambra that Stegner refers to in the last sentence of paragraph 11? Why is the idea of remodeling it with a bulldozer shocking? Explain Stegner's use of the Alhambra in paragraph 13.

BUILDING VOCABULARY

1. English converts nouns to verbs and to adjectives, and verbs and adjectives to nouns by using a variety of suffixes. The suffix *-ed* combined with a noun creates a verb, and *-less* combined with a noun produces an adjective. Similarly, a verb combined with *-tion* becomes a noun, as does an adjective combined with *-ness*. Create nouns, verbs, and adjectives from the following words: *leaf, track, dark, pollute, educate, explore, detonate, strange, dark, empty, big, shrill, initiate.* (All of the words to be created occur in Stegner's "The Gift of Wilderness.")
2. The words *breaks* (paragraph 4), referring to a geographical feature, and *packed* (paragraph 4) are particularly regional terms as Stegner uses them. What do they mean? Are they defined in your dictionary? Are they marked as regional or as informal?

SUGGESTIONS FOR WRITING

1. Strong convictions frequently develop out of personal experiences. Write an essay arguing for such a conviction of yours, recounting one or more personal experiences to support your argument.
2. Write an essay arguing for or against one of the issues Stegner raises in his final paragraph: automobile emission controls, liberalization of timber cutting in national forests, private concessions in public parks, allowing oil and mineral exploration in wilderness areas.

Chapter 10

A Life-and-Death Issue Debated: The Environment

Although the six essays that follow were not written in direct response to one another, they form a debate, offering differing arguments (as well as similar ones occasionally) on issues related to the environment—whether it is in danger; what, if anything, needs to be done to protect it; what may happen if nothing is done.

As you read the essays, you will notice that they often reach different conclusions because of the different assumptions on which they are based, and even when the essays agree, they differ in the emphasis they place on particular points. They differ in tone, as well, reflecting not only the different attitudes of the writers toward both their subjects and their audiences, but also how seriously the writers take the subject.

The essays afford excellent opportunities to see at work the several appeals discussed in the introduction to Chapter 9: the appeal to reason, the appeal to the reader's emotions and values, and the appeal to the credibility or authority of the one making the argument. Some of the six writers depend heavily—and some hardly at all—upon language freighted with emotional connotations. Some explicitly present themselves, or others for whom they speak, as authorities, whose views therefore deserve at least our very serious consideration; others give us hardly a clue about themselves, relying entirely on the force of the points they make and the evidence they can present.

All, however, are writers of intelligence, skill, and stature, who deserve to be read with an open mind; try as you read to set aside any preconceptions you may have about the environment. Give each writer his or her "day in court," and then judge the case as wisely and thoughtfully as you can. Each essay is followed by questions designed to help you consider its individual merits (and perhaps weaknesses). The "Suggestions for Discussion and Writing" at the end of the chapter focus for the most part on issues raised in several of the essays.

Confessions of a Nature Hater

Eugene V. Weinstock

Born in 1927, Eugene V. Weinstock received a Ph.D. in physics from the University of Pennsylvania and is associated with Brookhaven National Laboratories. He has published a number of articles on experimental reactor physics and nuclear safeguards, his most recent being an article on arms control verification. He also writes short stories, which are as yet unpublished. No stranger to nature, Weinstock has lived on a farm, backpacked, and canoed. When his leisure time is not occupied waging war on nature's annoyances, he enjoys tennis, music, and reading.

1   I have a terrible confession to make. I like man and his works better than nature. No doubt this will condemn me in the eyes of those who gush over the limited, repetitious, and near-mechanical activities of birds while disdaining the infinitely more varied repertoire of human beings.

2   Theirs is an essentially misanthropic view. Personally, I would rather sit in my car and watch the bustle of a busy supermarket parking lot than the flittings of birds in a salt marsh. A snatch of conversation overheard in a restaurant can engage my curiosity and arouse my imagination far more effectively than the mysteries of animal migration. And I find a promenade down Fifth Avenue incomparably more interesting than a safari in the Serengeti.

3   Oh, like everyone else I will watch Jacques Cousteau and his rubber-suited minions propelling themselves through submarine canyons, and David Attenborough bounding from continent to continent till my eyes drop out. But I never kid myself that what I am watching is reality, or that I would ever want to be a participant rather than a spectator. Long ago I learned that there is a world of difference between watching nature on television and actually experiencing it. Almost always, TV is better.

4   The camera condenses and prettifies things for us. Television, by telescoping a succession of seasons into 60 minutes and entire lives into a few climactic episodes—the charge of a lion or the mating of whales—cuts out the sheer tedium of "natural" existence. It selects those moments in life that dramatize it or seem to endow it with meaning, while discarding the rest, by far the bulk of it, as irrelevant or boring. Sometimes it achieves its effect by magnifying the microscopic—for example, by filling the screen with a close-up of a bee entering a flower—thereby transforming the humdrum into the wondrous. But an ordinary observer, unequipped with a macro zoom lens, is apt to find the same scene, in its true scale, surpassingly dull.

But there is more to my lack of enthusiasm for "unspoiled" nature (by   5
which is meant, of course, nature unspoiled by man) than that. The truth is,
as anyone with half an eye can see, the natural state of living things—that is,
of things living in the wild—is to be diseased, undernourished, or hunted, and
sometimes, all three. For both plants and animals life is a grim struggle for
survival, one in which, until the rise of modern technology and medicine, man
was as often a victim as a victor.

The view that nature is red in tooth and claw is no longer a fashionable   6
one. Instead, we now take the Panglossian position that the natural world is
the best of all possible worlds. So, as we watch the lioness tearing out the
throat of a gazelle, the unctuous voice of the narrator, safe in his studio in
Cambridge, assures us that this is merely nature's way of weeding out the sick
and the weak, thus preventing overpopulation and improving the species. To
appreciate fully the reality underlying this bland assurance one has only to
imagine the savannah as Central Park, the lion as a mugger, and the bleating
victim as an elderly woman. Since man is also a part of nature, is the mugger, in the larger view, also improving the species?

The fact is, we enjoy these scenes and can watch them with detached in-   7
terest only because we ourselves, thanks to industrialization, are no longer
threatened by nature in the raw. Munching potato chips, we sit entranced as
the snake swallows the rat alive, inch by inch, and the voice from *Nova* drones
on soothingly about the important role of predators in preserving the precious
balance of nature. The last thing we want, however, is to become part of that
balance ourselves. Nature may be neither cruel nor benign, but she most as-
suredly isn't merciful, either.

Of course, boredom and gore aren't all there is to nature. There are also   8
mosquitoes and biting flies, those maddening spoilers of the wild that take
such a consuming interest in whatever warm-blooded creature has the misfortune to wander into their particular corner of paradise and which, in the
far North, can torment caribou into headlong, suicidal flight. Thoreau, in all
his rhapsodizing about the wilderness, discreetly ignores them, but my theory
is that they were what drove him out of Walden after only two years.

Don't get me wrong, though. I don't actually *hate* nature. There's noth-   9
ing I like better than a stroll through a tree-lined park on a summer evening,
observing young lovers passing by and children from the surrounding apartment houses chasing each other across the grass. Nature's fine, as long as you
don't let her get the upper hand.

✳

ANALYZING THE ARGUMENT

1. What can the reader infer from Weinstock's first paragraph about the argument
    that will follow? Point to specifics in the paragraph that suggest the nature of the
    argument.

2. What is Weinstock's thesis? Summarize the main points Weinstock makes in support of this thesis, and show where each is presented in the essay.

3. Weinstock makes three points about why he thinks civilization is preferable to nature. What are they?

4. Weinstock makes a large concession toward the end of the essay. What is it, and why is it placed at the end? [5e and 5g]

5. Show where Weinstock uses appeals primarily to the emotions and values of the reader, and where primarily to reason. [5f]

6. What clues does the essay contain about the audience for whom Weinstock intended it? Are there indications Weinstock was not writing for those he says disdain the "varied repertoire of human beings"? Describe Weinstock's intended audience. [1g(2)]

7. In paragraph 6, Weinstock draws an analogy between a lion and a mugger. What similarities does Weinstock see? What differences between the lion and the mugger are essential from the point of view of the environmentalist?

Buying In
Eve Pell

Eve Pell, a native New Yorker, was born in 1937 and earned a bachelor's degree from Bryn Mawr College in 1958. She has been a staff reporter for the Center for Investigative Reporting and has authored articles for *Nation, New West,* and *In These Times.* In 1971 she co-edited *To Serve the Devil,* a two-volume history of ethnic groups in the United States, and in 1972 edited *Maximum Security,* a collection of letters by convicts describing conditions in California's prisons. She teaches English at the Sara Dix Hamlin School in San Francisco, California.

If the 1980s taught us anything, it is that almost everything is for sale. 1
Even the environmental movement now risks slipping under the influence of some of the most powerful corporations in the United States.

As the public increasingly supports environmental activism, corporate ex- 2
ecutives are gaining access to environmental organizations. Governing boards of some major environmental groups now include the chair of the New York Stock Exchange as well as executives of such corporations as Exxon, Stroh Brewery, Philip Morris, and the giant paper and pulp maker, Union Camp Corporation. Moreover, as the competition for foundation grants intensifies, corporations are giving more and more money to conservation groups. Consider that:

- The World Wildlife Fund/Conservation Foundation, one of the top ten environmental groups in the country, now lists as major donors Chevron and Exxon, which each donated more than $50,000 in 1988, as well as Philip Morris, Mobil, and Morgan Guaranty Trust.
- The National Audubon Society, which in 1986 received only $150,000 in corporate contributions, expects to receive nearly $1 million in such funds in 1989.
- The National Wildlife Federation recently added three new members to its Corporate Council. It costs each company $10,000 to join. Among the fourteen members are Arco, DuPont, and Ciba-Geigy. The Council promotes cooperation between industry leaders and environmentalists.
- The Sierra Club, after considerable agonizing, turned down $700,000 from McDonald's, which wanted to sponsor an environmental education project. McDonald's sought another environmental organization to fund. The National Audubon Society turned down a similar offer shortly afterward.

Businesses say they are just being good citizens, and the environmental   3
groups claim they can remain independent while taking corporate money. But
critics charge that the reality is far more sinister. "These corporations claim to
be environmentalists, but they are buying off the groups who are opposing
them," says David Rapaport of Greenpeace. "And the corporations are buying
legitimacy as well. Dow funds environmental groups and schools in Michigan,
and the chemical companies do the same in the Louisiana chemical corridor."

The relationship between Waste Management, Inc. (WMI) and the   4
Environmental Grantmakers Association (EGA) is a prime example of the
growing connection between big business and the environmental movement.
Perhaps the most sophisticated of the corporate infiltrators, WMI is a world-
wide conglomerate with an annual gross income of more than $3 billion and
nearly nine hundred subsidiaries. Although WMI is the nation's largest and
most advanced handler of wastes, it is also known for its leaky landfills, its
conviction for price-fixing, and its violations of environmental regulations that
resulted in more than $30 million in fines being assessed from 1982 to 1987.
For those reasons it has become a prime target for many grassroots activists
around the country.

Strange as it may seem, Waste Management has been admitted to the   5
Environmental Grantmakers Association, an association of foundation executives who have studied, worked with, and financially supported most of the
varied organizations that make up the U.S. environmental movement today.
The diversity of the funders mirrors the diversity of the environmental movement itself, which spans a wide spectrum of environmental policies and goals—
from simple preservation of rain forests to lawsuits against polluters. By deciding which organizations get money, the grant-makers help set the agenda
of the environmental movement and influence the programs and strategies that
activists carry out.

A latecomer to philanthropy, WMI, in the past three years, has donated   6
more than $900,000 to organizations such as the National Wildlife Federation,
the National Audubon Society, and the Trust for Public Land. Because of
these contributions to environmental causes, WMI's public affairs director,
Dr. William Y. Brown, was invited to attend the EGA's 1988 meeting in
Princeton; his presence there made several funders very uncomfortable.

Admission to the EGA gives the controversial WMI unusual access to the   7
inner sanctum of the environmental movement. Since the funders hold frank,
detailed discussions about the activists they are considering for support, EGA
members learn the movement's plans and tactics. As a major target of some
of those activist groups, WMI is now in the position that the fox might envy:
guarding, and even financing, the henhouse.

Dr. Brown says that his company likes to fund legislative advocacy, espe-   8
cially laws to strengthen regulations governing hazardous waste. If, for instance, laws prohibit dumping waste at sea, that means more business for
WMI. "Stricter legislation is environmentally good and it also helps our
business," he says. Conceding that his company "is not perfect," he says that

because of the nature of its operations, it can't have "a squeaky clean record as if we made yogurt." And Brown readily admits, "The EGA has been useful for me to share information about environmental groups."

That's just what some environmentalists fear. "We don't want to be worried about giving information to the enemy," says a funder who wishes to remain anonymous. The debate over WMI has polarized the EGA into groups roughly paralleling divisions in the environmental movement, where groups that favor compromising with polluters square off against those that favor confrontation. Some funders feel that to keep lines of communication open to all, WMI must be included. Others, who believe that the EGA should hew to higher standards, refuse to attend any meeting where Dr. Brown shows up. "I have met with the parents who come from the bedsides of kids in hospitals as a result of pollution," says another foundation officer. "It's a matter of conscience for me that if he is admitted, I will leave."

Greenpeace, which accepts neither corporate nor foundation money, took the unprecedented step of picketing the Environmental Grantmakers' November 1989 meeting in San Francisco. There, Greenpeace activists marched around with placards telling EGA members about the local groups across the United States that are currently battling to keep WMI landfills out of their communities. Among the signs: "People for Clean Air and Water Is Fighting WMI in Kettleman, CA"; "Dumpstoppers Are Fighting WMI, Inc., in Ft. Wayne, IN"; "Alabamans for a Clean Environment Is Fighting WMI, Inc., in Emelle, AL"; "Citizens United to Recover the Environment Is Fighting WMI, Inc., in Chicago, IL."

To many, the question of whether to exclude WMI from the EGA dramatizes the issues facing the environmental movement in the United States today: where is its soul? And can money buy that soul?

Grassroots groups, such as the Citizen's Clearinghouse for Hazardous Wastes, Inc., are already suspicious of the three-way revolving door connecting many large environmental organizations (like the National Wildlife Federation and the National Audubon Society), government regulatory agencies, and big business. For example, William Ruckelshaus, the Environmental Protection Agency's first director, now chairs Browning-Ferris Industries, second in size only to WMI in the waste disposal field. Ruckelshaus also sits on the governing board of the World Wildlife Fund/Conservation Foundation. The current EPA head, William Reilly, joined the Bush administration from the World Wildlife Fund/Conservation Foundation, which he headed. This revolving door allows established Beltway insiders to move so easily from one sector to another that it is not always clear just whose interests they are serving.

For those who say that the dangers of accepting corporate money are exaggerated, critics point to the way WMI appeared to benefit from its relationship with the National Wildlife Federation. In 1987, WMI began giving money to the NWF. That same year, WMI chief executive officer Dean Buntrock was appointed a director of the NWF, a development that caused considerable controversy. NWF director Jay D. Hair, a figure in the upper

reaches of the environmental elite, defended Buntrock and, in letters to critics of the appointment, called WMI's environmental records "responsible."

Buntrock then parlayed his connection with Hair into a cozy breakfast   14
meeting with EPA chief William Reilly. Afterward, Reilly softened an EPA position on waste disposal regulations, to the benefit of WMI.

The events leading up to that meeting illustrate the workings of the in-   15
sider network. Last March, NWF director Hair, a friend of Reilly's, suggested
that Reilly meet with him and Buntrock. The invitation was written on a newspaper clipping describing a South Carolina state regulation that spelled trouble for WMI's business practices—and which the EPA had the power to affect. In the note, Hair suggested that Reilly discuss the "national implications"
of the South Carolina regulation and "get to know Dean." After the breakfast, Reilly said he was reversing the EPA policy WMI disliked, telling a
reporter that Buntrock had lobbied him to make the change. However, Reilly
later denied to in-house investigators that any lobbying had taken place.

Publicly, NWF director Hair opposed the EPA policy change, but the WMI   16
breakfast controversy shows the difficulty of determining whose side environmentalists are on once the corporate nose enters the environmental tent.

While corporations wishing to improve their images are able to saturate   17
the air waves with public-relations campaigns, corporate influence over environmental organizations through quiet funding is less easily detected.
Chevron's "People Do" campaign—which gives the impression that Chevron
is in the business of raising eagles rather than selling oil—may be offensive,
but at least viewers recognize it as a paid message.

Why have businesses suddenly begun funding some of their most effective   18
adversaries—groups that have cost them billions of dollars in government regulations, court actions, fines, and other headaches? The companies are buying
credibility and access to insider networks because they cannot win a free and
open war of ideas, and because nothing covers up depredations like large checks.

Not everyone agrees with the analysis. EGA president Joe Kilpatrick as-   19
serts, "Even if corporations have adopted what they call an 'enlightened strategy' to make grants to environmental groups in order to 'inject reason' into
their tactics, the grantees have their eyes open."

Nevertheless, it seems naive to believe that environmental groups will act   20
any differently than politicians or judges or journalists when confronted with
gobs of cold cash.

Do people *really* respond to large amounts of money? People do.   21

*

ANALYZING THE ARGUMENT

1. Does Pell oppose the funding of environmental groups by corporations, warn about
    the problems that may result, or both? Support your answer with evidence from
    the essay. In one sentence, state Pell's thesis as completely and exactly as you can.

2. Pell's thesis rests upon the premise that people do, indeed, respond to large amounts of money. What evidence of this assertion does she provide? [2b]

3. According to Pell, what are some reasons that corporate funding of environmental groups is dangerous? Can you think of any way an environmental group might elude this danger?

4. Is Pell's method in this argumentative essay primarily inductive or deductive? Is the other kind of reasoning also apparent? Explain [5h]

5. Which of the appeals—to reason, to emotion, to the writer's credibility or authority—does Pell rely on in this essay? Point to and discuss examples. [5f]

6. Where, if at all, does Pell acknowledge possible objections to what she is saying? If she does make such acknowledgement, does she attempt to refute the objection(s)? [5e and 5g]

7. This essay appeared first in *Mother Jones*, a publication that specializes in investigative reporting having a focus on progressive politics and the arts. What qualities of Pell's essay would appeal to the regular readers of a publication like *Mother Jones*? Would anything in the essay be likely to offend such readers? If so, what and why? If not, why not? [1g(2)]

8. Paragraph 2 of Pell's essay contains five examples of corporate gifts offered to environmental organizations. Could this paragraph be used in an argument defending the actions of corporations? If so, how? If not, why not?

Toward a Land Ethic
Aldo Leopold

Known as the "father of wildlife ecology," Aldo Leopold (1887–1948) is widely respected as a scientist, philosopher, teacher, and writer. After earning a degree in forestry from Yale University, Leopold served as the Deputy Forest Assistant for the U.S. Forestry Service in Arizona and was promoted to Associate Director of the U.S. Forestry Products Laboratory. In 1928, Leopold resigned from the national forestry service to conduct research in the Midwest and teach in, and later chair, the Game Management department of the University of Wisconsin. Along with his teaching and research, Leopold founded the Wilderness Society in 1934, and wrote *Game Management* and *A Sand County Almanac*, which are revered as literary landmarks in the evolution of conservation and environmentalism. "Toward a Land Ethic" originally appeared in *A Sand County Almanac*, published one year after Leopold's death.

1 When god-like Odysseus returned from the wars in Troy, he hanged all on one rope a dozen slave-girls of his household whom he suspected of misbehavior during his absence.

2 This hanging involved no question of propriety. The girls were property. The disposal of property was then, as now, a matter of expediency, not of right and wrong.

3 Concepts of right and wrong were not lacking from Odysseus' Greece: witness the fidelity of his wife through the long years before at last his black-prowed galleys clove the wine-dark seas for home. The ethical structure of that day covered wives, but had not yet been extended to human chattels. During the three thousand years which have since elapsed, ethical criteria have been extended to many fields of conduct, with corresponding shrinkages in those judged by expediency only. . . .

4 The first ethics dealt with the relation between individuals; the Mosaic Decalogue is an example. Later accretions dealt with the relation between the individual and society. The Golden Rule tries to integrate the individual to society; democracy to integrate social organization to the individual.

5 There is as yet no ethic dealing with man's relation to land and to the animals and plants which grow upon it. Land, like Odysseus' slave-girls, is still property. The land-relation is still strictly economic, entailing privileges but not obligations. . . .

The Community Concept.   All ethics so far evolved rest upon a single premise: that the individual is a member of a community of interdependent parts. 6

His instincts prompt him to compete for his place in the community, but his ethics prompt him also to cooperate (perhaps in order that there may be a place to compete for).

The land ethic simply enlarges the boundaries of the community to in- 7 clude soils, waters, plants, and animals, or collectively: the land.

This sounds simple: do we not already sing our love for and obligation 8 to the land of the free and the home of the brave? Yes, but just what and whom do we love? Certainly not the soil, which we are sending helter-skelter downriver. Certainly not the waters, which we assume have no function except to turn turbines, float barges, and carry off sewage. Certainly not the plants, of which we exterminate whole communities without batting an eye. Certainly not the animals, of which we have already extirpated many of the largest and most beautiful species. A land ethic of course cannot prevent the alteration, management, and use of these "resources," but it does affirm their right to continued existence, and, at least in sports, their continued existence in a natural state.

In short, a land ethic changes the role of *Homo sapiens* from conqueror 9 of the land-community to plain member and citizen of it. It implies respect for his fellow members, and also respect for the community as such.

In human history, we have learned (I hope) that the conqueror role is 10 eventually self-defeating. Why? Because it is implicit in such a role that the conqueror knows, *ex cathedra,* just what makes the community clock tick, and just what and who is valuable, and what and who is worthless, in community life. It always turns out that he knows neither, and this is why his conquests eventually defeat themselves. . . .

Substitutes for a Land Ethic. . . . One basic weakness in a conservation sys- 11 tem based wholly on economic motives is that most members of the land community have no economic value. Wildflowers and songbirds are examples. Of the 22,000 higher plants and animals native to Wisconsin, it is doubtful whether more than 5 percent can be sold, fed, eaten, or otherwise put to economic use. Yet these creatures are members of the biotic community, and if (as I believe) its stability depends on its integrity, they are entitled to continuance.

When one of these noneconomic categories is threatened, and if we hap- 12 pen to love it, we invent subterfuges to give it economic importance. At the beginning of the century songbirds were supposed to be disappearing. Ornithologists jumped to the rescue with some distinctly shaky evidence to the effect that insects would eat us up if birds failed to control them. The evidence had to be economic in order to be valid.

It is painful to read these circumlocutions today. We have no land ethic 13 yet, but we have at least drawn nearer the point of admitting that birds should continue as a matter of biotic right, regardless of the presence or absence of economic advantage to us.

A parallel situation exists in respect of predatory mammals, raptorial birds, 14 and fish-eating birds. Time was when biologists somewhat overworked the evidence that these creatures preserve the health of game by killing weaklings, or that they control rodents for the farmer, or that they prey only on "worthless" species. Here again, the evidence had to be economic in order to be valid. It is only in recent years that we hear the more honest argument that predators are members of the community, and that no special interest has the right to exterminate them for the sake of a benefit, real or fancied, to itself. Unfortunately this enlightened view is still in the talk stage. In the field the extermination of predators goes merrily on. . . .

Some species of trees have been "read out of the party" by economics-minded foresters because they grow too slowly, or have too low a sale value to pay as timber crops: white cedar, tamarack, cypress, beech, and hemlock are examples. In Europe, where forestry is ecologically more advanced, the noncommercial tree species are recognized as members of the native forest community, to be preserved as such, within reason. Moreover some (like beech) have been found to have a valuable function in building up soil fertility. The interdependence of the forest and its constituent tree species, ground flora, and fauna is taken for granted. 15

Lack of economic value is sometimes a character not only of species or groups, but of entire biotic communities: marshes, bogs, dunes, and "deserts" are examples. Our formula in such cases is to relegate their conservation to government as refuges, monuments, or parks. The difficulty is that these communities are usually interspersed with more valuable private lands; the government cannot possibly own or control such scattered parcels. The net effect is that we have relegated some of them to ultimate extinction over large areas. If the private owner were ecologically minded, he would be proud to be the custodian of a reasonable proportion of such areas, which add diversity and beauty to his farm and to his community. 16

In some instances, the assumed lack of profit in these "waste" areas has proved to be wrong, but only after most of them had been done away with. The present scramble to reflood muskrat marshes is a case in point. . . . 17

To sum up: a system of conservation based solely on economic self-interest is hopelessly lopsided. It tends to ignore, and thus eventually to eliminate, many elements in the land community that lack commercial value, but that are (as far as we know) essential to its healthy functioning. It assumes, falsely, I think, that the economic parts of the biotic clock will function without the uneconomic parts. It tends to relegate to government many functions eventually too large, too complex, or too widely dispersed to be performed by government. 18

An ethical obligation on the part of the private owner is the only visible remedy for these situations. 19

The Land Pyramid.   An ethic to supplement and guide the economic relation to land presupposes the existence of some mental image of land as a biotic mechanism. We can be ethical only in relation to something we can see, feel, understand, love, or otherwise have faith in. 20

The image commonly employed in conservation education is "the balance 21
of nature." For reasons too lengthy to detail here, this figure of speech fails
to describe accurately what little we know about the land mechanism. A much
truer image is the one employed in ecology: the biotic pyramid. I shall first
sketch the pyramid as a symbol of land, and later develop some of its implications in terms of land-use.

Plants absorb energy from the sun. This energy flows through a circuit 22
called the biota, which may be represented by a pyramid consisting of layers.
The bottom layer is the soil. A plant layer rests on the soil, an insect layer on
the plants, a bird and rodent layer on the insects, and so on up through various animal groups to the apex layer, which consists of larger carnivores.

The species of a layer are alike not in where they came from, or in what 23
they look like, but rather in what they eat. Each successive layer depends on
those below it for food and often for other services, and each in turn furnishes
food and services to those above. Proceeding upward, each successive layer
decreases in numerical abundance. Thus, for every carnivore there are hundreds of his prey, thousands of their prey, millions of insects, uncountable
plants. The pyramidal form of the system reflects this numerical progression
from apex to base. Man shares an intermediate layer with the bears, raccoons,
and squirrels which eat both meat and vegetables.

The lines of dependency for food and other services are called food chains. 24
Thus soil-oak-deer-Indian is a chain that has now been largely converted to
soil-corn-cow-farmer. Each species, including ourselves, is a link in many
chains. The deer eats a hundred plants other than oak, and the cow a hundred plants other than corn. Both, then, are links to a hundred chains. The
pyramid is a tangle of chains so complex as to seem disorderly, yet the stability of the system proves to be a highly organized structure. Its functioning
depends on the cooperation and competition of its diverse parts.

In the beginning, the pyramid of life was low and squat; the food chains 25
short and simple. Evolution has added layer after layer, link after link. Man
is one of thousands of accretions to the height and complexity of the pyramid. Science has given us many doubts, but it has given us at least one certainty: the trend of evolution is to elaborate and diversify the biota.

Land, then, is not merely soil; it is a fountain of energy flowing through 26
a circuit of soils, plants, and animals. Food chains are the living channels
which conduct energy upward; death and decay return it to the soil. The circuit is not closed; some energy is dissipated in decay, some is added by ab-
sorption from the air, some is stored in soils, peats, and long-lived forests; but
it is a sustained circuit, like a slowly augmented revolving fund of life. There
is always a net loss by downhill wash, but this is normally small and offset
by the decay of rocks. It is deposited in the ocean and, in the course of geological time, raised to form new lands and new pyramids.

The velocity and character of the upward flow of energy depend on the 27
complex structure of the plant and animal community, much as the upward
flow of sap in a tree depends on its complex cellular organization. Without

this complexity, normal circulation would presumably not occur. Structure means the characteristic numbers, as well as the characteristic kinds and functions, of the component species. This interdependence between the complex structure of the land and its smooth functioning as an energy unit is one of its basic attributes.

When a change occurs in one part of the circuit, many other parts must adjust themselves to it. Change does not necessarily obstruct or divert the flow of energy; evolution is a long series of self-induced changes, the net result of which has been to elaborate the flow mechanism and to lengthen the circuit. Evolutionary changes, however, are usually slow and local. Man's invention of tools has enabled him to make changes of unprecedented violence, rapidity, and scope.   28

One change is in the composition of floras and faunas. The larger predators are lopped off the apex of the pyramid; food chains, for the first time in history, become shorter than longer. Domesticated species from other lands are substituted for wild ones, and wild ones are moved to new habitats. In this world-wide pooling of faunas and floras, some species get out of bounds as pests and diseases, others are extinguished. Such effects are seldom intended or foreseen; they represent unpredicted and often untraceable readjustments in the structure. Agricultural science is largely a race between the emergence of new pests and the emergence of new techniques for their control.   29

Another change touches the flow of energy through plants and animals and its return to the soil. Fertility is the ability of soil to receive, store, and release energy. Agriculture, by overdrafts on the soil, or by too radical a substitution of domestic for native species in the superstructure, may derange the channels of flow or deplete storage. Soils depleted of their storage, or of the organic matter which anchors it, wash away faster than they form. This is erosion.   30

Waters, like soil, are part of the energy circuit. Industry, by polluting waters or obstructing them with dams, may exclude the plants and animals necessary to keep energy in circulation.   31

Transportation brings about another basic change: the plants or animals grown in one region are now consumed and returned to the soil in another. Transportation taps the energy stored in rocks, and in the air, and uses it elsewhere; thus we fertilize the garden with nitrogen gleaned by the guano birds from the fishes of seas on the other side of the equator. Thus the formerly localized and self-contained circuits are pooled on a world-wide scale.   32

The process of altering the pyramid for human occupation releases stored energy, and this often gives rise, during the pioneering period, to a deceptive exuberance of plant and animal life, both wild and tame. These releases of biotic capital tend to becloud or postpone the penalties of violence.   33

This thumbnail sketch of land as an energy circuit conveys three basic ideas: 34

1. That the land is not merely soil.
2. That the native plants and animals keep the energy circuit open; others may or may not.

3. That man-made changes are of a different order than evolutionary changes, and have effects more comprehensive than is intended or foreseen. . . .

Land Health and the A-B Cleavage.   A land ethic, then, reflects the existence   35
of an ecological conscience, and this in turn reflects a conviction of individual responsibility for the health of the land. Health is the capacity of the land for self-renewal. Conservation is our effort to understand and preserve this capacity.

Conservationists are notorious for their dissensions. Superficially these   36
seem to add up to mere confusion, but a more careful scrutiny reveals a single plane of cleavage common to many specialized fields. In each field one group (A) regards the land as soil, and its function as a commodity-production; another group (B) regards the land as a biota, and its function as something broader. How much broader is admittedly in a state of doubt and confusion.

In my own field, forestry, Group A is quite content to grow trees like   37
cabbages, with cellulose as the basic forest commodity. It feels no inhibition against violence; its ideology is agronomic. Group B, on the other hand, sees forestry as fundamentally different from agronomy because it employs natural species, and manages a natural environment rather than creating an artificial one. Group B prefers natural reproduction on principle. It worries on biotic as well as economic grounds about the loss of species like chestnut, and the threatened loss of the white pines. It worries about a whole series of secondary forest functions: wildlife, recreation, watersheds, wilderness areas. To my mind, Group B feels the stirrings of an ecological conscience.

In the wildlife field, a parallel cleavage exists. For Group A the basic com-   38
modities are sport and meat; the yardsticks of production are ciphers of take in pheasants and trout. Artificial propagation is acceptable as a permanent as well as a temporary recourse—if its unit costs permit. Group B, on the other hand, worries about a whole series of biotic side-issues. What is the cost in predators of producing a game crop? Should we have further recourse to exotics? How can management restore the shrinking species, like prairie grouse, already hopeless as shootable game? How can management restore the threatened rarities, like trumpeter swan and whooping crane? Can management principles be extended to wildflowers? Here again it is clear to me that we have the same A-B cleavage as in forestry. . . .

In all these cleavages, we see repeated the same basic paradoxes: man the   39
conqueror versus man the biotic citizen; science the sharpener of his sword versus science the searchlight on his universe; land the slave and servant versus land the collective organism. . . .

The Outlook.   It is inconceivable to me that an ethical relation to land can   40
exist without love, respect, and admiration for land, and a high regard for its value. By value, I of course mean something far broader than mere economic value; I mean value in the philosophical sense.

Perhaps the most serious obstacle impeding the evolution of a land ethic   41
is the fact that our educational and economic system is headed away from,
rather than toward, an intense consciousness of land. Your true modern is
separated from the land by many middlemen, and by innumerable physical
gadgets. He has no vital relation to it; to him it is the space between cities on
which crops grow. Turn him loose for a day on the land, and if the spot does
not happen to be a golf links or a "scenic" area, he is bored stiff. If crops
could be raised by hydroponics instead of farming, it would suit him very
well. Synthetic substitutes for wood, leather, wool, and other natural land
products suit him better than the originals. In short, land is something he has
"outgrown."

Almost equally serious as an obstacle to a land ethic is the attitude of the   42
farmer for whom the land is still an adversary, or a taskmaster that keeps him
in slavery. Theoretically, the mechanization of farming ought to cut the farmer's
chains, but whether it really does is debatable. . . .

The "key-log" which must be moved to release the evolutionary process   43
for an ethic is simply this: quit thinking about decent land-use as solely an
economic problem. Examine each question in terms of what is ethically and
esthetically right, as well as what is economically expedient. A thing is right
when it tends to preserve the integrity, stability, and beauty of the biotic community. It is wrong when it tends otherwise.

It of course goes without saying that economic feasibility limits the tether   44
of what can or cannot be done for land. It always has and it always will.
The fallacy the economic determinists have tied around our collective neck,
and which we will now need to cast off, is the belief that economics determines *all* land-use. This is simply not true. An innumerable host of actions
and attitudes, comprising perhaps the bulk of all land relations, is determined by the land-users' tastes and predilections, rather than by his purse.
The bulk of all land relations hinges on investments of time, forethought,
skill, and faith rather than on investments of cash. As a land-user thinketh,
so is he. . . .

The evolution of a land ethic is an intellectual as well as emotional process.   45
Conservation is paved with good intentions which prove to be futile, or even
dangerous, because they are devoid of critical understanding either of the land,
or of economic land-use. I think it is a truism that as the ethical frontier advances from the individual to the community, its intellectual content increases.

The mechanism of operation is the same for any ethic: social approbation   46
for right actions: social disapproval for wrong actions.

By and large, our present problem is one of attitudes and implements. We   47
are remodeling the Alhambra with a steam shovel, and we are proud of our
yardage. We shall hardly relinquish the shovel, which after all has many good
points, but we are in need of gentler and more objective criteria for its successful use.

✳

ANALYZING THE ARGUMENT

1. What does Leopold's opening anecdote accomplish? How is it related to the rest of the essay? [3b(1)]
2. How does Leopold define the "land ethic"? What alternative motive for conservation does Leopold discuss? How does he characterize this viewpoint? Support your answer with evidence from the essay.
3. From paragraphs 21 through 34, the essay is given over to Leopold's description of the land pyramid and how he believes it works. Briefly summarize how this system works. What consequences does Leopold attribute to the introduction of man-made changes into this ecosystem?
4. On which of these appeals—to reason, to emotion, to personal credibility or authority—does Leopold's essay chiefly rely? On which does it least rely? Explain. [5f]
5. Reread paragraphs 36 through 39, in which Leopold discusses the dissension among conservationists, and determine whether Leopold favors one group of conservationists more than the other. How can you tell?
6. Leopold identifies several obstacles to the evolution of a land ethic. What are they? Explain how Leopold proposes that his readers begin to eliminate these impediments.
7. Does Leopold object to the economic motive for conservation, warn about the problems that may result from this basis for conservation, or both? Point to evidence from the essay to support your answer. In one sentence, state Leopold's thesis as completely and exactly as you can. [2b]
8. What basic assumptions does Leopold make about his audience? Explain. [1g(2)]

Environment for Sale
Brian Tokar

An activist in the peace, antinuclear, and environmental movements since the 1970s, Brian Tokar holds degrees from MIT in biology and physics and from Harvard University in biophysics. He is currently a faculty member at Goddard College and the Institute for Social Ecology in Plainfield, Vermont, and has lectured throughout the U.S. as well as internationally. He is the author of *The Great Alternative: Creating an Ecological Future* (1987, revised 1992) and *Earth for Sale: Reclaiming Ecology in the Age of Corporate Greenwash* (1997), and the editor of *Redesigning Life? The Worldwide Challenge to Genetic Engineering* (2001). Tokar's articles on environmental politics and emerging ecological movements appear frequently in *Z Magazine* (where this selection was first published), as well as in *The Ecologist, Food & Water Journal, Synthesis/Regeneration, Toward Freedom,* and numerous other publications.

Few international environmental issues in recent years have raised as 1 much widespread concern or as much passion as the fate of the world's tropical forests. Tropical forests are the earth's greatest reservoir of biological diversity, housing up to three-quarters of all living species. They hold massive amounts of organic carbon and release globally-significant quantities of oxygen. Their human inhabitants include many of the last remaining tribal people whose traditional ways have not been compromised by the intrusion of civilization. The crippling indebtedness of many tropical nations, especially Brazil, has brought pressure for a wave of new development schemes, in which vast tracts of rainforest are being destroyed to satisfy the demands of international banks. Rainforest activists predict that if the destruction continues at present rates, there will be no tropical forests left in just 20 or 30 years.

In the 1980s, several Third World countries began to resist continuing 2 debt payments. Citing the effects of foreign debt on their national economies and the fact that many loans have already been paid several times over in exorbitant interest payments, several countries have threatened to default on their loans. Others have slowed debt payments to a trickle, forcing banks to admit that many Third World loans will simply never be repaid.

Anxious to keep these countries "in the system," the banks continue to 3 loan countries money to support debt payments, while proposing new, more destructive development projects and imposing ever-stricter austerity measures. In an effort to squeeze some tangible benefit from these increasingly dubious loans, banks have become increasingly involved in international debt-swapping. They are directly trading portions of various countries' debt for equity in debtor countries, stakes in future development and, most significantly for environmentalists, commitments for the preservation and "sustainable management" of parcels of tropical forest land. Organizations like the World Wildlife Fund, Conservation International, and the Nature Conservancy are actively sponsoring so-called "debt-for-nature swaps," promoting them as vehicles for "The Greening of International Finance."

Vehicle for Exploitation.   The first, and by far the best publicized, of all these   4
"swaps" was launched in 1987 when the Frank Weeden Foundation of Connecticut granted $100,000 to Conservation International for the purchase of $650,000 in unpaid debt from a Citibank affiliate in Bolivia. In exchange, the Bolivian government had agreed to support the expansion of the Beni Biological Reserve, an ecologically unique area containing some of the world's largest remaining reserves of mahogany and tropical cedar. The Reserve itself would become protected "to the maximum extent possible under Bolivian law," according to CI, and would be surrounded by a much larger "multiple use and conservation" buffer zone, for a total of almost 4 million acres. The Bolivian government agreed to allocate $250,000 (mostly from funds generated through US-sponsored food aid) toward the management of the project. CI would provide training, technical support and other forms of international assistance for the project, and advise local agencies on the "sustainable use" of the precious mahogany forests.

Supporters of the project assert that the entire area might have been   5
stripped of trees before the next century had Conservation International not intervened, while critics argue that the entire project is merely a vehicle for the more rational exploitation of the area. Some accounts report that logging in the buffer zone has increased tremendously since the project began: twice as many mahogany trees were removed in 1988 as in 1987, for example. Contracts for several new sawmills in the area were approved immediately before the debt swap went into effect. Residents of the area were not consulted before the debt-swap agreement was signed, even though much of the land was already in dispute between logging companies and the area's 5,000 native inhabitants.

Experts in so-called "sustainable development"—one of the key catch-   6
phrases of corporate environmentalism—have carved the land up into experimental parcels which will experience varying degrees of tree harvesting, from the most limited to the most intensive. For the native people, these are trees that would have been used to build homes and canoes, and to shelter local wildlife for countless generations to come. The Moxeno and Chimane people have seen environmentalists thwart their efforts to manage the land as a community—the project's needs were apparently better served by continuing the Bolivian government's practice of maintaining native lands in isolated private plots, the perferred model in much of Latin America.

Debt-for-nature swaps, like the equity swaps upon which they were mod-   7
eled, raise serious questions about both local and national sovereignty. The
land ostensibly remains under the host country's control, but patterns of use
are determined by international organizations. . . . Of course, most of the
countries involved remain indebted to international banks to the tune of many
billions of dollars.

African Concerns.   Concerns about the impact of such schemes have arisen in   8
Africa, where several countries are discussing plans for future debt-for-nature
arrangements. Africans have already had some difficult experiences with North
American conservationists. In 1909 Teddy Roosevelt went there and reportedly shot a third of the rhinos in Uganda. Groups like the World Wildlife
Fund, with encouragement from wealthy big game hunters and safari enthu-
siasts, have been involved in the creation of National Parks in several African
countries. The parks, conceived on the American model, are seen as pristine
places where wild animal habitats can be preserved without human distur-
bance. This often happens at the expense of native peoples, who have been
living alongside wild animals for countless generations and, in many cases,
fought to keep slave traders, poachers and colonialists out of these areas.
Without native protection wildlife habitats might be designated for preservation today, but can be eliminated tomorrow at the stroke of a pen or the roll
of a bulldozer. The damage could be done before international wildlife groups
knew what was happening.

In Kenya and Tanzania, the pastoral Masaai people have protected ele-   9
phants and other animals from hunters since the beginnings of European colonialism, but are being systematically excluded from National Parks planned
with support from U.S. environmentalists. Moringe Parkipuny, a Masaai elder
who represents his people in the national parliament of Tanzania, explains:
"To us in Africa, the disappearance of the elephant is just one aspect of the
major problem of colonialism. . . . The conflict, as we see it, is between indigenous peoples and the policies imposed on them by foreign governments.
These policies discriminate against us by making wild animals more important than indigenous peoples. They have also turned our people against wild
animals, because they feel that wildlife is now being used as a weapon to
destroy us."

By blinding themselves to underlying political factors, US-based environ-   10
mental organizations become unwitting agents of imperialism overseas, just
as they sometimes help to rationalize polluting practices at home.

✳

ANALYZING THE ARGUMENT

1. What purpose is served by Tokar's opening with a discussion of tropical forests?
   How is it related to the rest of the essay? [3b(1)]

2. How would you described Tokar's tone in this essay? For example, does it reveal strong feelings on his part about the issue he is discussing, or is the tone more dispassionate, objective? Would you say he addresses his reader in a voice that is formal, conversational, or something in between? Does he seem to assume an audience hostile to his views, sympathetic with them, or perhaps undecided but willing to hear him out? Point to specifics in the essay that support your answer. [3a(3)]

3. What is Tokar's thesis? Does he state it explicitly? If so, where? [2b]

4. On which of the three appeals—to reason, to emotion, to personal credibility or authority—does Tokar's essay chiefly rely? On which does it least rely? Explain. [5f]

5. What basic assumptions does Tokar make about U.S. corporations? What is the relationship of the final sentence of paragraph 3 to those assumptions? Explain.

6. What does Tokar say are the real objections to "debt-for-nature swaps"? Would you say that his distrust of financial interest is more important to him than his defense of the environment itself? Why or why not?

7. Does Tokar offer any alternatives to "debt-for-nature swaps"? If so, what are they? If not, why not?

Government Intervention Can Protect the Environment
Robert Gottlieb and Helen Ingram

Robert Gottlieb and Helen Ingram are both professors—Gottlieb in the Urban Planning Program at UCLA and Ingram at the University of Arizona. Gottlieb is well known for his writing on public policy issues and is the author of several books, among them *A Life of Its Own: The Politics and Power of Water.* Ingram holds a bachelor's degree from Oberlin College (1959) and a Ph.D. from Columbia University (1967). Professor Ingram has taught at the University of New Mexico as well as the University of Arizona, and she has directed the Udall Center for Studies in Public Policy. She is the author of several books and is book review editor for the *American Political Science Review.*

Environmental policy today is at a crossroads. Attempts . . . to undo the legislation and regulatory policies established during the 1970s have backfired. Environmental groups have grown in numbers and reach, and Congressional initiatives have increased. In some cases, this has led to more legislation, greater funding for environmental programs, and increased regulations. 1

Yet environmental problems have, for the most part, remained intractable. Legislative and regulatory approaches have often been inadequate in addressing a growing set of concerns that touch the very fabric of our urban and industrial society. Target dates, such as those established by the Clean Air Act, have come and gone, without anticipated goals having been reached. While the current regulatory approaches look to tradeoffs, cost-benefit analysis, and risk assessment procedures, among others, to try to reduce or at least contain the degradation at hand, it is not even clear whether such goals will ever be met for particular contaminants, such as ozone, in those cities, such as Los Angeles or Denver, where dirty air appears to have become a permanent fixture of the urban design. 2

The basis for environmental policy continues to evolve around how best to accommodate the dual objectives of environmental protection and economic growth. Government policymakers are continually beset by the apparently conflicting pressures regarding environmental degradation, reindustrialization (whether high tech or old tech), job creation, and community fears regarding environmental and/or economic decline. Policy questions frequently are posed as a choice between contrasting objectives: jobs versus community versus environment. Those environmental groups who accept such a framework are 3 faced with either selecting the route of tradeoffs and compromise, and accepting some level of degradation as an inevitable byproduct of industrialization, or choosing the environment over jobs and economic growth; that is, either enter the corridors of power and likely alienate part of the environmental constituency or be considered marginal in terms of the present political discourse. It is an unhappy predicament somehow incommensurate with the overwhelming public sentiment in favor of large-scale and more definitive action to address hazardous wastes, air and water contamination, pesticide use, solid waste disposal, and countless other environmental problems of our contemporary urban/industrial society.

Protective Laws.   The established environmental movement of the 1970s and   4
1980s prided itself on developing a legislative and regulatory agenda over the years. This consisted of specific initiatives in a range of policy areas, much of which translated into laws and administrative programs designed to protect the natural environment. Efforts, such as the 1985 *Environmental Agenda for the Future* put together by the ten largest established environmental groups, represented an elaboration of this already developed program. Their approach, furthermore, has been dictated by the politics of the lobbyist, where agreements are crafted by various interest groups in a give-and-take process in which the giving often exceeds the taking when the power of money is involved.

There is, however, a more grassroots-oriented environmentalism on both   5
a more local and unyielding basis. These movements will frequently insist that a particular project such as an incinerator or a power plant be stopped. They exhibit less willingness to compromise, although their focus is usually limited to the specific matter at hand. Thus, they develop little by way of national program or agenda. Still, many of these movements have begun to make tentative efforts toward developing networks and coalitions. In the process, they have established the outlines of a statewide or national approach, albeit one confined to particular issues.

A national environmental strategy and set of policy goals and objec-   6
tives remain imperative in the face of a declining environment and untempered forms of industrialization. Between the political constraints of the national lobbyist and the limits of a localized campaign, there needs to emerge a form of action—and theory—that links grassroots mobilization with attacking the structure of the problem on the state, national, and even international levels. Such an approach—a new environmental politics—would indeed entail the obvious ("think globally, act locally"), as well as the less obvious ("think globally, act globally") and the most immediate ("think locally, act locally").

Programs and improvements come about largely through the influence of   7
social movements and community action. Legislative initiatives, regulatory actions, and court interventions have been framed in part by the public's concern and activity; such is likely to be the case in the future as well.

Environmental "improvements" in this light reflect the state of environmental politics. . . .

Government Acts.   During the 1970s, environmental organizations were suc-   8
cessful in establishing what came to be called the "environmental agenda,"
aided largely by the enormous swelling of public environmental sentiment.
This included the major legislative initiatives of the decade such as the Clean
Air Act, Safe Drinking Water Act, the Endangered Species Protection Act, the
Resource Recovery and Conservation Act, and the Comprehensive Environmental
Response, Conservation, and Liabilities Act (better known as Superfund). These
bills and several others signed into law during the 1970s sought to address the
problems of pollution and contamination as well as the protection of scenic
and natural resources.

Environmental organizations also developed a series of complex and in-   9
teractive relationships with a host of new administrative bureaucracies such
as the Environmental Protection Agency and the Council on Environmental
Quality, complementing the relations established by the previous generation of conservationists and preservationists with such agencies as the
National Park Service, the Soil Conservation Service, and the U.S. Forest
Service. Environmental groups were also successful in transforming a range
of legal rulings and legislative initiatives, such as the California Friends of
Mammoth ruling in 1972 and the 1969 National Environmental Policy Act,
into a whole new field of environmental law where, for example, the production and review of environmental impact statements became an industry unto itself.

The election of Ronald Reagan seemed to threaten that agenda. The new   10
administration, under the banner of deregulation, attempted to either reduce
or restructure bureaucracies, limit spending levels for "clean up" legislation,
and separate certain key constituencies such as hunters and fishermen and the
tourism trade as a whole from the scenic protectionists among the environmental groups. While Jimmy Carter had overestimated the clout and reach of
the environmental groups, particularly in the West, Ronald Reagan underes-
timated the elevation of environmental values among the public at large. The
hard-edged rhetoric used by the President and certain of his key officials, such
as James Watt and Anne Gorsuch, during much of Reagan's first term, had
the immediate effect of reinvigorating environmental organizations, many of
which had been ready to proclaim the end of the Environmental Decade. Most
of the administration's attempts to halt expenditures, roll back legislation, or
delay implementation of regulations had only limited success. In certain instances, such as passage of the Safe Drinking Water Act Amendments in 1986,
Congress, responding to the strong public concerns that had evolved around
the issue of groundwater contamination, restructured this legislation initiative
to forestall Reagan administration regulatory backbiting, specifically referring
to the efforts of the Office of Management and Budget to undermine EPA
standard-setting.

Environmental Standstill.   For the most part, however, environmentally   11
sensitive legislators were too busy fighting the Reagan administration's attempts to march backward to push forward with new laws or approaches.
Reauthorizations of existing laws became pitched battles, with changes
mostly a matter of detail. Much of the significant policymaking of the Reagan
years took place within the bureaucracy, far from public, and often from
Congressional, scrutiny. It is not surprising that the development interests
tended to fare best in restricted forums where legal and technical expertise,
which can be purchased, are at a premium.

Rather than insisting upon opening agency forums and broadening con-   12
flict, some environmental groups actually cooperated in restricting public access. A great deal was made of new opportunities for negotiation and environmental mediation. Emphasis was put upon finding common ground for
agreement, not upon distinguishing environmental and development viewpoints. Leaders of environmental groups were congratulated for their growing maturity, reasonableness, and sound management of what had become
large-scale organizations. Instead of publicly regretting the lack of substantial
accomplishment in cleaning up the environment, environmental leaders satisfied themselves that the network of regulatory laws put in place in the 1970s
was not dismantled.

The apparent failure at full-blown deregulation and dismantling of legis-   13
lation, however, did not prevent the emergence of a number of new or revised
approaches, some of which were embraced by both Reaganites and environmental groups. These placed the environmental issue on the level of competing technologies and reallocation of resources and minimized the role of both
the government and public action. Reaganites emphasized the move toward
privatization and private markets in place of government intervention, a
position which attracted those environmentalists who had come to focus on
government subsidies as a major source of environmental abuse. In the area
of solid waste management, for example, growing environmental concerns
over landfills, which in turn contributed to the price escalation of the fees per
pound of waste, helped stimulate the reappearance of the incineration industry. Privatization-oriented measures, such as tax breaks and the reduction of
federal grants, aided that shift, which the environmental movement was slow
to address. During the late 1970s, in fact, several environmental groups even
welcomed the development of this "waste-to-energy" technology, only to modify their positions later as community and neighborhood groups, worried about
air contaminants, hazardous ash residue, and local neighborhood impacts,
took the lead in opposing this newly touted technical solution.

The Private Sector.   The focus began to shift to the private sector as the prob-   14
lems of regulation, expensive and inefficient subsidies, and the costs of cleanup
multiplied. Water markets, for one, were identified by some in the water
industry—that unique collection of public agencies and private interests—as
the best way to salvage long-standing water policies designed to stimulate

irrigated agricultural production and urban development. A number of environmental groups identified with this approach, calling it a "win-win" alternative to the construction of new and potentially environmentally destructive facilities. Yet markets also allowed pricing inequities to continue, even providing an additional benefit for those landowners wishing to either bail out of the system or maneuver to obtain an additional profit from arrangements that had amounted to billions of dollars in federal transfer payments to western agriculture. The buyers, meanwhile—the rapidly expanding urban complexes in places like San Diego, Denver, and Phoenix—saw markets as the way to sustain development plans in the face of newly emerging "slow growth" movements. These movements were different from the environmental constituencies, more distinctly neighborhood- and community-oriented, focused on the urban and industrial environment, though not unsympathetic to fears about abuse of the natural environment.

These new social movements have compounded the complexity of the environmental agenda. They have raised concerns about toxics and hazardous wastes. They worry about residential groundwater contamination and carcinogenic water disinfection byproducts more than protecting in-stream flows. They have placed questions of housing, transportation, air quality, and even economic development on the agenda, which the traditional environmental agenda either had failed to address or addressed inadequately. These questions, however, are fundamental environmental issues. They reflect patterns of industrialization and urbanization, the primary sources of environmental degradation.   15

Environmental issues are social issues; the natural environment and the human environment are intricately linked in this industrial age. Some groups have begun to connect apparently disparate concerns such as environmentalism and feminism into a new discourse that places the abuses of industrialization in the context of daily life. Furthermore, unlike the traditional agendas of the nationally-oriented environmental organizations, the focus of many of these community, neighborhood, and various "single issue" groups is local. Their issues are as much about community and democratic control as about "natural" environmental degradation, where the focus tends to be on national and bureaucratic solutions.   16

These divergent forms of environmental politics help to develop larger perspectives on the environment and future political approaches. Traditional environmentalism, aside from its long-standing interest in scenic protection, has developed as a crisis-oriented, reactive form of politics, seeking to address questions of "clean-up" and more effective regulation of the extraordinary brew of new products and production processes that have heightened the potential of large-scale environmental deterioration. Though this environmentalism also seeks to promote concepts of conservation and "source reduction," these are often articulated in the form of programs to make urban and industrial interests more efficient in their operations, rationalizing rather than restructuring the production process.   17

The Grassroots Movement. In contrast, the more populist grassroots envi- 18
ronmentalism promotes the concept that the needs of the community, and, in
its more radical form, the workplace, take precedence. Traditional environmentalism has focused primarily on protecting nature and rationalizing the system
while reducing its more obvious environmental abuses. Grassroots environmentalism, dealing with everyday problems from toxics to growth, has questioned
how the system functions, at least on a local and single-issue level. . . .

What is most striking about these grassroots movements is their demo- 19
cratic thrust, similar in some ways to the emergence of the student, civil rights,
and women's movements a generation earlier. Instead of embracing expertise,
they have become examples of how to develop "self-taught experts." Instead
of seeking to lobby or litigate more effectively, they have become advocates of
popular action and citizen lawsuits, influencing legislative debate by their mo-
bilizing efforts rather than lobbying skills. They have become organizations of
members, in neighborhoods and communities, rather than groups with organized mailing lists and membership dues which are situated in offices that take
the place of communities. Most important, they have begun to demand an accounting of how actions by industries and developers, the government as well
as the private sector, affect people in their day-to-day lives and impact both
the environments around us and the larger natural—and social—environment.

There is a rich historical tradition related to what can be called a demo- 20
cratic and populist environmentalism. These were the movements that emerged
in the late 19th century to address the extraordinary abuses of early industrialization and urbanization, when issues of foul air, dirty water (which killed
thousands of people in countless epidemics of infectious diseases), the horrendous noises and din of the new industrial and urban order, the suffocat-
ing and overcrowded cities, and the problems of rotting and infected foods
dominated the urban and industrial landscape. Rivers, streams, mountains,
and wilderness were, to be sure, casualties of this new order, part of the same
package of development. The movements that emerged—public sanitarians,
municipal housekeepers, social feminists, both "sewer socialists" and radical
syndicalists, and a range of other reformist and revolutionary movements of
the moment—represented an environmental tradition much as John Muir and
Gifford Pinchot did with their romantic and utilitarian impulses.

Today, the issues of the industrial and urban order are more complex and 21
yet more extensive in their impact on peoples' lives and environments. The
new grassroots movements of the 1980s are part of a range of efforts that
seek to address the consequences of this order, whether in terms of nuclear
politics, economic dislocation, or the problems of the environment writ large
or small. In this sense, environmentalism can be seen not as an "interest group"
seeking better regulation or protection of scenic resources, but as an essential
component of a new democratic politics. It is a politics where "risk" is no
longer just a question of what contaminant we are prepared or not prepared
to live with, but a question of dealing with the hazards of an undemocratic
society where the decisions that affect our lives are made elsewhere.

✳

ANALYZING THE ARGUMENT

1. Gottlieb and Ingram's essay is divided into five points: protective laws, governmental acts, environmental standstill, the private sector, and the grassroots movement. Explain how each of these sections is related to the point they make.

2. Where do you first discover Gottlieb and Ingram's thesis? State it in as few words as you can. [2b]

3. What opposing arguments, if any, do Gottlieb and Ingram acknowledge? How do they deal with them? [5e and 5g]

4. In "Government Intervention Can Protect the Environment" do Gottlieb and Ingram rely primarily on the appeal to credibility, the appeal to reason, or the appeal to the emotions and values of their readers? Are all three appeals present? Supply evidence to support your answer. [5f]

5. How effective is Gottlieb and Ingram's introduction to this argument? Does their use of the crossroads image at the beginning of paragraph 1 support the thesis? If so, how? If not, why not? [3b(1)]

6. Comment upon the meaning and rhetorical effect of each of the following phrases: *backfired* (paragraph 1), *tradeoffs* (paragraph 2), *high tech* (paragraph 3), *clout* (paragraph 10), *privatization* (paragraph 13), *bail out* (paragraph 14), *brew* (paragraph 17), *impact* (paragraph 19). [23a and 24a]

7. Do Gottlieb and Ingram rely primarily upon inductive or deductive reasoning, or do they make use of another model? Explain. [5h]

The Environmental Mindset
Rush Limbaugh III

In 1983, long-time radio broadcaster Rush Hudson Limbaugh III (1951–)
launched his talk show, *The Rush Limbaugh Show*. Limbaugh's on-air persona as an outspoken critic of liberals, feminists, and social activists
immediately made him a controversial media figure, but it also brought him
nationwide attention. His talk show soon emerged as a nationally syndicated radio and television program, reaching millions of listeners and
viewers. Recently, Limbaugh introduced a new nationally syndicated radio
program, the *Rush Limbaugh Morning Update*. Limbaugh also visits 45
cities across the nation in his Rush to Excellence Tour each year. The
following selection is from Limbaugh's book of social commentary, *The Way
Things Ought to Be*.

1 I used to think environmentalists were a bunch of political liberals who
were just using a different angle to advance their cause. Some of that goes on.
But it goes beyond merely advancing liberalism. There are two groups of people that have made environmentalism their new home: socialists and enviro-
religious fanatics. And they have chosen two new constituencies which cannot speak or disagree and therefore cannot refuse their "help and assistance":
animals and trees.

2 With the collapse of Marxism, environmentalism has become the new
refuge of socialist thinking. The environment is a great way to advance a political agenda that favors central planning and an intrusive government. What
better way to control someone's property than to subordinate one's private
property rights to environmental concerns.

3 The second group that has latched on to the environmental movement are
people who believe it is a religion; that God is the earth and that God is nothing more than the earth. Actually, it is a modern form of pantheism, where
nature is divine. This group wants to preserve the earth at all costs, even if it
means that much of the Third World will be forever condemned to poverty.
Rather than elevate the Third World, they want to move us closer to Third
World conditions. That's somehow cleaner, and purer. It's the way things were
before Western white people came along and terrorized the earth by inventing things. They want to roll us back, maybe not to the Stone Age, but at
least to the horse-and-buggy era.

4 Both of these groups are consumed with egocentricity. They behave as
though they believe the world began the day they were born and that it's going to end the day they die.

Now, I've spoken about the leaders of the radical environmental move- 5
ment. The followers are also interesting. They are the people who just want
to feel good; the people who want to receive accolades for their perceived care
and concern for the environment. Then we have the media who willingly serve
as conduits for all of these predictions, studies, prophecies, and tall tales that
the environmentalist wackos disseminate.

But there are also many average Americans who consider themselves en- 6
vironmentalists. It is quite natural to want a clean planet, with clean water and
air for ourselves and our children. It is quite commendable to not want to destroy that which enables us to live. So, if some scientist comes along and is
given credibility by the media, it is not surprising that a lot of people believe
him. That is how hundreds of thousands of people are mobilized for the cause
and end up on the Mall in Washington and in Central Park in New York.

What these decent people have to realize is that regardless of what per- 7
spective they have—socialist, religious, or whatever—a common characteristic of those in the radical environmental movement is the belief that private
property rights will have to be severely curbed in this country. That's what is
behind the move to take private land out of circulation to preserve wetlands,
and the efforts to save the spotted owl. If it rains in your backyard one day
and you have an inch of water there, all of a sudden your yard becomes a
wetland and you can't build anything there.

This hostility to private property, my friends, is based on the belief that 8
human beings can't be trusted to own very much of the land; that we are selfish and cursed with the desire to change nature. We are 4 percent of the world's
population here in America and we use 25 percent of the world's resources.
How dare we be so selfish. Never mind the fact that our country feeds the
world. Never mind the fact that our technology has improved life everywhere
on this planet.

I believe that many environmental leaders are quite sincere, but that they 9
all operate from a fundamentally different viewpoint than most other people.
You and I and the vast majority of other people work for a living. We hold jobs
in which we produce something or perform a service. We create commerce.

Most of the people running environmental groups don't work. What they 10
do is persuade other people to donate to their cause. They live well, with a
fair amount being siphoned off for expenses, conferences, and high salaries.
They've become dependent on the income from donations. These people want
to improve their standard of living and so they have to build up their donations. There are only so many people who will give to create bird sanctuar-
ies in this country. That's why some environmentalists have gone into crisis
mongering to increase the level of their donations. Their appeals and their
scare tactics are designed to transform people into foot soldiers in the army
of doomsday environmentalism.

It's interesting to note which environmental hazards these people really 11
worry about. It is those that are caused by business or man-made things.

Consider the danger of radon gas. If there is one environmental problem that is real, it is radon. Some Easterners have homes where radon seeps in from under the ground and reaches levels many times beyond what is considered safe. But there is no hysteria over radon. Why? Because it's natural, man didn't put it there. There are no dramatic calls for radon studies, nor any calls for evacuations. Everything that happens in their deified nature is somehow acceptable. Things will work themselves out. Well, man-made disasters can also work themselves out. Take the *Exxon Valdez* spill. We were told that the cleanup would take hundreds of years. Now we see that through natural processes and the incredibly resilient powers of the planet, the tide has taken care of much of the damage that man didn't clean up. And, would you believe that more fish were caught last year than ever before in Prince William Sound?

My friends, the earth is a remarkable creation and is capable of great re-   12
juvenation. We can't destroy it. It can fix itself. We shouldn't go out of our way to do damage, but neither should we buy into the hysteria and mono-mania which preaches, in essence, that we don't belong here. We have a right to use the earth to make our lives better.

✳

ANALYZING THE ARGUMENT

1. What can a reader infer from the first paragraph about the argument that will follow? Point to specifics in the paragraph that suggest the nature of the argument.
2. Limbaugh focuses on two types of environmentalists. What are they? How does he characterize them? Does he view environmentally minded "average Americans" in the same way? Why or why not?
3. Are there any underlying assumptions upon which the argument is based? If so, what are they? If not, how can you tell?
4. Comment upon the kind of appeal that Limbaugh makes in "The Environmental Mindset." Is the primary appeal to logic? to the attitudes and values of the reader? to Limbaugh's credibility? to more than one of these? Point to evidence in the essay to support your answer. [5f]
5. What is Limbaugh's thesis and why does it occur where it does? What would be the effect if it came in the middle of the essay? at the end? [2b]
6. How would you describe Limbaugh's tone in this essay? Does he address the topic from an objective viewpoint or from his own strong beliefs about it? Does he address his readers in a formal voice? a conversational voice? or something in between? [3a(3)]
7. Does the argument contain any concessions to those who would be likely to disagree? If so, where and what are the concessions? If not, why? [5e and 5g]
8. What does Limbaugh's use of *my friends, we,* and *you and I* suggest about his intended audience? Does Limbaugh reveal other assumptions about his audience? If so, what are they? How can you tell? [1g(2)]

SUGGESTIONS FOR DISCUSSION AND WRITING: A LIFE-AND-DEATH ISSUE DEBATED

1. With your classmates—in discussion groups or, if your instructor prefers, as a whole class—list (1) all the specific arguments leveled against private involvement in environmental action in the six essays just presented, and (2) all the specific arguments presented in favor of it in the essays. (You might also want to list points for and against government involvement.) After each point, write in parentheses the names of the essayists who advance it. This analysis will help you to see the essays in relation to one another and should also help you carry out the other suggestions that follow here.

2. With your classmates, list as many possible arguments as you can think of—both for and against private/government involvement in environmental action—that are not advanced by any of the writers in this section.

3. In his essay, "Toward a Land Ethic," Aldo Leopold asserts that conservationists can be classified according to their view of nature as either a commodity or a biotic system. Analyze the essays in this section to discover which of these views informs the arguments set forth by each essayist. Which of these views of nature would you say predominates in the arguments in this chapter? Which of these views do the essayists find most objectionable?

4. Whatever positions they may take on who should control environmental action, a number of the authors focus either mainly or partly on ways that policies and regulations have been evaded. Summarize these objections and then argue either that such objections can or that they cannot be conclusive as arguments concerning who should control environmental action.

5. Choose any practice you encounter frequently that you consider potentially harmful to the environment (for instance, packaging fast food in styrofoam containers, dumping old engine oil in the garbage) and argue as convincingly as you can for the discontinuation of that practice. (You may need to do a little research.)

6. Several of the essays in this chapter discuss the reasons why people become active in environmentalism. Working in small groups, or if your instructor prefers, as a whole class, identify and discuss what motives for environmental action are revealed in the essays written by Leopold, Limbaugh, Pell, and Ingram and Gottlieb. Which motives, if any, appear to be based solely on assumptions made by the authors? How can you tell? How would you characterize environmental activists?

7. The majority of essays in this section discuss environmental protection in terms of economic issues; however, as Leopold has shown, economic concerns are not the only reason (or even the primary reason) for protecting the environment. Danger to all of life as we know it from pollution and unsound use of the environment is a far more urgent issue. Write an essay for an audience of your classmates arguing for or against a government tax on air conditioners (which uses large amounts of environmentally damaging freon). As with the essays you have read, you will need to consider such questions as whether the benefits to the society balance the effects on the environment, whether the preservation of the environment overrides any perceived benefit to society, who would be most damaged by such a tax, whether such a tax would actually reduce use of freon (an analogous situation is the gasoline tax)—and there are undoubtedly other considerations. You may use any evidence you draw from these essays, and you may wish to consult other sources.

Chapter 11

The Essay Examination: A Student Writer across the Disciplines

Essay examinations impose a variety of constraints on the writer. Pressure of time is the most obvious, but others are important as well. In the time allowed (usually fifty minutes, rarely more than two or three hours), you must produce answers that are

Exactly responsive to the question asked,

Complete and factually accurate,

Convincingly supported by specific details,

Coherent and well organized,

Clearly and concisely written, and

Free of grammatical and mechanical errors.

Faced with these requirements, obviously you should do everything you can in advance to make the task go smoothly. And there is much that you can do. From the first day of the course, discipline yourself to *think critically* about the material presented in class and in your reading rather than merely trying to absorb it all. As you take notes in class, jot down reminders ("TEST?") to yourself about points that could become the basis for essay-examination questions. If you listen (and watch) closely, you will usually be able to discern what information your instructor considers especially important. Unlike instructors, written texts cannot raise their voices or punctuate the air with gestures, but they have their own ways of providing emphasis. Which topics are given the most space? Which topics are explicitly mentioned in chapter titles or in headings within the chapters? What terms are italicized for emphasis or defined at length, or both? In your textbooks look at the beginnings of chapters for lists of "learning objectives," the concepts or subjects you should have mastered when you read the chapter. Also pay particular attention to material at the ends of chapters that may summarize key points. Thinking critically also means looking for relationships among the facts or concepts you encounter; essay questions very often focus on such relationships, as the three essays by Anne

Nishijima in this section illustrate. If you do all of these things, you will find there is a benefit besides being prepared for examinations: you will learn a great deal more from the course than you would have otherwise.

Your notebook can be an important resource. Use it not only as a place to deposit information gained from lectures and class discussions but also as a journal in which you anticipate questions and try out answers. A few days before the examination, review your notes to sort out again what is most important, searching for relationships you might have missed earlier in the semester. See if you can develop new questions, and plan answers to them.

When the examination begins, take a few minutes before starting to write to budget your time. Some experts advise about 20 percent of the time you allocate to a question should be spent in planning, about 70 percent in writing, and about 10 percent in reviewing and revising what you have written. Glance through the entire examination before you begin to do anything else. If the examination requires that you answer several questions, budget the most time for the questions that are worth the most points. It is usually a good idea to answer those questions first. However, if you draw a blank about them at that moment, working on another question may stimulate your thinking and help you recall the information you need.

Essay-examination questions are usually carefully worded and often specify the method you should use in your answer: compare, define, analyze, explain, argue, and so on. However the question is phrased, make sure your answer responds to it exactly. Even if you feel insecure about your ability to answer well, resist the temptation to wander from the question asked to discuss a topic you think you can handle better; such digressions will almost always cost you more than you could hope to gain. As you plan your answer, try jotting down (inconspicuously in the margin or a corner of the page) a few key words or phrases that stand for the main ideas you intend to cover; such a list—a small working plan—will help to ensure that you don't skip anything important, an easy thing to do when you are writing under pressure.

When you begin writing, get right to the point in your first paragraph. Your reader should be able to see immediately that you have grasped the question and are on your way to answering it. For example, a common type of essay question quotes an assertion from one of the assigned readings and asks you to agree or disagree, defending your position with evidence drawn from the course. In such a situation, begin your essay with a clear statement of the position you are taking. Not only will such a statement up-front demonstrate to your reader that you are on the right track; it will also help you *stay* on the track as you write the essay.

Be sure to support any generalizations with specifics: details, examples, illustrations, quotations. It is these particulars, not your general statements, that will convince your instructor that you really know what you are talking about. Be direct and confident in your tone; an answer written with assurance is more likely to convince a reader than one that is larded with unnecessary qualifications or that seems apologetic.

In the time you have set aside for revision, reread your essay and make corrections and any other changes you think will improve it. Don't hesitate to cross out or insert material, but make the changes as neatly as possible. Check to make sure your sentences are clear and grammatical and that spelling and punctuation are correct.

The following pages present Anne Nishijima's answers to essay-examination questions in three courses: American Intellectual History, Introduction to Shakespeare, and Vertebrate Zoology. The answers for the history and Shakespeare tests show Nishijima's revisions, visible as crossed-out and inserted material.

Examination 1:
American Intellectual History
Anne Nishijima

The question in this examination is unusually broad, offering little guidance, but Anne Nishijima quickly finds a topic she wishes to pursue and writes directly to that point. Nishijima sets herself a difficult task: to argue the importance of environment in the determination of an individual's worldview, an exploration of the nature-nurture theme. In fact, the choice is probably too ambitious—forcing her to sacrifice the kind of specific detail that a more restricted, and therefore more manageable, topic would have permitted; however, she carries it off remarkably well. Notice that her primary method of development is that of cause and effect; for further discussion of this development strategy, see Chapter 5.

QUESTION: This examination is in two parts. The first, consisting of a series of short-answer questions, is to be completed and handed in before going on to the second part, and in any event after thirty minutes of the exam have lapsed. *The second part is to be answered in the form of an essay, drawing upon the readings, lectures, discussions, and your own considered reflections on American intellectual life during the Age of Henry Adams and William James.*

ESSAY

What determines a person's point of view? Why does one thinker see fit to agree with his colleagues' philosophy, or his society's philosophy, when another feels called upon to choose a different, possibly new, direction? ~~While Henry Adams was prophesying the doom of mankind and others of his social and intellectual ilk were Specifically, why how did William James happen of Pragmatism his philosophy of Pragmatism when all about him, men of equal intelligence were bogged down still caught up in still bogged down with Social Darwinism?~~ If biography is ~~construed to mean~~ defined as one's temperament and heritage, then biography alone cannot explain innovation. The influence of people, ideas, and experience must be brought to bear on temperament ~~and the mind~~ before it can be inspired to originate anything of its own. Genetic makeup, which is the only part of heritage that is not

388

~~brought~~ shown to the individual by people, ideas, and experience, is not sufficient. ~~Twins~~ Many people of vastly different genetic background can hold the same opinions, and identical twins often think very differently from one another. Clearly, other factors must be involved.

William James's life and development as a philosopher illustrate the way in which outside influences shape the individual's thought. Although he grew up in and was, by virtue of his role as an intellectual, exposed to a high degree to Social Darwinism, ~~the prevalent philosop~~ he was not content to believe ~~what so many others~~ in it, for several reasons.

James's first influence was his father, who taught him to think and to reason. Henry James, Sr., stayed home during the day, having no trade that would keep him away, and amused himself by inventing *games* ~~things~~ to keep his children busy. On Sundays, they would be sent to the different churches in town to listen to the sermons so they could report *to their father*ʌwhat had been said. Already, then, when most children are jealously ~~being brought up to in the "best" creed by their parents and are~~ being protected from subversive ʌ*creeds* ~~ideas~~ while their minds are still in the formative stage, the James children were being exposed to different interpretations of religion and philosophy.

~~As James grew older, he was educated in the proper and orthodox ways~~

~~When James came face to face with~~

~~When the time came for James to choose his avocation, he was undecided. He seemed only to know that he did not want to be a Social Darwinist.~~

~~Yet more than anything, James, when he began writing, was reacting against the ideas of his time.~~

~~This~~ Such exposure allowed William James to realize that options exist; the solution to a problem is not necessarily a given. ~~And~~ This concept was to become the foundation for his philosophy of Pragmatism.

We see, then, that the philosopher's upbringing is important. (Had Adams, for instance, been raised to think freely rather than to listen to the conversations of his elders and betters, he might have had a shot at leading a more optimistic life.) But James also shows us that the prevailing intellectual climate is at least as important.

Pragmatism was, to a large extent, a direct reaction against Social Darwinism. James held that, given a set of data, it is often possible to reach several conclusions and, therefore, choose one of several different directions. The Darwinist believed, however, that given the same set of data, only one conclusion could possibly result. Furthermore, that result would come about by itself. The Grand Pooh-Bah of Natural Selection would see to it that each course was continued to its end. To some, like Adams, the end was cold, lethargic doom. To others, it was the creation of a single perfect species. ~~But to James, even if events were controlled by unavoidable fate, the end might be either perfection or doom. Or it might be something entirely different.~~

Social Darwinism, then, had ^{OK} ~~run its course.~~ "Whatever is to happen," said the Darwinist, "there is nothing you or I can do about it. In fact, there's really no point in thinking about it." What philosophy could be more stultifying to an active, intelligent mind such as James's? Furthermore, the separation between rich and poor was getting rapidly wider, and social injustices were getting more and more horrifying. ^{OK} ~~Society~~ was ripe for conversion. Society embraced Progressivism, and philosophers were prepared to consider Pragmatism.

Social and intellectual climate, personal experience, all are part of the process by which a thinker like William James devises his philosophy. The influence of individuals also plays a part. The writings of Charles S. Peirce and Clifford both helped James refine his philosophic method, though in very different ways. Even the writers who criticized or objected outright to James's ideas aided him in straightening out any logical errors he may have made.

Although the nature-nurture question will never be answered satisfactorily, it is evident that outside influences are necessary to development. In the case of William James, I have endeavored to show some of these influences and their effects. Undoubtedly, temperament played a large role in determining these effects, ~~but temperament must in part~~ but equally, influences must determine the actions of the temperament. Biography, i.e., heritage and temperament, cannot act alone.

> **INSTRUCTOR'S COMMENT:** On balance, an attractive, even persuasive, answer, though one a bit short of the kind of illustrative detail that goes far to tie down any argument on behalf of a, at the least, disputable view. Still, an interesting response.

✳

Examination 2:
Introduction to Shakespeare
Anne Nishijima

———————

Nishijima's task in her Shakespeare test is considerably more clearly defined than in the history test. Having considered the question carefully, she states her approach to it in her first sentence, then devotes most of the rest of the essay to supporting her case with specific details, illustrations, and examples. Her method of development—specified in the examination question—is that of comparison and contrast; for further discussion of this development strategy, see Chapter 6.

QUESTION: Choose two important characters from different plays you have read so far in the term, and explore their essential similarities and differences. (40 points)

ESSAY

Shakespeare's Richard III and Brutus are, in a sense, ~~mirror images~~ *opposites* of each other. Where the former is entirely self-directed, doing all he can to further his own cause, the latter puts aside his own desires and natural judgment to further what he believes is the cause of Rome and her citizens. Richard is savage and twisted, physically as well as mentally; Brutus is, above all, an honorable man. Yet two so different characters wind up in similar plights, fighting to maintain hold on a crown illegally seized.

One is tempted, to cite a closer parallel. Richard's mock refusal of the crown is inescapably similar to Caesar's refusal. Shakespeare himself asks us to make the comparison when he has Richard discuss how Julius Caesar built the Tower of London, a place of which Richard himself makes great use.

Yet there are similarities between Richard and Brutus. Both, it is true, are ambitious, though for different causes. Both are willing to kill those in power to get power for themselves. Both fight bravely and desperately in the end (assuming that the horse King Richard calls for is to be used to join the fray, not flee from it, and granting that Brutus' suicide is a brave act).

There the similarities end. The differences, which are more widespread, can be seen clearly in, for example, their relationships with their allies and co-conspirators. Richard uses Hastings and Buckingham (and anyone else he can) for his own ends, fully intending to get rid of them permanently when their usefulness is ended. Brutus, on the other hand, remains faithful to his co-conspirators and even treats his enemy, Marc Antony, with fairness and consideration. And whereas Richard kills everyone ~~who might get~~ *who stands* in his way, Brutus, at some risk to himself, persuades the conspirators not to kill Antony, whose presence on the scene is certainly dangerous to Brutus.

A very clear difference is seen in their treatment of their women. Brutus loves his wife, and mourns her death with despair and convincing restraint. Richard woos and marries Anne with scorn, for political reasons only, does her in, and then proposes to go after young Elizabeth. One can easily imagine him reacting to Anne's death with a show *of* crocodile tears in contrast to Brutus' reluctance to show *and succumbs to* his more plausible grief.

Richard, of course, is capable of acting as though he were every bit as honorable as Brutus. Before others he is always the injured party, longing to be friends with Elizabeth's brothers who refuse, unjustly, to trust him. He is the noble lord protector who must explain, ever so sadly, to the young princes that they must not trust their uncles. But Shakespeare is careful to provide us with frequent monologues from Richard in which he states his true aims, lest we too may be taken in by him.

One could try to read Brutus' character in the same way, and see him as a clever, ambitious man eager to take advantage of his fellow citizens' ~~discontent~~ disenchantment ~~of~~ with Caesar. One could believe Antony that Caesar put aside the crown deliberately and sincerely, not disingenuously. But such a reading is hard to maintain in the absence of Richard-like monologues, and overt glimpses of Brutus' dissembling.

Finally, there is the argument between Brutus and Cassius towards the end of *Julius Caesar*. It is rare in drama, where time and space are limited by the confines of the stage and the audience's attention span, to have two characters have ~~an arg~~ a dispute that is amicably settled, unless that is the main subject of a comedy. But the argument *in Julius Caesar* and its subsequent peaceful conclusion, prove beyond all doubt the essential differences between Brutus and Richard. It is very characteristic of Brutus to keep his temper and make friends again ~~to~~ *with* Cassius, even though Cassius (unbeknownst to Brutus) has deceived him. On the other hand, it would be greatly out of character for Richard to back down in an argument, or to wish to make peace, even with so loyal an ally as Buckingham.

Richard and Brutus are, therefore, like parallel arrows that point in opposite directions. The similarity in their circumstances is brought about by opposite goals and intentions.

INSTRUCTOR'S COMMENT: You write well and knowingly about the two characters, and on balance one certainly agrees with you about the essential differences between the two. Yet there is a good deal of similarity, too, and I think you could go further in acknowledging and exploring the parallels. It is not just a forced reading of *Caesar* that sees Brutus as somewhat self-congratulatory and self-deceived in believing that murder is good. He is human and appealing, in contrast to Richard, but his actions don't seem all that different, whatever his intentions.

✳

Examination 3:
Vertebrate Zoology
Anne Nishijima

Nishijima's zoology test provides the most specific directions, though she must still choose the particular groups of animals she will write about. Note, incidentally, that this essay contains no obvious revisions. It was, however, revised. The examination was of a special kind you may sometimes be given: the "take home" examination. In such a test, you are allowed to write at home, referring to notes and books as necessary. Obviously, more time——typically a day or two—is available, and a clean copy can be handed in. In developing her answer, Nishijima combines several methods, especially description, comparison and contrast, and classification and division—all of which she handles extremely well. (For discussions of these strategies, see Chapters 3, 6, and 7.)

QUESTION: Describe the adaptations of a group of predators that allow them to hunt effectively, and the adaptations of prey that help them elude carnivores. Discuss the relationships between these adaptations of adversary animals.

ESSAY

The big cats of Africa, the lion and cheetah in particular, have like all cats developed a set of adaptations which allow them to chase down their prey. Aside from the forward-oriented eyes and sharp tearing and shearing teeth that are universal in mammalian carnivores, felines have exceedingly flexible backbones and strong shoulder musculature. With this kind of physique, a running cat can reach forward with its fore paws, pull itself rapidly over the ground, bend its back to reach forward with the hind paws, and then straighten the back to begin another stride with its fore paws. In this way, the feline is permitted a long stride for fast sprinting. However, such a strategy is a compromise. What a cat gains in speed it loses in endurance. The animal tires quickly and cannot run long distances because much of the forward force created by the hind limbs against the ground is lost to the flexibility of the vertebral column.

It is here that the ungulates have "found" their advantage. They are provided with stiff backbones that transmit the force of the hind legs against the ground into forward motion. Thus, although the animal cannot run as fast as its feline predator, and does not have as long a stride, it can run farther. If it becomes aware that it is being stalked, it can outrun a would-be killer fairly handily. To aid in perceiving prey, ungulates have laterally oriented eyes, large ears, and a tendency to form herds in which some animals are keeping watch at any given time.

Perhaps in response to these defensive mechanisms, various cats have developed ways of quite literally catching their prey by surprise. Lions are colored like the sun-dried grass in which they hunt. The males, with their impressive and conspicuous manes, do not hunt. It is the more inconspicuous females who do the hunting, and though they are less speedy than some felines, they make up for it with strategy, hunting in groups.

The cheetah, hunting in the same environment as the lion, also has concealing coloration, being dappled with small black spots on a dun background. Such dappling helps to mask the outline of an animal. Its claws are not fully retractable so that it has good traction, and it has particularly large scapulae and strong pectoral musculature on a long and supple body. With such assets, it does not need to hunt in groups, and so it is a solitary creature by and large, though its cubs spend an unusually long time with their mother learning hunting techniques.

Thus, predators and prey have developed skills and strengths that complement each other. Which developed in response to what is a chicken-and-egg question; probably they evolved in leap-frog fashion, each kind of animal responding to the other simultaneously. In the end, they reached a balance that allows predators to catch enough prey for their species to survive, and the prey sufficient means of escaping to perpetuate their species. Both, in the long run, are successful.

INSTRUCTOR'S COMMENT: Nicely done. Excellent choice of subject. Your command of species is impressive, and the whole is *very* well written.

✳

✳

Chapter 12

Writing from Research

Preparing a research paper can be a highly rewarding experience that you will remember with a sense of achievement long after college. The key is, first of all, to choose a subject that genuinely interests you and that you would like to learn more about; next, to limit and focus the subject so that you can do a thorough job with it in the time and space you have; and, finally, to work systematically, following time-tested procedures that will help you avoid becoming disorganized or overwhelmed.

The two research chapters of *Writer's* (6 and 7) guide you through the process in detail. This chapter of *The Resourceful Reader* is intended to help you by supplementing handbook chapters with additional examples, particularly a "case study" of one student's progress from a rough idea to a finished paper.

Between *Writer's* and *The Resourceful Reader* you have seven researched papers available to you as examples, five by students and two by professional scholars. The student papers are Dietrich Bohn's and Adrienne Harton's in *Writer's* 7f and 7i, the student essay in *Writer's* 9g, and those by Bill Wallace and Barbara Kiger in this chapter. The professionally written examples are both in this text: "The Harlem Renaissance: One Facet of an Unturned Kaleidoscope" by Darwin Turner in Chapter 2 and "'We Can't Dance Together'" by María Rosa Menocal in Chapter 9. As you examine these essays, however, bear in mind that they do not all employ the same documentation style or even the same level of documentation. Five of the student essays and the essay by Menocal use the documentation style of the Modern Language Association of America (MLA), the style you are most likely to be asked to use in a college composition course. Turner's essay follows an older documentation style that uses *ibid.* and traditional footnotes for citations. Kiger's and Harton's essays follow the style of the American Psychological Association (APA), the most widely used style in the social sciences.

One of the most important challenges in writing a research paper is finding an appropriate subject. The advice and the questioning methods discussed in *Writer's* 2a can help you. Whatever subject you choose, it should be something that genuinely interests you. If a subject is assigned to you, of course, you may have a problem unless you are lucky; however, even a subject that seems to leave you cold can often be given an interesting focus if you consider it from different angles. Try some of the procedures described in *Writer's* 2a.

Finding a general subject was fairly difficult for Bill Wallace, whose research paper appears in this chapter. His assignment was vague—write a research paper on a literary topic using at least five different sources. Wallace conferred with the instructor and with other students to try to pin down something he would be interested in doing. Noting a possible connection between his interest in fantasy fiction, information from a mythology course he was taking, and an assignment in the previous semester's English literature course, he decided to write about J. R. R. Tolkien's use of northern European mythology to create his mythic world.

Wallace began his research by consulting the library's online computer catalog. He found several books by Tolkien that seemed to be suitable and that his library had. He printed out the bibliographic information for each source—author, title (and subtitle, if any), and quite a bit of publishing information including whatever he would need if he later decided to use that source. He then switched to the MLA and *Reader's Guide* online databases to see what he could find on Tolkien's mythology in journals and magazines.

As he discovered possible sources, Wallace built his working bibliography, cutting and pasting from the database to his word processing program. (Instead of using a computer, he could have gone to the library and written the information on index cards or in a notebook, as researchers have done for years.) When he looked at the books and articles themselves, he added to each entry a one-sentence statement of what the book or article was about. This would come in handy when he decided to limit his topic to the mythological associations as revealed in a comparison of *Beowulf* and *The Hobbit*.

A sample entry that he printed for his working bibliography from a database follows.

> AUTHOR: Provost, William.
> TITLE: Language and myth in the fantasy writings of J. R. R. Tolkien.
> SOURCE: Modern Age v. 33 (Spring '90) p. 42–52.

In creating his "works cited" list, Wallace carefully followed MLA style, which was the style specified by his instructor. [*Writer's* 6f and 7, especially 7c and 7d] To do so, he cut and pasted from his working bibliography, making whatever adjustments were required to conform to MLA style. If Wallace had been using cards, he would have entered information for each source, carefully following MLA style, which would later have enabled him to type the information from his cards directly into his final list of "works cited." When Wallace completed his working bibliography, he had seventeen entries representing material that seemed promising.

Wallace had found a number of sources but still lacked a clear direction for his research project. Wisely, he decided to consult a biographical dictionary of literary topics, which included a substantial essay on Tolkien. He found a reference to Tolkien's efforts to make his fantasy world seem real. This reference suggested the direction Wallace's essay finally took—the role played by the mythology of northern Europe in the creation of Tolkien's world. Wallace was lucky to find a way to focus his project so quickly. A good rule of thumb is that if you find dozens of sources on your topic, your subject is too broad; if you find fewer than a dozen, it may be too narrow.

With this focus, Wallace was on his way. He also found—a pleasant surprise after his initial frustration—that he was more excited about this topic than he had expected. In fact, this is not surprising; it is almost always easier to be interested in specifics than in generalities. He began to read the source materials and take notes. The key to successful note taking is to find and evaluate useful passages quickly and efficiently, checking tables of contents and indexes and then skimming the pertinent pages for information related to the chosen topic. Wallace created computer files to hold bits of information or comments that he thought he would be able to use in his paper, a new file for each source. In each case, he had to decide how he would write down what he found—whether to summarize, paraphrase, or quote. [7b] Each note file contained the author's name flush left on the first line and the page number from which the note came on the right margin. Additionally, Wallace entered a descriptive heading, such as "weapon" or "dragon," to help him classify and arrange his information.

Bill Wallace

Professor McLeod

English 102.A9

November 10, 1999

J. R. R. Tolkien's Mythology

If history were to be forgotten and our concept of God along with it, people would still require something to believe in. The stories of J. R. R. Tolkien could record myths as readily believed in as were those the ancients found in the stories of Homer and Vergil. As Augustus M. Kolich notes in the <u>Concise Dictionary of British Literary Biography,</u>

> [t]he driving passion of John Ronald Ruel Tolkien's literary
> life was to make his "fairy stories" so complete in
> description and detail, so varied in character and action, so
> expansive in philosophy and religion, as to be "real." (369)

This strong sense of reality derives in large part from familiarity. Tolkien used familiar childhood tales and traditional legends as a core around which he solidified a mythology for western civilization that in its conception is truly northern European, a coalescence of Teutonic and Celtic myth:

> A number of the beings in Tolkien's works are completely
> supernatural. These include the Valar, Wizards, Elves,
> Dwarves, Bombadil and Goldberry, Ents, and such evil
> creatures as Sauron, the Orcs, and the Balrog. They belong
> to the classes of beings which, at one time or another and
> in one form or another, were worshipped as gods by Celts,
> Teutons, and indeed most European peoples. Beings analogous
> to them were revered in most parts of the world. (Noel 98)

The creation of this mythic world grounded in the northern European mythos, that rich lode of legend, fable, and "fairy stories," was a task for which Tolkien was uniquely prepared, for Anglo-Saxon language and literature and its sources in myth and legend were his area of scholarly expertise.

A comparison of the Anglo-Saxon poem <u>Beowulf</u> with <u>The Hobbit</u> clearly reveals the origins of Tolkien's fables. Beginning with the monsters in both works, one easily finds similarities between Grendel and Gollum. For instance, each has his own underground lake habitat. Tolkien describes Gollum's in <u>The Hobbit:</u>

There were strange things living in the pools and lakes in
the hearts of mountains. . . . Deep down here by the dark
water lived old Gollum, a small, slimy creature. (78-79)

Although we are not shown Grendel's lair immediately when we meet
him, we soon find that he, too, like Gollum and like everything
else dark and slimy, has his home in an underground lake:

He went before with a few wise-men to spy out the country,
until suddenly he found mountain trees leaning out over
hoary stone, a joyless wood: water lay beneath, bloody and
troubled. (Tuso 25)

We see the true nature of Grendel's habitat only when Beowulf
fights Grendel's mother:

Then the earl saw that he was in some hostile hall where no
water harmed him at all, and the floods' onrush might not
touch him because of the hall roof. (27)

But Grendel and Gollum share other similarities besides the
underground habitat. Both use stealth to attack, though each
employed his own style. In The Hobbit Gollum had the One Ring,
which made him invisible. This, coupled with his natural stealth,
made him a dangerous opponent indeed. But the Gollum that we are
most familiar with, the Gollum from Lord of the Rings, no longer
has the ring and must rely on his natural instinct, much like
Grendel. Grendel used the cloak of night to hide his actions, being
thereby both visible and invisible. "There came gliding in the
black night the walker of darkness" (Tuso 13). Clearly, if size
were to be overlooked, the descriptions of the two monsters are
virtually interchangeable.

A comparison of The Hobbit and Beowulf can also clearly show
that Tolkien probably based much of his characterization of Smaug on
the dragon from the final episode of Beowulf. To be specific, the
generic worm of Beowulf inhabits a barrow—a burial mound (39). Early
Germanic peoples often buried their kings and mighty heroes in
barrows with all their treasure. The well-characterized (and well-
heeled) dragon of The Hobbit, Smaug, lived in the same kind of place,
the kind of place the Beowulf Poet called the "lonely mountain" (35).

Furthermore, the word "barrow" is derived from the Old English
word "beorg" which is related to the German word "berg" meaning

"mountain" (Noel 168). This language connection supports the
assertion that a close relationship can be drawn between <u>Beowulf</u>
and "The King Under the Mountain," the chapter from <u>The Hobbit</u>
describing Smaug. If we substitute the word "barrow" for
"mountain," the connection is obvious: "The King Under the Barrow."

A study of the weapons that helped both Bilbo and Beowulf defeat
their monsters supports the idea that Tolkien derived many of his
ideas for <u>The Hobbit</u> from Anglo-Saxon sources. Sting, Bilbo's blade,
is instrumental in allowing its owner to defeat Gollum at playing the
game of riddles and so save his life (80). Sting is thus comparable
to the victory-blessed blade that allows Beowulf to finally put an end
to the Grendel family (27). Both tales make much of named, magical,
ancestral weapons, and Tolkien emphasizes the theme by endowing Bard
with a similar weapon named "Black Arrow." Furthermore, "Black Arrow"
gives Bard the edge he needs to finally slay Smaug (237), just as the
magical giant sword aids Beowulf (although luck also plays an
important part in the deaths of both Smaug and Grendel's mother).

A further symmetry can be seen in the characterizations of the
heroes themselves. In both tales, there are actually two key
heroes, the young hero and the old hero. In <u>Beowulf,</u> the old hero
and the young hero are the same person revealed to us at different
times of life, whereas in <u>The Hobbit,</u> the young hero and the old
hero are separate characters, Bilbo and Thorin, respectively. Both
stories show how the young hero triumphs and how the old hero dies.
Bilbo, the young hero of <u>The Hobbit,</u> lies in wait invisibly to
triumph over Gollum, just as Beowulf lies in wait for Grendel to
attack Heorot once more. The young Beowulf triumphs over Grendel
and the water hag, but the old Beowulf is killed fighting the
barrow dragon and with his death buys the dragon's treasure for his
people. Although the old hero of <u>The Hobbit,</u> Thorin, does not die
fighting the dragon, he is killed in the battle of the five armies
defending his people's claim to Smaug's halls of gold.

In <u>Beowulf</u> the young warrior Wiglaf provides the lucky
assistance that allows Beowulf to finally kill the dragon and win
its treasure for his people, though Beowulf dies in the attempt. In
<u>The Hobbit</u> it is the young warrior, Bard, who actually kills the
dragon, allowing Thorin's friends and fellow dwarves to claim the
enormous treasure of Smaug's huge barrow-mound. These echoes of

<u>Beowulf</u> that are found in <u>The Hobbit</u> clearly show the strong
influence of Anglo-Saxon/Teutonic myth and legend in Tolkien's first
work, an influence that can be continuously seen throughout his
later works.

Tolkien also draws upon northern European roots for the poetry
which gives vigor to his world and his characters. Primarily
through kennings, Tolkien's poetry shows influence not only of
Teutonic sources, but also of medieval Celtic sources (Rogers 33).
Including these recreations of early Germanic and Celtic forms
allowed Tolkien to make his fiction seem more real, a technique
only now being used by a few end-of-the-century writers. Perhaps it
was Tolkien's view of himself as a philologist first that inspired
him to do so (Kolich 372).

Tolkien captures and molds the amorphous legends and tales of
ancient Europe into a solid mythology that captures the modern
spirit (Provost 42). But, alas, mythologies must be built over
time. It took Tolkien his whole life to concentrate the scattered
myths of Europe into an all-encompassing work, <u>The Silmarillion</u>
(Kroeber 522). Undoubtedly the culmination of his life's work, the
development of a modern Western mythology that began with <u>The
Hobbit</u> reached its culmination in this last and final book which
allows us a glimpse of the reservoir from which flowed <u>The Hobbit</u>
and <u>The Lord of the Rings.</u>

Works Cited

Kolich, Augustus M. "J. R. R. Tolkien." <u>Concise Dictionary of British
Literary Biography: Modern Writers.</u> Vol. 6. Detroit: Gale, 1991.

Kroeber, Karl, "J. R. R. Tolkien." <u>British Writers.</u> Sup. II. New
York: Scribner's, 1992.

Noel, Ruth S. <u>The Mythology of Middle Earth.</u> Boston: Houghton,
1977.

Provost, William. "Language and Myth in the Fantasy Writings of
J. R. R. Tolkien." <u>Modern Age</u> 33 (1990): 42-52.

Rogers, Deborah W. "Literary Backgrounds." <u>J. R. R. Tolkien.</u>
Boston: Twayne, 1980.

Tolkien, J. R. R. <u>The Hobbit.</u> New York: Ballantine, 1937.

Tuso, Joseph F., ed. <u>Beowulf: A Norton Critical Edition.</u> New York:
Norton, 1975.

America's Forgotten People

Barbara Kiger

Sociology 243

Professor Ortega

March 3, 1999

Running Head: Forgotten People

America's Forgotten People

Living in the inner city, I witnessed a great number of
homeless people struggling to survive the winter months. Each time
I passed one of their cardboard homes or noticed them sleeping in
the doorways of abandoned shops, I became more and more interested
in the impact of homelessness; but it was really not until I
learned that the younger sister of one of my high school friends
had become homeless that I was motivated to look into the problem
carefully.

"Widespread homelessness in the U.S. may be dated back from the
period immediately following the Civil War" when men whose platoons
had been disbanded were on the move (Hopper, 1990, p. 13). At this
time, the homeless men were referred to as "hoboes, tramps, gandy
dancers, and knights of the road; only later were 'bums' and
'derelicts' common epithets" (p. 13). Today, homelessness affects
all types of people, cutting across race, gender, and age barriers.
Frequently homeless people have been "stripped of traditional social
roles and brutalized in a variety of ways" (D'Ercole & Struening,
1990, p. 141). On the street, these people lack adequate shelter,
clothing, and food. They are often robbed and victimized physically
and sexually. Struening and Padgett (1990) assert that "many
homeless persons are afflicted by both mental and physical
comorbidities, imposing a tremendous burden on their lives" (p. 66).
In fact, many homeless people suffer from alcoholism, drug abuse,
and such chronic diseases as AIDS as well.

These days, men are not the only homeless people. Women, too,
who live on the streets endure this victimization and disease, yet
most of them have fled to the streets to avoid the same experiences
in the home. For instance, most women become homeless due to
domestic violence and eviction. And because of the victimization
regularly directed at homeless women, they experience higher levels
of fear than do homeless men (D'Ercole & Struening, 1990, p. 141).
And not only does this social problem impact women; many women are
forced to bring their children to the streets with them and to try
to nurture these children in this dangerous environment. That a
woman is responsible for caring for children no doubt also raises
her level of fear, often leading to depression or other mental
illnesses. D'Ercole and Struening's study confirms that sixty-three

percent of a shelter sample of homeless women were mothers, of whom twenty-seven percent had some college education or were college graduates (p. 145). The education and marital status of these women varied greatly, yet most had children, and several had their children with them on the street. Although D'Ercole and Struening focus on homeless women in their study, their findings imply a significant problem regarding homeless children, concerning whom there are few studies.

One study, however, was completed by Janice Molnar, William R. Rath, and Tovah Klein (1990). In their article, "Constantly Compromised: The Impact of Homelessness on Children," Molnar et al. claim that "one in four preschoolers lives in poverty" and that within the rising number of homeless, the number of homeless children is increasing the fastest (p. 109). In fact, the 1989 U.S. Conference of Mayors reported that children and families account for thirty-eight percent of homeless people. In addition to safety hazards, homeless children encounter many health hazards while living on the streets. For instance, a large number of homeless children have high lead levels in their blood and suffer from vitamin and mineral deficiencies, leading to anemia and slow wound-healing (Molnar et al., 1990, p. 111). These children are extremely susceptible to disease and receive little health care and few immunizations because the parents do not know where to take the children for medical help (p. 113).

However, physical distress is only one facet of children's life on the street. Most of these children are exposed to this harmful environment during the stages of cognitive and social development. In a New York City shelter sample of preschool children, Phillips and Hartigan observed "language delays, problems in conceptualizing cause-and-effect relationships and time sequencing, difficulty in organizing behavior (especially in transitions), and a lack of empathy and the difficulty in the ability to share" (Molnar et al., 1990, p. 115). The effects of homelessness on children are many, especially during the preschool years; yet homelessness affects adolescents in much the same way.

Homeless adolescents consist of both throwaways and runaways. Throwaways are socially rejected teens who have generally experienced prolonged abuse and neglect and are finally forced to leave home. In a study of homeless adolescents, Thomas Gullota (1978) discovered that the average age that a youngster is expelled from the home is about fifteen (p. 545). Because these adolescents are rejected by their parents and usually have few friends, they often choose to commit delinquent acts in an attempt to be accepted by their peer group on the streets (Heir, Korboot, & Schweitzer, 1990, p. 763). Heir et al. assert that although "both runaways and throwaways [in an Australian sample] were found to have high scores on hostility, antisocial tendency, depression, and social isolation," throwaways were generally less aggressive than runaways, and female throwaways were more socially isolated than female runaways (pp. 769-770). Runawayas, teens between the ages of eleven and seventeen who decide to leave home without parental consent (Brennan, Huizinga, & Elliott, 1978, p. 2), generally run away from home to escape family conflicts or to get the attention of their alienated parents. Most of these teens leave home with "no specific destination" in mind, and, therefore, end up on the streets (Orten & Soll, 1980, p. 252). Often these girls and boys become delinquent, especially those with low self-esteem, powerlessness, normlessness and high societal estrangement (Brennan et al. 1978, p. 242). However, Henggeler, Edwards, and Borduin (1987) contend that "families of female delinquents are more dysfunctional than those of male delinquents" (p. 200), and the study completed by D'Ercole and Struening (1990) shows that most homeless women were once runaways or lived in a foster home (p. 143).

In any case, none can deny that the quality of life the homelessness experience deteriorates. Not only those who have left home to find a better situation but also those who are forced to move to the streets are often disappointed to find life on the streets so difficult. The physical and emotional hardships quickly take their toll leaving these people destitute, trying to cope with mental illness, alcoholism, drug abuse, and poor health. Because of the large number of homeless, solutions to the problem are far in the future. Although many health and housing programs have been instated, most of these people end up in prisons or stay on the streets. Perhaps early intervention or better communication could decrease the number of runaways, now at 1.2 million a year (Hersch, 1988, p. 31), but the problems of those who are mentally ill or who have been evicted from their homes are entirely different from those of runaways. Breakley and Fischer (1990) suggest that "service planners must consider the diversity of the people affected and the variety of problems that compound their difficulties" (p. 43).

Perhaps the answer does lie in the hands of policy makers, but that certainly looks like just another instance of buck-passing. No one seems to be considering how the problem of homelessness will proliferate; homelessness appears to beget homelessness. Unless everybody takes some responsibility to do something practical about the problem now, in the long run, homelessness may be everybody's problem.

References

Breakley, W., & Fischer, P. (1990). Homelessness: the extent of the problem. *Journal of Social Issues, 46*(4), 31-47.

Brennan, T., Huizinga, D., & Elliott, D. (1978). *The social psychology of runaways.* Lexington, MA: Lexington Books.

D'Ercole, A., & Struening, E. (1990). Victimization among homeless women: implications for service delivery. *Journal of Community Psychology, 18,* 141-152.

Gullota, T. (1978). Runaway: reality or myth. *Adolescence, 13*(52), 15-20.

Heir, S. J., Korboot, P. J., & Schweitzer, R. D. (1990). Social adjustment and symptomology in two types of homeless adolescents: runaways and throwaways. *Adolescence, 25*(100), 761-771.

Henggeler, S., Edwards, J., & Borduin, C. (1987). The family relations of female delinquents. *Journal of Abnormal Child Psychology, 15*(2), 199-209.

Hersch, P. (1988, January). Coming of age on city streets. *Psychology Today,* 28-37.

Hopper, K. (1990). Public shelter as "a hybrid institution": homeless men in historical perspective. *Journal of Social Issues, 46*(4), 13-29.

Molnar, J. M., Rath, W. R., & Klein, T. P. (1990). Constantly compromised: the impact of homelessness on children. *Journal of Social Issues, 46*(4), 109-124.

Orten, J. D., & Soll, S. K. (1980). Runaway children and their families. Journal of Family Issues, 1(2), 249-261.

Struening, E., & Padgett, D. (1990). Physical health status, substance use and abuse, and mental disorders among homeless adults. Journal of Social Issues, 46(4), 65-81.

＊

Chapter 13

For Further Reading: Some Classic Essays

The Allegory of the Cave
Plato

SOCRATES,
GLAUCON. The
den, the prisoners:
the light at a
distance;

the low wall, and
the moving figures
of which the
shadows are seen
on the opposite
wall of the den.

And now, I said, let me show in a figure how far our 1
nature is enlightened or unenlightened:—Behold! human beings living in an underground den, which has a mouth open
towards the light and reaching all along the den; here they
have been from their childhood, and have their legs and necks
chained so that they cannot move, and can only see before
them, being prevented by the chains from turning round their
heads. Above and behind them a fire is blazing at a distance,
and between the fire and the prisoners there is a raised way;
and you will see, if you look, a low wall built along the way,
like the screen which marionette players have in front of
them, over which they show the puppets.

I see. 2

And do you see, I said, men passing along the wall car- 3
rying all sorts of vessels, and statues and figures of animals
made of wood and stone and various materials, which appear over the wall? Some of them are talking, others silent.

You have shown me a strange image, and they are 4
strange prisoners.

Like ourselves, I replied; and they see only their own 5
shadows, or the shadows of one another, which the fire
throws on the opposite wall of the cave?

True, he said; how could they see anything but the shad- 6
ows if they were never allowed to move their heads?

411

And of the objects which are being carried in like man- 7
ner they would only see the shadows?

Yes, he said. 8

And if they were able to converse with one another, 9
would they not suppose that they were naming what was
actually before them?

Very true. 10

And suppose further that the prison had an echo which 11
came from the other side, would they not be sure to fancy
when one of the passers-by spoke that the voice which they
heard came from the passing shadow?

No question, he replied. 12

To them, I said, the truth would be literally nothing but 13
the shadows of the images.

That is certain. 14

And now look again, and see what will naturally fol- 15
low if the prisoners are released and disabused of their error. At first, when any of them is liberated and compelled
suddenly to stand up and turn his neck round and walk and
look towards the light, he will suffer sharp pains; the glare
will distress him, and he will be unable to see the realities
of which in his former state he had seen the shadows; and
then conceive some one saying to him, that what he saw before was an illusion, but that now, when he is approaching
nearer to being and his eye is turned towards more real existence, he has a clearer vision—what will be his reply? And
you may further imagine that his instructor is pointing to
the objects as they pass and requiring him to name them,—
will he not be perplexed? Will he not fancy that the shadows which he formerly saw are truer than the objects which
are now shown to him?

Far truer. 16

And if he is compelled to look straight at the light, will 17
he not have a pain in his eyes which will make him turn
away to take refuge in the objects of vision which he can
see, and which he will conceive to be in reality clearer than
the things which are now being shown to him?

True, he said. 18

And suppose once more, that he is reluctantly dragged 19
up a steep and rugged ascent, and held fast until he is forced
into the presence of the sun himself, is he not likely to be
pained and irritated? When he approaches the light his eyes
will be dazzled, and he will not be able to see anything at
all of what are now called realities.

*The prisoners
would mistake
the shadows for
realities.*

*And when
released, they
would still persist
in maintaining the
superior truth of
the shadows.*

*When dragged
upwards, they
would be dazzled
by excess of light.*

Not all in a moment, he said. 20

He will require to grow accustomed to the sight of the 21
upper world. And first he will see the shadows best, next
the reflections of men and other objects in the water, and
then the objects themselves; then he will gaze upon the light
of the moon and the stars and the spangled heaven; and he
will see the sky and the stars by night better than the sun
or the light of the sun by day?

Certainly. 22

At length they will Last of all he will be able to see the sun, and not mere 23
see the sun and reflections of him in the water, but he will see him in his
understand his own proper place, and not in another, and he will contem-
nature. plate him as he is.

Certainly. 24

He will then proceed to argue that this is he who gives 25
the season and the years, and is the guardian of all that is in
the visible world, and in a certain way the cause of all things
which he and his fellows have been accustomed to behold?

Clearly, he said, he would first see the sun and then rea- 26
son about him.

They would then And when he remembered his old habitation, and the 27
pity their old wisdom of the den and his fellow prisoners, do you not sup-
companions of pose that he would felicitate himself on the change, and pity
the den. them?

Certainly, he would. 28

And if they were in the habit of conferring honors 29
among themselves on those who were quickest to observe
the passing shadows and to remark which of them went before, and which followed after, and which were together;
and who were therefore best able to draw conclusions as to
the future, do you think that he would care for such honors and glories, or envy the possessors of them? Would he
not say with Homer,

Better to be the poor servant of a poor master,

and to endure anything, rather than think as they do and
live after their manner?

Yes, he said, I think that he would rather suffer any- 30
thing than entertain these false notions and live in this miserable manner.

Imagine once more, I said, such a one coming suddenly 31
out of the sun to be replaced in his old situation; would he
not be certain to have his eyes full of darkness?

To be sure, he said.   32

And if there were a contest, and he had to compete in   33
measuring the shadows with the prisoners who had never
moved out of the den, while his sight was still weak, and
before his eyes had become steady (and the time which
would be needed to acquire this new habit of sight might
be very considerable), would he not be ridiculous? Men
would say of him that up he went and down he came without his eyes; and that it was better not even to think of as-
cending; and if any one tried to loose another and lead him
up to the light, let them only catch the offender, and they
would put him to death.

No question, he said.   34

This entire allegory, I said, you may now append, dear   35
Glaucon, to the previous argument; the prison house is the
world of sight, the light of the fire is the sun, and you will
not misapprehend me if you interpret the journey upwards
to be the ascent of the soul into the intellectual world according to my poor belief, which, at your desire, I have expressed—whether rightly or wrongly God knows. But,
whether true or false, my opinion is that in the world of
knowledge the idea of good appears last of all, and is seen
only with an effort; and, when seen, is also inferred to be
the universal author of all things beautiful and right, parent of light and of the lord of light in this visible world, and
the immediate source of reason and truth in the intellectual;
and that this is the power upon which he who would act
rationally either in public or private life must have his eye
fixed.

I agree, he said, as far as I am able to understand you.   36

Moreover, I said, you must not wonder that those who   37
attain to this beatific vision are unwilling to descend to human affairs; for their souls are ever hastening into the upper world where they desire to dwell; which desire of theirs
is very natural, if our allegory may be trusted.

Yes, very natural.   38

And is there anything surprising in one who passes from   39
divine contemplations to the evil state of man, misbehaving
himself in a ridiculous manner; if, while his eyes are blink-
ing and before he has become accustomed to the surrounding darkness, he is compelled to fight in courts of law, or in
other places, about the images or the shadows of images of
justice, and is endeavoring to meet the conceptions of those
who have never yet seen absolute justice?

Marginal notes:

But when they returned to the den they would see much worse than those who had never left it.

The prison is the world of sight, the light of the fire is the sun.

Nothing extraordinary in the philosopher being unable to see in the dark.

Anything but surprising, he replied. 40

Anyone who has common sense will remember that the 41 bewilderments of the eyes are of two kinds, and arise from two causes, either from coming out of the light or from going into the light, which is true of the mind's eye, quite as much as of the bodily eye; and he who remembers this when he sees anyone whose vision is perplexed and weak, will not be too ready to laugh; he will first ask whether that soul of man has come out of the brighter life, and is unable to see because unaccustomed to the dark, or having turned from darkness to the day is dazzled by excess of light. And he will count the one happy in his condition and state of being, and he will pity the other; or, if he have a mind to laugh at the soul which comes from below into the light, there will be more reason in this than in the laugh which greets him who returns from above out of the light into the den.

That, he said, is a very just distinction. 42

But then, if I am right, certain professors of education 43 must be wrong when they say that they can put a knowledge into the soul which was not there before, like sight into blind eyes.

They undoubtedly say this, he replied. 44

Whereas, our argument shows that the power and ca- 45 pacity of learning exists in the soul already; and that just as the eye was unable to turn from darkness to light without the whole body, so too the instrument of knowledge can only by the movement of the whole soul be turned from the world of becoming into that of being, and learn by degrees to endure the sight of being, and of the brightest and best of being, or in other words, of the good.

Very true. 46

And must there not be some art which will effect con- 47 version in the easiest and quickest manner; not implanting the faculty of sight, for that exists already, but has been turned in the wrong direction, and is looking away from the truth?

Yes, he said, such an art may be presumed. 48

And whereas the other so-called virtues of the soul seem 49 to be akin to bodily qualities, for even when they are not originally innate they can be implanted later by habit and exercise, the virtue of wisdom more than anything else contains a divine element which always remains, and by this conversion is rendered useful and profitable; or, on the other

The eyes may be blinded in two ways, by excess or by defect of light.

The conversion of the soul is the turning round the eye from darkness to light.

The virtue of wisdom has a divine power which may be turned either towards good or towards evil.

hand, hurtful and useless. Did you never observe the narrow intelligence flashing from the keen eye of a clever rogue—how eager he is, how clearly his paltry soul sees the way to his end; he is the reverse of blind, but his keen eyesight is forced into the service of evil, and he is mischievous in proportion to his cleverness?

Very true, he said.   50

But what if there had been a circumcision of such na-   51
tures in the days of their youth; and they had been severed from those sensual pleasures, such as eating and drinking, which, like leaden weights, were attached to them at their birth, and which drag them down and turn the vision of their souls upon the things that are below—if, I say, they had been released from these impediments and turned in the opposite direction, the very same faculty in them would have seen the truth as keenly as they see what their eyes are turned to now.

Very likely.   52

Neither the uneducated nor the overeducated will be good servants of the State.

Yes, I said; and there is another thing which is likely,   53
or rather a necessary inference from what has preceded, that neither the uneducated and uninformed of the truth, nor yet those who never make an end of their education, will be able ministers of State; not the former, because they have no single aim of duty which is the rule of all their actions, private as well as public; nor the latter, because they will not act at all except upon compulsion, fancying that they are already dwelling apart in the islands of the blessed.

Very true, he replied.   54

Then, I said, the business of us who are the founders of   55
the State will be to compel the best minds to attain that knowledge which we have already shown to be the greatest of all—they must continue to ascend until they arrive at the good; but when they have ascended and seen enough we must not allow them to do as they do now.

What do you mean?   56

Men should ascend to the upper world, but they should also return to the lower.

I mean that they remain in the upper world: but this   57
must not be allowed; they must be made to descend again among the prisoners in the den, to partake of their labors and honors, whether they are worth having or not.

But is not this unjust? he said; ought we to give them a   58
worse life, when they might have a better?

You have again forgotten, my friend, I said, the inten-   59
tion of the legislator, who did not aim at making any one

class in the State happy above the rest; the happiness was to be in the whole State, and he held the citizens together by persuasion and necessity, making them benefactors of the State, and therefore benefactors of one another; to this end he created them, not to please themselves, but to be his instruments in binding up the State.

True, he said, I had forgotten. 60

The duties of the philosophers.

Observe, Glaucon, that there will be no injustice in com- 61 pelling our philosophers to have a care and providence of others; we shall explain to them that in other States, men of their class are not obliged to share in the toils of politics: and this is reasonable, for they grow up at their own sweet will, and the government would rather not have them. Being self-taught, they cannot be expected to show any gratitude for a culture which they have never received. But we have brought you into the world to be rulers of the hive, kings of yourselves and of the other citizens, and have educated you far better and more perfectly than they have been educated, and you are better able to share in the double duty.

Their obligations to their country will induce them to take part in her government.

Wherefore each of you, when his turn comes, must go down to the general underground abode, and get the habit of seeing in the dark. When you have acquired the habit, you will see ten thousand times better than the inhabitants of the den, and you will know what the several images are, and what they represent, because you have seen the beautiful and just and good in their truth. And thus our State, which is also yours, will be a reality, and not a dream only, and will be administered in a spirit unlike that of other States, in which men fight with one another about shadows only and are distracted in the struggle for power, which in their eyes is a great good. Whereas the truth is that the State in which the rulers are most reluctant to govern is always the best and most quietly governed, and the State in which they are most eager, the worst.

Quite true, he replied. 62

And will our pupils, when they hear this, refuse to take 63 their turn at the toils of State, when they are allowed to spend the greater part of their time with one another in the heavenly light?

They will be willing but not anxious to rule.

Impossible, he answered; for they are just men, and the 64 commands which we impose upon them are just; there can be no doubt that every one of them will take office as a stern necessity, and not after the fashion of our present rulers of State.

The statesman
must be provided
with a better life
than that of a
ruler; and then he
will not covet
office.

Yes, my friend, I said; and there lies the point. You must   65
contrive for your future rulers another and a better life than
that of a ruler, and then you may have a well-ordered State;
for only in the State which offers this, will they rule who
are truly rich, not in silver and gold, but in virtue and wisdom, which are the true blessings of life. Whereas if they
go to the administration of public affairs, poor and hun-
gering after their own private advantage, thinking that hence
they are to snatch the chief good, order there can never be;
for they will be fighting about office, and the civil and domestic broils which thus arise will be the ruin of the rulers
themselves and of the whole State.

Most true, he replied.   66

And the only life which looks down upon the life of po-   67
litical ambition is that of true philosophy. Do you know of
any other?

Indeed, I do not, he said.   68

A Modest Proposal

Jonathan Swift

Clergyman, Irish patriot, critic, poet, Jonathan Swift (1667–1745) is considered by many to be the greatest satirist in the English language. Born in Ireland to English parents who had settled there, Swift spent much of his early career in London, where he wrote his first important satires, *A Tale of a Tub* and *The Battle of the Books* (both published in 1704). He became a leading writer for the Tory party and as a reward for his services was appointed Dean of St. Patrick's Cathedral in Dublin. He spent the rest of his life in that post, involving himself deeply in Irish politics. His masterpiece, *Gulliver's Travels* (1726), embodies Swift's increasing disgust with his fellow human beings. "A Modest Proposal," written in 1729, reflects his mordant view of callous British administrators and absentee landowners whose indifference to the sufferings of the Irish poor during a time of famine filled him with indignation.

FOR PREVENTING THE CHILDREN OF POOR PEOPLE IN IRELAND FROM BEING A BURDEN TO THEIR PARENTS OR COUNTRY, AND FOR MAKING THEM BENEFICIAL TO THE PUBLIC

It is melancholy object to those who walk through this great town or travel in the country, when they see the streets, the roads, and cabin doors, crowded with beggars of the female-sex, followed by three, four, or six children, all in rags and importuning every passenger for an alms. These mothers, instead of being able to work for their honest livelihood, are forced to employ all their time in strolling to beg sustenance for their helpless infants, who, as they grow up, either turn thieves for want of work, or leave their dear native country to fight for the Pretender in Spain, or sell themselves to the Barbadoes. 1

I think it is agreed by all parties that this prodigious number of children in the arms, or on the backs, or at the heels of their mothers, and frequently of their fathers, is in the present deplorable state of the kingdom a very great additional grievance; and therefore whoever could find out a fair, cheap, and easy method of making these children sound, useful members of the commonwealth would deserve so well of the public as to have his statue set up for a preserver of the nation. 2

But my intention is very far from being confined to provide only for the children of professed beggars; it is of a much greater extent, and shall take in the whole number of infants at a certain age who are born of parents in effects as little able to support them as those who demand our charity in the streets. 3

419

As to my own part, having turned my thoughts for many years upon this   4
important subject, and maturely weighed the several schemes of other projectors, I have always found them grossly mistaken in their computation. It is
true, a child just dropped from its dam may be supported by her milk for a
solar year, with little other nourishment; at most not above the value of two
shillings, which the mother may certainly get, or the value in scraps, by her
lawful occupation of begging; and it is exactly at one year old that I propose
to provide for them in such a manner as instead of being a charge upon their
parents or the parish, or wanting food and raiment for the rest of their lives,
they shall on the contrary contribute to the feeding, and partly to the clothing, of many thousands.

There is likewise another great advantage in my scheme, that it will pre-   5
vent those voluntary abortions, and that horrid practice of women murdering their bastard children, alas, too frequent among us, sacrificing the poor
innocent babes, I doubt, more to avoid the expense than the shame, which
would move tears and pity in the most savage and inhuman breast.

The number of souls in this kingdom being usually reckoned one million   6
and a half, of these I calculate there may be about two hundred thousand couple whose wives are breeders; from which number I subtract thirty thousand
couple who are able to maintain their own children, although I apprehend
there cannot be so many under the present distresses of the kingdom; but this
being granted, there will remain an hundred and seventy thousand breeders.
I again subtract fifty thousand for those women who miscarry, or whose children die by accident or disease within the year. There only remain an hundred and twenty thousand children of poor parents annually born. The question therefore is, how this number shall be reared and provided for, which, as
I have already said, under the present situation of affairs, is utterly impossible by all the methods hitherto proposed. For we can neither employ them in
handicraft or agriculture; we neither build houses (I mean in the country) nor
cultivate land. They can very seldom pick up a livelihood by stealing till they
arrive at six years old, except where they are of towardly parts; although I
confess they learn the rudiments much earlier, during which time they can
however be looked upon only as probationers, as I have been informed by a
principal gentleman in the county of Cavan, who protested to me that he never
knew above one or two instances under the age of six, even in a part of the
kingdom so renowned for the quickest proficiency in that art.

I am assured by our merchants that a boy or a girl before twelve years old   7
is no salable commodity; and even when they come to this age they will not
yield above three pounds, or three pounds and half a crown at most on the
Exchange; which cannot turn to account either to the parents or the kingdom,
the charge of nutriment and rags having been at least four times that value.

I shall now therefore humbly propose my own thoughts, which I hope   8
will not be liable to the least objection.

I have been assured by a very knowing American of my acquaintance in   9
London, that a young healthy child well nursed is at a year old a most delicious,

nourishing, and wholesome food, whether stewed, roasted, baked, or boiled; and I make no doubt that it will equally serve in a fricasse or a ragout.

I do therefore humbly offer it to public consideration that of the hundred 10 and twenty thousand children, already computed, twenty thousand may be reserved for breed, whereof only one fourth part to be males, which is more than we allow to sheep, black cattle, or swine; and my reason is that these children are seldom the fruits of marriage, a circumstance not much regarded by our savages, therefore one male will be sufficient to serve four females. That the remaining hundred thousand may at a year old be offered in sale to the persons of quality and fortune through the kingdom, always advising the mother to let them suck plentifully in the last month, so as to render them plump and fat for a good table. A child will make two dishes at an entertainment for friends; and when the family dines alone, the fore or hind quarter will make a reasonable dish, and seasoned with a little pepper or salt will be very good boiled on the fourth day, especially in winter.

I have reckoned upon a medium that a child just born will weigh twelve 11 pounds, and in a solar year if tolerably nursed increased to twenty-eight pounds.

I grant this food will be somewhat dear, and therefore very proper for 12 landlords, who, as they have already devoured most of the parents, seem to have the best title to the children.

Infant's flesh will be in season throughout the year, but more plentiful in 13 March, and a little before and after. For we are told by a grave author, an eminent French physician, that fish being a prolific diet, there are more children born in Roman Catholic countries about nine months after Lent than at any other season; therefore, reckoning a year after Lent, the markets will be more glutted than usual, because the number of popish infants is at least three to one in this kingdom; and therefore it will have one other collateral advantage, by lessening the number of Papists among us.

I have already computed the charge of nursing a beggar's child (in which 14 list I reckon all cottagers, laborers, and four fifths of the farmers) to be about two shillings per annum, rags included; and I believe no gentleman would repine to give ten shillings for the carcass of a good fat child, which, as I have said, will make four dishes of excellent nutritive meat, when he hath only some particular friend or his own family to dine with him. Thus the squire will learn to be a good landlord, and grow popular among the tenants; the mother will have eight shillings net profit, and be fit for work till she produces another child.

Those who are more thrifty (as I must confess the times require) may flay 15 the carcass; the skin of which artificially dressed will make admirable gloves for ladies, and summer boots for fine gentlemen.

As to our city of Dublin, shambles may be appointed for this purpose in 16 the most convenient parts of it, and butchers we may be assured will not be wanting; although I rather recommend buying the children alive, and dressing them hot from the knife as we do roasting pigs.

A very worthy person, a true lover of his country, and whose virtues I highly 17
esteem, was lately pleased in discoursing on this matter to offer a refinement
upon my scheme. He said that many gentlemen of this kingdom, having of late
destroyed their deer, he conceived that the want of venison might be well supplied by the bodies of young lads and maidens, not exceeding fourteen years of
age nor under twelve, so great a number of both sexes in every county being
now ready to starve for want of work and service; and these to be disposed of
by their parents, if alive, or otherwise by their nearest relations. But with due
deference to so excellent a friend and so deserving a patriot, I cannot be altogether in his sentiments; for as to the males, my American acquaintance assured
me from frequent experience that their flesh was generally tough and lean, like
that of our schoolboys, by continual exercise, and their taste disagreeable; and
to fatten them would not answer the charge. Then as to the females, it would,
I think with humble submission, be a loss to the public, because they soon would
become breeders themselves: and besides, it is not improbable that some scrupulous people might be apt to censure such a practice (although indeed very unjustly) as a little bordering upon cruelty; which, I confess, hath always been with
me the strongest objection against any project, how well soever intended.

But in order to justify my friend, he confessed that this expedient was put 18
into his head by the famous Psalmanazar, a native of the island Formosa, who
came from thence to London above twenty years ago, and in conversation
told my friend that in his country when any young person happened to be
put to death, the executioner sold the carcass to persons of quality as a prime
dainty; and that in his time the body of a plump girl of fifteen, who was crucified for an attempt to poison the emperor, was sold to his Imperial Majesty's
prime minister of state, and other great mandarins of the court, in joints from
the gibbet, at four hundred crowns. Neither indeed can I deny that if the same
use were made of several plump young girls in this town, who without one
single groat to their fortunes cannot stir abroad without a chair, and appear
at the playhouse and assemblies in foreign fineries which they never will pay
for, the kingdom would not be the worse.

Some persons of a desponding spirit are in great concern about that vast 19
number of poor people who are aged, diseased, or maimed, and I have been
desired to employ my thoughts what course may be taken to ease the nation
of so grievous an encumbrance. But I am not in the least pain upon that matter, because it is very well known that they are every day dying and rotting
by cold and famine, and filth and vermin, as fast as can be reasonably expected. And as to the younger laborers, they are now in almost as hopeful a
condition. They cannot get work, and consequently pine away for want of
nourishment to a degree that if at any time they are accidentally hired to common labor, they have not strength to perform it; and thus the country and
themselves are happily delivered from the evils to come.

I have too long digressed, and therefore shall return to my subject. I think 20
the advantages by the proposal which I have made are obvious and many, as
well as of the highest importance.

For first, as I have already observed, it would greatly lessen the number   21
of Papists, with whom we are yearly overrun, being the principal breeders of
the nation as well as our most dangerous enemies; and who stay at home on
purpose to deliver the kingdom to the Pretender, hoping to take their advantage by the absence of so many good Protestants, who have chosen rather to
leave their country than to stay at home and pay tithes against their conscience
to an Episcopal curate.

Secondly, the poorer tenants will have something valuable of their own,   22
which by law may be made liable to distress, and help to pay their landlord's
rent, their corn and cattle being already seized and money a thing unknown.

Thirdly, whereas the maintenance of an hundred thousand children, from   23
two years old and upwards, cannot be computed at less than ten shillings a
piece per annum, the nation's stock will be thereby increased fifty thousand
pounds per annum, besides the profit of a new dish introduced to the tables
of all gentlemen of fortune in the kingdom who have any refinement in taste.
And the money will circulate among ourselves, the goods being entirely of our
own growth and manufacture.

Fourthly, the constant breeders, besides the gain of eight shillings sterling   24
per annum by the sale of their children, will be rid of the charge of maintaining them after the first year.

Fifthly, this food would likewise bring great custom to taverns, where the   25
vintners will certainly be so prudent as to procure the best receipts for dressing it to perfection, and consequently have their houses frequented by all the
fine gentlemen, who justly value themselves upon their knowledge in good
eating; and a skillful cook, who understands how to oblige his guests, will
contrive to make it as expensive as they please.

Sixthly, this would be a great inducement to marriage, which all wise   26
nations have either encouraged by rewards or enforced by laws and penalties. It would increase the care and tenderness of mothers toward their children, when they were sure of a settlement for life to the poor babes, provided in some sort by the public, to their annual profit instead of expense.
We should see an honest emulation among the married women, which of
them could bring the fattest child to the market. Men would become as fond
of their wives during the time of their pregnancy as they are now of their
mares in foal, their cows in calf, or sows when they are ready to farrow;
nor offer to beat or kick them (as is too frequent a practice) for fear of a
miscarriage.

Many other advantages might be enumerated. For instance, the addition   27
of some thousand carcasses in our exportation of barreled beef, the propagation of swine's flesh, and improvement in the art of making good bacon, so
much wanted among us by the great destruction of pigs, too frequent at our
tables, which are no way comparable in taste or magnificence to a well-grown,
fat, yearling child, which roasted whole will make a considerable figure at a
lord mayor's feast or any other public entertainment. But this and many others I omit, being studious of brevity.

Supposing that one thousand families in this city would be constant cus-   28
tomers for infants' flesh, besides others who might have it at merry meetings,
particularly weddings and christenings, I compute that Dublin would take off
annually about twenty thousand carcasses, and the rest of the kingdom (where
probably they will be sold somewhat cheaper) the remaining eighty thousand.

I can think of no one objection that will possibly be raised against this   29
proposal, unless it should be urged that the number of people will be thereby
much lessened in the kingdom. This I freely own, and it was indeed one principal design in offering it to the world. I desire the reader will observe, that
I calculate my remedy for this one individual kingdom of Ireland and for no
other that ever was, is, or I think ever can be upon earth. Therefore let no
man talk to me of other expedients: of taxing our absentees at five shillings
a pound: of using neither clothes nor household furniture except what is of
our own growth and manufacture: of utterly rejecting the materials and instruments that promote foreign luxury: of curing the expensiveness of pride,
vanity, idleness, and gaming in our women: of introducing a vein of parsi-
mony, prudence, and temperance: of learning to love our country, in the want
of which we differ even from Laplanders and the inhabitants of Topinamboo:
of quitting our animosities and factions, nor acting any longer like the Jews,
who were murdering one another at the very moment their city was taken: of
being a little cautious not to sell our country and conscience for nothing: of
teaching landlords to have at least one degree of mercy toward their tenants:
lastly, of putting a spirit of honesty, industry, and skill into our shopkeepers;
who, if a resolution could now be taken to buy only our native goods, would
immediately unite to cheat and exact upon us in the price, the measure, and
the goodness, nor could ever yet be brought to make one fair proposal of just
dealing, though often and earnestly invited to it.

Therefore I repeat, let no man talk to me of these and the like expedients,   30
till he hath at least some glimpse of hope that there will ever be some hearty
and sincere attempt to put them in practice.

But as to myself, having been wearied out for many years with offering   31
vain, idle, visionary thoughts, and at length utterly despairing of success, I
fortunately fell upon this proposal, which, as it is wholly new, so it hath something solid and real, of no expense and little trouble, full in our own power,
and whereby we can incur no danger in disobliging England. For this kind of
commodity will not bear exportation, the flesh being of too tender a consis-
tence to admit a long continuance in salt, although perhaps I could name a
country which would be glad to eat up our whole nation without it.

After all, I am not so violently bent upon my own opinion as to reject   32
any offer proposed by wise men, which shall be found equally innocent, cheap,
easy, and effectual. But before something of that kind shall be advanced in
contradiction to my scheme, and offering a better, I desire the author or authors will be pleased maturely to consider two points. First, as things now
stand, how they will be able to find food and raiment for an hundred thousand useless mouths and backs. And secondly, there being a round million of

creatures in human figure throughout this kingdom, whose sole subsistence put into a common stock would leave them in debt two millions of pounds sterling, adding those who are beggars by profession to the bulk of farmers, cottagers, and laborers, with their wives and children who are beggars in effect; I desire those politicians who dislike my overture, and may perhaps be so bold to attempt an answer, that they will first ask the parents of these mortals whether they would not at this day think it a great happiness to have been sold for food at a year old in the manner I prescribe, and thereby have avoided such a perpetual scene of misfortunes as they have since gone through by the oppression of landlords, the impossibility of paying rent without money or trade, the want of common sustenance, with neither house nor clothes to cover them from the inclemencies of the weather, and the most inevitable prospect of entailing the like or greater miseries upon their breed forever.

I profess, in the sincerity of my heart, that I have not the least personal 33 interest in endeavoring to promote this necessary work, having no other motive than the public good of my country, by advancing our trade, providing for infants, relieving the poor, and giving some pleasure to the rich. I have no children by which I can propose to get a single penny; the youngest being nine years old, and my wife past childbearing.

Liberty or Death
Patrick Henry

Patrick Henry (1736–1799) was a shopkeeper who educated himself to become one of Virginia's leading trial lawyers. Having started his law practice in 1760 at the age of twenty-four, Henry—always sharp-tongued—became a public figure three years later when, in arguing "The Parson's Cause" case, he denounced King George III as a tyrant for reversing a law passed by the Virginia House of Burgesses. Two more years found him in the House of Burgesses himself and at the center of the Stamp Act crisis; it was Henry who presented the seven "Virginia resolutions" against the act, reportedly closing his speech with a statement that George III should profit from the example of Julius Caesar (who was assassinated by members of his senate). When this raised cries of "Treason!" from the assembly, Henry is supposed to have answered, "If this be treason, make the most of it." His most famous statement, however, is the one with which the following selection concludes. The speech, calling for an armed militia, was delivered on March 23, 1775, in St. John's Church, Richmond, to the second Virginia Convention.

Mr. President: No man thinks more highly than I do of the patriotism, as 1 well as abilities, of the very worthy gentlemen who have just addressed the House. But different men often see the same subject in different lights; and, therefore, I hope it will not be thought disrespectful to those gentlemen if, entertaining as I do opinions of a character very opposite to theirs, I shall speak forth my sentiments freely and without reserve. This is no time for ceremony. The question before the House is one of awful moment to this country. For my own part, I consider it as nothing less than a question of freedom or slavery; and in proportion to the magnitude of the subject ought to be the freedom of the debate. It is only in this way that we can hope to arrive at truth, and fulfill the great responsibility which we hold to God and our country. Should I keep back my opinions at such a time, through fear of giving offense, I should consider myself as guilty of treason towards my country, and of an act of disloyalty toward the Majesty of Heaven, which I revere above all earthly kings.

Mr. President, it is natural to man to indulge in the illusions of hope. We 2 are apt to shut our eyes against a painful truth, and listen to the song of that siren till she transforms us into beasts. Is this the part of wise men, engaged in a great and arduous struggle for liberty? Are we disposed to be of the number of those who, having eyes, see not, and, having ears, hear not, the things which so nearly concern their temporal salvation? For my part, whatever anguish of spirit it may cost, I am willing to know the whole truth to know the worst, and to provide for it.

I have but one lamp by which my feet are guided, and that is the lamp of experience. I know of no way of judging of the future but by the past. And judging by the past, I wish to know what there has been in the conduct of the British ministry for the last ten years to justify those hopes with which gentlemen have been pleased to solace themselves and the House. Is it that insidious smile with which our petition has been lately received? Trust it not, sir; it will prove a snare to your feet. Suffer not yourselves to be betrayed with a kiss. Ask yourselves how this gracious reception of our petition comports with those warlike preparations which cover our waters and darken our land. Are fleets and armies necessary to a work of love and reconciliation? Have we shown ourselves so unwilling to be reconciled that force must be called in to win back our love? Let us not deceive ourselves, sir. These are the implements of war and subjugation; the last arguments to which kings resort. I ask gentlemen, sir, what means this martial array, if its purpose be not to force us to submission? Can gentlemen assign any other possible motive for it? Has Great Britain any enemy, in this quarter of the world, to call for all this accumulation of navies and armies? No, sir, she has none. They are meant for us: they can be meant for no other. They are sent over to bind and rivet upon us those chains which the British ministry have been so long forging. And what have we to oppose to them? Shall we try argument? Sir, we have been trying that for the last ten years. Have we anything new to offer upon the subject? Nothing. We have held the subject up in every light of which it is capable; but it has been all in vain. Shall we resort to entreaty and humble supplication? What terms shall we find which have not been already exhausted? Let us not, I beseech you, sir, deceive ourselves longer. Sir, we have done everything that could be done to avert the storm which is now coming on. We have petitioned; we have remonstrated; we have supplicated; we have prostrated ourselves before the throne, and have implored its interposition to arrest the tyrannical hands of the ministry and Parliament. Our petitions have been slighted; our remonstrances have produced additional violence and insult; our supplications have been disregarded; and we have been spurned, with contempt, from the foot of the throne! In vain, after these things, may we indulge the fond hope of peace and reconciliation. There is no longer any room for hope. If we wish to be free—if we mean to preserve inviolate those inestimable privileges for which we have been so long contending—if we mean not basely to abandon the noble struggle in which we have been so long engaged, and which we have pledged ourselves never to abandon until the glorious object of our contest shall be obtained—we must fight! I repeat it, sir, we must fight! An appeal to arms and to the God of Hosts is all that is left us!

They tell us, sir, that we are weak; unable to cope with so formidable an adversary. But when shall we be stronger? Will it be the next week, or the next year? Will it be when we are totally disarmed, and when a British guard shall be stationed in every house? Shall we gather strength by irresolution and inaction? Shall we acquire the means of effectual resistance by lying supinely on our backs and hugging the delusive phantom of hope, until our enemies shall have bound us hand and foot? Sir, we are not weak if we make a proper use of those means which the God of nature hath placed in our power. Three millions of people, armed in the holy cause of liberty, and in such a country as that which we possess, are invincible by any force which our enemy can send against us. Besides, sir, we shall not fight our battles alone. There is a just God who presides over the destinies of nations, and who will raise up friends to fight our battles for us. The battle, sir, is not to the strong alone; it is to the vigilant, the active, the brave. Besides, sir, we have no election. If we were base enough to desire it, it is now too late to retire from the contest. There is no retreat but in submission and slavery! Our chains are forged! Their clanking may be heard on the plains of Boston! The war is inevitable—and let it come! I repeat it, sir, let it come.

It is in vain, sir, to extenuate the matter. Gentlemen may cry, Peace, Peace—   5 but there is no peace. The war is actually begun! The next gale that sweeps from the north will bring to our ears the clash of resounding arms! Our brethren are already in the field! Why stand we here idle? What is it that gentlemen wish? What would they have? Is life so dear, or peace so sweet, as to be purchased at the price of chains and slavery? Forbid it, Almighty God! I know not what course others may take, but as for me, give me liberty or give me death!

The Declaration of Independence
Thomas Jefferson

A man with an astonishing range of talents, Thomas Jefferson (1743–1826) served as a member of the Virginia House of Burgesses, as a delegate to the Continental Congress (where he drafted the Declaration of Independence), as governor of Virginia, as ambassador to France, and then as our first secretary of state (under George Washington), our second vice-president (under John Adams), and, from 1801 to 1809, our third president. He was also a scientist, an inventor, an architect, a farmer, a historian, and one of the most original political and social philosophers of his day, becoming president of the American Philosophical Society in 1797. Retiring to his beloved Monticello in 1809, he went on to found the University of Virginia, whose campus and buildings he designed. It was only logical that Jefferson's colleagues in the Second Continental Congress of 1775–1776 should choose him to draft the Declaration of Independence, for he was already one of the most articulate men of his—or any—time. Jefferson's complete draft is reproduced here as Garry Wills has reconstructed it from Jefferson's published papers. Brackets and underlining indicate the parts of Jefferson's original draft that were struck out by the Congress (one member of which was Benjamin Franklin). Revisions that were inserted appear either in the margin or in a parallel column.

A Declaration by the representatives of the United states 1
of America, in [General] Congress assembled.

When in the course of human events it becomes neces- 2
sary for one people to dissolve the political bands which have
connected them with another, and to assume among the powers of the earth the separate & equal station to which the
laws of nature and of nature's god entitle them, a decent respect to the opinions of mankind requires that they should
declare the causes which impel them to the separation.

We hold these truths to be self evident: that all men are 3
created equal; that they are endowed by their creator with ∧
certain   [inherent and] inalienable rights; that among these are life, liberty & the pursuit of happiness: that to secure these rights,
governments are instituted among men, deriving their just
powers from the consent of the governed; that whenever any
form of government becomes destructive of these ends, it is
the right of the people to alter or to abolish it, & to institute

new government, laying it's foundation on such principles, &
organising it's power in such form, as to them shall seem most
likely to effect their safety & happiness. Prudence indeed will
dictate that governments long established should not be
changed for light & transient causes; and accordingly all experience hath shewn that mankind are more disposed to suffer while evils are sufferable than to right themselves by
abolishing the forms to which they are accustomed. But
when a long train of abuses & usurpations [begun at a distinguished period and] pursuing invariably by the same object, evinces a design to reduce them under absolute des-
potism it is their right, it is their duty to throw off such
government, & to provide new guards for their future security. Such has been the patient sufferance of these colonies;
& such is now the necessity which constrains them to ∧
alter   [expunge] their former systems of government. The history
of the present king of Great Britain is a history of ∧ [un-
repeated   remitting] injuries & usurpations, [among which appears no
solitary fact to contradict the uniform tenor of the rest but
all having   all have] ∧ in direct object the establishment of an absolute
tyranny over these states. To prove this let facts be submit-
ted to a candid world [for the truth of which we pledge a
faith yet unsullied by falsehood].

He has refused his assent to laws the most wholesome &   4
necessary for the public good.

He has forbidden his governors to pass laws of imme-   5
diate & pressing importance, unless suspended in their operation till his assent should be obtained; & when so suspended, he has utterly neglected to attend to them.

He has refused to pass other laws for the accommo-   6
dation of large districts of people, unless those people
would relinquish the right of representation in the legislature, a right inestimable to them, & formidable to
tyrants only.

He has called together legislative bodies at places un-   7
usual, uncomfortable, and distant from the depository of
their public records, for the sole purpose of fatiguing them
into compliance with his measures.

He has dissolved representative houses repeatedly [&   8
continually] for opposing with manly firmness his invasions
on the rights of the people.

He has refused for a long time after such dissolutions   9
to cause others to be elected, whereby the legislative powers, incapable of annihilation, have returned to the people

at large for their exercise, the state remaining in the mean time exposed to all the dangers of invasion from without & convulsions within.

He has endeavored to prevent the population of these states; for that purpose obstructing the laws for naturalization of foreigners, refusing to pass others to encourage their migrations hither, & raising the conditions of new appropriations of lands.   10

obstructed by   He has ∧ [suffered] the administration of justice [totally to cease in some of these states] ∧ refusing his assent to laws for establishing judiciary powers.   11

He has made [our] judges dependant on his will alone, for the tenure of their offices, & the amount & payment of their salaries.   12

He has erected a multitude of new offices [by a self assumed power] and sent hither swarms of new officers to harrass our people and eat out their substance.   13

He has kept among us in times of peace standing armies [and ships of war] without the consent of our legislatures.   14

He has affected to render the military independent of, & superior to the civil power.   15

He has combined with others to subject us to a jurisdiction foreign to our constitutions & unacknowledged by our laws, giving his assent to their acts of pretended legislation for quartering large bodies of armed troops among us; for protecting them by a mock-trial from punishment for any murders which they should commit on the inhabitants of these states; for cutting off our trade with all parts of the world; for imposing taxes on us without our consent;   *in many cases*   for depriving us ∧ of the benefits of trial by jury; for transporting us beyond seas to be tried for pretended offences; for abolishing the free system of English laws in a neighboring province, establishing therein an arbitrary government, and enlarging its boundaries, so as to render it at once an example and fit instrument for introducing   *colonies*   the same absolute rule and these ∧ [states]; for taking away our charters, abolishing our most valuable laws, and altering fundamentally the forms of our governments; for suspending our own legislatures, & declaring themselves invested with power to legislate for us in all cases whatsoever.   16

by declaring us out of his protection & waging war against us   He has abdicated government here ∧ [withdrawing his governors, and declaring us out of his allegiance & protection].   17

He has plundered our seas, ravaged our coasts, burnt   18
our towns, & destroyed the lives of our people.

He is at this time transporting large armies of foreign,   19
mercenaries to compleat the works of death, desolation &
tyranny already begun with circumstances of cruelty and
perfidy ∧ unworthy the head of a civilized nation.

scarcely
paralleled in the
most barbarous
ages, & totally

He has constrained our fellow citizens taken captive on   20
the high seas to bear arms against their country, to become
the executioners of their friends & brethren, or to fall themselves by their hands.

excited domestic
insurrections
amongst us, &
has

He has ∧ endeavored to bring on the inhabitants of our   21
frontiers the merciless Indian savages, whose known rule of
warfare is an undistinguished destruction of all ages, sexes,
& conditions [of existence].

[He has incited treasonable insurrections of our fellow   22
citizens, with the allurements of forfeiture & confiscation
of our property.

He has waged cruel war against human nature itself, vi-   23
olating it's most sacred rights of life and liberty in the
persons of a distant people who never offended him, capti-
vating & carrying them into slavery in another hemisphere
or to incur miserable death in their transportation thither.
This piratical warfare, the opprobrium of *infidel* powers, is
the warfare of the *Christian* king of Great Britain. Determined
to keep open a market where *Men* should be bought & sold,
he has prostituted his negative for suppressing every legislative attempt to prohibit or to restrain this execrable commerce. And that this assemblage of horrors might want no
fact of distinguished die, he is now exciting those very people to rise in arms among us, and to purchase that liberty
of which he has deprived them, by murdering the people
on whom he also obtruded them: thus paying off former
crimes committed against the *Liberties* of one people, with
crimes which he urges them to commit against the *lives* of
another].

In every stage of these oppressions we have petitioned   24
for redress in the most humble terms: our repeated petitions
have been answered only by repeated injuries. A prince
whose character is thus marked by every act which may de-

free

fine a tyrant is unfit to be the ruler of a ∧ people [who
mean to be free. Future ages will scarcely believe that the
hardiness of one man adventured, within the short compass
of twelve years only, to lay a foundation so broad & so
undisguised for tyranny over a people fostered & fixed in
principles of freedom].

25

Nor have we been wanting in attentions to our British brethren. We have warned them from time to time of attempts by their legislature to extend ∧ [a] jurisdiction over ∧ [these our states]. We have reminded them of the circumstances of our emigration & settlement here, [no one of which could warrant so strange a pretension: that these were effected at the expense of our own blood & treasure, unassisted by the wealth or the strength of Great Britain: that in constituting indeed our several forms of government, we had adopted one common king, thereby laying a foundation for perpetual league & amity with them: but that submission to their parliament was no part of our constitution, nor ever in idea, if history may be credited: and,] we ∧ appealed to their native justice and magnanimity ∧ [as well as to] the ties of our common kindred to disavow these usurpations which ∧ [were likely to] interrupt our connection and correspondence. They too have been deaf to the voice of justice & of consanguinity, [and when occasions have been given them, by the regular course of their laws, of removing from their councils the disturbers of our harmony, they have, by their free election, re-established them in power. At this very time too they are permitting their chief magistrate to send over not only soldiers of our common blood, but Scotch & foreign mercenaries to invade & destroy us. These facts have given the last stab to agonizing affection, and manly spirit bids us to renounce for ever these unfeeling brethren. We must endeavor to forget our former love for them, and to hold them as we hold the rest of mankind enemies in war, in peace friends. We might have been a free and a great people together; but a communication of grandeur & of freedom it seems is below their dignity. Be it so, since they will have it. The road to happiness & to glory is open to us too. We will tread it apart from them, and] ∧ acquiesce in the necessity which denounces our [eternal] separation ∧ !

Marginal notes:

an unwarrantetable
us

have and we have
conjured them by
would inevitably

we must therefore
and hold them as
we hold the rest
of mankind,
enemies in war, in
peace friends

26

We therefore the representatives of the United States of America in General Congress assembled do in the name, & by the authority of the good people of these [states reject & renounce all allegiance & subjection to the kings of Great Britain & all others

We therefore the representatives of the United States of America in General Congress assembled, appealing to the supreme judge of the world for the rectitude of our intentions, do in the name, & by the authority of the good people of these colonies,

who may hereafter claim by, through or under them: we utterly dissolve all political connection which may theretofore have subsisted between us & the people or parliament of Great Briian: & finally we do assert & declare these colonies to be free & independant states,] & that as free & independant states, they have full power to levy war, conclude peace, contract alliances, establish commerce, & to do all other acts & things which independant states may of right do. And for the support of this declaration we mutually pledge to each other our lives, our fortunes & our sacred honour.

solemnly publish & declare that these United colonies are & of right ought to be free & independant states; that they are absolved from all allegiance to the British crown, and that all political connection between them & the state of Great Britain is, & ought to be, totally dissolved; & that as free & independant states they have full power to levy war, conclude peace, contract alliances, establish commerce & to do all other acts & things which independant states may of right do.

And for the support of this declaration, with a firm reliance on the protection of divine providence we mutually pledge to each other our lives, our fortunes & our sacred honour.

The Prevailing Opinion of a Sexual Character Discussed

Mary Wollstonecraft

Mary Wollstonecraft (1759–1797), a major figure in the history of the struggle for women's rights, was well known in her own time not only as an advocate of women's rights but as a political thinker on a more comprehensive scale. In an age when it was notoriously difficult for a woman to support herself financially, Wollstonecraft (whose father's drinking had ruined the family) supported herself first as a governess, the traditional occupation for single women, and then by working for a London publisher, James Johnson. After spending several years in France observing the French Revolution at first hand, she returned to London and again worked for Johnson, becoming part of the group of influential radicals he gathered about himself, of which William Blake, William Wordsworth, and William Godwin were also members. Eventually she married Godwin, and not long afterward she died giving birth to a daughter, Mary (who later became the wife of the poet Percy Bysshe Shelley and wrote the novel *Frankenstein*). *A Vindication of the Rights of Woman*, from which the following section is taken, argues mainly for intellectual rather than social or political rights for women.

1 To account for, and excuse the tyranny of man, many ingenious arguments have been brought forward to prove, that the two sexes, in the acquirement of virtue, ought to aim at attaining a very different character: or, to speak explicitly, women are not allowed to have sufficient strength of mind to acquire what really deserves the name of virtue. Yet it should seem, allowing them to have souls, that there is but one way appointed by Providence to lead *mankind* to either virtue or happiness.

2 If then women are not a swarm of ephemeron triflers, why should they be kept in ignorance under the specious name of innocence? Men complain, and with reason, of the follies and caprices of our sex, when they do not keenly satirize our headstrong passions and groveling vices.—Behold, I should answer, the natural effect of ignorance? The mind will ever be unstable that has only prejudices to rest on, and the current will run with destructive fury when there are no barriers to break its force. Women are told from their infancy, and taught by the example of their mothers, that a little knowledge of human weakness, justly termed cunning, softness of temper, *outward* obedience, and a scrupulous attention to a puerile kind of propriety, will obtain for them protection of man; and should they be beautiful, every thing else is needless, for, at least, twenty years of their lives.

Thus Milton describes our first frail mother; though when he tells us that   3
women are formed for softness and sweet attractive grace, I cannot compre-
hend his meaning, unless, in the true Mahometan strain, he meant to deprive
us of souls, and insinuate that we were beings only designed by sweet attractive grace, and docile blind obedience, to gratify the senses of man when he
can no longer soar on the wing of contemplation.

How grossly do they insult us who thus advise us only to render ourselves   4
gentle, domestic brutes? For instance, the winning softness so warmly, and
frequently, recommended, that governs by obeying. What childish expressions,
and how insignificant is the being—can it be an immortal one? who will con-
descend to govern by such sinister methods! "Certainly," says Lord Bacon,
"man is of kin to the beasts by his body; and if he be not of kin to God by
his spirit, he is a base and ignoble creature!" Men, indeed, appear to me to
act in a very unphilosophical manner when they try to secure the good conduct of women by attempting to keep them always in a state of childhood.
Rousseau [whom Wollstonecraft argues against earlier, in a passage omitted
here] was more consistent when he wished to stop the progress of reason in
both sexes, for if men eat of the tree of knowledge, women will come in for
a taste; but, from the imperfect cultivation which their understandings now
receive, they only attain a knowledge of evil.

Children, I grant, should be innocent; but when the epithet is applied to   5
men or women, it is but a civil term for weakness. For if it be allowed that
women were destined by Providence to acquire human virtues, and by the exercise of their understandings, that stability of character which is the firmest
ground to rest our future hopes upon, they must be permitted to turn to the
fountain of light, and not forced to shape their course by the twinkling of a
mere satellite. Milton, I grant, was of very different opinion; for he only bends
to the indefeasible right of beauty, though it would be difficult to render two
passages which I now mean to contrast, consistent. But into similar inconsis-
tencies are great men often led by their senses.

> To whom thus Eve with *perfect beauty* adorn'd
> "My Author and Disposer, what thou bidst
> *Unargued* I obey; So God ordains;
> God is *thy law, thou mine:* to know no more
> Is Woman's *happiest* knowledge and her *praise.*

These are exactly the arguments that I have used to children; but I have   6
added, your reason is now gaining strength, and, till it arrives at some degree
of maturity, you must look up to me for advice—then you ought to *think,*
and only rely on God.

Yet in the following lines Milton seems to coincide with me; when he   7
makes Adam thus expostulate with his Maker.

> Hast thou not made me here thy substitute,
> And these inferior far beneath me set?

Among *unequals* what society
Can sort, what harmony or true delight?
Which must be mutual, in proportion due
Giv'n and receiv'd; but in *disparity*
The one intense, the other still remiss
Cannot well suit with either, but soon prove
Tedious alike: of *fellowship* I speak
Such as I seek, fit to participate
All rational delight—

In treating, therefore, of the manners of women, let us, disregarding sensual arguments, trace what we should endeavour to make them in order to cooperate, if the expression be not too bold, with the supreme Being. 8

By individual education, I mean, for the sense of the word is not precisely defined, such an attention to a child as will slowly sharpen the senses, form the temper, regulate the passions as they begin to ferment, and set the understanding to work before the body arrives at maturity; so that the man may only have to proceed, not to begin, the important task of learning to think and reason. 9

To prevent any misconstruction, I must add, that I do not believe that a private education can work the wonders which some sanguine writers have attributed to it. Men and women must be educated, in a great degree, by the opinions and manners of the society they live in. In every age there has been a stream of popular opinion that has carried all before it, and given a family character, as it were, to the century. It may then fairly be inferred, that, till society be differently constituted, much cannot be expected from education. It is, however, sufficient for my present purpose to assert, that, whatever effect circumstances have on the abilities, every being may become virtuous by the exercise of its own reason; for if but one being was created with vicious inclinations, that is positively bad, what can save us from atheism? or if we worship a God, is not that God a devil? 10

Consequently, the most perfect education, in my opinion, is such an exercise of the understanding as is best calculated to strengthen the body and form the heart. Or, in other words, to enable the individual to attain such habits of virtue as will render it independent. In fact, it is a farce to call any being virtuous whose virtues do not result from the exercise of its own reason. This was Rousseau's opinion respecting men: I extend it to women, and confidently assert that they have been drawn out of their sphere by false refinement, and not by an endeavour to acquire masculine qualities. Still the regal homage which they receive is so intoxicating, that till the manners of the times are changed, and formed on more reasonable principles, it may be impossible to convince them that the illegitimate power, which they obtain, by degrading themselves, is a curse, and that they must return to nature and equality, if they wish to secure the placid satisfaction that unsophisticated affections impart. But for this epoch we must wait—wait, perhaps, till kings and nobles, enlightened by reason, and, preferring the real dignity of man to childish state, throw off their gaudy hereditary trappings: and if then women do not resign the arbitrary power of beauty—they will prove that they have *less* mind than man. 11

Where I Lived, and What I Lived For
Henry David Thoreau

Henry David Thoreau (1817–1862) remains for many Americans the most appealing of those nineteenth-century writers and thinkers known as the Transcendentalists (of whom Thoreau's friend Ralph Waldo Emerson was the most eminent). Well educated in the Greek and Latin classics and also in the modern languages, Thoreau briefly taught school and then worked as a tutor in his hometown of Concord, Massachusetts. In 1845 he built his now-famous cabin on some property belonging to the Emerson family near Walden Pond and began his experiment in simplifying his life to understand its real values. *Walden,* from which the following selection is taken, records and reflects upon that experience. Begun in 1846, *Walden* was not published until 1854, seven years after Thoreau had left the cabin. During those years he had published his first book, *A Week on the Concord and Merrimack Rivers,* based on his journal of a trip with his brother John, and his famous essay "Civil Disobedience," whose doctrine of nonviolent resistance was later to influence both Mahatma Gandhi in his struggle for an independent India and the Reverend Martin Luther King, Jr., in his struggle for civil rights for black Americans.

1   I went to the woods because I wished to live deliberately, to front only the essential facts of life, and see if I could not learn what it had to teach, and not, when I came to die, discover that I had not lived. I did not wish to live what was not life, living is so dear, nor did I wish to practice resignation, unless it was quite necessary. I wanted to live deep and suck out all the marrow of life, to live so sturdily and Spartan-like as to put to rout all that was not life, to cut a broad swath and shave close, to drive life into a corner, and reduce it to its lowest terms, and, if it proved to be mean, why then to get the whole and genuine meanness of it, and publish its meaness to the world; or if it were sublime, to know it by experience, and be able to give a true account of it in my next excursion. For most men, it appears to me, are in a strange uncertainty about it, whether it is of the devil or of God and have *somewhat hastily* concluded that it is the chief end of man here to "glorify God and enjoy him forever."

2   Still we live meanly, like ants; though the fable tells us that we were long ago changed into men; like pygmies we fight with cranes; it is error upon error, and clout upon clout, and our best virtue has for its occasion a superfluous and inevitable wretchedness. Our life is frittered away by detail. An honest man has hardly need to count more than his ten fingers, or in extreme

438

cases he may add his ten toes, and lump the rest. Simplicity, simplicity, simplicity! I say, let your affairs be as two or three, and not a hundred or a thousand; instead of a million count half a dozen, and keep your accounts on your thumb-nail. In the midst of this chopping sea of civilized life, such are the clouds and storms and quicksands and thousand-and-one items to be allowed for, that a man has to live, if he would not founder and go to the bottom and not make his port at all, by dead reckoning, and he must be a great calculator indeed who succeeds. Simplify, simplify. Instead of three meals a day, if it be necessary eat but one; instead of a hundred dishes, five; and reduce other things in proportion. Our life is like a German Confederacy, made up of petty states, with its boundary forever fluctuating, so that even a German cannot tell you how it is bounded at any moment. The nation itself, with all its so-called internal improvements, which, by the way, are all external and superficial, is just such an unwieldy and overgrown establishment, cluttered with furniture and tripped up by its own traps, ruined by luxury and heedless expense, by want of calculation and a worthy aim, as the million households in the land; and the only cure for it, as for them, is in a rigid economy, a stern and more than Spartan simplicity of life and elevation of purpose. It lives too fast. Men think that it is essential that the *Nation* have commerce, and export ice, and talk through a telegraph, and ride thirty miles an hour, without a doubt, whether *they* do or not; but whether we should live like baboons or like men, is a little uncertain. If we do not get out sleepers, and forge rails, and devote days and nights to the work, but go to tinkering upon our *lives* to improve *them*, who will build railroads? And if railroads are not built, how shall we get to Heaven in season? But if we stay at home and mind our business, who will want railroads? We do not ride on the railroad; it rides upon us. Did you ever think what those sleepers are that underlie the railroad? Each one is a man, an Irishman, or a Yankee man. The rails are laid on them, and they are covered with sand, and the cars run smoothly over them. They are sound sleepers, I assure you. And every few years a new lot is laid down and run over; so that, if some have the pleasure of riding on a rail, others have the misfortune to be ridden upon. And when they run over a man that is walking in his sleep, a supernumerary sleeper in the wrong position, and wake him up, they suddenly stop the cars, and make a hue and cry about it, as if this were an exception. I am glad to know that it takes a gang of men for every five miles to keep the sleepers down and level in their beds as it is, for this is a sign that they may sometime get up again.

Why should we live with such hurry and waste of life? We are determined to be starved before we are hungry. Men say that a stitch in time saves nine, and so they take a thousand stitches to-day to save nine tomorrow. As for *work*, we haven't any of any consequence. We have the Saint Vitus' dance, and cannot possibly keep our heads still. If I should only give a few pulls at the parish bell-rope, as for a fire, that is, without setting the bell, there is hardly a man on his farm in the outskirts of Concord, notwithstanding that press of engagements which was his excuse so many times this morning, nor a boy, nor a woman, I might almost say, but would forsake all and follow that sound, not mainly to save property from the flames, but, if we will confess the truth, much more to see it burn, since burn it must, and we, be it known, did not set it on fire,—or to see it put out, and have a hand in it, if that is done as handsomely; yes, even if it were the parish church itself. Hardly a man takes a half-hour's nap after dinner, but when he wakes he holds up his head and asks, "What's the news?" as if the rest of mankind had stood his sentinels. Some give directions to be waked every half-hour, doubtless for no other purpose; and then, to pay for it, they tell what they have dreamed. After a night's sleep the news is as indispensable as the breakfast. "Pray tell me anything new that has happened to a man anywhere on this globe,"—and he reads it over his coffee and rolls, that a man has had his eyes gouged out this morning on the Wachito River, never dreaming the while that he lives in the dark unfathomed mammoth cave of this world, and has but the rudiment of an eye himself.

For my part, I could easily do without the post-office. I think that there 4 are very few important communications made through it. To speak critically, I never received more than one or two letters in my life—I wrote this some years ago—that were worth the postage. The penny-post is, commonly, an institution through which you seriously offer a man that penny for his thoughts which is so often safely offered in jest. And I am sure that I never read any memorable news in a newspaper. If we read of one man robbed, or murdered, or killed by accident, or one house burned, or one vessel wrecked, or one steamboat blown up, or one cow run over on the Western Railroad, or one mad dog killed, or one lot of grasshoppers in the winter,—we never need read of another. One is enough. If you are acquainted with the principle, what do you care for a myriad instances and applications? To a philosopher all *news,* as it is called, is gossip and they who edit and read it are old women over their tea. Yet not a few are greedy after this gossip. There was such a rush, as I hear, the other day at one of the offices to learn the foreign news by the last arrival, that several large squares of plate glass belonging to the establishment were broken by the pressure,—news which I seriously think a ready wit might write a twelvemonth, or twelve years, beforehand with sufficient accuracy. As for Spain, for instance, if you know how to throw in Don Carlos and the Infanta, and Don Pedro and Seville and Granada, from time to time in the right proportions,—they may have changed the names a little since I saw the papers,—and serve up a bull-fight when other entertainments fail, it will be true to the letter, and give us as good an idea of the exact state or ruin of things in Spain as the most succinct and lucid reports under this head in the newspapers: and as for England, almost the last significant scrap of news from that quarter was the revolution of 1649, and if you have learned the history of her crops for an average year, you never need attend to that thing again, unless your speculations are of a merely pecuniary character. If one may judge who rarely looks into the newspapers, nothing new does ever happen in foreign parts, a French revolution not excepted.

What news! how much more important to know what that is which was   5
never old! "Kieou-he-yu (great dignitary of the state of Wei) sent a man to
Khoung-tseu to know his news. Khoung-tseu caused the messenger to be seated
near him, and questioned him in these terms: What is your master doing? The
messenger answered with respect: My master desires to diminish the number
of his faults, but he cannot come to the end of them. The messenger being
gone, the philosopher remarked: What a worthy messenger! What a worthy
messenger!" The preacher, instead of vexing the ears of drowsy farmers on
their day of rest at the end of the week,—for Sunday is the fit conclusion of
an ill-spent week, and not the fresh and brave beginning of a new one,—with
this one other draggle-tail of a sermon, should shout with thundering voice,
"Pause! Avast! Why so seeming fast, but deadly slow?"

Shams and delusions are esteemed for soundest truths, while reality is fab-   6
ulous. If men would steadily observe realities only, and not allow themselves
to be deluded, life, to compare it with such things as we know, would be like
a fairy tale and the Arabian Nights' Entertainments. If we respected only what
is inevitable and has a right to be, music and poetry would resound along the
streets. When we are unhurried and wise, we perceive that only great and worthy things have any permanent and absolute existence, that petty fears and
petty pleasures are but the shadow of the reality. This is always exhilarating
and sublime. By closing the eyes and slumbering, and consenting to be deceived by shows, men establish and confirm their daily life of routine and
habit everywhere, which still is built on purely illusory foundations. Children,
who play life, discern its true law and relations more clearly than men, who
fail to live it worthily, but who think that they are wiser by experience, that
is, by failure. I have read in a Hindoo book, that "there was a king's son,
who, being expelled in infancy from his native city, was brought up by a
forester, and growing up to maturity in that state, imagined himself to belong
to the barbarous race with which he lived. One of his father's ministers having discovered him, revealed to him what he was, and the misconception of
his character was removed, and he knew himself to be a prince. So soul," continues the Hindoo philosopher, "from the circumstances in which it is placed,
mistakes its own character, until the truth is revealed to it by some holy teacher,
and then it knows itself to be *Brahma*." I perceive that we inhabitants of New
England live this mean life that we do because our vision does not penetrate
the surface of things. We think that this *is* which *appears* to be. If a man
should walk through this town and see only the reality, where, think you,
would the "Mill-dam" go to? If he should give us an account of the realities
he beheld there, we should not recognize the place in his description. Look at
a meeting-house, or a court-house, or a jail, or a shop, or a dwelling-house,
and say what that thing really is before a true gaze, and they would all go to
pieces in your account of them. Men esteem truth remote, in the outskirts of
the system, behind the farthest star, before Adam and after the last man. In
eternity there is indeed something true and sublime. But all these times and
places and occasions are now and here. God himself culminates in the present

moment, and will never be more divine in the lapse of all the ages. And we are enabled to apprehend at all what is sublime and noble only by the perpetual instilling and drenching of the reality that surrounds us. The universe constantly and obediently answers to our conceptions; whether we travel fast or slow, the track is laid for us. Let us spend our lives in conceiving then. The poet or the artist never yet had so fair and noble a design but some of his posterity at least could accomplish it.

Let us spend one day as deliberately as Nature, and not be thrown off the track by every nutshell and mosquito's wing that falls on the rails. Let us rise early and fast, or break fast, gently and without perturbation; let company come and let company go, let the bells ring and the children cry,—determined to make a day of it. Why should we knock under and go with the stream? Let us not be upset and overwhelmed in that terrible rapid and whirlpool called a dinner, situated in the meridian shallows. Weather this danger and you are safe, for the rest of the way is down hill. With unrelaxed nerves, with morning vigor, sial by it, looking another way, tied to the mast like Ulysses. If the engine whistles, let it whistle till it is hoarse for its pains. If the bell rings, why should we run? We will consider what kind of music they are like. Let us settle ourselves, and work and wedge our feet downward through the mud and slush of opinion, and prejudice, and tradition, and delusion, and appearance, that alluvion which covers the globe, through Paris and London, through New York and Boston and Concord, through Church and State, through poetry and philosophy and religion, till we come to a hard bottom and rocks in place, which we can call *reality*, and say, This is, and no mistake; and then begin, having a *point d'appui*, below freshet and frost and fire, a place where you might found a wall or a state, or set a lamppost safely, or perhaps a gauge, not a Nilometer, but a Realometer that future ages might know how deep a freshet of shams and appearances had gathered from time to time. If you stand right fronting and face to face to a fact, you will see the sun glimmer on both its surfaces, as if it were a cimeter, and feel its sweet edge dividing you through the heart and marrow, and so you will happily conclude your mortal career. Be it life or death, we crave only reality. If we are really dying, let us hear the rattle in our throats and feel cold in the extremities; if we are alive, let us go about our business.

Time is but the stream I go a-fishing in. I drink at it; but while I drink I see the sandy bottom and detect how shallow it is. Its thin current slides away, but eternity remains. I would drink deeper; fish in the sky, whose bottom is pebbly with stars. I cannot count one. I know not the first letter of the alphabet. I have always been regretting that I was not as wise as the day I was born. The intellect is a cleaver; it discerns and rifts its way into the secret of things. I do not wish to be any more busy with my hands than is necessary. My head is hands and feet. I feel all my best faculties concentrated in it. My instinct tells me that my head is an organ for burrowing, as some creatures use their snout and fore paws, and with it I would mine and burrow my way through these hills. I think that the richest vein is somewhere hereabouts; so by the divining-rod and thin rising vapors I judge; and here I will begin to mine.

The Death of the Moth
Virginia Woolf

Virginia Woolf (1882–1941) is best known for experimental novels such as *Mrs. Dalloway, The Waves,* and *To The Lighthouse,* but she was also influential as a critic and essayist. Born in London, the daughter of the eminent scholar Sir Leslie Stephen, Woolf was educated at home and read voraciously in her father's large library. She married journalist Leonard Woolf in 1912 and with him founded the Hogarth Press, which published works by several prominent artists, intellectuals, and writers known as the Bloomsbury group. Introspective and prone to depression, Woolf drowned herself in 1941. "The Death of the Moth," published posthumously, reveals her powers of observation and echoes a recurrent theme in her fiction, the interaction of time and consciousness.

Moths that fly by day are not properly to be called moths; they do not   1
excite that pleasant sense of dark autumn nights and ivy-blossom which the commonest yellow-underwing asleep in the shadow of the curtain never fails to rouse in us. They are hybrid creatures, neither gay like butterflies nor sombre like their own species. Nevertheless the present specimen, with his narrow hay-coloured wings, fringed with a tassel of the same colour, seemed to be content with life. It was a pleasant morning, mid-September, mild, benignant, yet with a keener breath than that of the summer months. The plough was already scoring the field opposite the window, and where the share had been, the earth was pressed flat and gleamed with moisture. Such vigour came rolling in from the fields and then down beyond that it was difficult to keep the eyes strictly turned upon the book. The rooks too were keeping one of their annual festivities; soaring round the tree tops until it looked as if a vast net with thousands of black knots in it had been cast up into the air; which, after a few moments sank slowly down upon the trees until every twig seemed to have a knot at the end of it. Then, suddenly, the net would be thrown into the air again in a wider circle this time, with the utmost clamour and vociferation, as though to be thrown into the air and settle slowly down upon the tree tops were a tremendously exciting experience.

The same energy which inspired the rooks, the ploughmen, the horses,   2
and even, it seemed, the lean bare-backed downs, sent the moth fluttering from side to side of his square of the window pane. One could not help watching him. One was, indeed, conscious of a queer feeling of pity for him. The possibilities of pleasure seemed that morning so enormous and so various that to have only a moth's part in life, and a day moth's at that, appeared a hard

fate, and his zest in enjoying his meagre opportunities to the full, pathetic. He flew vigorously to one corner of his compartment, and, after waiting there a second, flew across to the other. What remained for him but to fly to a third corner and then to a fourth? That was all he could do, in spite of the size of the downs, the width of the sky, the far-off smoke houses, and the romantic voice, now and then, of a steamer out at sea. What he could do he did. Watching him, it seemed as if a fibre, very thin but pure, of the enormous energy of the world had been thrust into his frail and diminutive body. As often as he crossed the pane, I could fancy that a thread of vital light became visible. He was little or nothing but life.

Yet, because he was so small, and so simple a form of the energy that was   3
rolling in at the open window and driving its way through so many narrow and intricate corridors in my own brain and in those of other human beings, there was something marvelous as well as pathetic about him. It was as if someone had taken a tiny bead of pure life and decking it as lightly as possible with down and feathers, had set it dancing and zigzagging to show us the true nature of life. Thus displayed one could not get over the strangeness of it. One is apt to forget all about life, seeing it humped and bossed and garnished and cumbered so that it has to move with the greatest circumspection and dignity. Again, the thought of all that life might have been he been born in any other shape caused one to view his simple activities with a kind of pity.

After a time, tired by his dancing apparently, he settled on the window   4
ledge in the sun, and, the queer spectacle being at an end, I forgot about him. Then, looking up, my eye was caught by him. He was trying to resume his dancing, but seemed either so stiff or so awkward that he could only flutter to the bottom of the windowpane; and when he tried to fly across it he failed. Being intent on other matters I watched these futile attempts for a time without thinking, unconsciously waiting for him to resume his flight, as one waits for a machine, that has stopped momentarily, to start again without considering the reason of its failure. After perhaps a seventh attempt he slipped from the wooden ledge and fell, fluttering his wings, on to his back on the window sill. The helplessness of his attitude roused me. It flashed upon me that he was in difficulties; he could no longer raise himself; his legs struggled vainly. But, as I stretched out a pencil, meaning to help him to right himself, it came over me that the failure and awkwardness were the approach of death. I laid the pencil down again.

The legs agitated themselves once more. I looked as if for the enemy against   5
which he struggled. I looked out of doors. What had happened there? Presumably it was midday, and work in the fields had stopped. Stillness and quiet had replaced the previous animation. The birds had taken themselves off to feed in the brooks. The horses stood still. Yet the power was there all the same, massed outside indifferent, impersonal, not attending to anything in particular. Somehow it was opposed to the little hay-coloured moth. It was useless to try to do anything. One could only watch the extraordinary efforts made by those tiny legs against an oncoming doom which could, had it chosen,

have submerged an entire city, not merely a city, but masses of human beings; nothing, I knew, had any chance against death. Nevertheless after a pause of exhaustion the legs fluttered again. It was superb this last protest, and so frantic that he succeeded at last in righting himself. One's sympathies, of course, were all on the side of life. Also, when there was nobody to care or to know, this gigantic effort on the part of an insignificant little moth, against a power of such magnitude, to retain what no one else valued or desired to keep, moved one strangely. Again, somehow, one saw life, a pure bead. I lifted the pencil again, useless though I knew it to be. But even as I did so, the unmistakable tokens of death showed themselves. The body relaxed, and instantly grew stiff. The struggle was over. The insignificant little creature now knew death. As I looked at the dead moth, this minute wayside triumph of so great a force over so mean an antagonist filled me with wonder. Just as life had been strange a few minutes before, so death was now as strange. The moth having righted himself now lay most decently and uncomplainingly composed. O yes, he seemed to say, death is stronger than I am.

Copyrights and Acknowledgments

Index of Authors and Titles